The Critical Edition of Q

Synopsis including the Gospels of Matthew and Luke, Mark and Thomas with English, German, and French Translations of Q and Thomas

Edited by
James M. Robinson
Paul Hoffmann
John S. Kloppenborg

Managing Editor
Milton C. Moreland

Fortress Press
Minneapolis

Peeters Publishers
Leuven

The Critical Edition of Q:
Synopsis including the Gospels of Matthew and Luke, Mark and Thomas
with English, German, and French Translations of Q and Thomas

Cover and interior design by Kenneth Hiebert

Library of Congress Cataloging-in-Publication Data

The critical edition of Q: a synopsis including the Gospels of Matthew and Luke and Thomas with English, German, and French translations of Q and Thomas / edited by James M. Robinson, Paul Hoffmann, John S. Kloppenborg; managing editor, Milton C. Moreland.
p. cm. — (Hermeneia—a critical and historical commentary on the Bible)
English, French, German, and Greek.
ISBN 0-8006-3149-8 (alk. paper)
1. Q hypothesis (synoptics criticism) 2. Bible. N.T. Gospels—Criticism, interpretation, etc. I. Robinson, James McConkey, 1924- II. Hoffmann, Paul, 1933- III. Kloppenborg, John S., 1951- IV. Series.

BS2555.2 .C73 2000
226'.066—dc21

00-022716

Photo Credits: The photo of the Gospel of Thomas (P.Qxy. 655) is provided by the Houghton Library, Harvard University, Cambridge, Mass., and used with permission. The photo of Codex Sinaiticus (located in the British Museum, London, England) is provided by T. C. Skeat and used with permission.

The paper used in this publication meets the minimum requirements of American National Standard for Information Sciences—Permanence of Paper for Printed Library Materials, ANSI Z329.48-1984.

AF 1–6031

04 03 02 01 00 1 2 3 4 5 6 7 8 9 10

Table of Contents

Q Texts in Matthean Order ix
Foreword by Frank Moore Cross and Helmut Koester xiii
Preface by James M. Robinson, Paul Hoffmann, and John S. Kloppenborg xv
Acknowledgements xvii

History of Q Research by James M. Robinson

Introduction xix
Papias' Aramaic λόγια
  From Schleiermacher and Weisse to Holtzmann xx
Matthew without Q
  Schweitzer's Jesus the Apocalypticist xxxiii
Q as the Essence of Christianity or the Kerygma
  Harnack vs. Wellhausen, Barth, and Bultmann xxxviii
Proclamation and Redaction
  Bornkamm, Tödt, Steck, and Lührmann xlvii
Sapiential Origins of Q and *Thomas*
  Koester, Robinson, and Kloppenborg lix
The Critical Edition of Q
  The International Q Project lxvi

Technical Data by James M. Robinson

The Synopsis Format in Eight Columns lxxii
  List of Matthean and Lukan Doublets lxxii
  List of Markan Parallels lxxv
  List of Parallels from the *Gospel of Thomas* lxxvii
  List of Texts from the LXX lxxviii
  List of Texts from the Gospel of John lxxix
  List of Texts from the Rest of the New Testament lxxix
  List of Texts from the *Didache* lxxix
  Lists of Texts from Other Early Christian Literature lxxix
Sigla in the Page Layout lxxx
Divergences from the Lukan Sequence lxxxix
  List of Sayings not in Lukan Sequence lxxxix
Text Critical Notes xc
  Excursus on the Scribal Error in Q 12:27 xcix
Endpapers cvii

The Critical Text of Q

Q 3:⟦0⟧ ⟦Incipit⟧ 2
Q 3:~~1a~~, 2b-3a, ~~3b-4~~ The Introduction of John 4
Q 3:7-9 John's Announcement of Judgment 8
Q 3:16b-17 John and the One to Come 14
Q 3:⟦21-22⟧ ⟦The Baptism of Jesus⟧ 18
Q 4:1-4, 9-12, 5-8, 13 The Temptations of Jesus 22
Q 4:16, ~~31~~ Nazara 42
Q 6:20-21 Beatitudes for the Poor, Hungry, and Mourning 44
Q 6:22-23 The Beatitude for the Persecuted 50
Q 6:~~24-26 The Woes against the Rich~~ 54
Q 6:27-28, 35c-d Love Your Enemies 56
Q 6:29, ⟦29↔30/Matt 5:41⟧, 30 Renouncing One's Own Rights 60
Q 6:31 The Golden Rule 66
Q 6:32, 34 Impartial Love 68
Q 6:36 Being Full of Pity like Your Father 72
Q 6:37-38 Not Judging 74
Q 6:39 The Blind Leading the Blind 76
Q 6:40 The Disciple and the Teacher 78
Q 6:41-42 The Speck and the Beam 80
Q 6:43-45 The Tree Is Known by its Fruit 84
Q 6:46 Not Just Saying Master, Master 94
Q 6:47-49 Houses Built on Rock or Sand 96
Q 7:1, ~~2~~, 3, ~~4-6a~~, 6b-9, ?10? The Centurion's Faith in Jesus' Word 102
Q 7:18-19, ~~20-21~~, 22-23 John's Inquiry about the One to Come 118
Q 7:24-28 John – More than a Prophet 128
Q 7:⟦29-30⟧ ⟦For and Against John⟧ 138
Q 7:31-35 This Generation and the Children of Wisdom 140
Q 9:57-60, ⟦~~61-62~~⟧ Confronting Potential Followers 150
Q 10:~~1 Sending on the Mission~~ 158
Q 10:2 Workers for the Harvest 160
Q 10:3 Sheep among Wolves 162
Q 10:4 No Provisions 164
Q 10:5-9 What to Do in Houses and Towns 166
Q 10:10-12 Response to a Town's Rejection 176
Q 10:13-15 Woes against Galilean Towns 182
Q 10:16 Whoever Takes You in Takes Me in 188
Q 10:21 Thanksgiving that God Reveals Only to Children 190
Q 10:22 Knowing the Father through the Son 192
Q 10:~~22↔23/Matt 11:28-30 The Invitation to Come for Rest~~ 194
Q 10:23-24 The Beatitude for the Eyes that See 196
Q 10:~~25-28 The Law's Love of God and Neighbor~~ 200
Q 11:~~1-2a~~, 2b-4 The Lord's Prayer 206
Q 11:⟦~~5-8~~⟧ ⟦~~The Friend at Midnight~~⟧ 212

Q 11:9-13 The Certainty of the Answer to Prayer 214
Q 11:14-15, 17-20 Refuting the Beelzebul Accusation 222
Q 11:⟦21-22⟧ ⟦Looting a Strong Person⟧ 234
Q 11:23 The One not with Me 236
Q 11:24-26 The Return of the Unclean Spirit 238
Q 11:?27-28? ?Hearing and Keeping God's Word? 244
Q 11:16, 29-30 The Sign of Jonah for This Generation 246
Q 11:31-32 Something More than Solomon and Jonah 252
Q 11:33 The Light on the Lampstand 256
Q 11:34-35, ⟦~~36~~⟧ The Jaundiced Eye Darkens the Body's Light 258
Q 11:?39a?, 42, 39b, ⟦~~40~~⟧, 41, 43-44 Woes against the Pharisees 264
Q 11:46b, 52, 47-48 Woes against the Exegetes of the Law 278
Q 11:49-51 Wisdom's Judgment on This Generation 284
Q 12:2-3 Proclaiming What Was Whispered 290
Q 12:4-5 Not Fearing the Body's Death 296
Q 12:6-7 More Precious than Many Sparrows 300
Q 12:8-9 Confessing or Denying 304
Q 12:10 Speaking against the holy Spirit 308
Q 12:11-12 Hearings before Synagogues 312
Q 12:~~12‹ ›33/Matt 10:23~~ ~~Fleeing among the Towns of Israel~~ 318
Q 12:~~13-15~~ ~~Against Covetousness~~ 320
Q 12:⟦~~16-20~~⟧, ~~21~~ ⟦~~The Rich Fool~~⟧ 324
Q 12:33-34 Storing up Treasures in Heaven 328
Q 12:22b-31, ~~32~~ Free from Anxiety like Ravens and Lilies 334
Q 12:⟦~~35-38~~⟧ ⟦~~Like Slaves Waiting up for Their Master~~⟧ 356
Q 12:39-40 The Son of Humanity Coming as a Robber 360
Q 12:42-46 The Faithful or Unfaithful Slave 366
Q 12:⟦49⟧, ~~50~~, 51, ~~52~~, 53 Children against Parents 376
Q 12:⟦54-56⟧ ⟦Judging the Time⟧ 388
Q 12:~~57~~, 58-59 Settling out of Court 392
Q 13:18-19 The Mustard Seed 400
Q 13:20-21 The Yeast 404
Q 13:24-27 I Do not Know You 406
Q 13:29, 28 Many Will Come from Sunrise and Sunset 414
Q 13:⟦30⟧ ⟦The Reversal of the Last and the First⟧ 418
Q 13:34-35 Judgment over Jerusalem 420
Q 14:~~1-4~~, ~~5~~, ~~6~~ ~~The Ox in the Pit~~ 424
Q 14:⟦11⟧ ⟦The Exalted Humbled and the Humble Exalted⟧ 430
Q 14: ~~15~~, 16-18, ?19-20?, 21, ~~22~~, 23, ~~24~~ The Invited Dinner Guests 432
Q 14:26 Hating One's Family 450
Q 14:27 Taking One's Cross 454
Q 17:33 Finding or Losing One's Life 456
Q 14:34-35 Insipid Salt 458
Q 16:13 God or Mammon 462

Q 16:16 Since John the Kingdom of God 464
Q 16:17 No Serif of the Law to Fall 468
Q 16:18 Divorce Leading to Adultery 470
Q 17:1-2 Against Enticing Little Ones 472
Q 15:4-5a, ~~5b-6~~, 7 The Lost Sheep 478
Q 15:⟦8-10⟧ ⟦The Lost Coin⟧ 484
Q 17:3-4 Forgiving a Sinning Brother Repeatedly 488
Q 17:6 Faith like a Mustard Seed 492
Q 17:⟦20-21⟧ ⟦The Kingdom of God within You⟧ 494
Q 17:~~22~~, 23-24, ~~25~~ The Son of Humanity like Lightning 500
Q 17:37 Vultures around a Corpse 510
Q 17:26-27, ?28-29?, 30, ~~31-32~~ As in the Days of Noah 512
Q 17:34-35 One Taken, One Left 522
Q 19:12-13, ~~13‹ ›15/Matt 25:15c-18~~, 14, 15-24, ~~25~~, 26, ⟦~~27~~⟧ The Entrusted Money 524
Q 22:28, ~~29~~, 30 You Will Judge the Twelve Tribes of Israel 558

Concordance of Q by John S. Kloppenborg

Introduction 563
Concordance 565

Q Texts in Matthean Order

Matthew	Matthean Doublet	Q (Luke)	Gospel of Thomas	Page
3:⟦0⟧				2-3
3:1, ~~2-4~~, 5, ~~6~~	3:13; 11:10b	3:~~1a~~, 2b-3a, ~~3b-4~~		4-7
3:7-10	7:19	3:7-9		8-13
3:11-12		3:16b-17		14-17
3:⟦13, 16-17⟧	3:5-6; 17:5b-c	3:⟦21-22⟧		18-21
4:1-11		4:1-4, 9-12, 5-8, 13		22-41
4:13		4:16, ~~31~~		42-43
5:1-4, 6	4:25	6:20-21	54; 69.2	44-49
5:11-12		6:22-23	69.1a; 68.1	50-53
—	5:3, 6, 4, 11-12	6:~~24-26~~		54-55
5:13		14:34-35		458-61
5:15		11:33	33.2-3	256-57
5:18	24:34a, 35, 34b	16:17		468-69
5:25-26		12:~~57~~, 58-59		392-99
5:32	19:9	16:18		470-71
5:~~38-39a~~, 39b-40	5:42b	6:29		60-61
5:⟦41⟧		6:⟦29↔30/Matt 5:41⟧		62-63
5:42	5:40	6:30	95	64-65
5:~~43~~, 44		6:27-28		56-57
5:45	5:48	6:35c-d		58-59
5:47	5:46	6:34	95	70-71
5:48	5:45	6:36		72-73
6:~~7-8~~, 9-13		11:~~1-2a~~, 2b-4		206-11
—		11:⟦~~5-8~~⟧		212-13
6:19-21	19:21b	12:33-34	76.3	328-33
6:22-23a		11:34	24.3	258-59
—		11⟦~~36~~⟧		262-63
6:24		16:13	47.2	462-63
6:25-33		12:22b-31	36	334-53
6:~~34~~		12:~~32~~		354-55
7:1-2		6:37-38		74-75
7:3-5		6:41-42	26	80-83
7:7-11		11:9-13	92.1; 94	214-21

Matthew	Matthean Doublet	Q (Luke)	Gospel of Thomas	Page
7:12	22:40	6:31	6.3	66-67
7:13-14		13:24		406-07
7:~~15~~, 16b, 18-~~19~~		6:43	45.1	84-89
7:21	12:50a	6:46		94-95
7:22-23		13:26-27		410-13
7:24-27		6:47-49		96-101
7:28a		7:1a		102-03
8:5-10, ?13?	15:21-23a, 25-28	7:1b, ~~2~~, 3, ~~4-6a~~, 6b-9, ?10?		102-17
8:11-12		13:29, 28		414-17
8:~~18~~, 19-22		9:57-60	86	150-55
9:32-34	12:22-24	11:14-15		222-25
9:37-38		10:2	73	160-61
10:5-6	10:1	10:~~1~~		158-59
10:7-8	4:17	10:9	14.4c	174-75
10:10b-11	10:12	10:7-8	14.4a-b	170-71
10:14		10:10-11		176-79
10:15	11:24	10:12		180-81
10:16		10:3	39.3	162-63
10:~~17-18~~, 19	10:20	12:11-12		312-17
10:~~23~~		12:~~12‹ ›33/Matt 10:23~~		318-19
—		12:~~13-14~~	72.1-2	320-21
—		12:~~15~~		322-23
—		12:⟦~~16-20~~⟧	63.1-3	324-25
—	6:19-20	12:~~21~~		326-27
10:24-25a		6:40		78-79
10:26		12:2	5.2 = 6.5	290-91
10:27		12:3	33.1	292-95
10:28-31		12:4-7		296-303
10:32-33	16:27	12:8-9		304-07
—	10:34	12:⟦49⟧	10	376-77
—		12:~~50~~		378-79
10:34		12:51	16.1-2	380-81
—	10:35a, 36b	12:~~52~~	16.3a	382-83
10:35-36		12:53	16.3b	384-87
10:37	19:29a	14:26	55; 101.1-2	450-53
10:38	16:24b	14:27	55.2	454-55
10:39	16:25	17:33		456-57
10:40	18:5	10:16		188-89
11:2-6		7:18-19, ~~20-21~~, 22-23		118-27
11:7-10		7:24-27	78	128-35
11:11		7:28	46	136-37

Matthew	Matthean Doublet	Q (Luke)	Gospel of Thomas	Page
11:12-13		16:16		464-67
11:16-19		7:31-35		140-49
11:21-24	11:23b, 21b; 10:15	10:13-15		182-87
11:25-27		10:21-22	61.3b	190-93
11:~~28-30~~		10:~~22‹ ›23/Matt 11:28-30~~	90	194-95
12:~~11~~	12:9-10, 12-14	14:~~1-4~~, ~~5~~, ~~6~~		424-29
12:25-28		11:17-20		226-33
12:⟦29⟧		11:⟦21-22⟧	35	234-35
12:30		11:23		236-37
12:32a-b	12:31, 32c	12:10	44	308-11
12:33	7:17, 20a; 20b=16a	6:44	45.1	84-89
12:34-35	3:7b	6:45	45.2-4	90-93
12:38-40	16:1, 2a, 4	11:16, 29-30		246-51
12:41-42		11:32, 31		252-55
12:43-45		11:24-26		238-43
—		11:?27-28?	79.1-2	244-45
13:16-17		10:23-24		196-99
13:31-32		13:18-19	20	400-03
13:33		13:20-21	96.1-2	404-05
15:14		6:39	34	76-77
16:⟦3b⟧		12:⟦56⟧	91.2	390-91
17:20b	21:21	17:6	48	492-93
18:6-7		17:2, 1		472-77
18:12-13, ~~14~~	18:10	15:4-5a, ~~5b-6~~, 7	107	478-83
—	18:10, 12-14	15:⟦8-10⟧		484-87
18:15, 21, ~~22~~		17:3-4		488-91
19:28		22:28, ~~29~~, 30		558-61
20:⟦16⟧	19:30	13:⟦30⟧	4.2	418-19
21:⟦32⟧	21:25c, 29	7:⟦29-30⟧		138-39
22:~~1~~, 2-10, ~~11-14~~		14:~~15~~,16-18, ?19-20?, 21, ~~22~~, 23, ~~24~~	64	432-49
22:~~34-40~~, ~~46~~	19:16	10:~~25-28~~		200-05
23:?1-2a?		11:?39a?		264-65
23:4		11:46b		278-79
23:5-7		11:43		274-75
23:⟦12⟧	18:4	14:⟦11⟧		430-31
23:13		11:52	39.1-2	280-81
23:23		11:42		266-67
23:25, ⟦26a⟧, 26b		11: 39b, ⟦40⟧, 41	89	268-73

Matthew	Matthean Doublet	Q (Luke)	Gospel of Thomas	Page
23:27-28		11:44		276-77
23:29-32		11: 47-48		282-83
23:34-36		11: 49-51		284-89
23:37-39	21:9b	13:34-35		420-23
24:~~17-18~~		17:~~31-32~~		520-21
—		17:⟦20⟧	113.1-2	494-95
24:⟦23⟧	24:26	17:⟦21⟧	113.3-4; 3	496-99
24:26-27	24:23	17:23	3.1-2	502-05
24:28		17:37		510-11
24:37-39a		17:26-27		512-15
—		17:?28-29?		516-17
24:39b		17:30		518-19
24:40-41	24:18	17:34-35	61.1	522-23
24:43		12:39	21.5; 103	360-63
24:45-51	25:21b	12:42-46		366-75
25:⟦~~1-13~~⟧	24:46, 42	12:⟦~~35-38~~⟧	21.7	356-59
25:10-12		13:25		408-09
25:14-15b, ~~15c-18~~, 19-29, ~~30~~	25:20-26; 13:12; 8:~~12~~; 22:~~13b-c~~	19:12-13, ~~13‹ ›15/ Matt 25:15c-18~~, ~~14~~, 15-24, ~~25~~, 26, ⟦~~27~~⟧	41	524-57

Foreword

Hermeneia is a commentary series that is based upon the interpretation of the original texts of the biblical books and other literature closely related to the Bible. The Foreword to the *Hermeneia* commentaries states:

> *Hermeneia* is designed for the serious student of the Bible. It will make full use of ancient Semitic and classical languages. … Insofar as possible, the aim is to provide the student or scholar with full critical discussion of each problem of interpretation and with the primary data upon which the discussion is based.

As the work on the commentaries proceeded, it became clear that texts and translations of important biblical texts and their sources as well as related materials from the world of Israel and early Christianity are not always readily available. Moreover, in-depth scholarly research is often desirable in order to enable the expeditious writing of a commentary without burdening the commentary itself with detailed preliminary studies. The editorial boards of *Hermeneia* therefore decided to begin a series of publications under the title *Hermeneia Supplements*.

Volumes of this supplement series will appear from time to time whenever it seems evident that the publication of texts and studies can provide resources that will assist the scholarly work that is a prerequisite for the writing of commentaries. Such supplementary volumes will also inform the reader about texts and studies that are vital for the understanding of biblical books and the world and history to which they belong.

The editors of *Hermeneia* are heavily indebted to Fortress Press for its energy and courage that has supported the expensive and long-term project of the *Hermeneia* commentaries for the last several decades. We are also grateful for the willingness of Fortress Press to take on the additional burden of publishing the *Hermeneia Supplements*.

The editor responsible for this first volume of the supplements is James M. Robinson of the Claremont Graduate University.

Frank Moore Cross
For the Old Testament
Editorial Board

Helmut Koester
For the New Testament
Editorial Board

Preface

The Critical Edition of Q is in the form of a *Synopsis including the Gospels of Matthew and Luke, Mark and Thomas with English, German, and French Translations of Q and Thomas*. It is intended to function as a standard research tool for the study of Q in the future.

The text of Q need no longer be just an imaginary black box lurking somewhere behind certain Matthean and Lukan verses as their source, but can emerge as a text in its own right.

The parallel texts are laid out in as nearly a parallel way as possible, so that their interrelationships are readily visible: Eight columns, on facing pages, present, from left to right: (1) any Markan parallel to Matthew; (2) any Matthean doublet; (3) the Matthean text derived from Q; (4) the critical text of Q; (5) the Lukan text derived from Q; (6) any Lukan doublet; (7) any Markan parallel to Luke; (8) any parallel from the *Gospel of Thomas*. (For details and exceptions, see the section on The Synopsis Format in Eight Columns in the Technical Data that follows the History of Q Research, pp. lxxii-lxxix.)

The critical text of Q (column 4) is highlighted in light grey tones for ready reference. It is the result of the teamwork of the International Q Project and has been edited by the General Editors. A critical apparatus beneath the columns lists divergent readings by the International Q Project when it worked through Q as a committer of the whole (1989-1996), as well as minority views among the General Editors as they carried through the final establishment of the text.

In the few instances when uncertainties about the Matthean or Lukan text influence the establishing of the critical text of Q, a Text Critical Note follows, listing the manuscript evidence provided in the 27th edition of the *Novum Testamentum Graece* of Nestle-Aland. (The relevance of this manuscript evidence for the text of Q is discussed in the section on Text Critical Notes in the Technical Data, pp. xc-cvi.)

The critical text of Q and the Matthean and Lukan texts derived from Q are formatted with numbered sigla that define each variation unit calling for decision in reconstructing the text of Q. (See the section on Sigla in the Page Layout in the Technical Data, pp. lxxx-lxxxviii.) Beneath the columns, similarly numbered definitions of each variation unit are provided, to clarify what is involved in each decision. The Databases and Evaluations leading to the decision regarding each variation unit are being published progressively in the multi-volume companion series *Documenta Q: Reconstructions of Q Through Two Centuries of Gospel Research Excerpted, Sorted, and Evaluated* (Leuven: Peeters Press, 1996–).

The fully formatted text of Q in column 4 makes use of the many sigla needed to analyze in detail the decision-making process. Hence a simplified text of Q, containing only the very few sigla relevant to the degree of certainty ascribed to the critical text, is also presented below the eight parallel columns, with similar highlighting, as a convenience to those whose interest is less in the critical process of reconstructing the text than in its outcome. This Q text is accompanied by English, German, and French translations.

In cases when column eight presents a parallel from the *Gospel of Thomas*, there is, still further below the columns, a retroversion of the Coptic text into Greek, and, when extant, the Greek text of the Oxyrhynchus papyri, each with English, German, and French translations, to facilitate inclusion of this extra-canonical Sayings Gospel in one's study of the Q text.

The History of Q Research (pp. xix-lxxi) sketches the major turning points in the study of Q, especially as they relate to the present undertaking of producing *The Critical Text of Q*.

A Concordance of Q at the conclusion of the volume (pp. 563-581) provides ready access to specific terms one seeks to locate in the vocabulary of Q.

James M. Robinson   Paul Hoffmann   John S. Kloppenborg

Acknowledgements

An expression of gratitude is due first of all to the members of the International Q Project, who have amassed and sorted the Databases, prepared the Evaluations, participated in the discussions and voting of the meetings, and thereby provided the foundation upon which *The Critical Edition of Q* is built: Josef E. Amon, Stanley D. Anderson, William E. Arnal, Jon Ma. Asgeirsson, Ulrich Bauer, Sterling G. Bjorndahl, M. Eugene Boring, Stefan H. Brandenburger, Shawn Carruth, Amos (Joon Ho) Chang, Jon B. Daniels, Robert A. Derrenbacker, Jr., Rees Conrad Douglas, Claudio Ettl, Carmen Feldmeier, Harry T. Fleddermann, Albrecht Garsky, Heinz O. Guenther, Patrick J. Hartin, Christoph Heil, Thomas Hieke, Paul Hoffmann, Michael Humphries, Clayton N. Jefford, Steven R. Johnson, Ronald L. Jolliffe, Neal Kelsey, Alan Kirk, John S. Kloppenborg, Helmut Koester, Bradley H. McLean, Milton C. Moreland, Stephen J. Patterson, Ronald A. Piper, Jonathan L. Reed, James M. Robinson, Andreas Schmidt, Philip H. Sellew, Saw Lah Shein, Daniel A. Smith, Ky-Chun So, Michael G. Steinhauser, Darla Dee Turlington, Risto Uro, Leif E. Vaage, John Y. H. Yieh, and Linden E. Youngquist.

The Greek text is that of the *Novum Testamentum Graece*, 1993[27], edited by Barbara Aland et al., Deutsche Bibelgesellschaft, Stuttgart. We thank Barbara Aland and Joachim Lange for their cooperation in this undertaking.

The English translation of Q has been provided by James M. Robinson, the German by Paul Hoffmann and the French by Frédéric Amsler of the Faculté de Théologie of the University of Geneva, in each case in consultation with each other and with others of the same mother tongue. We especially wish to express our thanks to Bernard Bouvier, professeur honoraire of the Faculté des Lettres of the University of Geneva, for his invaluable careful reading of the Greek texts and his fine stylistic retouches to the French translation.

Parallels from the *Gospel of Thomas* have been provided in Coptic and with Greek, English, and German translations by the Berliner Arbeitskreis für koptisch-gnostische Schriften under the responsibility of Hans-Gebhard Bethge, published in the *Synopsis Quattuor Evangeliorum: Locis parallelis evangeliorum apocryphorum et patrum adhibitis editit Kurt Aland* (Stuttgart: Deutsche Bibelgesellschaft, 15. redivierte Aufl. 1996, 2. korrigierter Druck 1997, see the Vorwort zur fünfzehnten Auflage by Barbara Aland xi, and the appendix Evangelium Thomae Copticum, Vorbemerkung by Hans-Gebhard Bethge [517-18], and the text of the *Gospel of Thomas* [519-46]). The French translation is provided by Paul-Hubert Poirier of the Québec Bibliothèque Copte de Nag Hammadi. Both Bethge and Poirier have coordinated their translations with the English, German, and French translations of Q. We wish to express to all involved our appreciation for permission to make use of these texts.

Eldon J. Epp provided expert advice concerning the Text Critical Notes, for which we express here our gratitude.

Donald S. Deer has supplied technical assistance for the volume, especially with regard to the translations, for which we are also very grateful.

T. C. Skeat and Harold W. Attridge collaborated in making important improvements in the transcription and translation of *Gos. Thom.* 36.3 in *P. Oxy.* 655, 10-13 at Q 12:27, 25[1]: κ̣[αὶ] / ἓν ἔχ̣ο̣ντ[ες ἔ]νδ[υ-]/μα, τί ἐν[.....]..αι ὑμεῖς; "[And] having *one* clothing, ... you ...?

We would like to express appreciation to those who made invaluable suggestions during the final preparation of this volume, especially to Frans Neirynck[2] and Jozef Verheyden[3] of the University of Leuven, who met with our Editorial Board 28 July 1998 to advise us about the structuring of *The Critical Edition of Q*.

Subsequently Jozef Verheyden has worked through the text with great penetration, careful detail, and substantive suggestions that have led to many improvements in the published volume. We are all very much in his debt for this expert and kind assistance.

---

[1] In other regards the text and translation of *Gos. Thom.* 36 in *P. Oxy* 655 at Q 12:22b, 25, 27, 28 is that of Harold W. Attridge, in *Nag Hammadi Codex II,2-7 together with XIII, 3*, Brit. Lib. Or. 4926(1), and P. Oxy. 1, 654, 655* (ed. Bentley Layton; NHS 20; Leiden: Brill, 1989) 1. 121-22, 127.

[2] See also his announcement "The International Q Project," *EThL* 69 (1993) 221-25, reprinted in his *Q-Synopsis: The Double Tradition Passages in Greek*, Revised Edition with Appendix (Leuven: University Press and Peeters, 1995) 75-79, and his essays "Q: From Source to Gospel," *EThL* 71 (1995) 430, nn. 52-53 and "Note on Q 4,1-2," *EThL* 73 (1997) 94-102, and helpful reviews of the volumes published in the series Documenta Q: *Q 11:2b-4*: The Lord's Prayer (Leuven: Peeters, 1996), in *EThL* 72 (1996) 418-24; *Q 12:49-59: Children against Parents – Judging the Time – Settling out of Court* (Leuven: Peeters, 1997), in *EThL* 73 (1997) 458-59; and *Q 12:8-12: Confessing or Denying – Speaking against the Holy Spirit – Hearings before Synagogues* (Leuven: Peeters, 1997), in *EThL* 74 (1998) 433-36.

[3] See also his helpful reviews of Documenta Q: *Q 11:2b-4: The Lord's Prayer* (Leuven: Peeters, 1996), in *LouvSt* 22 (1997) 183-86; *Q 4:1-13, 16: The Temptations of Jesus – Nazara*, in *LouvSt* 23 (1998) 283-86; *Q 12:49-59: Children against Parents – Judging the Time – Settling out of Court*, in *LouvSt* 23 (1998) 286-87; *Q 12:8-12: Confessing or Denying – Speaking against the Holy Spirit – Hearings before Synagogues* (Leuven: Peeters, 1997), in *LouvSt* 24 (1999) 80-83; and *Q 22:28, 30: You Will Judge the Twelve Tribes of Israel* (Leuven: Peeters, 1998 [1999]), *EThL* 76 (2000) forthcoming.

History of Q Research
James M. Robinson

Introduction

The purpose of this Introduction is to document the major turning points in the history of Q research, with particular attention to the problem of establishing a critical text of Q.[1]

Throughout the nineteenth century, the study of Q was facilitated by a cluster of factors that succeeded in accrediting Q as the most viable solution to the Synoptic problem, and yet in such a way that the reconstruction of a critical text of Q hardly came in question: The point of departure of Q studies was the assumption that Q was composed by the apostle Matthew in Aramaic, of which nothing has survived. This view, though theologically quite appealing, turned out to make it quite impossible to gain access to Q itself, that is to say, to move behind the canonical Greek Gospels of Matthew and Luke to a purely hypothetical Aramaic source, attested at best by an occasional Aramaism sensed to lurk behind the Greek text. The Aramaic text of Q itself would forever remain undocumented and unattainable. On these terms, Q would never be more than a hypothesis.

Only gradually, especially in the latter part of the twentieth century, were such arguments, whose tenacious appeal lay in their apologetic value, completely replaced by objective criteria, based on empirical observation of Matthean and Lukan redactional traits. For once these are inferred from their redaction of Mark, they can be applied to the sayings of Q.[2] Now Q need no longer remain purely hypothetical, a mere postulate lurking unattainably behind Matthew and Luke. The result in more recent times has been a multiplication of reconstructions of the Greek text of Q, in whole or in part. The present *Critical Edition of Q* is based on the collaboration in this effort of a team of scholars who have been working together since 1985 as the International Q Project.

---

1 For a more detailed presentation see John S. Kloppenborg Verbin, *Excavating Q: The History and Setting of the Sayings Gospel* (Minneapolis: Fortress, 2000). For a focused presentation limited to the twentieth century, see the 1996 Toronto dissertation of his student, Alan Kirk, *The Composition of the Sayings Source: Genre, Synchrony, and Wisdom Redaction in Q* (NovTSup 91; Leiden: Brill, 1998), "Compositional Analysis of Q in the History of Scholarship," 2-64.

2 This argument, though greatly expanded as a result of redaction criticism, is in principle not new. See Kirsopp Lake, "The Date of Q," *The Expositor*, Seventh Series, 7 (1909) 494-507: 495-96:

If we look at their treatment of Mark, we can see that Matthew and Luke both used it with a considerable degree of fidelity, except in small points of diction, such as altering the characteristic historic present of Mark to the more literary past tense. It is unusual for them both to alter Mark at the same place in the same way, and the number of places where they seem to do so ought probably [496] to be considerably reduced by textual criticism. Therefore we have good reason for believing that as a rule the original Q is preserved either in Matthew or Luke, and an intelligent criticism ought to enable us generally to be right in our discrimination between the two.

Papias' Aramaic λόγια
From Schleiermacher and Weisse to Holtzmann

In 1832 Friedrich Schleiermacher interpreted Papias[3] to the effect that his term λόγια referred to Jesus' sayings. For Papias wrote a work entitled Λογίων κυριακῶν ἐξήγησις, and reported: Ματθαῖος μὲν οὖν Ἑβραΐδι διαλέκτῳ τὰ λόγια συνετάξατο, ἡρμήνευσεν δ' αὐτὰ ὡς ἦν δυνατὸς ἕκαστος. Schleiermacher took this to mean that Papias wrote a work entitled *Exegesis of the Lord's Sayings*, in which he reported that Matthew "composed the sayings in the Hebrew dialect [= Aramaic] and each interpreted them as one was able." Schleiermacher argued that the reference was not to the canonical Gospel of Matthew (as Papias mistakenly thought), but to a lost Aramaic source written by the apostle Matthew lying behind (and thus giving its apostolic name and authority to) the Greek canonical Gospel of Matthew, consisting of "*logia*," (mis)understood by Schleiermacher as referring to "sayings":

> Matthew wrote a collection of utterances of Christ, be they individual sayings, or longer discourses, or both, as is doubtless most probable. For the expression of Papias itself cannot have meant anything else.[4]

Since Schleiermacher thought Matthew's sayings collection was not used by the other canonical Gospels, and hence not by Luke,[5] he does not deserve credit for having discovered Q. But, building on such early patristic evidence, he did suggest the collection had apostolic authorship. The weight of these arguments throughout the nineteenth century is hard to exaggerate. And he launched Papias' term *logia* as the *terminus technicus* for what only much later came to be known as Q.

In 1838 the Leipzig philosopher Ch. Hermann Weisse first presented the argument basic to establishing the existence of Q, to the effect that Matthew and Luke used, in addition to Mark, a sayings collection:

> If we maintain of this just-mentioned work [the Gospel of Luke] that it stands in a similar relation [56] to Mark as does the Gospel of Matthew, that it, like the latter [Matthew], only even more freely, and seeking a certain pragmatism of narration, wove into the thread of Mark's narrative the λόγια of Matthew, and in addition an impressive series of other communications, yet in the process remaining completely independent of our Gospel of Matthew, as [Matthew] of [Luke] – one will find no preliminary *external* justification needed for this view, insofar as it stands in no contradiction with the historical reports about the Gospel of Luke. Luke himself tells us in the opening words of his work that he has used outside communications about the life history of the Redeemer which stand nearer the first source [Mark]. … But after all that has been noted thus far, it lies so near at hand to presuppose that among the sources he used were to be found the writings of Mark and of the genuine Matthew [i.e. Q], that we would have to be extremely surprised, if it had not been the case. Hence we can confidently pursue further the path we have entered upon, in rela-

---

3 Eusebius, *Hist. eccl.* 3.39.16 (ed. E. Schwartz), GCS 9,1. The Papias texts are conveniently available in *Synopsis Quattuor Evangeliorum: Locis parallelis evangeliorum apocryphorum et patrum adhibitis edidit Kurt Aland* (Stuttgart: Deutsche Bibelgesellschaft, 15. redivierte Aufl. 1996, 2. korrigierter Druck 1997) 547.

4 Friedrich Schleiermacher, "Ueber die Zeugnisse des Papias von unsern beiden ersten Evangelien," *ThStKr* 5 (1832) 735-68: 738:

> Matthäus hat eine Sammlung von Aussprüchen Christi geschrieben, das mögen nun einzelne Sprüche gewesen sein, oder längere Reden, oder beides, wie es wohl am wahrscheinlichsten ist. Denn etwas anderes kann einmal der Ausdrukk des Papias nicht bedeuten.

5 Schleiermacher, "Ueber die Zeugnisse des Papias von unsern beiden ersten Evangelien," 757.

tion to Luke as well, with the consciousness that precisely in this way we remain in the best possible agreement with the historical witnesses.[6]

This leads us to reflect briefly on the mutual relationship of the two other Synoptics to one another apart from their shared connection to Mark. We have already noted that we regard this relationship as an independent one, independent, that is to say, in the use of the common sources by each of the two, but not in the sense that each of them, throughout or for the most part, had used sources that the other had not used. It is our most certain conviction that not only Mark but also Matthew's collection of sayings is a source common to both.[7]

In 1863 Heinrich Julius Holtzmann presented a detailed comparison of the sayings in Matthew and Luke in such a convincing way as to gain for Q general acceptance.[8] For, in spite of various continuing minority views, it has remained the dominant position, of course improved in various regards, down to the present.

Holtzmann, still in deference to Papias' *logia*, designated this sayings source as Λ:

> Rather, we stay with the quite simple assumption of a further Greek source shared by

---

6 Ch. Hermann Weisse, *Die evangelische Geschichte kritisch und philosophisch bearbeitet* (2 vols.; Leipzig: Breitkopf und Härtel, 1838) 1.55-56:

> Wenn wir von diesem letztgenannten [canonical Luke] behaupten, dass es zu Marcus in einem [56] entsprechenden Verhältniss steht, wie das Matthäusevangelium, dass es gleich diesem, nur in noch freierer Behandlung und mit dem Streben nach einem gewissen Pragmatismus der Erzählung, die λόγια des Matthäus, und ausserdem noch eine ansehnliche Reihe anderer Mittheilungen, dem Faden der Erzählung des Marcus einverwebt, dabei aber von unserem Matthäusevangelium, so wie dieses von ihm, völlig unabhängig bleibt: so wird man für diese Ansicht insofern keine vorläufige *äusserliche* Rechtfertigung nöthig finden, als sie mit den historischen Nachrichten über das Lukasevangelium in keinem Widerspruche steht. Dass Lukas fremde, der ersten Quelle [Mark] näher stehende Mittheilungen über die Lebensgeschichte des Erlösers benutzt habe, sagt er uns selbst in den Eingangsworten seines Werkes. … Dass aber unter den Quellen, die er benutzte, die Schriften des Marcus und des ächten Matthäus [i.e. Q] sich befanden: dies vorauszusetzen liegt nach allem bisher Bemerkten so nahe, dass wir uns höchlich zu verwundern hätten, wenn es nicht geschehen wäre. Wir können also auch in Bezug auf Lukas mit dem Bewusstsein, gerade so in bestmöglicher Uebereinstimmung mit den geschichtlichen Zeugnissen zu bleiben, getrost den eingeschlagenen Pfad weiter verfolgen.

7 Weisse, *Die evangelische Geschichte kritisch und philosophisch bearbeitet*, 1.83:

> Dies führt uns darauf, noch mit Wenigem des gegenseitigen Verhältnisses der beiden andern Synoptiker zu einander, abgesehen von ihrer gemeinschaftlichen Beziehung auf Marcus, zu gedenken. Wir haben bereits angemerkt, dass wir dies Verhältniss für ein unabhängiges erkennen, unabhängig nämlich in der Benutzung der gemeinschaftlichen Quellen durch jeden der beiden, nicht aber in dem Sinne, als ob jeder von beiden, durchgehends oder dem grössern Theile nach, andere Quellen, als der andere, benutzt hätte. Nicht nur Marcus ist beiden gemeinschaftliche Quelle, sondern, unserer bestimmtesten Überzeugung nach, auch die Spruchsammlung des Matthäus.

This is the decisive passage for the origin of the Q hypothesis quoted by Werner Georg Kümmel, *Das Neue Testament: Geschichte der Erforschung seiner Probleme* (Orbis Academicus 3/3: Problemgeschichten der Wissenschaft in Dokumenten und Darstellungen; Freiburg and München: Karl Alber, 1958) 185. ET: *The New Testament: The History of the Investigation of Its Problems* (Nashville and New York: Abingdon, 1972) 151. (The English translation is edited to render it more precise).

8 Heinrich Julius Holtzmann, *Die synoptischen Evangelien: Ihr Ursprung und geschichtlicher Charakter* (Leipzig: Engelmann, 1863).

Matthew and Luke, which we, pending the demonstration of its more precise nature, want to indicate in what follows with the *siglum* Λ (λόγια).[9]

The publication by Bernard P. Grenfell and Arthur S. Hunt in 1897 of *P. Oxy.* 1, fragments from an unknown sayings collection (which we now know to be the *Gospel of Thomas*), as ΛΟΓΙΑ ΙΗΣΟΥ,[10] illustrated the broadly based acceptance of the designation *logia* for such a sayings collection. They summarized the initial reception of their publication in its republication a year later:

> Lastly, with regard to the questions of origin and history, we stated in our edition our belief in four points: (1) that we have here part of a collection of sayings, not extracts from a narrative gospel; (2) that they were not heretical; (3) that they were independent of the Four Gospels in their present shape; (4) that they were earlier than 140 A.D., and might go back to the first century. These propositions, especially the first, have, as is natural, been warmly disputed. Attempts have been made to show that the "Logia" were extracts from the Gospel according to the Egyptians (Harnack), the Gospel according to the Hebrews (Batiffol), or the Gospel of the Ebionites (Zahn); and Gnostic, mystic, Ebionite, or Therapeutic tendencies, according to the point of view, have been discovered in them. On the other hand our position has received the general support of critics such as Swete, Rendel Harris, Heinrici, and Lock; and so far the discussion has tended to confirm us in our original view.

This publication did of course create considerable discussion. J. Rendel Harris drew attention to the quotation formula repeated with each saying in *P. Oxy.* 1, λέγει Ἰ(ησοῦ)ς, for he related it to the quotation formula in Acts 20:5: μνημονεύειν τε τῶν λόγων τοῦ κυρίου Ἰησοῦ ὅτι αὐτὸς εἶπεν. Since almost the same formula occurs in *1 Clem.* 13.1; 46.7; Polycarp *Phil.* 2.3, he concluded:

> Here we have the same peculiarity – viz., a quotation of *Logia*, not from our Gospels, with a prologue about the remembrance of what He said. And we have noticed the phenomenon four times. We conclude that it was the introductory formula of the book, which must have ran something like this:
>
> "We ought to remember what things our Lord said in His teaching, for He said ..." and then probably follows the first *Logion*.[11]

Although the remembrance formula turned out to be absent from the *incipit* of the *Gospel of Thomas*, Rendell Harris was right to sense that the standard quotation formula that introduces each saying was picked up in the *incipit*. But he overlooked completely the fact that this remembrance formula only speaks of λόγοι, never λόγια (though Polycarp *Phil.* 2.3 uses neither). But Walter Lock, also stimulated by *P. Oxy.* 1, published the same year a very similar position, while conjecturing as the title more logically Λόγοι Ἰησοῦ:

> Further, there are two points on which I would enter a caveat, – a caveat which the history of the discussion seems to render necessary. I think first that we should sit loosely to the exact title Λόγια; I do not say that it is wrong, but we need to remember that it has no authority as the title of this document; many will think it a very probable suggestion, but considering that the phrase λόγια Ἰησοῦ never occurs, that the phrase

[9] Holtzmann, *Die synoptischen Evangelien,* 128:
> Vielmehr verbleiben wir bei der ganz einfachen Annahme einer weiteren, dem Matthäus und Lucas gemeinsamen, griechischen Quelle, die wir vorbehältlich des Erweises ihres näheren Charakters im Folgenden mit dem Zeichen Λ (λόγια) andeuten wollen.

[10] Bernard P. Grenfell and Arthur S. Hunt, *ΛΟΓΙΑ ΙΗΣΟΥ: Sayings of our Lord* (London: Henry Frowde for the Egypt Exploration Fund, 1897), republished as "1. ΛΟΓΙΑ ΙΗΣΟΥ," *The Oxyrhynchus Papyri,* 1 (London: Egyptian Exploration Fund, 1898) 1-3: 2.

[11] J. Rendell Harris, "The Logia and the Gospels," *Contemporary Review* (1897) 346-48: 348.

λόγια or τὰ λόγια with Θεοῦ or τοῦ Κυρίου or Κυριακά most frequently seems to mean both in the first and second centuries *either* the Old Testament *or* the whole Gospel message, and considering such passages as Acts xx.35, Apoc xxi.5, Clem. Rom. xiii, and the πιστοὶ λόγοι of the Pastoral Epistles, it seems to me at least as probable that the real title was Λόγοι Ἰησοῦ. At any rate if Logia is right, "Sayings" is scarcely an adequate translation; "Solemn Utterances" or "Oracles" would better reproduce the authoritative associations of the word.[12]

Thereupon, already in 1902, J. Armitage Robinson rejected the use of *logia* for Q as "question-begging":

> I would here put in a warning, which is sorely needed, against the confusion introduced by the attempt to give this lost document a name. It is true that the characteristic feature which distinguishes it from St Mark's Gospel is that it contains a very large amount of discourse and a comparatively small amount of narrative. Now Papias, as we have already seen, writing in the [69] first half of the second century, says that "Matthew composed the oracles of the Lord in the Hebrew tongue"; and the word which he uses for "oracles" is *logia*, the primary meaning of which is "sayings." But it is the word which St Paul uses in Rom. iii 2, when he says of the Jews that "to them were committed the oracles of God"; and in the technical meaning of inspired scriptures it is found in both Jewish and Christian writers. We need have no hesitation in saying that when Papias spoke of "the oracles of the Lord" he meant simply "the scriptures about the Lord," or, in other words, the Gospel. But because *logia* originally meant "sayings," and because in St Matthew's Gospel we have a large amount of teaching uttered by our Lord, many persons have hastily concluded that Papias knew of a book of *logia* or sayings of the Lord, which consisted of discourses, and from which the writer of our first Gospel largely drew. That, however, is a guess – and, I think, a bad guess – based on the misunderstanding of the usage of a Greek word. We have no evidence that there ever was a book entitled *Logia*, and to apply this name to the document which we are considering is to beg [70] the question and prejudice our study. We must be content to speak of our lost document as the non-Marcan Greek document which was used by St Matthew and St Luke. *Logia* is a question-begging name: I could wish that we might hear no more of it in this connection.[13]

But it was only the publication in 1904 of *P. Oxy.* 654, containing the *incipit* of the sayings collection already attested by *P. Oxy.* 1, thereby showing it to be the *Gospel of Thomas,* that made the rejection of λόγια in favor of λόγοι inescapable.[14]

---

12 Walter Lock, "Interpretation of the Text," Ch. 3 in Walter Lock and William Sanday, *Two Lectures on the "Sayings of Jesus" Recently Discovered at Oxyrhynchus* (Oxford: Clarendon, 1897) 15-27: 16.

13 J. Armitage Robinson, *The Study of the Gospels* (London, New York: Longmans, Green, and Co., 1902, fifth impression [quoted here] 1909), 68-70. The criticism of "question-begging" was repeated by Benjamin W. Bacon, "A Turning Point in Synoptic Criticism," *HTR* 1 (1908) 55 and *Studies in Matthew* (London: Henry Holt, 1930) 92, in criticism of taking Papias' σύνταξις τῶν λογίων to designate Q as a "Spruchsammlung."

14 To be sure, this was rendered difficult by two scribal errors in the Greek text that could have obscured the nature of the *incipit*: OITOIOIOILOGOIOI[...], i. e. ο<ὗ>τοι οἱ {οι} λόγοι οἱ [...]. Grenfell and Hunt, *New Sayings of Jesus and Fragment of a Lost Gospel from Oxyrhynchus* (London: Henry Frowde, and New York: Oxford University Press American Branch, 1904), republished as "**654**. New Sayings of Jesus," and "**655**. Fragment of a Lost Gospel," *The Oxyrhynchus Papyri*, 4 (London: Egyptian Exploration Fund, 1904), 1-22, 22-28. Grenfell and Hunt mistranscribed: {οἱ} τοῖοι οἱ λόγοι οἱ [...].

For the *incipit* of *P. Oxy.* 654 uses λόγοι: ο<ὖ>τοι οἱ {οι} λόγοι οἱ [ἀπόκρυφοι οὓς ἐλά-]λησεν Ἰη(σοῦ)ς ὁ ζῶν … . Thereupon Grenfell and Hunt, in view of the arguments of Rendell Harris and Lock, formally retracted the term they had used in the title of their first publication:

> There is considerable resemblance between the scheme of II. 1-3, "the words…which Jesus spake … and he said," and the formulae employed in introducing several of the earliest citations of our Lord's Sayings.
>
> … all questions concerning the meaning of the latter term [λόγια] may therefore be left out of account in dealing with the present series of Sayings.[15]

Kirsopp Lake[16] immediately threw his support to this shift in terminology:

> … few criticisms have ever been more completely justified. The title has been found, and it is *Logoi*, not *Logia*.

Adolf Harnack promptly proposed as the title of Q: Λόγοι τοῦ κυρίου Ἰησοῦ.[17]

One may summarize the documentation from the last half of the first century for the usage of λόγοι, not λόγια, to designate sayings of Jesus as follows:

The *explicit* of the Inaugural Sermon in Q (Q 6:47-49), where one might expect something comparable to a title or *incipit*, contains the exhortation not only to hear but also to keep Jesus' λόγοι (πᾶς ὁ ἀκούων μου τοὺς λόγους καὶ [μὴ] ποιῶν αὐτούς …). Clearly this is a designation for the immediately preceding sayings that constitute the Inaugural Sermon. This formulation is retained as the *explicit* in Matthew's Sermon on the Mount (Matt 7:24-27) and Luke's Sermon on the Plain (Luke 6:47-49).

The formula of Q 7:1 (καὶ ἐγένετο ὅτε ἐπλήρωσεν .. τοὺς λόγους τούτους …), which was adopted by Matthew as a stereotypical conclusion for three of his five major discourses (Matt 7:28; 19:1; 26:1), uses the term λόγοι to designate these collections of Jesus' sayings. The Centurion's Faith in Jesus' Word, which immediately follows in Q, has its point in the Centurion's faith in the authority of Jesus' λόγος (Q 7:7).

Paul (1 Thess 4:15) uses λόγος in the quotation formula (ἐν λόγῳ κυρίου) to introduce a saying he ascribes to the Lord.

Acts 20:35 uses λόγοι in what appears to have become a stereotypical formula for introducing sayings of Jesus: … μνημονεύειν τε τῶν λόγων τοῦ κυρίου Ἰησοῦ ὅτι αὐτὸς εἶπεν. It recurs *1 Clem.* 13.1: … μεμνημένοι τῶν λόγων τοῦ κυρίου Ἰησοῦ, οὓς ἐλάλησεν …, followed by the injunction (*1 Clem.* 13.3) to be obedient to Jesus' holy sayings (τοῖς ἁγιοπρεπέσι λόγοις), where again Jesus' sayings are referred to as his λόγοι. Similarly *1 Clem.* 46.7: μνήσθητε τῶν λόγων τοῦ κυρίου Ἰησοῦ.

Revelation 22:6 refers to the resurrected Christ's revelation: καὶ εἶπεν μοι· οὗτοι οἱ λόγοι πιστοὶ καὶ ἀληθινοί.

Didache 1.2-3a is quite similar. For the *Didache* obtained its title by making use in its *incipit* of a formula for presenting sayings (λόγοι) followed by their interpretation (in this case διδαχή). For the *Didache* begins with the core of Jesus' sayings

---

15 Grenfell and Hunt, *New Sayings of Jesus and Fragment of a Lost Gospel from Oxyrhynchus*, 13, 25.

16 Kirsopp Lake, "The New Sayings of Jesus and the Synoptic Problem," *HibJ* 3 (1905) 332-41: 333. For a full quotation of his quite definitive statement, see my essay, "The *Incipit* of the Sayings Gospel Q," *RHPhR* 75 (1995) 9-33: 23-24.

17 Adolf Harnack, *Sprüche und Reden Jesu. Die zweite Quelle des Matthäus und Lukas* (Beiträge zur Einleitung in das Neue Testament, 2; Leipzig: Hinrichs'sche Buchhandlung, 1907) 132. ET: *The Sayings of Jesus: The Second Source of St. Matthew and St. Luke* (London: Williams and Norgate, and New York: Putnam, 1908) 188. Harnack noted, 132, n. 1 (ET: 189, n. 1) that Rendell Harris and Lake had anticipated his view. Athanasius Polag, *Fragmenta Q: Textheft zur Logienquelle* (Neukirchen-Vluyn: Neukirchener Verlag, 1979^1, 1982^2) 28, followed Harnack.

(λόγοι) found, according to *Did* 1.2, in the combination of love of God and neighbor (Mark 12:30-31) plus the (negative) Golden Rule (Q 6:31), with the formula: τούτων δὲ τῶν λόγων ἡ διδαχή ἐστιν αὕτη·, "now the teaching of these sayings is this:" (*Did* 1.3a). This is much the same formula as is found in the similarly-placed introductory saying of the *Gospel of Thomas*: [ὃς ἄν τὴν ἑρμηνεί]αν τῶν λόγων τούτ[ων εὕρῃ, ...],[18] "[whoever finds] the [interpretation] of these sayings ...".[19] Indeed Rufinus' Latin translation of the term διδαχή in the *incipit* of the *Didache* is *interpretatio*.[20]

The *incipit* of *P. Oxy.* 654 (*Gospel of Thomas*) surely belongs in this list in its use of λόγοι: ο<ὗ>τοι οἱ {οι} λόγοι οἱ [ἀπόκρυφοι οὓς ἐλά]-λησεν Ἰη(σοῦ)ς ὁ ζῶν ... .

The frequency of the use of λόγοι in this quasi-technical sense, and the complete absence of the use of λόγιον or λόγια for sayings of Jesus in the first century, make it clear that one should speak of Q as λόγοι rather than as λόγια.

For its part, λόγια is used in its standard meaning (Liddell and Scott: "oracle, esp. one preserved from antiquity, ... more freq. in pl.") in Rom 3:2; Acts 7:38; Heb 5:12; 1 Pet 4:11 – and presumably also in Papias.[21] Dieter Lührmann has made it clear that Papias did not record the original terminology, but rather introduced a new meaning for the sayings of Jesus, and with it a new terminology:

> The thesis of this study is that at the beginning of Q-research there was a misunderstanding, namely Schleiermacher's interpretation of Papias' comments on the gospels of Matthew and Mark. The two-document hypothesis was developed in the 19th [98] century in part independently of this, and in part appealing to it. At the end of the 19th century it became separated from this interpretation, but to some extent was now substantiated by new discoveries of apocryphal gospels. ...
>
> But in that Papias understood the sayings of Jesus as λόγια in the strict sense, he gave a new significance to *them*, not to the Greek word λόγιον. He thus stands at the beginning of a development which can be traced in the 2nd century. ...
>
> Papias was the first to understand the sayings of Jesus as oracles preserved from antiquity, but down to his own time found only poor or even false translations and/or interpretations of such oracles, and wished himself to supply the inter-

[18] The restoration of the lacunae is assured by the here fully extant Coptic translation (Nag Hammadi II 2: 32.13), where the Greek ἑρμηνεία is used as a loan word, and ϣⲁϫⲉ is the standard Sahidic translation of λόγος, for example both here and in the *incipit* itself, where the Greek is also extant in *P. Oxy.* 654.

[19] See also the synonym for διδαχή, ἐπίλυσις, presupposed in Mark 4:34, the "resolution" of Jesus' obscure "parables": χωρὶς δὲ παραβολῆς οὐκ ἐλάλει αὐτοῖς, κατ' ἰδίαν δὲ τοῖς μαθηταῖς ἐπέλυεν πάντα. Similarly the term παρρησία is used for this plainness of speech on the higher level (Mark 8:32): καὶ παρρησίᾳ τὸν λόγον ἐλάλει. John 16:25, 29 employs the similar contrast between παροιμία and παρρησία for Jesus' obscure sayings and their enlightened interpretation. The hermeneutical formula involved in the pesher exegesis in Qumran is similar. For the rôle this concept of interpreting Jesus' sayings played in the development of the genre of the Gospels, see James M. Robinson, "Einleitung," *Messiasgeheimnis und Geschichtsverständnis: Zur Gattungsgeschichte des Markus-Evangeliums* (Theologische Bücherei 81; München: Chr. Kaiser, 1989) v-ix: ix.

[20] Eusebius, *Hist. eccl.* 2.1.253.

[21] John Caesar Hawkins, *Horae Synopticae* (Oxford: Clarendon, 1899, second edition revised and supplemented 1909 [quoted here], reprinted 1968) xiii, translated Papias' reference: "Matthew composed the oracles ...." Kirsopp Lake, *Eusebius: The Ecclesiastical History with an English Translation* (LCL, 2 vols; London: Heinemann and Cambridge, Mass.: Harvard University Press, 1926, reprint 1959 [quoted here], 291, 297), translated "Interpretation of the Oracles of the Lord," "Matthew collected the oracles ... ."

pretation which with oracles is always necessary.[22]

In fact this is evident even in the usage of Papias himself. He uses λόγοι when referring to sayings, be they sayings of the presbyters (τοὺς τῶν πρεσβυτέρων ἀνέκρινον λόγους), the apostles (τοὺς μὲν τῶν ἀποστόλων λόγους) or Aristion's interpretation of Jesus' sayings (τῶν τοῦ κυρίου λόγων διηγήσεις).[23] Then Papias shifts to λόγια to refer to Peter's, and hence Mark's, lack of an arrangement of the Lord's oracles (οὐχ ὥσπερ σύνταξιν τῶν κυριακῶν ποιούμενος λογίων).[24] Since the λόγια of Mark are surely not limited to Jesus' sayings, the immediately following reference to Matthew collecting the oracles (τὰ λόγια συνετάξατο) should not be taken to refer to sayings only, but to the whole scope of the Gospel of Matthew.[25] Papias' book, which Eusebius referred to in terms of its title as Λογίων κυριακῶν ἐξηγήσεως,[26] was not limited to sayings of Jesus, for it included "marvels and other details,"[27] including the resurrection of a corpse in connection with the daughters of Philip, another miracle associated with Justus Barsabas, and a millenarianism that offended the intelligence of Eusebius.[28] Hence Papias' vocabulary provides no valid reason to consider his reference to the Gospel of Matthew as consisting of λόγια to be a mistake on his part for what should have been a reference to a prior sayings collection. In fact, he provides no documentation for λόγια as the *terminus technicus* for sayings of Jesus in primitive Christianity, which could then justify the use of λόγια in modern scholarship to designate the sayings source used by Matthew and Luke.

Yet, in fact, neither the discovery of the formula of "remembering" Jesus' λόγοι by Rendell Harris and Lock, nor the discovery of the *incipit* of the collection of Jesus' λόγοι by Grenfell and Hunt in *P. Oxy.* 654, which is actually the *incipit* of the *Gospel of Thomas*, nor Harnack's elevation of λόγοι into the title of Q led to a replacement of *Logia* with *Logoi* as the *terminus technicus* in scholarship. Instead, the designation Q emerged as a replacement for Λ (which, after all, could have been redefined as an abbreviation for Λόγοι.)

"Q." (with a period making it clear that it was meant as an abbreviation, representing *Quelle*) was first used in 1880,[29] but "Q" came to be used sim-

---

22 Dieter Lührmann, "Q: Sayings of Jesus or Logia?" *The Gospel behind the Gospels: Current Studies on Q* (Ronald A. Piper, ed.; NovTSup 75; Leiden: Brill, 1995) 97-116: 97-98, 108, 111.

23 Eusebius, *Hist. eccl.* 3.39.4, 7, 14.

24 Eusebius, *Hist. eccl.* 3.39.4, 15.

25 Eusebius, *Hist. eccl.* 3.39.16.

26 Eusebius, *Hist. eccl.* 3.39.1.

27 Eusebius, *Hist. eccl.* 3.39.8: παράδοξά τινα ἱστορεῖ καὶ ἄλλα.

28 Eusebius, *Hist. eccl.* 3.39.9-13.

29 The history of the designation Q has been worked out in debate with other suggested derivations by Frans Neirynck, "The Symbol Q (=Quelle)," *EThL* 54 (1978) 119-25; "Once More: The Symbol Q," *EThL* 55 (1979) 382-83, both republished in his collected essays *Evangelica: Gospel Studies – Études d'Évangile* (Leuven: Peeters and Leuven University Press, 1982) 683-89, 689-90, where the usage is traced back to Johannes Weiss in 1890, and then a "Note on the Siglum Q" in the second volume of collected essays, *Evangelica II: 1982–1991* (Leuven: University Press and Peeters, 1991) 474, tracing it back to Eduard Simons in 1880: *Hat der dritte Evangelist den kanonischen Matthäus benutzt?* (Bonn: Universitäts-Buchdruckerei von Carl Georgi). Simons used it as an abbreviation for *Quelle* in a dissertation at the Kaiser-Wilhelm-Universität Strassburg that persuaded his professor, Heinrich Julius Holtzmann, to give up his Urmarkus theory: Holtzmann, *Lehrbuch der historisch-kritischen Einleitung in das Neue Testament* (Freiburg i. Br.: Mohr-Siebeck, 1886²) 339. Neirynck quotes Simons to make clear that Simons normally used Λ, especially when envisaging Holtzmann's position. But when the position of Bernhard Weiss is involved, Simons can speak of "Λ (resp. Q.)" (p. 29), "Λ (Q)" (p. 30), or just "Q. (Die apostolische Quelle nach W.)" (p. 22), "Die W.'sche Q." (p. 95), or simply "Q." (p. 68). But Weiss' source was much more extensive than what we

ply as a symbol first in the 1890s, beginning with Johannes Weiss:

> … a dependence on Urmarkus (A) is excluded, since Luke is here not reflecting on Mark at all. Rather both are following another shared source, namely Q.[30]

Paul Wernle then accepted this symbol in 1899: "Let this – hypothetical – source be denoted with Q."[31]

John Caesar Hawkins illustrates the way in which this shift to "Q" replaced a shift to *Logoi*. For in 1909 he wrote:

> THE SOURCE LARGELY USED BY MATTHEW AND LUKE, APART FROM MARK. In the first edition of this book (1899) the title of the present Section was "The Logia of Matthew as a probable source." Since then the scholars of England and America have largely followed those of Germany in designating this source as Q (= *Quelle*). For it has been generally admitted that to call it "the Logia of Matthew" was unfairly "question-begging," as assuming that Matthew and Luke certainly used the document named by Papias … . But the abandonment of that name in favour of the neutral symbol Q need not involve any intention of begging the question in the other direction, by ignoring the reasons for holding that the only two documents named by the earliest writer who deals with sources at all are the two which bulk so largely in our First and Third Gospels.[32]

Yet from this it is clear that Hawkins still identified Papias' λόγια with Q. The "question-begging" simply went underground, hidden beneath the innocuously objective symbol Q. Indeed Hawkins still proposed as late as 1911 the title based on Papias, Κυριακὰ Λόγια.[33]

The result of this anomaly has been that the argument has needed to be repeated half a century later. In 1965 Roger Gryson gave a full report on research on the Papias issue to conclude:

> The result of these observations is that the usage of the word λόγιον in the fathers of the Second Century would not be able to serve to accredit the theories according to which, in the Testimony of Papias about Matthew, the words τὰ λόγια have in view sayings of Jesus or Old Testament oracles. It could be appealed to as an argument, on the other hand, by those who think that these words designate the ensemble of the material "put in order" by Matthew to compose his Gospel, and that these λόγια, like the κυριακὰ λόγια of which Mark has left us a remembrance in his work, are not only sayings of

now mean by Q, e.g., it included much narrative material: "Die Aufstellung der Matthäusquelle (Q)," *Die Quellen der synoptischen Überlieferung* (TU 32,3; Leipzig: J. C. Hinrichs'sche Buchhandlung, 1908) 1-75.

30 Johannes Weiss, "Die Verteidigung Jesu gegen den Vorwurf des Bündnisses mit Beelzebul," *ThStKr* 63 (1890) 557, cited by Neirynck, "The Symbol Q (= Quelle)," 686, n. 17:

> … eine Abhängigkeit vom Urmarkus (A) ist ausgeschlossen, weil Lukas hier auf Markus gar nicht reflektiert; weithin folgen beide einer andern gemeinsamen Quelle, nämlich Q.

The period had by then disappeared. See further Johannes Weiss, "Die Parabelrede bei Markus," *ThStKr* 64 (1891) 291; "Die Komposition der synoptischen Wiederkunftsrede," *ThStKr* 65 (1892) 248; *Die Predigt Jesu vom Reiche Gottes* (Göttingen: Vandenhoeck und Ruprecht, 1892) 8; ET: *Jesus' Proclamation of the Kingdom of God*, (Philadelphia: Fortress, 1971) 60. "Q" is then used in his *Evangelium des Lukas*, in Bernhard and Johannes Weiss, *Die Evangelien des Markus und Lukas* (KEK 1,2; 8th ed.; Göttingen: Vandenhoeck und Ruprecht, 1892) iii-iv, 279-83.

31 Paul Wernle, *Die synoptische Frage* (Leipzig, Freiburg im Breisgau, Tübingen: Mohr-Siebeck, 1899) 44: "Diese – hypothetische – Quelle sei mit Q bezeichnet."

32 Hawkins, *Horae Synopticae*^{2}, 107.

33 John Caesar Hawkins, "Probabilities as to the so-called Double Tradition of St. Matthew and St. Luke," *Studies in the Synoptic Problem: By Members of the University of Oxford* (ed. William Sanday; Oxford: Clarendon Press, 1911), 95-140: 119.

the Lord (τὰ λεχθέντα), but also narrations of his deeds and actions (τὰ πραχθέντα).[34]

That is to say, the language Eusebius uses (*Hist. eccl.* 3.39.15) with regard to the Gospel of Mark: οὐ μέντοι τάξει τὰ ὑπὸ τοῦ κυρίου ἢ λεχθέντα ἢ πραχθέντα ... οὐχ ὥσπερ σύνταξιν τῶν κυριακῶν ποιούμενος λογίων, seems to make clear that λόγια would include both λεχθέντα and πραχθέντα, and hence would not suggest a sayings collection when used in referring to the Gospel of Matthew in the continuation that immediately follows (Eusebius, *Hist. eccl.* 3.39.16).

The translation (that is to say, the interpretation) of Papias' cryptic comments has continued to be discussed. With regard to the title of Papias' work, Josef Kürzinger translated κυριακὰ λόγια as "'Words (statements) about the Lord' or 'related to the Lord,'" and ἐξήγησις in its basic meaning, "'presentation, depiction, communication.'"[35] But the interpretation of Papias' comment about Matthew is even more complex. In this regard Wayne Meeks sought to move beyond Kürzinger:

> Josef Kürzinger goes so far as to say that *hebrais dialektos* in the Papias report ... does not mean "Hebrew language" at all, but "a Jewish style." This is not convincing, but Kürzinger does make some very important observations about the way the sentence from Papias is to be understood. First, Eusebius has interrupted the continuity by inserting his own comment: "This is reported by Papias about Mark, and about Matthew this was said. ..." Read without the interruption, the Papias quotation does not present an independent statement about Matthew, but rather contrasts Mark, who did not make a literary composition, with Matthew, who did. Thus the emphasis is not on *hebraidi dialekto*, whatever it may mean, but on *synetaxato* ("composed"). Moreover, the contrastive clause that follows, which has so baffled modern interpreters, is not talking about translation at all. "Each" still refers to Matthew and Mark, *hermēneusen* means "presented, expounded, reported," and the meaning is that Matthew and Mark each expounded the gospel as best he could. Thus, if [166] Papias did know about a Semitic Gospel of Matthew, he does *not* describe its translation into Greek, *nor is a translation of*

---

[34] Roger Gryson, "A propos du Témoignage de Papias sur Matthieu: Le sens du mot λόγιον chez les Pères du second siècle," *EThL* 41 (1965) 530-47: 547:

> Il résulte de ces observations que l'usage du mot λόγιον, chez les Pères du second siècle, ne saurait servir à accréditer les théories selon lesquelles, dans le Témoignage de Papias sur Matthieu, les mots τὰ λόγια visent des paroles de Jésus ou des oracles vétéro-testamentaires. Il pourrait être invoqué comme argument, par contre, par ceux qui estiment que ces mots désignent l'ensemble de la matière "mise en ordre" par Matthieu pour composer son Évangile et que ces λόγια, comme les κυριακὰ λόγια dont Marc nous a consacré le souvenir dans son œuvre, ne sont pas seulement des dits du Seigneur (τὰ λεχθέντα) mais aussi des récits de ses faits et gestes (τὰ πραχθέντα).

A similar view was repeatedly advocated by Josef Kürzinger, "Das Papiaszeugnis und die Erstgestalt des Matthäusevangeliums," *BZ*, n.F. 4 (1960) 19-38; "Die Aussage des Papias von Hierapolis zur literarischen Form des Markusevangeliums," *BZ*, n.F. 21 (1977) 245-64; "Papias von Hierapolis: Zu Titel und Art seines Werkes," *BZ*, n.F. 23 (1979) 172-86: 176 (where he presents the same quotation from Gryson). These essays are reprinted in his collected essays: *Papias von Hierapolis und die Evangelien des Neuen Testaments: Gesammelte Aufsätze, Neuausgabe und Übersetzung der Fragemente, kommentierte Bibliographie* (Eichstätter Materialien, Abt. Philosophie und Theologie, 4; Regensburg: Pustet, 1983): *BZ* 1960 = 1983, 9-32; *BZ* 1977 = 1983, 43-67; *BZ* 1979 = 1983, 69-87:73. Citation is from the original publication.

[35] Kürzinger, "Papias von Hierapolis: Zu Titel und Art seines Werkes," 175, 179 (reprint 72, 76): "'Worte (Aussagen) über den Herrn' oder 'bezüglich des Herrn'"; "'Darbietung, Darstellung, Mitteilung.'"

Matthew ever described by the writers who report Papias' testimony.[36]

Ron Cameron, in his Harvard dissertation on the *Apocryphon of James* (Nag Hammadi Codex I 2), used this text, contemporary with Papias, to interpret Papias:

> But in terms of Papias's understanding of the history of the tradition, the reference to Matthew is designed to locate Matthew's testimony at the earliest state of transmission. By stating that Matthew "composed" (συνετάξατο) the λόγια "in the Hebrew language," Papias means that it was not in Greek, but in what was thought to be the language of Jesus himself. The import of [111] this statement is on the proximity of Matthew's written words with the original sayings of Jesus. The emphasis is thus not on an alleged Semitic Gospel of Matthew, nor on its putative translation into Greek, but on the earliness of the tradition and the reliability of its testimony. …
>
> The apologetic statement that "each interpreted" (ἡρμήνευσεν … ἕκαστος) that tradition as best he could is also designed to emphasize its written mode of transmission. This would seem to be confirmed by the passages in Lucian (*Hist. conscr.* 6, 47-48), which speak of the historians' "putting [112] facts into words" (ἑρμηνεῦσαι) in presenting or expounding their materials. Neither Mark, the ἑρμηνευτής of Peter, nor the unnamed interpreter(s) of Matthew is presented as a "translator"; each is rather understood as an "expositor," an exegete.[37]

Helmut Koester commented:

> It is noteworthy that the incipit of the *Apocryphon of James* says that the book was [34] written "in the Hebrew alphabet." Papias's reference to Matthew writing in Hebrew may rest upon such a statement in the original incipit of the book. Thus Papias would not be a witness to the existence for a Semitic original, but would simply report that such a reference occurred in the title of the book.[38]

In spite of such a variety of alternatives to the traditional interpretation of Papias, something approaching a consensus has tended to emerge. Werner Georg Kümmel concluded:

> It is in order to leave the Papias references out of consideration – in spite of their great age – when studying the literary relationships between the Gospels.[39]

Helmut Merkel agreed that Kümmel "must be reproducing the view widespread in the historical-critical camp":

> There is surely agreement today that the interpretation, advocated again and again since Schleiermacher, as referring to the sayings source, is inaccurate; after all, the fragment about Mark speaks also of λόγια κυριακά.[40]

---

36 Wayne Meeks, "Hypomnemata from an Untamed Sceptic: A Response to George Kennedy," *The Relationships Among the Gospels: An Interdisciplinary Dialogue* (ed. William O. Walker, Jr.; TUMSR 5; San Antonio, Tex.: Trinity University Press, 1978) 157-72: 165-66.

37 Ron Cameron, *Sayings Traditions in the Apocryphon of James* (HTS 34; Philadelphia: Fortress, 1984) 110-12.

38 Helmut Koester, *Ancient Christian Gospels: Their History and Development* (London: SCM, and Philadelphia: Trinity Press International, 1990) 33-34, n. 6. One may compare what is perhaps a similar apologetic interest both in the *incipit* and in a passage shortly thereafter in the *Gospel of Philip* (NHC II, 3: 51,29-30; 52,21-24):

> A Hebrew makes another Hebrew, and such a person is called "proselyte." …
>
> When we were Hebrews we were orphans and had only our mother, but when we became Christians we had both father and mother.

39 Werner Georg Kümmel, *Einleitung in das Neue Testament* (Heidelberg: Quelle & Meyer, 1980[20]) 29:

> … es ist daher geraten, die Papiasnotizen trotz ihres hohen Alters bei der Untersuchung der literarischen Beziehung der Synopt. ausser Betracht zu lassen.

ET: *Introduction to the New Testament* (Nashville: Abingdon, rev. ed. 1973) 55.

40 Helmut Merkel, "Die Überlieferungen der alten Kirche über das Verhältnis der Evangelien," *The*

Dieter Lührmann concurs in this view:

> The modern solution of the Synoptic Problem thus freed itself from the early church tradition. …
>
> Nobody today argues for the existence of Q on the basis of the Papias quotation in Eusebius. For all who follow the two-document hypothesis, it results from the analysis of the Synoptic Gospels.[41]

The misinterpretation of the Papias reference as attestation for an Aramaic Q has been largely responsible for the widespread assumption that it would be futile to seek to reconstruct a Greek, much less an Aramaic, archetype behind the Q texts of the Matthean and Lukan communities. But once Papias is no longer a factor in the study of Q, one impediment to its reconstruction is for all practical purposes eliminated.

Yet Wellhausen had argued for an Aramaic origin of Q, now less on the authority of Papias than on his own authority in Semitic linguistics:

> If these sayings are derived from Q, this source must have been available to both Evangelists still in Aramaic. In addition they both, to a large extent, used one and the same Greek translation, whereby admittedly the degree of their agreement in the Greek wording fluctuates for whole pericopes. Whether it suffices as an explanation for this unusual situation to say that they at times repeated an available translation each according to one's assessment and preference, at times literally, at times somewhat altered, and at times replaced by a new translation from the original, strikes me as somewhat problematic.[42]

Wellhausen then modified somewhat his concept of the Aramaic origin of Q, seeking to make more sense out of "this unusual situation" that he had quite rightly recognized as "somewhat problematic":

> That the pieces that agree in sequence in Matthew and Luke come from one source, i.e.

Interrelations of the Gospels (ed. David L. Dungan; Macon, Ga.: Mercer University Press, 1990) 566-90: 566, 571:

> … dürfte er die im historisch-kritischen Lager verbreitete Stimmung wiedergeben. …
>
> Einigkeit besteht wohl heute darüber, dass die seit Schleiermacher immer wieder vertretene Deutung auf die Logienquelle unzutreffend ist; spricht doch das Markusfragment ebenfalls von λόγια κυριακά.

41 Lührmann, "Q: Sayings of Jesus or Logia?" 101. This is in spite of the fact that Lührmann disagreed (109, n. 20) with the dissertation of his pupil, Ulrich H. J. Körtner, *Papias von Hierapolis* (FRLANT 133; Göttingen: Vandenhoeck und Ruprecht, 1983), who argued from Papias' comments on Mark that λόγια refers not specifically to sayings, but to deeds as well. Frans Neirynck, "Q: From Source to Gospel," *EThL* 71 (1995) 421-30: 422, n. 7, though agreeing to exclude Papias from the discussion, points out that Lührmann's "nobody" is a slight exaggeration, with reference to Helmut Koester, *Einführung in das Neue Testament* (Berlin and New York: Walter de Gruyter, 1980) 608; ET: *Introduction to the New Testament*. Vol. 2, *History and Literature of Early Christianity* (Hermeneia, Foundations and Facets; Philadelphia: Fortress, and Berlin and New York: de Gruyter, 1982) 172; Koester, *Ancient Christian Gospels*, 33, 189. But Koester once translates the title of Papias' work "Interpretations of the Oracles of the Lord," 337, n. 3 (though 33, 316: "Sayings").

42 Wellhausen, *Einleitung in die drei ersten Evangelien* (Berlin: Reimer, 1905[1]) 68:

> Wenn diese Sprüche aus Q stammen, so muss diese Quelle beiden Evangelisten noch aramäisch zugänglich gewesen sein. Daneben haben sie aber in grossem Umfange beide eine und die selbe griechische Übersetzung benutzt, wobei freilich der Grad ihrer Übereinstimmung im griechischen Wortlaut bei ganzen Perikopen schwankt. Ob man zur Erklärung dieses sonderbaren Tatbestandes damit auskommt, dass sie eine vorhandene Übersetzung je nach Ermessen und Belieben bald wörtlich wiederholten, bald etwas veränderten, und bald durch eine neue aus dem Original ersetzten, kommt mir etwas problematisch vor.

from Q, must be retained, although the degree of their agreement in the Greek wording fluctuates, and some variants can be satisfactorily derived only from a different reading or interpretation of an Aramaic original. [60] This fact is admittedly unusual, and in need of explanation: It is not to be assumed that the sources lay before both Evangelists in Greek (hence the agreement) as well as in Aramaic (hence the difference). Rather they both knew them only in Greek translation. This was originally one and the same, but it then separated into recensions, which arose from subsequent corrections, in part based on the Aramaic original, much as is the case, e.g., in the Septuagint. Matthew used a different recension than did Luke.[43]

The English tradition shared the prevalent assumption of an Aramaic origin of Q, including the appeal to an Aramaic Q to explain the divergences between Matthew and Luke. Representative of the first half of the century is T. W. Manson:

> We have already seen that the tradition of the teaching circulated at first in Aramaic, and that probably the first considerable collections of it would be made in the original language. There is nothing improbable in the supposition that several Greek versions of such a document might be made. We know that at least four Greek versions of the Old Testament were made at various times and for various reasons. These, however, are possibilities: we must look now at the facts. We have two versions of Q – Q according to Matthew and Q according to Luke. The differences between them can be explained in part as editorial – stylistic or other "improvements" carried out by the Evangelist. But after we have allowed for these there is still a certain amount of difference in wording, and some of it at least can be explained on the supposition that we have before us two different renderings of a single Aramaic original.[44]

In the second half of the century it was Matthew Black who most authoritatively presented the argument for an Aramaic origin of Q, by maintaining that Q reflected (mis)translations of Aramaic. Yet it is striking to what a large extent he had already reduced the claims for an Aramaic origin, even though at this time he was the main advocate of this view:

> This evidence of "non-translation Greek" in Q is just as important as the evidence of translation; and it points to something more than minor editorial improvements by the Evangelists. In the light of it, it is doubtful if we are justified in describing Q, without qualification, as a translation of Aramaic. Certainly it seems clear that the most the Aramaic element can *prove* is an Aramaic origin, not always translation of an Ara-

[43] Wellhausen, *Einleitung in die drei ersten Evangelien*, 1911², the second revised edition reprinted with the same pagination in Wellhausen's *Evangelienkommentare* (Berlin, New York: de Gruyter, 1987) 59-60:

> Dass die in der Reihenfolge bei Matthäus und Lukas übereinstimmenden Stücke aus Einer Quelle, also aus Q stammen, muss festgehalten werden, obgleich der Grad ihrer Übereinstimmung im griechischen Wortlaut schwankt und einige Varianten nur aus verschiedener Lesung oder Deutung eines aramäischen Originals be-[60]friedigend abgeleitet werden können. Diese Tatsache ist freilich sonderbar und bedarf der Erklärung. Es ist nicht anzunehmen, dass die Quellen beiden Evangelisten sowohl griechisch (daher die Übereinstimmung) als auch aramäisch (daher die Differenz) vorgelegen haben. Sie haben sie vielmehr beide nur in griechischer Übersetzung gekannt. Diese war ursprünglich eine und die selbe, ging aber dann in Rezensionen aus einander, die aus nachträglichen Korrekturen, zum teil nach dem aramäischen Original, entstanden sind, ähnlich wie es z. B. in der Septuaginta der Fall ist. Matthäus benutzt eine andere Rezension als Lukas.

[44] H. D. A. Major, T. W. Manson, C. J. Wright, *The Mission and Message of Jesus: An Exposition of the Gospels in the Light of Modern Research* (New York: Dutton, 1938, 1953⁶ [quoted here]) 18.

maic original; and *it is the Greek literary factor which has had the final word with the shaping of the Q tradition.*

The evidence from the Gospels themselves for the existence of an Aramaic document is necessarily speculative.[45]

John S. Kloppenborg drew the inference, constitutive of the current efforts to reconstruct a critical text of Q, that the divergences between Matthew and Luke in the wording of Q are not to be explained in terms of (mis)translations, but rather in terms of the Evangelists' redaction:

> While Black has convincingly demonstrated the presence of Semitisms in Q, the case for a mistranslation hypothesis is insecure at best. Moreover, this type of explanation hinges on so many imponderables – such as both Matthew and Luke knowing Aramaic, and only occasionally using that knowledge – that in comparison with the redactional solution it is clearly the more cumbersome one. To be convincing a translation hypothesis would have to explain not only the occasional variation but extensive portions of the Matthew-Luke disagreements. Moreover, it would have to show that the variations cannot be accounted for by the more proximate explanation, namely, redactional modification. In the absence of such demonstrations, we are obligated to conclude that while parts of Q betray a Semitizing Greek style, and possibly an origin in an Aramaic-speaking milieu, there is no convincing proof of a literary formulation in Aramaic.[46]

To this Black in turn responded:

> That this complicated issue is not so easily disposed of, I have argued in a recent article; Papias may well be referring to a "Hebrew", i.e. Aramaic Chreiae (Sayings, etc.) collection of [34] which Q is the Greek equivalent and for which it is the main source. … [36]
>
> What I sought to do was to indicate those *parts* of Q which were originally composed in Aramaic; I would now add, parts transmitted *either* orally *or* in written form, and that this was the Aramaic *Vorlage* of Q. We may not be able to prove that there was an Aramaic Chreiae collection identical with parts of Q, but we cannot, as Kloppenborg does, reject the hypothesis altogether.[47]

Kloppenborg responded with the conclusion:

> The thesis of an Aramaic origin of Q is extraordinarily weak. The origin of the speculation, Papias's statement about Matthew, is legendary at best. The linguistic data employed to demonstrate an Aramaic origin is scant and what little there is admits of more economical explanations that avoid having to posit yet another document. Finally, the dazzlingly improbable logistics needed to account for Matthew's *and* Luke's occasional revision of their Greek Q by recourse to a *written* Aramaic version that *both* had (and could read!) reduce the likelihood of demonstrating an Aramaic Q to near zero.[48]

The trend away from interpreting Papias' reference to "Hebrew" λόγια as a reference to Jesus' λόγοι in Q, the dwindling number of (mis)transla-

---

45 Matthew Black, *An Aramaic Approach to the Gospels and Acts* (Oxford: Clarendon Press, 1946¹, 1954², 1967³ [quoted here]), "Synoptic Variants from Aramaic," 186-96: 191 (introduced first among the "Supplementary Notes" in 1954², 270-78: 274, i.e. absent in 1946¹); and "Mistranslation and Interpretation of Aramaic," 197-243, including "The Source Q," 203-8.

46 John S. Kloppenborg, *The Formation of Q: Trajectories in Ancient Wisdom Collections* (Studies in Antiquity and Christianity; Philadelphia: Fortress, 1987; reprint, Trinity Press International, 2000), "The Original Language of Q," 51-64: 59.

47 Matthew Black, "The Aramaic Dimension in Q with Notes on Luke 17.22 Matthew 24.26 (Luke 17.23)," *JSNT* 40 (1990) 33-41: 33-34, 36. He refers to his article, "The Use of Rhetorical Terminology in Papias on Mark and Matthew," *JSNT* 37 (1989) 31-41.

48 Kloppenborg Verbin, *Excavating Q*, 66-73: "The Language of Q," 80.

tions from a postulated written Aramaic Q to which one could appeal to explain divergences of wording between Matthew and Luke, as well as Q's use of the LXX,[49] have led to the general abandonment of the conjecture that Q was originally in Aramaic and then translated differently into Greek. Rather Q is a Greek text whose archetype, lying behind both Matthew and Luke, one might well try to reconstruct.

Matthew without Q
Schweitzer's Jesus the Apocalypticist

Of course the central position that Q had attained a century ago in Protestant Liberalism's quest of the historical Jesus in terms of ethical idealism did not go unchallenged at the time. It was Albert Schweitzer who carried to its ultimate consequences a dramatic renunciation of that quest, as a modernization of Jesus by projecting our ideology back on him.

Central to Schweitzer's own solution was his assumption that Q did not exist. For he preferred Ferdinand Christian Baur's prioritizing of Matthew to the alternative of a document Q that had established itself in the intervening trajectory from Weisse to Holtzmann:

> Research was initially spared having to experience the problem in its whole weight, in that it, under the influence of Christian Hermann Weiße, *Die Evangelienfrage* (1856), and Heinrich Julius Holtzmann, *Die synoptischen Evangelien* (1863), gives up the view advocated by Ferdinand Christian Baur (1792-1860) and the Tübingen School, to the effect that the Gospel of Matthew is the oldest and most original, and regards the Gospel of Mark to be this. The preference for the shorter Gospel made it possible for it to evaluate the significant material that Matthew offers above and beyond that of Mark to be not fully valid. And it is precisely this that contains the discourses and reports in which Jesus' thought world is shown to belong to that of late Jewish eschatology. It is especially the Sermon on the Mount (Matthew 5-7), the great discourse at the sending out of the disciples (Matthew 10), the inquiry of the Baptist and the statements of Jesus it called forth (Matthew 11), the discourse on the coming of the Son of man and the judgment he will hold (Matthew 25). ...
>
> For the quest of the historical Jesus, the point is not which of the two oldest Gospels could be a little bit older than the other. Incidentally, this literary question will hardly ever be solved. With the fragmentary report of Mark, the historical problem of the life of Jesus could not be resolved, indeed would not even come in view. The reports of the two oldest Gospels are in their way of equal value. That of Matthew is, however, as the more complete, of more value. In substance, Ferdinand Christian Baur and his school, in preferring it, are still right.[50]

---

[49] Siegfried Schulz, *Q: Die Spruchquelle der Evangelisten* (Zürich: Theologischer Verlag, 1972), "Die Septuaginta-Benutzung," 27-28, 49-50. For a critical review of Schulz' book see Paul Hoffmann, *BZ* 19 (1975) 104-15, and with regard to the exaggerated importance of the LXX, 108-9.

[50] Albert Schweitzer, *Von Reimarus zu Wrede: Eine Geschichte der Leben-Jesu-Forschung* (Tübingen: Mohr-Siebeck, 1906). The second edition, entitled only *Die Geschichte der Leben-Jesu-Forschung* (Tübingen: Mohr-Siebeck, 1913), is considerably revised, especially in the concluding sections under discussion here. The quotations are from the first edition with the pagination in the second edition, when parallel (though, even then, copyedited to produce a smoother text), given in parentheses, both according to 1951[6] and to the republication as Siebenstern-Taschenbuch 77/78, München, 1966. A retrospective "Vorrede," dated 1950, included only in the German editions, beginning with 1951[6], is quoted, here, vi, xii (1951) and 30, 36 (1966):

> Das Problem in seiner ganzen Schwere erfahren zu müssen bleibt der Forschung vorerst

Though Schweitzer was guarded in his statements (Holtzmann had, after all, been his professor in Strassburg), the position that he took on the sources only makes sense if he considered the canonical Gospel of Matthew to be the product of an eyewitness, which amounts to treating it as a definitive work of the apostle Matthew, the prevalent pre-critical view ever since Papias. He simply dismissed as absurd efforts to dismantle into its sources Matthew's Mission Instructions, whose detailed historicity was decisive for his own interpretation of Jesus' public ministry. Whereas one maintained, then as now, that material from the Markan apocalypse was interpolated into the Mission Instructions of Mark and Q, which were conflated both with each other and with other Q and special Matthean material, Schweitzer maintained:

> Thus this discourse [Matt 10] is historical as a whole and down to the smallest detail precisely because, according to the view of modern theology, it must be judged unhistorical. …
>
> That being so, we may judge with what right the modern psychological theology dismisses the great Matthean discourses off-hand as mere "composite structures." Just let any one try to show how the Evangelist when he was racking his brains over the task of making a "discourse at the sending forth of the disciples," half by the method of piecing it together out of traditional sayings and "primitive theology," and half by inventing it, lighted on the curious idea of making Jesus speak entirely of inopportune and unpractical matters; and of then going on to provide the evidence that they never happened.[51]

> dadurch erspart, dass sie unter dem Einfluss von Christian Hermann Weisses "Die Evangelienfrage" (1856) und Heinrich Julius Holtzmanns "Die synoptischen Evangelien" (1863) die von Ferdinand Christian Baur (1792-1860) und der Tübingerschule vertretene Ansicht, daß das Matthäusevangelium das älteste und ursprünglichste sei, aufgibt und als solches das Markusevangelium ansieht. Die Bevorzugung dieses kürzeren Evangeliums erlaubt es ihr, das bedeutende Material, das Matthäus über das des Markus hinaus bietet, nicht als ganz vollgültig zu bewerten. Und gerade dieses enthält die Reden und Berichte, in denen sich die Zugehörigkeit der Gedankenwelt Jesu zu der der spätjüdischen Eschatologie bekundet. Vornehmlich sind dies die Bergpredigt (Mt 5-7), die grosse Rede bei der Aussendung der Jünger (Mt 10), die Anfrage des Täufers und die durch sie veranlassten Äusserungen Jesu (Mt 11), die Rede vom Kommen des Menschensohnes und des von ihm abzuhaltenden Gerichts (Mt 25). …
>
> Für die Leben-Jesu-Forschung kommt es nicht darauf an, welches der beiden ältesten Evangelien ein klein wenig älter sein könnte als das andere. Diese literarische Frage wird sich überdies kaum je entscheiden lassen. Mit dem lückenhaften Bericht des Markus wäre das historische Problem des Lebens Jesu nicht zu lösen, ja nicht einmal zu erkennen gewesen. Die Berichte der beiden ältesten Evangelien sind ihrer Art nach gleichwertig. Das des Matthäus ist aber als das vollständigere das wertvollere. Sachlich haben Ferdinand Christian Baur und seine Schüler mit ihrer Bevorzugung desselben Recht behalten.

(In the sixth edition Baur's last name is omitted, but is added in the 1966 edition.) ET: *The Quest of the Historical Jesus: A Critical Study of Its Progress from Reimarus to Wrede* (New York: Macmillan, 1910, paperback edition 1961, reprint 1968), does not include this "Vorrede" of 1950. (Otherwise, it is the 1968 edition that is quoted.)

51 Schweitzer, *Von Reimarus zu Wrede*, 360 (*Die Geschichte der Leben-Jesu-Forschung*, 410 [1951] and 420 [1966]):

> So ist die Aussendungsrede als Ganzes und bis in das kleinste Detail geschichtlich, gerade weil sie nach der Auffassung der modernen Theologie als ungeschichtlich erfunden werden muss. …
>
> Danach beurteile man, mit welchem Recht die modern-psychologische Theologie die grossen matthäischen Reden kurzerhand als "Redekompositionen" hinstellt. Man beweise doch einmal, wie der Evangelist, der an seiner Feder saugte, um eine Aussendungsrede aus überlieferten Sprüchen und aus der "Gemeindetheologie" halb zusammenzustellen,

Schweitzer proposed going beyond Johannes Weiß' discovery of the eschatological nature of Jesus' preaching about the kingdom,[52] by carrying this eschatological interpretation consistently through all of Jesus' "conduct and action" down to the very end of the public ministry:

> Johannes Weiß demonstrates the thoroughly eschatological character of Jesus' proclamation of the kingdom of God. My contribution consists primarily in that I proceed to make comprehensible not only his proclamation but also his conduct and action as conditioned by the eschatological expectation.[53]

This led to Schweitzer's own "life of Jesus," with which his *Quest of the Historical Jesus* concluded. His point of departure is Jesus' fascination with parables of harvest:

> If this genuinely "historical" interpretation of the mystery of the Kingdom of God is correct, Jesus must have expected the coming of the Kingdom at harvest time. And that is just what He did expect. It is for that reason that He sends out His disciples to make known in Israel, as speedily as may be, what is about to happen.[54]

Jesus intended the Mission of the Twelve as his final act before the end:

> He tells them in plain words (Matt. x. 23), that He does not expect to see them back in the present age. The Parousia of the Son of Man, [359] which is logically and temporally identical with the dawn of the kingdom, will take place before they shall have completed a hasty journey through the cities of Israel to announce it.[55]

Schweitzer described "the significance of the sending forth of the disciples and the discourse which Jesus uttered upon that occasion" as follows:

> Jesus' purpose is to set in motion the eschatological development of history, to let loose the final woes, the confusion and strife, from which shall issue the Parousia, and so to introduce the supra-mundane phase of the eschatological drama.[56]

> halb zu erfinden, auf den seltsamen Gedanken kommen konnte, Jesum von lauter unzeitgemässen und unsachlichen Dingen reden zu lassen und nachher selber zu konstatieren, daß sie nicht in Erfüllung gingen.

ET: *The Quest of the Historical Jesus*, 363.

52 Weiss, *Die Predigt Jesu vom Reiche Gottes*. ET: *Jesus' Proclamation of the Kingdom of God*.

53 Schweitzer, *Die Geschichte der Leben-Jesu-Forschung*, "Vorrede zur sechsten Auflage," viii [1951] and 32 [1966]:

> Johannes Weiss weist den durchaus eschatologischen Charakter der Verkündigung Jesu vom Reiche Gottes nach. Mein Beitrag besteht hauptsächlich darin, dass ich dazu fortschreite, nicht nur seine Verkündigung sondern auch sein Verhalten und Handeln als durch die eschatologische Erwartung bedingt begreiflich zu machen.

54 Schweitzer, *Von Reimarus zu Wrede*, 355 (*Die Geschichte der Leben-Jesu-Forschung*, 405 [1951] and 415 [1966]):

> Ist diese in Wahrheit "historische" Deutung des Geheimnisses des Reiches Gottes richtig, so muss Jesus zur Erntezeit den Anbruch des Reiches Gottes erwartet haben. Das hat er wirklich getan. Darum sendet er ja die Jünger aus, damit sie eilend in Israel verkünden, was kommen soll.

ET: *The Quest of the Historical Jesus*, 358.

55 Schweitzer, *Von Reimarus zu Wrede*, 355 (*Die Geschichte der Leben-Jesu-Forschung*, 405 [1951] and 416 [1966]):

> Jesus sagt den Jüngern in dürren Worten, Mt 10, 23, daß er sie in diesem Äon nicht mehr zurückerwartet. Die Parusie des Menschensohnes, die mit dem Einbruch des Reiches logisch und zeitlich identisch ist, wird stattfinden, ehe sie mit ihrer Verkündigung die Städte Israels durcheilt haben.

ET: *The Quest of the Historical Jesus*, 358-59.

56 Schweitzer, *Von Reimarus zu Wrede*, 367:

> Diese Erwägungen über den besonderen Charakter der synoptischen Eschatologie waren notwendig, um die Bedeutung der Aussendung und der sie begleitenden Rede zu verstehen. Jesus will die eschatologische Geschichte in Gang bringen, die Enddrangsal, die Verwirrung und den Aufruhr, aus denen die Parusie hervorgehen soll, entfesseln und die überirdische Phase des eschatologischen Dramas einleiten.

ET: *The Quest of the Historical Jesus*, 371.

He was convinced that "at the time of their mission," Jesus "did not expect them to return before the Parousia."[57] But that is in fact just what happened:

> There followed neither the sufferings, nor the outpouring of the Spirit, nor the Parousia of the Son of Man. The disciples returned safe and sound and full of a proud satisfaction; for one promise had been realized – the power which had been given them over the demons.[58]

Schweitzer drew the inevitable consequence:

> It is equally clear, and here the dogmatic considerations which guided the resolutions of Jesus become still more prominent, that this prediction was not fulfilled. The disciples returned to Him; and the appearing of the Son of Man had not take place. The actual history disavowed the dogmatic history on which the action of Jesus had been based. An event of supernatural history which must take place, and must take place at that particular point of time, failed to come about. That was for Jesus, who lived wholly in the dogmatic history, the first "historical" occurrence, the central event which closed the former period of His activity and gave the coming period a new character.[59]

The failure of the apocalyptic end to come before the end of the mission must have been a terrible letdown for Jesus. He felt compelled to change his strategy:

> This change was due to the non-fulfillment of the promises made in the discourse at the sending forth of the Twelve. He had thought then to let loose the final tribulation and so compel the coming of the Kingdom. And the cataclysm had not occurred. He had expected it also after the return of the disciples. …
>
> In leaving Galilee He abandoned the hope that the final tribulation would begin of itself. If it delays, that means that there is still something to be done, and yet another of the violent must lay violent hands upon the Kingdom of God. The movement of repentance had not been sufficient. When, in accordance with His commission, by sending forth the disciples with their message, he hurled the fire-brand which should

---

57 Schweitzer, *Von Reimarus zu Wrede*, 383:

> …zur Zeit der Aussendung, als er sie vor der Parusie nicht mehr zurückerwartete… .

ET: *The Quest of the Historical Jesus*, 386.

58 Schweitzer, *Von Reimarus zu Wrede*, 360 (*Die Geschichte der Leben-Jesu-Forschung*, 411 [1951] and 421 [1966]):

> Es traf aber weder das Leiden, noch die Geistesausgiessung, noch die Parusie des Menschensohnes ein, sondern gesund und frisch, voll stolzer Genugtuung kehrten die Jünger zum Herrn zurück. Eine Verheissung war real geworden: die Vollmacht, die er ihnen über die Dämonen gegeben.

ET: *The Quest of the Historical Jesus*, 364. (Schweitzer did not point out that this anti-climactic return of the disciples from their mission is not in Matthew, but only in Mark 6:30 and Luke 10:17-20. Indeed the "proud satisfaction" in "the power which had been given them over the demons" is only in Luke, althrough Schweitzer had confidence primarily in Matthew, and to a lesser extent in Mark, and even less in Luke.)

59 Schweitzer, *Von Reimarus zu Wrede*, 355 (*Die Geschichte der Leben-Jesu-Forschung*, 406 [1951] and 416 [1966]):

> Ebenso klar ist aber, und hier tritt das Dogmatische der Entschliessungen Jesu noch stärker hervor, dass diese Weissagung nicht in Erfüllung ging. Die Jünger kehrten zu ihm zurück und die Erscheinung des Menschensohnes fand nicht statt. Die natürliche Geschichte desavourierte die dogmatische, nach welcher Jesus gehandelt hatte. Ein Ereignis der übernatürlichen Geschichte, welches stattfinden mußte, in jenem Zeitpunkte stattfinden mußte, blieb aus. Das war für Jesus, der einzig in der dogmatischen Geschichte lebte, das erste "geschichtliche" Ereignis, das Zentralereignis, welches seine öffentliche Tätigkeit nach rückwärts abschliesst, nach vorn neu orientiert.

ET: *The Quest of the Historical Jesus*, 359.

kindle the fiery trials of the Last Time, the flame went out.[60]

So Jesus determined to go to Jerusalem for Passover, in order to provoke there his own martyrdom as an alternate way to compel God to bring in the end:

> … His death must at last compel the Coming of the Kingdom. … [391]
>
> The new thought of His own passion has its basis therefore in the authority with which Jesus was armed to bring about the beginning of the final tribulation. … For now He identifies his condemnation and execution, which are to take place on natural lines, with the predicted pre-Messianic tribulations. This imperious forcing of eschatology into history is also its destruction; its assertion and abandonment at the same time.[61]

This heroic resolve ended in a second, even more painful encounter with actual history, leading to his last anguished cry: "My God, my God, why have you abandoned me?"

> The Baptist appears, and cries: "Repent, for the Kingdom of Heaven is at hand." Soon after that comes Jesus, and in the knowledge that He is the coming Son of Man lays hold of the wheel of the world to set it moving on that last revolution which is to bring all ordinary history to a close. It refuses to turn, and He throws [391] Himself upon it. Then it does turn; and crushes Him. Instead of bringing in the eschatological conditions, He has destroyed them. The wheel rolls onward, and the mangled body of the one immeasurably great Man, who was strong enough to think of Himself as the spiritual ruler of mankind and to bend history to His purpose, is hanging upon it still. That is His victory and His reign.[62]

Subsequent scholarship has shied away from Schweitzer's all-too-apocalyptic public ministry of Jesus. Such a picture of a deluded fanatic is hardly appetizing. Instead, it has preferred Weiss' limitation to the eschatological preaching of Jesus, exemplified perhaps most clearly in Rudolf Bultmann's

---

60 Schweitzer, *Von Reimarus zu Wrede*, 385-86:

> Die Wandlung beruht auf dem Nichteintreten der Verheissungen der Aussendungsrede. Er hatte damals die Enddrangsal zu entfachen gemeint, um damit das Reich herbeizuzwingen. Und der Aufruhr war ausgeblieben. Er hatte ihn auch nach der Rückkehr der Jünger noch erwartet. … [386]
>
> Mit dem Verlassen des Bodens Galiläas gibt er die Hoffnung auf, dass sich die Drangsal von sich aus einstellen werde. Wenn sie ausbleibt, will dies besagen, dass noch eine Leistung fehlt und noch ein Gewalttätiger zu den Vergewaltigern des Reiches Gottes hinzutreten müsse. Die Bussbewegung hatte nicht ausgereicht. Als er seiner Vollmacht gemäss bei der Aussendung den Feuerbrand, der die Drangsal zum Auslodern bringen sollte, in die Welt schleuderte, erlosch er.

ET: *The Quest of the Historical Jesus*, 389.

61 Schweitzer, *Von Reimarus zu Wrede*, 387, 388:

> … sein Tod — endlich — das Reich herbeizwingt. … [388]
>
> Der neue Leidensgedanke ist also seinem Wesen nach begründet in der auf das Heraufführen der Drangsal gehenden Vollmacht, mit welcher Jesus in der Welt auftritt. … Denn jetzt identifiziert er seine natürliche Verurteilung und Hinrichtung mit der geweissagten vormessianischen Drangsal. Dieses gewaltsame Hineinzerren der Eschatologie in die Geschichte ist zugleich ihre Aufhebung; ein Bejahen und Preisgeben zugleich.

ET: *The Quest of the Historical Jesus*, 390-91.

62 Schweitzer, *Von Reimarus zu Wrede*, 367:

> Da erscheint der Täufer und ruft: Tuet Busse! das Reich Gottes ist nahe herbeigekommen! Kurz darauf greift Jesus, als der, welcher sich als den kommenden Menschensohn weiss, in die Speichen des Weltrades, dass es in Bewegung komme, die letzte Drehung mache und die natürliche Geschichte der Welt zu Ende bringe. Da es nicht geht, hängt er sich dran. Es dreht sich und zermalmt ihn. Statt die Eschatologie zu bringen, hat er sie vernichtet. Das Weltrad dreht sich weiter und die Fetzen des Leichnams des einzig unermesslich großen Menschen, der gewaltig genug war, um sich als den geistigen Herrscher der Menschheit zu erfassen und die Geschichte zu vergewaltigen, hängen noch immer daran. Das ist sein Siegen und Herrschen.

ET: *The Quest of the Historical Jesus*, 370-71.

Jesus and the Word.[63] But Schweitzer was in a sense correct, that such an apocalyptic message must have meant something in Jesus' actual practise.

Yet Schweitzer's position was untenable for ongoing critical scholarship, especially because his methodological presuppositions, such as the non-existence of Q, were already out of date. His attempt at a life of Jesus based on an eye-witness account by Matthew only serves to illustrate the price one pays for such a reversion from critical scholarship to a more traditional view of the sources, at least if one were to operate with the remorseless consistency of a genius such as Schweitzer.

Q as the Essence of Christianity or the Kerygma Harnack vs. Wellhausen, Barth, and Bultmann

Once William Wrede had removed Mark from the status of a historically accurate report on which the quest of the historical Jesus could confidently build,[64] it was Q to which critical scholarship had naturally turned. For it was upon the sayings of Jesus that Adolf von Harnack had built his "essence of Christianity":

> If, however, we take a general view of Jesus' teaching, we shall see that it may be grouped under three heads. They are each of such a nature as to contain the whole, and hence it can be exhibited in its entirety under any one of them.
>
> *Firstly, the kingdom of God and its coming.*
> *Secondly, God the Father and the infinite value of the human soul.*
> *Thirdly, the higher righteousness and the commandment of love.*[65]
>
> But the fact that the whole of Jesus' message may be reduced to these two heads – God as the Father, and the human soul so ennobled that it can and does unite with Him – shows us that the Gospel is in no wise a positive religion like the

63 Rudolf Bultmann, *Jesus* (Tübingen: Mohr-Siebeck, 1926[1], 1929[2] (with many subsequent reprints), ET: *Jesus and the Word* (New York: Scribner's Sons, 1934). In the "Translators' Preface to the New Edition" of 1958, Louise Pettibone Smith and Erminie Huntress Lantero explain the enlarged title: "It was felt by both publishers and translators that the title, *Jesus and the Word*, would convey a more definite idea of the content and viewpoint of the book than the original title, *Jesus*. This change was made with the approval of the author."

64 William Wrede, *Das Messiasgeheimnis in den Evangelien* (Göttingen: Vandenhoeck & Ruprecht, 1901). ET: *The Messianic Secret* (Cambridge and London: Clarke, 1971).

65 Adolf Harnack, *Das Wesen des Christentums: 16 Vorlesungen vor Studierenden aller Fakultäten im Wintersemester 1899/1900 an der Universität Berlin* (Leipzig: Hinrichs'sche Buchhandlung, 1900) 33. A student, Walther Becker, took down the lectures in shorthand, which Harnack edited for publication. It was an immediate best-seller: 1900[3] (11th to 15th thousand [quoted here]), 45th to 50th thousand 1903, 56th to 60th thousand 1908, 70th thousand 1925; more recent reprints: Adolf Harnack, *Das Wesen des Christentums*: Neuauflage zum fünfzigsten Jahrestag des ersten Erscheinens mit einem Geleitwort von Rudolf Bultmann (Stuttgart: Klotz, 1950); Adolf Harnack, *Das Wesen des Christentums*: Mit einem Geleitwort von Wolfgang Trillhaas (Gütersloher Taschenbücher / Siebenstern 227; Gütersloh: Gütersloher Verlagshaus Mohn, 1985); Adolf Harnack, *Das Wesen des Christentums*: Herausgegeben und kommentiert von Trutz Rendtorff (Gütersloh: Kaiser / Gütersloher Verlagshaus, 1999) 33 (1900), 40 (1985), and 87 (1999):

> Überschauen wir aber die Predigt Jesu, so können wir drei Kreise aus ihr gestalten. Jeder Kreis ist so geartet, dass er die *ganze* Verkündigung enthält; in jedem kann sie daher vollständig zur Darstellung gebracht werden:
>
> *Erstlich, das Reich Gottes und sein Kommen,*
> *Zweitens, Gott der Vater und der unendliche Wert der Menschenseele,*
> *Drittens, die bessere Gerechtigkeit und das Gebot der Liebe.*

ET: *What Is Christianity* (London, Edinburgh, Oxford: Williams and Norgate, and New York: Putnam, 1901, 3rd rev. ed. [quoted here] 1904) 52.

rest; that it contains no statutory or particularistic elements; *that it is, therefore, religion itself*.[66]

But Wellhausen understood Q much more in analogy to Wrede's Mark. For, in his view, Q was later than Mark, hence hardly more reliable:

> Just as Mark has priority for the narrative material, just so he also has it for the discourse material. He is the oldest Gospel author. … [88].
>
> What is most important for the comparison is what appears to be only a superficial difference: the source [Q], which in Mark is narrowly contained, in Matthew and Luke trickles through on all sides. This is enough to prove the priority of Mark, also prior to Q.[67]
>
> So Q is also from Jerusalem, and indeed (with regard to Jesus himself) more explicit than is Mark, but younger than it is. If one may claim for this document the verse Matt 23:35 (Luke 11:50), then it was first composed only a rather long time after A. D. 67 or 68, … .[68]

Harnack's reconstruction of Q complete with commentary was in large measure intended as a refutation of Wellhausen:

> I, on the contrary, believe that I can show in the following pages that Wellhausen in his characteristic of Q has unconsciously allowed himself to be influenced by the tendencies of St. Matthew and St. Luke, that he has attributed to Q what belongs to these gospels, and that in not a few passages he has preferred St. Mark on insufficient grounds. The conclusions at which I have arrived stand therefore in strong opposition to the results of his criticism.[69]

Yet he nonetheless retained the assumption of a hypothetical Aramaic origin. For this was involved in ascribing to it apostolic Matthean authorship, which in turn justified his according to Q ultimate authority:

> Seeing that our St. Matthew cannot have been [249] composed by an Apostle, and that the tradition: Ματθαῖος Ἑβραΐδι διαλέκτῳ τὰ λόγια συνετάξατο, already dates from about A. D. 100, there is a strong balance of probability that Q is a work of St. Matthew; but more cannot be said. … But whoever the author, or rather the redactor, of Q may have been, he was a man deserving of the highest respect. To his reverence and faith-

---

66 Harnack, *Das Wesen des Christentums*, 41 (1900), 47 (1985), and 96 (1999):

> Indem man aber die ganze Verkündigung Jesu auf diese beiden Stücke zurückführen kann – Gott als der Vater, und die menschliche Seele so geadelt, dass sie sich mit ihm zusammenzuschliessen vermag und zusammenschliesst –, zeigt es sich, dass das Evangelium überhaupt keine positive Religion ist wie die anderen, dass es nichts Statuarisches und Partikularistisches hat, *dass es also die Religion selbst ist*.

ET: *What Is Christianity*, 65.

67 Wellhausen, *Einleitung in die drei ersten Evangelien*, 1905¹: 84; 1911²: 75:

> Für die Vergleichung ist am wichtigsten der scheinbar nur äusserliche Unterschied, dass die Quelle, die bei Markus eng eingefasst ist, bei Matthäus und Lukas nach allen Seiten durchsickert. Er genügt zum Beweise der Priorität des Markus, auch vor Q.

68 Wellhausen, *Einleitung in die drei ersten Evangelien*, 1905^1: 87-88 (similar also 1911^2: 78-79):

> Wie Markus die Priorität für den Erzählungsstoff hat, so hat er sie auch für den Redestoff. Er ist der älteste evangelische Schriftsteller. … [88].
>
> Q ist also ebenfalls jerusalemisch und zwar (in Bezug auf Jesus selber) ausgesprochener als Markus, aber jünger als er. Wenn man den Vers Mt. 23,35 (Lc. 11,50) für diese Schrift in Anspruch nehmen darf, so ist sie erst längere Zeit nach A. D. 67 oder 68 abgefasst ….

69 Harnack, *Sprüche und Reden Jesu*, 136:

> Dem gegenüber glaube ich in dem Folgenden zeigen zu können, dass Wellhausen sich bei seiner Charakteristik von Q unwillkürlich von den Tendenzen des Matth. (und Luk.) hat bestimmen lassen, dass er jenem aufgebürdet hat, was diesen gehört, und dass er ohne zureichenden Grund an nicht wenigen Stellen Markus bevorzugt. Die Ergebnisse, zu denen ich gelangt bin, stehen daher in starkem Widerspruch zu den Resultaten seiner Kritik.

ET: *The Sayings of Jesus*, 194.

fulness, to his simple-minded common-sense, we owe this priceless compilation of the sayings of Jesus. …

On the one hand St. Mark – wherein page by page the student is reduced to despair by the incon-[250]sistencies, the discrepancies, and the incredibilities of the narrative – and yet without this gospel we should be deprived of every thread of consistent and concrete historical information concerning the life of Jesus; and on the other hand, this compilation of sayings, which alone affords us a really exact and profound conception of the teaching of Jesus, and is free from bias, apologetic or otherwise, and yet gives us no history. …

Which is the more valuable? Eighteen centuries of Christianity have answered this question, and their answer is true. *The portrait of Jesus as given in the sayings of Q has remained in the foreground. … The collection of sayings and St. Mark must remain in power, but the former takes precedence.* Above all, the tendency to exaggerate the apocalyptic and eschato-[251]logical element in our Lord's message, and to subordinate to this the purely religious and ethical elements, will ever find its refutation in Q. This source is the authority for that which formed the central theme of the message of our Lord – that is, the revelation of the knowledge of God, and the moral call to repent and to believe, to renounce the world and to gain heaven – this and nothing else.[70]

Wellhausen then published a second edition in which he repeated, indeed strengthened, his earlier position.[71]

Between the two World Wars, the form critics Rudolf Bultmann and Martin Dibelius both assumed the existence of Q, though their point of departure was more nearly that of Wellhausen than that of Harnack. For it was Wellhausen[72]

---

70 Harnack, *Sprüche und Reden Jesu*, 172-73:

Kann unser Matth. nicht von einem Apostel verfasst sein und stammt die Nachricht: Ματθαῖος Ἑβραΐδι διαλέκτῳ τὰ λόγια συνετάξατο, bereits aus der Zeit um d. J. 100, so ist es überwiegend wahrscheinlich, dass Q ein Werk des Matthäus ist; aber mehr lässt sich nicht sagen. … Wer aber auch immer der Verfasser bez. der Redactor von Q gewesen sein mag – er war ein Mann, dem die grösste Anerkennung gebührt. Seiner Pietät und Treue, seiner Schlichtheit und Besonnenheit verdanken wir die unschätzbare Sammlung von Sprüchen Jesu. … [173]

… Hier dieser Markus, der Seite für Seite durch Widersprüche, Unstimmigkeiten und Unglaubliches den Forscher zur Verzweiflung bringt und ohne den uns doch jeder Faden und jede konkrete Anschauung von Jesus fehlen würde, und dort die Spruchsammlung, die uns allein ein bestimmteres und tieferes Bild von der Verkündigung Jesu gewährt, von apologetischen und partikularen Tendenzen frei ist, aber keine Geschichte bietet. …

Wer ist wertvoller? Seit 1800 Jahren ist diese Frage entschieden, und mit Recht entschieden. Das Bild Jesu, welches Q in den Sprüchen gegeben hat, ist im Vordergrunde geblieben. … Die Spruchsammlung und Markus müssen in Kraft bleiben, aber jene steht voran. Vor allem wird die Übertreibung des apokalyptisch-eschatologischen Elements in der Verkündigung Jesu und die Zurückstellung der rein religiösen und moralischen Momente hinter jenes immer wieder ihre Widerlegung durch die Spruchsammlung finden. Sie bietet die Gewähr für das, was in der Verkündigung Jesu die Hauptsache gewesen ist: Die Gotteserkenntnis und die Moral zu Busse und Glauben, zum Verzicht auf die Welt und zum Gewinn des Himmels – nichts anderes.

ET: *The Sayings of Jesus*, 248-51.

71 Wellhausen, *Einleitung in die drei ersten Evangelien*[2], 170-176: In an appended "Corrolarium" he refuted the argument of Kirsopp Lake, "The Date of Q," that Q was written no later than 50 C. E.

72 Martin Hengel, in his "Einleitung" to *Evangelienkommentare*, vi-vii:

Er endet mit einer harschen Kritik der Leben-Jesu-Forschung des 19. Jh.s, die wesentlich über die A. Schweitzers, mit dem er sich kritisch auseinandersetzt, hinausgeht und die sich in manchen Punkten mit Martin Kähler und der frühen dialektischen Theologie

who had anticipated the new kerygmatic orientation:

> It is as the crucified, resurrected and returning one that Jesus is the Christian Messiah, not as religious teacher. The apostolic gospel, which preaches faith in the Christ, is the real one, and not the gospel of Jesus which prescribes to the church its moral. … And the expression purportedly committed by Harnack, "not the Son, but only the Father belongs in the Gospel," is basically false, if it is intended to claim a fact and not merely expresses a postulate.[73]

Harnack had indeed said: "*The Gospel, as Jesus proclaimed it, has to do with the Father only and not with the Son.*"[74] Wellhausen, apparently quoting from hearsay, left out the decisive "*as Jesus proclaimed it.*"[75] The "Gospel" that Wellhausen has in

> K. [vii] Barths und R. Bultmanns berührt. In der dadurch befruchteten kritischen Evangelienforschung zwischen den beiden Weltkriegen wird die Wirkung des Neutestamentlers Wellhausen am ehesten sichtbar.

Bultmann's only essay on Q, written before World War I, only two years after Wellhausen's second edition, built explicitly on him rather than on Harnack: "Was lässt die Spruchquelle über die Urgemeinde erkennen?" *Oldenburgisches Kirchenblatt* 19 (1913) 35-37, 41-44: 35:

> Den folgenden Ausführungen liegt also eine bestimmte Auffassung der synoptischen Frage zu Grunde, die ich natürlich hier nicht näher entwickeln kann. Ich verweise auf B. Weiss, A. Jülicher und J. Wellhausen.

ET: "What the Sayings Source Reveals about the Early Church," in *The Shape of Q: Signal Essays on the Sayings Gospel* (ed. John S. Kloppenborg; Minneapolis: Fortress, 1994) 23-34: 23, n. 1:

> The following explication presupposes a definite solution to the Synoptic problem, which obviously I cannot pursue in more detail here. I refer the reader to B. Weiss 1908; Jülicher 1904; and Wellhausen 1905, 1911.

Rudolf Bultmann, *Jesus* (Die Unsterblichen: Die geistigen Heroen der Menschheit in ihrem Leben und Wirken mit zahlreichen Illustrationen, 1; Berlin: Deutsche Bibliothek, n. d. [1926]), 18 (reprint Tübingen: Mohr-Siebeck, 1951, 16):

> Die Übersetzung der evangelischen Texte schliesst sich oft an die von J. Wellhausen an.

Martin Dibelius, *Die Formgeschichte des Evangeliums* (Tübingen: Mohr-Siebeck, 1919, revised 1933[2], 1966[5] ed. Günther Bornkamm [quoted here]) 236, n. 1. ET: *From Tradition to Gospel*, tr. Bertram Lee Woolf (New York: Scribners, n.d.), 235, n. 1, appeals to Wellhausen, *Einleitung in die drei ersten Evangelien*[1], 66-67, for his own skepticism (quoted below) regarding Q.

73 Wellhausen, *Einleitung in die drei ersten Evangelien*[2], 153, Quoted by Hengel, *Evangelienkommentare*, "Einleitung," vii:

> Als der Gekreuzigte, Auferstandene und Wiederkommende ist Jesus der christliche Messias, nicht als Religionslehrer. Das apostolische Evangelium, welches den Glauben an den Christus predigt, ist das eigentliche, und nicht das Evangelium Jesu, welches der Kirche ihre Moral vorschreibt. … Und der angeblich von Harnack getane Ausspruch: "nicht der Sohn, sondern nur der Vater gehört ins Evangelium" ist grundfalsch, wenn damit ein Faktum behauptet und nicht nur ein Postulat ausgesprochen werden soll.

Hengel, vi, inaccurately states that chapter 17 of the second edition ("Das Evangelium und das Christentum," 147-53) corresponds to chapter 12 of the first edition, which, however, in fact corresponds to chapter 10 of the second ("Das Evangelium und Jesus von Nazareth," 98-104). There is in the first edition no chapter equivalent to chapter 17 of the second edition. Hence the quotation is not in the first edition at all.

74 Harnack, *Das Wesen des Christentums*, 91 (1900), 90 (1985), and 154 (1999):

> *Nicht der Sohn, sondern allein der Vater gehört in das Evangelium, wie es Jesus verkündigt hat, hinein.*

ET: *What Is Christianity*, 147.

75 Harnack, *Das Wesen des Christentums*, in the endnotes added to the 1908 edition (56th to 60th thousand), drew attention to this omission distorting his position (on p. 183 of the 1950 edition and p. 154-55, n. 22, of the 1999 edition):

> Dieses Wort ist von vielen Seiten aufs schärfste bekämpft, aber nicht widerlegt worden. Ich habe nichts an ihm zu ändern. Nur sind die Worte: "Wie es Jesus verkündigt hat", hier kursiv gesetzt worden, weil sie von vielen Gegnern übersehen worden sind. Dass

view is of course that of the church, i.e. the kerygma, which became more nearly what one could refer to as "the essence of Christianity" down through history, e.g., in the form of the *Apostolicum* and subsequent creeds, whereas Jesus' message was largely overlooked, though occasionally rediscovered, as by Francis of Assisi.

This debate between Wellhausen and Harnack was to a remarkable extent repeated in 1923 in a debate between Karl Barth and Harnack. Here it is quite clear that dialectic theology created a theological climate in which Wellhausen's position regarding the relative unimportance, not to say illegitimacy, of Q would have the ascendancy.[76]

Harnack spoke of

> the close connection, even equating, of love for God and love for one's neighbor which constitutes the heart of the gospel,[77]

to which Barth replied:

> Does anything show more clearly than this heart (not of the gospel, but of the law), that God does not make alive unless he first slays?[78]

Thus the central sayings of Jesus (Mark 12:28-34 parr.) that Harnack hailed as "gospel" were for Barth "law," over against which he appealed to the "gospel" of God granting life only after death. The implication of the history-of-religions classification of Jesus as Jew by Wellhausen[79] and Bultmann[80] was heard theologically as the dialectic of

---

> Jesus in das Evangelium, wie es Paulus und die Evangelisten verkündigt haben, nicht nur hineingehört, sondern den eigentlichen Inhalt dieses Evangeliums bildet, braucht nicht erst gesagt zu werden.

76 This exchange was published in *Die christliche Welt*, 1923, as follows: Harnack: "Fünfzehn Fragen an die Verächter der wissenschaftlichen Theologie unter den Theologen," 6-8; Barth: "Fünfzehn Antworten an Herrn Professor von Harnack," 89-91; Harnack: "Offener Brief an Herrn Professor K. Barth," 142-44; Barth: "Antwort auf Herrn Professor von Harnacks offenen Brief," 244-52; and Harnack: "Nachwort zu meinem offenen Brief an Herrn Professor Karl Barth," 305-6. This debate has been republished in Barth's *Gesammelte Vorträge*, vol. 3: *Theologische Fragen und Antworten* (Zollikon: Evangelischer Verlag, 1957) 7-31: 7-9, 9-13, 13-17, 18-30, 30-31 (quoted here). ET in *The Beginnings of Dialectic Theology*, volume 1 (ed. James M. Robinson; Richmond, Va: John Knox, 1968): Harnack: "Fifteen Questions to Those Among the Theologians Who Are Contemptuous of the Scientific Theology," 165-66; Barth: "Fifteen Answers to Professor von Harnack," 167-70; Harnack: "An Open Letter to Professor Karl Barth," 171-74; Barth: "An Answer to Professor von Harnack's Open Letter," 175-85; and Harnack: "Postscript to My Open Letter to Professor Karl Barth," 186-87.

77 Harnack, "Fünfzehn Fragen," 8: "... die enge Verbindung, ja Gleichsetzung der Gottes- und Nächstenliebe, welche den Kern des Evangeliums bildet, ...". ET: "Fifteen Questions," 165.

78 Barth, "Fünfzehn Antworten," 11: "Was zeigt deutlicher als dieser 'Kern' (nicht des Evangeliums, aber des Gesetzes), dass Gott nicht lebendig macht, er töte denn zuvor?" ET: "Fifteen Answers," 168.

79 Julius Wellhausen, *Einleitung in die drei ersten Evangelien*, 1905[1]: 113; 1911[2]: 102: "Jesus war kein Christ, sondern Jude."

80 Rudolf Bultmann, "Das Verhältnis der urchristlichen Christusbotschaft zum historischen Jesus," SHAW.PH, Jg. 1960, Abh. 3 (Heidelberg: Winter, 1960, 1962[3]) 8:

> Nun werde ich ferner angegriffen, weil ich in meinem Buch 'Das Urchristentum im Rahmen der antiken Religionen' die Verkündigung Jesu nicht in dem Kap. 'Das Urchristentum', sondern im Kapitel 'Das Judentum' dargestellt, Jesus also als Juden aufgefasst habe. Im gleichen Sinne hat man beanstandet, dass ich in meiner Theologie des Neuen Testaments' gesagt habe, die Verkündigung Jesu gehöre zu den *Voraussetzungen* der Neutestamentlichen Theologie. Gegenüber dem Vorwurf, dass ich Jesus als Juden verstehe und ihn in den Bereich des Judentums rechne, habe ich zunächst einfach zu fragen: war Jesus – der historische Jesus! – denn ein Christ? Nun, wenn christlicher Glaube der Glaube an ihn als den Christus ist, doch gewiss nicht, und selbst wenn er sich als den Christus ('Messias') gewusst haben und gar den Glau-

law and gospel, in which sense Q is by definition not gospel, but law.

Whereas Q refers to its sayings as "evangelizing the poor" (Q 7:22), Paul makes clear that any other gospel than his kerygma, even if it come from an angel, is anathema (Gal 1:8-9). This tension persists down to the present, as the theological background of the discussion as to whether Sayings Gospels such as Q and the Gospel of Thomas should be called Gospels at all.[81]

In other regards as well, the form critics played down the importance of Q. For the focus of attention had shifted to the oral transmission of traditions under the influence of their social settings, rather than remaining on written sources incorporated in later texts. Therefore whether Q was a single written Greek document, conceivably subject to reconstruction in a critical edition, was not relevant.

Bultmann retained Wellhausen's hypothesis of an Aramaic Q, though giving up the concept of a single Greek translation:

> We have to conclude that Q, which originally appeared in an Aramaic version, was variously translated into Greek, because it obviously was known to Matthew and Luke in different versions[82].

Dibelius abandoned the hypothetical Aramaic Q behind the Greek Q, but nonetheless was very skeptical about Q being a tangible Greek document:

> ben an sich als den Christus gefordert haben sollte, so wäre er immer noch kein Christ und nicht als Subjekt des christlicher Glaubens, dessen Objekt er doch ist, zu bezeichenen.

ET: "The Primitive Christian Kerygma and the Historical Jesus," *The Historical Jesus and the Kerygmatic Christ* (ed. Carl E. Braaten and Roy A. Harrisville; Nashville: Abingdon, 1964) 15-42: 19:

> I am further attacked because in my book *Primitive Christianity* I have not described Jesus' preaching in the chapter on 'Primitive Christianity,' but rather in the chapter on 'Judaism,' and hence have conceived of Jesus as a Jew. Similarly, the objection has been raised that in my *Theology of the New Testament* I have stated that Jesus' preaching belongs to the presuppositions of New Testament theology. Over against the reproach that I conceive of Jesus as a Jew and assign him to the sphere of Judaism I must first of all simply ask: Was Jesus – the historical Jesus! – a Christian? Certainly not, if Christian faith is faith in him as the Christ. And even if he should have known that he was the Christ ('Messiah') and should actually have demanded faith in himself as the Christ, then he would still not have been a Christian and ought not to be described as the subject of Christian faith, though he is nevertheless its object.

81 For the resultant discussion about the legitimacy of calling Q a "Sayings Gospel," see Frans Neirynck, "Q: From Source to Gospel," *EThL* 71 (1995) 421-34; Kloppenberg Verbin, *Excavating Q*, "Q as a 'Gospel': What's in a Name," 398-408.

82 Bultmann, *Die Geschichte der synoptischen Tradition* (FRLANT, NF 12; 1921, 1931[2] revised, cited here), 354:

> Dass Q, ursprünglich aramäisch verfasst, verschiedentlich ins Griechische übersetzt wurde, muss man daraus schliessen, dass es dem Mt und Lk offenbar in verschiedenen Übersetzungen vorgelegen hat.

ET: *The History of the Synoptic Tradition* (New York and Evanston: Harper and Row, 1963, 1968[2] [the heavily corrected translation of the second edition quoted here]) 328. In a footnote Bultmann refers not only to Wellhausen, *Einleitung in die drei ersten Evangelien*[2], 59-60, but, in first place, to Adolf Jülicher, *Einleitung in das Neue Testament* (ed. Erich Fascher; Tübingen: Mohr-Siebeck, 1904[7]), 340-341. The relevance of the dependence on Jülicher and Fascher is made evident by Günther Bornkamm, "Evangelien, synoptische," *RGG*[3] 2(1958), 753-66: 755-56, 758-60: 756:

> Auf keinen Fall also darf Q in derselben Weise wie Mk als eine schon fest umrissene literarische Grösse vorgestellt werden. Vielmehr ist sie als eine 'Traditionsschicht' (Fascher) zu denken, die der in Unterweisung und Gottesdienst beheimateten mündlichen Tradition noch erheblich näher stand und ihrem Wandlungsprozess stärker ausgesetzt war und blieb als Mk.

The text used by Matthew and Luke was Greek, otherwise there would have been no such agreement. All the genuine sayings of Jesus were once translated [234]. But it seems possible to conceive this process in such a way that even in bilingual Churches it was handed on in Greek, and that these Greek sayings were brought together in a Greek-speaking region. This is much more probable than the other case, that the Aramaic words were first assembled and then translated as a connected writing. For in this case we shall have to assume even for the earliest Christian generation a certain literary activity – and that is out of the question. …

But the greatest doubts arise when we consider the literary category of Q, for we have not the slightest idea whether and in what way this writing, deduced piecemeal, can have constituted a book. … In these, as in other questions, we must be careful not to speak with too great self-confidence of Q as a definitely ascertained entity. [235]

As long as we leave this fact out of sight we run the danger of reckoning with as much certainty upon the source which we do not know as upon Mark which we can see in front of us. We tend to forget that we are dealing with a hypothetical entity. …

By such a systematic self-limitation, we abandon the possibility of reconstructing the source in its fullness. For even in the case of sections which can be reconstructed, we must earnestly ask the question whether they all really belonged to the same "writing." This may appear doubtful and has, in fact, been doubted. The present position of research into the source Q warrants our speaking rather of a stratum than of a document. We clearly recognize the effort of the churches to gather together words of Jesus in the manner of Q, but we do not know whether the result of these efforts was one or more books or indeed any books at all.[83]

---

[83] Dibelius, *Die Formgeschichte des Evangeliums,* 234-36:

Der Text, den Matthäus und Lukas benutzten, war griechisch; sonst [235] würde sich nicht eine solche Übereinstimmung ergeben haben. Alle echten Worte Jesu sind einmal übersetzt worden. Aber es liegt nahe, diesen Vorgang so zu denken, dass sie in zweisprachigen Gemeinden bald auch griechisch weitergegeben und dass diese griechischen Worte dann auf griechischem Sprachboden gesammelt wurden. Das ist bei weitem wahrscheinlicher als der andere Fall: Dass die aramäischen Worte erst gesammelt und dann als Sammlung übersetzt wurden. Dann müsste schon für die älteste Generation ein gewisses literarisches Bemühen vorausgesetzt werden – und damit ist nicht zu rechnen. …

Das allerstärkste Bedenken aber erhebt sich, wenn wir die literarische Gattung von Q überdenken. Denn wir haben überhaupt keine Vorstellung davon, ob und in welcher Weise diese stückweis erschlossenen Texte ein Buch gebildet haben könnten. … [236] In dieser wie in anderen Fragen müssen wir uns jedenfalls davor hüten, mit allzu grosser Selbstverständlichkeit von Q als von einer gesicherten Grösse zu reden.

Solange wir dies ausser acht lassen, laufen wir Gefahr, mit der Quelle, die wir nicht kennen, ebenso sicher zu rechnen wie mit Markus, den wir vor uns sehen, und vergessen, dass wir es mit einer hypothetischen Grösse zu tun haben. …

Wir verzichten mit solcher methodischen Selbstbeschränkung freilich auf die Möglichkeit, die Quelle in ihrem ganzen Umfang zu rekonstruieren. Denn es muss ja auch für die rekonstruierbaren Abschnitte ernstlich gefragt werden, ob sie alle wirklich zu derselben "Schrift" gehören, das kann zweifelhaft scheinen und ist in der Tat bezweifelt worden. Was wir bei dem heutigen Stande der Forschung von der Quelle Q wissen, berechtigt uns eher von einer *Schicht* als von einer *Schrift* zu reden; wir erkennen deutlich das Bestreben der Gemeinden, Worte Jesu in der Weise von Q zu sammeln, wir wissen aber nicht, ob das Ergebnis dieser Bemühungen ein oder mehrere Bücher und ob es überhaupt Bücher waren.

ET: *From Tradition to Gospel,* 233-35. (The

The nature of this «stratum» is for Dibelius the paraenesis prevalent in the first generation of Christianity, prior to a christological rearrangement of the sayings into a more biographical cast:

> Hence we can say that at an early date, viz. already in the time of Paul, words of Jesus had been collected for hortatory purposes. ... [244]
>
> In the whole of the Q material recognizable by us there is no reference to the story of the Passion. If the tendency of our source was toward narrative, we ought surely to expect a Passion story. ... Thus the Q material which we have received shows in its essential content no narrative inference. We must infer as this source little else than speeches, mostly indeed isolated, i.e. sayings without context. ... [245]
>
> Thus the total content of the groups of material which we deal with in Q still shows clearly the original tendency of such collections. Their purpose is not to deal with the life of Jesus, but to give His words in order that they may be followed and in order that they may instruct.[84]

Bultmann, for his part, in distinction from Dibelius, apparently conceived of Q as more than a stratum, but rather as a single document with ascertainable beginning and conclusion:

> Q, finally, the collection of Jesus' sayings that goes back to the earliest Church, testifies to the same belief [of the primitive community that it is the eschatological community]. It is prefaced by the eschatological preaching of John the Baptist; the beatitudes, full of eschatological consciousness, follow; the close is constituted by sayings dealing with the parousia.[85]

In either case, the result is that during the period of form criticism there was no single Greek archetype that one might hope to reconstruct. For since Bultmann considered Q to be an Aramaic text variously translated into Greek, and Dibelius thought Q might be actually an indeterminate number of separate texts,[86] rather than a single text, and hence better conceived of as a stratum than as a written text, the possibility of reconstructing a critical text of Q seemed precluded.

The English tradition, on the other hand, was largely uninvolved in form criticism at the time, and hence continued by and large its high level of assur-

---

misleading translation of "einmal" as "at the same time" is here corrected to "once.")

84 Dibelius, *Die Formgeschichte des Evangeliums,* 244-45:

> So können wir behaupten, dass man frühzeitig, nämlich schon zu des Paulus Zeit, Worte Jesu gesammelt hat zum Zweck der Paränese. ... Einmal fehlt in dem gesamten uns erkennbaren Q-Material jede Andeutung einer Leidensgeschichte. Wenn aber die Tendenz unserer Quelle auf Erzählung ginge, so müssten wir vor allem eine Leidensgeschichte erwarten. ... [245] Sodann verrät der uns erhaltene Q-Stoff nach seinem wesentlichen Gehalt überhaupt kein erzählendes Interesse. Es sind fast nur Redestücke, zumeist sogar isolierte, d. h. ungerahmte Sprüche, die wir für diese Quelle erschließen müssen. ...
>
> So blickt in der Gesamthaltung der Stoffgruppen, die wir für Q erschließen, die ursprüngliche Tendenz solcher Sammlungen noch deutlich durch: sie wollen nicht aus dem Leben Jesu erzählen, sondern seine Worte zur Befolgung und zur Belehrung mitteilen.

ET: *From Tradition to Gospel*, 243-45.

85 Rudolf Bultmann, *Theologie des Neuen Testaments* (Tübingen: Mohr-Siebeck, 1. Lieferung 1948, 43; 1958^1, 1965^5, 44:

> Solcher Glaube [of the primitive community that it is the eschatological community] wird endlich bezeugt durch Q, die auf die Urgemeinde zurückgehende Sammlung von Herrenworten. Vorangestellt ist diesen die eschatologische Täuferpredigt; es folgen dann die vom eschatologischen Bewusstsein getragenen Makarismen; den Schluss bilden Worte, die von der Parusie handeln.

ET: *Theology of the New Testament* (New York: Scribners, 2 vols, 1951, 1955), 1. 42.

86 This conjecture was carried through by W. L. Knox, *The Sources of the Synoptic Gospels*, volume 2, *St. Luke and St. Matthew* (Cambridge: Cambridge University Press, 1957).

ance as to the existence of a reliable Q document, the position which Hawkins had reached by the turn of the century.[87] For this approach was carried forward by Burnett Hillman Streeter,[88] and reached its standard form and widest dissemination in T. W. Manson's "The Sayings of Jesus," which included a commentary on Q.[89] Yet Manson's commentary is not based on a critical text of Q, but only on the text of Matthew and Luke printed in parallel columns, somewhere behind which Q must lurk.

With regard to the sequence of Q, there was high confidence that the order of Luke was that of Q. For there had been a traditional lack of confidence in Matthew's sequence, based on the then-current perception of Matthew's use of Mark:

> Matthew has entirely rearranged the order of practically every section in the first six chapters of Mark. If, therefore, he completely disregards the order of a document [146] relating a series of events, narrated presumably in their historical sequence, we may assume he would be still more indifferent to the original order of a document which was plainly only a loose collection of sayings. ...[147]
>
> It follows that we should *a priori* expect that where Matthew and Luke differ the original order of Q is to be presumed to be that of Luke unless in a particular case a reason to the contrary can be assigned, e.g. a desire to connect with other sayings on a similar topic.[90]

Quite apart from such dated presuppositions as those reflected in describing Mark as relating events "in their historical sequence" and Q being "a loose collection of sayings," the precedent of Matthew's use of Mark, on which the working hypothesis was based, is inadequately presented. For Matthew 12–28 follows Markan order with hardly any exceptions, at least as faithfully as does Luke. It is Matthew 3–11 which does not (hence the Matthean rearrangement of Mark 1–6). For in this first major redactional unit within Matthew, his attention is not directed to Mark so much as to Q, into which Markan material (as well as much subsequent Q material, cf. Matthew 5–7; 10) is imbedded when useful to carry forward Q's agenda.[91]

Vincent Taylor carried the argument for Lukan order one step further, by providing what he considered compelling new evidence that it was that of Q, with the objective of putting the Q hypothesis on a sound foundation.[92] He argued that Matthew, when composing his five discourses (and indeed when composing the "Rest of Matthew"), each time went through Q in the Q sequence, presumably to extract sayings that fitted the topic of the given discourse (though in many cases the relation to a unifying

87 Hawkins, *Horae Synopticae* (1899¹, 1909²) and "Probabilities as to the So-called Double Tradition of St. Matthew and St. Luke" (1911).

88 Burnett Hillman Streeter, "On the Original Order of Q," and "The Original Extent of Q," both in *Studies in the Synoptic Problem: By Members of The University of Oxford* (ed. William Sanday; Oxford: Clarendon Press, 1911) 141-64, 185-208; and *The Four Gospels* (London: Macmillan, 1924, reprint 1951).

89 Major, Manson, and Wright, *The Mission and Message of Jesus*. Manson's "The Sayings of Jesus" is Book II, 301-639: "3. The Sources: (a) The Document Q," 307-12; "Text and Commentary: I. — The Document Q," 331-440. Manson's contribution to the volume was published as a separate volume, *The Sayings of Jesus as recorded in the Gospels according to St. Matthew and St. Luke arranged with introduction and commentary* (London: SCM, 1949; reprint 1971): "3. The Sources: (a) The Document Q," 15-21; "Text and Commentary: I. — The Document Q," 39-148.

90 This view of the sequence was the working hypothesis and conclusion of the basic study by Streeter, "On the Original Order of Q," 145-47.

91 James M. Robinson, "The Matthean Trajectory from Q to Mark," *Ancient and Modern Perspectives on the Bible and Culture: Essays in Honor of Hans Dieter Betz* (ed. Adela Yarbro Collins; Atlanta: Scholars, 1998 [1999]) 122-54.

92 Vincent Taylor, "The Order of Q," *JTS*, n. s. 4 (1953) 27-31, reprinted in Taylor, *New Testament Essays* (Grand Rapids: Eerdmans, 1972) 90-94.

"topic" is hard to detect). For, as Taylor's thesis ran, the Q material in each discourse is used in the Lukan sequence, which thus is validated as the Q sequence.

Yet the overwhelming quantity of exceptions to this very straightforward thesis renders such a schematism highly unreliable, in spite of a second essay intended to provide detailed support.[93] When his rule does not in many instances actually apply, even if one grants that Matthew could have gone through Q several times in composing a single discourse, Taylor explains the divergences of sequence in various ways: The preference for the Markan position; or the preference for the position of M (thought to be a written source and hence with a fixed sequence); or the omission of sayings already used in a previous discourse; or simply Matthean interpretation. Though some of these are no doubt correct explanations of exceptions to his rule, they cumulatively become special pleading.

Today the point of departure continues to be the Lukan sequence, but without a prejudice in its favor; the sequence is an open question that must in each case be tested.[94] A List of Sayings not in Lukan Sequence is given in the section of the Technical Data on Divergences from the Lukan Sequence, below, p. lxxxix.

Proclamation and Redaction
Bornkamm, Tödt, Steck, and Lührmann

The revival of the study of Q after World War II took place primarily in Heidelberg, under the leadership of Bultmann's student and Dibelius' successor Günther Bornkamm, one of the founders of the distinctively post-war innovation, redaction criticism, initiated by his redaction critical analysis of the Stilling of the Storm in Matt 8:23-27:

> This characterization of the story of the stilling of the storm as a "nature miracle" does not, however, exhaust its meaning for Matthew. By inserting it into a definite context and by his own presentation of it, he gives it a new meaning which it does not yet have with the other evangelists. … [51]
>
> Matthew is not only a hander-on of the narrative, but also its oldest exegete, and in fact the first to interpret the journey of the disciples with Jesus in the storm and the stilling of the storm with reference to discipleship, and that means with reference to the little ship of the Church.[95]

---

93 Taylor, "The Original Order of Q," *New Testament Essays: Studies in Memory of T. W. Manson, 1893-1958* (ed. A. J. B. Higgins; Manchester: Manchester University Press, 1959) 246-69, reprinted in Taylor, *New Testament Essays*, 95-118.

94 James M. Robinson, "The Sequence of Q: The Lament over Jerusalem," *Von Jesus zum Christus: Christologische Studien. Festgabe für Paul Hoffmann zum 65. Geburtstag* (ed. Rudolf Hoppe and Ulrich Busse; BZNW 93; Berlin and New York: Walter de Gruyter, 1998) 225-60.

95 Günther Bornkamm, "Die Sturmstillung im Matthäusevangelium," *Wort und Dienst*: Jahrbuch der Theologischen Schule Bethel, NF 1 (1948) 49-54, reprinted in Günther Bornkamm, Gerhard Barth and Heinz Joachim Held, *Überlieferung und Auslegung im Matthäusevangelium* (WMANT 1; Neukirchen: Neukirchener Verlag, 1960), 48-53: 49, 51.

> Aber diese Kennzeichnung der Sturmstillungsgeschichte als "Naturwunder" erschöpft bei Matthäus nicht ihren Sinn. Er gibt ihr durch die Einordnung in einen bestimmten Zusammenhang und durch die Darstellung selbst einen neuen Sinn, den sie bei den andern Evangelisten noch nicht hat. …
>
> Matthäus ist nicht nur Tradent der Erzählung, sondern auch ihr ältester Exeget, und zwar der erste Ausleger, der die Sturmfahrt der Jünger mit Jesus und die Stillung des Sturmes auf die Nachfolge und damit auf das Schifflein der Kirche deutet.

ET: *Tradition and Interpretation in Matthew* (London: SCM, and Philadelphia: Westminster, 1963), 52-57: 53, 55.

The approach of redaction criticism made it methodologically more possible to reconstruct the critical text of Q, by identifying distinctive Matthean and Lukan traits of syntax, vocabulary, and theology (broadly understood), identified by studying their redaction of Mark, and then using these traits as objective criteria for identifying the redactional alterations in Q. These Matthean and Lukan "fingerprints" on the Q sayings facilitate the reconstruction of the Q text, in that one is often able to identify and peel off the Matthean and Lukan redaction. The reconstruction of a critical text thereby becomes a more feasible undertaking.

Dibelius had already anticipated this development in the case of Q, by distinguishing between the bulk of early Q material and later accretions added by the Q redaction:

> Nevertheless it may be granted that the collection used by Matthew and Luke already shows traces of a more advanced development.
>
> Thus passages appear to have been included which, though of totally different origin, have still the same office in this connection, viz. the handing down of the sayings of Jesus, to show and to prove who He was whose word had been gathered in the churches. … [246]
>
> All this is naturally conceived not in a historical, or biographical, but in a practical interest. But this particular practical interest outweighs the one which brought about the gathering of the sayings of Jesus as already discussed. The immediate object was to obtain from the words of Jesus not only solutions of problems or rules for one's own life, but also to derive from them some indications about the nature of the Person who had uttered them. … It is even not altogether out of the question that these special features of the source Q came into being under the influence of the Gospel of Mark. Granted, we cannot say anything certain about the matter, because the date of Q, and especially the chronology for its development, is altogether unknown to us.[96]

Dibelius had in fact shared the then-prevalent placing of Q around the middle of the century:

> The first congregations, let us say about C.E. 50, required a summary of the Lord's teaching in order to have rules of conduct for their own life. This gives us evidence that they believed in Jesus Christ not only as the Redeemer but also as a teacher who brought with him the new commandments of the Kingdom of Heaven. … [29]
>
> Probably there was more than one collection of sayings; at all events the existence of collections such as that contained in our alleged document Q is entirely probable, even at the time when Paul was receiving his missionary training from those who were believers before him, i.e., in

[96] Dibelius, *Die Formgeschichte des Evangeliums*, 245-47:

> Immerhin kann man zugeben, dass die [246] von Matthäus und Lukas benutzte Sammlung schon Spuren einer fortgeschrittenen Entwicklung zeigt. Es scheinen hier nämlich bereits Stücke aufgenommen zu sein, die bei ganz verschiedenartiger Herkunft in diesem Zusammenhang doch die gleiche Aufgabe haben: die Überlieferung der Sprüche Jesu zu deuten, zu zeigen, wer der war, dessen Worte man in den Gemeinden gesammelt hatte. … Dies alles geschah natürlich nicht im geschichtlichen oder biographischen, sondern im praktischen Interesse. Nur ging *dieses* praktische Interesse über dasjenige hinaus, was zunächst, wie wir sahen, zur Sammlung der Sprüche Jesu geführt hatte: man wollte nun den Worten Jesu nicht nur Lösungen und Regeln für das eigene Leben entnehmen, sondern man wollte von ihnen auch Aufschluss erhalten über das Wesen dessen, der sie gesprochen. … Es ist auch nicht völlig ausgeschlossen, dass diese Besonderheiten der sogenannten Quelle Q unter dem Einfluss des Markus-Evangeliums zustande kamen. Freilich können wir darüber nichts Sicheres sagen, da uns die [247] Entstehungszeit von Q und vollends die Chronologie seiner Entwicklung völlig unbekannt ist.

ET: *From Tradition to Gospel*, 245-46.

the thirties or at the beginning of the forties of the first century C.E.[97]

But by dating Q, or collections it contained, back to 50 C. E. or even earlier, and the redaction of Q to 70 C. E. or even later (thus, in a way, doing justice both to Harnack and to Wellhausen), Dibelius invited the effort to distinguish the tendency at work in the redaction from that at work in the original collection(s). The redaction criticism of Q became inevitable.

Heinz Eduard Tödt's Heidelberg dissertation of 1956 focused attention upon the problem that Q lacked sayings about the Son of man dying and rising:

> Harnack rightly stresses again and again that the concept of Jesus' passion which is present in the Gospel of Mark as his so-called Paulinism is absent in Q. How is this absence comprehensible in material which was transmitted by a community which after all must have been acquainted with Jesus' passion?[98]

Tödt recognized that the logical answer for the form critics to give would be to emphasize the kerygma's centrality and to play down the importance of the sayings of Jesus, and hence to classify Q as secondary:

> The masters of the method of form-criticism, Bultmann and Dibelius, both established, each in his own specific way, the theological priority of the community's kerygma of the passion over the Q material.
>
> ... The faith of the first Christians was that the passion and resurrection meant the beginning of the new era. Accordingly they were living in expectation of an imminent end. The point from which they took the direction of their life was exclusively what God had done at the cross and the resurrection. Only after it had become evident that the end had been delayed did the Christians realize that they needed valid moral instructions for the regulation of their life in the world. So the sayings were compiled at this later stage as a secondary supplement to the unique central core, the kerygma of the passion.[99]

---

97 Martin Dibelius, *Botschaft und Geschichte: Gesammelte Aufsätze*, Vol. 1: *Zur Evangelienforschung* (ed. Günther Bornkamm; Tübingen: Mohr-Siebeck, 1953) 97-98:

> Die ersten Gemeinden, sagen wir um 50 n. Chr., verlangten eine Zusammenfassung der Lehre des Herrn, um ein Gesetz für ihre Lebensführung zu haben. Das zeigt uns, dass sie an Christus nicht nur als an den Erlöser glaubten, sondern auch als an den Lehrer, der die neuen Gebote für das himmlische Reich brachte. ... [98]
>
> Wahrscheinlich gab es mehr als nur *eine* Sammlung von Sprüchen; auf alle Fälle ist das Vorhandensein von Sammlungen, so wie die in dem von uns angeführten Dokument Q enthaltene, durchaus wahrscheinlich, sogar zu einer Zeit, als Paulus seine missionarische Unterweisung von denen erhielt, die vor ihm Gläubige geworden waren, d. h. im dritten oder im Anfang des vierten Jahrzehnts des ersten Jahrhunderts n. Chr.

ET: *The Sermon on the Mount* (New York: Scribners, 1940) 28-29.

98 Heinz Eduard Tödt, *Der Menschensohn in der synoptischen Überlieferung* (Gütersloh: Gütersloher Verlagshaus Mohn, 1959) 217:

> Mit Recht betont Harnack immer wieder, dass der Gedanke an die Passion Jesu, der sogenannte Paulinismus bei Markus, in Q fehlt. Wie ist das verständlich in dem Traditionsgut einer Gemeinde, die doch zweifellos von der Passion Jesu Kenntnis hatte?

ET: *The Son of Man in the Synoptic Tradition* (London: SCM; Philadelphia: Westminster, 1965) 237.

99 Tödt, *Der Menschensohn in der synoptischen Überlieferung*, 218:

> Die Meister der formgeschichtlichen Methode, Bultmann und Dibelius, fanden jeder einen besonderen Weg, die theologische Priorität des Passions-Kerygmas der Gemeinde vor den Stoffen der Logienquelle sicherzustellen. ... Denn nach dem Glauben der ersten Christen hat mit der Passion und Auferstehung das neue Zeitalter begonnen. So lebt die Gemeinde im Zustand der Naherwartung und orientiert sich ausschliesslich an der Tat Gottes, die in Kreuz und Auferstehung geschehen ist. Erst als das

Such a later stage for sayings collections over against the kerygma would not necessitate a dating as late as that of Wellhausen, but was primarily a logical, i.e. theological, position of being secondary to the kerygma. For if Dibelius had emphasized the presence of such paraenetic collections even in Paul's experience, Bultmann also ascribed Q to the primitive community:

> It seems to me that the sayings source (*Spruchquelle*) employed by Matthew and Luke is the nearest to the primitive community.[100]

Yet Tödt sensed that Bultmann, by drawing attention to the church's proclamation of Jesus' sayings from the very beginning on, had by implication restructured the either-or choice between Q and kerygma that had dominated the period between the two World Wars:

> A momentous step towards an appropriate understanding of this Q material was taken by Bultmann. He realized that the primitive community gathered up Jesus' proclamation and continued to proclaim it. And, in fact, there are many passages the preservation and collection of which can easily be understood as being due to an urge to do this. Of course this idea upsets the prevailing notion that the earliest and central message was the passion kerygma alone. Instead this idea assumes that there was a community which accepted as its central commission the passing on of Jesus' message.[101]

Tödt was thus the first to draw explicitly the inference that Q was not just the paraenetic material of the primitive church and thus subservient to its standard kerygma,[102] but rather the central message of a distinct Q community, whose "kerygma" was itself the sayings of Jesus:

> There are two spheres of tradition, distinguished both by their concepts and by their history. The centre of the one sphere is the passion kerygma; the centre of the other sphere is the intention to take up again the proclamation of Jesus' message. The Q material belongs to the second sphere. ... [269] The concepts of the passion kerygma remained outside this sphere. Thus

---

> Ende sich verzögert, erkennen die Christen, dass sie zur Regelung ihres Lebens in der Welt gültiger sittlicher Weisungen bedürfen. Erst in diesem späteren Stadium entsteht die Spruchsammlung – als sekundäre Ergänzung zu der einzig zentralen Grösse, dem Passionskerygma.

ET: *The Son of Man in the Synoptic Tradition*, 238.

100 Bultmann, "Was läßt die Spruchquelle über die Urgemeinde erkennen?" 35:

> Der Urgemeinde am nächsten scheint mir die von Mt. und Lk. benutzte Spruchquelle (Q) zu stehen ... .

ET: "What the Sayings Source Reveals about the Early Church," 23.

101 Tödt, *Der Menschensohn in der synoptischen Tradition*, 225-26:

> Einen wichtigen Schritt zum sachgemässen Verständnis dieser Q-Stoffe hat [226] Bultmann getan, erkannte er doch, dass die Urgemeinde die Verkündigung Jesu wieder aufgenommen und weiterverkündigt hat. In der Tat ist die Aufbewahrung und Sammlung vieler Stücke unschwer aus diesem Bestreben abzuleiten. Freilich zerbricht man mit diesem Gedanken die herrschende Auffassung, dass einzig das Passionskerygma der älteste und zentrale Gegenstand der Verkündigung gewesen ist, und nimmt an, dass es eine Gemeinde gab, welche die Weitergabe der Botschaft Jesu als ihren zentralen Auftrag betrachtete.

ET: *The Son of Man in the Synoptic Tradition*, 247. The translation here has been edited to make it more literal. For the English-language preference for the idiom "teachings of Jesus" obscures Tödt's point: The message of Jesus is a kind of proclamation in its own right, not just ethical teaching for catechumens who had been baptized on the basis of faith in the kerygma of cross and resurrection.

102 For this standard view cf., e.g., Manson, *The Mission and Message of Jesus*, 308:

> The most probable explanation is that there is no Passion-story because none is required, Q being a book of instruction for people who are already Christian and know the story of the Cross by heart.

the Q material proved to be an independent source of Christological cognition.[103]

Ever since Tödt, the study of Q has had a sociological concomitant, the Q community, a previously overlooked outcome of the impact of Jesus on his hearers and beneficiaries in Galilee.

Ulrich Wilckens' Heidelberg dissertation, also of 1956, emphasized the distinctively sapiential orientation of much of Q:

> The motif that Wisdom abandons the earth is also found in a Q saying, Jesus' threat against Jerusalem: Matt 23:37-39 par. Luke 13:34-35. In Matthew this saying follows upon another threat against "this generation," Matt 23:34-36 par. Luke 11:49-51, where Matthew has retained from Q the sequence of both sayings and Luke the introduction to this last threat (διὰ τοῦτο καὶ ἡ σοφία τοῦ θεοῦ εἶπεν). Hence the saying Matt 23:37ff was originally in Q a saying of Wisdom that Matthew put on Jesus' tongue. … Here an echo of the myth in 1 Enoch 42 becomes clear: In resignation, Wisdom withdraws back into heaven. She wanted to collect to herself the children of Jerusalem as her children, but they did not want it. Now she withdraws from them and will leave them to themselves until the parousia of the Messiah.[104]
>
> The situation is similar for the saying Matt 11:16-19 (Luke 7:31-35). … [198] These "children of Wisdom" are precisely hers, who in contrast to the *massa perditionis* of "this generation" have turned to her. With them, Wisdom has found recognition, whereas she otherwise was rejected on all sides. But how can "Wisdom" be introduced here, where, after all, the talk is about John and Jesus? Well, John and Jesus are her messengers who represent her and through whom she speaks, just as Wisdom in Wis 7:27 "from generation to generation passes into holy souls and equips them as friends of God and prophets."[105]

---

103 Tödt, *Der Menschensohn in der synoptischen Tradition*, 244-45:

> … unsere These, dass traditionsgeschichtlich und sachlich zwei Traditionskreise unterschieden werden müssen: der eine ist durch das Passionskerygma bestimmt, beim anderen steht die Absicht einer erneuten Verkündigung der Botschaft Jesu im Mittelpunkt. Die Q-Stoffe gehören zum zweiten Kreis. … Die Gedanken des Passionskerygmas blieben ausgeschlossen. So erwiesen [245] die Stoffe der Logienquelle sich als ein selbständiges Ursprungsgebiet christologischer Erkenntnis.

ET: *The Son of Man in the Synoptic Tradition*, 268-69. The translation of "Verkündigung der Botschaft" as "teaching of what Jesus had taught" again obscures Tödt's emphasis, to the effect that it was Jesus' proclamation that continued to be proclaimed, as an alternative to, rather than an ethical, catechetical application of, the proclamation of the Easter kerygma. The translation has again been edited to make it more literal and thus clarify this point

104 Ulrich Wilckens, *Weisheit und Torheit: Eine exegetisch-religionsgeschichtliche Untersuchung zu 1. Kor. 1 und 2* (BHTh 26; Tübingen: Mohr-Siebeck, 1959) 163-64:

> Das Motiv, dass die Weisheit die Erde verlässt, findet sich auch in einem Q-Spruch, dem Drohwort Jesu gegenüber Jerusalem: Mt. 23,37-39; Luk. 13,34f. Dies Wort folgt bei Mt. auf ein anderes Drohwort gegen "dies Geschlecht", Mt. 23,34-36; Luk. 11,49-51, wobei Mt. die Reihenfolge beider Worte und Lukas die Einleitung zu diesem letzten [164] Drohwort aus Q erhalten hat (διὰ τοῦτο καὶ ἡ σοφία τοῦ θεοῦ εἶπεν). Das Wort Mt. 23,37ff. ist also ursprünglich in Q ein Wort der Weisheit gewesen, das Mt. Jesus in den Mund gelegt hat. … Hier haben wir deutlich einen Anklang an den Mythos 1. Hen. 42: Die Weisheit zieht sich resignierend in den Himmel zurück; sie wollte die Kinder Jerusalems als ihre Kinder bei sich sammeln, aber diese wollten nicht; nun entzieht sie sich ihnen und wird sie allein lassen bis zur Parusie des Messias.

See also his article σοφία, *TWNT* 7 (1964) 465-529, especially "Die Logienquelle," 515-18. ET: *TDNT* 7 (1971) 465-526, especially "The Logia," 515-17.

105 Wilckens, *Weisheit und Torheit*, 197-98:

> Ähnlich verhält es sich mit dem Wort Mt. 11,16-19 (Luk. 7,31-35). … [198] Diese

It is quite similar in the case of Matt 11:25-27 = Q 10:21-22:

> ... Jesus speaks as revealer, as does Wisdom. ... [199] The pericope thus stands in very close proximity to the Wisdom speculations in Sir and Wis. ... [200] Matt 11:25ff can without further ado be fitted into this development. In our context it is only interesting that here the person of Jesus is merged with the figure of Wisdom.[106]

Hence I, participating in this Heidelberg discussion while on sabbatic leave in Heidelberg 1959-60, suggested that the literary *genre* of Q might be sapiential.[107]

Odil Hannes Steck, in his 1965 dissertation in Heidelberg (where he was also an assistant), traced throughout the Bible the deuteronomistic view of history, which served to vindicate God with regard to disasters that fell upon Israel, especially the fall of Jerusalem in 586 B.C.E., as the inevitable result of Israel having killed the prophets God had sent. This deuteronomistic view of history cropped up in Judaism in texts taken over into primitive Christianity, where it is found primarily in Q 6:23c; 11:49-51; and 13:34-35:

> Luke 6:22-23, Matt 23:29-31, and Luke 11:49-51 do show that this relation is not limited to the isolated element of the violent fate of the prophets. In Matt 23:29-31 the conceptual relation of this element to Late[108] Judaism's tradition of the deuteronomistic view of history is taken over; in Luke 6:22-23 the coherence of the concepts of the suffering of the righteous and the deuteronomistic statements about prophets points to the conceptual content of this area of tradition; and in Luke 11:49-51

> "Kinder der Weisheit" sind eben die Ihrigen, die sich im Gegensatz zur massa perditionis "dieses Geschechtes" ihr zugewendet haben. Von ihnen hat die Weisheit Anerkennung gefunden, während sie sonst allenthalben abgelehnt wurde. Aber wie kann hier "die Weisheit" eingeführt werden, wo doch von Johannes und Jesus die Rede ist? Nun, Johannes und Jesus sind ihre Boten, die sie repräsentieren und durch die sie spricht, ähnlich wie die Weisheit in Sap. Sal. 7,27 "von Generation zu Generation in heilige Seelen übergeht und sie zu Freunden Gottes und Propheten ausrüstet".

106 Wilckens, *Weisheit und Torheit*, 198-200:

> ... Jesus als Offenbarer wie die Weisheit spricht. ... [199] Die Pericope steht damit in nächster Nähe zu den Weisheitsspekulationen in Sir. und Sap. Sal. ... [200] Mt. 11,25ff. lässt sich ohne weiteres in diese Entwicklung einfügen. Interessant in unserem Zusammenhang ist dabei nur, dass hier die Person Jesu mit der Gestalt der Weisheit verschmolzen ist.

(Wilckens includes here Matt 11:28-30, which, absent from Luke, was apparently not in Q).

107 James M. Robinson, "Basic Shifts in German Theology," *Interpretation* 16 (1962) 76-97: 82-86, and "ΛΟΓΟΙ ΣΟΦΩΝ: Zur Gattung der Spruchquelle Q," *Zeit und Geschichte: Dankesgabe an Rudolf Bultmann zum 80. Geburtstag* (ed. Erich Dinkler; Tübingen: Mohr-Siebeck, 1964) 77-96, then in a revised and enlarged edition *Entwicklungslinien durch die Welt des frühen Christentums* (edd. Helmut Koester and James M. Robinson; Tübingen: Mohr-Siebeck 1971) 67-106. In English it was also revised and enlarged, and published as "*Logoi Sophōn*: On the *Gattung* of Q," *The Future of Our Religious Past: Essays in Honour of Rudolf Bultmann* (ed. James M. Robinson; London: SCM; New York: Harper and Row, 1971) 84-130, then as "LOGOI SOPHON: On the Gattung of Q," *Trajectories through Early Christianity* (edd. James M. Robinson and Helmut Koester; Philadelphia: Fortress, 1971; paperback edition, 1979) 71-113. The concluding section "Jewish Wisdom Literature and the Gattung LOGOI SOPHON," was reprinted in *The Shape of Q: Signal Essays on the Sayings Gospel*, 51-58.

108 The idiom "Late Judaism" was until recently carried over inappropriately to refer to Judaism contemporary with "Late Antiquity" as itself "Late." (See already in the case of Albert Schweitzer n. 50 above.) But in fact during the period of Late Antiquity one had to do with Early Judaism.

even a firmly formulated unit of tradition is derived from it.[109]

Whereas Q 11:49 is actually introduced as a saying of Wisdom, and her sending of emissaries beginning with the foundation of the world would not fit a human speaker, not even Jesus, it is actually Q 13:34-35 whose language most clearly presupposes personified Wisdom. Steck found its roots, as in the case of Q 11:49-51, to lie in Jewish wisdom literature:

> Thus, after all, it seems most likely to me, along with many scholars, [231] that personified Wisdom was the original subject of the saying. … [232] *The subject of the Jerusalem saying is hence the Wisdom of Sir 24 residing in Jerusalem, which has received from God Israel as its abode, and is identical with the law*! Hence Luke 13:34-35 shows how, going beyond 11:49-50, now also this element of the concept of Wisdom has been connected with the tradition of the deuteronomistic view of history. If already in Sir 24 the myth of Wisdom plays a role, in that Wisdom, despised by the nations, has found precisely in Israel its place, then again in Luke 13:35bα ["you will not see me …"], to the extent that, after all, in the background stands the concept of the ascent of Wisdom, resigning herself. Thus in the Jerusalem saying there is present a further development of the tradition of Sir 24, more radical than which one can hardly imagine: It is precisely the Wisdom which has no abode among the nations, but has found its dwelling in Israel, which will now also abandon Israel![110]

Such a drastic application of the deuteronomistic view of history can, in Steck's view, only fit the siege of Jerusalem, a time when Jewish sources reported similar forebodings:

> But is such a horrendous word of judgment conceivable at all in Jewish tradition? The difficulties in explaining the saying as a Christian creation, but also the outcome of our analysis in terms of the history of traditions, according to which one has to do with a connection of sapiential and deuteronomistic tradition, each in its Late Jewish formulation, without a single specifically Christian element emerging, point after all in this direction. This Jewish word of judgment, which takes away any future for one's own peo-

[109] Odil Hannes Steck, *Israel und das gewaltsame Geschick der Propheten: Untersuchungen zur Überlieferung des deuteronomistischen Geschichtsbildes im Alten Testament, Spätjudentum und Urchristentum* (WMANT 23; Neukirchen-Vluyn: Neukirchener Verlag, 1967) 286:

> Lk 6,22f; Mt 23,29-31; Lk 11,49-51 zeigen ja, dass sich diese Beziehung nicht auf das isolierte Moment vom gewaltsamen Geschick der Propheten beschränkt; Mt 23,29-31 ist auch die Vorstellungsrelation dieses Moments zu der spätjüdischen Tradition des dtrGB [deuteronomistischen Geschichtsbildes] übernommen, Lk 6,22f weist der Zusammenbestand der Vorstellungen Leiden des Gerechten – dtrPA [deuteronomistische Prophetenaussage] in den Vorstellungsbestand dieses Traditionsbereichs, und Lk 11, 49f ist gar ein festformuliertes Traditionsstück aus ihm aufgenommen.

[110] Steck, *Israel und das gewaltsame Geschick der Propheten*, 230-32:

> So scheint mir doch mit vielen Forschern das Nächstliegende, [231] dass die personifizierte Weisheit das ursprüngliche Subjekt des Wortes war. … [232] *Das Subjekt des Jerusalemwortes ist also die in Jerusalem wohnende Weisheit von Sir 24, die Israel von Gott zur Bleibe erhalten hat und mit dem Gesetz identisch ist!* Lk 13,34f zeigt also, wie sich über 11,49f hinaus nun auch dieses Moment der Weisheitsvorstellung mit der Tradition des dtrGB [deuteronomistischen Geschichtsbildes] verbunden hat. Wirkt schon Sir 24 der Weisheitsmythos ein, insofern die von den Völkern verschmähte Weisheit eben in Israel ihre Stätte gefunden hat, so in Lk 13,35bα wieder, insofern im Hintergrund doch die Vorstellung vom resignierenden Ascensus der Weisheit steht. Im Jerusalemwort liegt somit eine Weiterbildung der Tradition von Sir 24 vor, wie sie radikaler nicht gedacht werden kann: eben die Weisheit, die bei den Völkern keine Bleibe, aber in Israel ihre Wohnung gefunden hat, wird nun auch Israel verlassen!

ple, is more understandable if one reflects that it must have been spoken under the unmediated impression of the impending catastrophe of Jerusalem. ... [238]

Accordingly everything does speak for the view that the Jerusalem saying is a Jewish word of judgment spoken between C.E. 66 and 70 in or near Jerusalem. If one looks at the listed parallels, then the assumption that [239] a *vaticinium ex eventu* is at hand is quite unnecessary, it even has obvious historical facts against it. If one looks at the various factions in Jerusalem at the time of the Jewish war, then the author of the Jerusalem saying can be sought neither among the Zealots, nor generally among the war party; he must rather have belonged to the peace party, which saw in the resistance movement the reason for their fear of God's judgment in the capture and destruction of the city. The situation in terms of the history of traditions suggests that Luke 13:34-35 arose in the same circles, led by wisdom teachers, as did the admittedly older judgment saying Luke 11:49-50.[111]

This led Steck to the somewhat awkward conclusion that Matt 23:37-39 par. Luke 13:34-35, in spite of such a high degree of verbal identity between Matthew and Luke that this text would otherwise be ascribed with certainty to Q, nonetheless cannot have belonged to Q, since Q was traditionally dated much earlier:

> Here we bracket out the Jerusalem saying, since, in spite of the extensive agreement of the Matthean and Lukan formulations, its relation to the sayings source is not clear. ... The motive for taking the saying up into Christian tradition may have been the expectation of the fall of Jerusalem also among Palestinian Christians, who take the saying over and ascribe it to Jesus.[112]

The revival of the deuteronomistic view of history at the time leading up to the siege of Jerusalem nonetheless provided Steck with the key to understanding Q:

---

[111] Steck, *Israel und das gewaltsame Geschick der Propheten*, 237-39:

> Aber ist ein so horrendes Gerichtswort in jüdischer Tradition überhaupt vorstellbar? Die Schwierigkeiten, das Wort als christliche Bildung zu erklären, aber auch das Ergebnis unserer traditionsgeschichtlichen Analyse, wonach eine Verbindung von Weisheits- und dtr Tradition je in ihrer spätjüdischen Ausprägung vorliegt, ohne dass ein einziges spezifisch christliches Moment aufträte, weisen jedoch in diese Richtung. Begreiflicher wird dieses jüdische Gerichtswort, das dem eigenen Volk alle Zukunft nimmt, wenn man bedenkt, dass es unter dem unmittelbaren Eindruck der bevorstehenden Katastrophe Jerusalems gesprochen sein muss. ... [238]
>
> Demnach scheint doch alles dafür zu sprechen, dass das Jerusalemwort ein zwischen 66 und 70 n. Chr. in oder nahe Jerusalem gesprochenes jüdisches Gerichtswort ist. Blickt man auf die gegebenen Parallelen, so ist die Annahme, es [239] liege ein vaticinium ex eventu vor, ganz unnötig, ja sie hat offenkundige historische Tatbestände gegen sich. Sieht man auf die verschiedenen Richtungen in Jerusalem zur Zeit des jüdischen Krieges, so kann der Verfasser des Jerusalemwortes weder unter den Zeloten noch überhaupt in den Reihen der Kriegspartei gesucht werden; er muss vielmehr zur Friedenspartei gehört haben, die in der Aufstandsbewegung den Grund für ihre Befürchtung des Gottesgerichts in Einnahme und Zerstörung der Stadt sah. Der traditionsgeschichtliche Befund legt nahe, dass Lk 13, 34f in denselben von Weisheitslehrern geführten Trägerkreisen entstanden ist wie das freilich ältere Gerichtswort Lk 11,49f.

[112] Steck, *Israel und das gewaltsame Geschick der Propheten*, 283, n. 1:

> Das Jerusalemwort klammern wir hier aus, da trotz der weitgehenden Übereinstimmung der Mt- und Lk-Fassung sein Verhältnis zur Logienquelle nicht deutlich ist. ... Das Motiv für die Aufnahme des Wortes in christliche Tradition dürfte die Erwartung des Untergangs Jerusalem auch bei den palästinischen Christen gewesen sein, die das Wort übernehmen und es auf Jesus zurückführen.

The deuteronomistic view of history, in its Late Jewish formulation, is admittedly not presented thematically as such in Q. As is indeed also the case in Late Jewish tradition, it can stand, as the known, only in the background of the presentation, and nevertheless be presupposed as the comprehensive conceptual framework in which the individual statements stand and to whose conceptual structure they are related.[113]

Whereas Steck did not carry through an analysis of other Q texts on the basis of this working hypothesis (with the exception of Q 6:23c[114]), Dieter Lührmann (assistant in Heidelberg from 1965-1968), in his habilitation of 1968 dedicated to Bornkamm, did elevate Steck's thesis into the *Tendenz* characteristic of the whole redaction of Q.[115] Lührmann realized that Steck's exclusion from Q of Matt 23:37-39 par. Luke 13:34-35 was not defensible, given their high verbal identity:

His reasons (absence of a context, late dating) say nothing about whether it belongs to Q.[116]

Rather one would have to adjust the standard mid-century date of Q[117] into a later time frame:

All these observations point to the fact that the redaction of Q is not to be put all too early, but rather in the Hellenistic congregation of about the 50s or 60s.[118]

The gradual shift for the assumed dating of Q from around 50 CE to around 70 CE that has taken place over the last generation has in a subtle way produced a new weighting for some of the perennial issues of Q research. If Q were not composed a generation prior to Mark, but is contempory with Mark, then Mark's use of Q is correspondingly less probable.[119]

But such a late dating for the redaction of Q made it all the more necessary to assume that earlier compositions were imbedded in Q, as Dibelius had argued.

This intensive period of research on Q reached its preliminary conclusion in 1972 with the Q

113 Steck, *Israel und das gewaltsame Geschick der Propheten*, 286:

Das dtrGB in seiner spätjüdischen Ausprägung wird freilich als solches in Q nicht thematisch dargeboten; es kann wie ja auch in spätjüdischer Tradition als das Bekannte nur im Hintergrund der Darstellung stehen und trotzdem als der umfassende Vorstellungsrahmen vorausgesetzt sein, in dem die Einzelaussagen stehen und auf dessen Vorstellungsstruktur sie bezogen sind.

114 Steck, *Israel und das gewaltsame Geschick der Propheten*, 257-60.

115 Dieter Lührmann, *Die Redaktion der Logienquelle* (WMANT 33; Neukirchen-Vluyn: Neukirchener Verlag, 1969).

116 Lührmann, *Die Redaktion der Logienquelle*, 44, n. 5:

Seine Gründe (Fehlen eines Kontextes, späte Entstehungszeit) besagen nichts über die Zugehörigkeit zu Q.

117 Representative of the many that could be listed is Manson, *The Mission and Message of Jesus*, 312:

Concerning the date and place of origin of Q we can do no more than make more or less probable conjectures. If it had its origin as a book of instruction for converts from Gentile paganism, it would be natural to connect it with Antioch, the first headquarters of the Gentile mission, and to date it about the middle of the first century, probably rather before than after A. D. 50.

118 Lührmann, *Die Redaktion der Logienquelle*, 88:

Alle diese Beobachtungen weisen darauf hin, dass die Redaktion von Q nicht allzu früh, sondern in der hellenistischen Gemeinde etwa der 50er oder 60er Jahre anzusetzen ist.

119 The most thorough recent presentation of the case for Mark's use of Q is that of Harry T. Fleddermann, *Mark and Q: A Study of the Overlap Texts* (BETL 122; Leuven: University Press and Peeters, 1995). But the "Assessment" by Frans Neirynck, published in the same volume, 261-307, and the review article by Jozef Verheyden, "Mark and Q," *EThL* 72 (1996) 408-17, refute the details with sufficient cogency to leave this theory still a minority view.

monograph of Siegfried Schulz.[120] He regarded Q as a written, Greek text, making it reasonable to weigh the probability of Matthean versus Lukan redaction of Q in the case of each divergence of vocabulary:

> The striking agreements in wording within the Q material permit one to infer a source collection composed in Greek, just as the sequence and doublets lead one to think of a written source which Matthew and Luke had before them. Which of the two Evangelists has preserved the original Q text, whether Matthew or Luke, can certainly not be known in advance, but must be verified from case to case, in fact primarily with the help of an investigation of word statistics.[121]

Unfortunately he did not follow through with a reconstruction of the text of Q itself.[122]

By this time a revival of interest in Q was documented on all sides. It is especially in Roman Catholic scholarship where this is prominent, once the encyclical *Divino afflante Spiritu*, issued in 1943, followed in 1965 by Vatican II's *Constitutio dogmatica de divina revelatione*, "*Dei Verbum*," had opened the door to scholarship presupposing the existence of Q.[123] Athanasius Polag produced in Trier a licentiate on Q in 1966, and a doctorate in 1968.[124] Paul Hoffmann's Münster habilitation in 1968 worked through the theological dimensions of Q more systematically.[125]

Of the impressive number of beginning Q scholars from the late '50s to the early '70s, Hoffmann is the only one who has consistently continued Q research down to the present, and whose views have as a result kept in step with ongoing Q research. He was initially hesitant about the feasibility of a redactional theory, since he presupposed the early dating of Q, in terms of which there is not only less time, but indeed less need, for a redaction distinct from the ongoing informal collecting of sayings into smaller clusters of tradition.[126] But he has come to advocate Lührmann's redactional theory, along with his later dating:

> My present occupation with redactional history is at the same time an attempt to repair a

---

[120] Siegfried Schulz, *Q: Die Spruchquelle der Evangelisten*, based on Q seminars he had conducted, beginning in 1960.

[121] Schulz, *Q: Die Spruchquelle der Evangelisten*, 41:

> Die auffallenden Übereinstimmungen im Wortlaut innerhalb der Q-Stoffe lassen auf eine griechisch abgefasste Quellensammlung ebenso schliessen, wie die Reihenfolge und Dubletten es nahelegen, an eine schriftliche Quelle zu denken, die Matthäus und Lukas vorgelegen hat. Wer den ursprünglichen Q-Text von beiden Evangelien bewahrt hat, ob Matthäus oder Lukas, kann auf keinen Fall von vornherein, sondern muss von Fall zu Fall verifiziert werden, und zwar vornehmlich mit Hilfe der vokabelstatistischen Untersuchung.

[122] Siegfried Schulz, *Griechisch-deutsche Synopse der Q-Überlieferungen* (Zürich: Theologischer Verlag, 1972), is a booklet printed separately to accompany the monograph. But it merely prints out the parallel Matthean and Lukan texts, as had Manson before him.

[123] To be sure, there had been precursors, such as Josef Schmid, *Matthäus und Lukas: Eine Untersuchung des Verhältnisses ihrer Evangelien* (BS[F] 23/2-4; Freiburg i. Br.: Herder, 1930).

[124] Athanasius Polag, "Der Umfang der Logienquelle" (typescript 1966), and "Die Christologie der Logienquelle" (typescript 1968); *Die Christologie der Logienquelle* (WMANT 45; Neukirchen-Vluyn: Neukirchener Verlag, 1977); and finally *Fragmenta Q: Textheft zur Logienquelle* (Neukirchen-Vluyn: Neukirchener Verlag, 1979[1], 1982[2]).

[125] Paul Hoffmann, *Studien zur Theologie der Logienquelle* (NTAbh, NF 8; Münster: Aschendorff, 1972[1], 1975[2], 1982[3]).

[126] Lührmann, *Die Redaktion der Logienquelle*, 8:

> Wegen des Frühansatzes von Q rechnet H. [Hoffmann] offenbar nicht mit einem längeren Überlieferungsprozess. Deshalb differenziert er m. E. nicht stark genug zwischen *Tradition* und *Redaktion* und nennt manches redaktionell, was ich der Tradition zurechnen würde.

deficit in my Habilitationsschrift, *Studien zur Theologie der Logienquelle*. ... [191-92, n. 50]

I would, however, depart from my discussion in the *Studien* in seeing [192] as correct the reference to the situation in the Jewish-Roman war, which Steck expounds. ... [193, n. 56]

The question of the age and origins of the genuine SM [Son of man] sayings, as assembled especially in Q 17, is in need of further investigation in this context. In doing so, we should take final leave from the often too "self-evident" assumption that in the SM sayings we are dealing with the oldest Christian or even dominical tradition. In this respect I wish expressly to correct my own position.[127]

The result is a new understanding of Q's theology in that late setting:

The saying [Q 13:34-35] looks back to the vain efforts on Israel's behalf and reflects the imminently expected, or perhaps already completed(?), destruction of Jerusalem in the framework of the deuteronomistic view of history as the consequence of the rejection of the envoys. ...

If we assume this to be QR's [Q redaction's] situation, various characteristics of QR find a plausible explanation. I would mention first of all the intensification of imminent expectation. ... It seems more plausible to relate them to the final phase of the Jewish-Roman war. In the situation of political crisis in Jewish, especially Zealot circles, but also in the Christian groups, as the reworked Palestinian piece of tradition in Mk 13 shows, that phase brought about the expectation of the imminent in-breaking of the end times. ... [193] The reception of the partly traditional statements in Q that are characterized by the imminent expectation is then less the legacy of an eschatological fervour that has been going on for decades, but rather an indication of a renaissance of the early Christian imminent expectation in response to the challenge of the general sociopolitical situation of crisis in the late 60s. This would also correspond better with the general sociology-of-religions insight that apocalyptic expectations generally appear in waves and are reactions to concrete crisis situations.

The Palestinian tradition from the time of the Jewish-Roman war, preserved in Mk 13, which – apart from Q – represents the earliest evidence of the Christian reception of the SM expectation of Dan 7 (though already transformed in its own way), now also sheds light on the appearance of

---

[127] Paul Hoffmann, "QR und der Menschensohn: Eine vorläufige Skizze," *The Four Gospels 1992: Festschrift Frans Neirynck* (ed. F. Van Segbroeck, C. M. Tuckett, G. Van Belle, J. Verheyden; 3 vols.; Leuven: University Press and Peeters, 1992) 1. 421-56: 421, 451, n. 50, 452, n. 56 (quoted here). This is reprinted in his collected essays, *Tradition und Situation: Studien zur Jesusüberlieferung in der Logienquelle und den synoptischen Evangelien* (NTAbh NF 28; Münster: Aschendorff, 1995) 243-78: 243, 273, n. 51, 274-75, n. 57. The quotations are from the first publication, but pagination refers to both:

> Wenn ich hier auf die Redaktionsgeschichte eingehe, versuche ich zugleich ein Defizit meiner Habilitationsschrift *Studien zur Theologie der Logienquelle* aufzuarbeiten. ... [451, n. 50 and 273, n. 51]
>
> Im Unterschied zu meinen Ausführungen in den *Studien* möchte ich jedoch den Bezug auf die Situation des jüdischen-römischen Kriegs, den Steck herausarbeitet, für richtig halten. ... [452, n. 56 and 274, n. 57]
>
> Die Frage des Alters und der Herkunft der genuinen MS[Menschensohn]-Worte, wie sie vor allem in QLk 17 zusammengeordnet sind, bedarf weiterer Untersuchungen. Nur sollte in der Diskussion nicht wie es häufig geschieht, zu "selbstverständlich" vorausgesetzt werden, dass es sich in den Menschensohn-Worten um die älteste christliche oder gar um jesuanische Tradition handelt. Hier möchte ich auch meine eigene Position ausdrücklich korrigieren.

ET: "The Redaction of Q and the Son of Man: A Preliminary Sketch," *The Gospel Behind the Gospels: Current Studies on Q*, 159-98: 159, 191-92, n. 50, 193, n. 56.

the SM sayings in Q. … Nonetheless, the parallel appearance of this expectation in Mk 13 and QR could indicate that the SM concept gained special significance for Christian circles during this late phase in the transmission of Q, i.e. in the period around 70 CE, and that it was then that there took place its reception and theological integration into the traditional Q material that was not previously characterized by it. … [195]

The "late dating" of QR proposed here would, finally, provide an explanation for the currency of the SM concept in Christian circles in the second half of the first century. … [197]

The above considerations presuppose a fair proximity, in both space and time, to the Gospel of Matthew. If we suppose the period around 70 for QR and the 80s for MtR [Matthean redaction], we are dealing with a span of ten or at most twenty years. It thus becomes clear again, that QR indeed represents only an "intermediate stage" in the process of early Christian tradition from the Jesus of history through to the Gospel of Matthew. Perhaps this is also one of the reasons why Q has not survived as an independent document but only in its reception by the great evangelists.[128]

---

[128] Hoffmann, "QR und der Menschensohn: Eine vorläufige Skizze," 451-53, 456 (*Tradition und Situation*, 273-74, 276, 278):

> Das Wort [Q 13:34-35] schaut auf die vergeblichen Bemühungen um Israel zurück und reflektiert die unmittelbar erwartete oder bereits erfolgte(?) Zerstörung Jerusalems im Rahmen des deuteronomistischen Geschichtsbildes als Folge der Abweisung der Boten. …
>
> Setzen wir diese Situation für QR [Q-Redaktion] voraus, finden verschiedene Eigentümlichkeiten von QR eine plausible Erklärung. Ich nenne zunächst die Intensivierung der Naherwartung, … [274] Plausibler scheint mir zu sein, sie mit der Endphase des jüdisch-römischen Kriegs in Verbindung zu bringen. Diese hat in der politischen Krisensituation in jüdischen, vor allem zelotischen Kreisen, aber auch in den christlichen Gruppen, wie das in Mk 13 verarbeitete palästinische Traditionsstück zeigt, die Erwartung des unmittelbaren bevorstehenden Anbruchs der Endzeit ausgelöst. … Die Rezeption der zum Teil sicher [452] traditionellen von der Naherwartung bestimmten Aussagen in Q ist dann weniger der Beleg einer Jahrzehnte andauernden eschatologischen Hochstimmung, sondern eher Indiz einer Wiederbelebung der frühchristlichen Naherwartung unter der Herausforderung der allgemein gesellschaftlich-politischen Krisensituation der 60iger Jahre. Dies entspräche auch besser der allgemein religionssoziologischen Einsicht, dass apokalyptische Erwartungen meist in einer Wellenbewegung auftreten und Reaktionen auf konkrete Krisensituationen sind.
>
> Die in Mk 13 erhaltene palästinische Überlieferung aus der Zeit des jüdisch-römischen Kriegs, die – von Q abgesehen – den ältesten Beleg für die christliche Rezeption der MS-Erwartung von Dan 7 (allerdings bereits in eigentümlicher Transformation) darstellt, wirft nun auch Licht auf das Auftauchen der MS-Sprüche in Q. … Dennoch könnte das parallele Auftreten dieser Erwartung in Mk 13 und in QR darauf hinweisen, dass in dieser Spätphase der Q-Überlieferung, also in der Zeit vor 70 n. Chr., die MS-Vorstellung für christliche Kreise besondere Bedeutung gewann und es zu ihrer Rezeption und theologischen Integration in das von ihr nicht geprägte Überlieferungsgut von Q kam. … [453 and 276]
>
> Durch die vorgeschlagene "Spätdatierung" von QR gewänne schliesslich auch die Aktualität der MS-Vorstellung in christlichen Kreisen der zweiten Hälfte des 1. Jahrhunderts eine Erklärung. … [456 and 278]
>
> Die obigen Überlegungen setzen nicht nur räumlich, sondern auch zeitlich eine ziemliche Nähe zum Matthäusevangelium voraus. Wenn wir für QR die Zeit um 70 und für MtR die 80iger Jahre voraussetzen, handelt es sich um eine Spanne von zehn bis maximal zwanzig Jahren. Dadurch wird nochmals deutlich, dass QR in dem frühchristlichen Traditionsprozess von Jesus der Geschichte hin zum Matthäusevangelium tatsächlich nur

Lührmann's definition of Q's redaction has by now gained general acceptance among Q scholars, and functions as the presupposition for the next step in the history of Q research.[129]

Sapiential Origins of Q and *Thomas* Koester, Robinson, and Kloppenborg

Helmut Koester, a pupil of Bultmann,[130] became Bornkamm's Heidelberg assistant from 1954-56, where he completed his habilitation in 1956 and continued as Dozent until 1959, by which time he had moved to Harvard, already as a visiting professor in 1958, bringing with him the Heidelberg tradition:

> The predecessor of the Christian collection and transmission of one particular aspect of Jesus' sayings was the Gattung *logoi sophon*, primarily developed in the Jewish wisdom movement. [138] This existing form served as a focus of crystallization for the preservation of one particular aspect of Jesus' historical appearance and work: his teachings. It is not possible to discuss here the complex questions regarding historical and primitive sayings or groups of sayings in these early pre-Q and pregospel collections. It is highly probable, however, that such collections were dominated by wisdom sayings, legal statements (critique of old conduct and pronouncements regarding new conduct), prophetic sayings (including some I-words, beatitudes, and woes), and parables, just as in Jesus' own teaching. As is partly evident from Q, sayings predicting Jesus' suffering, death, and resurrection, and the material reflecting the development of a christological evaluation of the person of Jesus, were still absent; detailed apocalyptic predictions, such as those contained in Mark 13, were not part of such primitive collections; specific regulations for the life of the church (*Gemeinderegeln*) were equally absent.
>
> What was the theological tendency of such collections of *logoi*? The answer to this depends entirely upon the christological post-Easter frame to which they were subjected. Q domesticated the *logoi* through a kind of apocalypticism which identified Jesus with the future Son of man. Mark (and subsequently Matthew and Luke) were able to incorporate the *logoi* in the "gospel" developed on the basis of the early Hellenistic (Pauline) kerygma. Neither of these developments seems to have touched the *logoi* tradition that found its way into the *Gospel of Thomas*. The criterion controlling Thomas's *logoi* is apparently closely connected with the internal principle of this Gattung as it gave focus to the transmission of Jesus' sayings: the authority of the word of wisdom as such, which rests in the assumption

eine "Zwischenetappe" darstellt. Vielleicht ist dies auch eine der Ursachen dafür, dass uns Q nicht als selbständiges Dokument, sondern nur in der Rezeption durch die Grossevangelisten erhalten ist.

ET: "The Redaction of Q and the Son of Man: A Preliminary Sketch," 192-93, 195, 197. The view that the Q redaction took place after the Jewish War, at about 75 C.E., has been advocated by Burton L. Mack, *The Lost Gospel: The Book of Q and Christian Origins* (San Francisco: HarperSanFrancisco, 1993) 177, and Matti Myllykoski, "The Social History of Q and the Jewish War," *Symbols and Strata: Essays on the Sayings Gospel Q* (ed. Risto Uro; Helsinki: SESJ 65, and Göttingen: Vandenhoeck und Ruprecht, 1996) 144-99: 199.

129 John S. Kloppenborg, "The Sayings Gospel Q and the Quest of the Historical Jesus," *HTR* 89 (1996) 307-44: 321, n. 66, has given an impressive list of those accepting Lührmann's redactional thesis. It includes most of the important Q scholars of today.

130 Koester's Marburg dissertation of 1954 already focussed attention on the non-canonical sayings tradition: *Synoptische Überlieferung bei den apostolischen Vätern* (TU 65; Berlin: Akademie-Verlag, 1957).

that Wisdom [139] is present in the teacher of the word.[131]

Building on Philipp Vielhauer's view that the apocalyptic Son of man sayings do not go back to Jesus himself,[132] he argued that they are late in the Q trajectory (and completely absent from the *Gospel of Thomas)*, and only serve to obscure the earlier sapiential focus of Q:

> The basis of the *Gospel of Thomas* is a sayings collection which is more primitive than the canonical gospels, even though its basic principle is not related to the creed of the passion and res-

[131] Helmut Koester, "GNOMAI DIAPHOROI: The Origin and Nature of Diversification in the History of Early Christianity," *HTR* 58 (1965) 279-318: 300-301. German publication: "GNOMAI DIAPHOROI: Ursprung und Wesen der Mannigfaltigkeit in der Geschichte des frühen Christentums," *ZThK* 65 (1968) 160-203: 184-85. The German text was republished in Koester and Robinson, *Entwicklungslinien durch die Welt des Frühchristentums* (ed. Koester and Robinson; Tübingen: Mohr-Siebeck, 1971) 107-46: 129-30:

> Der Vorläufer der christlichen Sammlung und Überlieferung der Sprüche Jesu war die Gattung "Logoi Sophon", die vor allem in der jüdischen Weisheitsbewegung entwickelt wurde. Diese bereits bestehende Überlieferungsform diente als Kristallisationspunkt für die Aufbewahrung einer besonderen Eigenart des historischen Wirkens Jesu: seines Lehrens. Es ist hier nicht tunlich, die schwierige Frage der Historizität und Ursprünglichkeit bestimmter Sprüche und Spruchgruppen zu erörtern, die in diesem frühen, den Evangelien und auch der Spruchquelle noch vorausliegenden Spruchsammlungen enthalten waren. In jedem Falle muss man damit rechnen, dass Weisheitsworte, Gesetzesworte (soweit sie eine Kritik des alten Wandels darstellen und den neuen Wandel verkünden), prophetische Worte (einschliesslich einiger Ich-Worte, Makarismen und Weherufe) und Gleichnisse deshalb in diesen Sammlungen vorherrschten, weil das dem Lehren des historischen Jesu entsprach. Auf der anderen Seite wird wenigstens teilweise aus Q deutlich, dass Leidensankündigungen sowie solche Sprüche, die von Jesus christologisch reden, zunächst der Spruchüberlieferung nicht angehörten; ebenso fehlten spezifische apokalyptische Weissagungen, sowie natürlich die Gemeinderegeln.
>
> Die theologische Tendenz solcher Spruchsammlungen wird entscheidend von dem nachösterlichen christologischen Rahmen abhängig, dem sie untergeordnet werden. Q zähmte die Logoi durch seine besondere Apokalyptik, derzufolge Jesus mit dem kommenden Menschensohn gleichgesetzt wurde. [130] Markus (und nach ihm Matthäus und Lukas) passten die Logoi dem Rahmen des "Evangeliums" an, der aus dem frühen hellenistischen (paulinischen) Passionskerygma entwickelt worden war. Weder der erstere noch der letztere Vorgang scheint diejenige Überlieferung der Logoi, die ihren Weg ins Thomasevangelium fand, berührt zu haben. Der Massstab, der die theologische Tendenz dieser Logoi prägte, ist offenbar eng verwandt mit dem inneren Prinzip dieser Gattung selbst, durch das sie zum Kristallisationspunkt der Sprüche Jesu wurde: die Vollmacht des Weisheitswortes selbst, die darin begründet ist, dass die Weisheit im Lehrer des Wortes da ist.

The English text was republished in Robinson and Koester, *Trajectories through Early Christianity* (ed. Robinson and Koester; Philadelphia: Fortress, 1971), 114-57: 137-39, quoted here. (The last sentence is edited to make it more literal.)

[132] Koester, "GNOMAI DIAPHOROI," *Trajectories through Early Christianity*, 138, n. 66:

> Whether any apocalyptic Son of man sayings were existent at this stage is very doubtful. Cf. Philipp Vielhauer, "Gottesreich und Menschensohn in der Verkündigung Jesu," ... idem, "Jesus und der Menschensohn."

German text: *Entwicklungslinien durch die Welt des Frühchristentums*, 129, n. 66:

> Es ist sehr zweifelhaft, ob die apokalyptischen Menschensohnsprüche schon zum frühesten Stadium der Überlieferung gehörten, vgl. *Ph. Vielhauer*, Gottesreich und Menschensohn in der Verkündigung Jesu ...; *ders.*, Jesus und der Menschensohn ...; ferner *N. Perrin*, Rediscovering the Teaching of Jesus (1967), passim.

urrection. Its principle is nonetheless theological. Faith is understood as belief in Jesus' words, a belief which makes what Jesus proclaimed present and real for the believer. The catalyst which has caused the crystallization of these sayings into a "gospel" is the view that the kingdom is uniquely present in Jesus' eschatological preaching and that eternal wisdom about man's true self is disclosed in his words. ...

The relation of this "sayings gospel," from which the *Gospel of Thomas* is derived, to the synoptic sayings source Q, is an open question. Without doubt, most of its materials are Q sayings (including some sayings which appear occasionally in Mark). But it must have been a version of Q in which the apocalyptic expectation of the Son of man was missing, and in which Jesus' radicalized eschatology of the kingdom and his revelation of divine wisdom in his own words were dominant motifs.[133]

This primarily German revival of Q studies more than a generation ago, once transplanted to America, came into focus largely through the synthesis produced by John S. Kloppenborg in his Toronto dissertation of 1984.[134] He built upon Lührmann's identification of the Q redactor, my identification of the sapiential *genre*, and Koester's focus on sources behind Q and *Thomas*. Indeed the later one is obliged to place the redaction of Q, down to the time around 70 C.E., the more some explanation is required to explain what would

[133] "One Jesus and Four Primitive Gospels," *HTR* 61 (1968) 203-47: 229-30, reprinted in *Trajectories through Early Christianity* [quoted here] 158-204: 186. The German text was published in Koester and Robinson, *Entwicklungslinien durch die Welt des Frühchristentums*, 147-90: 172-73:

> Die Grundlage des Thomasevangeliums war eine Spruchsammlung, die ursprünglicher als die kanonischen Evangelien ist, obgleich ihr Grundprinzip mit dem Bekenntnis von Leiden und Auferstehung nichts zu tun hat. Dennoch unterstehen solche Spruchsammlungen dem ihnen eigenen theologischen Grundprinzip. Danach wird der Glaube verstanden als ein Glaube an die Worte Jesu; in diesem Glauben wird das, was Jesus verkündet hat, für den Glaubenden wirklich und gegenwärtig. Der Katalysator, der diese Kristallisation der Sprüche zu einem Spruchevangelium verursacht hat, ist die Sicht, dass die Gottesherrschaft in Jesu eschatologischer Predigt in einzigartiger Weise gegenwärtig und dass göttliche Weisheit über des Menschen wahres Selbst in Jesu Worten erschlossen ist. ...
>
> Das Verhältnis dieses Spruchevangeliums, das dem Thomasevangelium zugrunde liegt, zur synoptischen Spruchquelle Q ist eine offene Frage. Bei dem darin enthaltenen Material handelt es sich ohne Zweifel weithin um Q-Sprüche (einschliesslich jener Sprüche, die gelegentlich bei Markus ihre Parallelen haben). Aber wir haben es mit einer Fassung der Spruchquelle zu tun, [173] in der die apokalyptische Menschensohnerwartung der synoptischen Spruchquelle noch nicht enthalten und in der Jesu radikalisierte Eschatologie der Gottesherrschaft und seine Offenbarung göttlicher Weisheit in seinen Worten die beherrschenden Züge waren.

In his more recent book, *Ancient Christian Gospels: Their Histsory and Development* (London: SCM and Philadelphia: Trinity Press International, 1990), Koester works out in more detail the relation between "Thomas and the Synoptic Sayings Source (Q)" (86-95), to conclude (95):

> Thus, the *Gospel of Thomas* is either dependent upon the earliest version of Q or, more likely, shares with the author of Q one or several very early collections of Jesus' sayings.

A telling critique is provided by Christopher M. Tuckett, "Q and Thomas: Evidence of a Primitive 'Wisdom Gospel'? A Response to H. Koester," *EThL* 67 (1991) 346-60. Yet see the discussion below of Q 12:22b-31 (Free from Anxiety like Ravens and Lilies).

[134] Published as: John S. Kloppenborg, *The Formation of Q: Trajectories in Ancient Wisdom Collections* (Studies in Antiquity and Christianity; Philadelphia: Fortress, 1987).

seem to be early, pre-redactional (non-deuteronomistic) collections of sapiential material. Lührmann himself had, in passing, called attention to such early collections:

> Collecting of this sort is found in other parts of the Synoptic tradition as well as in Q, for example, in the programmatic speech that forms the basis of the Lukan Sermon on the Plain and the Matthaean Sermon on the Mount (Luke 6:20-49 // Matt 5:1-7:29), in Q 12:22-32, 33-34, in Q 12:2-7, or in Luke 11:33, 34-36. ... Examples of this kind could be multiplied.
>
> The presence of such collections suggests that Q is already the (provisional) result of a long process of tradition and that, correspondingly, the content of Q is not homogeneous. Rather, just as is the case elsewhere in the Synoptic tradition, Q reflects various stages in the assimilation of the preaching of Jesus by the early church.[135]

But Lührmann, building on Steck, placed the sapiential orientation of Q nearest to the final redaction, where Wisdom is personified:

> One set of sayings that are clearly influenced by late Jewish wisdom turns out to be the latest stratum, and therefore the stratum that is chronologically, although not necessarily tradition-historically, nearest the redaction of Q. That datum may not at first glance [98] be surprising, since the influence of this current on the preaching of Jesus is recognizable elsewhere in the Synoptic tradition. But the frequency and the special character of these sayings and the patterning of Q as a whole on a *genre* deriving from sapiential literature indicate that this influence had considerable importance in the transmission of Q.[136]

Kloppenborg, on the other hand, identified, as an early formative stage in the emergence of Q, not personified Wisdom, but six "sapiential speeches," which he argued came together into an early written layer of Q, since it is into them that the later material reflecting the deuteronomistic redaction was interpolated, not vice versa:

> Alongside the large complexes which evince the motifs of judgment and polemic there are substantial units whose primary redactional intent is paraenetic, hortatory and instructional, and indeed compare favorably in their structure with the "instruction," a widely attested genre of wisdom literature. They include:

---

[135] Lührmann, *Die Redaktion der Logienquelle*, 84:

> "Sammlung" findet sich wie in der sonstigen synoptischen Tradition auch in Q, z.B. in der der lukanischen Feldrede und der matthäischen Bergpredigt zugrundeliegenden programmatischen Rede Lk 6,20-49/Mt 5,1-7,29, in Lk 12,22-33f/Mt 6,25-34.20f, in Lk 12,2-7/Mt 10,26-31 oder in Lk 11,33.34-36, ... Die Beispiele liessen sich vermehren.
>
> Das Vorliegen solcher Sammlungen deutet darauf hin, dass Q bereits am (vorläufigen) Ende eines längeren Überlieferungsvorgangs steht und dass dementsprechend das in Q aufgenommene Material nicht einheitlich ist, sondern in der allenthalben in der synoptischen Tradition nachweisbaren Weise die verschiedenen Stufen der Aufnahme der Verkündigung Jesu durch die frühe Gemeinde spiegelt.

ET: "Q in the History of Early Christianity," *The Shape of Q: Signal Essays on the Sayings Gospel*, 59-73: 59.

[136] Lührmann, *Die Redaktion der Logienquelle*, 97-98:

> Als späteste und damit zeitlich, wenn auch nicht unbedingt traditionsgeschichtlich der Redaktion von Q nächste Schicht ergab sich eine Reihe von Logien, die deutlich von der spätjüdischen Weisheit geprägt sind. Das mag auf den ersten Blick nicht ver-[98]wundern, denn der Einfluss gerade dieser Strömung schon auf die Verkündigung Jesu ist ja in der synoptischen Tradition allenthalben erkennbar. Doch sprechen die Häufigkeit und die spezielle Prägung dieser Worte und die Gestaltung der Logienquelle als Ganzer nach einer der Weisheitsliteratur entstammenden Gattung dafür, dass gerade dieser Einfluss erhebliches Gewicht in der Überlieferung der Logienquelle hatte.

ET: "Q in the History of Early Christianity," 69.

1. Q 6:20b-23b, 27-35, 36-45, 46-49,
2. Q 9:57-60, (61-62); 10:2-11, 16,
3. Q 11:2-4, 9-13,
4. Q 12:2-7, 11-12,
5. Q 12:22b-31, 33-34 and probably
6. Q 13:24; 14:26-27; 17:33; 14:34-35.

Since some of these blocks contain secondary interpolations that express the perspective of the polemical redaction, it is reasonable to assume that the hortatory instructions were literarily antecedent to the polemical materials and that at some point in the development of Q the instructional material was edited in accordance with the later perspective.[137]

It has been pointed out[138] that Kloppenborg's thesis is one of several alternate and independent expressions of a rather widespread recognition that the clusters he identified are indeed early clusters, composed before the final redaction:

> Three of these are among the early pre-redactional "collections" listed by Lührmann.[139]
>
> Five are listed by Siegfried Schulz as going back to "the kerygma of the oldest Q congregations of the Palestinian-Syrian border areas."[140]
>
> Five are included by Dieter Zeller in his list of "six larger groups of sayings that may have grown up around a kernel of admonitions."[141]
>
> Four are among the pre-Q collections of aphoristic sayings, each displaying a similar structure, presented by Ronald A. Piper in his London dissertation.[142]
>
> Four are in the Sermon on the Mount dated to around 50 C. E. as a result of the Jerusalem Council by Hans Dieter Betz.[143]

It is striking that such very divergent studies, in method and orientation, tend to agree to such a large extent about there having been such sapiential clusters at an early stage of the development. Indeed two, Q 6:20-49 (the Inaugural Sermon) and Q 12:22b-31 (Free from Anxiety Like Ravens and Lilies), are actually on each of these lists.

Kloppenborg has welcomed such drawing of "attention to the convergence of the results obtained by Zeller, Kloppenborg and Piper,"[144] and himself has added Heinz Schürmann to the list:

> It might also be noted that Schürmann, while hesitant to follow the stratigraphical model of

---

[137] John S. Kloppenborg, "The Sayings Gospel Q: Literary and Stratigraphic Problems," *Symbols and Strata: Essays on the Sayings Gospel Q*, 1-66: 48.

[138] James M. Robinson, "The Q Trajectory: Between John and Matthew via Jesus," in *The Future of Early Christianity: Essays in Honor of Helmut Koester* (ed. Birger A. Pearson; Minneapolis: Fortress, 1991) 173-94: 185-89.

[139] Lührmann, *Die Redaktion der Logienquelle*, 84: 1, 4 (only Q 12:2-7) and 5.

[140] Siegfried Schulz, *Q: Die Spruchquelle der Evangelisten*, "Das Kerygma der ältesten Q-Gemeinde des palästinensisch-syrischen Grenzraumes," 57-175: 1 (except Q 6:43-49), 3, 4 (only Q 12:4-9), 5 and 6 (only Q 16:17-18).

[141] Dieter Zeller, *Die weisheitlichen Mahnsprüche bei den Synoptikern* (FzB 17; Würzburg: Echter Verlag, 1977) 191: "6 grössere Spruchgruppen, die um einen Kern von Mahnung herumgewachsen sein dürften": 1 (except Q 6:34-35a,37b-38a, 39-40), 2 (except Q 9:57-62; 10:8b,11b, but with Q 10:12), 3 (except Q 11:9-13) 4 (except Q 12:11-12, but with Q 12:9-10), 5. However Zeller has not appropriated Kloppenborg's theory of a first, sapiential edition of Q. See Zeller, "Redaktionsprozesse und wechselnder 'Sitz im Leben' beim Q-Material," *Logia - Les paroles de Jésus - The Sayings of Jesus: Mémorial Joseph Coppens* (ed. J. Delobel; BEThL 59; Leuven: Peeters and Leuven University Press, 1982) 395-409; Zeller, "Eine weisheitliche Grundschrift in der Logienquelle?" *The Four Gospels 1992: Festschrift Frans Neirynck*, 1. 389-401.

[142] Ronald A. Piper, *Wisdom in the Q-Tradition: The Aphoristic Teaching of Jesus:* 1 (except Q 6:20b-23b, 46-49), 3 (except Q 11:2-4), 4 (adding Q 12:8-9), 5 (except Q 12:33-34).

[143] Hans Dieter Betz, *The Sermon on the Mount* (Hermeneia; Minneapolis: Fortress, 1995): 1, 3, 5 and 6 (only Q 13:24-27).

[144] Kloppenborg, "The Sayings Gospel Q: Literary and Stratigraphic Problems," 52.

Kloppenborg, has now recognized the impor-[54]tance of the six topically organized instructional speeches in the composition of Q and acknowledges that such "speeches" were already "finished" units prior to the final redaction of Q.[145]

To this list of advocates of early sapiential clusters can also be added Migaku Sato, though also a rather unwilling supporter:

> Here, more as a concession, precisely those sayings collections are named that Zeller and Kloppenborg had worked out as the sapiential collections 1, 2, 3 and 5 of the first edition of Q.[146]

Kloppenborg went on to argue that these sapiential collections had been assembled into what amounted to a first edition of Q prior to the deuteronomistic redaction:

> Given the techniques of interpolation and insertion, it is reasonable to assume that the "wisdom speeches" were *already in a written form* when they were glossed. Otherwise one would expect a greater degree of homogeneity and fewer abrupt transitions.[147]

This is the dimension of Kloppenborg's thesis that has met with the most resistance, which at times has even obscured the nigh-consensus as to the existence of such early sapiential collections. This is partly due to the widespread view that the first period was dominated by apocalypticism, with the inference that it was only the delay of the parousia mitigating that apocalyptic "enthusiasm" which made it necessary in a second phase to come to grips with the ongoing realities of normal life (see Tödt's criticism of this inference, above). For this is what one has, all too uncritically, associated with the term "sapiential."[148] But that concept of sapiential in the time frame in question has been outdated by John G. Gammie's studies of the trajectories in Jewish wisdom literature,[149] from which Kloppenborg draws the conclusion:

---

[145] Kloppenborg, "The Sayings Gospel Q: Literary and Stratigraphic Problems," 53-54. He refers to Heinz Schürmann, "Zur Kompositionsgeschichte der Redenquelle: Beobachtungen an der lukanischen Q-Vorlage," *Der Treue Gottes trauen: Beiträge zum Werk des Lukas: Für Gerhard Schneider* (edd. C. Bussmann and W. Radl; Freiburg: Herder, 1991) 325-42: 327-28, 332. Reprinted in Schümann, *Jesus - Gestalt und Geheimnis: Gesammelte Beiträge* (ed. Klaus Scholtissek; Paderborn: Bonifatius, 1994) 398-419: 400-402, 406-407.

[146] James M. Robinson, "Die Logienquelle: Weisheit oder Prophetie? Anfragen an Migaku Sato, Q und Prophetie," *EvTh* 53 (1993) 367-89: 385:

> Hier werden gleichsam als Konzession gerade die Spruchsammlungen genannt, die Zeller und Kloppenborg als die weisheitlichen Sammlungen 1, 2, 3 und 5 der ersten Auflage von Q herausgearbeitet hatten.

See Martin Ebner, *Jesus — ein Weisheitslehrer? Synoptische Weisheitslogien im Traditionsprozess* (Herders Biblische Studien / Herder's Biblical Studies 15; Freiburg: Herder, 1998) 32:

> Es ist Robinson ausserdem gelungen zu zeigen, dass Sato – ohne das in seiner Gesamtkonzeption zur Geltung kommen zu lassen – mit den weisheitlichen Kompositionen, die er als Vorstufen seines prophetischen Buches durchaus anerkennt, ziemlich nahe an die sechs 'sapiential speeches' herankommt, die nach Kloppenborg – übrigens schon von Zeller 1977 so ausgesondert – den ältesten Grundbestand von Q ausmachen: programmatische Rede (Q 6), Aussendungsrede (Q 10), Gebetsinstruktion (Q 11), Aufruf zur Sorglosigkeit (Q 12) und schliesslich Schlussmahnungen (Q 13f).

[147] Kloppenborg, *The Formation of Q*, 244.

[148] For a summary of scholarly literature correcting that inference and documenting the sapiential sayings in Q see Robinson, "Die Logienquelle: Weisheit oder Prophetie?" 374-77.

[149] John D. Gammie, "The Sage in Sirach" and "From Prudentialism to Apocalypticism: The Houses of the Sages Amid the Varying Forms of Wisdom," both in *The Sage in Israel and the Ancient Near East* (ed. John G. Gammie and Leo G. Perdue; Winona Lake: Eisenbrauns, 1990) 355-72, 479-97, and "Paraenetic Literature: Toward the Morphology of a Secondary Genre" [within wisdom literature], *Paraenesis: Act and Form* [= *Semeia* 50], 1990, 41-77.

> Although some of the *literary forms* – the instruction, for example – adopted by sages demonstrate remarkable stability over a millennium or more, the *content* of the wisdom tradition is itself remarkably diverse and adaptable. ...
>
> To characterize Q as "sapiential" is not, therefore, to imply a depiction of Jesus as a teacher of this-worldly, prudential wisdom, still less to imply an intellectual world that was hermetically sealed against eschatology, prophetic traditions, and the epic traditions of Israel.[150]

Quite apart from how one assesses the initially very obscure beginning of the Q community, Kloppenborg goes on to make clear that his analysis is literary, without necessarily involving historical inferences or presuppositions:

> To say that the wisdom components were formative for Q and that the prophetic judgment oracles and apophthegms describing Jesus' conflict with "this generation" are secondary is not to imply anything about the ultimate tradition-historical provenance of any of the sayings. It is indeed possible, indeed probable, that some of the materials from the secondary compositional phase are dominical or at least very old, and that some of the formative elements are, from the [245] standpoint of authenticity or tradition-history, relatively young. Tradition-history is not convertible with *literary history*, and it is the latter which we are treating here.[151]

Kloppenborg has concluded his recent detailed *Forschungsbericht* as follows:

> It may not be too bold to suggest that in addition to the existing consensus, initiated by Lührmann's study, that the polemic against "this generation" and the announcement of judgment provide organizing motifs at one level of the redaction of the Sayings Gospel, a second consensus point has emerged: Key to the understanding of the formation of Q is the recognition of the presence of large blocks of topically organized "sapiential" sayings, each exhibiting a similar structure, and Sitz im Leben, rhetorical intention.[152]

In fact one such sapiential collection shared by all those listed above, Free from Anxiety like Ravens and Lilies (Q 12:22b-31), has been traced back to a written Greek text that antedates the archetype of the Q text used by Matthew and Luke. It is found in the *Gospel of Thomas* 36, as preserved in *P. Oxy.* 655, a very early form of this small sayings collection. For the fragmentary papyrus attests a reading o]ὐ ξα[ί]νει, "not card," free of a scribal error found in the canonical texts: Matthew 6:28: αὐξάνουσιν par. Luke 12:27: αὐξάνει, "grow." The correct reading is otherwise attested only in the original hand of Codex Sinaiticus at Matt 6:28 (οὐ ξένουσιν, itacism for οὐ ξαίνουσιν), which was erased by the first corrector in favor of the standard Matthean reading αὐξάνουσιν (i. e., "not card" was "corrected" into "grow").[153]

On closer examination, it turns out that Saying 36 of the *Gospel of Thomas* in *P. Oxy.* 655 does not yet display other traits that critical scholarship throughout this century (but without consulting *P. Oxy.* 655) has rightly identified as secondary intrusions into that very old pre-Q collection:

> In Q 12:22b, food and clothing will be provided by God, as the ravens (Q 12:24) and lilies (Q 12:27) exemplify. But Q 12:23 interrupts this expected flow of the little collection by

150 Kloppenborg Verbin, *Excavating Q*, 385, 388.

151 Kloppenborg, *The Formation of Q*, 245.

152 Kloppenborg, "The Sayings Gospel Q: Literary and Stratigraphic Problems," 55.

153 James M. Robinson and Christoph Heil, "Zeugnisse eines schriftlichen, griechischen vorkanonischen Textes: Mt 6,28b א*, *P. Oxy.* 655 I,1-17 (EvTh 36) und Q 12,27," *ZNW* 89 (1998) 30-44. In the present volume, one may consult, for a fuller statement, the Excursus in the Text Critical Notes in the Technical Data that follows this History of Q Research, and the Endpapers, which reproduce photographs of the relevant texts in Codex Sinaiticus and *P. Oxy.* 655.

degrading food and clothing in favor of higher values, ψυχή and σῶμα, a spiritual value structure in no way exemplified by ravens and lilies. Hence Q 12:23, and the references to ψυχή and σῶμα in Q 12:22b, have seemed to be secondary intrusions, and indeed turn out to be missing from Saying 36 in *P. Oxy.* 655!

Q 12:25, expressing morose resignation as to one's inability to raise oneself by one's own bootstraps (literally: to increase one's stature or life-span), not only separates off the lilies (Q 12:27) from the ravens (Q 12:24) in the sequence of Q, making it necessary to recreate the original context by inserting the redactional verse Q 12:26, but also stands in sharp contrast to the glowing trust in God's caring that is characteristic of the collection as a whole. But in Saying 36 in *P. Oxy.* 655, the saying continues the theme of trust in God: "And as for you, who might add to your stature? He will give you your clothing."

The original climax, that your Father will surely provide the basic necessities of food, drink, and clothing (Q 12:29,30b), thereby returned appropriately as an *inclusio* to the point of departure in Q 12:22b. But this is then followed by a second climax, bringing for the first time the kingdom of God into the collection, which hence has been considered secondary. Now this anti-climactic reference to the kingdom is also absent from P. Oxy. 655![154]

Even apart from this one striking instance of documentation, the assumption of early sapiential collections embedded in Q, once justifying an early dating of Q, followed by a deuteronomistic layer corresponding to the final redaction of Q, and justifying the current trend toward a later dating of the archetype shared by Matthew and Luke, seems to have become a general assumption of the present status of Q scholarship.

The Critical Edition of Q
The International Q Project

The emergence of Q as a text originally written in Greek, whose Matthean and Lukan redaction can often be detected and discounted by applying the methods and results of redaction criticism in identifying Matthean and Lukan redactional traits in their treatment of Mark, made a critical edition of Q seem at least a possibility. Yet that undertaking itself, modeled after papyrology and textual criticism, has sought to maintain its objectivity to the particular *status quaestionis* at the time it was first undertaken by the International Q Project, in order that *The Critical Edition of Q* be equally usable for scholars of all opinions[155] and thus function as a

---

[154] For details see James M. Robinson, "The Pre-Q Text of the (Ravens and) Lilies: Q 12:22b-31 and *P. Oxy.* 655 (*Gos. Thom.* 36)," *Text und Geschichte: Facetten theologischen Arbeitens aus dem Freundes- und Schülerkreis. Dieter Lührmann zum 60. Geburtstag* (ed. Stefan Maser and Egbert Schlarb; MThSt.NF 50, 1999, 143-80); for a more readable summary see James M. Robinson, "A Written Greek Sayings Cluster Older than Q: A Vestige," *HTR* 92 (1999) 61-77.

[155] Current opinion is of course widely divided: "Der Entwurf von J. M. Robinson und H. Köster und die darauf aufbauende amerikanische Position" is the title of a sub-section, and a main focus of the polemic, of Jens Schröter, *Erinnerung an Jesu Worte: Studien zur Rezeption der Logienüberlieferung in Markus, Q und Thomas* (WMANT 76; Neukirchen: Neukirchener Verlag, 1997), 132-36. A position somewhat similar to that of Schröter is that of Richard A. Horsley with Jonathan A. Draper, *Whoever Hears You Hears Me: Prophets, Performance, and Tradition in Q* (Harrisburg, Pa.: Trinity Press International, 1999). The converse position is that of Thomas Zöckler, *Jesu Lehren im Thomasevangelium* (NHMS 47; Leiden: Brill, 1999) 2, n. 4: "Zwar behandelt Schröter nur einen Teil der Thomas-Logien, er setzt sich aber intensiv mit der Forschungsgeschichte zu Thomas und

standard tool in our discipline.[156] Hence its method has neither presupposed a view as to the layering of the text of Q, nor a view as to what extent or in what way Q reflects the sayings of Jesus and/or of the Q community. The only presupposition is the general outcome of the history of Q research that has rendered the undertaking possible at all, namely the conclusion that there was a written Greek text of Q which functioned as an archetype, copies of which were available to the Matthean and Lukan communities and used by their Evangelists. It is that archetype which *The Critical Edition of Q* seeks to reconstitute and thus to make more readily available to scholarship.

This undertaking began as a research project entitled "Q: A Lost Collection of Jesus' Sayings," launched at the Institute for Antiquity and Christianity in 1983,[157] and at the Annual Meetings of the Society of Biblical Literature as "Study of Q Consultations" (1983-1984). One of its initial policies has now become standard usage in Q research, namely the use of Lukan chapter and verse references when quoting Q.[158] The consultations developed into a Q Seminar (1985-1989), which in turn was given the status of the International Q Project[159] by the Research and Publications Committee of the Society of Biblical Literature in 1989.[160]

With the help of Leif Vaage and Jon Daniels, Research Associates of the Q Project of the Institute for Antiquity and Christianity, a brochure (entitled *Pap. Q*) was prepared to inaugurate the Project at

Q auseinander und übt in diesem Zusammenhang teilweise scharfe Kritik an den Forschungsansätzen von Köster und Robinson, an denen sich die vorliegende Arbeit massgeblich orientiert." According to Ebner, *Jesus – ein Weisheitslehrer? Synoptische Weisheitslogien im Traditionsprozess*, 31, "erscheint die Annahme eines weisheitlichen Kerns von Q als die plausiblere und textgerechtere Lösung."

156 Those who deny the existence of Q as a whole will of course not be satisfied: Michael Goulder, "Is Q a Juggernaut?" *JBL* 115 (1996) 667-81; Goulder, "Self-contradiction in the IQP," *JBL* 118 (1999) 506-17. The IQP has indeed refrained from entering into the never-ending discussion over the existence of Q, and has preferred to concentrate its energy (Goulder: "enormous industry," 506) on seeking to reconstruct the text of Q, on the assumption that this may in the end be a more compelling and useful argument for its existence.

157 "New Project Launched," *Bulletin of the Institute for Antiquity and Christianity* 10/4 (1983) 6.

158 James M. Robinson, "The Sermon on the Mount/Plain: Work Sheets for the Reconstruction of Q," SBL.SP 22 (1983) 451-54: 451-52:

> We might adopt the policy of citing Q as follows: Q 6:20 (rather than Lk 6:20 par., or Luke 6:20 //, or Mt 5:3 // Lk 6:20). This practice would mean that one regards something in Lk 6:20 as coming from Q (though not necessarily implying that Luke, rather than Matthew or some wording or sequence diverging in part from both, preserves the wording or sequence of Q). This would be a crisp way of referring to Q as an entity in its own right, without the problem of numbering the Q sayings in a different numbering system than that of Luke (e.g., like the numeration of the 114 sayings in the *Gospel of Thomas*). Thus we could refer to a specific verse without prematurely settling upon a numeration system that would soon become antiquated, or without the problem of constantly renumbering (both of which problems have emerged in the case of the *Gospel of* [452] *Thomas*).

In fact none of the various numbering systems that have been proposed have gained general acceptance other than the one based on Luke proposed here.

159 All who have been members are listed in the Acknowledgements above.

160 For further details of the beginning of the project see James M. Robinson, "A Critical Text of the Sayings Gospel Q," *RHPhR* 72 (1992) 15-22 (a paper presented at the SNTS meeting of 1991), and Frans Neirynck, "The International Q Project," *EThL* 69 (1993) 221-25, reprinted in his *Q-Synopsis: The Double Tradition Passages in Greek*, Revised Edition with Appendix (Leuven: University Press and Peeters, 1995) 75-79.

the Annual Meeting of SBL in Anaheim, Cal., in November, 1985. It contained the text shared by Matthew and Luke, letter by letter (though in transliteration, since Greek was not yet readily available on word processors), with sigla identifying the lacunae caused by divergences due to Matthean and/or Lukan redaction. A brief introduction explained:

> The following pages present a modern simulation of the quire of a tattered papyrus, with the surviving letters enmeshed within a *lacunae*-ridden web of fibre-like *sigla*. This printout, like a unique papyrus, contains the only extant vestiges of the otherwise lost collection of Jesus' sayings familiarly known as Q.
>
> Reworked by Matthew and Luke as they incorporated it in differing ways into their Gospels, the text of Q was in the process "corrupted" by the "moth" of Luke and the "rust" of Matthew. For when Luke or Matthew made a change in it, we are left with an awkward situation: At places where the two Gospels are so alike that a shared dependence on Q is to be assumed, but where Luke and Matthew nonetheless diverge in some details of wording or order, it is unclear which has altered and which has retained Q. Hence both readings become suspect, resulting in a fragmented text like a tattered papyrus shot through with *lacunae*. By the painstaking process of analyzing the syntax, vocabulary and theology of the canonical Gospels Luke and Matthew and the pre-canonical Gospel Q, one may seek to fill the *lacunae*, as one would seek to edit a papyrus.[161]

This "minimal Q" text was considered the point of departure for the work ahead:

> It is to be hoped that this printout of Pap. Q can be replaced by succeeding drafts of Q, as the work moves from its point of departure at the level of a tattered papyrus, toward a critical text constantly being improved.[162]

However, from its inception, this narrowly focused exercise was cast in a much broader and more important context. For it provided new access to Jesus and his first followers:

> The resultant critical text of Q is (at least) one step removed from Jesus himself, in that the sayings it ascribes to Jesus (and to John) are actually those proclaimed in Jesus' name by his Galilean successors. This critical text will however be (at least) one step nearer to Jesus than are Luke and Matthew, to the extent that most of the sayings they ascribe to Jesus are their reworkings of the Q text. A critical text of Q is thus indispensable for advances in our understanding of Jesus, of his immediate followers, and of the Gospels of Luke and Matthew. Thus the all-but-impossible critical task is thoroughly matched by its unrivaled importance: Quite frankly, the "shock" of the Jesus movement is less blunted when not imbedded in the cushioning provided by the next generation.[163]

A Q Section in SBL's Annual Program itself has continued without interruption, intended for a wider public, while the members of the International Q Project, co-chaired by James M. Robinson and John S. Kloppenborg, have met annually just prior to the Annual Meeting of SBL for one or two days of concentrated work (1989-1996),[164] as well

161 James M. Robinson, Leif Vaage and Jon Daniels, *Pap. Q* (Claremont, Cal.: The Institute for Antiquity and Christianity, 1985). The Introduction (pp. 1-2) was composed by Robinson, the transcription of the lacunae-laden minimal Q text (pp. 3-20) by Vaage and Daniels. The quotation is the opening of the Introduction, 1.

162 *Pap. Q.* 2.

163 *Pap. Q.* 1.

164 The meeting at Anaheim 17 xi 1989 was attended by 21 members, that at New Orleans 16 xi 1990 by 23 members, that at Kansas City 22 xi 1991 by 24 members, that at San Francisco 20 xi 92 by 24 members, that at Washington, D.C. 18-19 xi 1993 by 29 members, that at Chicago 17-18 xi 1994 by 26 members, that at Philadelphia 16 xi 1995 by 23 members, and that at New Orleans 23 xi 1996 by 25 members.

as once or twice each summer at one of the Project's centers (1991-1994).[165] The General Editors have met regularly (1995-1999)[166] to revise and edit the critical text of Q.

In 1992 Paul Hoffmann proposed a German branch of the International Q Project to be located in Bamberg. Ever since the first organizational meeting held there (21-25 vi 1993), the Bamberg members have participated in the work and attended the meetings of the International Q Project.

In 1994 Peeters Press offered to publish the Databases, Evaluations, and resultant Critical Text developed by the International Q Project. A contract to this effect was signed in Bamberg in 1995. To date there have appeared five volumes in this series entitled Documenta Q: Reconstructions of Q Through Two Centuries of Gospel Research Excerpted, Sorted, and Evaluated.[167]

The production of the critical text has been structured so as to minimize subjectivity and attain a degree of overall objectivity. The collaboration of more than forty scholars in establishing the first draft,[168] followed by the joint work of the three General Editors in refining that into the text here published, provides a check-and-balance protection against the subjectivity of an individual scholar. The critical text also has the advantage of being somewhat less the product of a given generation, in that the Database, stretching back to the discovery of Q in 1838, provides a certain balance to the inherent danger of over-emphasizing the present.

Whereas in previous generations the trend had been to leave open the exact wording, and refer only to the verses "behind" which a Q saying lurks, there has been, during the time when the International Q Project has been doing its work, a striking escalation of efforts, even outside that context, to reconstruct the actual wording of Q.

In *The Critical Edition of Q*, the English, German, and French translations both of Q and of parallel sayings from the *Gospel of Thomas* are included, saying by saying, below the eight-column synopsis format. These translations have, to the extent possible, been coordinated with each other: The translations into the three languages normally diverge from one another only when the style of each language requires, though occasionally divergences in the understanding of the text by the translators also come to expression (e.g., Q 12:25; 17: ⟦21⟧). Similarly, when it seems to be the case that Q and the *Gospel of Thomas* have the same *Vorlage*, the attempt is made to use the same language, so that divergences in the wording of the translations not be misleading, but serve to call attention to real divergences between Q and the *Gospel of Thomas*.

The style of the translations is intended to reflect the style of the text of Q itself. To be avoided is the improvement of the Q text's style, begun already by Matthew and Luke and continuing in the liturgical cadence of most translations. For it is Q itself that is being translated. Conversely, what may have been intended by Jesus, John, or those involved in oral transmission is not what determines the translation (e.g., Q 3:16b). Rather, the translation seeks to reflect the saying as the redactor of Q might have understood it.

165 The meeting at Claremont 12-14 vii 1991 was attended by 15 members, that at Claremont 31 vii-2 viii 1992 by 15 members, that at Toronto 6-8 viii 1993 by 19 members, that at Claremont 23-27 v 1994 by 15 members, and that at Rattenbach, Germany 22-26 viii 1994 by 16 members.

166 The General Editors met 1-10 vi 1995 (Bamberg), 16 xi 1995 (Philadelphia), 11-21 viii 1996 (Bamberg), 22 xi 1996 (New Orleans), 20-25 vii 1998 (Bamberg), and 27-31 vii 1999 (Bamberg).

167 *Q 11:2b-4 (The Lord's Prayer)* 1996; *Q 4:1-13,16: The Temptations of Jesus – Nazara*, 1996; *Q12:49-59: Children against Parents – Judging the Time – Settling out of Court*, 1997; *Q 12:8-12: Confessing and Denying – Speaking against the Holy Spirit – Hearings before Synagogues*, 1997; *Q 22:28, 30: You Will Judge the Twelve Tribes of Israel*, 1998.

What is offered is a fresh translation, seeking to avoid language that is so familiar (at times so offensive) that one no longer listens to what the text has to say, but also seeking to avoid language that is so bold that it would distract from what the text has to say and instead attract attention to itself.[169] Thus it seeks to facilitate the intention of the text itself: "Everyone hearing my words *and acting on them* ..." (Q 6:47).

Inclusive language is preferred, again in such a way as not to attract attention to the language itself, and so as to respect the cultural limitations of the text as given. It is not assumed that Jesus or the Q movement transcended intellectually their culture in such regards.[170] Hence, patriarchal references to God as a benevolent Father are left as such (Q 6:35c, 36; 10:21 *bis*, 22 *tris*; 11:2b, 13; 12:6, 30), rather than, for example, opening the Lord's Prayer with a politically more correct form of address: "Mother-Father," or "Parent."

Designations for Jesus pose their own problems. The perhaps all-too-familiar "Son of man" is not retained (Q 6:22; 7:34; 9:58; 11:30; 12:8, 10, 40; 17:24, 26, 30), but the somewhat more inclusive and still recognizable "son of humanity" is preferred, rather than the freer translation, "human," which would obscure the Semitic idiom as such. "Son of Humanity" is capitalized only when the saying in question suggests a superhuman person (Q 12:40; 17:24, 26, 30), in analogy to the capitalization of "God" and "Father."

"Son" is also retained in references to God's Son (Q 3:22; 4:3, 9; 10:22 *tris*). When used of God-like humans in general, "son" is used (Q 6:35c), rather than the familiar modulation "child." For "child," while more inclusive, obscures the continuity in terminology from God-like humans to Jesus.

---

168 The International Q Project has published in the October issue of *JBL* almost each year from 1990-1997 the sayings whose critical text was established the previous year: 109 (1990) 499-501; 110 (1991) 494-98; 111 (1992) 500-508; 112 (1993) 500-506; 113 (1994) 495-99; 114 (1995) 475-85; 116 (1997) 521-25. These reports did not contain the sayings in a reconstructed Q sequence, but rather in the order in which the Databases and Evaluations were prepared, discussed, and voted on. Hence decisions as to sequence were indeed involved in the process, when Matthew and Luke disagree on the positioning, but were not included in the annual reports. The members in attendance at each meeting are listed in these annual reports.

169 By way of illustration: *The Complete Gospels: Annotated Scholars Version* (ed. Robert J. Miller; Santa Rosa, CA: Polebridge, 1992; revised and expanded edition, third edition = first Harper Collins paperback edition, San Francisco: HarperSanFrancisco, 1994), contains a "Cameo Essay" (p. 448) explaining the policy of translating μακάριοι and οὐαί with "Congratulations" and "Damn": It is "performative language" that should be translated with the modern equivalent rather than the traditional language that is "archaic language and now nearly empty of meaning." But since, at least in this case, the dominant focus of attention and discussion has unfortunately become the bold new language itself, thereby actually distracting from the meaning the text seeks to convey, such potentially provocative and thus distracting translations tend to be avoided.

170 Luise Schottroff, *Itinerant Prophetesses: A Feminist Analysis of the Sayings Source Q* (Occasional Papers 21; Claremont, Ca.: Institute for Antiquity and Christianity, 1991); Schottroff, "Wanderprophetinnen: Eine feministische Analyse der Logienquelle," *EvTh* 51 (1991) 332-44. Helga Melzer-Keller, *Jesus und die Frauen: Eine Verhältnisbestimmung nach den synoptischen Überlieferungen* (Herders biblische Studien 14; Freiburg: Herder, 1997), Teil IV: "Jesus und die Frauen in der Logienquelle," 330-53; Melzer-Keller, "Frauen in der Logienquelle und ihrem Trägerkreis: Ist Q das Zeugnis einer patriarchatskritischen, egalitären Bewegung?" *Wenn Drei das Gleiche sagen ... Studien zu den ersten drei Evangelien* (ed. Stefan H. Brandenburger and Thomas Hieke; Theologie 14; Münster: Lit, 1998) 37-62; Melzer-Keller, "Wie frauenfreundlich ist die Logienquelle?" *BiKi* 54 (1999) 89-92.

Similarly in the case of κύριος one normally has the standard Jewish (LXX) usage referring to God as "Lord" (Q 4:12, 8; 10:2, 21; 13:35; 16:13), whereas in other instances it is a matter of a human "master," as the householder or slave-owner (Q 12:42, 43, 46; 13:25; 14:21; 19:16, 18, 20), or as the teacher (Q 6:46; 9:59), though such human designations no doubt acquired progressively an indeterminate degree of theologizing of a christological kind.

"Spirit" poses similar problems: If Q 3:16b is old Baptist tradition, ἐν πνεύματι ἁγίῳ καὶ πυρί, referring to God's apocalyptic action, could have meant "in holy wind and fire," i.e. with devastating hurricanes and bolts of lightning, as acts of God in judgment. But since Q interpreted the prediction of Q 3:16b to be referring to Jesus as the one to come (Q 7:19, 22), ἐν πνεύματι would refer to the Spirit present with Jesus and his followers (Q 4:1; 12:10, 12). But this in turn is not yet as advanced as the trinitarian associations suggested by "the Holy Spirit." Hence an intermediate translation is used: "in holy Spirit" and "the holy Spirit" (except in *Gos. Thom.* 44, parallel to Q 12:10, where a more trinitarian development does seem to be presupposed). Capital letters are not used for other superhuman forces, such as evil spirits (Q 11:24, 26), demons (Q 7:33; 11:14 *bis*, 15 *bis*, 19, 20) or angels (Q 4:10; 12:8, 9).

It is not to be assumed that the present critical text is a last word. Technological advances in the use of the computer make the assimilation of a mass of diverse data increasingly attainable, from which methodological advances are emerging.[171] Many serious differences of opinion have characterized efforts to reconstruct the text of Q in the past, as has been made quite clear from the two centuries of Gospel research that has been excerpted, sorted and evaluated by members of the International Q Project, as well as from the critical apparatus in *The Critical Edition of Q* itself. Such diversity will no doubt continue in the Q studies of the future, though advances that gain general acceptance should also result.

The layout of the present volume, in the form of a synopsis, putting parallel material in parallel lines, is intended to facilitate the study of Q, and thus to stimulate this ongoing process. Similarly the series Documenta Q, publishing the Databases and Evaluations, will make clear how the decisions presupposed in *The Critical Text of Q* were reached, as well as making a mass of relevant material scattered over two centuries, in three or more languages, and often in inaccessible journals and out-of-print books, more readily available. It is thus to be hoped that the refinement of the text of Q will continue unabated, in the ongoing series Documenta Q and elsewhere, indeed at an accelerated tempo, with the help of *The Critical Edition of Q*, so as to make an electronic and/or printed revision of the present work from time to time desirable.

[171] Computer-engendered tools are already in preparation: *Synoptic Concordance: A Greek Concordance to the First Three Gospels in Synoptic Arrangement, statistically evaluated, including occurrences in Acts; Griechische Konkordanz zu den ersten drei Evangelien in synoptischer Darstellung, statistisch ausgewertet, mit Berücksichtigung der Apostelgeschichte*, ed. Paul Hoffmann, Thomas Hieke, Ulrich Bauer, Vol. 1: *Introduction α-δ* (Berlin and New York: de Gruyter, 1999). See the review by Frans Neirynck, "A New Synoptic Tool," *EThL* 75 (1999) 407-18. The 4-volume series continues: Vol. 2: *ε-ι* (2000), Vol. 3: *κ-ο* (forthcoming), Vol. 4: *ψ-ω* (due 2001). Conversely, the dissertation of Thomas Bergemann, *Q auf dem Prüfstand: Die Zuordnung des Mt/Lk-Stoffes zu Q am Beispiel der Bergpredigt* (FRLANT 158; Göttingen: Vandenhoeck & Ruprecht, 1993) is not to be regarded as a methodological advance, in spite of its appeal to recent computer technology. See Adelbert Denaux, "Criteria for Identifying Q-Passages: A Critical Review of a Recent Work by T. Bergemann," *NovT* 37 (1995) 105-29, reprinted in *The Synoptic Problem and Q: Selected Studies From Novum Testamentum* (Brill's Readers in Biblical Studies 4; ed. David E. Orton; Leiden: Brill, 1999) 243-67; the book review by Thomas Hieke, *BiKi* 54 (1999) 95-96; and Kloppenborg Verbin, *Excavating Q*, 62-66.

Technical Data
James M. Robinson

The Synopsis Format in Eight Columns

The Critical Edition of Q presents the text of Q in the context of the relevant parallel texts, as the subtitle indicates: *Synopsis including the Gospels of Matthew and Luke, Mark and Thomas.*

Parallel wording in the different gospels is put, to the extent possible, on the same line. This presentation of parallel material in parallel columns is not intended to imply any theory as to the relation of the texts to each other. The form of presentation is simply intended to be user-friendly. The scholarly literature discusses such parallel material, and hence it is helpful to have it readily at hand, to make the comparison of the relevant texts more convenient for the user.

There are four columns on each of two facing pages, a total of eight columns. Column 4, highlighed in a light grey tone, contains the text of Q itself. Adjacent to it on each side, in columns 3 and 5, are the texts of Matthew and Luke that are based on Q, and hence from which the Q text has been reconstructed.

If there is a doublet, or even only a partial doublet or relevant parallel, in Matthew and/or Luke, it is put in column 2 and/or 6 respectively, adjacent to the text based on Q, separated from the main Matthean or Lukan column by a vertical dotted line.

The Matthean and Lukan materials included in these doublet columns are as follows:

Q 3:~~1a~~, 2b-3a, ~~3b-4~~: Matt 3:13; 11:10b is in column 2 and Luke 3:7a; 7:27b in column 6. In the case of Matt 11:10b par. Luke 7:27b, they are presented here, in the position of the Markan parallel, though there is no Q parallel here, and then repeated in their Q position at Q 7:27.

Q 3:9: Matt 7:19 is in column 2.

Q 3:⟦21⟧: Matt 3:5-6 is in column 2.

Q 3:⟦22⟧: Through Matt 17:5b-c and Luke 9:35 are not, strictly speaking, a parallel, but a distinct incident (a voice at the Transfiguration, rather than at the Baptism), they are included for comparison in columns 2 and 6.

Q 6:20: Matt 4:25 is in column 2 and Luke 6:17a-b in column 6.

Q 6:20-23, ~~24-26~~: The Woes in the Lukan Sermon (Luke 6:24-26) are not really doublets to the Beatitudes, but rather the inversion of the Beatitudes into Woes. Yet the shared vocabulary is relevant to the discussion of the language of the Beatitudes. Hence they are included parallel to the Beatitudes, and the Beatitudes parallel to the Woes:

> Q 6:20: Luke 6:24 is in column 6, and (by way of exception) Luke 4:18a-b in column 7.
> Q 6:21: Luke 6:24-25 is in column 6.
> Q 6:22: Luke 6:26a is in column 6.
> Q 6:23: Luke 6:26b is in column 6.
> Q 6:~~24-26~~: Matt 5:3, 6, 4, 11-12 is in column 2 and Luke 6:20b-23 in column 6.

Q 6:27-28: Luke 6:35a-b is in column 6.

Q 6:35c-d: Matt 5:48 is in column 2 and Luke 6:36 in column 6. They are not actually doublets to Matt 5:45 par. Luke 6:35c-d, but are similar in structure and concept. Also Matt 5:48 and Luke 6:35c share ἔσεσθε, as well as Matt 5:45 reading γένησθε and Luke 6:36 γίνεσθε.

Q 6:29: Matt 5:42b is in column 2 and Luke 6:30b in column 6. The two similarly formulated instances of Renouncing One's Own Rights are not actually doublets, since they are different instances, but are placed side by side for comparison of language and structure.

Q 6:30: Matt 5:40 is in column 2 and Luke 6:29b in column 6. As in the case of Q 6:29, the two similarly formulated instances of Renouncing One's Own Rights are not actually doublets, since they are different instances, but are placed side by side for comparison of language and structure.

Q 6:31: Matt 22:40 is in column 2.

Q 6:32, 34: The two instances of Impartial Love in Matt 5:46, 47 and the three instances in Luke 6:32, 33, 34 apparently represent not a doublet, but rather two distinct instances, though in the case of Luke the second of the three seems to be no more than a variant of the first, and hence is treated as a redactional doublet, not an independent saying. The layout attempts to make this visually clear:

Q 6:32: Matt 5:47 is in column 2, Luke 6:33 in column 6, and Luke 6:34 (by way of exception) in column 7.

Q 6:34: Matt 5:46 is in column 2, Luke 6:32 in column 6 and Luke 6:33 (by way of exception) in column 7.

Q 6:36: Matt 5:45 is in column 2 and Luke 6:35c-d in column 6. They are not actually doublets to Matt 5:48 par. Luke 6:36, but are similar in structure and concept. Also Matt 5:45 reads γένησθε and Luke 6:36 γίνεσθε, as well as Matt 5:48 and Luke 6:35c sharing ἔσεσθε.

Q 6:43-44: Matt 7:17, 20a, 20b=16a are in column 2. They are Matthean redundancies.

Q 6:45: Through Matt 3:7b is not, strickly speaking, a parallel, but a distinct incident (the proclamation of John, rather than of Jesus), it is included for comparison in column 2.

Q 6:46: Matt 12:50a is in column 2.

Q 7:1, ~~2~~, 3, ~~4-6a~~, 6b-9, ?10?: As exceptions to the normal practice, two Markan healings and their Matthean and Lukan parallels are included even where there is no literary relation to Q under consideration (and hence not even passive formatting is involved), but where their striking parallel structuring indicates that they are form-critically relevant to the reconstruction of the Q narrative. One is a different but comparable Gentile healing from a distance, the Syro-Phoenician (Mark) or Canaanite (Matthew) woman's daughter (Mark 7:24a, 25-30 par. Matt 15:21-28):

Q 7:1: Matt 15:21 is in column 2.

Q 7:~~2~~, 3, ~~4-6a~~: Matt 15:22-23a, 25-26 is in column 2.

Q 7:6b-c: Matt 15:27 is in column 2.

Q 7:?10?: Matt 15:28 is in column 2.

The other is the first part of the story of the healing of Jairus' daughter (Mark 5:22-23 par. Matt 9:18 par. Luke 8:41-42a):

Q 7:~~2~~, 3, ~~4-6a~~: Luke 8:41-42a is in column 6. (Matt 9:18 is here omitted due to lack of space.)

Q 7:⟦29-30⟧: Matt 21:25e, 29 is in column 2.

Q 10:~~1~~: Matt 10:1 is in column 2 and Luke 9:1-2a in column 6.

Q 10:4: Luke 9:3 is in column 6.

Q 10:5: Matt 10:11a-b is in column 2 and Luke 9:4a in column 6.

Q 10:6: Matt 10:11b is in column 2.

Q 10:7-8: Matt 10:12 is in column 2 and Luke 9:4 in column 6.

Q 10:9: Luke 9:2b is in column 6. Though Matt 4:17 is not, strictly speaking, a parallel, but a distinct incident (Jesus' proclamation, rather than that of his followers), it is included for comparison in column 2.

Q 10:10: Luke 9:5a is in column 6.

Q 10:11: Luke 9:5b is in column 6.

Q 10:12: Matt 11:24 is in column 2.

Q 10:13: Matt 11:23b is in column 2.

Q 10:15: Matt 11:21b; 10:15 is in column 2.

Q 10:16: Matt 18:5 is in column 2 and Luke 9:48a-b in column 6.

Q 10:~~25-26~~: Matt 19:16 is in column 2 and Luke 18:18 in column 6.

Q 10:~~28~~: Luke 20:39, 10:37b, and 20:40 are in column 6.

Q 11:14: Matt 12:22-23 is in column 2.

Q 11:15: Matt 12:24 is in column 2.

Q 11:23: Luke 9:50c is in column 6, though it is not actually a doublet, but rather the reverse of Q 11:23.

Q 11:16 (between Q 11:?26-27? and Q 11:29): Matt 16:1 is in column 2.

Q 11:29: Matt 16:2a, 4 is in column 2.

Q 11:33: Luke 8:16 is in column 6.

Q 11:?39a?: Luke 20:45 is in column 6.

Q 11:43: Luke 20:46 is in column 6.

Q 12:2: Luke 8:17 is in column 6.

Q 12:4: Matt 10:28b is in column 2 and Luke 12:5a-b in column 6, though they are not actually doublets, but rather the reverse of Q 12:4.

Q 12:5: Matt 10:28a is in column 2 and Luke 12:4 in column 6, though they are not actually doublets, but rather the reverse of Q 12:5.

Q 12:7: Luke 21:18 is in column 6.

Q 12:9: Matt 16:27 is in column 2 and Luke 9:26 in column 6.

Q 12:10: Matt 12:31, 32c is in column 2.

Q 12:11: Luke 21:12-14 is in column 6.

Q 12:12: Matt 10:20 is in column 2 and Luke 21:15 in column 6.

Q 12:~~21~~: Matt 6:19-20 is in column 2.

Q 12:33 (between Q 12:2-12, ~~12‹ ›33/Matt 10:23~~, ~~13-15~~, ⟦~~16-20~~⟧, ~~21~~ and Q 12:34, 22b-31): Matt 19:21b is in column 2 and Luke 12:21; 18:22b in column 6.

Q 12:30: Matt 6:7-8 is in column 2.

Q 12:⟦35-38⟧: Matt 24:46, 42 is in column 2 and Luke 12:43 in column 6.

Q 12:40: Matt 24:42 is in column 2.

Q 12:42: Matt 25:21b is in column 2.

Q 12:43: Luke 12:37a is in column 6.

Q 12:44: Luke 12:37b is in column 6.

Q 12:⟦49⟧: Matt 10:34 is in column 2 and Luke 12:51 in column 6. They are not actually doublets, but are only rather similar to Q 12:⟦49⟧.

Q 12:51: Luke 12:49 is in column 6. This is not actually a doublet, but is only rather similar to Q 12:51.

Q 12:~~52~~: Matt 10:35a, 36b is in column 2.

Q 13:24: Luke 13:23 is in column 6.

Q 13:⟦30⟧: Matt 19:30 is in column 2.

Q 13:35: Matt 21:9b is in column 2 and Luke 19:38 in column 6.

Q 14: ~~1-4~~, ~~5~~, ~~6~~: Matt 12:9-10, 12-14 is in column 2 and Luke 6:6-8; 13:15b; 6:9-11 in column 6.

Q 14:⟦11⟧: Matt 18:4 is in column 2 and Luke 18:14b in column 6.

Q 14:21: Matt 22:9 is in column 2, Luke 14:23a-b in column 6, and (by way of exception) Luke 14:13b in column 7.

Q 14:23: Matt 22:10a is in column 2 and Luke 14:21b-c in column 6.

Q 14:26: Matt 19:29a is in column 2 and Luke 18:29b in column 6.

Q 14:27: Matt 16:24b is in column 2 and Luke 9:23b in column 6.

Q 17:33 (between Q 14:27 and Q 14:34): Matt 16:25 is in column 2 and Luke 9:24 in column 6.

Q 16:17: Matt 24:34a, 35, 34b is in column 2 and Luke 21:32a, 33, 32b in column 6.

Q 16:18: Matt 19:9 is in column 2.

Q 15:4-5a, ~~5b-6~~, 7 (between Q 17:1-2 and Q 15:⟦8-10⟧; 17:3-4): Matt 18:10 is in column 2 and Luke 15:8-10 in column 6, though it is not actually a doublet, but rather another quite parallel parable.

Q 15:⟦8-10⟧ (between Q 17:1-2; 15:4-5a, ~~5b-6~~,7 and Q 17:3-4): Matt 18:10, 12-14 is in column 2 and Luke 15:4-7 in column 6, though the latter is not actually a doublet, but rather another quite parallel parable.

Q 17:6: Matt 21:21 is in column 2.

Q 17:⟦21⟧: Matt 24:26 is in column 2 and Luke 17:23 in column 6.

Q 17:23: Matt 24:23 is in column 2 and Luke 17:21 in column 6.

Q 17:24: Luke 17:30 is in column 6.

Q 17:~~25~~: Luke 9:22 is in column 6.

Q 17:26: Luke 17:28a is in column 6.

Q 17:27: Luke 17:28b-29 is in column 6.

Q 17:?28-29?: Luke 17:26a, 27 is in column 6.

Q 17:30: Luke 17:26b is in column 6, and (by way of exception) Luke 17:24b in column 7.

Q 17:34: Matt 24:18 is in column 2.

In the Entrusted Money (Q 19:12-26), the presentations of each slave's activity and his resultant treatment are strikingly parallel, and so are presented in parallel columns:

> Q 19:16: Matt 25:24a, 25 is (by way of exception) in column 1, Matt 25:22 in column 2, Luke 19:18 in column 6, and Luke 19:20 (by way of exception) in column 7.

Q 19:17: Matt 25:26 is (by way of exception) in column 1, Matt 25:23 in column 2, Luke 19:19 in column 6, Luke 19:22 (by way of exception) in column 7, and Luke 16:10a (by way of exception) in column 8.

Q 19:18: Matt 25:20 is in column 2 and Luke 19:16 in column 6.

Q 19:19: Matt 25:26 is (by way of exception) in column 1, Matt 25:21 in column 2, Luke 19:17 in column 6, Luke 19:22 (by way of exception) in column 7, and Luke 16:10a (by way of exception) in column 8.

Q 19:20-21: Matt 25:20 is (by way of exception) in column 1, Matt 25:22a, 26b, 22b in column 2, Luke 19:22b in column 6, Luke 19:16 (by way of exception) in column 7, and Luke 19:18 (by way of exception) in column 8.

Q 19:22: Matt 25:21 = 25:23 is (by way of exception) in column 1, Matt 25:24 in column 2, Luke 19:19 in column 6, Luke 19:17 (by way of exception) in column 7 and Luke 19:21 (by way of exception) in column 8.

Q 19:26: Matt 13:12 is in column 2 and Luke 8:18 in column 6.

Q 19:⟦~~27~~⟧: Matt 8:12 is in column 2 and (by way of exception) Matt 22:13b-c in column 1.

Q 22:28: Luke 18:29a is in column 6.

Q 22:~~29~~, 30: Matt 25:31 is in column 2 and Luke 12:32 in column 6.

Some instances of doublets or parallel formulations are in adjoining verses in columns 3 and/or 5, and hence are not explicitly noted in columns 2 and/or 6: Q 4:1-4, 9-12, and 5-8; Q 6:20b, 21a, and 21b; Q 6:47-48 and 49; Q 7:24b, 25, and 26; Q 7:33 and 34; Q 9:57-58, 59-60, and ⟦61-62⟧; Q 10:8 and 10-11; Q 11:31 and 32; Q 11:42a, 39b, 43, 44, 46b, 52, and 47-48; Q 12:24 and 27; Q 13:18-19 and 20-21; Q 14:26 and 27; and Q 17:24 and 26.

If there is a Markan parallel, it is put in column 1 (if reflected by Matthew) and/or 7 (if reflected by Luke). The Markan column is separated from the Matthean, Q and Lukan columns (columns 2 through 6) by a vertical line.

The Markan materials that are included are as follows:[1]

Q 3:~~1a~~, 2b-3a, ~~3b-4~~: Mark 1:9a, 4, 15, 2a, 3, 6, 5, 2b is in column 1 and Mark 1:4a, 5a, 4b, 2a, 3, 5b, 2b in column 7. Mark 1:2b is put here, though there is no Q parallel in this Markan position, as well as in its Q position at Q 7:27.

Q 3:7: Mark 1:5 is in columns 1 and 7.

Q 3:16b: Mark 1:8a, 7b, 8b is in columns 1 and 7.

Q 3:⟦21⟧: Mark 1:9-10a is in column 1 and Mark 1:5, 9 in column 7.

Q 3:⟦22⟧: Mark 1:10b-11 is in column 1. Though Mark 9:7b-c is not, strictly speaking, a parallel, but a distinct incident (a voice at the Transfiguration, rather than at the Baptism), it is included for comparison, but without sigla, in column 7 (as in the case of Q 7:1, ~~2~~, 3, ~~4-6a~~, 6b-9, ?10?, see below).

Q 4:1-2: Mark 1:12-13a is in columns 1 and 7.

Q 4:13: Mark 1:13b is in column 1.

Q 4:16, ~~31~~: Mark 1:21a is in column 1 and Mark 6:1-2a; 1:21 in column 7.

Q 6:20: Mark 3:7-9, 13; 1:21b is in column 1 and Mark 3:7-9 in column 7.

Q 6:37-38: Mark 4:24 is in columns 1 and 7.

Q 6:46: Mark 3:35a is in column 1.

Q 7:1: Mark 2:1a in column 7.

Q 7:1, ~~2~~, 3, ~~4-6a~~, 6b-9, ?10?: As exceptions to the normal practice, two Markan healings are included even where there is no literary relation to Q under consideration (and hence not even passive formatting is involved), but where their striking parallel structuring indicates they are form-critically relevant to the recon-

[1] There is a similar list of Markan parallels in Athanasius Polag, *Fragmenta Q: Textheft zur Logienquelle* (Neukirchen-Vluyn: Neukirchener Verlag, 1979, 1982[2]), "Anhang III: Parallelstellen aus dem Markusevangelium," 92-98, and "Übersicht: Synopsis Mk — Q," 99; ET: "Appendix III: Marcan Passages Parallel to Q" and "Synopsis of Mk and Q Traditions," in Ivan Havener, *Q: The Sayings of Jesus* (Wilmington, Del.: Michael Glazier, 1987) 153-60, 160-61.

struction of the Q narrative. One is a different but comparable Gentile healing from a distance, the Syro-Phoenician (Mark) or Canaanite (Matthew) woman's daughter (Mark 7:24a, 25-30 par. Matt 15:21-28):

Q 7:1: Mark 7:24a is in column 1 and Mark 2:1a in column 7.

Q 7:~~2~~, 3, ~~4-6a~~: Mark 7:25-27 is in column 1 and Mark 5:22-23 in column 7.

Q 7:6b-c: Mark 7:28 is in column 1.

Q 7:?10?: Mark 7:29 is in column 1 and Mark 7:30 in column 7.

The other is the first part of the healing of Jairus' daughter:

Q 7:~~2~~, 3, ~~4-6a~~: Mark 5:22-23 is in column 7.

Q 7:~~21~~: Mark 3:10 is in column 7.

Q 7:27: Mark 1:2 is in column 7.

Q 9:57: Mark 4:35 is in column 1.

Q 10:~~1~~: Mark 6:7a,c,b, 8a is in column 1 and Mark 6:7a,c,b in column 7.

Q 10:4: Mark 6:8-9 is in columns 1 and 7.

Q 10:5: Mark 6:10a-b is in columns 1 and 7.

Q 10:7-8: Mark 6:10b-c is in columns 1 and 7.

Q 10:9: Mark 6:12-13 in column 7. Though Mark 1:14b-15 is not, strictly speaking, a parallel, but a distinct incident (Jesus' proclamation, rather than that of his disciples), it is included for comparison, but without sigla, in column 1 (as in the case of Q 7:1,~~2~~, 3, ~~4-6a~~, 6b-9, ?10?, see above).

Q 10:10: Mark 6:11a is in columns 1 and 7.

Q 10:11: Mark 6:11b is in columns 1 and 7.

Q 10:16: Mark 9:37 is in columns 1 and 7.

Q 10:~~25-26~~: Mark 12:28-29a is in column 1 and Mark 10:17 in column 7.

Q 10:~~27~~: Mark 12:29b-30, 28c, 31 is in column 1 and Mark 12:29b-31 in column 7.

Q 10:~~28~~: Mark 12:34c, 29b-30 is in column 1 and Mark 12:32-34 in column 7.

Q 11:15: Mark 3:22 is in columns 1 and 7.

Q 11:17: Mark 3:23-25 is in columns 1 and 7.

Q 11:18: Mark 3:26 is in columns 1 and 7.

Q 11:⟦21-22⟧: Mark 3:27 is in column 1.

Q 11:23: Mark 9:40 is in column 7.

Q 11:16 (between Q 11:?26-27? and Q 11:29): Mark 8:11 is in columns 1 and 7.

Q 11:29: Mark 8:12 is in columns 1 and 7.

Q 11:33: Mark 4:21 is in columns 1 and 7.

Q 11:?39a?: Mark 12:37b-38a is in column 1 and Mark 7:6a in column 7.

Q 11:43: Mark 12:39b,a, 38c is in column 1 and Mark 12:38b-39 in column 7.

Q 12:2: Mark 4:22 is in columns 1 and 7.

Q 12:9: Mark 8:38 is in columns 1 and 7.

Q 12:10: Mark 3:28-29 is in column 1 and Mark 3:29a in column 7.

Q 12:11: Mark 13:9-11a is in columns 1 and 7.

Q 12:12: Mark 13:11b-c is in columns 1 and 7.

Q 12:33: Mark 10:21b is in columns 1 and 7.

Q 12:⟦35-38⟧: Mark 13:37, 35 is in column 1 and Mark 13:33-34, 37, 35-36 in column 7.

Q 12:40: Mark 13:35a-b is in columns 1 and 7.

Q 12:43: Mark 13:36 is in columns 1 and 7.

Q 12:~~50~~: Mark 10:38b is in column 7.

Q 12:53: Mark 13:12 is in column 7.

Q 13:18-19: Mark 4:30-32 is in columns 1 and (by way of exception) 6.

Q 13:⟦30⟧: Mark 10:31 is in columns 1 and 7.

Q 13:35: Mark 11:9b-10 is in columns 1 and 7.

Q 14:~~1-4~~, ~~5~~, ~~6~~: Mark 3:1-6 is in columns 1 and 7.

Q 14:26: Mark 10:29b is in column 1.

Q 14:27: Mark 8:34b is in columns 1 and 7.

Q 17:33 (between Q 14:27 and Q 14:34): Mark 8:35 is in columns 1 and 7.

Q 14:34: Mark 9:49-50a is in columns 1 and 7.

Q 16:17: Mark 13:30a, 31, 30b is in columns 1 and 7.

Q 16:18: Mark 10:11-12 is in columns 1 and 7.

Q 17:2: Mark 9:42 is in column 1 and Mark 9:42b,a in column 7.

Q 17:6: Mark 11:22-23 is in columns 1 and 7.

Q 17:⟦21⟧: Mark 13:21 is in column 1.

Q 17:23: Mark 13:21 is in columns 1 and 7.

Q 17:~~25~~: Mark 8:31 is in column 7.

Q 17:~~31-32~~: Mark 13:15-16 is in columns 1 and 7.

Q 17:34-35: Mark 13:16 is in columns 1 and 7.

Q 19:12: Mark 13:34a is in column 1.

Q 19:13: Mark 13:34b is in columns 1 and 7.

Q 19:26: Mark 4:25 is in columns 1 and 7.

Q 22:28: Mark 10:29a is in columns 1 and 7.

If there is a parallel in the *Gospel of Thomas*, it is put in column 8, separated from column 7 by a heavier vertical line.

The sayings from the *Gospel of Thomas* are as follows:[2]

Q 6:20: *Gos. Thom.* 54 (Nag Hammadi II 2).

Q 6:21: *Gos. Thom.* 69.2 (Nag Hammadi II 2).

Q 6:22: *Gos. Thom.* 69.1a (by way of exception in column 7) and 68.1 (both Nag Hammadi II 2).

Q 6:30: *Gos. Thom.* 95 (Nag Hammadi II 2).

Q 6:31: *Gos. Thom.* 6.3 (Nag Hammadi II 2; *P. Oxy.* 654).

Q 6:34: *Gos. Thom.* 95 (Nag Hammadi II 2).

Q 6:39: *Gos. Thom.* 34 (Nag Hammadi II 2).

Q 6:41: *Gos. Thom.* 26.1 (Nag Hammadi II 2).

Q 6:42: *Gos. Thom.* 26.2 (Nag Hammadi II 2; *P. Oxy.* 1).

Q 6:43-44: *Gos. Thom.* 45.1 (Nag Hammadi II 2).

Q 6:45: *Gos. Thom.* 45.2-4 (Nag Hammadi II 2).

Q 7:24: *Gos. Thom.* 78.1 (Nag Hammadi II 2).

Q 7:25 *Gos. Thom.* 78.2-3 (Nag Hammadi II 2).

Q 7:28: *Gos. Thom.* 46 (Nag Hammadi II 2).

Q 9:58: *Gos. Thom.* 86 (Nag Hammadi II 2).

Q 10:2: *Gos. Thom.* 73 (Nag Hammadi II 2).

Q 10:3/Matt 10.16~~b~~: *Gos. Thom.* 39.3 (Nag Hammadi II 2; *P. Oxy.* 655).

Q 10:7-8: *Gos. Thom.* 14.4a-b (Nag Hammadi II 2).

Q 10:9: *Gos. Thom.* 14.4c (Nag Hammadi II 2).

Q 10:22: *Gos. Thom.* 61.3b (Nag Hammadi II 2).

Q 10:~~22‹ ›23/Matt 11:28-30~~: *Gos. Thom.* 90 (Nag Hammadi II 2).

Q 11:9: *Gos. Thom.* 92.1 (Nag Hammadi II 2).

Q 11:10: *Gos. Thom.* 94 (Nag Hammadi II 2).

Q 11:⟦21-22⟧: *Gos. Thom.* 35 (Nag Hammadi II 2).

Q 11:?27-28?: *Gos. Thom.* 79.1-2 (Nag Hammadi II 2).

Q 11:33: *Gos. Thom.* 33.2-3 (Nag Hammadi II 2).

Q 11:34: *Gos. Thom.* 24.3 (Nag Hammadi II 2; *P. Oxy.* 655).

Q 11:39b: *Gos. Thom.* 89.1 (Nag Hammadi II 2).

Q 11:⟦~~40~~⟧: *Gos. Thom.* 89.2 (Nag Hammadi II 2).

Q 11:52: *Gos. Thom.* 39.1-2 (Nag Hammadi II 2; *P. Oxy.* 655).

Q 12:2: *Gos. Thom.* 5.2; 6.5 (Nag Hammadi II 2; *P. Oxy.* 654).

Q 12:3: *Gos. Thom.* 33.1 (Nag Hammadi II 2; *P. Oxy.* 1).

Q 12:10: *Gos. Thom.* 44 (Nag Hammadi II 2).

Q 12:~~13-14~~: *Gos. Thom.* 72.1-2 (Nag Hammadi II 2).

Q 12:⟦~~16-20~~⟧: *Gos. Thom.* 63.1-3 (Nag Hammadi II 2).

Q 12:33 (between Q 12:12 and Q 12:34, 21b-31): *Gos. Thom.* 76.3 (Nag Hammadi II 2).

Q 12:22b, 25, 27, 28: *Gos. Thom.* 36 has a much more complete text in the relatively extant original Greek of *P. Oxy.* 655 than in the Coptic translation of Nag Hammadi II 2. For this reason *P. Oxy.* 655 is put in column 8, whereas Nag Hammadi II 2, which has a parallel only to Q 12:22b, is put below. This is the reverse of the usual procedure, which is that the more fully extant text of Nag Hammadi II 2 is put in column 8, though it is a translation from Greek into Coptic, and the text of *P. Oxy.* 1, 654, 655, though in the original Greek, is put below, since the texts are usually very fragmentary.

> Q 12:22b: *Gos. Thom.* 36.1 (*P. Oxy.* 655; Nag Hammadi II 2).
>
> Q 12:25: *Gos. Thom.* 36.4 (*P. Oxy.* 655).
>
> Q 12:27: *Gos. Thom.* 36.2-3 (*P. Oxy.* 655).
>
> Q 12:28: *Gos. Thom.* 36.2 (*P. Oxy.* 655).

Q 12:⟦~~35-38~~⟧: *Gos. Thom.* 21.7 (Nag Hammadi II 2).

Q 12:39: *Gos. Thom.* 21.5 (by way of exception in column 7); 103 (both Nag Hammadi II 2).

[2] There are similar lists of parallels from the *Gospel of Thomas* in Helmut Koester, *Ancient Christian Gospels: Their History and Development* (London: SCM, and Philadelphia: Trinity Press International, 1990) 87-89, and Harold W. Attridge, "Reflections on Research into Q," *Early Christianity, Q and Jesus* (ed. John S. Kloppenborg with Leif E. Vaage; *Semeia* 55; Atlanta: Scholars Press, 1992) 223-34: 231-32, the latter broken down in terms of two editions of Q.

Q 12:⟦49⟧: *Gos. Thom.* 10 (Nag Hammadi II 2).
Q 12:51: *Gos. Thom.* 16.1-2 (Nag Hammadi II 2).
Q 12:~~52~~: *Gos. Thom.* 16.3a (Nag Hammadi II 2).
Q 12:53: *Gos. Thom.* 16.3b (Nag Hammadi II 2).
Q 12:⟦56⟧: *Gos. Thom.* 91.2 (Nag Hammadi II 2).
Q 13:18-19: *Gos. Thom.* 20 (Nag Hammadi II 2).
Q 13:20-21: *Gos. Thom.* 96.1-2 (Nag Hammadi II 2).
Q 13:⟦30⟧: *Gos. Thom.* 4.2 (Nag Hammadi II 2; *P. Oxy.* 654).
Q 14:~~15~~, 16: *Gos. Thom.* 64.1a (Nag Hammadi II 2).
Q 14:17: *Gos. Thom.* 64.1b (Nag Hammadi II 2).
Q 14:18, ?19-20?: *Gos. Thom.* 64.2-5, 8-9, 6-7 (Nag Hammadi II 2).
Q 14:21: *Gos. Thom.* 64.10-11a (Nag Hammadi II 2).
Q 14:23: *Gos. Thom.* 64.11b (Nag Hammadi II 2).
Q 14:~~24~~: *Gos. Thom.* 64.12 (Nag Hammadi II 2).
Q 14:26: *Gos. Thom.* 55 (by way of exception in column 7); 101.1-2 (both Nag Hammadi II 2).
Q 14:27: *Gos. Thom.* 55.2 (Nag Hammadi II 2).
Q 16:13: *Gos. Thom.* 47.2 (Nag Hammadi II 2).
Q 15:4-5a, ~~5b-6~~, 7 (between Q 17:2 and Q 15:⟦8-10⟧; 17:3): *Gos. Thom.* 107 (Nag Hammadi II 2).
Q 17:6: *Gos. Thom.* 48 (Nag Hammadi II 2).
Q 17:⟦20⟧: *Gos. Thom.* 113.1-2 (Nag Hammadi II 2).
Q 17:⟦21⟧: *Gos. Thom.* 113.3-4 (by way of exception in column 7); 3.1-3 (both Nag Hammadi II 2; Saying 3 also *P. Oxy.* 654).
Q 17:23: *Gos. Thom.* 3.1-2 (Nag Hammadi II 2; *P. Oxy.* 654).
Q 17:34: *Gos. Thom.* 61.1 (Nag Hammadi II 2).
Q 19:26: *Gos. Thom.* 41 (Nag Hammadi II 2).

At times, columns are not needed for their primary purpose, since there is no Matthean and/or Lukan doublet, or no Markan parallel, or no parallel in the *Gospel of Thomas*. Such unused columns normally remain empty. But sometimes such empty columns are used for a text that falls outside the assigned rôle of that column, when there is a parallel text useful in analyzing the passage at hand, such as a LXX parallel, or another sayings parallel, e.g. from the Gospel of John, or from the rest of the New Testament, or from the *Didache,* or other early Christian literature. In such cases a heavier vertical line separates these columns from the more central columns. There follow lists of other instances of a column being thus used for a text that is not the normal text expected in that column.

First, texts from the LXX:[3]
Q 3:~~1a~~, 2b-3a, ~~3b-4~~: Isa 40:3 LXX is in column 8.
Q 3:⟦22⟧: Ps 2:7b-d LXX is in column 8.
Q 4:4: Deut 8:3 LXX is in column 8.
Q 4:10: Ps 90:11 LXX is in column 8.
Q 4:11: Ps 90:12 LXX is in column 8.
Q 4:12: Deut 6:16 LXX is in column 8.
Q 4:8 (between Q 4:9-12, 5-7 and Q 4:13): Deut 6:13a = 10:20a LXX is in column 8.
Q 6:20: Isa 61:1a-b LXX is in column 7.
Q 6:21: Isa 61:2 LXX is in column 7.
Q 6:27-28: Lev 19:18c LXX is in column 1.
Q 6:29: Exod. 21:24a-b LXX = Lev 24:20b-c LXX = Deut 19:21c-d LXX are in column 1.
Q 7:22: Isa 61:1 LXX is in column 6, Isa 42:7, 18; 26:19a LXX in column 7, and Isa 35:5-6a; 29:18-19a LXX in column 8.

[3] There is a similar list of LXX parallels in Polag, *Fragmenta Q,* "Anhang IV: Schriftstellen aus der Septuaginta," 100-102; ET: "Appendix IV: Septuagint Passages Appearing in Q," in Havener, *Q: The Sayings of Jesus,* 163-65.

Q 7:27: Exod 23:20a-b LXX is in column 1 and Mal 3:1a LXX in column 2.

Q 9:⟦~~61-62~~⟧: 3 Kgdms 19:19a, 20 LXX is in column 8.

Q 10:4: 4 Kgdms 4:29 LXX is in column 8.

Q 10:15: Isa 14:13a-c, 15 LXX is in columns 1 and 8.

Q 10:21: Sir 51:1a, 2a-b LXX is in column 1.

Q 10:~~22↔23/Matt 11:28-30~~: Sir 51:23a, 26a-b, 27b LXX is in column 1.

Q 10:~~27~~: Deut 6:4b-5 LXX and Lev 19:18c LXX are in column 8.

Q 12:42: Ps 103:27 LXX is in column 1.

Q 12:53: Mic 7:6 LXX is in column 1.

Q 13:18-19: Ps 103: 12a LXX is in column 7.

Q 13:27: Ps 6:9a LXX is in columns 1 and 8.

Q 13:35: Ps 117:26a LXX is in column 1 and Jer 22:5 LXX in column 2.

Q 17:?28-29?: Gen 19:24 LXX is in column 8.

Q 17:~~31-32~~: Gen 19:26 LXX is in column 8.

Next, there are texts from the Gospel of John:

Q 6:40: John 13:16b = 15:20b is in column 8.

Q 7:1, ~~2~~, 3, ~~4-6a~~, 6b-9, ?10?: The Johannine narration of the same Gentile healing from a distance, the Centurion's (Q) or Royal Official's boy (John 4:46b-53), is included in column 8, since its parallel structure is relevant to the reconstruction of the Q narrative.

Q 7:1: John 4:46b is in column 8.

Q 7:~~2~~, 3, ~~4-6a~~: John 4:46b-48 is in column 8.

Q 7:6b-c: John 4:51a, 49 is in column 8.

Q 7:?10?: John 4:50-53 is in column 8.

Q 10:2: John 4:35 is in column 7.

Q 10:16: John 13:20 is in column 8.

Q 10:22: John 13:3a; 10:15 is in column 7.

Q 11:9: John 16:24b is in column 7.

Q 12:12: John 14:26 is in column 8.

Q 13:35: John 12:13b in column 8.

Q 17:33 (between Q 14:27 and Q 14:34): John 12:25 is in column 8.

There are a few texts from the the rest of the New Testament:

Q 10:7-8: 1 Tim 5:18b is in column 1.

Q 10:~~27~~: Gal 5:14b = Rom 13:9c are in column 8.

Q 12:39: Rev 3:3b is in column 1.

Q 16:18: 1 Cor 7:10-11 is in column 6.

There are a number of texts from the *Didache*:

Q 6:27-28: *Did* 1.3d,b is in column 7.

Q 6:29: *Did* 1.4b,d is in column 7.

Q 6:⟦29↔30/Matt 5:41⟧: *Did* 1.4c is in column 1.

Q 6:30: *Did* 1.5a is in column 7.

Q 6:31: *Did* 1.2d is in column 1.

Q 6:32: *Did* 1.3c is in column 1.

Q 10:~~27~~: *Did* 1.2b-c is in column 6.

Q 11:~~1-2a~~, 2b: *Did* 8.2a is in column 1.

Q 11:3: *Did* 8.2b is in column 1.

Q 11:4: *Did* 8.2c is in column 1.

Q 12:59: *Did* 1.5-6 is in column 1.

There are a few texts from other early Christian literature:

Q 16:13: *2 Clem.* 6.1 is in column 7.

Q 16:18: *Herm. Man.* 4.1.6c is in column 8.

Q 17:1: *1 Clem.* 46.8a is in column 8.

Q 17:2: *1 Clem.* 46.8b-c is in column 8.

Q 16:16: Justin, *Dial.* 51.3a is in column 8.

Beneath the eight columns, one below the other, there are broader panels containing (when applicable): a critical apparatus of divergent views within the International Q Project; text critical notes to the biblical texts; definitions of the individual variation units; an unformatted text of Q, again highlighted in a light grey tone, in Greek, English, German, and French (with only degrees of certainty indicated by sigla); translations of the Coptic translation of the *Gospel of Thomas* (Nag Hammadi II 2) in Greek (a retroversion), English, German, and French; and the Greek original of the *Gospel of Thomas* (*P. Oxy.* 1, 654, 655), with English, German, and French translations. These panels are broader than the eight columns, usually two columns in width, except for the text critical notes, which are four columns in width.

Sigla in the Page Layout

The International Q Project began by delimiting the discrete variation units in the text of Q. "Variation unit" is a concept borrowed from textual criticism to define precisely the extent of alteration that a single scribal error would bring with it. For what is involved is often not just one word or a few letters, but includes whatever cluster of changes is set in motion by that error, such as a change in a noun's case necessitated by a change of the preposition governing it. Of course in the case of Q it is not a matter of scribal error, but rather of Matthean and/or Lukan redactional "improvements," but the need to delimit in terms of variation units is the same.

Each variation unit is evaluated {A}, {B}, {C}, {D}, or {U} (indeterminate), in a descending scale of certainty, based upon a procedure familiar from textual criticism.[1]

An initial selection was made as to which sayings are most probably in Q, to avoid the endless task of discussing all the verses in Matthew and Luke. The initial sifting was that of John S. Kloppenborg.[2] Items he included without question, and those he considered doubtful, but probably in Q, were included; doubtful items which he thought are probably not in Q were initially excluded, though some were later examined.

Sigla Used in Columns 3 (Matthew), 4 (Q), and 5 (Luke)

(αβγ) Parentheses in the text of Matthew and Q enclose wording or lettering found in Matthew but not in Luke.

[αβγ] Square brackets in the text of Luke and Q enclose wording or lettering found in Luke but not in Matthew.

{αβγ} Braces in the text of Matthew, Q, and Luke enclose wording or lettering found in Mark (columns 1 and/or 7).

$^{0}/\ \backslash^{0}$ The number zero is normally used for a variation unit concerning whether or not a relatively large unit of Matthean and/or Lukan text is to be included in the text of Q. When the reason for uncertainty is simply significant dissimilarity between Matthew and Luke, slashes are used to delimit the extent of the material being discussed, $^{0}/\ \backslash^{0}$. When the reason for uncertainty is that it is a matter of Matthean special material, Lukan special material, or Markan overlap, then parentheses $^{0}(\ )^{0}$, square brackets $^{0}[\ ]^{0}$, or braces $^{0}\{\ \}^{0}$, respectively, are used to delimit the extent of the material being discussed.

ʃ ʅ Raised squiggles (which are short wavy twists) surround divergences in the sequence of

[1] *The Greek New Testament*, ed. Kurt Aland, Matthew Black, Bruce M. Metzger, Allen Wikgren (New York: American Bible Society; London: British and Foreign Bible Society; Edinburgh: National Bible Society of Scotland; Amsterdam: Netherlands Bible Society; Stuttgart: Württemberg Bible Society, 1966^{1}) x-xi:

> By means of the letters A, B, C, and D, enclosed within "braces" { } …, the Committee has sought to indicate the relative degree of certainty… . The letter A signifies that the text is virtually certain, [xi] while B indicates that there is some degree of doubt. The letter C means that there is considerable degree of doubt …, while D shows that there is a very high degree of doubt.

[2] John S. Kloppenborg, *Q Parallels: Synopsis, Critical Notes and Concordance* (Sonoma, Calif.: Polebridge, 1988).

Matthew's and Luke's shared material. The position where one evangelist has placed the thus-delimited material is marked at the equivalent position in the other Gospel with the sigla ⸂ ⸃, but enclosing no text. Though one or the other position is chosen in the reconstructed text of Q (column 4), the sigla are retained in Q at both locations, even in the position where the text does not occur in Q, so as to indicate what the other alternative would have been. No space between ⸂ and ⸃ in the text of Q means that this position was excluded with a certainty of {A} or {B}. Space between ⸂ and ⸃ in the text of Q means that this position was excluded with a certainty only of {C} or {D}, or is left indeterminate {U} (in which case the text of Q uses, by default, the Lukan position). For example:

> ⸂αβγ⸃ χψω ⸂⸃ means that αβγ precedes χψω in Q with an evaluation of {A} or {B}.
>
> ⸂αβγ⸃ χψω ⸂ ⸃ means that αβγ precedes χψω in Q with an evaluation of {C} or {D}, or an evaluation is indeterminate {U}.

^{1}, ^{2}, ^{3} Small raised numerals following the closing siglum are used to number the variation units within a verse (or longer text needing to be treated as a verse). The numeration follows the sequence established for the text of Q (column 4). The numbers are normally appended only to the closing siglum. However, when a smaller variation unit falls within the position markers ⸂ and ⸃ that delimit a larger variation unit having to do with sequence, the number precedes the first position marker as well as following the last position marker. This is done so that the numeration of the variation unit marked by ⸂ and ⸃ comes first and so automatically receives a higher number than the numeration of the smaller variation unit that falls between the position markers. For example: ⸂^{2} [αβγ]^{3} ⸃^{2} makes clear that variation unit 2, the discussion of the position, comes prior to variation unit 3, the discussion of whether Luke's text αβγ is in Q.

$^{1.2}$ When two raised numbers refer to distinct variation units (since distinct decisions are involved), but yet the two numbers are adjacent, they are separated by a dot.

⇒ When a closing siglum is in a different verse from the corresponding opening siglum, an arrow in the first verse, placed at the end of the texts of Matthew, Q and Luke, refers the reader to the subsequent verse where the respective closing siglum is found. For example:

> \\$^{1}$⇒ Q 12:12, on a line by itself at the end of the verse Q 12:11, means that the variation unit ^{1} (which in such cases usually has to do with the position of the whole pericope in Q) continues to the end of Q 12:12.
>
> \\Q 12:11^{1}, on a line by itself at the end of the verse Q 12:12, is the corresponding reference back, to indicate where this variation unit began.

( ) [ ] Since in Matthew or Luke parentheses or square brackets enclose wording or lettering that does not appear in the other Gospel, empty parentheses or square brackets (with space between them) are used at the equivalent position in the other Gospel, to indicate that the same text or at least some comparable text is here missing. If both Gospels have comparable but divergent material in the same position, parentheses enclose such material in Matthew and square brackets enclose it in Luke, without the use of empty sigla in either Gospel.

Sigla Used in Column 4 (Q) Only

(αβγ) [αβγ] When the Matthean and Lukan texts diverge from each other, the text of one or the other Gospel is normally present in Q within the appropriate sigla.

( ) [ ] If it has been decided with an evaluation no higher than {D}, or the decision remains indeterminate, as to whether the wording or lettering that is found in Matthew or Luke is in Q, the parentheses or square brackets are retained in the reconstructed text of Q to mark where that text would be, were it in Q, but with an empty space between the two sigla to indicate that no strong opinion for preferring this reading over the alternate reading has been established.

() [] If it has been decided with an evaluation of {A} or {B} that the wording or lettering that is found in Matthew or Luke is not in Q, the parentheses or square brackets are retained in the reconstructed text of Q to mark where that text would be, were it in Q, but without an empty space between them, to indicate that no text is assumed to be here in Q.

⟦(δέ)⟧ ⟦[δέ]⟧ Double square brackets are used in the reconstructed text of Q to enclose reconstructions that are probable but uncertain, {C}. Issues of sequence are excepted from the use of double square brackets, i.e., ⟦ʃ⟧, ⟦ʅ⟧, and ⟦ʃʅ⟧ do not occur.

Q 12:⟦54-56⟧ The verse numbers of whole verses that are probably in Q, but only with an evaluation of {C}, are enclosed in double square brackets, to indicate the uncertainty, as is the text of such verses, as well as the title of the pericope as a whole, if the whole pericope has an evaluation of {C}. For example:

Q 12:⟦54-56⟧ ⟦Judging the Time⟧

This means that in such verses no variation unit can show an evaluation higher than {C}, even though, apart from the overall evaluation, some variation units might seem to deserve a higher evaluation (as would of course be the case with material present in both Matthew and Luke). For a saying, or a larger pericope such as a parable, would either be completely in Q or completely absent from Q. Thus distinctions between hypothetical evaluations of {A}, {B}, or {C} are not indicated in the text of individual variation units, in view of the overarching evaluation of {C}. But evaluations lower than {C}, i.e. {D} or {U}, can, in spite of the overarching double square brackets, be appropriately indicated in the text.

⟦()⟧ ⟦[]⟧ If it has been decided with an evaluation of {C} that the wording or lettering that is found in Matthew or Luke is not in Q, the parentheses or square brackets are retained in the reconstructed text of Q, thus marking the place where Matthew or Luke had such material, but the space between them is removed, and double square brackets enclose the parentheses or square brackets.

[()] ⟦[()]⟧ [( )] If there is divergent but comparable wording or lettering at the same position in both Matthew and Luke, but it is decided that neither that of Matthew nor that of Luke is in Q, then the space is removed [()] for an evaluation of {A} or {B}, or ⟦[()]⟧ for an evaluation of {C}. But if it is decided (pro *or* con) with an evaluation of {D}, or it is left indeterminate, {U}, then the space is retained, [( )], since no strong opinion for inclusion or exclusion has been established.

~~οὐ δέ~~ Identical wording or lettering in similar usage in both Matthew and Luke would seem initially to belong to Q, indeed to be part of a "minimal Q" text. But if the context in Matthew and Luke proves on further analysis not to be in Q, with a negative evaluation as high as {A} or {B}, such shared lettering is marked out, if it could not have stood alone in Q without that now-excluded context. (Such marked-out wording or lettering is omitted completely from the unformatted Greek text and from the translations, see below, p. lxxxvii.)

Q 22:~~29~~-30 If it is decided that a verse (or a pericope) is not in Q, with a negative evaluation as high as {A} or {B}, the verse numeration is retained, but marked out, as is the title in the running header, if it has to do with a whole pericope. (Such marked-out verse numbers and titles are thereby distinguished from the many verses of Matthew and Luke that can on face value be excluded from Q with sufficient clarity that a detailed examination is not necessary, which are hence passed over in silence.) For example:

Q 22:~~29~~-30 means that there is not a verse of Q used in Luke 22:29, but that there is a verse of Q used in Luke 22:30.

Q 6:~~24-26~~ ~~The Woes against the Rich~~ means that this Lukan pericope is not in Q.

(Such marked-out verses and pericopes are omitted completely from the unformatted Greek text and from the translations, see below.)

Q 12:⟦~~35-38~~⟧ The verse numbers of verses that are probably not in Q, but are excluded only with an evaluation of {C}, are also marked out, as is the title of the pericope as a whole, if it has an evaluation of {C}. But such material is enclosed in double square brackets, to indicate the degree of uncertainty. For example:

> Q 12:⟦~~35-38~~⟧ ⟦~~Like Slaves Waiting up for Their Master~~⟧.

(Such material probably to be omitted is also omitted completely from the unformatted Greek text and from the translations, see below, p. lxxxvii.)

Q 11:?27-28? When there is serious uncertainty as to whether a verse is or is not included in Q, as indicated by evaluations of {D} (either to include *or* exclude) or {U}, the verse numbers, and the titles, are enclosed in question marks. For example:

> Q 11:?27-28? ?Hearing and Keeping God's Word?

This indicates that these verses are very uncertain, even though they have not been fully excluded with evaluations of {A}, {B}, or {C}. (In the unformatted Greek text and the translations, such texts are suggested as mere possibilities in that they are only represented by two dots: .., see below, p. lxxxvii.)

< > Angle brackets indicate that the text is an emendation found as such neither in Matthew nor in Luke. If the Q stem of a word is in one Gospel but the Q ending in the other, that Q ending, though in one text, is nonetheless considered an emendation, since the stem and the ending do not occur in the same word.

«» Double angle brackets indicate that there is a Greek text derived from Q only in one Gospel, and hence that a critical text cannot be established by the usual comparison of both Gospels. This text is thus considered pre-critical, and hence only an approximation or gist.

> Instances occur e. g. in Q 6:⟦29↔30/Matt 5:41⟧ and 12:49.

Reminiscences of Q

Verses in Matthew or Luke which are not from Q, but adjoin a verse derived from Q, may contain a reminiscence that has strayed from the text of Q into the adjoining Matthean or Lukan context. Such an adjoining verse is included in the layout in the Matthean or Lukan column 3 or 5, so that the possibility of a reminiscence may be taken into consideration in establishing the critical text of Q. But it is not considered a text primarily derived from Q, and hence is not formatted in the normal way that Q-based verses are presented in columns 3 and 5. Hence this divergence in the formatting needs to be clarified explicitly:

To avoid unnecessary clutter and confusion in the formatting of the Matthean and Lukan texts derived from Q, and of the Q text itself, the very numerous divergent readings of the Matthean and/or Lukan adjoining verses are not given the normal formatting with sigla, since that mass of sigla then would need to be repeated in the relevant positions in the Matthean and Lukan texts primarily dependent on Q, and in the Q text itself. However, in order to facilitate the visual assessment of the extent to which Q material may have strayed into these adjoining verses, they receive "passive" formatting, which is intended to draw attention to material in these adjoining verses which is shared with the Matthean and/or Lukan Q verses themselves. Such formatting makes readily visible, by means of braces { }, what material in the adjoining verses is shared with, and perhaps derived from, Mark (columns 1 and/or 7). And it makes readily visible, by means of parentheses ( ) embracing Matthean parallels and square brackets [ ] embracing Lukan parallels, what material in these adjoining verses is shared with the verses of Matthew and/or Luke that are based on Q. For such material may have strayed from Q into the context of the Matthean and/or Lukan Q verses, and hence may provide secondary attestation for the Q text itself. For example:

> Q 12:11: In Matt 10:19a (par. Q 12:11 par. Luke 12:11), an explicit reference to synagogues is missing, though present in Luke 12:11. Yet its anticipation in Matt 10:17, ἐν ταῖς συναγωγαῖς (par. Luke 21:12 εἰς τὰς συναγωγάς), would make a repetition in the position of Q 12:11 at Matt 10:19a superflu-

ous. The inclusion of Matt 10:17-18 with passive formatting renders the possibility of such secondary evidence for a Q reading readily visible.

Exclusions from Q

Many verses of Matthew and Luke can on face value be excluded from Q with sufficient clarity that a detailed examination is not necessary. They are passed over in silence. But there are borderline cases, usually resulting from the standard delimitation of Q material: That which is in Matthew and Luke but not in Mark. For sometimes a text is only in Matthew or Luke, and yet some scholars have nonetheless ascribed it to Q. Or sometimes a text is also in Mark, yet has been considered by some to be not just a saying derived from Mark, but rather a doublet that is both in Mark and in Q. Such borderline cases need to be included in the present analysis.

When the text is only in one Gospel, either Matthew or Luke, a breakdown into individual variation units of Matthean and Lukan disagreement is in any case not possible. Hence there is only a single variation unit, as to whether the text is in Q (usually variation unit [0]). If the overall decision is to the effect that the material was not in Q, no text is in the Q column, and a horizontal line is drawn through the verse numbers (and their titles): Q 6:~~24-26~~; 7:~~4-6a~~; 7:~~20-21~~; 9:~~61-62~~; 10:~~22‹ ›23/ Matt 11:28-30~~; 10:~~28~~; 11:~~1-2a~~; 11:⟦~~5-8~~⟧; 11:~~36~~; 12:~~12‹ ›33/Matt 10:23~~; 12:~~13-15~~; 12:⟦~~16-20~~⟧, ~~21~~; 12:~~50~~; 12:~~52~~; 12:~~57~~; 14:~~22~~; 14: ~~24~~; 15:~~5b-6~~; 17:~~22~~; 17:~~25~~; 17:~~28-29~~; 19:~~13‹ ›15/Matt 25:15c-18~~; 19:~~14~~; 19:~~25~~; 22:~~29~~. A less certain instance is Q 11: ?27-28?.

In other cases the text is in both Matthew and Luke, and hence there are a number of variation units, but the decision regarding whether the text is in Q at all (variation unit [0]), is, after working inductively through the individual variation units, to the effect that the text as a whole is not in Q. Hence no text is in the Q column. In these instances, the full formatting of the Matthean and Lukan texts is retained, along with their definitions, to facilitate a repetition of that inductive procedure if needed, even though the individual variation units would seem to be otiose, in view of the negative conclusion about the verse as a whole: Q 3:~~1~~; 3:~~3b-4~~; 4:~~31~~; 7:~~2~~; 10:~~1~~; 10:~~25-27~~; 11:~~40~~; 14:~~1-4~~, ~~5~~, ~~6~~; 14:~~15~~; 17:~~31-32~~. Less certain instances are Q 11:?39a?; 14:?19-20?; 19:⟦~~27~~⟧. In the case of Q 12:⟦~~35-38~~⟧, the widely divergent texts (Matt 25:1-13 and Luke 12:35-38) do not lend themselves to formatting in terms of individual variation units, but the shared vestiges of words are simply entered in the Q column with a horizontal line drawn through them.

Sigla Used in Columns 2 and 6 (Matthean and Lukan Doublets)

At times there are doublets in Matthew (column 2) or Luke (column 6), since an Evangelist uses twice, in different locations, a saying found both in Q and in Mark (or in special material, or from the Evangelist's own redaction), rather than fusing the two instances into a single saying. In such instances, a vestige of Q may well stray from the Matthean or Lukan verse primarily derived from Q (column 3 or 5) into the secondary doublet (column 2 or 6). (It is this practical consideration that determines what is included here, rather than the theoretical question of whether a text is literally a doublet, or perhaps a redactional contrast, or other kind of relevant parallel.) For example:

Matt 10:9-10a par. Q 10:4 par. Luke 10:4: The stick (ῥάβδον) one is forbidden to carry (Q 10:4) is listed in Matt 10:10a as forbidden (μηδὲ ῥάβδον), but is omitted completely from Luke 10:4, though listed as forbidden in the doublet Luke 9:3 (μήτε ῥάβδον). Though the doublet is primarily based on Mark 6:8-9, the forbidding of the stick can hardly have been derived from Mark 6:8, since there the stick is mentioned as permitted (εἰ μὴ ῥάβδον μόνον). So it may derive from Q, but was used by Luke not in the primary Q location, but in the doublet primarily based on Mark.

"Passive" formatting is used for such material (see also above, *Reminiscences of Q*), so as to make readily visible, by means of braces { }, what material in the doublet is shared with, and often derived from, Mark (columns 1 and/or 7), but also what material may be from Q, by means of parentheses ( ) in Luke embracing Matthean parallels and square brackets [ ] in Matthew embracing Lukan parallels. In this way attention is drawn visually to material that may be from Q, by means of parentheses ( ) put in Luke to embrance Matthean parallels found in column 3 and square brackets [ ] put in Matthew to embrance Lukan parallels found in column 5. In this way attention is drawn visually to material that may be from Q. Instances of such passive formatting in columns 2 and/or 6 occur at Q 3:~~1a~~, 2b-3a, ~~3b-4~~, 9, ⟦21⟧; 6:20-23, ~~24-26~~, 27-28, 35c-d, 29, 30, 31, 32, 34, 36, 43-44, 46; 7:⟦29-30⟧; 10:~~1~~, 4, 5, 6, 7-8, 10, 11, 12, 13, 15, 16, ~~25-26~~, ~~28~~; 11:14, 15, 23, 16, [between 11:?27-28? and 11:29], 29, 33, ?39a?, 43; 12:2, 4, 5, 7, 9, 10, 11, 12, ~~21~~, 33 [between Q 12:2-12, 12↔33/Matt 10:23, 13-15, ⟦16-20⟧, ~~21~~ and Q 12:34, 22b-31], 30, ⟦35-38⟧, 42, 43, 44, ⟦49⟧, 51, ~~52~~; 13:24, ⟦30⟧, 35; 14:~~1-4~~, ~~5~~, ~~6~~, ⟦11⟧, 21, 23, 26, 27; 17:33 [between 14:27 and 14:34-35]; 16:17, 18; 15:4-5a, ~~5b-6~~, 7, ⟦8-10⟧ [between 17:1-2 and 17:3-4], 17:6, ⟦21⟧, 23, 34; 19:16, 17, 18, 19, 20-21, 22, 26; 22:28, 30. Some of these instances call for special comment:

Q 6:27-28 and Q 6:32: The variation unit ^{0}, normally reserved for the question as to whether a larger unit in columns 3 and/or 5 belongs in Q, is also used in column 6 with the doublets Luke 6:35a-b and Luke 6:33 respectively, since there is a question as to whether they, rather than being redactional doublets with, at most, vestiges of Q, might actually themselves belong in Q.

Q 10:~~1~~: The variation unit ^{0} is also used in columns 2 and 6 with the alternate beginnings of the Mission Instructions, Matt 10:1 and Luke 9:1-2a, since there is a question as to whether they, rather than being simply based on Mark 6:7-8a, actually contain material that is in Q.

Q 13:24: In Luke 13:24 (par. Q 13:24 par. Matt 7:13-14) ὀλίγοι is missing, though present in Matt 7:14. Indeed, it is needed as a concluding contrast to the πολλοί who seek to enter. Actually, there may be an anticipation of ὀλίγοι in Luke 13:23 (εἰ ὀλίγοι οἱ σῳζόμενοι;), to which the conclusion of Luke 13:24 may by implication refer: πολλοί ... ζητήσουσιν εἰσελθεῖν καὶ οὐκ ἰσχύσουσιν. This might suggest an underlying Q text such as καὶ ὀλίγοι <εἰσέρχονται δι'> αὐτῆ<ς>, meaning that many seek to enter, but in vain, for only a few actually enter. The conclusion of Matt 7:14 (καὶ ὀλίγοι εἰσὶν οἱ εὑρίσκοντες αὐτήν) would be a slight stylistic variation from such a conclusion in Q, since Q's language was already anticipated in Matt 7:13 (πολλοί εἰσιν οἱ εἰσερχόμενοι δι' αὐτῆς). Thus the text of Q here may be missing in its Q position, since it was in part anticipated both by Luke (just prior to the saying, for which reason Luke 13:23 is treated as a reminiscence rather than itself a Q text) and by Matthew (in the middle of the Q saying). Such a reconstruction is of course quite hypothetical, {C}.

Q 14:21: The itemization of the needy found in Luke 14:21c, but not in the parallel texts (Matt 22:9; Luke 14:23b; and *Gos. Thom.* 64.11b), does recur as a Lukan doublet in Luke 14:13b. Hence Luke 24:13b is to be put in the parallel position. But it cannot be put in column 6, the normal column for Lukan doublets, since that is already occupied by Luke 14:23, and so had to be put in column 7.

Q 15:4-5a, ~~5b-6~~, 7, ⟦8-10⟧: Matt 18:12-14 (par. Q 15:4-5a, 7 par. Luke 15:4-7) is directly introduced by Matt 18:10 (since Matt 18:11 does not exist in the critical text of Matthew). Matt 18:10 shares terminology with Matt 18:14, the application of the Parable of the Lost Sheep (τοῦ πατρός ... τοῦ ἐν οὐρανοῖς). This familiar Mattheanism could reflect in both instances Matthean redaction, and obviously so if Matt

18:14 were not in Q; or, if Matt 18:14 were in Q, Matt 18:10 could be Matthean redaction or a reminiscence of Q. Further, Matt 18:10 shares "in heaven" with Luke 15:7 and "the angels" with Luke 15:10. Though the Parable of the Lost Coin is completely absent from Matthew, Matt 18:10 could be a reminiscence, which would indicate that Matthew knew of the Parable of the Lost Coin. This would support the argument that this parable is in Q.

When columns 2 and/or 6 would otherwise be blank, because there are no doublets, these columns are at times used for other parallel texts. In such cases not even passive formatting is used, so as to make clear that they are not places into which the Q text could have strayed. A list of such exceptional uses of columns 2 and/or 6 is found in the section of the Technical Data on The Synopsis Format in Eight Columns (see above, pp. lxxviii-lxxix).

In the case of Q 7:1-10, this absence even of passive formatting applies not only to John 4:46b-53, but also to Mark 7:24a, 25-30 par. Matt 15:21-28, and Mark 5:22-23 par. Matt 9:18 (here omitted due to lack of space) par. Luke 8:41-42a. For in these instances the Synoptic parallels are in completely independent stories, the healing of the Syro-Phoenician (Mark) or Canaanite (Matthew) woman's daughter, and the healing of Jairus' daughter. They are included only because of the striking similarities between the two healings of a Gentile from a distance, and the first part of the story of the healing of Jairus' daughter, without there being a question of mutual dependence. To avoid giving the impression that these parallels are taken to be doublets, no formatting at all is introduced. For the same reason passive formatting is also absent from columns 2 and/or 6 at Q 3:⟦22⟧, 6:45, and 10:9.

Sigla Used in Column 8 (*Gospel of Thomas*)

The usual sigla for editing papyri at times occur:

[ ] In lacunae, restored lettering is put in square brackets.

{ } Braces indicate a possible dittography, though in *Gos. Thom.* 33.1 at Q 12:3 the translations seek to make sense of the text as given (see the footnotes there).

. A dot is put under a letter that is not visually unambiguous.

[.....].. At Q 12:27, dots within square brackets indicate the number of letters lost in a lacune, and dots outside the square brackets indicate the number of letters whose vestiges are illegible.

Sigla Used Below the Eight Columns

Critical Apparatus

The critical text of Q, fully formatted in column 4, and, below, unformatted in Greek, English, German and French, is that of the majority of the General Editors, or, when all three diverge, a median position. The initial evaluations of the International Q Project reached in the years 1989–1996,[3] and/or minority evaluations among the General Editors, when they diverge from the critical text presented here, are listed in a critical apparatus. They are identified as follows: IQP refers to such earlier evaluations of the International Q Project, followed by the year that evaluation was reached; and, in the case of the evaluations of the General Editors: JMR refers to James M. Robinson, PH to Paul Hoffmann, and JSK to John S. Kloppenborg.

Text Critical Notes

When text critical uncertainties in the canonical texts influence the reconstruction of the critical text

[3] These results were published the subsequent year: *JBL* 109 (1990) 499-501; 110 (1991) 494-98; 111 (1992) 500-508; 112 (1993) 500-506; 113 (1994) 495-99; 114 (1995) 475-85; 116 (1997) 521-25.

of Q, the manuscript evidence given in Nestle-Aland[27] is listed. An explanation of the relevance of this manuscript evidence for the reconstruction of Q is found in the section of the Technical Data on Text Critical Notes (see below, pp. xc-cvi).

Definitions

The variation units identified in columns 3, 4, and 5 by means of sigla are numbered in those columns in the sequence in which they occur in the text of Q, so that each variation unit may be identified for full discussion in the series Documenta Q and elsewhere. The decision that is called for in each variation unit is defined in the list of definitions, to clarify the issue under discussion in each case.

The Unformatted Text of Q in Greek, English, German, and French

The sigla and numbers identifying variation units in columns 3, 4 and 5 are indispensable in discussing the establishment of the critical text of Q. But for those whose interest is focused instead on the text of Q thus established, rather than upon the process leading to that outcome, the critical text of Q is printed here as a continuous text, without such sigla. For the only sigla used here are those indicating the degree of certainty ascribed to the text, which is important for every user to realize:

< > Angle brackets embrace an emendation in the text.

« » Double angle brackets, guillemets, are used in the Greek text to indicate that there is a text from Q only in one Gospel, and hence that a critical text cannot be established by the usual comparison of both Gospels: Q 6:⟦29↔30/Matt 5:41⟧; 10:7, 8; 12:33, ⟦49⟧; 14:21; 15:⟦8-10⟧; 17:⟦20⟧, ⟦21b⟧. In the translations, guillemets also embrace a gist or flow of thought, or the most probable terms, which may well be rather clear, even though the Greek text could not be reconstructed: Q 4:2; 6:37, 42; 7:⟦29-30⟧; 10:21; 11:⟦21-22⟧, 48; 12:33, ⟦54⟧, 58; 14:18, ?19?; 15:4; 17:⟦21a⟧. Further, these sigla identify words needed for a smooth rendering in the modern language, even though there is no explicit equivalent in the Greek text behind the translation, e.g. in the English translation: 3:8, 17; 6:20, 21, 23, 30, 34, 40, 45; 7:8, 26, 28; 11:14, 19, 25, 26, 34, 35, 46b, 52, 47, 48, 51; 12:3, 6, ⟦55⟧; 13:26, 35; 16:16.

... Three dots indicate that there is some text here that cannot be reconstituted, and not even a gist is suggested.

.. Two dots indicate that there may be some text here that cannot be reconstituted, though even this remains uncertain. These are instances where in the fully formatted text of Q one finds the sigla [( )], ( ) or [ ]. Texts that are thought not to be in Q, even with a degree of uncertainty {C}, are not indicated at all.

Translations of the Coptic Gospel of Thomas (Nag Hammadi II 2) in Greek, English, German, and French

[ ] In lacunae, restored lettering is put in square brackets.

( ) The Coptic translation of the *Gospel of Thomas* (Nag Hammadi II 2), found in column 8, is retranslated into Greek (since the missing original was in Greek), with English, German, and French translations beside it. Material not actually present in the Coptic text that is needed for a smooth formulation in the translation is simply put in parentheses.

sa In notes to the Greek retroversion, sa refers to the Coptic translation of the New Testament in the Sahidic dialect, *Gos. Thom.* 78.2 at Q 7:25.

The Greek Original of the Gospel of Thomas (P. Oxy. 1, 654, 665) with English, German, and French Translations

In the rare instances when the Greek original of the *Gospel of Thomas* is extant, fragmentarily documented in *P. Oxy.* 1, 654 and 655, it is presented in the last panel at the bottom of the facing pages, with English, German, and French translations beside it. The more complex sigla are not used here.

Rather, the usual sigla for editing papyri at times occur:

[ ] In lacunae, restored lettering is put in square brackets.

. A dot is put under a letter that is not visually unambiguous.

[.....].. At Q 12:27, dots within square brackets indicate the number of letters lost in a lacuna, and adjoining dots outside the square brackets indicate the number of letters whose vestiges are illegible. In the English, German, and French translations, three dots indicate where, as a result, a translation cannot be provided.

( ) Parentheses surround lettering abbreviated in the Greek original but spelled out in the transcription, such as in the case of *nomina sacra,* e.g. 'I(ησοῦ)ς in the standard quotation formula. In translations, material not actually present in the Greek original that is needed for a smooth formulation is put in parentheses.

< > Angle brackets indicate the editor's correction of a scribal omission or error: *Gos. Thom.* 33.1 (*P. Oxy.* 1) at Q 12:3.

~~with~~ A conjectural emendation deleting some of the text in the translations is indicated by drawing a line through that text: Notes [2], [3] and [4] to *Gos. Thom.* 33.1 (Nag Hammadi II 2) at Q 12:3.

Only in the *Gospel of Thomas*, Saying 36, is *P. Oxy.* 655 much more complete in the otherwise very fragmentary Greek original than in the Coptic translation of Nag Hammadi II 2. (See the Excursus on the Scribal Error in Q 12:27, and the explanation of the Endpapers, below, pp. xcix-ci, cvii.) Hence, in column 8 of Q 12:22b, 25, 27, 28, the Greek original rather than the Coptic translation is presented, and then repeated in the last panel below, where it normally occurs. In this pericope the Coptic text of Saying 36 is limited to Q 12:22b. In this one case, at Q 12:22b, the Coptic text of Nag Hammadi II 2 is printed not in column 8, but below, just above its translation into Greek, English, German, and French.

Abbreviations

Abbreviations in references to scholarly literature are those found in Siegfried M. Schwertner, *Internationales Abkürzungsverzeichnis für Theologie und Grenzgebiete* (Berlin and New York: Walter de Gruyter, 1992[2]). (*HTR* for *HThR*, HTS for HThS, NTAbh for NTA and *NovT*Sup for NT.S are exceptions.)

Divergences from the Lukan Sequence

It has been generally assumed that Matthew tended to rearrange the sequence of Q in order to create the longer Matthean discourses, but that Luke tended to retain the sequence of Q. In preparing *The Critical Edition of Q*, such divergences of sequence between Matthew and Luke were examined when they occur. Indeed, in most cases, the Lukan rather than the Matthean order did seem to reflect that of Q. Hence one can normally follow Lukan sequence to find a text in *The Critical Edition of Q*.[1] But in cases where it became clear that the Matthean rather than the Lukan order is that of Q, it is this reconstructed sequence of Q, rather than the Lukan sequence, that is followed. A cross reference has been inserted at the bottom of the pages preceding and concluding the insertion of text that breaks the Lukan sequence, as well as at the bottom of the page just before a Q text is missing from the Lukan sequence due to it having been shifted to its correct Q position. With the help of such cross references, one can readily determine the Q position, and hence the position in this volume, of Q material one does not find in the Lukan sequence. One may also consult the Table of Contents and the Q Text in Matthean Order (above, pp. ix-xii) for such information.

Instances where the Lukan sequence is not that of Q are as follows:[2]

Q 4:5-8: Between Q 4:9-12 and Q 4:13.

Q 6:35c-d: Between Q 6:27-28 and Q 6:29, ⟦29↔30/Matt 5:41⟧, 30-32, 34.

Q 11:16: Between Q 11:17-20, ⟦21-22⟧, 23-26, ?27-28? and Q 11:29-30.

Q 11:42: Between Q 11:34-35, ⟦~~36~~⟧, ?39a? and Q 11:39b, ⟦~~40~~⟧, 41.

Q 11:52: Between Q 11:46b and Q 11:47-51; 12:2-3.

Q 12:33-34: Between Q 12:2-12, ~~12↔33/Matt 10:23~~, ~~13-15~~, ⟦~~16-20~~⟧, ~~21~~ and Q 12:22b-31, ~~32~~.

Q 13:29: Between Q 13:27 and Q 13:28, ⟦30⟧.

Q 17:33: Between Q 14:26-27 and Q 14:34-35.

Q 15:4-5a, ~~5b-6~~, 7, ⟦8-10⟧: Between Q 17:1-2 and Q 17:3-4.

Q 17:37: Between Q 17:23-24, ~~25~~ and Q 17:26-27.

The positions of Q 6:39 and Q 6:40 are very uncertain. As a convention, they are presented in their Lukan position.

Material considered for inclusion in Q that is only in Matthew, but not in Luke, is put in the sequence of the adjoining Matthean material that does have a Lukan parallel from Q, as its hypothetical position in Q:

Matt 5:⟦41⟧: Between Q 6:29 and Q 6:30.

Matt ~~10:23~~: Between Q 12:12 and Q 12:~~13-21~~, 33-34.

Matt ~~11:28-30~~: Between Q 10:22 and Q 10:23-24.

Matt ~~25:15c-18~~: Between Q 19:12-13 and Q 19:~~14~~, 15.

[1] This is the justification for the now widely accepted convention of quoting Q by Lukan chapter and verse numbers, a policy first introduced in the initial planning for the present volume. See James M. Robinson, "The Sermon on the Mount/Plain: Work Sheets for the Reconstruction of Q," SBL.SP 22 (1983) 451-54: 451-52, quoted above in the History of Q Research, p. lxvii, n. 158.

[2] See the discussion in James M. Robinson, "Instances of Matthew = Q Order," in: "The Sequence of Q: The Lament over Jerusalem," *Von Jesus zum Christus: Christologische Studien. Festgabe für Paul Hoffmann zum 65. Geburtstag.* BZNW 93 (ed. Rudolf Hoppe and Ulrich Busse; Berlin and New York: Walter de Gruyter, 1998) 225-60: 227-32.

Text Critical Notes

Text critical notes are rarely included, in that users are assumed to have at hand standard editions of the New Testament text where this information is provided in adequate detail.[1] Textual uncertainties

---

[1] The abbreviated names and/or short titles used here refer to the following:

Aland 1996^{15}: *Synopsis Quattuor Evangeliorum: Locis parallelis evangeliorum apocryphorum et patrum adhibitis* (ed. Kurt Aland; Stuttgart: Deutsche Bibelgesellschaft, 15. revidierte Auflage 1996, 2. korrigierter Druck 1997). The critical text is that of NA^{26}= NA^{27}, but the constantly improved critical apparatus moves even beyond that of NA^{27}.

BJ: *La Bible de Jérusalem: La Sainte Bible traduite en français sous la direction de l'École biblique de Jérusalem* (Paris: Les éditions du Cerf, 1961^{1}, 1973^{2}).

Boismard-Lamouille: M.-E. Boismard and A. Lamouille, *Synopsis Graeca Quattuor Evangeliorum* (Leuven and Paris: Peeters, 1986).

EÜ: *Die Heilige Schrift: Einheitsübersetzung* (Stuttgart: Katholisches Bibelwerk and Deutsche Bibelgesellschaft, 1981).

GNT: *The Greek New Testament* (in the case of the first edition: ed. Kurt Aland, Matthew Black, Bruce M. Metzger, Allen Wikgren; New York: American Bible Society; London: British and Foreign Bible Society; Edinburgh: National Bible Society of Scotland; Amsterdam: Netherlands Bible Society; Stuttgart: Württemberg Bible Society, 1966^{1}, 1968^{2}, 1975^{3}, 1983^{4}).

Huck-Greeven: Albert Huck, *Synopse der drei ersten Evangelien mit Beigabe der johanneischen Parallelstellen, Synopsis of the First Three Gospels with the Addition of the Johannine Parallels* (Tübingen: Mohr-Siebeck, 13. Auflage, völlig neu bearbeitet von Heinrich Greeven, 13th edition, fundamentally revised by Heinrich Greeven, 1981).

Lutherbibel: Die Bibel nach der Übersetzung Martin Luthers (Stuttgart: Deutsche Bibelgesellschaft, 1985).

Metzger: Bruce M. Metzger, *A Textual Commentary on the Greek New Testament* (London and New York: United Bible Societies, 1971^{1} [based on *GNT*^{3}, which however only appeared 1975]; Stuttgart: Deutsche Bibelgesellschaft and United Bible Societies, 1994^{2} [based on *GNT*^{4}]). Metzger presents the view of the Committee, which normally includes his own view, but on occasion he expresses, with his initials, a diverging view.

NA^{25}, NA^{26}, NA^{27}: *Novum Testamentum Graece* (in the case of the 27th edition: post Eberhard et Erwin Nestle editione vicesima septima revisa communiter ediderunt Barbara et Kurt Aland, Johannes Karavidopoulos, Carlo M. Martini, Bruce M. Metzger; Stuttgart: Deutsche Bibelgesellschaft, 25. Auflage 1963; 26., neu bearbeitete Auflage 1979; 27. revidierte Auflage 1993). In the case of each edition, the date and number is listed. The present critical text itself replaced that of NA^{25} in NA^{26}, and is retained unaltered in NA^{27}, though the critical apparatus has been revised in NA^{27}.

NEB: *The New English Bible: New Testament* (Oxford: Oxford University Press, and Cambridge: Cambridge University Press, 1961).

NRSV: *The Holy Bible containing the Old and New Testaments with the Apocryphal / Deuterocanonical Books: New Revised Standard Version* (Nashville, Tenn.: Thomas Nelson, 1989).

Rahlfs: Alfred Rahlfs, *Septuaginta: Id Est Vetus Testamentum Graece juxta LXX Interpretes* (Stuttgart: Privilegierte Württembergische Bibelanstalt, 1935, 1952^{5}).

REB: *The Revised English Bible with the Apocrypha* (Oxford: Oxford University Press, Cambridge: Cambridge University Press, 1989).

RSV: *The Holy Bible: Revised Standard Version, containing the Old and New Testaments* (Toronto, New York, London: Thomas Nelson and Sons, 1952). The New Testament appeared already in 1946.

that may affect the reconstruction of Q, and variant readings that have been ascribed prominently to Q, are included.[2]

In the course of transmission, the text of one Gospel influenced that of the other (more often Matthew influencing Luke than the converse). This insight indicates an area where textual criticism can reduce the quantity of agreements between Matthew and Luke that on first glance might seem to suggest the wording of Q.[3]

Only very rarely do the General Editors diverge from the text of NA[27], at Q 11:13, 33 (bis) and 12:31, though with serious doubts also at Q 11:24, 46b (on which passages especially, see below). We are indebted to the expert competence of Eldon J. Epp in textual criticism for advice on many details.

The Critical Edition of Q quotes New Testament texts according to NA[26.27] = *GNT*[3.4], since this text has in effect become a modern *textus receptus*. The critical apparatus of NA[27] is reproduced as a Text Critical Note beneath the eight-column layout where relevant. This manuscript evidence, since presented there, is presupposed here, and hence is not repeated. The uncertainty expressed in NA[27] by inclusion in square brackets [ ] comes to expression in *GNT* also as [ ].[4] Huck-Greeven, Boismard-Lamouille, NA[25], and modern translations[5] are often mentioned in order to give a rough approximation of the *status quaestionis* and in some cases to suggest a trend in recent years. Since these alternate readings may also have been presupposed especially in older scholarly literature, it may be helpful to have them readily available.[6] References to the secondary literature are usually given only when they have played an important role in establishing the text of Q.[7]

Tasker: R. V. G. Tasker, *The Greek New Testament: Being the text translated in The New English Bible 1961* (Oxford: Oxford University Press, Cambridge: Cambridge University Press, 1964).

TOB: *Traduction Oecuménique de la Bible, Édition intégrale: Nouveau Testament* (Paris: Cerf and Les Bergers et les Mages, 1972).

2 John S. Kloppenborg, *Q Parallels: Synopsis, Critical Notes and Concordance* (Sonoma, Calif.: Polebridge, 1988) presents similar text critical notes.

3 This has long been noted in the case of apparent agreements of Matthew and Luke in changing Mark, the number of which minor agreements "ought probably [496] to be considerably reduced by textual criticism," as explained, e.g., by Kirsopp Lake, "The Date of Q," *The Expositor*, Seventh Series, Volume 7 (1909) 494-507: 495-96 and 496, note 1:

> The main point in favour of this contention is that in early times the text of Matthew was on the whole the norm to which the others were adapted, and that on the whole Luke has suffered more from this cause than Mark, which often escaped, because it was the least widely used. The result is that when Luke was corrected so as to agree with Matthew it often produced a false appearance of an agreement between Matthew and Luke against Mark.

4 Square brackets cannot simply be taken over from NA and *GNT* into *The Critical Edition of Q*, since here they have another meaning: "Square brackets in the text of Luke and Q enclose wording or lettering found in Luke but not in Matthew." See the section of the Technical Data on Sigla in the Page Layout (above, p. lxxx).

5 Translations can be used only to a limited extent. Synonyms are indistinguishable, and the requirements of the language into which one is translating influence the translation. Caution must be especially used when it is a matter of the sequence of the Greek words, since the word order in the language into which one is translating, rather than the Greek word order, should have been determinative.

6 For a fuller listing of earlier editions of the Greek text (Tischendorf[8], Westcott and Hort text and margin, von Soden, Vogels, Merk, Bover, Nestle-Aland[25]) see NA[27], appendix III Editionum Differentiae, pp. 748-56 for the Synoptic Gospels, and of the Greek text and translations *GNT*[4] in the second apparatus at the foot of each page.

7 For fuller documentation in such instances one may consult the relevant volume in the series Documenta Q: Reconstructions of Q Through Two Centuries of Gospel Research Excerpted, Sorted, and Evaluated (Leuven: Peeters, 1996–).

Punctuation is less a matter of textual criticism, in view of its normal absence from the manuscript tradition, than a matter of decisions by editors. But, for completeness sake, two important instances affecting decisively the meaning and hence the translation may be mentioned:

Q 7:~~2~~, 3, ~~4-6a~~: In Matt 8:7 NA^{27}, Huck-Greeven and Boismard-Lamouille conclude Jesus' answer with a period, making it an affirmative statement, as do Tasker (with a note: "αὐτόν;"), *Lutherbibel*, *BJ*, *REB*, *RSV*, *NRSV*, *NEB* (with a note: "*Or* Am I to come and cure him?"), and *EÜ* (with a note: "Andere Übersetzungsmöglichkeit: Soll *ich* etwa kommen und ihn gesund machen?"), whereas, according to most current exegesis, and hence in *The Critical Edition of Q*, it is to be concluded with a question mark. For Matt 8:7 is to be understood as a question expressing reserve, in the light of Luke 7:3-5 (the appeal of the Jewish elders to persuade Jesus to overcome such reserve and help a Gentile) and John 4:48 (Jesus' rebuff to the Gentile official for demanding a sign, in the same healing narrative), and the analogous reserve of Jesus toward the Syrophoenician (Mark) or Canaanite (Matthew) woman (Mark 7:27 par. Matt 15:26), in a structurally parallel, but distinct healing of a Gentile from a distance. Thus *TOB*: "Moi, j'irai le guérir?" with a note: "Autre traduction, que pourrait recommander le contexte (8,17): *Oui, je vais aller le guérir.*"

Q 7:24b-26a: In Matt 11:7b-9a par. Luke 7:24b-26a the punctuation of NA is followed in *GNT*, Huck-Greeven, and Boismard-Lamouille, and hence is reflected in the text and translation here: Q 7:24b "What did you go out into the wilderness to look at? A reed shaken by the wind? 25 If not, what *did* you go out to see? A person arrayed in finery? Look, those wearing finery are in kings' houses. 26a But «then» what did you go out to see? A prophet?" *TOB*, *Lutherbibel*, and *EÜ* follow NA *et al.* in both Matthew and Luke.

Yet an alternate punctuation of Matt 11:7b-9a par. Luke 7:24b-26a is possible: τί ἐξήλθατε εἰς τὴν ἔρημον; θεάσασθαι …; 8/25 ἀλλὰ τί ἐξήλθατε; ἰδεῖν ...; … 9a/26a ἀλλὰ τί ἐξήλθατε; ἰδεῖν …;

RSV follows this second alternative for the second and third instances in Matt 11:7b-9a: "7b What did you go out into the wilderness to behold? A reed shaken by the wind? 8 Why then did you go out? To see a man (note: "Or*: What then did you go out to see? A man* …") clothed in soft raiment? Behold, those who wear soft raiment are in kings' houses. 9a Why then did you go out? To see a prophet?" (note: "Other ancient authorities read *What they did you go out to see? A prophet?*"). But *RSV* follows NA *et al.* at Luke 7:24b-26a. Then *NRSV* follows NA *et al.* in both Matthew and Luke, with converse footnotes at Matt 11:8 and 9a.

In Matt 11:7b-9a Tasker follows NA *et al.* in the first two instances, but in the third reads ἀλλὰ τί ἐξήλθατε; ἰδεῖν …; similarly *NEB* and *REB* follow NA *et al.* in the first two instances, but in the third read: "But why did you go out? To see a prophet?" Similarly *BJ*: "Alors qu'êtes-vous allés faire? Voir un prophète?"

In Luke 7:24b-26a Tasker, *NEB*, *REB,* and *BJ* follow NA *et al.* in all three instances.

Only in *Gos. Thom.* 78.1b-2a is the alternate punctuation actually required by the absence of the resumption of an equivalent to ἀλλὰ τί ἐξήλθατε in *Gos. Thom.* 78.2a: (78.1b) "To look at a reed shaken by the wind, (78.2a) and to see…."

This punctuation is also required in the text-critical variant at Matt 11:9a: προφήτην ἰδεῖν; is in ℵ* B^{1} W Z 0281^{vid} 892 pc, but ἰδεῖν; προφήτην; in ℵ^{1} B$^{*.2}$ C D L Θ 0233 $f^{1.13}$ 33 𝔐 latt sy sa. Metzger summarized the reasons for grading with {B} ἰδεῖν προφήτην rather than προφήτην ἰδεῖν as follows:

> The textual problem is complicated by the possibility of taking τί as meaning either "what?" or "why?" The printed text of verses 7 and 8 may be translated either (*a*) "What did you go out into the wilderness to behold? A reed shaken by the wind? (8) What they did you go out to see? A man dressed in soft clothing?" or (*b*) "Why did you go out into the wilderness? To behold a reed shaken by the wind? (8) But why did you go out? To see a man dressed in soft clothing?" (The second

interpretation is represented in the Gospel of Thomas, Logion 78.)

In ver. 9 the Committee decided that the reading ἰδεῖν προφήτην, which involves the previously mentioned ambiguity, is more likely to be original than the reading προφήτην ἰδεῖν, which, in the context, has to be taken in only one way, namely, "Why then did you go out? To see a prophet?"

A comparable agreement between א* and the *Gospel of Thomas*, then corrected in א[1] to conform to the dominant Matthean text, occurs also in Matt 6:28 at Q 12:27, which corresponds to *Gos. Thom.* 36 in P. Oxy. 655 (see below, pp. xcix-ci).

Orthography is also not normally considered a part of textual criticism, and hence divergences are usually not included in a critical apparatus. But one example is included:

Q 12:4: In Luke 12:4 NA[25] and Tasker read ἀποκτεννόντων, but *GNT*, Huck-Greeven, and Boismard-Lamouille read ἀποκτεινόντων, as does NA[27], but without mentioning the change in the critical apparatus. Both alternatives are echoed in the scholarly literature.

The list of manuscripts in the critical apparatus of NA[27] (more advanced than that of NA[26]) is placed in the Text Critical Notes beneath the eight-column layout of the relevant Q texts, to draw attention to the alternatives influencing the establishment of the critical text of Q.[8] This text critical data regarding the New Testament itself (and occasionally the LXX) is now to be briefly assessed in terms of modern critical editions and translations

Q 3:⟦22⟧: In Luke 3:22 the reading υἱός μου εἶ σύ, ἐγὼ σήμερον γεγέννηκά σε is that of Ps 2:7 LXX. It is advocated for Luke by Huck-Greeven and Boismard-Lamouille, and even for Q by Harnack,[9] Dibelius,[10] Streeter,[11] and Polag.[12] *BJ*[2] reads: "'Tu es mon fils; moi, aujourd'hui, je t'ai engendré,'" with a note: "Var.: 'Tu es mon Fils bien-aimé, tu as toute ma faveur', suspecte d'harmonisation avec Mt Mc. La teneur probablement originale de la voix céleste chez Luc ne fait pas référence à Is 42 comme chez Mt Mc, mais au Ps 2 7: plutôt que de reconnaître en Jésus le 'Serviteur', elle le présente comme le Roi-Messie du Psaume, intronisé au Baptême pour établir le Règne de Dieu dans le monde." *TOB* reads the same, with the note: "De nombreux témoins lisent ici la même formule que chez Mc: *il m'a plu de te choisir*. Mais le texte ici traduit est attesté chez de très anciens témoins et correspond particulièrement à la pensée de Lc. Il reproduit le Ps 2,7 et signifie l'intronisation messianique de Jésus, le début de sa mission auprès du peuple de Dieu. Le fait que cette parole soit prononcé par le Père en fait la révélation par excellence du mystère de Jesus." *GNT, Lutherbibel* and *EÜ* do not use the reading from Ps 2:7 LXX, nor does *BJ*[1], with a note: "Var.: 'Tu es mon Fils, je t'ai moi-même engendré aujourd'hui' (Ps 2 7). – Dans

[8] In one instance, Luke 14:27, the attestation for αὐτοῦ is for the first time presented in the critical apparatus of Aland 1996[15], which hence is of necessity what is put in the Text Critical Note beneath the eight-column layout.

[9] Adolf Harnack, *Sprüche und Reden Jesu: Die zweite Quelle des Matthäus und Lukas* (Beiträge zur Einleitung in das Neue Testament 2; Leipzig: Hinrichs, 1907) 216-19. ET: *The Sayings of Jesus* (New York: Putnam, and London: Williams and Norgate, 1908) 310-14.

[10] Martin Dibelius, *Die urchristliche Überlieferung von Johannes dem Täufer* (FRLANT 15; Göttingen: Vandenhoeck & Ruprecht, 1911) 62; Dibelius, *Die Formgeschichte des Evangeliums* (Tübingen: Mohr-Siebeck, 1919, revised 1933[2], 1966[5] ed. Günther Bornkamm [quoted here]) 271: "In der vorkanonischen Gestalt dieser Geschichte …." ET: *From Tradition to Gospel* (New York: Scribners, paperback reprint, n.d. [quoted here]) 272: "In the pre-canonical form of this story …."

[11] Burnett Hillman Streeter, *The Four Gospels: A Study of Origins treating of the Manuscript Tradition, Sources, Authorship and Dates* (London: Macmillan,1924, revised 1930[4], 1936[5] [quoted here]) 143, 188, 276.

[12] Athanasius Polag, *Fragmenta Q: Textheft zur Logienquelle* (Neukirchen-Vluyn: Neukirchener Verlag, 1979[1], 1982[2] [quoted here]) 30.

Lc et Mc, à la difference de Mt, la voix du ciel s'adresse à Jésus." Tasker puts two alternatives in a footnote reading "[*a*] Σὺ εἶ ὁ Υἱός μου ὁ ἀγαπητός, [*b*] Υἱός μου εἶ σύ, ἐγὼ σήμερον γεγέννηκά σε," and comments on the second that it "was regarded as an early adaptation of the passage to Ps. 2.7." There are similar notes in *RSV, NRSV, NEB, REB.* Metzger does not use Ps 2:7 LXX {B}: "The Western reading, 'This day I have begotten thee,' which was widely current during the first three centuries, appears to be secondary, derived from Ps 2.7. The use of the third person ('This is ... in whom ...') in a few witnesses is an obvious assimilation to the Matthean form of the saying (Mt 3.17)."

Q 4:2: In Matt 4:2 NA[25], Tasker, and Huck-Greeven, and hence many earlier interpreters, read (with the LXX: Exod 34:28; Deut 9:9, 18) τεσσεράκοντα νύκτας, but NA[26, 27] and Boismard-Lamouille read νύκτας τεσσεράκοντα. In translations, this alternative of the Greek word order is not visible. The complete omission of the forty nights is too weakly attested in Matthew to be considered Matthean, though it would bring Matthew into agreement with Luke, and hence would strengthen the case for the omission in Q.

Q 4:8: In Codex Alexandrinus, Deut 6:13a = 10:20a LXX is identical with Matt 4:10b par. Luke 4:8b, and hence with Q 4:8b. But Rahlfs (in both cases), preferring Vaticanus and Sinaiticus, reads κύριον τὸν θεόν σου φοβηθήσῃ καὶ αὐτῷ λατρεύσεις. Rather than Q attesting a rarely documented LXX reading found in Codex Alexandrinus, the reading of Codex Alexandrinus may have been adapted under Christian influence to the canonical Matthean/Lukan text.[13]

Q 6:32: In Luke 6:33 most manuscripts that omit γάρ in Luke 6:33a insert it in 33b, and most that insert γάρ in Luke 6:33a omit it in 33b. The manuscript evidence is fairly balanced, making a decision difficult (Epp). In Luke 6:33a *GNT* and NA[27] put γάρ within square brackets, which were not used in NA[25]. But γάρ is completely omitted in Luke 6:33a by Tasker, Huck-Greeven and Boismard-Lamouille. It is apparently absent in *RSV, NRSV, NET, RET, BJ, TOB, Lutherbibel,* and *EÜ.* The absence of γάρ in this Lukan doublet at Luke 6:33a would influence the decision as to whether γάρ is in Q, since γάρ is present in Matt 5:46 but absent in Luke 6:32a (and present in Luke 6:32b).

Q 7:~~2~~, 3, ~~4-6a~~: In Matt 8:7, regarding the punctuation (see above, p. xcii).

Q 7:6b-c: In Matt 8:8a NA[25] and Tasker read ἀποκριθεὶς δέ, but NA[27], Huck-Greeven, and Boismard-Lamouille read καὶ ἀποκριθείς. Since Luke 7:6b reads δέ, a reading of δέ in Matt 8:8a would strengthen somewhat the reading δέ for Q. But this could also be a matter of a textual corruption, assimilating the reading of one Gospel to that of the other, if indeed the quite divergent context in Luke 7:6b, the centurion's sending of his friends, does not make the use of δέ here irrelevant.

Q 7:24b-26a: In Matt 11:7b-9a par. Luke 7:24b-26a, regarding the punctuation, and in Luke 7:26a the text-critical variant (see above, pp. xcii-xciii).

Q 9:59: In Luke 9:59 NA[25] omit κύριε, but it is included within square brackets in NA[27] = *GNT* {C}. Tasker, Huck-Greeven, and Boismard-Lamouille omit it. *NEB, REB, EÜ* and *TOB* omit it, but *RSV, NRSV* and *Lutherbibel* include it. *BJ* omits it, but lists it in a note as a reading not adopted. Metzger includes it {C}:

> The omission of κύριε from B* D syr[s] *al* is puzzling; what motive would have prompted copyists to delete it? On the other hand, the word might well have been added, either from ver. 61 or from the parallel in Mt 8.21. Since, however, the absence of κύριε may have been due to a transcriptional blunder (ειπε̄ κ̄ε̄ επιτρεψον),

[13] See Robert Gundry, *The Use of the Old Testament in Matthew's Gospel* (NovTSup 18; Leiden: Brill, 1967) 68-69; Christopher M. Tuckett, "The Temptation Narrative in Q," *The Four Gospels 1992: Festschrift Frans Neirynck* (ed. F. Van Segbroeck, C. M. Tuckett, G. Van Belle, J. Verheyden; 3 vols.; Leuven: University Press and Peeters, 1992) 1. 479-507: 484.

it was thought safer to retain the word in the text, but to enclose it within square brackets indicating doubt that it has a right to stand there.

Epp favors κύριε on the basis of its earliest manuscript evidence. Since it is in Matt 8:21 also, its presence in Luke 9:59 would tend to assure its presence in Q.

Q 9:59: In Matt 8:21 αὐτοῦ is omitted by NA[25], Tasker, and Huck-Greeven, but included in square brackets by *GNT* {C} and NA[27]. Boismard-Lamouille includes it. It seems omitted in *RSV*, *TOB* and *Lutherbibel* ("… ein anderer unter den Jüngern…"), but included in *NEB*, *REB*, *NRSV*, and *EÜ*. *BJ*[1] omits it ("Un autre des disciples…,") but *BJ*[2] translates in a way that is nearer to including the person among Jesus' disciples, which is what the reading αὐτοῦ suggests: "Un autre, d'entre les disciples,…." Metzger includes it {C}: "Although the support of א B 33 it[a] cop[sa] for the omission of αὐτοῦ would usually be regarded as exceptionally strong evidence, in this case a majority of the Committee was impressed by the possibility that αὐτοῦ may have been deleted in order to prevent the reader from inferring that the γραμματεύς of ver. 19 was one of Jesus' disciples. On the other hand, it can be argued that it is because of the word ἕτερος, not αὐτοῦ, that a reader might infer that γραμματεύς of ver. 19 was a disciple of Jesus. Actually the absence of αὐτοῦ does not improve the sense, but rather makes the text more ambiguous. In order to represent these two opposing arguments the Committee decided to retain αὐτοῦ enclosed within square brackets." Epp: The stronger attestation argues for the omission.

Q 9:59: In Luke 9:59 NA[25], Tasker, *RSV* ("let me first go…"), *NRSV* ("First let me go…"), *REV* ("Let me first go…"), *Lutherbibel* ("… daß ich zuvor hingehe"), and *EÜ* ("Lass mich zuerst heimgehen") seem to read πρῶτον ἀπελθόντι, but *GNT*, Huck-Greeven, Boismard-Lamouille, *BJ* ("Permets-moi de m'en aller d'abord enterrer mon père"), *TOB* (similarly), and *NEB* ("Let me go and bury my father first") may read ἀπελθόντι πρῶτον.

Q 10:15: In Luke 10:15 Tasker, *GNT*, Huck-Greeven, Boismard-Lamouille, *RSV*, *NRSV*, *NEB*, *REB*, *BJ*, *TOB*, *Lutherbibel*, and *ËU* read μὴ ἕως οὐρανοῦ ὑψωθήσῃ;. In Matt 11:23 Tasker, *GNT*, Huck-Greeven, Boismard-Lamouille, *RSV*, *NRSV*, *NEB*, *REB*, *BJ*, *TOB*, *Lutherbibel*, and *EÜ* read μὴ ἕως οὐρανοῦ ὑψωθήσῃ;. Metzger μὴ ἕως οὐρανοῦ ὑψωθήσῃ; {B}:

> Palaeographically it is easy to see how the reading preserved in the earliest witnesses, which represent all the pre-Byzantine types of text, was accidentally modified. After Καφαρναούμ the first letter of μή was accidentally dropped, with the consequent alteration of the verb to either ὑψωθεῖσα or ὑψώθης depending on whether H was taken as the article ἡ or the relative ἥ. The strong external attestation for the presence of μή is supported also by intrinsic and transcriptional probability. The unexpected turn of expression, 'And you, Capernaum, will you be exalted to heaven?' is a sharp and startling interrogation, entirely in the manner of Jesus' use of vivid language. On the other hand, most copyists were likely to prefer the more commonplace statement, 'And you, Capernaum, that are exalted to heaven ….'

Q 10:15 In Luke 10:15 Tasker, *GNT* and Boismard-Lamouille read τοῦ before ᾅδου, but Huck-Greeven omits it.

Q 10:15: In Luke 10:15 Tasker, *GNT*[1.2], Huck-Greeven, and Boismard-Lamouille read καταβιβασθήσῃ. *GNT*[3.4] reads καταβήσῃ. (Translations cannot be distinguished clearly, as to the reading they presuppose, since καταβήσῃ can be translated as a passive, "be brought down."[14]) Metzger καταβήσῃ 1971[1] {D} 1993[2] {C}:

> It is difficult to decide between the merits of καταβήσῃ and καταβιβασθήσῃ. Did copyists

[14] Donald S. Deer, "The Interpretation and Translation of Constructions with a Passive Meaning in the Greek of the Synoptic Gospels" (doctoral dissertation, Faculté de théologie protestante de l'Université de Strasbourg, 1973) 151-52.

heighten the sense of the saying by replacing the former word with the latter; or did they replace the more rare verb (καταβιβάζεσθαι) with the much more usual verb (καταβαίνειν), thus also assimilating the quotation to the text of the Septuagint? A majority of the Committee, impressed by the superior external testimony of $\mathfrak{P}^{75}$ B D *al*, adopted καταβήσῃ.

In Matt 11:23 Tasker and Huck-Greeven read καταβιβασθήσῃ, but *GNT* and Boismard-Lamouille read καταβήσῃ. Metzger καταβήσῃ 1971^{1} {D} 1993^{2} {C}: "Whether the verb should read 'you shall go down' or 'you shall be brought down' is a difficult question to answer. Considerations of transcriptional probabilities – such as the heightening of the sense and the replacement of the rare verb with the more usual verb – are inconclusive. … Despite the possibility of assimilation to the text of Isa 14.15 (which reads καταβήσῃ), a majority of the Committee preferred this verb, supported as it is by the earliest representative of both the Alexandrian and the Western types of text."

Q 10:23: In Luke 10:23 NA^{27} considers καὶ ἀκούοντες ἃ ἀκούετε to be a scribal error of assimilation to Matt 13:16, ἀκούουσιν, rather than original in Luke. Tasker, Huck-Greeven, Boismard-Lamouille, *RSV*, *NRSV*, *NEB*, *REB*, *BJ*, *TOB*, *Lutherbibel*, and *EÜ* omit it. If the reading were in Luke, this might support the view that it and Matt 13:16b reflect a text of Q. (See also Q 10:24: καὶ ἀκοῦσαι ἃ ἀκούετε.)

Q 10:~~25-26~~: In Matt 22:35 Huck-Greeven and Boismard-Lamouille omit νομικός, but *RSV*, *NRSV*, *TOB*, *Lutherbibel*, and *EÜ* include it. NA^{27} and *GNT* put νομικός in square brackets {C}. Metzger includes it {C}: "Despite what seems to be an overwhelming preponderance of evidence supporting the word νομικός, its absence from family 1 as well as from widely scattered versional and patristic witnesses takes on addditional significance when it is observed that, apart from this passage, Matthew nowhere else uses the word. It is not unlikely, therefore, that copyists have introduced the word here from the parallel passage in Lk 10.25. At the same time, in view of the widespread testimony supporting its presence in the text, the Committee was reluctant to omit the word altogether, preferring to retain it enclosed within square brackets." *BJ* omits it, with a note: "Add.: 'un légiste', sans doute emprunté à Lc 10,25." "Tasker omits it with a note: «*add* νομικός," and "νομικός … was considered a later harmonization of the text with Lk 10:25."[15] *NEB* excludes it, with a note: "*Some witnesses insert* a lawyer," and *REB* excludes it, with a note: "*some witnesses add* an expert in the law."[16]

Q 11:2b: In Luke 11:2b Harnack[17] and Streeter[18] ascribe to Luke the reading ἐλθέτω τὸ πνεῦμά σου τὸ ἅγιον ἐφ᾽ ἡμᾶς καὶ καθαρισάτω ἡμᾶς (though Harnack, following Gregory of Nyssa, reads … τὸ ἅγιον πνεῦμά σου …). For Harnack, this, following directly upon πάτερ, is all that is in Luke 11:2b. For Streeter, the whole of the Lord's Prayer is not in Q, due to this and other wide divergences in the Matthean and Lukan texts, and the general availability of the Lord's Prayer to both Matthew and Luke in liturgical usage.[19] Tasker,

15 See Frans Neirynck, most recently "The Minor Agreements and Lk 10.25-28," *EThL* 71 (1995) 151-60: 156: "…copyists … possible heightened the similarity [between Matthew and Luke here] by adding νομικός in Matthew."

16 Ulrich Luz, *Das Evangelium nach Matthäus; 3. Teilband Mt 18-25* (EKK I/3; Zürich and Düsseldorf: Benziger Verlag and Neukirchen-Vluyn: Neukirchener Verlag, 1997) 269, n. 1: "Nur ganz wenige Textzeugen (f^{1}, e, sy^{s}, arm, geo, Or) streichen νομικός. Daß bei diesem Textbefund die Herausgeber des GNT und von Nestle^{26} νομικός in [ ] setzen, ist textkritisch unbegreiflich und nur von den Schwierigkeiten der Quellenscheidung her verständlich."

17 Harnack, *Sprüche und Reden Jesu*, 47-48, 94. ET: *The Sayings of Jesus*, 63-64, 136.

18 Streeter, *The Four Gospels*, 276-79, 291.

19 See the excursus in *Q 11:2b-4*: *The Lord's Prayer* (Documenta Q: Reconstructions of Q Through Two Centuries of Gospel Research Excerpted, Sorted, and Evaluated; Leuven: Peeters, 1996) 4-18. The Evaluations there favor inclusion of the Lord's Prayer in Q {A}.

with a note: "Marcionite in character," Huck-Greeven, and Boismard-Lamouille agree with NA[27] = *GNT* to read ἐλθέτω ἡ βασιλεία σου, as do: *RSV; NRSV,* with a note: "A few ancient authorities read *Your Holy Spirit come upon us and cleanse us*"; *NEB* and *REB*, both with a note: "*One witness reads* thy kingdom come upon us; *some others have* thy Holy Spirit come upon us and cleanse us; *Lutherbibel*; *EÜ; BJ*, with a note: "Var. (qui tire peut-être son origine de la liturgie baptismale): 'que ton Esprit Saint vienne sur nous et nous purifie'"; and *TOB*, with a note: "Chez Lc, quelques témoins anciens lisent: *Fais venir sur nous ton Règne*; quelques autres, plus récents, ont à la place de cette demande ou de la première: *Fais venir ton Esprit Saint sur nous, et qu'il nous purifie*. Cette formule pourrait avoir été introduite après coup dans le texte de Lc, sous l'influence d'une liturgie du baptême." Metzger ἐλθέτω ἡ βασιλεία σου {A}:

> Apparently, therefore, the variant reading is a liturgical adaptation of the original form of the Lord's Prayer, used perhaps when celebrating the rite of baptism or the laying on of hands. The cleansing descent of the Holy Spirit is so definitely a Christian, ecclesiastical concept that one cannot understand why, if it were original in the prayer, it should have been supplanted in the overwhelming majority of the witnesses by a concept originally much more Jewish in its piety.

Q 11:10: In Luke 11:10 Huck-Greeven, *BJ*, *RSV, NRSV, NEB, REB*, and *TOB* use the future. NA[27] prints ἀνοιγ[ήσ]εται. Boismard-Lamouille reads ἀνοίγεται. *Lutherbibel* and *EÜ* use the present. *GNT*[1] reads ἀνοίγεται {C}, but *GNT*[3.4] read ἀνοιγ[ήσ] εται {C}. Metzger ἀνοιγ[ήσ]εται {C}:

> It is difficult to decide between ἀνοιγήσεται and ἀνοίγεται. On the one hand, the former reading may have arisen as the result of scribal assimilation to the future tense at the end of ver. 9; on the other hand, the latter reading may be the result of assimilation to the present tense of ver. 10. In order to represent the balance of probabilities, a majority of the Committee decided to print ἀνοιγ[ήσ]εται.

Q 11:11-12: In Luke 11:11 Tasker reports in a note that the words referring to bread/stone "were considered an assimilation to Mt. 7.9." Huck-Greeven, Boismard-Lamouille, *RSV, NRSV, NEB, REB*, and *EÜ* agree with NA[27] in omitting the bread/stone formulation, as does *GNT*[1] {B}, but *GNT*[3.4] {C}. *BJ*[1] reads: "Quel est d'entre vous le père auquel son fils demande du pain et qui lui remettra une pierre? Ou s'il demande un poisson, à la place du poisson, lui remettra-t-il un serpent?" But *BJ*[2] reads: "Quel est d'entre vous le père auquel son fils demandera un poisson, et qui à la place du poisson lui remettra un serpent?" A note states: "Add. 'du pain, et qui lui remettra une pierre?' Harmonisation avec Mt 7,9." Similarly *TOB,* with a note: "Un grand nombre de témoins introduisent ici, sans doute d'après Mt 7,9: *du pain, est-ce qu'il lui présentera une pierre, ou....*" Similarly *Lutherbibel*, with a note: "In der späteren Überlieferung finden sich zusätzlich die Worte: 'ums Brot bitten, dafür einen Stein biete? Oder wenn er ...' (vgl. Mt 7,9.)" J. Delobel lists Luke 11:11 among "disputable passages."[20] Metzger omits bread/stone {B}: "It is difficult to decide (*a*) whether, like the Matthean account (7.9), Luke originally had two pairs of terms (but not the same two pairs as Matthew), and a third pair was incorporated from Matthew (bread and stone); or (*b*) whether Luke originally had three pairs and, through an accident in transcription, one of the pairs was omitted. A majority of the Committee, considering the longer readings to be the result of scribal assimilation to Matthew, preferred the shorter reading."

[20] J. Delobel, "The Sayings of Jesus in the Textual Tradition: Variant Readings in the Greek Manuscripts of the Gospels," *Logia – Les paroles de Jésus – The Sayings of Jesus*: *Mémorial Joseph Coppens* (ed. J. Delobel; *BETh L* 59; Leuven: Peeters and Leuven University Press, 1982) 431-57: 445 (see also 452). He bases this on the evaluation of {C} in *GNT*[3].

In Q 11:11-12: In Luke 11:11 NA[25], Tasker, and Huck-Greeven read μὴ ἀντὶ ἰχθύος, but *GNT* and Boismard-Lamouille read καὶ ἀντὶ ἰχθύος. Metzger[2] καὶ ἀντὶ ἰχθύος {C}: "The reading with καί … preserves a Semitism that most copyists replaced with μή, the usual Greek interrogative particle."

Q 11:13: In Luke 11:13 ὁ preceding ἐξ οὐρανοῦ is in Tasker, Huck-Greeven, and Boismard-Lamouille. In NA[27] it is included in brackets. The reading with ὁ is presupposed in *RSV, NEB, REB, Lutherbibel,* and in *NRSV*, but here with a note: "Other ancient authorities read *the Father give the Holy Spirit from heaven.*" It is included in *EÜ*, with a note: "Andere Übersetzungsmöglichkeit (nach einigen alten Textzeugen): wird der Vater denen, die ihn bitten, aus dem Himmel den Heiligen Geist geben." *GNT* includes ὁ {D}. Metzger 1971[1]{D}, 1993[2] {C}:

> In view of the Matthean parallel (7.11) ὁ πατὴρ ὑμῶν ὁ ἐν τοῖς οὐρανοῖς δώσει, it is easy to account for the rise of the variant readings ὑμῶν ὁ ἐξ οὐρανοῦ and ὁ οὐράνιος. It is much more difficult to decide between ἐξ οὐρανοῦ ('the Father will give *from heaven* the Holy Spirit to those who ask him') and ὁ ἐξ οὐρανοῦ, which seems to be a pregnant construction for ὁ ἐν οὐρανῷ ἐξ οὐρανοῦ. So evenly is the external evidence divided and so unconvincing are the arguments based on internal considerations that a majority of the Committee finally decided to include ὁ in the text, but to enclose it within square brackets, indicating doubt that it has a right to stand there.

BJ reads "le Père du ciel donnera-t-il," perhaps presupposing the absence of ὁ. *TOB* reads "le Père céleste," with a note: "Litt. *Le Père, celui du ciel.* Quelques bons témoins lisent: *Le Père donnera du ciel.*" The General Editors omit ὁ (with Epp), as an assimilation to Matt 7:11, where it is part of a standard Mattheanism. This weakens correspondingly the probability of it being in the text of Q.

Q 11:24: In Luke 11:24 τότε may be an assimilation to Matt 12:43. It is omitted in Tasker, Huck-Greeven, and Boismard-Lamouille. *Lutherbibel* includes it, but *EÜ* is unclear since unexpressed: "… und sucht einen Ort, wo er bleiben kann. Wenn er keinen findet, sagt er: …" NA[27] puts in square brackets and *NEB* evaluates {C}. Metzger [τότε] {C}: "On the basis of external evidence, a majority of the Committee preferred to include τότε, but, in view of the possibility that it may be a scribal assimilation to the parallel in Mt 12.44, decided to enclose the word within square brackets." The General Editors (and Epp) have serious doubt as to whether it is in Luke 11:24. This in turn weakens the probability of it being in the text of Q.

Q 11:33 In Luke 11:33 οὐδὲ ὑπὸ τὸν μόδιον is included in Huck-Greeven, *RSV, BJ, Lutherbibel* and *EÜ.* It is omitted in Boismard-Lamouille, *NEB, REB* and *NRSV.* Tasker puts it in a note, and describes it as "reflecting Mt. 5:15." *TOB* reads only "dans une cachette," with a note: "De nombreux témoins ajoutent: *ou sous le boisseau*, sans doute d'après Mt 5,15 ou Mc 4,21." But *GNT*[1-3] include it {D}; *GNT*[4] includes it {C}. Metzger 1971[1] {D} and 1994[2] {C}:

> Since Luke preferred not to use μόδιον in 8.16, a word that is present in the parallel in Mark (and Matthew), it may well be that the word, with its clause, was absent from the original form of the present passage also. On the other hand, since the clause is attested by weighty and diversified external evidence, a majority of the Committee was unwilling to drop it altogether and compromised by enclosing the words within square brackets.

NA[27] includes it in square brackets. The General Editors omit it.

Q 11:33: In Luke 11:33 φέγγος is read by NA[25], Tasker, Huck-Greeven, and Boismard-Lamouille. φῶς is read by NA[27] and probably *Lutherbibel*, though *EÜ* is unclear: "… damit alle, die eintreten, es leuchten sehen." Hoffmann and Kloppenborg read φέγγος, while Robinson prefers φῶς. (Epp agrees, even though φέγγος may be the *lectio difficilior.*)

Q 11:42: In Luke 11:42 Tasker includes ταῦτα δὲ ἔδει ποιῆσαι κἀκεῖνα μὴ παρεῖναι, but reports that the words "are not found in D d and Marcion, to whom they would obviously have been unacceptable." It is included in Huck-Greeven, Boismard-Lamouille, *RSV, NRSV, NEB, REB, BJ, Lutherbibel*, and *EÜ. TOB* includes it, but adds in a note: "Cette dernière phrase manque en plusieurs témoins anciens, sans doute choqués de ce qu'elle conserve une valeur aux pratiques légales." Metzger includes it {B}: "Marcion, finding these words entirely unacceptable, omitted them from his edition of Luke's Gospel; their absence from codex Bezae may be due to scribal oversight, or, more probably, to influence from the Marcionite form of text." The General Editors include it in the text of Luke and hence of Q.

Q 11:46b: In Matt 23:4 Tasker, *NEB, REB*, Huck-Greeven, Boismard-Lamouille, *BJ, TOB*, and *EÜ* omit καὶ δυσβάστακτα, but *RSV* and *NRSV* include it, with a note: "Other ancient authorities lack *hard to bear*." *Lutherbibel* includes it. *GNT*[1] omits it {C}, but *GNT*[3.4] include it {C}. Metzger includes it {C}:

> Impressed by the weight of the external evidence supporting the longer text, a majority of the Committee explained the absence … as perhaps due to stylistic refinement or an accidental oversight (the eye of the copyist passing from one καί to the other). Nevertheless, because it is possible that the words may be an interpolation from Lk 11.46, it was decided to enclose them within square brackets.

To this Metzger then appended with his initials his own dissenting view: "The words καὶ δυσβάστακτα should not stand in the text, for (*a*) if they were present originally, no good reason can account for their absence from such a wide variety of witnesses, and (*b*) the tendency of copyists to enhance the solemnity of Jesus' words accounts for the prefixing of μεγάλα before βαρέα in א, and for the interpolation after βαρέα of the synonymous expression καὶ δυσβάστακτα from Lk 11.46." The General Editors (and Epp) consider the presence of καὶ δυσβάστακτα in Matthew to be indeterminate. This in turn weakens the probability of it being in the text of Q.

Q 12:4: In Luke 12:4, regarding the orthography (see above, p. xciii).

Q 12:22b: In Matt 6:25a ἢ τί πίητε is in Tasker, *GNT* {C}, Boimard-Lamouille, *NEB*, *REB*, and *Lutherbibel*. But Huck-Greeven, *RSV*, *NRSV* (but with a note: "Other ancient authorities lack *or what you will drink*"), BJ, *TOB* and *EÜ* omit it. Metzger includes it {C}:

> In favor of the shorter reading, lacking ἢ τί πίητε, is the possibility that the text was assimilated to ver. 31. The variation between καί and ἤ can also be taken as an indication of the secondary nature of the addition. On the other hand, the similarity of the ending of φάγητε and πίητε may have occasioned a transcriptional oversight on the part of one or more copyists. To represent the balance of probabilities the Committee retained the words but enclosed them within square brackets.

Q 12:25: In Luke 12:25 ἐπὶ τὴν ἡλικίαν αὐτοῦ precedes προσθεῖναι in Tasker, *GNT*, and Boismard-Lamouille. But Huck-Greeven has the order προσθεῖναι ἐπὶ τὴν ἡλικίαν αὐτοῦ.

Q 12:25: In Luke 12:25 ἕνα is absent in Tasker, *GNT*, Huck-Lietzmann, Boismard-Lamouille, *RSV*, *NRSV*, *REB*, *BJ*, and *TOB*.

Q 12:27: A scribal error, already in Matt 6:28 par. Luke 12:27 and hence in Q, attests to Q having been a written Greek text, copied from a written Greek archetype. Hence an **Excursus on the Scribal Error in Q 12:27** is appropriate:

> In Matt 6:28 Tasker put the reading οὐ ξαίνουσιν οὐδὲ νήθουσιν οὐδὲ κοπιῶσιν in a note and explained: "א*, it would appear, has the interesting reading οὐ ξένουσιν (= ξαίνουσιν) οὐδὲ νήθουσιν οὐδὲ κοπιῶσιν. As ΟΥΞΕΝΟΥΣΙΝ, wrongly read as ΑΥΞΑΝΟΥΣΙΝ, could have given rise to the other variants, and as αὐξάνουσιν seemed

[21] This is a reference to T. C. Skeat, "The Lilies of the Field," *ZNW* 37 (1938) 211-14, to whom much credit is due for making this very difficult but important discovery.

unnatural in the present context, the translators thought that the possibility that the reading of א* is original should be left open, but αὐξάνουσιν was retained in the text. The passage should be compared with Lk. 12.27." NA[25] had a note at Matt 6:28: "οὐ ξένουσιν (= ξαίν-) οὐδὲ νήθουσιν οὐδὲ κοπιῶσιν א*vid. (cf. ZNW 1938, 211-214)."[21] The note in NA[27] has omitted completely the reference to T. C. Skeat's decisive essay, and reads only: "οὐ ξαίνουσιν οὐδὲ νήθουσιν οὐδὲ κοπιῶσιν א*vid." *GNT* has a note: "οὐ ξένουσιν [= ξαίνουσιν] οὐδὲ νήθουσιν οὐδὲ κοπιῶσιν א*vid." The reading αὐξάνουσιν is presupposed in *RSV*, *NRSV*, *BJ*, *TOB*, *Lutherbibel* and *EÜ*. This is also the case in *NEB* and *REB*, but with a note: "*one witness reads* Consider the lilies: they neither card, nor spin, nor work." Metzger αὐξάνουσιν {B}: "The original reading of codex Sinaiticus, which was detected when the manuscript was examined under an ultra-violet ray lamp, is οὐ ξένουσιν (= ξαίνουσιν) οὐδὲ νήθουσιν οὐδὲ κοπιῶσιν, 'they do not card neither do they spin nor toil.' This reading, though regarded as original by some scholars, doubtless arose as a scribal idiosyncrasy that was almost immediately corrected. Codex Koridethi, supported by the Curetonian Syriac, reverses the order of verbs, placing the specific word ('spin') before the general word ('toil')." Huck-Greeven reads as does NA[27], but refers in the critical apparatus to Athanasius, Chrysostom and the *Gospel of Thomas*. Boismard-Lamouille reads as does NA[27], but quotes in a note the *Gospel of Thomas*.

But, on the other hand, in the case of Luke 12:27 NA[25] had read πῶς οὔτε νήθει οὔτε ὑφαίνει. *BJ* reads "comme ils ne filent ni ne tissent," and in a note reads: "Var.: 'ils ne peinent ni ne filent,' cf. Mt 6 28." *EÜ*: "Seht euch die Lilien an: Sie arbeiten nicht und spinnen nicht." Then NA[27], Huck-Greeven and Boismard-Lamouille read: πῶς αὐξάνει· οὐ κοπιᾷ οὐδὲ νήθει. Metzger favors this reading 1971[1] {D}, 1994[2] {B}: "After some hesitation a majority of the Committee rejected the reading of D it[d] syr[c.s] *al*, οὔτε νήθει οὔτε ὑφαίνει ('they neither spin nor weave'), as a stylistic refinement introduced by copyists in view of the following reference to Solomon's clothing." *RSV* and *NRSV* read: "how they grow; they neither toil nor spin." (*Lutherbibel* presents an unattested mixed text: "Seht die Lilien an, wie sie wachsen: sie spinnen nicht, sie webern nicht.")

Thus the gradual recognition of the presence of αὐξάν- in both Matthew and Luke leads to the unavoidable conclusion that αὐξάν- was already in Q. As a result, one must infer that αὐξαν- is a scribal error already in the archetype of Q presupposed in Matthew and Luke. Hence an emendation of the text prior to Q is in place. The original text must have read οὐ ξαιν-, lilies "do not card," which was corrupted to read αὐξαν-, they "grow."

The *Gospel of Thomas* (*P. Oxy.* 655) documents a form of the sayings cluster Free from Anxiety like (Ravens and) Lilies (Q 12:22b-31) that itself pre-dates Q by presenting an even more archaic form. For it contains, in Saying 36, the reading ΑΤΙ[ΝΑΟ]ΥΞΑ[Ι] / ΝΕΙΟΥΔΕΝ[ΗΘ]ΕΙ (ἅτινα οὐ ξαίνει οὐδὲ νήθει, "which neither card nor spin"),[22] as well as other readings that are more archaic than those found in Q 12:22b-31.[23]

[22] James M. Robinson and Christoph Heil, "Zeugnisse eines schriftlichen, griechischen vorkanonischen Textes: Mt 6,28b א*, P. Oxy. 655 I,1-17 (EvTh 36) und Q 12,27," *ZNW* 89 (1998) 30-44.

[23] James M. Robinson, "The Pre-Q Text of the (Ravens and) Lilies: Q 12:22-31 and P. Oxy. 655 (*Gos. Thom.* 36)," in *Text und Geschichte: Facetten historisch-theologischen Arbeitens aus dem Freundes- und Schülerkreis, Dieter Lührmann zum 60. Geburtstag* (edd. Stefan Maser and Egbert Schlarb; MThSt 50, 1999) 143-80; and, in a more readable, simplified form, "A Written Greek Sayings Cluster Older than Q: A Vestige," *HTR* 92 (1999) 61-77. See also Jens Schröter, "Vorsynoptische Überlieferung auf P. Oxy. 655? Kritische Bemerkungen zu einer erneuerten These," *ZNW* 90 (1999) 265-72 and the reply by Robinson and Heil, "Noch einmal: Der Schreibfehler in Q 12,27," forthcoming in *ZNW*.

It was with the help of *P. Oxy.* 655 that Skeat had read at Matt 6:28 in Codex Sinaiticus, using ultraviolet light, an erased text below the familiar lines ΤΑΚΡΙΝΑΤΟΥ / ΑΓΡΟΥΠΩΣΑΥΞΑ / ΝΟΥΣΙΝΟΥΚΟΠΙ / ΩΣΙΝΟΥΔΕΝΗ> / ΘΟΥΣΙΝ (τὰ κρίνα τοῦ ἀγροῦ πῶς αὐξάνουσιν· οὐ κοπιῶσιν οὐδὲ νήθουσιν, "the lilies of the field, how they grow; they neither work nor spin"). The otherwise unattested reading, erased by the first corrector, read: ΤΑΚΡΙΝΑΤΟΥ / ΑΓΡΟΥΠΩΣΟΥΞΕ / ΝΟΥΣΙΝΟΥΔΕΝΗ / ΘΟΥΣΙΝΟΥΔΕΚΟΠΙ / ΩΣΙΝ (τὰ κρίνα τοῦ ἀγροῦ πῶς οὐ ξένουσιν [itacism for ξαίνουσιν[24]] οὐδὲ νήθουσιν οὐδὲ κοπιῶσιν, "the lilies of the field, how they do not card nor spin nor work").

These two manuscripts, *P. Oxy.* 655 (*Gos. Thom.* 36) and the original hand of Codex Sinaiticus, thus attest the original reading οὐ ξαίν-, already corrupted into αὐξαν- in Matthew and Luke, and hence presumably in Q, at least in the archetype of Q presupposed in Matthew and Luke.

A similar agreement between א* and the *Gospel of Thomas*, then corrected in א[1] to conform to the dominant Matthean text, just as in the present case, occurs also in Matt 11:9a at Q 7:26a, which corresponds to *Gos. Thom.* 78.1b-2a (see above, pp. xcii-xciii, in the discussion of punctuation).

Q 12:31: In Matt 6:33 Tasker, Huck-Greeven, *NEB*, *REB*, and *Lutherbibel* include τοῦ θεοῦ. But *EÜ* omits τοῦ θεοῦ and translates "sein Reich," as does similarly *RSV*, "his kingdom," but *NRSV* reads "kingdom of God," with a note: "Other ancient authorities lack *of God*." Boismard-Lamouille and *BJ* omit τοῦ θεοῦ. *TOB* translates "...le Royaume et la justice de Dieu," but has a note: "Litt. *de lui*. Il ne peut s'agir de la justice du Royaume, car en grec le pronom personnel est du genre masculin, alors que royaume est du féminin." NA[25] omitted τοῦ θεοῦ, but NA[27] includes it in square brackets. *GNT*[1] reads τὴν βασιλείαν καὶ τὴν δικαιοσύνην αὐτοῦ {C}, but *GNT*[3.4] read τὴν βασιλείαν [τοῦ θεοῦ] καὶ τὴν δικαιοσύνην αὐτοῦ {C}. Metzger τὴν βασιλείαν [τοῦ θεοῦ] καὶ τὴν δικαιοσύνην αὐτοῦ {C}: "The textual data are susceptible of quite diverse evaluations. On the one hand, according to the opinion of a minority of the Committee, the reading that best explains the rise of the other readings is that supported by א (B) it[1] *al*, inasmuch as the addition of τοῦ θεοῦ (or τῶν οὐρανῶν) after βασιλείαν seems to be an altogether natural supplement, which, if present originally, would not have been deleted. (The transposition of δικαιοσύνην and βασιλείαν in B is perhaps the result of the desire to suggest that righteousness is prerequisite to participation in the kingdom; compare 5.20). On the other hand, the majority of the Committee was impressed by the prevailing usage of Matthew, who almost never employs βασιλεία without a modifier (the instances in 8.12; 13.38; 24.7, 14 were regarded as special exceptions), and

[24] Skeat, in a letter of iv 99, points out why the shift from -αί- to -έ- in the case of οὐ ξένουσιν is to be considered a normal scribal fluctuation, whereas the shifts from οὐ to αὐ- and from -αί- to -ά- in the case of αὐξάνει are copyists' mistakes in writing:

> Vowels were certainly not 'carelessly interchanged' but were written to reflect current pronunciation. In the case of αὐξάνει for οὐ ξαίνει, αυ and ου were certainly not pronounced identically, nor were αι and α. αι and ε, however, were certainly pronounced identically, as in Modern Greek, and this explains the scribe of Sinaiticus writing ξενουσι for ξαινουσι.

On this last point see H. J. M. Milne and T. C. Skeat, *Scribes and Correctors of the Codex Sinaiticus* (London: British Museum, 1938) 54:

> The confusion of ε and αι can occur anywhere ... .

More recently, T. C. Skeat, "The Codex Sinaiticus, the Codex Vaticanus and Constantine," *JThS*, NS 50 (1999) 583-625: 585, n. 7:

> Caesarea is mentioned 15 times in Acts, and in 13 of these Scribe A [of Codex Sinaiticus] spells the name as here [Acts 8:5], Καισαρίᾳ. Twice, however (Acts x. 24, xxv. 6) the spelling is Κεσαρία. ... Cf. Matt 22:21, where he writes: λέγουσι Κέσαρος. τότε λέγει αὐτοῖς ἀπόδοτε οὖν τὰ Κέσαρος Καίσαρι κτλ.

explained the absence of a modifier in several witnesses as due to accidental scribal omission. In view of these conflicting interpretations, it was thought best to include the words in the text but to enclose them within square brackets." The General Editors (and Epp) do not include τοῦ θεοῦ.

Q 12:31: In Luke 12:31 τὴν βασιλείαν αὐτοῦ is in Tasker, Huck-Greeven, Boismard-Lamouille, *GNT*, *RSV* and *NRSV*, both with a note: "Other ancient authorities read *God's*," *NEB, REB, BJ, TOB, Lutherbibel*, and *EÜ*. Metzger τὴν βασιλείαν αὐτοῦ 1971[1] {C}, 1994[2] {B}: "It is more likely that αὐτοῦ was replaced by τοῦ θεοῦ (as has in fact happened in codex Bezae) than vice versa. The reading τοῦ θεοῦ καὶ τὴν δικαιοσύνην αὐτοῦ is an intrusion from the parallel in Mt 6.33. One of the idiosyncrasies of the scribe of 𝔓[75] is his tendency to omit personal pronouns."

Q 12:39: In Luke 12:39 Tasker, Huck-Greeven, Boismard-Lamouille, *BJ*, *TOB*, *NEB*, *REB*, *Lutherbibel*, and *EÜ* omit ἐγρηγόρησεν ἂν καί. *RSV* includes it, but *NRSV* and *GNT* omit it. Metzger omits it {B}: "The original Lukan text seems to have lacked ἐγρηγόρησεν ἂν καί. Scribes would have been almost certain to assimilate the shorter reading (preserved in 𝔓[75] ℵ* *al*) to the longer reading found in the parallel passage (Mt 24.43), whereas there is no good reason that would account for the deletion of the words had they been present originally." Epp agrees with Metzger. If original, ἐγρηγόρησεν ἂν καὶ οὐκ (ἄν) would present an assured Q reading. Hoffmann includes the reading in Luke 12:39, and hence in Q {C}.

Q 12:44: Luke 12:44 is omitted by Harnack, who conjectures it is an interpolation derived from Matt 24:47,[25] though there is no supporting manuscript evidence. Hence it is included by Tasker, *GNT*, Huck-Greeven, Boismard-Lamouille, *RSV*, *NRSV*, *NEB*, *REB*, *BJ*, *TOB*, *Lutherbibel*, and *EÜ*.

Q 12:53: In Mic 7:6,[26] editions of the LXX from van Ess (1835) and Tischendorf (1869) through Rahlfs (1936, 1952[5], reprint 1979), and hence much of the scholarly literature, read πάντες just prior to οἱ ἄνδρες, a reading no longer accepted by the Göttingen Septuagint project: *Duodecim Prophetae* (Septuaginta: Vetus Testamentum Graecum Auctoritate Academiae Scientiarum Gottingensis editum, 13. ed. Joseph Ziegler; Göttingen: Vandenhoeck & Ruprecht, 1943, 1984[3]) 224.

Q 12:54-55: In Matt 16:2b-3, Tasker omits the text, with a note: "This passage … was considered to be probably a later insertion from a source parallel to Lk. 12.54-56. Jerome knew of Greek MSS. that omitted it, but he retained it in the Vulgate." It is omitted in *NEB* and *REB*, with a note "*Some witnesses here insert*" the longer alternative. Huck-Greeven, Boismard-Lamouille, *RSV*, and *NRSV* include the text. *BJ* includes it, with a note: "Om.: 'Au crépuscule … pas capables'." *TOB* includes it, with a note: "D'importants manuscrits omettent la deuxième partie du v. 2 et le v. 3." *Lutherbibel* includes it, with a note: "Verse 2b.3 … finden sich bei einigen wichtigen Textzeugen nicht." *EÜ* omits it, with a note: "Spätere Textzeugen fügen hier ein" the longer text. *GNT*[1] includes within square brackets {C}, *GNT*[3] {D}, GNT[4] {C}. Metzger includes it 1971[1] {D}, 1994[2] {C}:

> The external evidence for the absence of these words is impressive, including ℵ B f^{13} 157 *al* syr$^{c.s}$ cop$^{sa.bomss}$ arm Origen and, according to Jerome, most manuscripts known to him (though he included the passage in the Vulgate). The question is how one ought to interpret this evidence. Most scholars regard the passage as a later insertion from a source similar to Lk 12.54-56, or from the Lukan passage itself, with an adjustment concerning the particular signs of the weather. On the other hand, it can be argued (as Shrivener and Lagrange do) that the words were omitted by copyists in climates (e.g. Egypt)

[25] Adolf Harnack, *Sprüche und Reden Jesu*, 28: "Der v. 44 ist in Luk. vielleicht Zusatz aus Matt. Dann hat man keine Gewähr, daß er in Q gestanden hat." ET: *The Sayings of Jesus*, 34: "The verse in St. Luke corresponding to St. Matthew, verse 44, is perhaps an interpolation from St. Matthew. If so, we cannot be sure that it stood in Q."

[26] Christoph Heil, "Die Rezeption von Micha 7,6 LXX in Q und Lukas," *ZNW* 88 (1997) 211-22.

where red sky in the morning does not announce rain. In view of the balance of these considerations it was thought best to retain the passage enclosed within square brackets.[27]

Q 13:19: In Luke 13:19 Tasker, *GNT,* Huck-Greeven, Boimard-Lamouille, *RSV, NRSV, NEB, REB, BJ, Lutherbibel,* and *EÜ* omit μέγα. *TOB* does so with a note: "D'assez nombreux témoins précisent: *un grand arbre.* Mais cet adjectif convient mal à l'arbuste qu'est la *moutarde,* et Lc n'insiste pas sur le contraste entre lui et sa graine, comme font Mt 13,32 et Mc 4,30-31." Metzger omits μέγα {B}:

> Although copyists may have deleted μέγα to harmonize Luke with the prevailing text of Matthew (13,32), it is much more probable that, in the interests of heightening the contrast between a mustard seed and a tree, μέγα was added — as it was added also in a few witnesses in the Matthean parallel (syr$^{p(1\ msc)}$ cop^{sa} eth geo^{B}).

Q 13:21: In Luke 13:21 Tasker and Huck-Greeven omit ἐν-, but Boismard-Lamouille and *GNT*^{1} include it, as does *GNT*^{4}, though in square brackets.

Q 13:27: In Luke 13:27 Boismard-Lamouille and *GNT* read ἐρεῖ λέγων ὑμῖν. Tasker, Huck-Greeven, *RSV, NEB, REB,* and *EÜ* read ἐρεῖ· λέγω ὑμῖν, but *BJ* ("Mais il vous répondra:"), *Lutherbibel* ("Und er wird zu euch sagen:"), and *NRSV* ("But he will say,") read ἐρεῖ λέγων ὑμῖν or only ἐρεῖ ὑμῖν, as is also the case of *TOB* ("et il vous dira:"), with a note: "De nombreux témoins lisent: *il dira: je vous le dis…* Celui qui parle ici est le juge du dernier jour, tandis qu'en Mt 7,23 c'est Jésus qui parle à la première person." Metzger ἐρεῖ λέγων ὑμῖν {C}:

> The reading adopted by the Committee, though narrowly attested, seems to account best for the origin of the other readings. The awkwardness of the participle λέγων (which probably represents the construction of the Hebrew infinitive absolute: 'he will *indeed* say to you') would have prompted copyists either to alter it to the indicative (λέγω) or to omit it as superfluous.

Q 13:27: In Luke 13:27 NA^{25}, Tasker, and Huck-Greeven omit ὑμᾶς, as do apparently *RSV, NRSV, NEB, REB, BJ, EÜ,* and as does *TOB*, with a note: "De nombreux témoins lisent: *Vous, je ne sais…*, comme au v. 25." But Boismard-Lamouille include it, as does *GNT* {C} and *Lutherbibel.* Metzger includes it {C}:

> The multiplicity of variant readings of these words in ver. 27 contrasts with the fidelity with which they have been transmitted in ver. 25 (where only Marcion seems to have omitted ὑμᾶς). The reading οὐδέποτε εἶδον ὑμᾶς of D arose because of influence from the Matthean parallel (οὐδέποτε ἔγνων ὑμᾶς, 7.23). The absence of πόθεν ἐστέ in several minuscules (56 61 71 291 692) appears to be the result of scribal oversight arising from homoeoteleuton with the following ἀπόστητε. Since both external evidence and internal probabilities concerning the presence or absence of ὑμᾶς are so evenly balanced, the Committee decided to retain the word in the text, but to enclose it within square brackets.

Q 13:35: In Matt 23:38 ἔρημος is omitted by NA^{25}. Tasker omits it, with a note "*add* ἔρημος," explaining that it "was considered a later insertion adapting the passage more closely to Jer. 22.5," as does *NEB,* with a note: "*Some witnesses add* and laid waste," and EÜ, with a note: "Wörtlich: Darum wird euch euer Haus überlassen." But it is present in *GNT,* Huck-Greeven, Boismard-Lamouille, *RSV,* with a note: "Other ancient authorities omit *and desolate," NRSV,* with a comparable note, *REB, BJ,* with a note: "om.: 'déserte,'" *TOB,* with a note: "Certains mss n'ont pas le mot *déserte* (cf. Jr 12,7). Le sens est le même (Jr 22,5)," and *Lutherbibel.* Metzger omits {B}:

27 See the excursus in *Q 12:49-59: Children against Parents – Judging the Time – Settling out of Court* (Documenta Q: Reconstructions of Q Through Two Centuries of Gospel Research Excerpted, Sorted, and Evaluated; Leuven: Peeters, 1997) 162-176. The Evaluations there all favor inclusion with the uncertain grade {C}, for the reasons given by Metzger.

On the one hand, it can be argued that copyists added ἔρημος in order to conform the quotation to the text of Jr 22.5. On the other hand, however, in view of what was taken to be the preponderant weight of external evidence a majority of the Committee preferred to include ἔρημος, explaining its absence in some witnesses as the result of deletion by copyists who thought the word superfluous after ἀφίεται.

Q 13:35: In Luke 13:35 δέ is present in Tasker, *GNT*, Huck-Greeven, Boismard-Lamouille, *RSV, NRSV, BJ, TOB*, and *Lutherbibel*, but is perhaps absent from *REB* and *EÜ*.

Q 13:35: In Luke 13:35 Tasker, NA^{25}, Huck-Greeven, Boismard-Lamouille and *GNT* read ἴδητέ με. The reading με ἴδητε seems to be a textual corruption assimilating Luke to Matt 23:38, rather than the original Lukan text, which would have made με ἴδητε a minimal Q reading.

Q 13:35: In Luke 13:35 ἥξει ὅτε is in Tasker, *GNT*^{1} {D}, *GNT*^{4} {C}, Huck-Greeven, and Boismard-Lamouille. It is omitted by *RSV*, but included in *NRSV*, with a note: "Other ancient authorities lack *the time comes when*," *NEB, REB, BJ, TOB*, with a note: "Plusieurs témoins lisent comme Mt 23,39: *jusqu'à ce que vous disiez…*," *Lutherbibel*, and *EÜ*. Metzger reads ἥξει ὅτε {C}: "The rarity of construing ὅτε with the subjunctive (Blass-Debrunner-Funk, ¶ 382 (2), as well as the temptation to assimilate to the Matthean parallel (23.39), seems to have prompted many copyists to omit ἥξει ὅτε, and, in some cases (Θ 1241 *al*), to prefix ἀπ᾽ ἄρτι (Δ conflates the Matthean and Lukan readings). Apart from the subsidiary problem involving variation in the presence or absence of ἄν after ἕως (with the corresponding change of ἥξει to ἥξῃ in Ψ *f*^{1} 565 700 *al*), the manuscript basis for the reading 'until the time [or, the day] comes when you will say …' includes A D W Ψ *f*^{1} 28 it$^{a, b, (c), d, ff2, l, q, rl}$ vg syr$^{c, s, h \text{ with } *}$ Marcion *al*."

Q 14:~~1-4~~, ~~5~~, ~~6~~: In Luke 14:5 Tasker reads ὄνος ἢ βοῦς, and in a note gives υἱὸς ἢ βοῦς, explaining: "The translators were agreed that the reading υἱὸς ἢ βοῦς, though attested by 𝔓^{45} B W 28 e f q, and Cop. sah., was almost certainly wrong, and decided to accept the variant ὄνος ἢ βοῦς, found in ℵ fam. 1 fam. 13, the rest of the Latin versions, and Cop. boh. Some of them were persuaded that the conjecture οἲς ἢ βοῦς would best explain the other readings (cf. πρόβατον in Mt. 12:11)." *NEB* reads "a donkey or an ox," but *REB* reads "a son or an ox." *RSV* reads "an ass or an ox," but *NRSV* reads "a child or an ox." NA^{27}, *GNT*, Huck-Greeven, and Boismard-Lamouille read υἱὸς ἢ βοῦς. *BJ* prefers "fils," with "âne" in a note, as does *TOB*, with a note: "D'assez nombreux témoins substituent ou ajoutent: *âne*, probablement sous l'influence de 13,15," as do also *Lutherbibel* and *EÜ*, the latter with a note: "seinen Sohn, andere Lesart: seinen Esel." Metzger υἱὸς ἢ βοῦς {B}: "The oldest reading preserved in the manuscripts seems to be υἱὸς ἢ βοῦς. Because the collocation of the two words appeared to be somewhat incongruous, copyists altered υἱός either to ὄνος (cf. 13.15) or to πρόβατον (cf. Mt 12.11). Several witnesses (Θ 2174 syr^{c}) conflate all three words." In a footnote Metzger comments: "It has been conjectured that υἱός is a corruption of the old Greek word ὄϊς ('a sheep'); see John Mill, *Novum Testamentum Graecum*, 2nd ed. (Leipzig, 1723), p. 44, ¶ 423." Mill: "Ex ὄϊς factum a scribis posterioribus υἱός quod in Codices multos transiit." (Epp favors Mill's emendation.) 𝔓^{75} uses for υἱός the *nomen sacrum* Υ̅Σ̅, of Jesus in Luke 9:44; 10:22 (*bis*); 22:70, not of Jesus Υ̅Ν̅ in Luke 9:41 and Υ̅Σ̅ in Luke 14:5. Without the superlinear stroke of a *nomen sacrum*, ΥΣ, "pig," could be an initial misunderstanding which then could have led to improvements to refer to clean animals.[28]

[28] Frans Neirynck, "Luke 14,1-6: Lukan Composition and Q Saying," *Der Treue Gottes trauen: Beiträge zum Werk des Lukas für Gerhard Schneider* (Freiburg: Herder, 1991) 243-63: 254-55. It is reprinted in his collected essays, *Evangelica II: 1982-1991* (BETL 99; Leuven: University Press and Peeters, 1991), 183-204: 196-98.

Q 14:26: In Luke 14:26 NA[25], Tasker, and Huck-Greeven read πατέρα αὐτοῦ, whereas NA[27] and Boismard-Lamouille read πατέρα ἑαυτοῦ. Epp: The evidence is very closely divided.

Q 14:27: In Luke 14:27 Tasker, NA[27], Huck-Greeven and Boismard-Lamouille read ἑαυτοῦ, and do not list αὐτοῦ as a variant reading in the critical apparatus. First Aland 1996[15], while retaining ἑαυτοῦ in the text, presents in the critical apparatus the attestation for αὐτοῦ. Since αὐτοῦ has the stronger attestation, is presumably represents the Lukan text. Yet since the Nestle-Aland and the Greek New Testament texts have been frozen in the form they had when they were brought together, it is apparently not possible to alter the text as a result of such new information. But one should be aware of the probability that here Matthew and Luke agree, and hence that the reading αὐτοῦ is the minimal Q text.

Q 15:4: Matt 18:11 is omitted in *GNT* {B}, Boismard-Lamouille, Huck-Greeven, *RSV, NRSV, NEB, REB, BJ.* It is omitted by Tasker, who explains: "This verse ... was regarded as an assimilation of the original text to Lk. 19.10." *TOB* omits it, with a note: "Cf. Lc 19,10." It is omitted in *Lutherbibel,* with a note: "Vers 11 findet sich erst in der späteren Überlieferung: ...," and in *EÜ* with a note: "Ein Teil der Textzeugen fügt hier ein: ..." Metzger omits {B}:

> There can be little doubt that the words ἦλθεν γὰρ ὁ υἱὸς τοῦ ἀνθρώπου (ζητῆσαι καὶ) σῶσαι τὸ ἀπολωλός are spurious here, being absent from the earliest witnesses representing several textual types (Alexandrian, Egyptian, Antiochian), and manifestly borrowed by copyists from Lk 19.10. The reason for the interpolation was apparently to provide a connection between ver. 10 and verses 12-14.

Q 17:21: In Luke 17:21 Tasker, *GNT*, Huck-Greeven, Boismard-Lamouille, *RSV*, *NRSV*, *NEB*, *REB*, *BJ*, *TOB*, *Lutherbibel*, and *EÜ* read ἰδοὺ ὧδε ἤ· ἐκεῖ. The variant reading ἰδοὺ ὧδε ἤ· ἰδοὺ ἐκεῖ would suggest a closer relation to Mark 13:21: ἴδε ὧδε ..., ἴδε ἐκεῖ.

Q 17:23: In Luke 17:23 ἰδοὺ ἐκεῖ, ἰδοὺ ὧδε is read by NA[25], Tasker, Huck-Greeven, and apparently *BJ*[2] ("Le voilà! Le voici!", though *BJ*[1], "Le voici! Le voilà!", may presuppose ἰδοὺ ὧδε, ἰδοὺ ἐκεῖ, see Mark 13:21), *TOB*, and *EÜ*, but NA[27] [ἤ·], *GNT* {C}, Boismard-Lamouille, and apparently *RSV*, *NRSV*, *NEB*, *REB*, and *Lutherbibel* read ἰδοὺ ἐκεῖ, ἤ· ἰδοὺ ὧδε, as does Metzger {C}:

> The great variety of readings has arisen partly from the circumstance that in later Greek ει, η, and ι came to be pronounced alike, thus facilitating alteration of the text, and partly from confusion arising from inattention on the part of copyists. Furthermore, recollection of the Markan sequence (ὧδε ... ἐκεῖ, 13:21) may also have exerted an influence on copyists. The Committee preferred the reading attested in 𝔓[75] and B as the earliest reading preserved in the extant witnesses, but in view of the absence of ἤ from such varied witnesses as D[gr] L W X Π 28 33 700 892 it[b, ff2, i, rl, s] vg syr[c, s, p, h with *], it was thought appropriate to enclose the word within square brackets.

Q 17:23: In Luke 17:23 Tasker, *GNT*, Huck-Greeven, Boismard-Lamouille, and apparently *RSV*, *NRSV*, *NEB*, *REB*, *BJ*, *TOB*, *Lutherbibel*, and *EÜ* read μὴ ἀπέλθητε μηδὲ διώξητε.

Q 17:24: In Luke 17:24 Tasker, Huck-Greeven, Boismard-Lamouille, *NEB*, *REB*, *RSV*, *NRSV*, *BJ*, *TOB*, *Lutherbibel*, and *EÜ* include ἐν τῇ ἡμέρᾳ αὐτοῦ. *GNT* includes it {C} in square brackets, as does NA[27]. Metzger includes it {C}:

> Although copyists may have inadvertently omitted the phrase ἐν τῇ ἡμέρᾳ αὐτοῦ because of homoeoteleuton (-που ... -του), the Committee was impressed by the combination of evidence for the shorter text in the best representatives of the Alexandrian and the Western types of text (𝔓[75] B D it[a.b.d.e.i]). The readings with παρουσία, a word that occurs nowhere else in the Gospel according to Luke, are the result of scribal assimilation to the parallel passage in Mt 24.27.

Q 17:26: In Matt 24:37 Tasker, *GNT*, Huck-Lietzmann, Boismard-Lamouille, *RSV*, *NRSV*,

NEB, *REB*, *JB*, *TOB* and *EÜ* omit καί after ἔσται, but *Lutherbibel* has καί. Since Luke 17:26 has καί at the equivalent position before ἐν ταῖς ἡμέραις, the Matthean καί could either reflect the influence of Q, if original in Matthew, or of the Lukan text, if a textual corruption.

Q 17:27: In Matt 24:38 Tasker, *GNT*[1], Huck-Greeven, *NEB*, *REB*, *Lutherbibel*, and *EÜ* omit ἐκείναις, but Boismard-Lamouille, *RSV*, *NRSV*, *JB*, *TOB* include it. *GNT*[3] includes it with an evaluation of {C} in square brackets, as does NA[27]. Metzger 1971[1] made no comment, but Metzger 1994[2] included it {C}:

> While it is possible that ἐκείναις was accidentally omitted in some witnesses because of the similarity in the terminations of words, yet because of the weight of the witnesses that support the inclusion, the Committee concluded that the word should be retained, but enclosed within square brackets.

Q 17:27: In Matt 24:38 Tasker, *GNT*, and Boismard-Lamouille read γαμίζοντες, but Huck-Greeven reads ἐκγαμίζοντες.

Q 17:30: In Matt 24:39b καί is omitted in Tasker and apparently in *RSV*, *NEB* and *REB*. It is put in square brackets in *GNT* and NA[27], but is included not in square brackets in NA[25], Huck-Greeven, and Boismard-Lamouille. It is presupposed in *NRSV*, *BJ*, *TOB*, *Lutherbibel*, and *EÜ*.

Q17:36: This verse is omitted from modern editions. Metzger *omit verse* {A}: "Although it is possible that ver. 36 ... may have been accidentally omitted through homoeoteleuton (an accident that happened to ver. 35 in א* and a few other witnesses), in view of the weighty manuscript authority supporting the shorter text ($\mathfrak{P}^{75}$ א A B L W Δ Θ Ψ f^1 28 33 565) it is more probable that copyists assimilated the passage to Mt 24.40."

Q 19:25: Luke 19:25 is included by Tasker, Huck-Greeven, Boismard-Lamouille, *RSV*, *NRSV*, *NEB*, *REB*, *BJ*, *Lutherbibel* and *EÜ*. *TOB* includes it with a note: "Ce verset manque chez plusieurs témoins anciens, sans doute parce qu'il ne se trouve pas chez Mt. Mais il est bien attesté chez Lc où il fait ressortir le caractère paradoxal du jugement royal." *GNT*[1] included the verse {D}, *GNT*[3] {C}, *GNT*[4] {A}. Metzger 1971[1] included it {C}, but Metzger 1994[2] {A} (with much the same comment as in Metzger[1]):

> Although it could be argued that ver. 25 was a marginal comment subsequently inserted by copyists into the text (but in that case the subject of εἶπαν would probably not have been left ambiguous – are they the bystanders of ver. 24, or those to whom Jesus was telling the parable?), a majority of the Committee considered it to be more probable that the words were omitted in several Western witnesses ... either (*a*) by assimilation to the Matthean parallel (25.28-29) or (*b*) for stylistic reasons, thereby providing a closer connection between verses 24 and 26. A majority of the Committee considered that, on balance, both external attestation and transcriptional probabilities favor the retention of the words in the text.

Endpapers

The endpaper on the right reproduces by permission of the Houghton Library, Harvard University, a photograph of papyrus fragments from a scroll dated to the late second or early third century that, unfortunately, do not come from Q, but rather from the somewhat similar Sayings Gospel, the *Gospel of Thomas* (*P. Oxy.* 655). For it documents a form of the archaic sayings cluster Free from Anxiety like (Ravens and) Lilies (Q 12:22b-31) that itself pre-dates Q in an even more archaic form: It contains, in Saying 36, the more original reading ΑΤΙ[ΝΑΟ]ΥΞΑ[Ι] / ΝΕΙΟΥΔΕΝ[ΗΘ]ΕΙ (ἅτινα οὐ ξαίνει οὐδὲ νήθει, "which neither card nor spin"), as well as other readings that are more archaic than those found in Q 12:22b-31.

The endpaper on the left reproduces (through the courtesy of T. C. Skeat) a photograph of Codex Sinaiticus at Matt 6:26-31, using ultraviolet light, where Skeat, "The Lilies of the Field," *ZNW* 37 (1938) 211-14, read the underlying text at Matt 6:28b, below the familiar lines ΤΑΚΡΙΝΑΤΟΥ / ΑΓΡΟΥΠΩΣΑΥΞΑ / ΝΟΥΣΙΝΟΥΚΟΠΙ / ΩΣΙΝΟΥΔΕΝΗ> / ΘΟΥΣΙΝ (τὰ κρίνα τοῦ ἀγροῦ πῶς αὐξάνουσιν· οὐ κοπιῶσιν οὐδὲ νήθουσιν, "the lilies of the field, how they grow; they neither work nor spin"): Underneath this familiar reading lies an otherwise unattested reading, erased by the first corrector: ΤΑΚΡΙΝΑΤΟΥ / ΑΓΡΟΥΠΩΣΟΥΞΕ / ΝΟΥΣΙΝΟΥΔΕΝΗ / ΘΟΥΣΙΝΟΥΔΕΚΟΠΙ / ΩΣΙΝ (τὰ κρίνα τοῦ ἀγροῦ πῶς οὐ ξένουσιν [itacism for ξαίνουσιν] οὐδὲ νήθουσιν οὐδὲ κοπιῶσιν, "the lilies of the field, how they neither card nor spin nor work").

In a letter of 15 July 1998 Skeat drew attention with his trained eye to the decisive details:

> The vital reading οὐ ξέ/νουσιν shows up very well because the scribe deleted only the omicron and the epsilon, leaving the intervening υξ untouched. The next three lines were completely erased and re-written because the scribe wished to reverse the order of νήθουσιν and κοπιῶσιν. The original eta of νήθουσιν can be seen at the end of the first line, and the πι of κοπιῶσιν (partly obscured by a filling-mark) can be seen at the end of the next line.

These two manuscripts thus attest the more original reading οὐ ξαίν-, already corrupted into αὐξαν- in Matthew and Luke, and hence presumably in Q, indeed in the archetype of Q presupposed in Matthew and Luke. This scribal error, since already in Q, attests to Q having been a written Greek text, copied from a written Greek archetype. For further details see James M. Robinson and Christoph Heil, "Zeugnisse eines schriftlichen, griechischen vorkanonischen Textes: Mt 6,28b א*, P. Oxy. 655 I,1-17 (EvTh 36) und Q 12,27," *ZNW* 89 (1998) 30-44; Robinson, "The Pre-Q Text of the (Ravens and) Lilies: Q 12:22-31 and P. Oxy. 655 (*Gos. Thom.* 36)," in *Text und Geschichte: Facetten theologischen Arbeitens aus dem Freundes- und Schülerkreis. Dieter Lührmann zum 60. Geburtstag* (ed. Stefan Maser and Egbert Schlarb; MThSt 50, 1999) 143-80; and Robinson, "A Written Greek Sayings Cluster Older than Q: A Vestige," *HTR* 92 (1999) 61-78. See the **Excursus on the Scribal Error in Q 12:27** in the section on Text Critical Notes in the Technical Data (above, pp. xcix-ci).

The Critical Text of Q

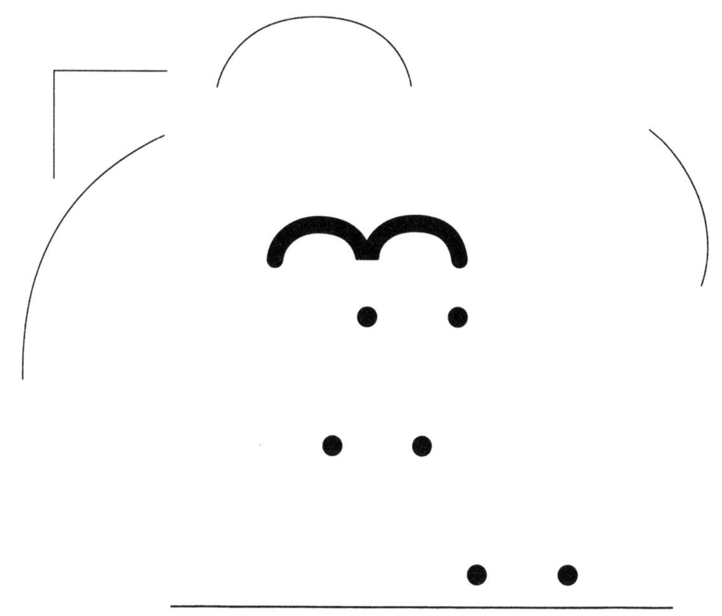

Q 3:⟦0⟧

Markan Parallel	Matthean Doublet	Matt 3:0	Q 3:⟦0⟧
			<>[1] ⟦< >[2] <’Ιησου>[3]< >[3]⟧

JMR: <>[1] ⟦< >[2] <λογ>[2]< >[2] <’Ιησου>[3]< >[3]⟧.

[1] Is τὰ λόγια in the incipit?

[2] Is οἱ λόγοι in the incipit?

Q

⟦<… ’Ιησου…>⟧	⟦<… Jesus…>⟧

Q 3:⟦0⟧

Luke 3:0	Lukan Doublet	Markan Parallel	Gospel of Thomas

[3] Can syntax, speaker(s) and context be determined?

⟦<… Jesus…>⟧	⟦<… Jésus…>⟧

Q 3:~~1a~~, 2b-3a, ~~3b-4~~

Mark 1:9a,4,15,2a,3,6,5,2b	Matt 3:13; 11:10b	Matt 3:1-6	Q 3:~~1a~~, 2b-3a, ~~3b-4~~
1:9a Καὶ ἐγένετο ἐν		**3:1** {Ἐν} [ ][1] δὲ	**3:~~1a~~** ~~ἐν~~ [][1] ~~δὲ~~
ἐκείναις ταῖς ἡμέραις		{(ταῖς ἡμέραις} {ἐκείναις)}[1]	[()][1]
1:4 ἐγένετο		(παρα)[2]{γ}(ί)[2]{νετ}(αι)[2]	**3:2b** [()][2]{~~γ~~}[()][2]{~~νετ~~}[()][2]
Ἰωάννης		{Ἰωάννη(ς)}[2]	{Ἰωάννη}[( )][2]
ὁ βαπτίζων		(ὁ βαπτι}στὴς)[3]	[({})][3]
ἐν τῇ ἐρήμῳ		⸉ {κηρύσσων}[4] ⸊[4]	⸉ ⸊[4]
καὶ κηρύσσων		{ἐν τῇ ἐρήμῳ}	{~~ἐν τῇ ἐρήμῳ~~}
βάπτισμα μετανοίας		(τῆς Ἰουδαίας)[5]	()[5]
εἰς ἄφεσιν ἁμαρτιῶν.			
1:15 καὶ λέγων		**3:2** ({καὶ λέγων}·	()[6]
ὅτι πεπλήρωται ὁ καιρὸς			
		{μετανοεῖτε}·	
καὶ ἤγγικεν		{ἤγγικεν} γὰρ	
ἡ βασιλεία		{ἡ βασιλεία	
τοῦ θεοῦ·		τ}ῶν οὐρανῶν.)[6]	
μετανοεῖτε καὶ πιστεύετε			
ἐν τῷ εὐαγγελίῳ.			
1:2a Καθὼς γέγραπται		**3:3** ⸉ (οὗτος γάρ ἐστιν	⸉⸊[7]
ἐν τῷ Ἠσαΐᾳ		ὁ ῥηθεὶς διὰ)[7] {Ἠσαΐ}ου	
τῷ προφήτῃ·		{τ}οῦ {προφήτ}ου (λέγοντος)[7]·	
1:3 φωνὴ βοῶντος		{φωνὴ βοῶντος	
ἐν τῇ ἐρήμῳ· ἑτοιμάσατε		ἐν τῇ ἐρήμῳ· ἑτοιμάσατε	
τὴν ὁδὸν κυρίου,		τὴν ὁδὸν κυρίου,	
εὐθείας ποιεῖτε		εὐθείας ποιεῖτε	
τὰς τρίβους αὐτοῦ,		τὰς τρίβους αὐτοῦ.} ⸊[7]	
1:6 καὶ ἦν ὁ Ἰωάννης		**3:4** (αὐτὸς δὲ {ὁ Ἰωάννης}	({})[8]
ἐνδεδυμένος		εἶχεν τὸ {ἔν}{δυ}μα αὐτοῦ	
τρίχας καμήλου		ἀπὸ {τριχ}ῶν {καμήλου	
καὶ ζώνην δερματίνην		καὶ ζώνην δερματίνην	
περὶ τὴν ὀσφὺν αὐτοῦ		περὶ τὴν ὀσφὺν αὐτοῦ},	
καὶ ἐσθίων		ἡ δὲ τροφὴ ἦν αὐτοῦ	
ἀκρίδας		{ἀκρίδ}ε{ς	
καὶ μέλι ἄγριον.		καὶ μέλι ἄγριον}.)[8]	

1 The divergent time references.

2 Does the narration begin with the word of God coming to John (Luke) or John himself coming (Matthew)?

3 The identification of John as the son of Zechariah (Luke) or as the Baptist (Matthew).

4 Is κηρύσσων in Q (and if so, in which position), or from Mark?

Q 3:~~1a~~, 2b-3a, ~~3b-4~~

Luke 3:1a, 2b, 3, 4	Luke 3:7a; 7:27b	Mark 1:4a,5a,4b,2a,3,5b,2b	Isa 40:3 LXX
3:1a Ἐν [ἔτει][1] δὲ [πεντεκαιδεκάτῳ τῆς ἡγεμονίας Τιβερίου Καίσαρος,][1]			
3:2b [{ἐ}][2]γ[έ][2]νετ[ο} ῥῆμα θεοῦ ἐπὶ][2]		**1:4a** ἐγένετο	
{Ἰωάννη}[ν][2] [τὸν Ζαχαρίου υἱὸν][3]		Ἰωάννης ὁ βαπτίζων	
⸉ ⸊[4]			
{ἐν τῇ ἐρήμῳ}.		ἐν τῇ ἐρήμῳ	
( )[5]			
( )[6]			
⸉ ⸊[7]			
			φωνὴ βοῶντος ἐν τῇ ἐρήμῳ· Ἑτοιμάσατε τὴν ὁδὸν κυρίου, εὐθείας ποιεῖτε τὰς τρίβους αὐτοῦ.
({ })[8]			

[5] Matthew's τῆς Ἰουδαίας.
[6] Is Matt 3:2 in Q or from Mark?
[7] Is Luke 3:4 par. Matt 3:3 in Q or from Mark, and, if in Q, in which position?
[8] Is Matt 3:4 in Q or from Mark?

Q 3:~~1a~~, 2b-3a, ~~3b-4~~

Mark 1:9a,4,15,2a,3,6,5,2b	Matt 3:13; 11:10b	Matt 3:1-6	Q 3:~~1a~~, 2b-3a, ~~3b-4~~
1:5 καὶ ἐξεπορεύετο πρὸς αὐτὸν πᾶσα ἡ Ἰουδαία χώρα καὶ οἱ Ἱεροσολυμῖται πάντες,	**3:13** (Τότε) παραγίνεται ὁ Ἰησοῦς ἀπὸ τῆς Γαλιλαίας	**3:5** (Τότε {ἐξεπορεύετο πρὸς αὐτὸν} {Ἱεροσόλυμ}α καὶ {πᾶσα ἡ Ἰουδαία} {καὶ})[9]	()[9]
		[ ][10] πᾶσα[ ][10]ἡ[ ][10] περί{χωρ}ο(ς)[10] τοῦ Ἰορδάνου, ʃ ʅ[4] [{ }][11] ʃ ʅ[7]	**3:3a** [][10] πᾶσα[ ][10]η[ ][10] περί{χωρ}ο[( )][10] τοῦ Ἰορδάνου **3:~~3b~~** ʃ {~~κηρύσσων~~}[4] ʅ[4] [{}][11] **3:4** ʃ [({})][7] {~~Ἠσαΐ~~}~~ου~~ {~~τ~~}~~οῦ~~ {~~προφήτ~~}~~ου~~()[7]· {~~φωνὴ βοῶντος~~ ~~ἐν τῇ ἐρήμῳ· ἑτοιμάσατε~~ ~~τὴν ὁδὸν κυρίου,~~ ~~εὐθείας ποιεῖτε~~ ~~τὰς τρίβους αὐτοῦ·~~} ʅ[7]
	ἐπὶ {(τ)}ὸν {(Ἰορδάνη)}ν πρὸς τὸν Ἰωάννην		
καὶ ἐβαπτίζοντο ὑπ' αὐτοῦ ἐν τῷ Ἰορδάνῃ ποταμῷ ἐξομολογούμενοι τὰς ἁμαρτίας αὐτῶν.	τοῦ {(βαπτι)}σθῆναι {(ὑπ' αὐτοῦ)}.	**3:6** ({καὶ ἐβαπτίζοντο} {ἐν τῷ Ἰορδάνῃ ποταμῷ} {ὑπ' αὐτοῦ} {ἐξομολογούμενοι τὰς ἁμαρτίας αὐτῶν}.)[12]	({})[12]
1:2b ἰδοὺ ἀποστέλλω τὸν ἄγγελόν μου πρὸ προσώπου σου, ὃς κατασκευάσει τὴν ὁδόν σου·	**11:10b** {ἰδοὺ} ἐγὼ {ἀποστέλλω τὸν ἄγγελόν μου πρὸ προσώπου σου, ὃς κατασκευάσει τὴν ὁδόν σου} ἔμπροσθέν σου.		

[9] Is Matt 3:5a in Q or from Mark?

[10] The function and hence the case of πᾶσα- -η- περίχωρο- τοῦ Ἰορδάνου: The place into which John came (Luke) or from which the people went to John (Matthew).

Q

2b <…> Ἰωάννη… **3a** <…> πᾶσα..η.. περίχωρο… τοῦ Ἰορδάνου <…>.

2b <…> John .. **3a** <…> all the region of the Jordan <…>.

Q 3:~~1a~~, 2b-3a, ~~3b-4~~

Luke 3:1a, 2b, 3, 4	Luke 3:7a; 7:27b	Mark 1:4a,5a,4b,2a,3,5b,2b	Isa 40:3 LXX
( )[9]	**3:7a** Ἔλεγεν οὖν τοῖς {ἐ}κ{πορευ}ομένοις ὄχλοις	**1:5a** καὶ ἐξεπορεύετο πρὸς αὐτὸν πᾶσα ἡ Ἰουδαία χώρα καὶ οἱ Ἱεροσολυμῖται πάντες,	
3:3 [καὶ ἦλθεν εἰς][10] πᾶσα[ν τ][10]ή[ν][10] περί{χωρ}ο[ν][10] τοῦ Ἰορδάνου			
⸉ {κηρύσσων}[4] ⸊[4] [{βάπτισμα μετανοίας εἰς ἄφεσιν ἁμαρτιῶν}][11],		**1:4b** καὶ κηρύσσων βάπτισμα μετανοίας εἰς ἄφεσιν ἁμαρτιῶν.	
3:4 ⸉ [{ὡς γέγραπται ἐν} βίβλῳ λόγων][7] {Ἠσαΐ}ου {τ}οῦ {προφήτ}ου· {φωνὴ βοῶντος ἐν τῇ ἐρήμῳ· ἑτοιμάσατε τὴν ὁδὸν κυρίου, εὐθείας ποιεῖτε τὰς τρίβους αὐτοῦ·} ⸊[7]		**1:2a** Καθὼς γέγραπται ἐν τῷ Ἠσαΐᾳ τῷ προφήτῃ· **1:3** φωνὴ βοῶντος ἐν τῇ ἐρήμῳ· ἑτοιμάσατε τὴν ὁδὸν κυρίου, εὐθείας ποιεῖτε τὰς τρίβους αὐτοῦ,	
({ })[12]	({βαπτι})σθῆναι ({ὑπ' αὐτοῦ})·	**1:5b** καὶ ἐβαπτίζοντο ὑπ' αὐτοῦ ἐν τῷ Ἰορδάνῃ ποταμῷ ἐξομολογούμενοι τὰς ἁμαρτίας αὐτῶν.	
	7:27b {ἰδοὺ ἀποστέλλω τὸν ἄγγελόν μου πρὸ προσώπου σου, ὃς κατασκευάσει τὴν ὁδόν σου} ἔμπροσθέν σου.	**1:2b** ἰδοὺ ἀποστέλλω τὸν ἄγγελόν μου πρὸ προσώπου σου, ὃς κατασκευάσει τὴν ὁδόν σου·	

[11] Is Luke's βάπτισμα μετανοίας εἰς ἄφεσιν ἁμαρτιῶν in Q or from Mark?

[12] Is Matt 3:6 in Q or from Mark?

2b <…> Johannes.. **3a** <…> die ganze Region des Jordan <…>.

2b <…> Jean.. **3a** <…> toute la région du Jourdain <…>.

Q 3:7

Mark 1:5	Matthean Doublet	Matt 3:7	Q 3:7
		^{0}/	^{0}/
		(’Ἰδὼν)^{1}	()^{1}
		ʃ ʅ^{2}	^{2}ʃ ⟦(εἶπεν)^{3}⟧ ()^{1} ʅ^{2}
καὶ		(δὲ)^{4}	[]^{4}
		[ ]^{5}	[τοῖς]^{5}
ἐξεπορεύετο πρὸς αὐτὸν		ʃ ʅ^{7}	^{7}ʃ ⟦(ἐρχ)^{6}⟧ομένο<ι>^{1}ςʅ^{7}
πᾶσα ἡ Ἰουδαία χώρα		(πολλοὺς τῶν Φαρισαίων	⟦[ὄχλοις]^{5}⟧
καὶ		καὶ Σαδδουκαίων)^{5}	
οἱ Ἱεροσολυμῖται πάντες,		^{7}ʃ (ἐρχ)^{6}ομένο(υ)^{1}ςʅ^{7}	ʃʅ^{7}
καὶ ἐβαπτίζοντο		(ἐπὶ τὸ)^{8} {βάπτι}σ(μα)^{8}	⟦()^{8}⟧ {βαπτι}σ⟦[θῆναι]^{8}⟧
ὑπ’ αὐτοῦ		{[ ]^{9} αὐτοῦ}^{9}	{[]^{9} ~~αὐτοῦ~~}^{9}
ἐν τῷ Ἰορδάνῃ ποταμῷ		^{2}ʃ (εἶπεν)^{3}	ʃʅ^{2}
ἐξομολογούμενοι		(αὐτοῖς)^{1}· ʅ^{2}	·
τὰς ἁμαρτίας αὐτῶν.		\$^{0}$	\$^{0}$
		γεννήματα ἐχιδνῶν,	γεννήματα ἐχιδνῶν,
		τίς ὑπέδειξεν ὑμῖν	τίς ὑπέδειξεν ὑμῖν
		φυγεῖν ἀπὸ τῆς	φυγεῖν ἀπὸ τῆς
		μελλούσης ὀργῆς;	μελλούσης ὀργῆς;

IQP 1992: ⟦(ἐπὶ τὸ)^{8}⟧ {βάπτι}σ⟦(μα)^{8}⟧ αὐτοῦ.

^{0} Is there an introductory quotation formula in Q?

^{1} Matthew's ἰδών, which determines the case of πολλοὺς … ἐρχομένους and necessitates the resumptive αὐτοῖς.

^{2} The position of ἔλεγεν at the beginning (Luke) or of εἶπεν αὐτοῖς at the end (Matthew) of the quotation formula.

^{3} Luke's ἔλεγεν or Matthew's εἶπεν.

^{4} Luke's οὖν or Matthew's δέ.

Q

⟦εἶπεν⟧ τοῖς ⟦ἐρχ⟧ομένο<ι>ς ⟦ὄχλοις⟧ βαπτισ⟦θῆναι⟧· γεννήματα ἐχιδνῶν, τίς ὑπέδειξεν ὑμῖν φυγεῖν ἀπὸ τῆς μελλούσης ὀργῆς;	He said to the ⟦crowds coming to be⟧ bapti⟦zed⟧: Snakes' litter! Who warned you to run from the impending rage?

Q 3:7

Luke 3:7	Lukan Doublet	Mark 1:5	Gospel of Thomas
[0]/			
( )[1]			
[2]ʃ ['Ελεγεν][3] ʅ[2]			
[οὖν][4]		καὶ	
[τοῖς][5]			
[7]ʃ [{ἐ}κ{πορευ}][6]ομένο[ι][1]ςʅ[7]		ἐξεπορεύετο πρὸς αὐτὸν	
[ὄχλοις][5]		πᾶσα ἡ Ἰουδαία χώρα	
		καὶ	
ʃ ʅ[7]		οἱ Ἱεροσολυμῖται πάντες,	
( )[8] {βαπτι}σ[θῆναι][8]		καὶ ἐβαπτίζοντο	
{[ὑπ'][9] αὐτοῦ}[9]		ὑπ' αὐτοῦ	
ʃ ʅ[2]		ἐν τῷ Ἰορδάνῃ ποταμῷ	
( )[1].		ἐξομολογούμενοι	
\[0]		τὰς ἁμαρτίας αὐτῶν.	
γεννήματα ἐχιδνῶν,			
τίς ὑπέδειξεν ὑμῖν			
φυγεῖν ἀπὸ τῆς			
μελλούσης ὀργῆς;			

5 Luke's τοῖς ... ὄχλοις or Matthew's πολλοὺς τῶν Φαρισαίων καὶ Σαδδουκαίων.

6 Luke's verb ἐκπορεύομαι or Matthew's ἔρχομαι (see also ἐξεπορεύετο Matt 3:5).

7 The position of the participle before (Luke) or after (Matthew) the noun(s) it modifies.

8 Luke's βαπτισθῆναι or Matthew's ἐπὶ τὸ βάπτισμα.

9 Is Luke's ὑπ' αὐτοῦ or Matthew's αὐτοῦ in Q or from Mark?

Er sagte zu der ⟦Volksmenge⟧, die ⟦kam, um sich⟧ taufe⟦n zu lassen⟧: Schlangenbrut! Wer hat euch in Aussicht gestellt, dass ihr dem bevorstehenden Zorn«gericht» entkommt?

Il dit aux ⟦foules⟧ qui ⟦venaient pour être⟧ baptis⟦ées⟧: Rejetons de vipères, qui vous a avertis de fuir devant la colère à venir?

Q 3:8

Markan Parallel	Matthean Doublet	Matt 3:8-9	Q 3:8
		3:8 ποιήσατε οὖν καρπὸ(ν)[1] ἄξιο(ν)[1] τῆς μετανοίας **3:9** καὶ μὴ (δό)[2]ξη(τε)[2] λέγειν ἐν ἑαυτοῖς· πατέρα ἔχομεν τὸν Ἀβραάμ. λέγω γὰρ ὑμῖν ὅτι δύναται ὁ θεὸς ἐκ τῶν λίθων τούτων ἐγεῖραι τέκνα τῷ Ἀβραάμ.	ποιήσατε οὖν καρπὸ(ν)[1] ἄξιο(ν)[1] τῆς μετανοίας καὶ μὴ (δό)[2]ξη(τε)[2] λέγειν ἐν ἑαυτοῖς· πατέρα ἔχομεν τὸν Ἀβραάμ. λέγω γὰρ ὑμῖν ὅτι δύναται ὁ θεὸς ἐκ τῶν λίθων τούτων ἐγεῖραι τέκνα τῷ Ἀβραάμ.

[1] Luke's καρποὺς ἀξίους or Matthew's καρπὸν ἄξιον.

[2] Luke's ἄρξησθε or Matthew's δόξητε.

Q

ποιήσατε οὖν καρπὸν ἄξιον τῆς μετανοίας καὶ μὴ δόξητε λέγειν ἐν ἑαυτοῖς· πατέρα ἔχομεν τὸν Ἀβραάμ. λέγω γὰρ ὑμῖν ὅτι δύναται ὁ θεὸς ἐκ τῶν λίθων τούτων ἐγεῖραι τέκνα τῷ Ἀβραάμ.

So bear fruit worthy of repentance, and do not presume to tell yourselves: We have as «fore»father Abraham! For I tell you: God can produce children for Abraham right out of these rocks!

Q 3:8

Luke 3:8	Lukan Doublet	Markan Parallel	Gospel of Thomas
ποιήσατε οὖν καρπο[ὺς][1] ἀξίο[υς][1] τῆς μετανοίας καὶ μὴ [ἄρ][2]ξη[σθε][2] λέγειν ἐν ἑαυτοῖς· πατέρα ἔχομεν τὸν Ἀβραάμ. λέγω γὰρ ὑμῖν ὅτι δύναται ὁ θεὸς ἐκ τῶν λίθων τούτων ἐγεῖραι τέκνα τῷ Ἀβραάμ.			

Bringt darum Frucht, die der Umkehr entspricht, und bildet euch nicht ein, sagen «zu können»: Wir haben Abraham zum Vater. Denn ich sage euch: Gott kann aus diesen Steinen dem Abraham Kinder erwecken.

Produisez donc du fruit digne d'une conversion et ne vous imaginez pas dire en vous-mêmes: Nous avons pour père Abraham! Car je vous dis que Dieu peut, de ces pierres, susciter des enfants à Abraham!

Q 3:9

Markan Parallel	Matt 7:19	Matt 3:10	Q 3:9
		ἤδη δὲ [ ][1] ἡ ἀξίνη	ἤδη δὲ [][1] ἡ ἀξίνη
		πρὸς τὴν ῥίζαν	πρὸς τὴν ῥίζαν
		τῶν δένδρων κεῖται·	τῶν δένδρων κεῖται·
	[(πᾶν)] [(δένδρον	πᾶν οὖν δένδρον	πᾶν οὖν δένδρον
	μὴ ποιοῦν καρπὸν καλὸν	μὴ ποιοῦν καρπὸν καλὸν	μὴ ποιοῦν καρπὸν καλὸν
	ἐκκόπτεται	ἐκκόπτεται	ἐκκόπτεται
	καὶ εἰς πῦρ βάλλεται.)]	καὶ εἰς πῦρ βάλλεται.	καὶ εἰς πῦρ βάλλεται.

[1] Luke's καί.

Q

ἤδη δὲ ἡ ἀξίνη πρὸς τὴν ῥίζαν τῶν δένδρων κεῖται· πᾶν οὖν δένδρον μὴ ποιοῦν καρπὸν καλὸν ἐκκόπτεται καὶ εἰς πῦρ βάλλεται.

And the ax already lies at the root of the trees. So every tree not bearing healthy fruit is to be chopped down and thrown on the fire.

Q 3:9

Luke 3:9	Lukan Doublet	Markan Parallel	Gospel of Thomas
ἤδη δὲ [καὶ][1] ἡ ἀξίνη πρὸς τὴν ῥίζαν τῶν δένδρων κεῖται· πᾶν οὖν δένδρον μὴ ποιοῦν καρπὸν καλὸν ἐκκόπτεται καὶ εἰς πῦρ βάλλεται.			

Schon ist aber die Axt an die Wurzel der Bäume gelegt; jeder Baum, der nicht gute Frucht bringt, wird daher herausgehauen und ins Feuer geworfen.

Et déjà la hache est posée contre la racine des arbres. Tout arbre donc qui ne produit pas de bon fruit va être abattu et jeté au feu.

Q 3:16b

Mark 1:8a, 7b, 8b	Matthean Doublet	Matt 3:11	Q 3:16b
		[0]{	[0]{
1:8a ἐγὼ		{᾽Εγὼ} μὲν	{ἐγὼ} μὲν
ἐβάπτισα		ʃ {ὑμᾶς} ʅ[1]	ʃ {ὑμᾶς} ʅ[1]
ὑμᾶς		{βαπτί}ζω	{βαπτί}ζω
ὕδατι,		[1]ʃ (ἐν)[2] {ὕδατι} ʅ[1]	[1]ʃ ⟦(ἐν)[2]⟧ {ὕδατι} ʅ[1]
		(εἰς μετάνοιαν)[3],	⟦()[3]⟧,
		ʃ {ὁ} ʅ[4]	ʃ {ὁ} ʅ[4]
		ʃ {δὲ} ʅ[5]	ʃ {δὲ} ʅ[5]
1:7b		({ὀπίσω μου})[6]	({ὀπίσω μου})[6]
ἔρχεται		{ἐρχ}(όμενος)[4]	{ἐρχ}(όμενος)[4]
		ʃ ʅ[5]	ʃʅ[5]
ὁ		ʃ ʅ[4]	ʃʅ[4]
ἰσχυρότερός μου ὀπίσω μου,		{ἰσχυρότερός μού} (ἐστιν)[4],	{ἰσχυρότερός μού} (ἐστιν)[4],
οὗ οὐκ εἰμὶ ἱκανὸς		{οὗ οὐκ εἰμὶ ἱκανὸς}	{οὗ οὐκ εἰμὶ ἱκανὸς}
κύψας λῦσαι		ʃ ʅ[7]	ʃʅ[7]
τὸν ἱμάντα		{[ ][7]	⟦[][7]⟧
τῶν ὑποδημάτων		τ}(ὰ)[7] {ὑποδήματ}(α)[7]	τ⟦(ὰ)[7]⟧ ὑποδήματ⟦(α)[7]⟧
αὐτοῦ.		{[ ]}[7]	⟦[][7]⟧
1:8b		ʃ (βαστά)[7]{σαι} ʅ[7]·	ʃ ⟦(βαστά)[7]⟧{σαι} ʅ[7]·
αὐτὸς δὲ βαπτίσει ὑμᾶς		{αὐτὸς} {ὑμᾶς} {βαπτίσει}	{αὐτὸς} {ὑμᾶς} {βαπτίσει}
ἐν πνεύματι		{ἐν}[8] {πνεύματι}[9]	{ἐν}[8] {πνεύματι}[9]
ἁγίῳ.		{ἁγίῳ}[10]	⟦{ἁγίῳ}[10]⟧
		καὶ[9] πυρί·	καὶ[9] πυρί·
		}[0]	}[0]

IQP 1992: {πνεύματι}[9] {ἁγίῳ}[10].

PH: ⟦{πνεύματι}[9] {}[10]⟧.

[0] Is Luke 3:16b par. Matt 3:11 in Q or from Mark?

[1] Do ὑμᾶς follow and (ἐν) ὕδατι precede βαπτίζω (Luke) or the reverse (Matthew)?

[2] Matthew's ἐν.

[3] Matthew's εἰς μετάνοιαν.

[4] Luke's construction with ὁ ἰσχυρότερος as the subject and ἔρχεται as the verb or Matthew's with ὁ … ἐρχόμενος as the subject and ἐστιν as the verb. The position of ὁ is part of this decision.

Q

ἐγὼ μὲν ὑμᾶς βαπτίζω ⟦ἐν⟧ ὕδατι, ὁ δὲ ὀπίσω μου ἐρχόμενος ἰσχυρότερός μού ἐστιν, οὗ οὐκ εἰμὶ ἱκανὸς τ⟦ὰ⟧ ὑποδήματ⟦α⟧ ⟦βαστά⟧σαι· αὐτὸς ὑμᾶς βαπτίσει ἐν πνεύματι ⟦ἁγίῳ⟧ καὶ πυρί·

I baptize you ⟦in⟧ water, but the one to come after me is more powerful than I, whose sandals I am not fit to ⟦take off⟧. He will baptize you in ⟦holy⟧ Spirit and fire.

Q 3:16b

Luke 3:16b	Lukan Doublet	Mark 1:8a, 7b, 8b	Gospel of Thomas
[0]{			
{ἐγὼ} μὲν		**1:8a** ἐγὼ	
⸂[1] ( )[2] {ὕδατι} ⸃[1]		ἐβάπτισα	
{βαπτί}ζω		ὑμᾶς	
⸂ {ὑμᾶς} ⸃[1].		ὕδατι,	
( )[3]			
⸂ ⸃[4]			
⸂ ⸃[5]			
({ })[6]		**1:7b**	
{ἔρχ[εται]}[4]		ἔρχεται	
⸂ {δὲ} ⸃[5]			
{⸂ὁ⸃[4]		ὁ	
ἰσχυρότερός μου} ( )[4],		ἰσχυρότερός μου ὀπίσω μου,	
{οὗ οὐκ εἰμὶ ἱκανὸς}		οὗ οὐκ εἰμὶ ἱκανὸς	
⸂ {[λῦ][7]σαι⸃[7]		κύψας λῦσαι	
[τὸν ἱμάντα][7]		τὸν ἱμάντα	
τ[ῶν][7] ὑποδημάτ[ων		τῶν ὑποδημάτων	
αὐτοῦ]}[7]		αὐτοῦ.	
⸂ ⸃[7].		**1:8b**	
{αὐτὸς} {ὑμᾶς} {βαπτίσει}		αὐτὸς δὲ βαπτίσει ὑμᾶς	
{ἐν}[8] {πνεύματι}[9]		ἐν πνεύματι	
{ἁγίῳ}[10]		ἁγίῳ.	
καὶ[9] πυρί·			
}[0]			

[5] The consistently postpositive position of δέ after ἔρχεται (Luke) or after ὁ (Matthew).

[6] Matthew's ὀπίσω μου.

[7] λῦσαι τὸν ἱμάντα τῶν ὑποδημάτων αὐτοῦ (Luke) or τὰ ὑποδήματα βαστάσαι (Matthew).

[8] Is ἐν in Q or from Mark?

[9] Is πνεύματι (and hence καὶ) in Q or from Mark?

[10] Is ἁγίῳ in Q or from Mark?

Ich taufe euch ⟦in⟧ Wasser; der nach mir kommt, ist jedoch stärker als ich. Ich bin nicht würdig, «ihm» die Sandalen zu ⟦tragen⟧. Er wird euch in ⟦heiligem⟧ Geist und Feuer taufen.

Moi, je vous baptise ⟦dans⟧ l'eau, mais celui qui vient après moi est plus fort que moi; de lui, je ne suis pas digne d'⟦enlever⟧ les sandales. Lui, il vous baptisera dans l'Esprit ⟦saint⟧ et le feu.

Q 3:17

Markan Parallel	Matthean Doublet	Matt 3:12	Q 3:17
		οὗ τὸ πτύον ἐν τῇ χειρὶ αὐτοῦ (καὶ)[1] διακαθαρ(ιεῖ)[1] τὴν ἅλωνα αὐτοῦ καὶ συνά(ξει)[1] τὸν σῖτον ⸉αὐτοῦ⸊[2] εἰς τὴν ἀποθήκην ⸉ ⸊[2], τὸ δὲ ἄχυρον κατακαύσει πυρὶ ἀσβέστῳ.	οὗ τὸ πτύον ἐν τῇ χειρὶ αὐτοῦ (καὶ)[1] διακαθαρ(ιεῖ)[1] τὴν ἅλωνα αὐτοῦ καὶ συνά(ξει)[1] τὸν σῖτον ⸉⸊[2] εἰς τὴν ἀποθήκην ⸉αὐτοῦ⸊[2], τὸ δὲ ἄχυρον κατακαύσει πυρὶ ἀσβέστῳ.

[1] Luke's διακαθᾶραι ... συναγαγεῖν or Matthew's καὶ διακαθαριεῖ ... συνάξει.

[2] The position of αὐτοῦ after ἀποθήκην (Luke) or after σῖτον (Matthew).

Q

οὗ τὸ πτύον ἐν τῇ χειρὶ αὐτοῦ καὶ διακαθαριεῖ τὴν ἅλωνα αὐτοῦ καὶ συνάξει τὸν σῖτον εἰς τὴν ἀποθήκην αὐτοῦ, τὸ δὲ ἄχυρον κατακαύσει πυρὶ ἀσβέστῳ.

His pitchfork «is» in his hand, and he will clear his threshing floor and gather the wheat into his granary, but the chaff he will burn on a fire that can never be put out.

Q 3:17

Luke 3:17	Lukan Doublet	Markan Parallel	Gospel of Thomas
οὗ τὸ πτύον ἐν τῇ χειρὶ αὐτοῦ ( )[1] διακαθᾶρ[αι][1] τὴν ἅλωνα αὐτοῦ καὶ συνα[γαγεῖν][1] τὸν σῖτον ʃ ʅ[2] εἰς τὴν ἀποθήκην ʃαὐτοῦʅ[2], τὸ δὲ ἄχυρον κατακαύσει πυρὶ ἀσβέστῳ.			

Seine Schaufel «ist» in seiner Hand, und er wird seinen Dreschplatz säubern und den Weizen in seine Scheune bringen, die Spreu aber wird er in einem Feuer verbrennen, das nicht erlischt.

Sa pelle à vanner «est» dans sa main et il nettoiera son aire et il recueillera le blé dans son grenier, mais la bale, il la brûlera d'un feu inextinguible.

Q 3:⟦21⟧

Mark 1:9-10a	Matt 3:5-6	Matt 3:13, 16a	Q 3:⟦21⟧
	3:5 (Τότε) ἐξεπορεύετο (πρὸς)	^{0}{	⟦^{0}{
1:9 Καὶ	αὐτὸν Ἱεροσόλυμα καὶ πᾶσα	**3:13** (Τότε)^{1}	( )^{1}
ἐγένετο	ἡ Ἰουδαία καὶ πᾶσα	(παρα)^{2}{γ}(ί)^{2}{νετ}(αι)^{2}	[( )]^{2}{~~γ~~}[( )]^{2}{~~νετ~~}[( )]^{2}
	ἡ περίχωρος τοῦ Ἰορδάνου,	[ ]^{1}	[ ]^{1}
ἐν ἐκείναις ταῖς ἡμέραις	**3:6** καὶ {ἐ([βαπτί])}ζοντο ἐν	[{ }]^{3}	[{ }]^{3}
	{τ}ῷ {Ἰορδάνῃ} ποταμῷ ({ὑπ'}		
ἦλθεν Ἰησοῦς	αὐτοῦ) ἐξομολογούμενοι	(ὁ {Ἰησοῦς	({ })^{4}
ἀπὸ Ναζαρὲτ τῆς Γαλιλαίας	τὰς ἁμαρτίας αὐτῶν.	ἀπὸ} {τῆς Γαλιλαίας}	
		ἐπὶ {τὸν Ἰορδάνην}	
καὶ ἐβαπτίσθη		πρὸς τὸν {Ἰωάνν}ην	
εἰς τὸν Ἰορδάνην		τοῦ {βαπτισθῆ}ναι	
ὑπὸ Ἰωάννου.		{ὑπ}' αὐτοῦ.)^{4}	
		3:16a ʃ ʅ^{5}	^{5}ʃ ()^{6}
			^{7}{Ἰησοῦ( )^{8}}^{7}
			ʅ^{5}
		{βαπτισθ}^{7}ε(ὶς)^{8}	{βαπτισθ}^{7}ε[( )]^{8}
		(δὲ)^{9}	()^{9}
		^{5}ʃ (ὁ)^{6}	ʃʅ^{5}
		^{7}{Ἰησοῦ(ς)^{8} }^{7}	
		ʅ^{5}	
1:10a καὶ εὐθὺς		({εὐθὺς ἀν}έ{β}η	({})^{10}
ἀναβαίνων ἐκ τοῦ ὕδατος		ἀπὸ {τοῦ ὕδατος}·)^{10}	
		[ ]^{11}	[]^{11}
εἶδεν		({καὶ} {ἰδ}ού)^{12}	({})^{12}
σχιζομένους		(ἠ)^{13}νεῴχθη^{14}(σαν)^{13}	[( )]^{13}νεῳχθη^{14}[( )]^{13}
		(αὐτῷ)^{15}	( )^{15}
τοὺς		[{ }]^{13}{ο}^{14}(ἰ)$^{13.16}$	[{ }]^{13} {ο}^{14}[( )]$^{13.16}$
οὐρανούς		{οὐρανο}^{14}(ί)$^{13.16}$,	{οὐρανο}^{14}[( )]$^{13.16}$,⟧
		}^{0}⇒ Matt 3:16b-17	}^{0}⇒ Q 3:⟦22⟧

IQP 1992, JSK: **3:21-22** is not in Q {D}.

0 Is Jesus' baptism in Q or from Mark?
1 Luke's δέ or Matthew's τότε.
2 Luke's ἐγένετο or Matthew's παραγίνεται.
3 Is Luke's baptizing of all the people in Q or from Mark 1:5 par. Matt. 3:5-6?
4 Is Matthew's narration of Jesus coming to be baptized in Q or from Mark?
5 Does Jesus' name precede (Luke) or follow (Matthew) the reference to being baptized?
6 Is there a definite article with Jesus' name?

Q

⟦.. Ἰησου.. βαπτισθε…νεωχθη…ο… οὐρανο…,⟧	⟦.. Jesus … baptized, heaven opened..,⟧

Q 3:⟦21⟧

Luke 3:21	Lukan Doublet	Mark 1:5, 9	Gospel of Thomas
[0]{ ( )[1] {[’Ε][2]γ[έ][2]νετ[ο][2]} [δὲ][1] [ἐν τῷ {βαπτι}σθῆναι ἅ{παντ}α τὸν λαὸν καὶ][3] ({ })[4]		**1:5** καὶ ἐξεπορεύετο πρὸς αὐτὸν πᾶσα ἡ ’Ιουδαία χώρα καὶ οἱ Ἱεροσολυμῖται πάντες, καὶ ἐβαπτίζοντο ὑπ’ αὐτοῦ ἐν τῷ ’Ιορδάνῃ ποταμῷ ἐξομολογούμενοι τὰς ἁμαρτίας αὐτῶν.	
[5]ʃ ( )[6] [7]{’Ιησοῦ( )[8]}[7] ʅ[5] {βαπτισθ}[7]έ[ντος][8] ( )[9] ʃ ʅ[5]		**1:9** Καὶ ἐγένετο ἐν ἐκείναις ταῖς ἡμέραις ἦλθεν ’Ιησοῦς ἀπὸ Ναζαρὲτ τῆς Γαλιλαίας καὶ ἐβαπτίσθη εἰς τὸν ’Ιορδάνην ὑπὸ ’Ιωάννου.	
({ })[10] [καὶ προσευχομένου][11] ({ })[12] [ἀ][13]νεῳχθῆ[14][ναι][13] ( )[15] {[τ][13]ὸ}[14][ν][13.16] {οὐρανὸ}[14][ν][13.16] }[0]⇒ Luke 3:22			

[7] Is the reference to Jesus in Q or from Mark?

[8] Is the reference to Jesus being baptized in the genitive (Luke) or the nominative (Matthew)?

[9] Is Matthew's δέ in Q?

[10] Is Matthew's εὐθὺς ἀνέβη ἀπὸ τοῦ ὕδατος in Q or from Mark?

[11] Is Luke's καὶ προσευχομένου in Q?

[12] Is Matthew's καὶ ἰδού in Q?

[13] The form of the verb ἀνοίγω and of the reference to heaven.

[14] Is the reference to the heaven(s) opening in Q?

[15] Is Matthew's αὐτῷ in Q?

[16] The singular (Luke) or the plural (Matthew) noun for heaven.

⟦.. Jesus getauft ..., öffnete sich der Himmel..,⟧

⟦.. Jésus ... baptisé, le ciel s'ouvrit..,⟧

Q 3:⟦22⟧

Mark 1:10b-11	Matt 17:5b-c	Matt 3:16b-17	Q 3:⟦22⟧
			⟦
1:10b καὶ		**3:16b** {καὶ}	{καὶ}
		({εἶδεν})^{1}	({})^{1}
		⸉ ⸊^{1}	⸉ {~~καταβ~~[( )]^{1}~~ν~~[( )}]^{1} ⸊^{1}
τὸ πνεῦμα		{τὸ πνεῦμα}^{2}	{τὸ πνεῦμα}^{2}
		το(ῦ θεοῦ)^{3}	~~το~~[( )]^{3}
		⸉ {καταβ(αῖ)^{1}ν(ον)^{1}} ⸊^{1}	⸉⸊^{1}
		[ ]^{4}	[]^{4}
ὡς περιστερὰν		{ὡς}^{5}(εὶ)^{5} {περιστερὰν}^{5}	{~~ὡς~~}^{5}( )^{5} {~~περιστερὰν~~}^{5}
καταβαῖνον		(καὶ ἐρχόμε{νον})^{6}	( )^{6}
εἰς αὐτόν·		ἐπ'^{7} {αὐτόν}·	ἐπ'^{7} {αὐτόν}·
1:11 καὶ	([{καὶ}] ἰδοὺ	**3:17** {καὶ}^{8} (ἰδοὺ)^{8}	{~~καὶ~~}^{8} ( )^{8}
φωνὴ ἐγένετο	[{φωνὴ}]	{φωνὴ}^{8}[ ]^{8}	{~~φωνὴ~~}^{8}[ ]^{8}
ἐκ τῶν	{[ἐ]κ)} τῆς	{ἐ(κ τῶν)^{9}	{~~ἐ~~[( )]^{9}( )^{9}
οὐρανῶν·	νεφέλης	οὐραν(ῶν)}^{9}	[(~~οὐραν~~)]^{9}[( )]^{9}
	(λέγουσα·	(λέγουσα)^{8}.	[( )]^{8}.
σὺ εἶ	οὗτός ἐστιν	(οὗτός ἐστιν)^{10}	[({)]^{10}
ὁ υἱός μου ὁ ἀγαπητός,	{[ὁ υἱός μου ὁ ἀγαπητός,	{ὁ υἱός μου ὁ ἀγαπητός,	~~ὁ υἱός μου ὁ ἀγαπητός,~~
ἐν σοὶ	ἐν]} ᾧ	ἐν}^{10} (ᾧ)^{10}	~~ἐν~~}^{10} [( )]^{10}
εὐδόκησα.	[{εὐδόκησα·}])	{εὐδόκησα}^{10}.	{~~εὐδόκησα~~}^{10}.
			⟧
		\Matt 3:13, 16a^{0}	\Q 3:⟦21^{0}⟧

IQP 1992, JSK: **3:21-22** not in Q {D}.

Text Critical Note (see the discussion in the front matter): In Luke 3:22 υἱός μου εἶ σύ, ἐγὼ σήμερον γεγέννηκά σε is in D it Ju (Cl) Meth Hil Aug; σὺ εἶ ὁ υἱός μου ὁ ἀγαπητός, ἐν ᾧ εὐδόκησα is in X *pc* f bo^{pt}; οὗτός ἐστιν ὁ υἱός μου ὁ ἀγαπητός, ἐν ᾧ εὐδόκησα is in 1574 *pc*; the rest of the manuscript evidence reads σὺ εἶ ὁ υἱός μου ὁ ἀγαπητός, ἐν σοὶ εὐδόκησα.

1 Luke's continuation of the infinitives from v. 21; Matthew's finite verb and circumstantial participle; the resultant position of the verb καταβαίνω.

2 Is τὸ πνεῦμα in Q or from Mark?

3 Luke's τὸ ἅγιον or Matthew's τοῦ θεοῦ.

4 Luke's σωματικῷ εἴδει.

5 Is Luke's ὡς περιστεράν or Matthew's ὡσεὶ περιστεράν in Q or from Mark?

Q

⟦καὶ .. τὸ πνεῦμα … ἐπ' αὐτόν … υἱ….⟧	⟦and .. the Spirit … upon him … Son ….⟧

Q 3:⟦22⟧

Luke 3:22	Luke 9:35	Mark 9:7b-c	Ps 2:7b-d LXX
{καὶ}			
( )[1]			
⸉ {καταβ}[ῆ][1]ν[αι][1] ⸊[1]			
{τὸ πνεῦμα}[2]			
τὸ [ἅγιον][3]			
⸉ ⸊[1]			
[σωματικῷ εἴδει][4]			
{ὡς( )[5] περιστερὰν}[5]			
( )[6]			
ἐπ'[7] {αὐτόν},			
{καὶ}[8] ( )[8]	[({καὶ})	καὶ	
{φωνὴ}[8][ν][8]	{(φωνὴ)] {ἐγένετο}	ἐγένετο φωνὴ	
{ἐ}[9][ξ][9] ( )[9]	{([ἐ]κ) τῆς	ἐκ τῆς	
{οὐραν}[9][οῦ][9]	νεφέλης}	νεφέλης	
[{γενέ}σθαι][8]·	(λέγουσα·		Κύριος εἶπεν πρός με
{[σὺ εἶ][10]	{οὗτός ἐστιν	οὗτός ἐστιν	Υἱός μου
ὁ υἱός μου ὁ ἀγαπητός,	[ὁ υἱός μου ὁ]}) ἐκλελεγμένος,	ὁ υἱός μου ὁ ἀγαπητός,	εἶ σύ,
ἐν[10] [σοὶ][10]	{αὐτοῦ}	ἀκούετε	ἐγὼ σήμερον
εὐδόκησα}[10].	{ἀκούετε}.	αὐτοῦ.	γεγέννηκά σε.
\Luke 3:21[0]			

[6] Matthew's καὶ ἐρχόμενον.

[7] Is the minor agreement ἐπ' in Q?

[8] Is Luke's καὶ φωνὴν … γενέσθαι or Matthew's καὶ ἰδοὺ φωνὴ … λέγουσα in Q or from Mark?

[9] Is ἐξ οὐρανοῦ (Luke) or ἐκ τῶν οὐρανῶν (Matthew) in Q or from Mark?

[10] Is Luke's σὺ εἶ ὁ υἱός μου ὁ ἀγαπητός, ἐν σοὶ εὐδόκησα or Matthew's οὗτός ἐστιν ὁ οἱός μου ὁ ἀγαπητός, ἐν ᾧ εὐδόκησα in Q or from Mark?

⟦und .. der Geist … auf ihn … Sohn ….⟧

⟦et .. l'Esprit … sur lui … Fils ….⟧

Q 4:1-2

Mark 1:12-13a	Matthean Doublet	Matt 4:1-2	Q 4:1-2
		[0]{	[0]{
1:12 Καὶ εὐθὺς		**4:1** (Τότε)[1]	**4:1** ()[1]
		(ὁ)[2]	⟦(ὁ)[2]⟧
		⸉ ⸊[2] Ἰησοῦς [2]⸉ [ ][1] ⸊[2]	[2]⸉ [δὲ][1] ⸊[2] Ἰησοῦς ⸉ ⸊[2]
τὸ πνεῦμα		[ ][3]	[][3]
αὐτὸν ἐκβάλλει		(ἀν)[4]ή(χθη)[5]	⟦(ἀν)[4]⟧ή⟦(χθη)[5]⟧
		⸉ ⸊[6]	⸉ ⸊[6]
εἰς τὴν ἔρημον.		{(εἰς)[7] τὴ(ν)[7] ἔρημ(ον)[7]}	⟦{(εἰς)[7]⟧ τὴ⟦(ν)[7]⟧ ἔρημ⟦(ον)[7]}
		[6]⸉ (ὑπὸ)[8] {τ(ο}ῦ)[8]	[6]⸉ (ὑπὸ)[8]⟧ {τ⟦(ο}ῦ)[8]⟧
		{πνεύμα}τ(ος)[8] ⸊[6]	{πνεύμα}⟦τ(ος)[8]⟧ ⸊[6]
		⸉ ⸊[9]	**4:2** ⸉⸊[9]
		{πειρα}(σθῆναι)[10]	{πειρα}⟦(σθῆναι)[10]⟧
		{ὑπὸ τοῦ} διαβόλου.	{ὑπὸ τοῦ} διαβόλου.
1:13a καὶ ἦν ἐν τῇ ἐρήμῳ		**4:2** {καὶ}	{καὶ}
		(νηστεύσας)[11]	[( )][11]
		[9]⸉ {ἡμέρας}	[9]⸉ {ἡμέρας}
τεσσεράκοντα ἡμέρας		{τεσσεράκοντα}	{τεσσεράκοντα}
		(καὶ νύκτας	()[12]
πειραζόμενος		τεσσεράκοντα)[12] ⸊[9]	⸊[9]
ὑπὸ τοῦ σατανᾶ,		[ ][9],	[][9],
		[ ][11]	[ ][11]
		(ὕστερον)[13]	( )[13]
		ἐπείνασεν.	ἐπείνασεν.
		}[0]	}[0]

JMR: ()[1] ⟦(ὁ)[2]⟧ [2]⸉ [ ][1] ⸊[2] Ἰησοῦς ⸉⸊[2].
IQP 1992: ⟦()[4]⟧ή[ ][5] [6]⸉ ⟦(ὑπὸ)[8]⟧ {τ⟦(ο}ῦ)[8]⟧ {πνεύμα⟦τ(ος)[8]⟧ ⸊[6].

IQP 1992: [{( )]][7] τη( )[7] ἐρημ[( )}]][7].
IQP 1992: {πειρα}(σθῆναι)[10].

Text Critical Note (see the discussion in the front matter): In Matt 4:2 καὶ τεσσεράκοντα νύκτας is in א D 892, but is omitted by *f* [1] *pc* sy[c]; and καὶ νύκτας τεσσεράκοντα is in B C L W 0233 *f* [13] 33 𝔐 sy[h].

[0] Is the framework of the story here and at 4:13 in Q or from Mark?
[1] Luke's δέ or Matthew's τότε.
[2] Matthew's ὁ and the resultant positioning of a possible δέ.
[3] Luke's πλήρης πνεύματος ἁγίου ὑπέστρεψεν ἀπὸ τοῦ Ἰορδάνου καί.
[4] Matthew's ἀν-.
[5] Luke's ἤγετο or Matthew's -ήχθη.
[6] The position of the phrase about the spirit, before (Luke) or after (Matthew) the phrase about the wilderness.

Q

1 ⟦ὁ⟧ δὲ Ἰησοῦς ⟦ἀν⟧ή⟦χθη⟧ ⟦εἰς⟧ τὴ⟦ν⟧ ἔρημ⟦ον ὑπὸ⟧ τ⟦οῦ⟧ πνεύμα⟦τος⟧ 2 πειρα⟦σθῆναι⟧ ὑπὸ τοῦ διαβόλου. καὶ … ἡμέρας τεσσεράκοντα, .. ἐπείνασεν.

1 And Jesus was led ⟦into⟧ the wilderness by the Spirit 2 ⟦to be⟧ tempted by the devil. And «he ate nothing» for forty days; .. he became hungry.

Q 4:1-2

Luke 4:1-2	Lukan Doublet	Mark 1:12-13a	Gospel of Thomas
[0]{			
4:1 ( )[1]		**1:12** Καὶ εὐθὺς	
( )[2]			
ʃ ʅ[2] Ἰησοῦς [2]ʃ [δὲ][1] ʅ[2]			
[πλήρης {πνεύμα}τος		ἐκβάλλει τὸ πνεῦμα αὐτὸν	
ἁγίου ὑπέστρεψεν ἀπὸ			
τοῦ Ἰορδάνου καὶ][3]			
( )[4]ἤ[γετο][5]			
[6]ʃ [ἐν][8] {τ}[ῷ][8]			
{πνεύμα}τ[ι][8] ʅ[6]			
{[ἐν][7] τῇ( )[7] ἐρήμ[ω][7]}		εἰς τὴν ἔρημον.	
ʃ ʅ[6]		**1:13a** καὶ ἦν ἐν τῇ ἐρήμῳ	
4:2 [9]ʃ {ἡμέρας}		τεσσεράκοντα	
{τεσσεράκοντα} ( )[12] ʅ[9]		ἡμέρας	
{πειρα[ζόμενος]}[10]		πειραζόμενος	
ὑπὸ τοῦ} διαβόλου.		ὑπὸ τοῦ σατανᾶ,	
{Καὶ}			
[οὐκ ἔφαγεν οὐδὲν][11]			
ʃ ʅ[9]			
[ἐν ταῖς ἡμέραις ἐκείναις][9],			
[καὶ][11]			
[συντελεσθεισῶν αὐτῶν][13]			
ἐπείνασεν.			
}[0]			

PH: **4:2** ʃʅ[9] ⟦{~~πειρα~~}[()][10] {~~ὑπὸ τοῦ~~} ~~διαβόλου~~⟧. καὶ ⟦(νηστεύσας)[11]⟧ … ⟦[][11]⟧. IQP 1992: ⟦[οὐκ ἔφαγεν οὐδὲν][11]⟧

[7] Luke's ἐν with the dative or Matthew's εἰς with the accusative.
[8] Luke's ἐν with the dative or Matthew's ὑπό with the genitive.
[9] The position of ἡμέρας τεσσεράκοντα. The Lukan position also determines the repetitive ἐν ταῖς ἡμέραις ἐκείναις.
[10] Luke's πειραζόμενος or Matthew's πειρασθῆναι.
[11] Luke's οὐκ ἔφαγεν οὐδέν … καί or Matthew's νηστεύσας.
[12] Matthew's καὶ νύκτας τεσσεράκοντα.
[13] Luke's συντελεσθεισῶν αὐτῶν or Matthew's ὕστερον.

1 Jesus aber wurde vom Geist ⟦in⟧ die Wüste geführt, 2 ⟦um⟧ vom Teufel versucht ⟦zu werden⟧. Und «er aß» vierzig Tage «nichts», .. er wurde hungrig.

1 Alors Jésus fut amené ⟦dans⟧ le désert par l'Esprit 2 ⟦pour être⟧ tenté par le diable. Et «il ne mangea rien» pendant quarante jours, .. il eut faim.

Q 4:3

Markan Parallel	Matthean Doublet	Matt 4:3	Q 4:3
		(καὶ)[1]	(καὶ)[1]
		(προσελθὼν)[2]	()[2]
		⸂ ⸃[3]	[3]⸂εἶπεν [][1] αὐτῷ⸃[3]
		ὁ (πειράζων)[4]	ὁ [διάβολος][4]
		[3]⸂εἶπεν [ ][1] αὐτῷ⸃[3].	⸂⸃[3].
		εἰ υἱὸς εἶ τοῦ θεοῦ, εἰπὲ	εἰ υἱὸς εἶ τοῦ θεοῦ, εἰπὲ
		⸂ ⸃[5]	⸂⸃[5]
		ἵνα	ἵνα
		[5]⸂ (οἱ)[5] λίθ(οι)[5] [ ][5]οὗτ(οι)[5] ⸃[5]	[5]⸂ (οἱ)[5] λίθ(οι)[5] [][5]οὗτ(οι)[5] ⸃[5]
		⸂ ⸃[6]	⸂⸃[6]
		ἄρτο(ι)[5]	ἄρτο(ι)[5]
		[6]⸂γέν(ων)[5]ται⸃[6].	[6]⸂γέν(ων)[5]ται⸃[6].

IQP 1992: [5]⸂ ⟦(οἱ)[5]⟧ λίθ⟦(οι)[5]⟧ ⟦[][5]⟧οὗτ⟦(οι)[5]⟧ ⸃[5] ⸂ ⸃[6] ἄρτο⟦(ι)[5]⟧ [6]⸂γέν⟦(ων)[5]⟧ται⸃[6].

1 Luke's δέ or Matthew's καί.
2 Matthew's προσελθών.
3 The relative sequence of subject and verb.
4 Luke's διάβολος or Matthew's πειράζων.
5 The position of the reference to stone(s) before (Luke) or after (Matthew) ἵνα, the different syntactic functions resul-

Q

καὶ εἶπεν αὐτῷ ὁ διάβολος· εἰ υἱὸς εἶ τοῦ θεοῦ, εἰπὲ ἵνα οἱ λίθοι οὗτοι ἄρτοι γένωνται.

And the devil told him: If you are God's Son, order that these stones become loaves.

Q 4:3

Luke 4:3	Lukan Doublet	Markan Parallel	Gospel of Thomas
( )[1] ( )[2] [3]⸂εἶπεν [δὲ][1] αὐτῷ⸃[3] ὁ [διάβολος][4] ⸂ ⸃[3]. εἰ υἱὸς εἶ τοῦ θεοῦ, εἰπὲ [5]⸂ [τῷ][5] λίθ[ῳ][5] [τ][5]ούτ[ῳ][5] ⸃[5] ἵνα ⸂ ⸃[5] [6]⸂γέν[η][5]ται⸃[6] ἄρτο[ς][5] ⸂ ⸃[6].			

ting in the different cases, and the divergent number of the stones and loaves.

6 The position of the verb before (Luke) or after (Matthew) the loaf / loaves.

Und der Teufel sagte ihm: Wenn du Gottes Sohn bist, befiehl, dass diese Steine Brote werden.

Et le diable lui dit: Si tu es Fils de Dieu, ordonne à ces pierres de devenir des pains.

Q 4:4

Markan Parallel	Matthean Doublet	Matt 4:4	Q 4:4
		[1]ʃὁ [ ][5] ʅ[1] (δὲ)[2] ἀπ(ο)[3]κριθ(εὶς εἶπεν)[3] [ ][4] ʃ ʅ[1]. γέγραπται [ ][6]. οὐκ ἐπ' ἄρτῳ μόνῳ ζήσεται ὁ ἄνθρωπος, (ἀλλ' ἐπὶ παντὶ ῥήματι ἐκπορευομένῳ διὰ στόματος θεοῦ)[7].	ʃʅ[1] [καὶ][2] ἀπ[ε][3]κρίθ[η][3] ⟦[][4] [αὐτ][4] <ῷ>[4]⟧ [1]ʃὁ ['Ιησοῦς][5] ʅ[1]. γέγραπται [ὅτι][6] οὐκ ἐπ' ἄρτῳ μόνῳ ζήσεται ὁ ἄνθρωπος ()[7] .

IQP 1992: ʃ ʅ[1].

JMR: ἀπ⟦[ε][3]⟧κρίθ⟦[η][3]⟧.

[1] The position of the subject after (Luke) or before (Matthew) the verb.

[2] Luke's *καί* or Matthew's postpositive δέ.

[3] Luke's ἀπεκρίθη or Matthew's ἀποκριθεὶς εἶπεν.

[4] Luke's πρὸς αὐτόν.

Q

καὶ ἀπεκρίθη ⟦αὐτ<ῷ>⟧ ὁ 'Ιησοῦς· γέγραπται ὅτι οὐκ ἐπ' ἄρτῳ μόνῳ ζήσεται ὁ ἄνθρωπος.	And Jesus answered ⟦him⟧: It is written: A person is not to live only from bread.

Q 4:5-8 is to be found below, between Q 4:9-12 and Q 4:13.

Q 4:4

Luke 4:4	Lukan Doublet	Markan Parallel	Deut 8:3 LXX
⸂ ⸃[1]			καὶ ἐκάκωσέν σε
[καὶ][2]			καὶ ἐλιμαγχόνησέν σε
ἀπ[ε][3]κρίθ[η][3]			καὶ ἐψώμισέν σε τὸ μαννα,
[πρὸς αὐτὸν][4]			ὃ οὐκ εἴδησαν
[1]⸂ὁ [Ἰησοῦς][5] ⸃[1]·			οἱ πατέρες σου,
γέγραπται [ὅτι][6]			ἵνα ἀναγγείλῃ σοι ὅτι
οὐκ ἐπ' ἄρτῳ μόνῳ			οὐκ ἐπ' ἄρτῳ μόνῳ
ζήσεται ὁ ἄνθρωπος			ζήσεται ὁ ἄνθρωπος,
( )[7]			ἀλλ' ἐπὶ παντὶ ῥήματι
			τῷ ἐκπορευομένῳ
.			διὰ στόματος θεοῦ
			ζήσεται ὁ ἄνθρωπος.

IQP 1992: [][4].

JMR: [ ][6].

[5] Luke's Ἰησοῦς.

[6] Luke's ὅτι.

[7] Matthew's ἀλλ' ἐπὶ παντὶ ῥήματι ἐκπορευομένῳ διὰ στόματος θεοῦ.

Da antwortete ⟦ihm⟧ Jesus: Es steht geschrieben: Nicht von Brot allein lebt der Mensch.

et Jésus ⟦lui⟧ répondit: Il est écrit: Personne ne vivra de pain seulement.

Q 4:5-8 is to be found below, between Q 4:9-12 and Q 4:13.

Q 4:9

Markan Parallel	Matthean Doublet	Matt 4:5-6a	Q 4:9
		[1]ʃ	[1]ʃ
		4:5 (Τότε)[2]	()[2]
		(παραλαμβάν)[3](ει)[4]	(παραλαμβάν)[3](ει) [4]
		[ ][2] αὐτὸν	[ ][2] αὐτὸν
		(ὁ διάβολος)[5]	⟦(ὁ διάβολος)[5]⟧
		εἰς (τὴν ἁγίαν πόλιν)[6]	εἰς ['Ιερουσαλὴμ][6]
		καὶ ἔστησεν (αὐτὸν)[7]	καὶ ἔστησεν (αὐτὸν)[7]
		ἐπὶ τὸ πτερύγιον τοῦ ἱεροῦ	ἐπὶ τὸ πτερύγιον τοῦ ἱεροῦ
		4:6a καὶ (λέγει)[8] αὐτῷ·	καὶ [εἶπεν][8] αὐτῷ·
		εἰ υἱὸς εἶ τοῦ θεοῦ,	εἰ υἱὸς εἶ τοῦ θεοῦ,
		βάλε σεαυτὸν	βάλε σεαυτὸν
		[ ][9] κάτω·	⟦[][9]⟧ κάτω·
		ʅ[1]⇒ Matt 4:7	ʅ[1]⇒ Q 4:12

IQP 1994: [( )][6].

IQP 1994: [( )][8].

[1] The order of the second and third temptations.
[2] Luke's δέ or Matthew's τότε.
[3] The choice of the verb: Luke's ἄγω or Matthew's παραλαμβάνω.
[4] The choice of the verb's tense: Luke's aorist or Matthew's present.
[5] Matthew's ὁ διάβολος.

Q

παραλαμβάνει αὐτὸν ⟦ὁ διάβολος⟧ εἰς 'Ιερουσαλὴμ καὶ ἔστησεν αὐτὸν ἐπὶ τὸ πτερύγιον τοῦ ἱεροῦ καὶ εἶπεν αὐτῷ· εἰ υἱὸς εἶ τοῦ θεοῦ, βάλε σεαυτὸν κάτω·

⟦The devil⟧ took him along to Jerusalem and put him on the tip of the temple and told him: If you are God's Son, throw yourself down.

Q 4:9

Luke 4:9	Lukan Doublet	Markan Parallel	Gospel of Thomas
¹ʃ ( )² [Ἤ]⁴[γαγ]³[εν]⁴ [δὲ]² αὐτὸν ( )⁵ εἰς [Ἰερουσαλὴμ]⁶ καὶ ἔστησεν ( )⁷ ἐπὶ τὸ πτερύγιον τοῦ ἱεροῦ καὶ [εἶπεν]⁸ αὐτῷ· εἰ υἱὸς εἶ τοῦ θεοῦ, βάλε σεαυτὸν [ἐντεῦθεν]⁹ κάτω· ʅ¹⇒ Luke 4:12			

6 Luke's Ἰερουσαλήμ or Matthew's τὴν ἁγίαν πόλιν.
7 Matthew's repetition of the pronoun.
8 Luke's εἶπεν or Matthew's λέγει.
9 Luke's ἐντεῦθεν.

⟦Der Teufel⟧ nahm ihn mit nach Jerusalem und stellte ihn an den Rand des Tempel«dache»s und sagte ihm: Wenn du Gottes Sohn bist, stürze dich hinab.

⟦Le diable⟧ le prit avec lui à Jérusalem et le plaça sur le pinacle du temple et lui dit: Si tu es Fils de Dieu, jette-toi en bas.

Q 4:10

Markan Parallel	Matthean Doublet	Matt 4:6b	Q 4:10
		γέγραπται γὰρ ὅτι τοῖς ἀγγέλοις αὐτοῦ ἐντελεῖται περὶ σοῦ [ ][1]	γέγραπται γὰρ ὅτι τοῖς ἀγγέλοις αὐτοῦ ἐντελεῖται περὶ σοῦ [][1]

[1] Luke's τοῦ διαφυλάξαι σε.

Q

γέγραπται γὰρ ὅτι τοῖς ἀγγέλοις αὐτοῦ ἐντελεῖται περὶ σοῦ	For it is written: He will command his angels about you,

Q 4:10

Luke 4:10	Lukan Doublet	Markan Parallel	Ps 90:11 LXX
γέγραπται γὰρ ὅτι τοῖς ἀγγέλοις αὐτοῦ ἐντελεῖται περὶ σοῦ [τοῦ διαφυλάξαι σε][1]			ὅτι τοῖς ἀγγέλοις αὐτοῦ ἐντελεῖται περὶ σοῦ τοῦ διαφυλάξαι σε ἐν πάσαις ταῖς ὁδοῖς σου·

Denn es steht geschrieben: Seinen Engeln wird er deinetwegen Befehl geben,

Car il est écrit: À ses anges, il donnera des ordres à ton sujet,

Q 4:11

Markan Parallel	Matthean Doublet	Matt 4:6c	Q 4:11
		καὶ [ ][1] ἐπὶ χειρῶν ἀροῦσίν σε, μήποτε προσκόψῃς πρὸς λίθον τὸν πόδα σου.	καὶ [][1] ἐπὶ χειρῶν ἀροῦσίν σε, μήποτε προσκόψῃς πρὸς λίθον τὸν πόδα σου.

[1] Luke's ὅτι.

Q

καὶ ἐπὶ χειρῶν ἀροῦσίν σε, μήποτε προσκόψῃς πρὸς λίθον τὸν πόδα σου.	and on their hands they will bear you, so that you do not strike your foot against a stone.

Q 4:11

Luke 4:11	Lukan Doublet	Markan Parallel	Ps 90:12 LXX
καὶ [ὅτι][1] ἐπὶ χειρῶν ἀροῦσίν σε, μήποτε προσκόψῃς πρὸς λίθον τὸν πόδα σου.			ἐπὶ χειρῶν ἀροῦσίν σε, μήποτε προσκόψῃς πρὸς λίθον τὸν πόδα σου.

und auf Händen werden sie dich tragen, damit du deinen Fuß nicht an einen Stein stößt.

et ils te porteront sur leurs mains, pour éviter que tu heurtes une pierre de ton pied.

Q 4:12

Markan Parallel	Matthean Doublet	Matt 4:7	Q 4:12
		[ ][1] [ ][2] (ἔφη)[3] αὐτῷ ὁ Ἰησοῦς· [ ][4] (πάλιν)[5] (γέγραπ)[6]ται· οὐκ ἐκπειράσεις κύριον τὸν θεόν σου. ꝛ Matt 4:5-6a[1]	[καὶ][1] ⟦[ἀποκριθεὶς][2]⟧ [εἶπεν][3] αὐτῷ ὁ Ἰησοῦς· ⟦[][4]⟧ ()[5] (γέγραπ)[6]ται· οὐκ ἐκπειράσεις κύριον τὸν θεόν σου. ꝛ Q 4:9[1]

IQP 1994: [καὶ][1] [ ][2] [( )][3] αὐτῷ.

JMR: [ ][4] ( )[5].

[1] Luke's καί.
[2] Luke's ἀποκριθείς.

[3] Luke's εἶπεν or Matthew's ἔφη.
[4] Luke's ὅτι.

Q

καὶ ⟦ἀποκριθεὶς⟧ εἶπεν αὐτῷ ὁ Ἰησοῦς· γέγραπται· οὐκ ἐκπειράσεις κύριον τὸν θεόν σου·

And Jesus ⟦in reply⟧ told him: It is written: Do not put to the test the Lord your God.

Q 4:13 is to be found below, between Q 4:5-8 and Q 4:16, ~~31~~.

Q 4:12

Luke 4:12	Lukan Doublet	Markan Parallel	Deut 6:16 LXX
[καὶ][1] [ἀποκριθεὶς][2] [εἶπεν][3] αὐτῷ ὁ Ἰησοῦς [ὅτι][4] ( )[5] [εἴρη][6]ται· οὐκ ἐκπειράσεις κύριον τὸν θεόν σου. ʅ Luke 4:9[1]			Οὐκ ἐκπειράσεις κύριον τὸν θεόν σου, ὃν τρόπον ἐξεπειράσασθε ἐν τῷ Πειρασμῷ.

5 Matthew's πάλιν.
6 Luke's εἴρηται or Matthew's γέγραπται.

Da ⟦antwortete⟧ Jesus «und» sagte ihm: Es steht geschrieben: Du sollst den Herrn, deinen Gott, nicht versuchen.

Et ⟦en réponse⟧ Jésus lui dit: Il est écrit: Ne mets pas à l'épreuve le Seigneur ton Dieu.

Q 4:13 is to be found below, between Q 4:5-8 and Q 4:16, ~~31~~.

Q 4:5-7

Markan Parallel	Matthean Doublet	Matt 4:8-9	Q 4:5-7
		4:8 (Πάλιν)[1]	**4:5** [καὶ][1]
		(παραλαμβάνει)[2] αὐτὸν	(παραλαμβάνει)[2] αὐτὸν
		⸂ὁ διάβολος⸃[3]	⸂ὁ διάβολος⸃[3]
		(εἰς ὄρος)[4]	(εἰς ὄρος)[4]
		(ὑψηλὸν)[5]	⟦(ὑψηλὸν)[5]
		(λίαν)[6]	(λίαν)[6]⟧
		(καὶ)[7]	(καὶ)[7]
		[ ][8]δεί(κνυσιν)[8] αὐτῷ	[][8]δεί(κνυσιν)[8] αὐτῷ
		πάσας τὰς βασιλείας	πάσας τὰς βασιλείας
		τ(οῦ κόσμου)[9]	τ(οῦ κόσμου)[9]
		⸂καὶ τὴν δόξαν αὐτῶν⸃[10]	⸂καὶ τὴν δόξαν αὐτῶν⸃[10]
		[ ][11]	[][11]
		4:9 καὶ εἶπεν αὐτῷ	**4:6** καὶ εἶπεν αὐτῷ
		⸂ ⸃[3].	⸂ ⸃[3].
		⸂ ⸃[12]	⸂⸃[12]
		⸂ ⸃[13]	⸂⸃[13]
		[ ][14] ταῦτ(ά)[14]	[][14] ταῦτ(ά)[14]
		⸂σοι⸃[12]	⸂σοι⸃[12]
		[ ][15]πά(ντ)[14]α[ ][14]	[][15]πά(ντ)[14]α[][14]
		⸂δώσω⸃[13]	⸂δώσω⸃[13]
		⸂ ⸃[10],	⸂⸃[10],
		[ ][16]	[][16]
		[ ][17]	**4:7** [][17]
		ἐὰν (πεσὼν)[18] προσκυνήσῃς	ἐὰν ()[18] προσκυνήσῃς
		[ ][19]	[][19]
		[ ][20]μο(ι)[19]	[][20]μο(ι)[19]
		[ ][17].	[][17].

IQP 1994: ⸂ ⟦ὁ διάβολος⟧ ⸃[3] (εἰς ὄρος)[4].

[1] Luke's καί or Matthew's πάλιν.
[2] Luke's ἀναγαγών or Matthew's παραλαμβάνει.
[3] The position of ὁ διάβολος only after καὶ εἶπεν αὐτῷ (Luke) or already after πάλιν παραλαμβάνει αὐτόν (Matthew).
[4] Matthew's εἰς ὄρος.
[5] Matthew's ὑψηλόν.
[6] Matthew's λίαν.
[7] Matthew's καί.
[8] Luke's ἔδειξεν or Matthew's δείκνυσιν.
[9] Luke's τῆς οἰκουνένης or Matthew's τοῦ κόσμου.
[10] The position of καὶ τὴν δόξαν αὐτῶν only after σοὶ δώσω τὴν ἐξουσίαν ταύτην ἅπασαν (Luke) or already after καὶ δείκνυσιν αὐτῷ πάσας τὰς βασιλείας τοῦ κόσμου (Matthew).

Q

5 καὶ παραλαμβάνει αὐτὸν ὁ διάβολος εἰς ὄρος ⟦ὑψηλὸν λίαν⟧ καὶ δείκνυσιν αὐτῷ πάσας τὰς βασιλείας τοῦ κόσμου καὶ τὴν δόξαν αὐτῶν **6** καὶ εἶπεν αὐτῷ· ταῦτά σοι πάντα δώσω, 7 ἐὰν προσκυνήσῃς μοι.

5 And the devil took him along to a ⟦very high⟧ mountain and showed him all the kingdoms of the world and their splendor, **6** and told him: All these I will give you, **7** if you bow down before me.

Q 4:5-7

Luke 4:5-7	Lukan Doublet	Markan Parallel	Gospel of Thomas

4:5 [Καὶ][1]
[ἀναγαγὼν][2] αὐτὸν
⸂ ⸃[3]
( )[4]
( )[5]
( )[6]
( )[7]
[ἔ][8]δει[ξεν][8] αὐτῷ
πάσας τὰς βασιλείας
τ[ῆς οἰκουμένης][9]
⸂ ⸃[10]
[ἐν στιγμῇ χρόνου][11]
4:6 καὶ εἶπεν αὐτῷ
⸂ὁ διάβολος⸃[3]·
⸂σοὶ⸃[12]
⸂δώσω⸃[13]
[τὴν ἐξουσίαν][14] ταύτ[ην][14]
⸂ ⸃[12]
[ἅ][15]πα[σ][14]α[ν][14]
⸂ ⸃[13]
⸂καὶ τὴν δόξαν αὐτῶν⸃[10],
[ὅτι ἐμοὶ παραδέδοται καὶ
ᾧ ἐὰν θέλω δίδωμι αὐτήν·][16]
4:7 [σὺ οὖν][17]
ἐὰν ( )[18] προσκυνήσῃς
[ἐνώπιον][19]
[ἐ][20]μο[ῦ][19],
[ἔσται σοῦ πᾶσα][17].

[11] Luke's ἐν στιγμῇ χρόνου.
[12] The position of σοι.
[13] The position of δώσω, between (Luke) or after (Matthew) the objects.
[14] Luke's τὴν ἐξουσίαν ταύτην ἅπασαν or Matthew's ταῦτά σοι πάντα.
[15] Luke's prefix ἅ-.
[16] Luke's ὅτι ἐμοὶ παραδέδοται καὶ ᾧ ἐὰν θέλω δίδωμι αὐτήν.
[17] Luke's σὺ οὖν … ἔσται σοῦ πᾶσα.
[18] Matthew's πεσών.
[19] Luke's ἐνώπιον with the genitive.
[20] Luke's prefix ἐ- with the pronoun.

5 Da nahm ihn der Teufel mit auf einen ⟦sehr hohen⟧ Berg und zeigte ihm alle Reiche der Welt und ihre Pracht, **6** und er sagte ihm: Das alles werde ich dir geben, **7** wenn du mich anbetest.

5 Et le diable le prend sur une ⟦très haute⟧ montagne et il lui fait voir tous les royaumes du monde et leur splendeur **6** et il lui dit: Tout cela, je te le donnerai, **7** si tu te prosternes devant moi.

Q 4:8

Markan Parallel	Matthean Doublet	Matt 4:10	Q 4:8
		(τότε)[1] [ ][2] ⸉ ⸊[3] (λέγει)[4] αὐτῷ ⸉ὁ Ἰησοῦς⸊[3]. (ὕπαγε, σατανᾶ·)[5] γέγραπται (γάρ)[6]· κύριον τὸν θεόν σου προσκυνήσεις καὶ αὐτῷ μόνῳ λατρεύσεις.	[καὶ][1] ⟦[ἀποκριθεὶς][2]⟧ ⸉ὁ Ἰησοῦς⸊[3] [εἶπεν][4] αὐτῷ ⸉⸊[3]. ()[5] γέγραπται ()[6]· κύριον τὸν θεόν σου προσκυνήσεις καὶ αὐτῷ μόνῳ λατρεύσεις.

IQP 1994: [ ][2] ⸉ὁ Ἰησοῦς⸊[3] [( )][4].

JMR: ⸉ ⸊[3].

Text Critical Note: See the discussion of Deut 6:13a = 10:20a LXX in the front matter.

[1] Luke's καί or Matthew's τότε.
[2] Luke's ἀποκριθείς.

[3] The position of the subject before εἶπεν αὐτῷ (Luke) or after λέγει αὐτῷ (Matthew).

Q

καὶ ⟦ἀποκριθεὶς⟧ ὁ Ἰησοῦς εἶπεν αὐτῷ· γέγραπται· κύριον τὸν θεόν σου προσκυνήσεις καὶ αὐτῷ μόνῳ λατρεύσεις.

And ⟦in reply⟧ Jesus told him: It is written: Bow down to the Lord your God, and serve only him.

Q 4:9-12 is to be found above, between Q 4:1-4 and Q 4:5-8.

Q 4:8

Luke 4:8	Lukan Doublet	Markan Parallel	Deut 6:13a = 10:20a LXX
[καὶ][1] [ἀποκριθεὶς][2] ⸂ὁ Ἰησοῦς⸃[3] [εἶπεν][4] αὐτῷ ⸂ ⸃3. ( )[5] γέγραπται ( )[6]· κύριον τὸν θεόν σου προσκυνήσεις καὶ αὐτῷ μόνῳ λατρεύσεις.			κύριον τὸν θεόν σου φοβηθήσῃ καὶ αὐτῷ λατρεύσεις.

IQP 1994: ⟦()[5]⟧.

[4] Luke's εἶπεν or Matthew's λέγει.
[5] Matthew's ὕπαγε, σατανᾶ·.
[6] Matthew's γάρ.

Da ⟦antwortete⟧ Jesus ⟦«und»⟧ sagte ihm: Es steht geschrieben: Den Herrn, deinen Gott, sollst du anbeten und allein ihm dienen.

Et ⟦en réponse⟧ Jésus lui dit: Il est écrit: Devant le Seigneur ton Dieu prosterne-toi et à lui seul rends un culte.

Q 4:9-12 is to be found above, between Q 4:1-4 and Q 4:5-8.

Q 4:13

Mark 1:13b	Matthean Doublet	Matt 4:11	Q 4:13
		⁰{	⁰{
		(Τότε)¹	[καὶ]¹
		[ ]²	⟦[]²⟧
		∫ ≀³	∫ὁ διάβολος≀³
		ἀ(φίησιν)⁴	ἀ(φίησιν)⁴
		αὐτὸ(ν)⁴	αὐτό(ν)⁴
		∫ὁ διάβολος≀³,	∫≀³
καὶ ἦν μετὰ τῶν θηρίων,			
καὶ οἱ ἄγγελοι		({καὶ} ἰδοὺ {ἄγγελοι}	[({})]⁵
		προσῆλθον καὶ	
διηκόνουν αὐτῷ.		{διηκόνουν αὐτῷ}).⁵	.
		}⁰	}⁰

JMR: []².

JMR: ∫ ≀³ ἀ(φίησιν)⁴ αὐτὸ(ν)⁴ ∫ὁ διάβολος≀³.

⁰ See Q 4:1–2⁰.
¹ Luke's καί or Matthew's τότε.

² Luke's συντελέσας πάντα πειρασμόν.
³ The position of ὁ διάβολος before ἀπέστη ἀπ' αὐτοῦ (Luke) or after ἀφίησιν αὐτόν (Matthew).

Q

καὶ ὁ διάβολος ἀφίησιν αὐτόν.	And the devil left him.

Q 4:13

Luke 4:13	Lukan Doublet	Markan Parallel	Gospel of Thomas
⁰{ [Καὶ][1] [συντελέσας πάντα πειρασμὸν][2] ⸉ὁ διάβολος⸊[3] ἀ[πέστη ἀπ'][4] αὐτο[ῦ][4] ⸉ ⸊[3] [ἄχρι καιροῦ][5] . }⁰			

[4] Luke's ἀπέστη ἀπ' αὐτοῦ or Matthew's ἀφίησιν αὐτόν.

[5] Luke's ἄχρι καιροῦ or Matthew's καὶ ἰδοὺ ἄγγελοι προσῆλθον καὶ διηκόνουν αὐτῷ.

Da verließ ihn der Teufel.

Et le diable le quitta.

Q 4:16, ~~31~~

Mark 1:21a	Matthean Doublet	Matt 4:13	Q 4:16, ~~31~~
		[0]/	[0]/
Καὶ		{καὶ}[1]	**4:16** { }[1]
		(καταλιπὼν)[2]	[( )][2]
		(τὴν)[3]	()[3]
		Ναζαρὰ	Ναζαρά
		[ ][4]	[][4]
		[ ][5]	[][5]
		[ ][6]	**4:~~31~~** [][6]
εἰσπορεύονται		(ἐ)[7]λθ(ὼν κατῴκησεν)[7]	[()][7]~~λθ~~[()][7]
εἰς Καφαρναούμ		{εἰς Καφαρναοὺμ}[8]	{~~εἰς Καφαρναοὺμ~~}[8]
		(τὴν παραθαλασσίαν ἐν ὁρίοις Ζαβουλὼν καὶ Νεφθαλίμ·)[9]	[()][9]
		[ ][10]	[][10]
		\\[0]	\\[0]

IQP 1990: ⟦{ }[1] [( )][2] ( )[3] Ναζαρά⟧.

PH: ⟦(καταλιπών)[2]⟧.

[0] Is (at least) Ναζαρά in Q?

[1] Is the καί at the opening of Luke and Matthew in Q or from Mark?

[2] Luke's ἦλθεν εἰς or Matthew's καταλιπών.

[3] Matthew's article with Ναζαρά.

[4] Luke's οὗ ἦν τεθραμμένος.

Q

<…> Ναζαρά <…>.	<…> Nazara <…>.

Q 4:16, ~~31~~

Luke 4:16, 31	Lukan Doublet	Mark 6:1-2a; 1:21	Gospel of Thomas
[0]/			
4:16 {Καὶ}[1]		**6:1** Καὶ ἐξῆλθεν ἐκεῖθεν	
[ἦλθεν {εἰς}][2]		καὶ ἔρχεται εἰς	
( )[3]		τὴν	
Ναζαρά,		πατρίδα αὐτοῦ,	
[οὗ ἦν		καὶ ἀκολουθοῦσιν	
τεθραμμένος,][4]		αὐτῷ οἱ μαθηταὶ αὐτοῦ.	
[{καὶ} εἰσῆλθεν		**6:2a** καὶ γενομένου	
κατὰ τὸ εἰωθὸς αὐτῷ		σαββάτου ἤρξατο	
ἐν τῇ ἡμέρᾳ		διδάσκειν	
τῶν {σαββάτ}ων			
εἰς {τὴ}ν {συναγωγὴ}ν		ἐν τῇ συναγωγῇ,	
καὶ ἀνέστη ἀναγνῶναι.][5]			
4:31 [{Καὶ}][6]		**1:21** Καὶ	
[κατῆ][7]λθ[εν][7]		εἰσπορεύονται	
{εἰς Καφαρναοὺμ}[8]		εἰς Καφαρναούμ·	
[πόλιν τῆς Γαλιλαίας.][9]			
[{καὶ} ἦν {διδάσκ}ων αὐτοὺς		καὶ εὐθὺς	
ἐν {τοῖς σάββασιν}·][10]		τοῖς σάββασιν εἰσελθὼν	
		εἰς τὴν συναγωγὴν	
\[0]		ἐδίδασκεν.	

PH: 4:~~31~~ [ ][7].

[5] Luke's statement about Jesus' reading.
[6] Is Luke's καί in Q or from Mark?
[7] Luke's κατῆλθεν or Matthew's ἐλθὼν κατῴκησεν.

[8] Is εἰς Καφαρναούμ in Q or from Mark?
[9] The different descriptions of the location of Capernaum.
[10] Is Luke's καὶ ἦν διδάσκων αὐτοὺς ἐν τοῖς σάββασιν in Q or from Mark?

<…> Nazara <…>.

<…> Nazara <…>.

Q 6:20

Mark 3:7-9, 13; 1:21b	Matt 4:25	Matt 5:1-3	Q 6:20
3:7 Καὶ ὁ Ἰησοῦς			
μετὰ τῶν μαθητῶν αὐτοῦ			
ἀνεχώρησεν			
πρὸς τὴν θάλασσαν,			
καὶ	{καὶ} {ἠκολούθησ}αν αὐτῷ		
πολὺ πλῆθος ἀπὸ τῆς	{(ὄχλο)}ι {πολ}λοὶ {ἀπὸ τῆς		
Γαλιλαίας ἠκολούθησεν,	Γαλιλαίας}		
καὶ ἀπὸ τῆς Ἰουδαίας	{καὶ} Δεκαπόλεως		
3:8 καὶ ἀπὸ Ἱεροσολύμων	{καὶ} {Ἱεροσολύμων}		
	καὶ {Ἰουδαίας}		
… καὶ πέραν	{καὶ πέραν		
τοῦ Ἰορδάνου …	τοῦ Ἰορδάνου}.		
πλῆθος πολὺ			
ἀκούοντες …			
3:9 καὶ εἶπεν			
τοῖς μαθηταῖς αὐτοῦ			
ἵνα πλοιάριον			
προσκαρτερῇ αὐτῷ			< >[1]
διὰ τὸν ὄχλον ἵνα		**5:1** (Ἰδὼν δὲ τοὺς {ὄχλο}υς	()[1]
μὴ θλίβωσιν αὐτόν·			
3:13 Καὶ ἀναβαίνει		{ἀν}έ{β}η	
εἰς τὸ ὄρος		{εἰς τὸ ὄρος},)[1]	
καὶ προσκαλεῖται		(καὶ καθίσαντος αὐτοῦ)[2]	()[2]
οὓς ἤθελεν αὐτός,			
καὶ ἀπῆλθον πρὸς αὐτόν.		[3]ʃ (προσῆλθαν αὐτῷ οἱ)[3]	ʃʅ[3]
		{μαθητα}(ὶ)[3] {αὐτοῦ}· ʅ[3]	

[1] Matthew's introduction ἰδὼν δὲ τοὺς ὄχλους ἀνέβη εἰς τὸ ὄρος.

[2] Matthew's καὶ καθίσαντος αὐτοῦ.

Q 6:20

Luke 6:20	Luke 6:17a-b, 24	Mark 3:7-9 Isa 61:1a-b LXX = Luke 4:18a-b	*Gos. Thom.* 54
	6:17a-b {Καὶ} καταβὰς {μετ'} αὐτῶν ἔστη ἐπὶ τόπου πεδινοῦ, {καὶ} {ὄχλο}ς {πολὺ}ς {(μαθητ)ῶν (αὐτοῦ)},	**3:7** Καὶ ὁ Ἰησοῦς μετὰ τῶν μαθητῶν αὐτοῦ ἀνεχώρησεν πρὸς τὴν θάλασσαν, καὶ πολὺ πλῆθος …	
	καὶ {πλῆθος πολὺ} τοῦ λαοῦ …	**3:8** … πλῆθος πολὺ ἀκούοντες … **3:9** καὶ εἶπεν τοῖς μαθηταῖς αὐτοῦ ἵνα πλοιάριον προσκαρτερῇ αὐτῷ διὰ τὸν ὄχλον ἵνα μὴ θλίβωσιν αὐτόν·	
( )[1]			
( )[2]			
⸂ ⸃[3]			

[3] The position and formulation of the reference to the disciples: Luke's phrase εἰς τοὺς μαθητὰς αὐτοῦ dependent upon ἐπάρας or Matthew's clause προσῆλθαν αὐτῷ οἱ μαθηταὶ αὐτοῦ.

Q 6:20

Mark 3:7-9, 13; 1:21b	Matt 4:25	Matt 5:1-3	Q 6:20
		5:2 καὶ [ ]^{4} (ἀνοίξ)^{5}ας τὸ[ ]^{5} (στόμα)^{5} αὐτοῦ ʃ ʅ^{3}	**6:20** καὶ []^{4} ⟦[ἐπάρ]^{5}⟧ας το⟦[ὺς ὀφθαλμοὺς]^{5}⟧ αὐτοῦ ^{3}ʃ ⟦[εἰς τοὺς]^{3}⟧ {μαθητὰ}⟦[ς]^{3}⟧ {αὐτοῦ}ʅ^{3}
1:21b καὶ εὐθὺς τοῖς σάββασιν εἰσελθὼν εἰς τὴν συναγωγὴν ἐδίδασκεν.		({ἐδίδασκεν} αὐτοὺς)^{6} [ ]^{7}λέγ(ων)^{7}· **5:3** Μακάριοι οἱ πτωχοὶ (τῷ πνεύματι)^{8}, ὅτι (αὐτῶν)^{9} ἐστιν ἡ βασιλεία τ(ῶν οὐρανῶν)^{10}.	()^{6} [ ]^{7}λεγ[< >]^{7}· μακάριοι οἱ πτωχοί ()^{8}, ὅτι ⟦[ὑμετέρα]^{9}⟧ ἐστὶν ἡ βασιλεία τ[οῦ θεοῦ]^{10}.

PH: καὶ ʃ ʅ^{3} []^{4} []^{5}~~ας το~~[]^{5} ~~αὐτοῦ~~ ()^{6} ⟦[ἔ]^{7}⟧λεγ⟦[εν]^{7}⟧ ʃ ⟦{τ<οῖς>^{3} μαθητ<αῖς>^{3}⟧ αὐτοῦ} ʅ^{3}.

IQP 1991: ⟦<εἶπεν>^{7}⟧; JSK: ⟦[]^{7}⟧λέγ⟦<εν>^{7}⟧; JMR: [ ]^{7}λεγ[< >]^{7} indeterminate.

^{4} Luke's pronoun αὐτός.
^{5} Luke's ἐπάρας τοὺς ὀφθαλμούς or Matthew's ἀνοίξας τὸ στόμα.
^{6} Matthew's ἐδίδασκεν αὐτούς.
^{7} Luke's ἔλεγεν or Matthew's λέγων.
^{8} Matthew's τῷ πνεύματι.

Q

<...> καὶ ⟦ἐπάρ⟧ας το⟦ὺς ὀφθαλμοὺς⟧ αὐτοῦ ⟦εἰς τοὺς⟧ μαθητὰ⟦ς⟧ αὐτοῦ ..λέγ...· μακάριοι οἱ πτωχοί, ὅτι ⟦ὑμετέρα⟧ ἐστὶν ἡ βασιλεία τοῦ θεοῦ.

<...> And ⟦rais⟧ing his ⟦eyes to⟧ his disciples he said: Blessed are ⟦«you»⟧ poor, for God's reign is for ⟦you⟧.

Gos. Thom. 54 (Nag Hammadi II 2)

Λέγει Ἰησοῦς· μακάριοι οἱ πτωχοί, ὅτι ὑμετέρα ἐστὶν ἡ βασιλεία τῶν οὐρανῶν.

Jesus says: Blessed are (you) poor, for heaven's reign is for you.

Q 6:20

Luke 6:20	Luke 6:17a-b, 24	Mark 3:7-9 Isa 61:1a-b LXX = Luke 4:18a-b	*Gos. Thom.* 54
6:20 Καὶ [αὐτὸς][4] [ἐπάρ][5]ας το[ὺς ὀφθαλμοὺς][5] αὐτοῦ [3]⸋ [εἰς τοὺς][3] {μαθητὰ}[ς][3] {αὐτοῦ}⸌[3]			
( )[6] [ἔ][7]λεγ[εν][7]· Μακάριοι οἱ πτωχοί ( )[8], ὅτι [ὑμετέρα][9] ἐστὶν ἡ βασιλεία τ[οῦ θεοῦ][10].	**6:24** Πλὴν οὐαὶ ὑμῖν τοῖς πλουσίοις, [(ὅτι)] ἀπέχετε τὴν παράκλησιν ὑμῶν.	**Isa 61:1a-b = Luke 4:18a-b** Πνεῦμα κυρίου ἐπ' ἐμέ, οὗ εἵνεκεν ἔχρισέν με εὐαγγελίσασθαι πτωχοῖς ἀπέσταλκέν με,	ⲡⲉϫⲉ ⲓⲥ̄ ϫⲉ ϩⲛ̄ⲙⲁⲕⲁⲣⲓⲟⲥ ⲛⲉ ⲛϩⲏⲕⲉ ϫⲉ ⲧⲱⲧⲛ̄ ⲧⲉ ⲧⲙⲛ̄ⲧⲉⲣⲟ ⲛⲙ̄ⲡⲏⲩⲉ'

[9] Luke's ὑμετέρα or Matthew's αὐτῶν. (See also Q 6:21, variation units [4] and [6].)

[10] Luke's τοῦ θεοῦ or Matthew's τῶν οὐρανῶν.

<...> Und er ⟦richtete⟧ seine ⟦Augen auf⟧ seine Jünger und sagte: Selig ⟦«ihr»⟧ Armen, denn ⟦euer⟧ ist das Reich Gottes.

<...> Et après avoir ⟦lev⟧é les ⟦yeux sur⟧ ses disciples, il dit: Bienheureux ⟦«vous»⟧ les pauvres, parce que le règne de Dieu est à ⟦vous⟧.

Jesus spricht: Selig (ihr) Armen, denn euer ist das Königreich der Himmel.

Jésus dit: Bienheureux (vous) les pauvres, parce que le royaume des cieux est à vous.

Q 6:21

<table>
<tr><th>Markan Parallel</th><th>Matthean Doublet</th><th>Matt 5:4, 6</th><th>Q 6:21</th></tr>
<tr><td></td><td></td><td>5:4 ^{1}ʃμακάριοι
οἱ (πενθ)^{5}ο(ῦ)^{5}ντες
[ ]^{3},
ὅτι (αὐτοὶ
παρακληθήσονται)^{6}. ʅ^{1}
<b>5:6</b> μακάριοι οἱ πεινῶντες
(καὶ διψῶντες
τὴν δικαιοσύνην)^{2}
[ ]^{3},
ὅτι (αὐτοὶ)^{4}
χορτασθήσ(ονται)^{4}.
ʃ ʅ^{1}</td><td>ʃʅ^{1}

μακάριοι οἱ πεινῶντες
()^{2}

[]^{3},
ὅτι ()^{4}
χορτασθήσ⟦[εσθε]^{4}⟧.
^{1}ʃμακάριοι
οἱ ⟦(πενθ)^{5}⟧ο⟦(ῦ)^{5}⟧ντες
[]^{3},
ὅτι ()^{6}
⟦(παρακληθήσ)^{6}<εσθε>^{4}⟧. ʅ^{1}</td></tr>
</table>

IQP 1991: χορτασθήσ[εσθε]^{4}.

IQP 1991: ⟦[κλαί]^{5}ο⟦()^{5}⟧ντες []^{3}, ὅτι ()^{6} [γελάσετε]^{6}.

1 The position of Q 6:21b after Q 6:21a (Luke) or the reverse (Matthew).

2 Matthew's καὶ διψῶντες τὴν δικαιοσύνην.

3 Luke's adverb νῦν (*bis*).

Q

μακάριοι οἱ πεινῶντες, ὅτι χορτασθήσ⟦εσθε⟧. μακάριοι οἱ ⟦πενθ⟧ο⟦ῦ⟧ντες, ὅτι ⟦παρακληθήσ<εσθε>⟧.	Blessed are ⟦«you»⟧ who hunger, for ⟦you⟧ will eat ⟦your⟧ fill. Blessed are ⟦«you»⟧ who ⟦mourn⟧, for ⟦<you> will be consoled⟧.

Gos. Thom. 69.2 (Nag Hammadi II 2)

μακάριοι οἱ πεινῶντες, ἵνα χορτασθῇ ἡ κοιλία τοῦ θέλοντος.

Blessed are those who hunger in order that the stomach of the one who craves for (it) may eat its fill.

Q 6:21

Luke 6:21	Luke 6:24-25	Isa 61:2 LXX	*Gos. Thom.* 69.2
ʃ ʅ[1]	**6:24** Πλὴν οὐαὶ ὑμῖν		
	τοῖς πλουσίοις,		
	[(ὅτι)] ἀπέχετε		
	(παράκλη)σιν ὑμῶν.		
μακάριοι οἱ πεινῶντες	**6:25** οὐαὶ ὑμῖν,		ϩⲙ̄ⲙⲁⲕⲁⲣⲓⲟⲥ ⲛⲉⲧϩⲕⲁⲉⲓⲧ’
( )[2]	[(οἱ)] ἐμπεπλησμένοι		
[νῦν][3],	[νῦν],		
ὅτι ( )[4]	[(ὅτι)]		ϣⲓⲛⲁ ⲉⲩⲛⲁⲧⲥⲓⲟ ⲛ̄ⲑϩⲏ
χορτασθήσ[εσθε][4].	[πειν]άσετε.		ⲙ̄ⲡⲉⲧⲟⲩⲱϣ
[1]ʃμακάριοι	οὐαί,	καλέσαι	
οἱ [κλαί][5]ο( )[5]ντες	[(οἱ)] [γελ]ῶ[(ντες)]	ἐνιαυτὸν κυρίου δεκτὸν	
[νῦν][3],	[νῦν],	καὶ ἡμέραν ἀνταποδόσεως,	
ὅτι ( )[6]	[(ὅτι)]	παρακαλέσαι πάντας	
[γελάσετε][6]. ʅ[1]	(πενθ)ήσετε καὶ κλαύσετε.	τοὺς πενθοῦντας	

JSK: ⟦[κλαί][5]⟧ο⟦()[5]⟧ντες [][3], ὅτι ()[6] ⟦[γελάσετε][6]⟧.

[4] Luke's χορτασθήσεσθε or Matthew's αὐτοὶ χορτασθήσονται. (See also Q 6:20 variation unit[5] and Q 6:21 variation unit[6]).

[5] Luke's κλαίοντες or Matthew's πενθοῦντες.

[6] Luke's γελάσετε or Matthew's αὐτοὶ παρακληθήσονται. (See also Q 6:20 variation unit[5] and Q 6:21 variation unit[6]).

Selig ⟦«ihr»⟧ Hungernden, denn ⟦ihr⟧ werde⟦t⟧ gesättigt werden. Selig, ⟦«ihr» Trauernden⟧, denn ⟦<ihr> werdet getröstet werden⟧.

Bienheureux ⟦«vous»⟧ les affamés, parce que ⟦vous⟧ ser⟦ez⟧ rassasiés. Bienheureux ⟦«vous»⟧ les ⟦endeuillés⟧, parce que ⟦<vous> serez consolés⟧.

Selig sind die Hungernden leiden, damit der Leib dessen gesättigt wird, der (es) wünscht.

Bienheureux (vous) les affamés, de sorte que soit rassasié le ventre de celui qui (le) veut.

Q 6:22

Markan Parallel	Matthean Doublet	Matt 5:11	Q 6:22
		μακάριοί ἐστε	μακάριοί ἐστε
		[ ][1]	⟦[][1]⟧
		[ ][2]	[][2]
		[ ][1]	⟦[][1]⟧
		ὅταν	ὅταν
		[3]ʃὀνειδίσʅ[3]ωσιν ὑμᾶς	ʃὀνειδίσʅ[3]ωσιν ὑμᾶς
		καὶ [3]ʃ (διώξ)[4]ʅ[3]ωσιν	καὶ [3]ʃ ⟦(διώξ)[4]⟧ʅ[3]ωσιν
		καὶ (εἴπ)[5]ωσιν	καὶ ⟦(εἴπ)[5]⟧ωσιν
		[ ][5]	⟦[][5]⟧
		ʃ ʅ[5] (πᾶν)[5] πονηρὸν	ʃʅ[5] ⟦(πᾶν)[5]⟧ πονηρὸν
		ʃ (καθ')[5] ὑμῶνʅ[5]	ʃ ⟦(καθ')[5]⟧ ὑμῶνʅ[5]
		(ψευδόμενοι)[6]	()[6]
		ἕνεκ(εν)[7]	ἕνεκ(εν)[7]
		(ἐμοῦ)[8].	[τοῦ υἱοῦ τοῦ ἀνθρώπου][8]·

IQP 1993: [ ][1] [][2] [ ][1].
JSK: ⟦[ὅταν μισήσωσιν ὑμᾶς][1]⟧ [][2] ⟦[καί][1]⟧.

[1] Luke's ὅταν μισήσωσιν ὑμᾶς … καί.
[2] Luke's οἱ ἄνθρωποι.

IQP 1993: καὶ [3]ʃ ( )[4] ʅ[3] ωσιν καὶ [( )][5]ωσιν [ ][5] ʃ ( )[5] ὑμῶνʅ[5] [ ][5] πονηρὸν ʃʅ[5] ()[6] ἕνεκ(εν)[7].

[3] In the ὅταν clause with three verbs is ὀνειδίσωσιν in second (Luke) or first place (Matthew)?
[4] Luke's ἀφορίσωσιν or Matthew's διώξωσιν.

Q

μακάριοί ἐστε ὅταν ὀνειδίσωσιν ὑμᾶς καὶ ⟦διώξ⟧ωσιν καὶ ⟦εἴπ⟧ωσιν ⟦πᾶν⟧ πονηρὸν ⟦καθ'⟧ ὑμῶν ἕνεκεν τοῦ υἱοῦ τοῦ ἀνθρώπου.

Blessed are you when they insult and ⟦persecute⟧ you, and ⟦say every kind of⟧ evil ⟦against⟧ you because of the son of humanity.

Gos. Thom. 69.1a (Nag Hammadi II 2)

Λέγει Ἰησοῦς· μακάριοι οἱ δεδιωγμένοι ἐν τῇ καρδίᾳ αὐτῶν.

Jesus says: Blessed are those who have been persecuted in their heart.[2]

[1] Possible conjecture: <ⲉⲩⲟⲩⲁⲁⲃ> ϩⲣⲁ ϊ ϩⲙ̅ ⲡⲟⲩϩⲏⲧ'.
[1] Mögliche Konjektur: <ⲉⲩⲟⲩⲁⲁⲃ> ϩⲣⲁ ϊ ϩⲙ̅ ⲡⲟⲩϩⲏⲧ'.
[1] Conjecture possible: <ⲉⲩⲟⲩⲁⲁⲃ> ϩⲣⲁ ϊ ϩⲙ̅ ⲡⲟⲩϩⲏⲧ'.

[2] Perhaps the text is corrupt and read originally in analogy to Matt 5:8: Blessed are the persecuted, <in so far as they are pure> in their hearts.

Gos. Thom. 68.1 (Nag Hammadi II 2)

Λέγει Ἰησοῦς· μακάριοί ἐστε ὅταν μισήσωσιν ὑμᾶς καὶ διώξωσιν ὑμᾶς.

Jesus says: Blessed are you when they hate you and persecute you.

Q 6:22

Luke 6:22	Luke 6:26a	*Gos. Thom.* 69.1a	*Gos. Thom.* 68.1
		ⲡⲉϫⲉ ⲓ̅ⲥ̅	ⲡⲉϫⲉ ⲓ̅ⲥ̅ ϫⲉ
μακάριοί ἐστε	οὐαὶ	ϩⲙ̅ⲙⲁⲕⲁⲣⲓⲟⲥ ⲛⲉ ⲛⲁⲉⲓ	ⲛ̅ⲧⲱⲧⲛ̅ ϩⲙ̅ⲙⲁⲕⲁⲣⲓⲟⲥ
[ὅταν μισήσωσιν	[(ὅταν)]		ϩⲟⲧⲁⲛ ⲉⲩϣⲁⲛⲙⲉⲥⲧⲉ
ὑμᾶς][1]	[(ὑμᾶς)]		ⲧⲏⲩⲧⲛ̅
	καλῶς (εἴπωσιν)		
[οἱ ἄνθρωποι][2]	πάντες [οἱ ἄνθρωποι]·		
[καὶ][1]			
ὅταν			
[3]ʃ [ἀφορίσ][4]ʅ[3]ωσιν ὑμᾶς			
καὶ [3]ʃὀνειδίσʅ[3]ωσιν		ⲛ̅ⲧⲁⲩⲇⲓⲱⲕⲉ ⲙ̅ⲙⲟⲟⲩ	ⲛ̅ⲥⲉⲣ̅ⲇⲓⲱⲕⲉ ⲙ̅ⲙⲱⲧⲛ̅
καὶ [ἐκβάλ][5]ωσιν			
[τὸ ὄνομα][5]		ϩⲣⲁ̈ⲓ ϩⲙ̅ ⲡⲟⲩϩⲏⲧ'[1]	
ʃ ( )[5] ὑμῶνʅ[5] [ὡς][5] πονηρὸν			
ʃ ʅ[5]			
( )[6]			
ἕνεκ[α][7]			
[τοῦ υἱοῦ τοῦ ἀνθρώπου][8]·			

JSK: καὶ ⟦[ἐκβάλ][5]⟧ωσιν ⟦[τὸ ὄνομα][5]⟧ ʃ ( )[5] ὑμῶνʅ[5] ⟦[ὡς][5]⟧ πονηρόν ʃ ʅ[5].

PH: ⟦[τοῦ υἱοῦ τοῦ ἀνθρώπου][8]⟧.

[5] Luke's ἐκβάλωσιν τὸ ὄνομα ὑμῶν ὡς πονηρόν or Matthew's εἴπωσιν πᾶν πονηρὸν καθ' ὑμῶν.

[6] Matthew's ψευδόμενοι.

[7] Luke's ἕνεκα or Matthew's ἕνεκεν.

[8] Luke's τοῦ υἱοῦ τοῦ ἀνθρώπου or Matthew's ἐμοῦ.

Selig seid ihr, wenn sie euch schmähen und ⟦verfolgen⟧ und ⟦alles mögliche⟧ Schlechte ⟦gegen⟧ euch ⟦sagen⟧ wegen des Menschensohnes.

Bienheureux êtes-vous lorsqu'ils vous injurient et vous ⟦persécut⟧ent et ⟦dis⟧ent ⟦toute sorte de⟧ mal ⟦contre⟧ vous à cause du fils de l'homme.

Jesus spricht: Selig sind die, die verfolgt wurden in ihrem Herzen.[3].

Jésus dit: Bienheureux sont ceux qui ont été persécutés dans leurs coeurs.[4]

[3] Möglicherweise ist der Text korrupt und lautete ursprünglich in Analogie zu Mt 5,8: Selig sind die Verfolgten, <sofern sie reinen> Herzens <sind>.

[4] Le passage doît peut-être être considéré comme corrumpu. On pourrait lire originalement d'une manière analogue à Matt 5,8: Bienheureux sont ceux qui sont persécutés, <dans la mesure où ils sont purs> dans leurs cœurs.

Jesus spricht: Selig seid ihr, wenn sie euch hassen und euch verfolgen.

Jésus dit: Bienheureux êtes-vous quand ils vous haïssent et vous persécutent.

Q 6:23

Markan Parallel	Matthean Doublet	Matt 5:12	Q 6:23
		χα(ί)[1]ρ(ε)[1]τε [ ][2] καὶ (ἀγαλλιᾶσθε)[3], (ὅτι)[4] ὁ μισθὸς ὑμῶν πολὺς ἐν τ(οῖς)[5] οὐραν(οῖς)[5]· (οὕτως)[6] γὰρ (ἐδίωξαν)[7] το(ὺ)[7]ς προφήτ(α)[7]ς (τοὺς πρὸ ὑμῶν)[8] [ ][9].	χα(ί)[1]ρ(ε)[1]τε [][2] καὶ ⟦(ἀγαλλιᾶσθε)[3]⟧, (ὅτι)[4] ὁ μισθὸς ὑμῶν πολὺς ἐν τ[ῷ][5] οὐραν[ῷ][5]· (οὕτως)[6] γὰρ ⟦(ἐδίωξαν)[7]⟧ το(ὺ)[7]ς προφήτ(α)[7]ς (τοὺς πρὸ ὑμῶν)[8] [][9].

IQP 1992: [ἐποίουν][7] το[ῖ][7]ς προφήτ[αι][7]ς ⟦(το<ῖ>ς πρὸ ὑμῶν)[8]⟧.

1 Luke's χάρητε or Matthew's χαίρετε.
2 Luke's ἐν ἐκείνῃ τῇ ἡμέρᾳ.
3 Luke's σκιρτήσατε or Matthew's ἀγαλλιᾶσθε.
4 Luke's ἰδοὺ γάρ or Matthew's ὅτι.
5 Luke's ἐν τῷ οὐρανῷ or Matthew's ἐν τοῖς οὐρανοῖς.
6 Luke's κατὰ τὰ αὐτά or Matthew's οὕτως.

Q

χαίρετε καὶ ⟦ἀγαλλιᾶσθε⟧, ὅτι ὁ μισθὸς ὑμῶν πολὺς ἐν τῷ οὐρανῷ· οὕτως γὰρ ⟦ἐδίωξαν⟧ τοὺς προφήτας τοὺς πρὸ ὑμῶν.

Be glad and ⟦exult⟧, for vast is your reward in heaven. For this is how they ⟦persecuted⟧ the prophets who «were» before you.

Q 6:23

Luke 6:23	Luke 6:26b	Markan Parallel	Gospel of Thomas
χά( )[1]ρ[η][1]τε [ἐν ἐκείνῃ τῇ ἡμέρᾳ][2] καὶ [σκιρτήσατε][3], [ἰδοὺ γὰρ][4] ὁ μισθὸς ὑμῶν πολὺς ἐν τ[ῷ][5] οὐραν[ῷ][5]· [κατὰ τὰ αὐτὰ][6] γὰρ [ἐποίουν][7] το[ῖ][7]ς προφήτ[αι][7]ς ( )[8] [οἱ πατέρες αὐτῶν][9].	 [κατὰ τὰ αὐτὰ (γὰρ) ἐποίουν (το)ῖ(ς)] ψευδο[(προφήτα)ι(ς)] οἱ πατέρες αὐτῶν.]		

[7] Luke's ἐποίουν τοῖς προφήταις or Matthew's ἐδίωξαν τοὺς προφήτας.

[8] Matthew's τοὺς πρὸ ὑμῶν.

[9] Luke's οἱ πατέρες αὐτῶν.

Freut euch und ⟦jubelt⟧, denn euer Lohn im Himmel ist groß; denn genauso ⟦verfolgten⟧ sie die Propheten vor euch.

Réjouissez-vous et ⟦soyez dans l'allégresse⟧, parce qu'une bonne récompense vous attend dans le ciel; car c'est ainsi qu'ils ⟦persécutèrent⟧ les prophètes qui «vécurent» avant vous.

Q 6:~~24-26~~

Markan Parallel	Matt 5:3, 6, 4, 11-12	Matthew	Q 6:~~24-26~~
	5:3 Μακάριοι οἱ πτωχοὶ τῷ πνεύματι, [ὅτι] αὐτῶν ἐστιν ἡ βασιλεία τῶν οὐρανῶν. **5:6** μακάριοι [οἱ] [πειν]ῶντες καὶ διψῶντες τὴν δικαιοσύνην, [ὅτι] αὐτοὶ χορτασθήσονται. **5:4** μακάριοι [οἱ] [πενθ]οῦ[ντες], [ὅτι] αὐτοὶ [παρακλη]θήσονται. **5:11** μακάριοί ἐστε [ὅταν] ὀνειδίσωσιν [ὑμᾶς] καὶ διώξωσιν καὶ [εἴπωσιν] πᾶν πονηρὸν καθ' ὑμῶν [ψευδό]μενοι ἕνεκεν ἐμοῦ. **5:12** χαίρετε καὶ ἀγαλλιᾶσθε, ὅτι ὁ μισθὸς ὑμῶν πολὺς ἐν τοῖς οὐρανοῖς· οὕτως [γὰρ] ἐδίωξαν [το]ὺ[ς] [προφήτα][ς] τοὺς πρὸ ὑμῶν.	[ ][0]	[][0]

JSK: The Woes in Q {C}.

[0] Are the Woes in Q?

Q 6:~~24-26~~

Luke 6:24-26	Luke 6:20b-23	Markan Parallel	Gospel of Thomas
[**6:24** Πλὴν οὐαὶ	**6:20b** Μακάριοι		
ὑμῖν τοῖς πλουσίοις,	οἱ πτωχοί,		
ὅτι ἀπέχετε	[ὅτι] ὑμετέρα ἐστὶν		
τὴν παράκλησιν ὑμῶν.	ἡ βασιλεία τοῦ θεοῦ.		
6:25 οὐαὶ ὑμῖν,	**6:21** μακάριοι		
οἱ ἐμπεπλησμένοι νῦν,	οἱ [πειν]ῶντες [νῦν,		
ὅτι πεινάσετε.	ὅτι] χορτασθήσεσθε.		
οὐαί,	μακάριοι		
οἱ γελῶντες νῦν,	[οἱ] κλαίο[ντες νῦν],		
ὅτι πενθήσετε	ὅτι] [γελ]ά[σετε].		
καὶ κλαύσετε.			
6:26 οὐαὶ	**6:22** μακάριοί ἐστε		
ὅταν ὑμᾶς καλῶς εἴπωσιν	[ὅταν] μισήσωσιν [ὑμᾶς]		
πάντες οἱ ἄνθρωποι·	[οἱ ἄνθρωποι]		
	καὶ ὅταν ἀφορίσωσιν ὑμᾶς		
	καὶ ὀνειδίσωσιν		
	καὶ ἐκβάλωσιν τὸ ὄνομα		
	ὑμῶν ὡς πονηρὸν		
	ἕνεκα τοῦ υἱοῦ		
	τοῦ ἀνθρώπου·		
	6:23 χάρητε		
	ἐν ἐκείνῃ τῇ ἡμέρᾳ		
	καὶ σκιρτήσατε,		
	ἰδοὺ γὰρ ὁ μισθὸς ὑμῶν		
	πολὺς ἐν τῷ οὐρανῷ·		
κατὰ τὰ αὐτὰ γὰρ	[κατὰ τὰ αὐτὰ γὰρ		
ἐποίουν	ἐποίουν		
τοῖς ψευδοπροφήταις	τοῖς] [προφήταις		
οἱ πατέρες αὐτῶν.]⁰	οἱ πατέρες αὐτῶν.]		

Q 6:27-28

Lev 19:18c LXX	Matthean Doublet	Matt 5:43-44	Q 6:27-28
		^{0}[	^{0}[
		5:43 ^{1}ʃ	**6:27** ^{1}ʃ
		('Ηκούσατε ὅτι ἐρρέθη· ἀγαπήσεις τὸν πλησίον σου καὶ μισήσεις τὸν ἐχθρόν σου. **5:44** ἐγὼ δὲ)^{2}	[()]^{2}
καὶ ἀγαπήσεις τὸν πλησίον σου ὡς σεαυτόν·			
		^{3}/ ʃ ʅ^{3} λέγω ʃὑμῖνʅ^{3} \\$^{3}$	^{3}/ ʃ~~ὑμῖν~~ʅ^{3} ~~λέγω~~ ʃʅ^{3} \\$^{3}$
		[ ]^{4}·	[]^{4}
		ἀγαπᾶτε τοὺς ἐχθροὺς ὑμῶν	ἀγαπᾶτε τοὺς ἐχθροὺς ὑμῶν
		[ ]^{5}	⟦[]^{5}⟧
			6:28 ⟦[]^{5}⟧
		(καὶ)^{6}	⟦(καὶ)^{6}⟧
		προσεύχεσθε (ὑ)^{7}πὲρ[ ]^{7}	προσεύχεσθε (ὑ)^{7}πὲρ[]^{7}
		τῶν (διωκ)^{8}όντων ὑμᾶς,	τῶν ⟦(διωκ)^{8}⟧όντων ὑμᾶς,
		ʅ^{1}⇒ Matt 5:45	ʅ^{1}⇒ Q 6:35c-d
		]^{0}	]^{0}

JSK: Q **6:35a-b** in Q after Q **6:27-34**.

JMR: Q **6:27-28, 35c-d** in Q after Q **6:29-31**.

^{0} Is Luke 6:35a-b in Q, or is it a redactional doublet?
^{1} The position of Q 6:27-28, 35c-d in Q 6:27-36.
^{2} Luke's ἀλλά or Matthew's antithetical introduction.
^{3} Are ὑμῖν and λέγω in Q, and if so, in which order?
^{4} Luke's τοῖς ἀκούουσιν.

Q

27 ἀγαπᾶτε τοὺς ἐχθροὺς ὑμῶν 28 ⟦καὶ⟧ προσεύχεσθε ὑπὲρ τῶν ⟦διωκ⟧όντων ὑμᾶς,	27 Love your enemies 28 ⟦and⟧ pray for those ⟦persecuting⟧ you,

Q 6:29, ⟦29↔30/Matt 5:41⟧, 30-32, 34 is to be found below, between Q 6:35c-d and Q 6:36.

Q 6:27-28

Luke 6:27-28	Luke 6:35a-b	*Did* 1.3d,b	Gospel of Thomas
[0][	[0][		
6:27 [1]ʃ			
[Ἀλλὰ][2]	πλὴν		
[3]/ ʃὑμῖνʅ[3] λέγω ʃ ʅ[3] \[3]			
[τοῖς ἀκούουσιν][4]·			
ἀγαπᾶτε	[(ἀγαπᾶτε	**1.3d** ὑμεῖς δὲ φιλεῖτε	
τοὺς ἐχθροὺς ὑμῶν,	τοὺς ἐχθροὺς ὑμῶν)]		
[καλῶς ποιεῖτε	καὶ ἀγαθο[ποιεῖτε]		
τοῖς μισοῦσιν ὑμᾶς,		τοὺς μισοῦντας ὑμᾶς,	
		καὶ οὐχ ἕξετε ἐχθρόν.	
6:28 εὐλογεῖτε		**1.3b** εὐλογεῖτε	
τοὺς καταρωμένους ὑμᾶς,][5]		τοὺς καταρωμένους ὑμῖν	
( )[6]	(καὶ)	καὶ	
προσεύχεσθε ( )[7]περ[ὶ][7]	δανίζετε	προσεύχεσθε ὑπὲρ	
	μηδὲν ἀπελπίζοντες·	τῶν ἐχθρῶν ὑμῶν,	
	καὶ ἔσται ὁ μισθὸς ὑμῶν	νηστεύετε δὲ ὑπὲρ	
τῶν [ἐπηρεαζ][8]όντων ὑμᾶς.	πολύς,	τῶν διωκόντων ὑμᾶς.	
ʅ[1]⇒ Luke 6:35c-d			
][0]	][0]		

IQP 1992: ⟦[ ][4]⟧.

IQP 1992: **6:28** ⟦[ἐπηρεαζ][8]⟧όντων.

[5] Luke's καλῶς ποιεῖτε τοῖς μισοῦσιν ὑμᾶς, εὐλογεῖτε τοὺς καταρωμένους ὑμᾶς.

[6] Matthew's καί.

[7] Luke's περί or Matthew's ὑπέρ.

[8] Luke's ἐπηρεαζόντων or Matthew's διωκόντων.

27 Liebt eure Feinde, 28 ⟦und⟧ betet für die, die euch ⟦verfolgen⟧,

27 Aimez vos ennemis 28 ⟦et⟧ priez pour ceux qui vous ⟦persécut⟧ent,

Q 6:29, ⟦29↔30/Matt 5:41⟧, 30-32, 34 is to be found below, between Q 6:35c-d and Q 6:36.

Q 6:35c-d

Markan Parallel	Matt 5:48	Matt 5:45	Q 6:35c-d
	[ἔσεσθε] οὖν ὑμεῖς τέλειοι ὡς (ὁ) (πατ)ὴ(ρ) (ὑμῶν) (ὁ) (οὐράν)ιος τέλειός [ἐστιν].	(ὅπως γένη)[1]σθε υἱοὶ (τοῦ πατρὸς ὑμῶν)[2] (τοῦ ἐν οὐρανοῖς)[3], ὅτι (τὸν ἥλιον)[4] αὐτο(ῦ ἀνατέλλει)[4] ἐπὶ ⸉πονηροὺς⸊[5] καὶ [5]⸉ (ἀγαθοὺς)[6] ⸊[5] (καὶ βρέχει ἐπὶ δικαίους καὶ ἀδίκους)[7]. ⸊Matt 5:43-44[1]	(ὅπως γένη)[1]σθε υἱοὶ (τοῦ πατρὸς ὑμῶν)[2] ()[3], ὅτι (τὸν ἥλιον)[4] αὐτο(ῦ ἀνατέλλει)[4] ἐπὶ ⸉πονηροὺς⸊[5] καὶ [5]⸉ ⟦(ἀγαθοὺς)[6] ⸊[5] (καὶ βρέχει ἐπὶ δικαίους καὶ ἀδίκους)[7]⟧. ⸊Q 6:27-28[1]

JSK: Q **6:35c-d** in Q after Q **6:27-35b**.

JSK: [καὶ ἔσε][1]σθε υἱοί.

[1] Luke's καὶ ἔσεσθε or Matthew's ὅπως γένησθε.

[2] Luke's ὑψίστου or Matthew's τοῦ πατρὸς ὑμῶν.

[3] Matthew's τοῦ ἐν οὐρανοῖς.

[4] Luke's ὅτι αὐτὸς χρηστός ἐστιν or Matthew's ὅτι τὸν ἥλιον αὐτοῦ ἀνατέλλει.

Q

ὅπως γένησθε υἱοὶ τοῦ πατρὸς ὑμῶν, ὅτι τὸν ἥλιον αὐτοῦ ἀνατέλλει ἐπὶ πονηροὺς καὶ ⟦ἀγαθοὺς καὶ βρέχει ἐπὶ δικαίους καὶ ἀδίκους⟧.

so that you may become sons of your Father, for he raises his sun on bad and ⟦good and rains on the just and unjust⟧.

Q 6:36 is to be found below, between Q 6:29, ⟦29↔30/Matt 5:41⟧, 30-32, 34 and Q 6:37-38.

Q 6:35c-d

Luke 6:35c-d	Luke 6:36	Markan Parallel	Gospel of Thomas
[καὶ ἔσε][1]σθε υἱοὶ [ὑψίστου][2] ( )[3], ὅτι ( )[4] αὐτὸ[ς χρηστός ἐστιν][4] ἐπὶ [5]⸂ [τοὺς ἀχαρίστους][6] ⸃[5] καὶ ⸂πονηρούς⸃[5] ( )[7] . ⸃Luke 6:27-28[1]	(Γ)ί(ν)ε[(σθε)] οἰκτίρμονες καθὼς καὶ ὁ (πατ)ὴ(ρ) (ὑμῶν) οἰκτίρμων [ἐστίν].		

IQP 1992: [( )][1]σθε υἱοί [(< >)][2] ()[3].
IQP 1992: [5]⸂ [( )][6] ⸃[5] (καὶ βρέχει)[7] ( )[7].

PH: [5]⸂ (ἀγαθοὺς)[6] ⸃[5] (καὶ βρέχει ἐπὶ δικαίους καὶ ἀδίκους)[7].

5 Is πονηρούς in first (Matthew) or second (Luke) position?
6 Luke's τοὺς ἀχαρίστους or Matthew's ἀγαθούς.
7 Matthew's second clause καὶ βρέχει ἐπὶ δικαίους καὶ ἀδίκους.

damit ihr Söhne eures Vaters werdet, denn er lässt seine Sonne aufgehen über Böse und ⟦Gute, und er lässt regnen über Gerechte und Ungerechte⟧.

afin que vous deveniez les fils de votre Père, parce qu'il fait lever son soleil sur les méchants et les ⟦bons, et qu'il fait pleuvoir sur les justes et les injustes⟧.

Q 6:36 is to be found below, between Q 6:29, ⟦29↔30/Matt 5:41⟧, 30-32, 34 and Q 6:37-38.

Q 6:29

Exod 21:24a-b LXX = Lev 24:20b-c LXX = Deut 19:21c-d LXX	Matt 5:42b	Matt 5:38-40	Q 6:29
		5:38 [1]⸂	[1]⸂
		(Ἠκούσατε ὅτι ἐρρέθη·	()[2]
ὀφθαλμὸν ἀντὶ ὀφθαλμοῦ, ὀδόντα ἀντὶ ὀδόντος,		ὀφθαλμὸν ἀντὶ ὀφθαλμοῦ καὶ ὀδόντα ἀντὶ ὀδόντος. **5:39** ἐγὼ δὲ λέγω ὑμῖν μὴ ἀντιστῆναι τῷ πονηρῷ· ἀλλ')[2]	
		(ὅστις)[3] ⸂σε⸃[4] (ῥαπίζ)[5](ει)[3] ⸂ ⸃[4] (εἰς)[6] τὴν (δεξιὰν)[7] σιαγόνα (σου)[8], (στρέψον)[9] (αὐτῷ)[3] καὶ τὴν ἄλλην·	⟦(ὅστις)[3]⟧ ⸂σε⸃[4] ⟦(ῥαπίζ)[5](ει)[3]⟧ ⸂ ⸃[4] (εἰς)[6] τὴν ()[7] σιαγόνα ⟦()[8]⟧, (στρέψον)[9] ⟦(αὐτῷ)[3]⟧ καὶ τὴν ἄλλην·
	([καὶ τ])ὸν (θέλοντ)α ἀπὸ ([σοῦ]) δανίσασθαι [μὴ] ἀποστραφῇς.	**5:40** καὶ (τῷ θέλοντί σοι κριθῆναι καί)[10] ⸂ ⸃[11] τὸν χιτῶνά ⸂σου⸃[11] (λαβεῖν, ἄφες αὐτῷ)[10] καὶ τὸ ἱμάτιον· ⸃[1]⇒ Matt 5:42	καὶ ⟦(τῷ θέλοντί σοι κριθῆναι καί)[10]⟧ ⸂⸃[11] τὸν χιτῶνά ⸂σου⸃[11] ⟦(λαβεῖν, ἄφες αὐτῷ)[10]⟧ καὶ τὸ ἱμάτιον. ⸃[1]⇒ Q 6:30

JMR: Q **6:29-30** before Q **6:27-28**.
IQP 1992: [( )][3] ⸂⸃[4] (ῥαπίζ)[5][( )][3] ⸂σε⸃[4].

IQP 1992: (στρέψον)[9] ( )[3] καὶ τὴν ἄλλην.

[1] The position of Q 6:29-30 in Q 6:27-36: After Q 6:28 and before Q 6:31 (Lukan order); or after Q 16:18 (Matt 5:32) and before Q 6:27 (Matt 5:44) (Matthean order).
[2] Matthew's antithetical introduction.
[3] Luke's τῷ or Matthew's ὅστις … αὐτῷ and the form of the verb.
[4] The position of σε after (Luke) or before (Matthew) the verb.

Q

⟦ὅς<>⟧ σε ⟦ῥαπίζει⟧ εἰς τὴν σιαγόνα, στρέψον ⟦αὐτῷ⟧ καὶ τὴν ἄλλην· καὶ ⟦τῷ θέλοντί σοι κριθῆναι καὶ⟧ τὸν χιτῶνά σου ⟦λαβεῖν, ἄφες αὐτῷ⟧ καὶ τὸ ἱμάτιον.

⟦The one who slaps⟧ you on the cheek, offer ⟦him⟧ the other as well; and ⟦to the person wanting to take you to court and get⟧ your shirt, ⟦turn over to him⟧ the coat as well.

Q 6:30 is to be found below, between Q 6:⟦29↔30/Matt 5:41⟧ and Q 6:31.

Q 6:29

Luke 6:29	Luke 6:30b	*Did* 1.4b,d	Gospel of Thomas
[1]ʃ			
( )[2]			
[τῷ][3]		**1.4b** ἐάν τίς	
ʃ ʅ[4] [τύπτ][5][οντί][3] ʃσεʅ[4]		σοι δῷ ῥάπισμα	
[ἐπὶ][6]		εἰς	
τὴν ( )[7] σιαγόνα		τὴν δεξιὰν σιαγόνα	
( )[8]			
[πάρεχε][9]		στρέψον	
( )[3] καὶ τὴν ἄλλην,		αὐτῷ καὶ τὴν ἄλλην,	
		καὶ ἔσῃ τέλειος.	
καὶ [ἀπὸ τοῦ αἴροντός][10]	[(καὶ) ἀπὸ (τ)οῦ αἴροντος]	**1.4d** ἐὰν ἄρῃ τις	
ʃσουʅ[11] τὸ ἱμάτιον ʃ ʅ[11]	τὰ [(σ)]ὰ	τὸ ἱμάτιόν σου,	
καὶ τὸν χιτῶνα		δὸς αὐτῷ	
[μὴ κωλύσῃς][10].	[μὴ] ἀπαίτει.	καὶ τὸν χιτῶνα·	
ʅ[1]⇒ Luke 6:30			

IQP 1992: [ ][10].

JSK: [( )][10].

[5] Luke's τύπτοντι or Matthew's ῥαπίζει.
[6] Luke's ἐπί or Matthew's εἰς.
[7] Matthew's δεξιάν.
[8] Matthew's σου.

[9] Luke's πάρεχε or Matthew's στρέψον.
[10] Luke's instance of violence or Matthew's court scene.
[11] Is σου before τὸ ἱμάτιον (Luke) or after τὸν χιτῶνα (Matthew)?

⟦Dem, der⟧ dich auf die Wange schlägt, ⟦dem⟧ halte auch die andere hin, und ⟦dem, der dich vor Gericht bringen und dir⟧ dein Untergewand ⟦nehmen will, dem überlass⟧ auch den Mantel.

⟦À celui qui⟧ te ⟦frappe⟧ à la joue, rends⟦-lui⟧ aussi l'autre; et ⟦à celui qui veut te traîner en justice et prendre⟧ ta chemise, ⟦laisse-lui⟧ aussi «ton» manteau.

Q 6:30 is to be found below, between Q 6:⟦29↔30/Matt 5:41⟧ and Q 6:31.

Q 6:⟦29↔30/Matt 5:41⟧

Did 1.4c	Matthean Doublet	Matt 5:41	Q 6:⟦29↔30/Matt 5:41⟧
ἐὰν ἀγγαρεύσῃ σέ τις μίλιον ἕν, ὕπαγε μετ᾽ αὐτοῦ δύο.		(καὶ ὅστις σε ἀγγαρεύσει μίλιον ἕν, ὕπαγε μετ᾽ αὐτοῦ δύο.)[0]	⟦(«καὶ ὅστις σε ἀγγαρεύσει μίλιον ἕν, ὕπαγε μετ᾽ αὐτοῦ δύο.»)[0]⟧

IQP 1992, JMR: ( )[0].

[0] Is Matt 5:41 in Q?

Q

⟦«καὶ ὅστις σε ἀγγαρεύσει μίλιον ἕν, ὕπαγε μετ᾽ αὐτοῦ δύο.»⟧	⟦«And the one who conscripts you for one mile, go with him a second.»⟧

Q 6:⟦29↔30/Matt 5:41⟧

Luke	Lukan Doublet	Markan Parallel	Gospel of Thomas
( )⁰			

⟦«Und mit dem, der dich zu einer Meile Frondienst zwingt, gehe zwei.»⟧

⟦«Et celui qui t'engagerait à faire un mille, fais-en deux avec lui.»⟧

Q 6:30

Markan Parallel	Matt 5:40	Matt 5:42	Q 6:30
		(τῷ)[1] αἰτοῦντί σε δ(ός)[2],	(τῷ)[1] αἰτοῦντί σε δ(ός)[2],
	([καὶ] [τ])ῷ (θέλοντ)ί σοι κριθῆναι καὶ [τ]ὸν χιτῶνά ([σ]οῦ) λαβεῖν, ἄφες αὐτῷ καὶ τὸ ἱμάτιον·	καὶ [ ][3] τ(ὸν θέλοντα ἀπὸ)[4] [ ][4] σ(οῦ δανίσασθαι)[4]	καὶ ⟦[ἀπὸ][3]⟧ τ⟦[οῦ][4] (δανι)[4] <ζομένου>[4], [τὰ][4]⟧ σ⟦[ὰ][4]⟧
		μὴ ἀπ(οστραφῇς)[3]. ⸂Matt 5:38[1]	μὴ ἀπ⟦[αίτει][3]⟧. ⸂Q 6:29[1]

IQP 1992: [ἀπὸ] τ⟦[οῦ][4] (δανισα)[4]<μένου>[4]⟧ [ ][4] σ[ ][4].

[1] Luke's παντί or Matthew's τῷ.

[2] Luke's δίδου or Matthew's δός.

Q

τῷ αἰτοῦντί σε δός, καὶ ⟦ἀπὸ⟧ τ⟦οῦ δανι<ζομένου>, τὰ⟧ σ⟦ὰ⟧ μὴ ἀπ⟦αίτει⟧.

To the one who asks of you, give; and ⟦from the one who borrows⟧, do not ⟦ask⟧ back ⟦«what is»⟧ yours.

Gos. Thom. 95 (Nag Hammadi II 2)

(1) [Λέγει Ἰησοῦς]· ἐὰν ἔχητε ἀργύριον, μὴ δανείζετε, (2) ἀλλὰ δίδοτε [αὐτὸ] παρ' οὗ οὐκ ἀπολήμψεσθε αὐτά.

(1) [Jesus says:] If you have money, do not lend out at interest. (2) Rather, give [it] to the one from whom you will not get it (back)[1] .

[1] Or: to the one from whom you will not get it (the interest).

Q 6:30

Luke 6:30	Luke 6:29b	*Did* 1.5a	*Gos. Thom.* 95
[παντὶ][1] αἰτοῦντί σε		παντὶ τῷ αἰτοῦντί σε	95.1 [ⲡⲉϫⲉ ⲓ̅ⲥ̅ ϫⲉ]
δ[ίδου][2],		δίδου	ⲉϣⲱⲡⲉ
καὶ [ἀπὸ][3]	[(καὶ) ἀπὸ	καὶ	ⲟⲩⲛ̄ⲧⲏⲧⲛ̄ ϩⲟⲙⲧ'
τ[οῦ	τοῦ		ⲙ̄ⲡⲣ̄ϯ ⲉⲧⲙⲏⲥⲉ
αἴροντος	αἴροντος]		95.2 ⲁⲗⲗⲁ ϯ [ⲙ̄ⲙⲟϥ]
τὰ][4] σ[ὰ][4]	([σ]ου) τὸ ἱμάτιον		ⲙ̣ⲡⲉⲧ̣[ⲉ]ⲧⲛⲁϫⲓⲧⲟⲩ
	καὶ τὸν χιτῶνα		
μὴ ἀπ[αίτει][3].	[(μὴ)] κωλύσῃς.	μὴ ἀπαίτει.	ⲁⲛ ⲛ̄ⲧⲟⲟⲧϥ'
↰Luke 6:29[1]			

[3] Luke's ἀπὸ … μὴ ἀπαίτει or Matthew's μὴ ἀποστραφῇς.

[4] Luke's τοῦ αἴροντος τὰ σά or Matthew's τὸν θέλοντα ἀπὸ σοῦ δανίσασθαι (see δανίσητε at Q 6:34 variation unit [1]).

Dem, der dich bittet, gib; und ⟦von dem, der sich leiht, fordere das⟧ Deine nicht zurück.

À celui qui te demande, donne; et ⟦à qui emprunte de⟧ tes ⟦biens⟧, ne réclame «rien».

(1) [Jesus spricht:] Wenn ihr Geld habt, gebt (es) nicht gegen Zins. (2) Vielmehr gebt [es] dem, von dem ihr es nicht (zurück)erhalten werdet[2].

[2] Oder: dem, von dem ihr sie (die Zinsen) nicht erhalten werdet.

(1) [Jésus dit:] Si vous avez de l'argent, ne (le) prêtez pas à intérêt. (2) Mais donnez[-le] à celui de qui vous ne le[3] recevrez pas (en retour).

[3] Ou: à celui de qui vous ne les (les intérêts) recevrez pas.

Q 6:31

Did 1.2d	Matt 22:40	Matt 7:12	Q 6:31
		¹⸀	¹⸀
πάντα δὲ ὅσα ἐὰν		(Πάντα οὖν ὅσα ἐὰν)²	[καὶ καθὼς]²
θελήσῃς μὴ γίνεσθαί		θέλ(η)²τε ἵνα ποιῶσιν	θέλ[ε]²τε ἵνα ποιῶσιν
σοι,		ὑμῖν οἱ ἄνθρωποι,	ὑμῖν οἱ ἄνθρωποι,
		³⸀ο(ὕτ)⁴ως⸃³	³⸀ο(ὕτ)⁴ως ⸃³
καὶ σὺ ἄλλῳ μὴ ποίει.		(καὶ ὑμεῖς)⁵ ποιεῖτε αὐτοῖς·	()⁵ ποιεῖτε αὐτοῖς
	ἐν ταύταις ταῖς δυσὶν	⸀ ⸃³	⸀⸃³
	ἐντολαῖς ὅλος (ὁ νόμος)	(οὗτος γάρ ἐστιν ὁ νόμος	
	κρέμαται (καὶ οἱ προφῆται).	καὶ οἱ προφῆται)⁶. ⸃¹	()⁶. ⸃¹

JMR: Q **6:31** after Q **6:29-30** and before Q **6:27-28**.

¹ The position of Q 6:31 in the Q Sermon: Between Q 6:30 and Q 6:32 (Lukan order); or after Q 11:13 (Matt 7:11) and before Q 13:24 (Matt 7:13) (Matthean order).

² Luke's καὶ καθὼς θέλετε or Matthew's πάντα οὖν ὅσα ἐὰν θέλητε.

Q

καὶ καθὼς θέλετε ἵνα ποιῶσιν ὑμῖν οἱ ἄνθρωποι, οὕτως ποιεῖτε αὐτοῖς.	And the way you want people to treat you, that is how you treat them.

Gos. Thom. 6.3 (Nag Hammadi II 2)

καὶ ὅ τι μισεῖτε μὴ ποιεῖτε.

And do not do what you hate.

Gos. Thom. 6.3 (P. Oxy. 654)

[καὶ ὅ τι μισ]εῖτε μὴ ποιεῖτ[ε·]

[and] do not do [what] you [hate].

Q 6:31

Luke 6:31	Lukan Doublet	Markan Parallel	*Gos. Thom.* 6.3
[1]⸂			
[Καὶ καθὼς][2]			ⲁⲩⲱ ⲡⲉⲧⲉⲧⲙ̄ⲙⲟⲥⲧⲉ
θέλ[ε][2]τε ἵνα ποιῶσιν			ⲙ̄ⲙⲟϥ’
ὑμῖν οἱ ἄνθρωποι			
⸂ ⸃[3]			
( )[5] ποιεῖτε αὐτοῖς			ⲙ̄ⲡⲣ̄ⲁⲁϥ
[3]⸂ὁ[μοί][4]ως⸃[3]			
( )[6]. ⸃[1]			

[3] The position of ὁμοίως (Luke) or οὕτως (Matthew) after the command (Luke) or before the command (Matthew).

[4] Luke's ὁμοίως or Matthew's οὕτως.

[5] Matthew's καὶ ὑμεῖς.

[6] Matthew's οὗτος γάρ ἐστιν ὁ νόμος καὶ οἱ προφῆται.

Und wie ihr wollt, dass euch die Menschen tun, so tut ihr ihnen.

Et comme vous voulez que les hommes agissent envers vous, ainsi vous agissez envers eux.

Und tut nicht das, was ihr hasst.

et ce que vous haïssez, ne le faites pas.

[und] tut nicht [das, was] ihr [hasst].

[et ce que] vous [haïssez], ne le faites pas.

Q 6:32

Did 1.3c	Matt 5:47	Matt 5:46	Q 6:32
		^{0}[	^{0}[
		^{1}∫	^{1}∫
ποία γὰρ χάρις ἐὰν	[καὶ] ([ἐὰν])	[ ]^{2} ἐ(ὰν)^{3} (γὰρ)^{2}	[ ]^{2} ε⟦[ὶ]^{3}⟧ ( )^{2}
ἀγαπᾶτε	ἀσπάσησθε	ἀγαπ(ήσῃ)^{3}τε	ἀγαπ⟦[ᾶ]^{3}⟧τε
τοὺς ἀγαπῶντας	[(τοὺς)] ἀδελφοὺς	τοὺς ἀγαπῶντας	τοὺς ἀγαπῶντας
ὑμᾶς;	([ὑμ])ῶν μόνον,	ὑμᾶς,	ὑμᾶς,
	(τί)	(τίνα)^{4}	(τίνα)^{4}
	περισσὸν ποιεῖτε;	(μισθὸν ἔχετε)^{5};	(μισθὸν ἔχετε)^{5};
οὐχὶ καὶ	(ουχὶ [καὶ	(οὐχὶ)^{6} καὶ [ ]^{6}	(οὐχὶ)^{6} καὶ []^{6}
τὰ ἔθνη	οἱ]) ἐθνικοὶ	οἱ (τελῶναι)^{7}	οἱ (τελῶναι)^{7}
τοῦτο	([τὸ αὐτὸ	τὸ[ ]^{8} αὐτὸ[ ]^{8}	τὸ[]^{8} αὐτὸ[]^{8}
ποιοῦσιν;	ποιοῦσιν]);	(ποιοῦ)^{8}σιν;	(ποιοῦ)^{8}σιν;
		≀^{1}⇒ Matt 5:47	≀^{1}⇒ Q 6:34
		]^{0}	]^{0}

JMR: Q **6:32, 34** in Q after Q **6:27-28, 35c-d.**

Text Critical Note (see the discussion in the front matter): In Luke 6:33 γάρ is absent in ℵ^{2} A D L W Θ Ξ Ψ *f* ^{13} 33 𝔐 latt sy co, but present in 𝔓^{75} ℵ* B. In Luke 6:33b γάρ follows καί in A D L Θ Ξ Ψ *f* ^{13} 33 𝔐 lat sy$^{P.h}$.

0 Are Luke 6:32, 33 both in Q, or is Luke 6:33 a redactional doublet?

1 The position of Q 6:32, 34 in Q: After Q 6:31 and before Q 6:35c-d, 36 (Lukan order); or after Q 6:27-28, 35c-d (Matt 5:43-45) and before Q 11:2b (Matt 6:9) (Matthean order).

2 Luke's καί or Matthew's postpositive γάρ (see also Luke 6:33: γάρ).

Q

.. ε⟦ὶ⟧ .. ἀγαπ⟦ᾶ⟧τε τοὺς ἀγαπῶντας ὑμᾶς, τίνα μισθὸν ἔχετε; οὐχὶ καὶ οἱ τελῶναι τὸ αὐτὸ ποιοῦσιν;	.. If you love those loving you, what reward do you have? Do not even tax collectors do the same?

Q 6:32

Luke 6:32	Luke 6:33	Luke 6:34	Gospel of Thomas
^{0}[	^{0}[		
^{1}ʃ			
[καὶ]^{2} ε[ἰ]^{3} ( )^{2}	[καὶ] (γὰρ) ([ἐ]ὰν)	[καὶ] ([ἐ]ὰν)	
ἀγαπ[ᾶ]^{3}τε	ἀγαθοποι(ῆ[τε]	δανίσῃ[(τε)]	
τοὺς ἀγαπῶντας	[τοὺς)] ἀγαθοποιοῦντας	παρ' ὧν ἐλπίζετε	
ὑμᾶς,	[(ὑμᾶς,)	λαβεῖν,	
[ποία]^{4}	ποία	[ποία	
[ὑμῖν χάρις ἐστίν]^{5};	ὑμῖν χάρις ἐστίν;	ὑμῖν χάρις ἐστίν;	
( )^{6} καὶ [γὰρ]^{6}	καὶ]	(καὶ)]	
οἱ [ἁμαρτωλοὶ]^{7}	[(οἱ) ἁμαρτωλοὶ	[ἁμαρτωλοὶ]	
το[ὺς ἀγαπῶντας]^{8} αὐτο[ὺς]^{8}	(τὸ] αὐτὸ	ἁμαρτωλοῖς δανίζουσιν	
[ἀγαπῶ]^{8}σιν.	ποιοῦ[σιν]).	ἵνα ἀπολάβωσιν τὰ ἴσα.	
ʅ^{1}⇒ Luke 6:34			
]^{0}	]^{0}		

3 Luke's εἰ ἀγαπᾶτε or Matthew's ἐὰν … ἀγαπήσητε (see also Luke 6:33: ἀγαθοποιῆτε).
4 Luke's ποία or Matthew's τίνα.
5 Luke's ὑμῖν χάρις ἐστίν or Matthew's μισθὸν ἔχετε.
6 Luke's postpositive γάρ or Matthew's οὐχί.
7 Luke's ἁμαρτωλοί or Matthew's τελῶναι.
8 Luke's τοὺς ἀγαπῶντας αὐτοὺς ἀγαπῶσιν or Matthew's τὸ αὐτὸ ποιοῦσιν (see also Luke 6:33 and Matt 5:47: τὸ αὐτὸ ποιοῦσιν).

.. Wenn ihr die liebt, die euch lieben, welchen Lohn habt ihr? Tun dasselbe nicht auch die Zöllner?

.. Si vous aimez ceux qui vous aiment, quelle récompense méritez-vous? Les collecteurs d'impôts aussi ne font-ils pas la même chose?

Q 6:34

Markan Parallel	Matt 5:46	Matt 5:47	Q 6:34
	[(ἐὰν)] γὰρ	καὶ ἐὰν	καὶ ἐὰν
	ἀγαπή([σητε]	(ἀσπάσησθε	⟦[δανίσητε
	τοὺς) ἀγαπωντας	τοὺς ἀδελφοὺς	παρ' ὧν ἐλπίζετε
	(ὑμ)ᾶς,	ὑμῶν μόνον)[1],	λαβεῖν][1],
	(τι)να	(τί	(τί)[3]<να
	μισθὸν ἔχετε;	περισσὸν ποιεῖτε)[2];	μισθὸν ἔχε>[2](τε)[2]⟧;
	(οὐχὶ [καὶ]	(οὐχὶ)[3] καὶ	(οὐχὶ)[3] καὶ
	οἱ) τελῶναι	(οἱ ἐθνικ)[4]οὶ	⟦(οἱ ἐθνικ)[4]⟧οὶ
	τὸ αὐτὸ	(τὸ αὐτὸ	(τὸ αὐτὸ
	ποιοῦσιν;)	ποι)[5]οῦσιν;	ποι)[5]οῦσιν;
		≀ Matt 5:46[1]	≀ Q 6:32[1]

IQP 1993 (based on Matt 5:47 par. Luke 6:33/34): καὶ ⟦[ ]⟧ ἐὰν [( )][1] (τοὺς ἀδελφοὺς ὑμῶν)[1], ⟦(τί)[2]<να μισθὸν ἔχε>[2](τε)[2]⟧;

[1] Luke's δανίσητε παρ' ὧν ἐλπίζετε λαβεῖν (see Matt 5:42 δανίσασθαι at Q 6:30, variation unit [4]), or Matthew's ἀσπάσησθε τοὺς ἀδελφοὺς ὑμῶν μόνον.

[2] Luke's ποία ὑμῖν χάρις ἐστίν or Matthew's τί περισσὸν ποιεῖτε.

[3] Matthew's οὐχί.

Q

καὶ ἐὰν ⟦δανίσητε παρ' ὧν ἐλπίζετε λαβεῖν, τί<να μισθὸν ἔχε>τε⟧; οὐχὶ καὶ ⟦οἱ ἐθνικ⟧οὶ τὸ αὐτὸ ποιοῦσιν;

And if you ⟦lend «to those» from whom you hope to receive, what <reward do> you <have>?⟧ Do not even ⟦the Gentiles⟧ do the same?

Gos. Thom. 95 (Nag Hammadi II 2)

(1) [Λέγει 'Ιησοῦς]· ἐὰν ἔχητε ἀργύριον, μὴ δανείζετε, (2) ἀλλὰ δίδοτε [αὐτὸ] παρ' οὗ οὐκ ἀπολήμψεσθε αὐτά.

(1) [Jesus says:] If you have money, do not lend out at interest. (2) Rather, give [it] to the one from whom you will not receive it (back)[1].

[1] Or: to the one from whom you will not receive it (the interest).

Q 6:35c-d is to be found above, between Q 6:27-28 and Q 6:29, ⟦29↔30/Matt 5:41⟧, 30-32, 34.

Q 6:34

Luke 6:34	Luke 6:32	Luke 6:33	*Gos. Thom.* 95
			95.1 [ⲡⲉϫⲉ ⲓ̅ⲥ̅ ϫⲉ]
καὶ ἐὰν	[(καὶ)] εἰ	([καὶ]) γὰρ ([ἐὰν])	ⲉϣⲱⲡⲉ
[δανίσητε	ἀγαπᾶτε	ἀγαθοποιῆτε	ⲟⲩⲛ̅ⲧⲏⲧⲛ̅ ϩⲟⲙⲧ'
παρ' ὧν ἐλπίζετε	(τοὺς) ἀγαπῶντας	(τοὺς) ἀγαθοποιοῦντας	ⲙ̅ⲡⲣ̅ϯ ⲉⲧⲙⲏⲥⲉ
λαβεῖν][1],	(ὑμ)ᾶς,	(ὑμ)ᾶς,	95.2 ⲁⲗⲗⲁ ϯ [ⲙ̅ⲙⲟϥ]
[ποία	[ποία	[ποία	ⲙ̣̅ⲡⲉⲧ̣[ⲉ]ⲧⲛⲁϫⲓⲧⲟⲩ
ὑμῖν χάρις ἐστίν][2];	ὑμῖν χάρις ἐστίν];	ὑμῖν χάρις ἐστίν;	
( )[3] καὶ	[(καὶ)] γὰρ	(καὶ]	ⲁⲛ ⲛ̅ⲧⲟⲟⲧϥ'
[ἁμαρτωλ][4]οὶ	(οἱ) [ἁμαρτωλοὶ]	οἱ) [ἁμαρτωλοὶ]	
[ἁμαρτωλοῖς δανίζ][5]ουσιν	τοὺς ἀγαπῶντας αὐτοὺς	(τὸ αὐτὸ	
[ἵνα ἀπολάβωσιν τὰ ἴσα.][5]	ἀγαπῶσιν.	ποιοῦσιν).	
ʅ Luke 6:32[1]			

JMR: ⟦(ἀσπάσησθε τοὺς ἀδελφοὺς ὑμῶν μόνον)[1]⟧.

PH: (οἱ ἐθνικ)[4]οί.

[4] Luke's ἁμαρτωλοί or Matthew's οἱ ἐθνικοί.

[5] Luke's ἁμαρτωλοῖς δανίζουσιν ἵνα ἀπολάβωσιν τὰ ἴσα or Matthew's τὸ αὐτὸ ποιοῦσιν (see Matt 5:46 and Luke 6:33: τὸ αὐτὸ ποιοῦσιν).

Und wenn ihr ⟦«denen» leiht, von denen ihr hofft, «es» zurückzubekommen, welchen <Lohn habt> ihr⟧? Tun dasselbe nicht auch ⟦die Heiden⟧?

Et si ⟦vous prêtez «à ceux» dont vous espérez récupérer, quelle <récompense méritez>-vous? Les Gentils⟧ aussi ne font-il pas la même chose?

(1) [Jesus spricht:] Wenn ihr Geld habt, gebt (es) nicht gegen Zins. (2) Vielmehr gebt [es] dem, von dem ihr es nicht (zurück)erhalten werdet[2].

[2] Oder: dem, von dem ihr sie (die Zinsen) nicht erhalten werdet.

(1) [Jésus dit:] Si vous avez de l'argent, ne (le) prêtez pas à intérêt. (2) Mais donnez[-le] à celui de qui vous ne le[3] recevrez pas (en retour).

[3] Ou: à celui de qui vous ne les (les intérêts) recevrez pas.

Q 6:35c-d is to be found above, between Q 6:27-28 and Q 6:29, ⟦29↔30/Matt 5:41⟧, 30-32, 34.

Q 6:36

Markan Parallel	Matt 5:45	Matt 5:48	Q 6:36
		₁⸉	₁⸉
	ὅπως [γ]έ[ν]η[σθε]	(ἔσ)²εσθε	⟦[γίν]²⟧εσθε
	υἱοὶ	(οὖν)³	()³
	τοῦ πατρὸς ὑμῶν	(ὑμεῖς)⁴	()⁴
	τοῦ ἐν οὐρανοῖς,	(τέλειοι)⁵	[οἰκτίρμονες]⁵
	ὅτι τὸν ἥλιον	[ ]⁶ὡς	[]⁶ὡς
	αὐτοῦ ἀνατέλλει	[ ]⁷	[ ]⁷
	ἐπὶ πονηροὺς καὶ ἀγαθοὺς	ὁ πατὴρ ὑμῶν	ὁ πατὴρ ὑμῶν
	καὶ βρέχει ἐπὶ δικαίους	(ὁ οὐράνιος)⁸	()⁸
	καὶ ἀδίκους.	(τέλειός)⁵ ἐστιν.	[οἰκτίρμων]⁵ ἐστίν.
		⸊¹	⸊¹

1 The position of Q 6:36 in Q: After Q 6:35c,d and before Q 6:37 (Lukan order); or after Q 6:34 (Matt 5:47) and before Q 11:2b-4 (Matt 6:9-13a) (Matthean order).

2 Luke's γίνεσθε or Matthew's ἔσεσθε.

3 Matthew's οὖν.

4 Matthew's ὑμεῖς.

Q

⟦γίν⟧εσθε οἰκτίρμονες ὡς .. ὁ πατὴρ ὑμῶν οἰκτίρμων ἐστίν.	Be full of pity, just as your Father .. is full of pity.

Q 6:36

Luke 6:36	Luke 6:35c-d	Markan Parallel	Gospel of Thomas
[1]⸂			
[Γίν][2]εσθε	καὶ (ἔσεσθε)		
( )[3]	υἱοὶ		
( )[4]	ὑψίστου,		
[οἰκτίρμονες][5]			
[καθ][6]ὡς	ὅτι		
[καὶ][7]			
ὁ πατὴρ ὑμῶν	αὐτὸς χρηστός ἐστιν		
( )[8]	ἐπὶ τοὺς ἀχαρίστους		
[οἰκτίρμων][5] ἐστίν.	καὶ πονηρούς.		
⸃[1]			

[5] Luke's οἰκτίρμονες ... οἰκτίρμων or Matthew's τέλειοι ... τέλειος.

[6] Luke's καθώς or Matthew's ὡς.

[7] Luke's καί.

[8] Matthew's ὁ οὐράνιος.

Seid barmherzig, wie .. euer Vater barmherzig ist.

Soyez miséricordieux, comme votre Père .. est miséricordieux.

Q 6:37-38

Mark 4:24	Matthean Doublet	Matt 7:1-2	Q 6:37-38
		[1]ʃ **7:1** [ ][2] Μὴ κρίνετε, (ἵνα)[3] μὴ κριθῆτε· **7:2** (ἐν ᾧ γὰρ κρίματι κρίνετε κριθήσεσθε,)[4] [ ][5]	[1]ʃ **6:37** [ ][2] μὴ κρίνετε, [( )][3] μὴ κριθῆτε· ⟦(ἐν ᾧ γὰρ κρίματι κρίνετε κριθήσεσθε,)[4]⟧ [][5]
			6:38
4:24 Καὶ ἔλεγεν αὐτοῖς· βλέπετε τί ἀκούετε. ἐν ᾧ μέτρῳ μετρεῖτε μετρηθήσεται ὑμῖν καὶ προστεθήσεται ὑμῖν.		ʃ (καὶ)[6] ʅ[6] [7]{(ἐν)[8] ᾧ ʃ [ ][6] ʅ[6] μέτρῳ μετρεῖτε [ ][9]μετρηθήσεται ὑμῖν}[7]. ʅ[1]	⟦ʃ (καὶ)[6] ʅ[6]⟧ [7]{(ἐν)[8] ᾧ ⟦ʃ [][6] ʅ[6]⟧ μέτρῳ μετρεῖτε [][9]μετρηθήσεται ὑμῖν}[7]. ʅ[1]

IQP 1992: [καὶ][2].

IQP 1992: **6:38** ⟦{(ἐν)}[8]⟧.

[1] The position of Q 6:37-38 in Q: After Q 6:36 and before Q 6:39 (Lukan order); or after Q 12:31 (Matt 6:33) and before Q 6:41 (Matt 7:3) (Matthean order).

[2] Luke's καί.

[3] Luke's paratactic formulation and negative, καὶ οὐ, or Matthew's ἵνα.

[4] Matthew's ἐν ᾧ γὰρ κρίματι κρίνετε κριθήσεσθε.

[5] The exhortation and promise of reward in Luke 6:37b-38a.

Q

37 .. μὴ κρίνετε, ... μὴ κριθῆτε· ⟦ἐν ᾧ γὰρ κρίματι κρίνετε κριθήσεσθε,⟧ **38** ⟦καὶ⟧ ἐν ᾧ μέτρῳ μετρεῖτε μετρηθήσεται ὑμῖν.

37.. Do not pass judgment, «so» you are not judged. ⟦For with what judgment you pass judgment, you will be judged.⟧ **38** ⟦And⟧ with the measurement you use to measure out, it will be measured out to you.

Q 6:37-38

Luke 6:37-38	Lukan Doublet	Mark 4:24	Gospel of Thomas
¹ʃ **6:37** [Καὶ]² μὴ κρίνετε, [καὶ οὐ]³ μὴ κριθῆτε· ( )⁴ [καὶ μὴ καταδικάζετε, καὶ οὐ μὴ καταδικασθῆτε. ἀπολύετε, καὶ ἀπολυθήσεσθε· **6:38** δίδοτε, καὶ δοθήσεται ὑμῖν· μέτρον καλὸν πεπιεσμένον σεσαλευμένον ὑπερεκχυννόμενον δώσουσιν εἰς τὸν κόλπον ὑμῶν·]⁵ ʃ ( )⁶ ʅ⁶ ( )⁸ {ᾧ}⁷ ʃ [γὰρ]⁶ ʅ⁶ {μέτρῳ μετρεῖτε}⁷ [ἀντι]⁹{μετρηθήσεται ὑμῖν}⁷. ʅ¹		**4:24** Καὶ ἔλεγεν αὐτοῖς· βλέπετε τί ἀκούετε. ἐν ᾧ μέτρῳ μετρεῖτε μετρηθήσεται ὑμῖν καὶ προστεθήσεται ὑμῖν.	

6 Luke's postpositive γάρ or Matthew's καί.
7 Are the agreements between Luke and Matthew in Q or from Mark?

8 Matthew's ἐν.
9 Luke's ἀντι-.

37 .. Richtet nicht, «so» werdet ihr nicht gerichtet; ⟦denn mit dem Richtspruch, mit dem ihr richtet, werdet ihr gerichtet werden,⟧ **38** ⟦und⟧ mit dem Maß, mit dem ihr messt, wird euch zugemessen werden.

37.. Ne jugez pas, «ainsi» vous n'êtes pas jugés. ⟦C'est selon le critère de jugement avec lequel vous jugez que vous serez jugés.⟧ **38** ⟦Et⟧ c'est la mesure avec laquelle vous mesurez qu'il vous sera mesuré.

Q 6:39

Markan Parallel	Matthean Doublet	Matt 15:14	Q 6:39
		^{0}/	^{0}/
		^{1}ʃ	^{1}ʃ
		[ ]^{2}	[]^{2}
		(ἄφετε αὐτούς· τυφλοί εἰσιν ὁδηγοὶ τυφλῶν·)^{3}	()^{3}
		[ ]^{4} τυφλὸς	[μήτι δύναται]^{4} τυφλὸς
		(δὲ)^{3} τυφλὸν	()^{3} τυφλὸν
		(ἐὰν)^{4} ὁδηγ(ῇ)^{4}, ἀμφότεροι	()^{4} ὁδηγ[εῖν; οὐχὶ]^{4} ἀμφότεροι
		εἰς βόθυνον [ ]^{5}πεσοῦνται.	εἰς βόθυνον []^{5}πεσοῦνται;
		ʅ^{1}	ʅ^{1}
		\\$^{0}$	\\$^{0}$

JMR, PH, JSK: The position of Q 6:39 is very uncertain.

^{0} Is Luke 6:39 par. Matt 15:14 in Q?

^{1} The position of Q 6:39 in Q: After Q 6:38 and before Q 6:40 (Lukan order); or after Q 13:20-21 (Matt 13:33) and before Q 12:⟦54-56⟧ (Matt 16:2-3b) (Matthean order).

Q

μήτι δύναται τυφλὸς τυφλὸν ὁδηγεῖν; οὐχὶ ἀμφότεροι εἰς βόθυνον πεσοῦνται;

Can a blind person show the way to a blind person? Will not both fall into a pit?

Gos. Thom. 34 (Nag Hammadi II 2)

Λέγει Ἰησοῦς· τυφλὸς ἐὰν προάγῃ τυφλόν, ἀμφότεροι πίπτουσιν εἰς βόθυνον.

Jesus says: If a blind person leads a blind person, both fall into a pit.

Q 6:39

Luke 6:39	Lukan Doublet	Markan Parallel	*Gos. Thom.* 34
0/ 1ʃ [Εἶπεν δὲ καὶ παραβολὴν αὐτοῖς·]2 ( )3 [μήτι δύναται]4 τυφλὸς ( )3 τυφλὸν ( )4 ὁδηγ[εῖν; οὐχὶ]4 ἀμφότεροι εἰς βόθυνον [ἐμ]5πεσοῦνται; ʅ1 \0			ⲡⲉϫⲉ ⲓ̅ⲥ̅ ϫⲉ ⲟⲩⲃⲗ̅ⲗⲉ ⲉϥϣⲁⲛ'ⲥⲱⲕ' ϩⲏⲧϥ' ⲛ̅ⲛⲟⲩⲃⲗ̅ⲗⲉ ϣⲁⲩϩⲉ ⲙ̅ⲡⲉⲥⲛⲁⲩ' ⲉⲡⲉⲥⲏⲧ' ⲉⲩϩⲓⲉⲓⲧ'

2 Luke's quotation formula εἶπεν δὲ καὶ παραβολὴν αὐτοῖς.
3 Matthew's introductory statement ἄφετε αὐτούς· τυφλοί εἰσιν ὁδηγοὶ τυφλῶν ... δέ.
4 Luke's double question or Matthew's conditional form.
5 Luke's verb prefix ἐμ-.

Kann etwa ein Blinder einen Blinden führen? Werden nicht beide in eine Grube fallen?

Un aveugle peut-il guider un aveugle? Tous les deux ne tomberont-ils pas dans un trou?

Jesus spricht: Wenn ein Blinder einen Blinden führt, fallen beide in eine Grube.

Jésus dit: Un aveugle, s'il conduit un aveugle, tous les deux tombent dans un trou.

Q 6:40

Markan Parallel	Matthean Doublet	Matt 10:24-25a	Q 6:40
		0/	0/
		1ʃ	1ʃ
		10:24 Οὐκ ἔστιν μαθητὴς ὑπὲρ τὸν διδάσκαλον (οὐδὲ δοῦλος ὑπὲρ τὸν κύριον αὐτοῦ)[2].	οὐκ ἔστιν μαθητὴς ὑπὲρ τὸν διδάσκαλον· ( )[2]
		10:25a (ἀρκετὸν τῷ μαθητῇ)[3] (ἵνα γένη)[4]ται ὡς ὁ διδάσκαλος αὐτοῦ (καὶ ὁ δοῦλος ὡς ὁ κύριος αὐτοῦ)[2].	⟦(ἀρκετὸν τῷ μαθητῇ)[3] (ἵνα γένη)[4]⟧ται ὡς ὁ διδάσκαλος αὐτοῦ ( )[2].
		ʅ1	ʅ1
		\0	\0

JMR; PH; JSK: The position of Q 6:40 is very uncertain.

PH: ⟦(οὐδὲ δοῦλος ὑπὲρ τὸν κύριον αὐτοῦ)[2]⟧ ... ⟦(καὶ ὁ δοῦλος ὡς ὁ κύριος αὐτοῦ)[2]⟧.

[0] Is Q 6:40 in Q?

[1] The position of Q 6:40 in Q: After Q 6:38, (39) and before Q 6:41 (Lukan order); or after Q 12:11-12 (Matt 10:19) and before Q 12:2 (Matt 10:36) (Matthean order).

Q

οὐκ ἔστιν μαθητὴς ὑπὲρ τὸν διδάσκαλον· ⟦ἀρκετὸν τῷ μαθητῇ ἵνα γένη⟧ται ὡς ὁ διδάσκαλος αὐτοῦ.

A disciple is not superior to «one's» teacher. ⟦It is enough for the disciple that he become⟧ like his teacher.

Q 6:40

Luke 6:40	Lukan Doublet	Markan Parallel	John 13:16b = 15:20b
⁰/ ₁ʃ οὐκ ἔστιν μαθητὴς ὑπὲρ τὸν διδάσκαλον· ( )[2] [κατηρτισμένος δὲ πᾶς][3] [ἔσ][4]ται ὡς ὁ διδάσκαλος αὐτοῦ ( )[2]. ʅ1 \0			οὐκ ἔστιν δοῦλος μείζων τοῦ κυρίου αὐτοῦ

IQP 1991: ⟦[κατηρτισμένος δὲ πᾶς][3]⟧ [ἔσ][4]ται.

[2] Matthew's slave-master correlation (*bis*).

[3] Luke's κατηρτισμένος δὲ πᾶς or Matthew's ἀρκετὸν τῷ μαθητῇ.

[4] Luke's ἔσται or Matthew's ἵνα γένηται.

Der Schüler ist nicht mehr als der Lehrer; ⟦es genügt für den Schüler, dass er⟧ wie sein Lehrer ⟦wird⟧.

Un disciple n'est pas au-dessus de «son» maître. ⟦Il suffit au disciple de devenir⟧ comme son maître.

Q 6:41

Markan Parallel	Matthean Doublet	Matt 7:3	Q 6:41
		τί δὲ βλέπεις τὸ κάρφος τὸ ἐν τῷ ὀφθαλμῷ τοῦ ἀδελφοῦ σου, τὴν δὲ ⸉ ⸊[1] ἐν τῷ (σ)[2]ῷ ὀφθαλμῷ ⸉δοκὸν [ ][1] ⸊[1] οὐ κατανοεῖς;	τί δὲ βλέπεις τὸ κάρφος τὸ ἐν τῷ ὀφθαλμῷ τοῦ ἀδελφοῦ σου, τὴν δὲ ⸉⸊[1] ἐν τῷ (σ)[2]ῷ ὀφθαλμῷ ⸉δοκὸν [][1] ⸊[1] οὐ κατανοεῖς;

[1] The position of δοκόν: before the prepositional phrase and with the repetition of the article (Luke), or δοκόν only, positioned after the prepositional phrase (Matthew).

[2] Luke's ἰδίῳ or Matthew's σῷ.

Q

τί δὲ βλέπεις τὸ κάρφος τὸ ἐν τῷ ὀφθαλμῷ τοῦ ἀδελφοῦ σου, τὴν δὲ ἐν τῷ σῷ ὀφθαλμῷ δοκὸν οὐ κατανοεῖς;

And why do you see the speck in your brother's eye, but the beam in your own eye you overlook?

Gos. Thom. 26.1 (Nag Hammadi II 2)

Λέγει Ἰησοῦς· τὸ κάρφος τὸ ἐν τῷ ὀφθαλμῷ τοῦ ἀδελφοῦ σου βλέπεις, τὴν δὲ δοκὸν τὴν ἐν τῷ ὀφθαλμῷ σου οὐ βλέπεις.

Jesus says: The speck in your brother's eye you see, but the beam in your own eye you do not see.

Q 6:41

Luke 6:41	Lukan Doublet	Markan Parallel	*Gos. Thom.* 26.1
Τί δὲ βλέπεις τὸ κάρφος τὸ ἐν τῷ ὀφθαλμῷ τοῦ ἀδελφοῦ σου, τὴν δὲ ⸉δοκὸν [τὴν][1] ⸆[1] ἐν τῷ [ἰδί][2]ῳ ὀφθαλμῷ ⸊ ⸆[1] οὐ κατανοεῖς;			ⲡⲉϫⲉ ⲓ̅ⲥ̅ ϫⲉ ⲡϫⲏ ⲉⲧϩⲙ̄ ⲡⲃⲁⲗ ⲙ̄ⲡⲉⲕ'ⲥⲟⲛ ⲕⲛⲁⲩ ⲉⲣⲟϥ' ⲡⲥⲟⲉⲓ ⲇⲉ ⲉⲧϩⲙ̄ ⲡⲉⲕⲃⲁⲗ' ⲕⲛⲁⲩ ⲁⲛ ⲉⲣⲟϥ'

Und was siehst du den Splitter im Auge deines Bruders, aber den Balken in deinem Auge bemerkst du nicht?

Et pourquoi vois-tu la paille qui est dans l'œil de ton frère, mais la poutre qui est dans ton œil ne la remarques-tu pas?

Jesus spricht: Den Splitter im Auge deines Bruders siehst du, den Balken aber in deinem Auge siehst du nicht.

Jésus dit: La paille qui est dans l'œil de ton frère, tu la vois, mais la poutre qui est dans ton œil, tu ne la vois pas.

Q 6:42

Markan Parallel	Matthean Doublet	Matt 7:4-5	Q 6:42
		(ἢ)[1] πῶς	()[1] πῶς
		(ἐρεῖς)[2]	[ ][2]
		τῷ ἀδελφῷ σου· [ ][3]	τῷ ἀδελφῷ σοῦ· [][3]
		ἄφες ἐκβάλω τὸ κάρφος	ἄφες ἐκβάλω τὸ κάρφος
		(ἐκ)[4]	⟦(ἐκ)[4]⟧
		τ(οῦ)[4] ὀφθαλμ(οῦ)[4] σου,	τ⟦(οὺ)[4]⟧ ὀφθαλμ⟦(οῦ)[4]⟧ σου,
		(καὶ ἰδοὺ)[5] ἡ[ ][5]	(καὶ ἰδοὺ)[5] ἡ[][5]
		[6]⸂δοκὸ(ς)[5] ⸃[6]	[6]⸂ δοκὸ(ς)[5] ⸃[6]
		ἐν τῷ ὀφθαλμῷ σοῦ	ἐν τῷ ὀφθαλμῷ σοῦ
		⸂ ⸃[6];	[6]⸂ [][5] ⸃[6];
		7:5 ὑποκριτά, ἔκβαλε	ὑποκριτά, ἔκβαλε
		πρῶτον ⸂ ⸃[7]	πρῶτον ⸂⸃[7]
		ἐκ τοῦ ὀφθαλμοῦ σου	ἐκ τοῦ ὀφθαλμοῦ σου
		⸂τὴν δοκόν⸃[7],	⸂τὴν δοκόν⸃[7],
		καὶ τότε διαβλέψεις	καὶ τότε διαβλέψεις
		⸂ἐκβαλεῖν⸃[8]	⸂ἐκβαλεῖν⸃[8]
		τὸ κάρφος (ἐκ)[9]	τὸ κάρφος [ ][9]
		τ(οῦ)[9] ὀφθαλμ(οῦ)[9]	τ[ ][9] ὀφθαλμ[ ][9]
		τοῦ ἀδελφοῦ σου	τοῦ ἀδελφοῦ σου
		⸂ ⸃[8].	⸂⸃[8].

IQP 1990: ⟦[δύνασαι λέγειν][2]⟧.

PH: ⟦(ἐρεῖς)[2]⟧.

[1] Matthew's ἤ.

[2] Luke's δύνασαι λέγειν or Matthew's ἐρεῖς.

[3] Luke's ἀδελφέ.

[4] Luke's τὸ ἐν τῷ ὀφθαλμῷ or Matthew's ἐκ τοῦ ὀφθαλμοῦ (see also variation unit [9]).

[5] Luke's αὐτὸς τὴν ... δοκὸν οὐ βλέπων or Matthew's καὶ ἰδοὺ ἡ δοκός.

Q

πῶς ... τῷ ἀδελφῷ σου· ἄφες ἐκβάλω τὸ κάρφος ⟦ἐκ⟧ τ⟦οῦ⟧ ὀφθαλμ⟦οῦ⟧ σου, καὶ ἰδοὺ ἡ δοκὸς ἐν τῷ ὀφθαλμῷ σου; ὑποκριτά, ἔκβαλε πρῶτον ἐκ τοῦ ὀφθαλμοῦ σου τὴν δοκόν, καὶ τότε διαβλέψεις ἐκβαλεῖν τὸ κάρφος ... τ... ὀφθαλμ... τοῦ ἀδελφοῦ σου.

How «can you» say to your brother: Let me throw out the speck ⟦from⟧ your eye, and just look at the beam in your own eye? Hypocrite, first throw out from your own eye the beam, and then you will see clearly to throw out the speck «in» your brother's eye.

Gos. Thom. 26.2 (Nag Hammadi II 2)

ὅταν ἐκβάλῃς τὴν δοκὸν ἐκ τοῦ ὀφθαλμοῦ σου, τότε διαβλέψεις ἐκβαλεῖν τὸ κάρφος ἐκ τοῦ ὀφθαλμοῦ τοῦ ἀδελφοῦ σου.

When you throw out the beam from your own eye, then you will see clearly to throw out the speck from your brother's eye.

Gos. Thom. 26.2 (P. Oxy. 1)

[...] καὶ τότε διαβλέψεις ἐκβαλεῖν τὸ κάρφος τὸ ἐν τῷ ὀφθαλμῷ τοῦ ἀδελφοῦ σου.

[...] and then you will see clearly to throw out the speck in your brother's eye.

Q 6:42

Luke 6:42	Lukan Doublet	Markan Parallel	*Gos. Thom.* 26.2
( )[1] πῶς [δύνασαι λέγειν][2] τῷ ἀδελφῷ σου· [ἀδελφέ][3], ἄφες ἐκβάλω τὸ κάρφος [τὸ ἐν][4] τ[ῷ][4] ὀφθαλμ[ῷ][4] σου, [αὐτὸς τ][5]ή[ν][5] ⸂ ⸃[6] ἐν τῷ ὀφθαλμῷ σου [6]⸂ δοκὸ[ν οὐ βλέπων][5] ⸃[6]; ὑποκριτά, ἔκβαλε πρῶτον ⸂τὴν δοκὸν⸃[7] ἐκ τοῦ ὀφθαλμοῦ σου ⸂ ⸃[7], καὶ τότε διαβλέψεις ⸂ ⸃[8] τὸ κάρφος [τὸ ἐν][9] τ[ῷ][9] ὀφθαλμ[ῷ][9] τοῦ ἀδελφοῦ σου ⸂ἐκβαλεῖν⸃[8].			ϨΟΤΑΝ ЄΚϢΑΝΝΟΥϪЄ ⲘⲠⲤⲞⲈⲒ ЄΒΟⲖ ϨⲘ ⲠЄΚ'ΒΑⲖ' ΤΟΤЄ ΚΝΑΝΑΥ ЄΒΟⲖ ЄΝΟΥϪЄ ⲘⲠϪΗ ЄΒΟⲖ ϨⲘ ⲠΒΑⲖ ⲘⲠЄΚⲤΟΝ

IQP 1990, PH: (ἐκ)[4] τ(οὺ)[4] ὀφθαλμ(οῦ)[4] σου.

PH: (ἐκ)[9] τ(οῦ)[9] ὀφθαλμ(οῦ)[9].

[6] The position of δοκόν after the prepositional phrase (Luke) or of δοκός before it (Matthew).

[7] The position of the second reference to τὴν δοκόν before the prepositional phrase (Luke) or after it (Matthew).

[8] The position of ἐκβαλεῖν after (Luke) or before (Matthew) what depends upon it.

[9] Luke's τὸ ἐν τῷ ὀφθαλμῷ or Matthew's ἐκ τοῦ ὀφθαλμοῦ. (See also variation unit[4])

Wie «kannst du» deinem Bruder sagen: Lass mich den Splitter ⟦aus⟧ deinem Auge herausziehen, und siehe, der Balken «ist» in deinem Auge? Heuchler, ziehe zuerst aus deinem Auge den Balken, und dann wirst du deutlich «genug» sehen, um den Splitter «im» Auge deines Bruders herauszuziehen.

Comment «peux-tu» dire à ton frère: Laisse-moi retirer la paille ⟦de⟧ ton œil, alors que la poutre est dans ton œil? Hypocrite, retire d'abord la poutre de ton œil, et alors tu verras clair pour retirer la paille «qui est dans» l'œil de ton frère.

Wenn du den Balken aus deinem Auge herausziehst, dann wirst du deutlich (genug) sehen, um den Splitter aus dem Auge deines Bruders herauszuziehen.

Quand tu auras enlevé la poutre de ton œil, alors tu verras clair pour retirer la paille de l'œil de ton frère.

[…] und dann wirst du deutlich (genug) sehen, um den Splitter, der in dem Auge deines Bruders ist, herauszuziehen.

[…] et alors tu verras clair pour retirer la paille qui est dans l'œil de ton frère.

Q 6:43-44

Markan Parallel	Matt 7:17, 20a; 20b=16a	Matt 7:15, 16b; 12:33a; 7:18-19; 12:33b	Q 6:43-44
		[1]⸂	**6:43** [1]⸂
		7:15 (Προσέχετε ἀπὸ τῶν ψευδοπροφητῶν, οἵτινες ἔρχονται πρὸς ὑμᾶς ἐν ἐνδύμασιν προβάτων, ἔσωθεν δέ εἰσιν λύκοι ἅρπαγες.)[2]	()[2]
		⸂ ⸃[3]	⸂⸃[3]
		7:16b [4]⸂ (μήτι)[15] ⸂συλλέγουσιν⸃[16] (ἀπὸ)[14] ἀκανθῶν ⸂ ⸃[16] [17]⸂σταφυλ(ὰς)[19] ⸃[17] (ἤ)[15] (ἀπὸ)[14] (τριβόλων)[18] ⸂σῦκα⸃[17] [ ][20]; ⸃[4]	⸂⸃[4]
	7:17 οὕτως πᾶν (δένδρον) ἀγαθὸν (καρπο)ὺς (καλο)ὺς (ποι)εῖ, (τὸ) δὲ (σαπρὸν) (δένδρον) (καρπο)ὺς πονηροὺς (ποι)εῖ.	**12:33a** (Ἢ ποιήσατε τὸ δένδρον καλὸν καὶ τὸν καρπὸν αὐτοῦ καλόν, ἢ ποιήσατε τὸ δένδρον σαπρὸν καὶ τὸν καρπὸν αὐτοῦ σαπρόν·)[5]	( )[5]

[1] The position of Q 6:43-44 in Q: After Q 6:42 and before Q 6:45 (Lukan position); or after Q 13:24 (Matt 7:14) and before Q 6:46 (Matt 7:21) (one Matthean position); or after Q 12:10 (Matt 12:32) and before Q 6:45 (Matt 12:34b-35) (the other Matthean position).

[2] Is Matt 7:15 (and the resultant orientation to false prophets and the plurality of fruits) in Q?

[3] Does the statement about being known by the fruit (Luke 6:44a; Matt 7:20b = 7:16a; 12:33b) come after the discussion of healthy and blighted trees and fruit (Luke 6:43;

Q 6:43-44

Luke 6:43-44	Lukan Doublet	Markan Parallel	*Gos. Thom.* 45.1
[1]⸢ ( )[2] ⸢ ⸣[3] ⸢ ⸣[4] ( )[5]			

Matt 7:17-19; 12:33a), or, as in the case of Matt 7:16a, before the discussion of the kinds of trees and fruit (Matt 7:16b)?

[4] Is the saying about figs and grapes at the end of the discussion of good and bad trees and fruit (Luke 6:44b), or at the beginning (Matt 7:16b)?

[5] Does the saying about a healthy tree producing healthy fruit and a blighted one producing blighted fruit stand in Q, and, if so, is its wording that of Matt 12:33a or Matt 7:17?

Q 6:43-44

Markan Parallel	Matt 7:17, 20a; 20b=16a	Matt 7:15, 16b; 12:33a; 7:18-19; 12:33b	Q 6:43-44
		7:18 οὐ [ ]^{6}	οὐ<κ> []^{6}
		(δύναται)^{7}	[ἐστιν]^{7}
		δένδρον (ἀγαθ)^{8}όν	δένδρον [καλ]^{8}όν
		⸂ ⸃^{7}	^{7}⸂ποι[οῦν]^{7} ⸃^{7}
		καρπο(ύς)^{9}	καρπὸ[ν]^{9}
		(πονη)^{10}ρο(ύς)^{9}	[σαπ]^{10}ρό[ν]^{9}
		^{7}⸂ποι(εῖν)^{7} ⸃^{7}	⸂⸃^{7},
		οὐδὲ [ ]^{11} δένδρον	οὐδὲ ⟦[πάλιν]^{11}⟧ δένδρον
		σαπρὸν	σαπρὸν
		⸂ ⸃^{7}	^{7}⸂ποι[οῦν]^{7} ⸃^{7}
		καρπο(ύς)^{9} καλο(ύς)^{9}	καρπὸ[ν]^{9} καλό[ν]^{9}
		^{7}⸂ποι(εῖν)^{7}⸃^{7}.	⸂⸃^{7}.
		7:19 (πᾶν δένδρον	()^{12}
		μὴ ποιοῦν καρπὸν καλὸν	
		ἐκκόπτεται	
		καὶ εἰς πῦρ βάλλεται.)^{12}	
		12:33b ^{3}⸂	**6:44** ^{3}⸂
		⸂ ⸃^{13}	⸂⸃^{13}
	7:20a ἄρα γε		
	7:20b = 7:16a ἀπὸ	ἐκ	ἐκ
		⸂γὰρ⸃^{13}	⸂γὰρ⸃^{13}
	[(τ)]ῶν	τοῦ	τοῦ
		[ ]^{13}	[]^{13}
	[(καρπ)]ῶν αὐτῶν	καρποῦ	καρποῦ
		^{13}⸂ (τὸ)^{13} δένδρον⸃^{13}	^{13}⸂ (τὸ)^{13} δένδρον⸃^{13}
	ἐπι[(γ)][(νώσ)]εσθε	γινώσκεται	γινώσκεται
	αὐτούς		
	.	.⸃^{3}	.⸃^{3}

6 Luke's γάρ.

7 Luke's ἐστιν with participles or Matthew's δύναται with infinitives, and the resultant divergence of positioning.

8 Luke's καλόν or Matthew's ἀγαθόν.

9 Luke's καρπόν or Matthew's καρπούς, and the corresponding number of the adjectives.

10 Luke's σαπρό- or Matthew's πονηρο-.

Q 6:43-44

Luke 6:43-44	Lukan Doublet	Markan Parallel	*Gos. Thom.* 45.1
6:43 Οὐ [γάρ][6] [ἐστιν][7] δένδρον [καλ][8]ὸν [7]⸆ποι[οῦν][7] ⸉[7] καρπὸ[ν][9] [σαπ][10]ρό[ν][9] ⸆ ⸉[7], οὐδὲ [πάλιν][11] δένδρον σαπρὸν [7]⸆ποι[οῦν][7] ⸉[7] καρπὸ[ν][9] καλό[ν][9] ⸆ ⸉[7]. ( )[12]			
6:44 [3]⸆ ⸆ [ἕκαστον][13] γὰρ δένδρον⸉[13] ἐκ τοῦ [ἰδίου][13] καρποῦ ⸆ ⸉[13] γινώσκεται .⸉[3]			

[11] Luke's πάλιν.
[12] Is Matt 7:19 here in Q (see Q 3:9b)?
[13] Luke's ἕκαστον ... δένδρον ... ἰδίου, with "tree" preceding "fruit," or Matthew's τὸ δένδρον (see also πᾶν δένδρον in Matt 7:17,19), with "tree" following "fruit," and the resultant position of γάρ. Or is the wording that of Matt 7:20b = 7:16a?

Q 6:43-44

Markan Parallel	Matt 7:17, 20a; 20b=16a	Matt 7:15, 16b; 12:33a; 7:18-19; 12:33b	Q 6:43-44
		ʃ4	4ʃ
			(μήτι)[14]
			ʃσυλλέγουσινʅ[15]
			[ἐξ][16] ἀκανθῶν
			ʃʅ[15]
			ʃσῦκαʅ[17]
			(ἢ)[14]
			[ἐκ][16]
			(τριβόλων)[18]
			[17]ʃσταφυλ⟦(άς)[19]⟧ ʅ[17]
			[][20];
			ʅ4
		ʅ1	ʅ1

IQP 1991: Matt 7:17 par. 12:35a not in Q {C}; PH: In Q {D}; JMR: Indeterminate; JSK: Not in Q {D}.

IQP 1991: [πάλιν][11].

[14] Luke's οὐ γάρ ... οὐδέ and the formulation as a statement or Matthew's μήτι ... ἤ and the formulation as a question.

[15] The position of συλλέγουσιν after ἐξ ἀκανθῶν (Luke) or before ἀπὸ ἀκανθῶν (Matthew).

Q

43 .. οὐ<κ> ἔστιν δένδρον καλὸν ποιοῦν καρπὸν σαπρόν, οὐδὲ ⟦πάλιν⟧ δένδρον σαπρὸν ποιοῦν καρπὸν καλόν. 44 ἐκ γὰρ τοῦ καρποῦ τὸ δένδρον γινώσκεται. μήτι συλλέγουσιν ἐξ ἀκανθῶν σῦκα ἢ ἐκ τριβόλων σταφυλ⟦άς⟧;

43 .. No healthy tree bears rotten fruit, nor ⟦on the other hand⟧ does a decayed tree bear healthy fruit. 44 For from the fruit the tree is known. Are figs picked from thorns, or grape⟦s⟧ from thistles?

Gos. Thom. 45.1 (Nag Hammadi II 2)

Λέγει Ἰησοῦς· οὐ τρυγῶσιν ἐξ ἀκανθῶν σταφυλὰς οὐδὲ συλλέγουσιν σῦκα ἀπὸ τριβόλων· οὐ γὰρ διδόασιν καρπόν.[1]

Jesus says: Grapes are not harvested from thorns, nor are figs picked from thistles, for they do not produce fruit.

[1] Instead of διδόασιν καρπόν, καρποφοροῦσιν or ποιοῦσιν καρπόν are also possible alternatives.

Q 6:43-44

Luke 6:43-44	Lukan Doublet	Markan Parallel	*Gos. Thom.* 45.1
4ʃ			ⲡⲉϫⲉ ⲓ̅ⲥ̅
[οὐ γὰρ][14]			ⲙⲁⲩϫⲉⲗⲉ
ʃ ʅ15			ⲉⲗⲟⲟⲗⲉ
[ἐξ][16] ἀκανθῶν			ⲉⲃⲟⲗ ϩⲛ̅ ϣⲟⲛⲧⲉ
ʃσυλλέγουσινʅ15			
ʃσῦκαʅ17			
[οὐδὲ][14]			ⲟⲩⲧⲉ ⲙⲁⲩⲕⲱⲧϥ'
[ἐκ][16]			ⲕⲛ̅ⲧⲉ ⲉⲃⲟⲗ ϩⲛ̅
[βάτου][18]			
17ʃσταφυλ[ὴν][19] ʅ17			
[τρυγῶσιν][20].			ⲥⲣ̅ϭⲁⲙⲟⲩⲗ'
ʅ4			ⲙⲁⲩϯ ⲕⲁⲣⲡⲟⲥ
ʅ1			ⲅⲁ̣ⲣ

IQP 1991: **6:44** ʃσυλλέγουσινʅ15 (ἀπὸ)[14] ἀκανθῶν ʃʅ15 ʃσῦκαʅ17 (ἤ)[14] [ἐκ][16] [βάτου][18] 17ʃσταφυλ[ήν][19] ʅ17.

JSK: **6:44** ʃσυλλέγουσινʅ15 (ἀπὸ)[14] ἀκανθῶν ʃʅ15 ʃσῦκαʅ17 (ἤ)[14] [ἐκ][16] ⟦[βάτου][18]⟧ 17ʃσταφυλ⟦[ήν][19]⟧ ʅ17.

16 Luke's ἐξ/ἐκ or Matthew's ἀπό (*bis*).
17 Is σῦκα first (Luke), or σταφυλήν/-άς first (Matthew)?
18 Luke's βάτου or Matthew's τριβόλων.
19 Luke's σταφυλήν or Matthew's σταφυλάς.
20 Luke's τρυγῶσιν.

43 .. Es gibt keinen guten Baum, der minderwertige Frucht bringt, und ⟦andererseits⟧ keinen minderwertigen Baum, der gute Frucht bringt. **44** Denn an der Frucht wird der Baum erkannt. Sammelt man etwa von Dornengestrüpp Feigen oder von Disteln Weintraube⟦n⟧?

43 .. Il n'y a pas de bel arbre qui produise du vilain fruit, ni⟦, à l'inverse,⟧ de vilain arbre qui produise de bel fruit. **44** Car c'est au fruit que l'arbre se reconnaît. Est-ce qu'on récolte des figues sur un buisson d'épines ou d⟦es⟧ raisin⟦s⟧ sur des chardons?

Jesus spricht: Weintrauben werden nicht von Dornengestrüpp geerntet, noch werden Feigen von Disteln gepflückt, denn sie geben keine Frucht.

Jésus dit: On ne récolte pas des raisins sur des buissons d'épines ni on ne ramasse des figues sur des chardons, car ils ne donnent pas de fruit.

1 Statt διδόασιν καρπόν wäre auch καρποφοροῦσιν oder ποιοῦσιν καρπόν möglich.

1 Au lieu de διδόασιν καρπόν, καρποφοροῦσιν ou ποιοῦσιν καρπόν seraient aussi possibles.

Q 6:45

Markan Parallel	Matt 3:7b	Matt 12:34-35	Q 6:45
		[1]⸂	[1]⸂
	(γεννήματα ἐχιδνῶν,) τίς ὑπέδειξεν ὑμῖν φυγεῖν ἀπὸ τῆς μελλούσης ὀργῆς;	**12:34** (γεννήματα ἐχιδνῶν, πῶς δύνασθε ἀγαθὰ λαλεῖν πονηροὶ ὄντες;)[2] ⸂ ⸃[3]	()[2]
			[3]⸂ὁ ἀγαθὸς ἄνθρωπος ἐκ τοῦ ἀγαθοῦ θησαυροῦ [][4] (ἐκβάλλ)[5]ει [][6] ἀγαθ(ά)[6], καὶ ὁ πονηρὸς ⟦(ἄνθρωπος)[7]⟧ ἐκ τοῦ πονηροῦ ⟦(θησαυροῦ)[8]⟧ (ἐκβάλλ)[5]ει [][6] πονηρ(ά)[6]. ⸃[3]
		ἐκ γὰρ (τοῦ)[9] περισσεύματος	ἐκ γὰρ ⟦()[9]⟧ περισσεύματος
		(τῆς)[10] καρδίας	⟦()[10]⟧ καρδίας
		⸂ ⸃[11] τὸ στόμα [ ][12] ⸂λαλεῖ⸃[11]. **12:35** [3]⸂ ὁ ἀγαθὸς ἄνθρωπος ἐκ τοῦ ἀγαθοῦ θησαυροῦ [ ][4] (ἐκβάλλ)[5]ει [ ][6] ἀγαθ(ά)[6], καὶ ὁ πονηρὸς (ἄνθρωπος)[7] ἐκ τοῦ πονηροῦ (θησαυροῦ)[8]	⸂λαλεῖ⸃[11] τὸ στόμα ⟦[αὐτοῦ][12]⟧ ⸂ ⸃[11]. ⸂⸃[3]

[1] The position of Q 6:45 in Q: After Q 6:44 and before Q 6:46 (Lukan order); or after Q 6:44a (Matt 12:33b) and before Q 11:16 (Matt 12:38) (Matthean order).

[2] Matthew's γεννήματα ἐχιδνῶν, πῶς δύνασθε ἀγαθὰ λαλεῖν πονηροὶ ὄντες;.

[3] The clause about the good person and the evil person before (Luke) or after (Matthew) the clause about the heart.

[4] Luke's τῆς καρδίας.

[5] Luke's προφέρει or Matthew's ἐκβάλλει (*bis*).

Q 6:45

Luke 6:45	Lukan Doublet	Markan Parallel	*Gos. Thom.* 45.2-4
[1]⸂			
( )[2]			
[3]⸂ὁ ἀγαθὸς ἄνθρωπος			45.2 ⲟ̣ⲩ̣ⲁ̣ⲅ̣ⲁ̣ⲑⲟⲥ ⲣ̄ⲣⲱⲙⲉ
ἐκ τοῦ ἀγαθοῦ			
θησαυροῦ [τῆς καρδίας][4]			ϣⲁϥⲉⲓⲛⲉ
[προφέρ][5]ει			ⲛ̄ⲟⲩⲁⲅⲁⲑⲟⲛ
[τὸ][6] ἀγαθ[όν][6],			ⲉⲃⲟⲗ ϩⲙ̣̄ ⲡⲉϥⲉϩⲟ
καὶ ὁ πονηρὸς			45.3 ⲟⲩⲕⲁⲕ̣[ⲟⲥ]
( )[7]			ⲣ̄ⲣⲱⲙⲉ
ἐκ τοῦ πονηροῦ			ϣⲁϥⲉⲓⲛⲉ
( )[8]			ⲛ̄ϩⲛ̄ⲡⲟⲛⲏⲣⲟⲛ
[προφέρ][5]ει			ⲉⲃⲟⲗ ϩⲙ̄ ⲡⲉϥⲉϩⲟ
[τὸ][6] πονηρ[όν][6]. ⸃[3]			ⲉⲑⲟⲟⲩ
			ⲉⲧϩⲛ̄ ⲡⲉϥϩⲏⲧ’
			ⲁⲩⲱ ⲛ̄ϥϫⲱ ⲛ̄ϩⲛ̄ⲡⲟ-
			ⲛⲏⲣⲟⲛ
ἐκ γὰρ ( )[9] περισσεύματος			45.4 ⲉⲃⲟⲗ ⲅⲁⲣ ϩⲙ̄
			ⲫⲟⲩⲟ
( )[10] καρδίας			ⲙ̄ⲫⲏⲧ’
⸂λαλεῖ⸃[11] τὸ στόμα			
[αὐτοῦ][12] ⸂ ⸃[11].			
⸂ ⸃[3]			

6 Luke's τὸ ἀγαθόν, … τὸ πονηρόν or Matthew's ἀγαθά, … πονηρά.
7 Matthew's ἄνθρωπος.
8 Matthew's θησαυροῦ.
9 Matthew's τοῦ.
10 Matthew's τῆς.
11 The position of λαλεῖ before (Luke) or after (Matthew) τὸ στόμα (αὐτοῦ).
12 Luke's αὐτοῦ.

Q 6:45

Markan Parallel	Matt 3:7b	Matt 12:34-35	Q 6:45
		(ἐκβάλλ)⁵ει [ ]⁶ πονηρ(ά)⁶.⸌3 ⸌1	⸌1

IQP 1991: ⟦(ἐκβάλλ)⁵⟧ει ... ⟦(ἐκβάλλ)⁵⟧ει.
PH: ⟦[]⁶⟧ ἀγαθ⟦(ά)⁶⟧, ... ⟦[]⁶⟧ πονηρ⟦(ά)⁶⟧.

IQP 1991: ( )⁷ ( )⁸.
PH: ( )⁹ ( )¹⁰.

Q

ὁ ἀγαθὸς ἄνθρωπος ἐκ τοῦ ἀγαθοῦ θησαυροῦ ἐκβάλλει ἀγαθά, καὶ ὁ πονηρὸς ⟦ἄνθρωπος⟧ ἐκ τοῦ πονηροῦ ⟦θησαυροῦ⟧ ἐκβάλλει πονηρά· ἐκ γὰρ περισσεύματος καρδίας λαλεῖ τὸ στόμα ⟦αὐτοῦ⟧.

The good person from «one's» good treasure casts up good things, and the evil ⟦person⟧ from the evil ⟦treasure⟧ casts up evil things. For from exuberance of heart ⟦one's⟧ mouth speaks.

Gos. Thom. 45.2-4 (Nag Hammadi II 2)

(2) ἀγαθὸς ἄνθρωπος προφέρει ἀγαθόν τι ἐκ τοῦ θησαυροῦ αὐτοῦ. (3) κακ[ὸς] ἄνθρωπος προφέρει πονηρὰ ἐκ τοῦ θησαυροῦ αὐτοῦ τοῦ κακοῦ, ὅς (ἐστιν) ἐν τῇ καρδίᾳ αὐτοῦ, καὶ λαλεῖ πονηρά. (4) ἐκ γὰρ τοῦ περισσεύματος τῆς καρδίας προφέρει πονηρά.

(2) A good person brings forth good from one's treasure. (3) A bad person brings forth evil things from the bad[1] treasure that is in one's heart, and (in fact) one speaks evil things. (4) For out of the exuberance of the heart one brings forth evil things.

[1] Literally: one's bad.

Q 6:45

Luke 6:45	Lukan Doublet	Markan Parallel	*Gos. Thom.* 45.2-4
⸉[1]			ϣⲁϥ'ⲉⲓⲛⲉ ⲉⲃⲟⲗ ⲛ̄ϩⲛ̄ⲡⲟⲛⲏⲣⲟⲛ

PH: The position of λαλεῖ indeterminate.
IQP 1991: [ ][12] {D}; PH: [ ][12] indeterminate.

Der gute Mensch holt aus dem guten Schatz Gutes hervor, und der böse ⟦Mensch⟧ holt aus dem bösen ⟦Schatz⟧ Böses hervor; denn ⟦sein⟧ Mund redet, wovon das Herz voll ist.

La personne bonne produit de bonnes choses les tirant de «son» bon trésor, et la ⟦personne⟧ mauvaise produit de mauvaises choses les tirant de «son» mauvais ⟦trésor⟧; car ⟦sa⟧ bouche exprime le trop-plein du cœur.

(2) Ein guter Mensch bringt Gutes aus seinem Schatz (hervor). (3) Ein schlechter Mensch bringt Böses aus dem schlechten[2] Schatz, der in seinem Herzen ist, hervor, und zwar redet er Böses. (4) Denn aus dem Überfluß des Herzens bringt er Böses hervor.

(2) Une personne bonne tire de bonnes choses de son trésor. (3) Une personne mauvaise tire de mauvaises choses de son méchant trésor qui est dans son cœur, et elle dit de mauvaises choses. (4) Car elle tire le mal du trop-plein du cœur.

[2] Wörtlich: seinem schlechten.

Q 6:46

Mark 3:35a	Matt 12:50a	Matt 7:21	Q 6:46
		^{0}/	^{0}/
		(Οὐ)^{1}	[τί]^{1}
		[ ]^{2}	[ ]^{2}
		(πᾶς ὁ λέγων)$^{1.3}$	()^{1} ()^{3}
		μ(οι)^{3}	μ[ε]^{3}
		[ ]^{3}[ ]^{1}·	[καλεῖ]^{3}[τε]^{1}·
		κύριε κύριε,	κύριε κύριε,
		(εἰσελεύσεται εἰς τὴν	()^{1}
		βασιλείαν τῶν οὐρανῶν,)^{1}	
		(ἀλλ')^{4}	[καὶ]^{4}
ὃς γὰρ ἂν ποιήσῃ	ὅστις {γὰρ ἂν {([ποι])ήσῃ	(ὁ)^{1} {ποι}(ῶν)^{1}	[οὐ]^{1} ποι[εῖτε]^{1}
τὸ θέλημα τοῦ θεοῦ,	(τὸ θέλημα τοῦ} πατρός	({τὸ θέλημα τοῦ} πατρός	[ἃ λέγω]^{5}
	μου τοῦ ἐν) (οὐρανοῖς)	μου τοῦ ἐν τοῖς οὐρανοῖς)^{5}.	;
		\\$^{0}$	\\$^{0}$

IQP 1990: μ⟦[ε]^{3} [καλεῖ]^{3}⟧[τε]^{1}.

^{0} Are the similarities due to Q or to coincidence? (See also Matt 7:22a).

^{1} Luke's τί … καλεῖτε … οὐ ποιεῖτε, or Matthew's οὐ πᾶς ὁ λέγων … εἰσελεύσεται εἰς τὴν βασιλείαν τῶν οὐρανῶν, … ὁ ποιῶν.

Q

τί .. με καλεῖτε· κύριε κύριε, καὶ οὐ ποιεῖτε ἃ λέγω;	.. Why do you call me: Master, Master, and do not do what I say?

Q 6:46

Luke 6:46	Lukan Doublet	Markan Parallel	Gospel of Thomas
[0]/ [Τί][1] [δέ][2] ( )[1.3] μ[ε][3] [καλεῖ][3][τε][1]· κύριε κύριε, ( )[1] [καὶ][4] [οὐ][1] ποι[εῖτε][1] [ἃ λέγω][5] ; \[0]			

2 Luke's δέ.
3 Luke's verb καλεῖν or Matthew's verb λέγειν, with the resultant case of the object.
4 Luke's καί or Matthew's ἀλλ'.
5 Luke's ἃ λέγω or Matthew's τὸ θέλημα τοῦ πατρός μου τοῦ ἐν τοῖς οὐρανοῖς.

.. Was ruft ihr mich: Herr, Herr, und tut nicht, was ich sage?

.. Pourquoi m'appelez-vous: Seigneur, Seigneur, et ne faites-vous pas ce que je dis?

Q 6:47

Markan Parallel	Matthean Doublet	Matt 7:24a	Q 6:47
		Πᾶς (οὖν)[1] (ὅστις)[2] [ ][3] ἀκού(ει)[2] μου τ(οὺς)[4] λόγ(ους)[4] (τούτους)[5] καὶ ποι(εῖ)[2] αὐτούς, [ ][6]	πᾶς ()[1] [ὁ][2] [][3] ἀκού[ων][2] μου τ( )[4] λόγ( )[4] ()[5] καὶ ποι[ῶν][2] αὐτούς, [][6]

IQP 1990: ⟦[ὁ][2]⟧ [][3] ἀκού⟦[ων][2]⟧ μου τ⟦[ῶν][4]⟧ λόγ⟦[ων][4]⟧ ( )[5] καὶ ποι⟦[ῶν][2]⟧.

[1] Matthew's οὖν.

[2] Luke's ὁ … ἀκούων … καὶ ποιῶν or Matthew's ὅστις ἀκούει … καὶ ποιεῖ.

[3] Luke's ἐρχόμενος πρός με καί.

[4] Luke's genitive or Matthew's accusative objects.

Q

πᾶς ὁ ἀκούων μου τ… λόγ… καὶ ποιῶν αὐτούς,	Everyone hearing my words and acting on them,

Q 6:47

Luke 6:47	Lukan Doublet	Markan Parallel	Gospel of Thomas
Πᾶς ( )[1] [ὁ][2] [ἐρχόμενος πρός με καὶ][3] ἀκού[ων][2] μου τ[ῶν][4] λόγ[ων][4] ( )[5] καὶ ποι[ῶν][2] αὐτούς, [ὑποδείξω ὑμῖν τίνι ἐστὶν ὅμοιος][6].			

PH: μου τ⟦(οὺς)[4]⟧ λόγ⟦(ους)[4]⟧.

[5] Matthew's τούτους.
[6] Luke's ὑποδείξω ὑμῖν τίνι ἐστὶν ὅμοιος.

Jeder, der meine Worte hört und sie tut,

Quiconque écoute mes paroles et les met en pratique,

Q 6:48

Markan Parallel	Matthean Doublet	Matt 7:24b-25	Q 6:48
		7:24b ὁμοι(ωθήσεται)[1] ἀν(δρὶ)[2] (φρονίμῳ)[3], (ὅστις ᾠ)[4]κοδόμ(ησεν)[4] (αὐτοῦ τὴν)[5] οἰκίαν [ ][6] ἐπὶ τὴν πέτραν· **7:25** (καὶ κατέβη ἡ βροχὴ καὶ ἦλθον)[7] ⸉ ⸊[7] ο(ἱ)[7] ποταμο(ὶ)[7] (καὶ ἔπνευσαν οἱ ἄνεμοι)[7] (καὶ)[7] ⸉προσέ(πεσαν)[7] ⸊[7] τῇ οἰκίᾳ ἐκείνῃ, καὶ οὐκ (ἔπε)[8]σεν [ ][8], (τε)[9] θεμελί(ωτο γὰρ ἐπὶ τὴν πέτραν)[9].	ὅμοι[ός ἐστιν][1] ἀν[θρώπῳ][2], ()[3] (ὃς)[4]⟦()[4]⟧ (ᾠ)[4]κοδόμ(ησεν)[4] ⟦(αὐτοῦ τὴν)[5]⟧ οἰκίαν ⟦[][6]⟧ ἐπὶ τὴν πέτραν· (καὶ κατέβη ἡ βροχὴ (καὶ ἦλθον)[7] ⸉ ⸊[7] ο(ἱ)[7] ποταμο(ὶ)[7] ⟦(καὶ ἔπνευσαν οἱ ἄνεμοι)[7]⟧ (καὶ)[7] ⸉προσέ(πεσαν)[7] ⸊[7] τῇ οἰκίᾳ ἐκείνῃ, καὶ οὐκ (ἔπε)[8]σεν [][8], (τε)[9] θεμελί(ωτο γὰρ ἐπὶ τὴν πέτραν)[9].

IQP 1990: ⟦()[5]⟧.

IQP 1990: [ ][6].

[1] Luke's ὅμοιός ἐστιν or Matthew's ὁμοιωθήσεται.
[2] Luke's ἀνθρώπῳ or Matthew's ἀνδρί.
[3] Matthew's φρονίμῳ.
[4] Luke's οἰκοδομοῦντι or Matthew's ὅστις ᾠκοδόμησεν.
[5] Matthew's αὐτοῦ τήν.
[6] Luke's ὃς ἔσκαψεν καὶ ἐβάθυνεν καὶ ἔθηκεν θεμέλιον (see also Matthew's τεθεμελίωτο at variation unit [9]).

Q

ὅμοιός ἐστιν ἀνθρώπῳ, ὃς ᾠκοδόμησεν ⟦αὐτοῦ τὴν⟧ οἰκίαν ἐπὶ τὴν πέτραν· καὶ κατέβη ἡ βροχὴ καὶ ἦλθον οἱ ποταμοὶ ⟦καὶ ἔπνευσαν οἱ ἄνεμοι⟧ καὶ προσέπεσαν τῇ οἰκίᾳ ἐκείνῃ, καὶ οὐκ ἔπεσεν, τεθεμελίωτο γὰρ ἐπὶ τὴν πέτραν.

is like a person who built ⟦one's⟧ house on bedrock; and the rain poured down and the flash-floods came, ⟦and the winds blew⟧ and pounded that house, and it did not collapse, for it was founded on bedrock.

Q 6:48

Luke 6:48	Lukan Doublet	Markan Parallel	Gospel of Thomas
ὅμοι[ός ἐστιν][1] ἀν[θρώπῳ][2] ( )[3] [οἰ][4]κοδομ[οῦντι][4] ( )[5] οἰκίαν [ὃς ἔσκαψεν καὶ ἐβάθυνεν καὶ ἔθηκεν][7] θεμέλι[ον][6] ἐπὶ τὴν πέτραν· [πλημμύρης δὲ γενομένης][7] ⸉προσέ[ρηξεν)[7] ⸊[7] ὁ( )[7] ποταμὸ[ς][7] ( )[7] ( )[7] ⸉ ⸊[7] τῇ οἰκίᾳ ἐκείνῃ, καὶ οὐκ [ἴσχυ][8]σεν [σαλεῦσαι αὐτὴν][8] [διὰ τὸ καλῶς οἰκοδομῆσθαι αὐτήν][9].			

IQP 1990: (καὶ)[7] ( )[7] (καὶ)[7] ( )[7] ὁ[ ][7] ποταμό[ ][7] προσέ⟦(πεσ)[7]⟧[ ][7]. IQP 1990: ⟦(ἔπε)[8]⟧σεν ⟦[][8]⟧.

[7] Luke's πλημμύρης δὲ γενομένης προσέρηξεν ὁ ποταμός or Matthew's καὶ κατέβη ἡ βροχὴ καὶ ἦλθον οἱ ποταμοὶ καὶ ἔπνευσαν οἱ ἄνεμοι καὶ προσέπεσαν.

[8] Luke's ἴσχυσεν σαλεῦσαι αὐτήν or Matthew's ἔπεσεν.

[9] Luke's διὰ τὸ καλῶς οἰκοδομῆσθαι αὐτήν or Matthew's τεθεμελίωτο γὰρ ἐπὶ τὴν πέτραν (see also Luke's ἔθηκεν θεμέλιον at variation unit [6]).

ist einem Menschen gleich, der ⟦sein⟧ Haus auf dem Felsen baute; und der Regen ging hernieder, und die Sturzbäche kamen, ⟦und die Winde stürmten⟧ und prallten gegen jenes Haus, es stürzte aber nicht ein, denn sein Fundament war auf den Felsen gelegt.

est semblable à une personne qui a bâti ⟦sa⟧ maison sur la roche; et la pluie est tombée et les torrents sont arrivés ⟦et les vents ont soufflé⟧ et ils se sont jetés contre cette maison et elle ne s'est pas écroulée, car ses fondations reposaient sur la roche.

Q 6:49

Markan Parallel	Matthean Doublet	Matt 7:26-27	Q 6:49
		7:26 (καὶ)[1]	(καὶ)[1]
		(πᾶς)[2] ὁ [ ][1]	⟦(πᾶς)[2]⟧ ὁ [][1]
		ἀκού(ων)[3]	ἀκού(ων)[3]
		(μου τοὺς λόγους)[4]	⟦(μου τοὺς λόγους)[4]⟧
		(τούτους)[5]	()[5]
		καὶ μὴ ποι(ῶν)[3]	καὶ μὴ ποι(ῶν)[3]
		(αὐτοὺς)[4]	⟦(αὐτοὺς)[4]⟧
		ὁμοι(ωθήσεται)[6]	ὅμοι[ός ἐστιν][6]
		ἀν(δρὶ)[7]	ἀν[θρώπῳ][7]
		(μωρῷ,)[8]	()[8]
		(ὅστις ᾠ)[9]κοδόμησ(εν)[9]	(ὃς)[9]⟦()[9]⟧ (ᾠ)[9]κοδόμησ(εν)[9]
		(αὐτοῦ τὴν)[10] οἰκίαν	⟦(αὐτοῦ τὴν)[10]⟧ οἰκίαν
		ἐπὶ τὴν	ἐπὶ τὴν
		(ἄμμον·)[11]	(ἄμμον·)[11]
		7:27 (καὶ κατέβη ἡ βροχὴ	(καὶ κατέβη ἡ βροχὴ
		καὶ ἦλθον)[12] ⸂ ⸃[12]	καὶ ἦλθον)[12] ⸂ ⸃[12]
		ο(ἱ)[12] ποταμο(ὶ)	ο(ἱ)[12] ποταμο(ὶ
		(καὶ ἔπνευσαν οἱ ἄνεμοι)[12]	⟦(καὶ ἔπνευσαν οἱ ἄνεμοι)[12]⟧
		(καὶ)[12] ⸂προσέ(κοψαν)[12] ⸃[12]	(καὶ)[12] ⸂προσέ(κοψαν)[12] ⸃[12]
		⸂τῇ[ ][13] οἰκίᾳ[ ][13] ἐκείνῃ[ ][13] ⸃[13],	⸂τῇ[][13] οἰκίᾳ[][13] ἐκείνῃ[][13] ⸃[13],
		καὶ [ ][14]	καὶ [εὐθὺς][14]
		[ ][15]ἔπεσεν καὶ	[][15]ἔπεσεν καὶ
		(ἦν)[16]	(ἦν)[16]
		(ἡ πτῶσις)[17]	⟦(ἡ πτῶσις)[17]⟧
		⸂ ⸃[13]	⸂⸃[13]
		(αὐτῆς)[13] μεγά(λη)[17].	(αὐτῆς)[13] μεγά⟦(λη)[17]⟧.

IQP 1990: ⟦(μου τ<ῶν> λόγ<ων>)[4]⟧.

IQP 1990: ⟦()[10]⟧ οἰκίαν.

1 Luke's postpositive δέ or Matthew's καί.
2 Matthew's πᾶς.
3 Luke's ἀκούσας … ποιήσας or Matthew's ἀκούων … ποιῶν.
4 Matthew's phrase μου τοὺς λόγους … αὐτούς.
5 Matthew's τούτους.
6 Luke's ὅμοιός ἐστιν or Matthew's ὁμοιωθήσεται.
7 Luke's ἀνθρώπῳ or Matthew's ἀνδρί.
8 Matthew's μωρῷ.
9 Luke's οἰκοδομήσαντι or Matthew's ὅστις ᾠκοδόμησεν.
10 Matthew's αὐτοῦ τήν.

Q

καὶ ⟦πᾶς⟧ ὁ ἀκούων ⟦μου τοὺς λόγους⟧ καὶ μὴ ποιῶν ⟦αὐτοὺς⟧ ὅμοιός ἐστιν ἀνθρώπῳ ὃς ᾠκοδόμησεν ⟦αὐτοῦ τὴν⟧ οἰκίαν ἐπὶ τὴν ἄμμον· καὶ κατέβη ἡ βροχὴ καὶ ἦλθον οἱ ποταμοὶ ⟦καὶ ἔπνευσαν οἱ ἄνεμοι⟧ καὶ προσέκοψαν τῇ οἰκίᾳ ἐκείνῃ, καὶ εὐθὺς ἔπεσεν καὶ ἦν ⟦ἡ πτῶσις⟧ αὐτῆς μεγά⟦λη⟧.

And ⟦everyone⟧ who hears ⟦my words⟧ and does not act on ⟦them⟧ is like a person who built ⟦one's⟧ house on the sand; and the rain poured down and the flash-floods came, ⟦and the winds blew⟧ and battered that house, and promptly it collapsed, and its ⟦fall⟧ was devastating.

Q 6:49

Luke 6:49	Lukan Doublet	Markan Parallel	Gospel of Thomas
( )[1] ( )[2] ὁ [δὲ][1] ἀκού[σας][3] ( )[4] ( )[5] καὶ μὴ ποι[ήσας][3] ( )[4] ὅμοι[ός ἐστιν][6] ἀν[θρώπῳ][7] ( )[8] [οἰ][9]κοδομήσ[αντι][9] ( )[10] οἰκίαν ἐπὶ τὴν [γῆν χωρὶς θεμελίου,][11] [ᾗ][12] ⸉προσέ[ρηξεν][12] ⸊[12] ὁ( )[12] ποταμό[ς,][12] ( )[12] ( )[12] ⸉ ⸊[12] ⸉ ⸊[13] καὶ [εὐθὺς][14] [συν][15]έπεσεν καὶ [ἐγένετο][16] [τὸ ῥῆγμα][17] ⸉τῆ[ς][13] οἰκία[ς][13] ἐκείνη[ς][13] ⸊[13] ( )[13] μέγα( )[17].			

IQP 1990: (καὶ)[12] ( )[12] (καὶ)[12] ( )[12] ⸉προσέ⟦(κοψ)[12]⟧( )[12] ⸊[12] ὁ( )[12] ποταμό( )[12] ⸉ ⸊[12].

[11] Luke's γῆν χωρὶς θεμελίου or Matthew's ἄμμον.

[12] Luke's ᾗ προσέρηξεν ὁ ποταμός or Matthew's καὶ κατέβη ἡ βροχὴ καὶ ἦλθον οἱ ποταμοὶ καὶ ἔπνευσαν οἱ ἄνεμοι καὶ προσέκοψαν.

[13] The position and construction of Luke's τῆς οἰκίας ἐκείνης or Matthew's τῇ οἰκίᾳ ἐκείνῃ ... αὐτῆς.

[14] Luke's εὐθύς.

[15] Luke's συν-.

[16] Luke's ἐγένετο or Matthew's ἦν.

[17] Luke's τὸ ῥῆγμα ... μέγα or Matthew's ἡ πτῶσις ... μεγάλη.

Und ⟦jeder⟧, der ⟦meine Worte⟧ hört und ⟦sie⟧ nicht tut, ist einem Menschen gleicht, der ⟦sein⟧ Haus auf den Sand baute; und der Regen ging hernieder, und die Sturzbäche kamen, ⟦und die Winde stürmten⟧ und prallten gegen jenes Haus, und sofort stürzte es ein und sein ⟦Einsturz⟧ war gewaltig.

Et ⟦quiconque⟧ écoute ⟦mes paroles⟧ et ne ⟦les⟧ met pas en pratique est semblable à une personne qui a bâti ⟦sa⟧ maison sur le sable; et la pluie est tombée et les torrents sont arrivés ⟦et les vents ont soufflé⟧ et ils ont battu cette maison, et aussitôt elle s'est écroulée et sa ⟦ruine⟧ fut totale.

Q 7:1, ~~2~~, 3, ~~4-6a~~, 6b-9, ?10?

Q 7:1

Mark 7:24a	Matt 15:21	Matt 7:28a; 8:5a	Q 7:1
		7:28a [0]/ (Καὶ ἐγένετο ὅτε)[1] ἐ(τέλε)[2]σεν (ὁ Ἰησοῦς)[3] [ ][4] τ(οὺς λόγους τούτους)[4] [ ][5],	[0]/ ⟦(καὶ ἐγένετο ὅτε)[1]⟧ ἐ⟦[πλήρω][2]⟧σεν ( )[3] [][4] τ(οὺς λόγους τούτους)[4] [][5],
Ἐκεῖθεν δὲ ἀναστὰς ἀπῆλθεν εἰς τὰ ὅρια Τύρου.	Καὶ ἐξελθὼν ἐκεῖθεν ὁ Ἰησοῦς ἀνεχώρησεν εἰς τὰ μέρη Τύρου καὶ Σιδῶνος.	\\[0] **8:5a** Εἰσ(ε)[6]λθ(ό)[6]ν(τος δὲ αὐτοῦ)[6] εἰς Καφαρναούμ	\\[0] εἰσ[ῆ][6]λθ[ε][6]ν()[6] εἰς Καφαρναούμ.

IQP 1994: / \\[0] in Q {C}.

IQP 1994: [][1] ( )[1] ἐ⟦[πλήρω][2]⟧σεν; JMR: (καὶ ἐγένετο ὅτε)[1] ἐ(τέλε)[2]σεν.

[0] Is Luke 7:1a par. Matt 7:28a in Q?
[1] Luke's ἐπειδή or Matthew's καὶ ἐγένετο ὅτε.

[2] Luke's ἐπλήρωσεν or Matthew's ἐτέλεσεν.
[3] Matthew's ὁ Ἰησοῦς.

Q

⟦καὶ ἐγένετο ὅτε⟧ ἐ⟦πλήρω⟧σεν .. τοὺς λόγους τούτους, εἰσῆλθεν εἰς Καφαρναούμ.

⟦And it came to pass when⟧ he .. ended these sayings, he entered Capernaum.

Q 7:1

Luke 7:1	Lukan Doublet	Mark 2:1a	John 4:46b
[0]/			
['Επειδὴ][1]			
ἐ[πλήρω][2]σεν			
( )[3]			
[πάντα][4]			
τ[ὰ ῥήματα			
αὐτοῦ][4]			
[εἰς τὰς ἀκοὰς			
τοῦ λαοῦ][5],			
\[0]			
εἰσ[ῆ][6]λθ[ε][6]ν( )[6]		Καὶ εἰσελθὼν	Καὶ ἦν τις βασιλικὸς
		πάλιν	οὗ ὁ υἱὸς ἠσθένει
εἰς Καφαρναούμ.		εἰς Καφαρναοὺμ	ἐν Καφαρναούμ.

IQP 1994: ()[3]; JSK: ( )[3] {D}; PH: ( )[3] indeterminate; JMR: ⟦(ὁ 'Ιησοῦς)[3]⟧.

IQP 1994: τ⟦(οὺς λόγους τούτους)[4]⟧.

[4] Luke's πάντα τὰ ῥήματα αὐτοῦ or Matthew's τοὺς λόγους τούτους.

[5] Luke's εἰς τὰς ἀκοὰς τοῦ λαοῦ.

[6] Luke's εἰσῆλθεν or Matthew's εἰσελθόντος δὲ αὐτοῦ. (See also Mark 1:21a parr.).

⟦Und es geschah, als⟧ er .. diese Worte beendete, ging er nach Kafarnaum.

⟦Et il arriva que lorsqu'⟧il .. eut achevé ces paroles, il entra dans Capharnaüm.

Q 7:1, ~~2~~, 3, ~~4-6a~~, 6b-9, ?10?

Q 7:~~2~~, 3, ~~4-6a~~

Mark 7:25-27	Matt 15:22-23a, 25-26	Matt 8:5b-7	Q 7:~~2~~, 3, ~~4-6a~~
		8:5b ʃ ʅ[1]	**7:~~2~~** ʃʅ[1]
7:25 ἀλλ’ εὐθὺς ἀκούσασα	**15:22** καὶ ἰδοὺ	[ ][2]	**7:3** ⟦[][2]⟧
γυνὴ περὶ αὐτοῦ,	γυνὴ Χαναναία		
	ἀπὸ τῶν ὁρίων ἐκείνων		
	ἐξελθοῦσα ἔκραζεν		
	λέγουσα· ἐλέησόν με,		
	κύριε υἱὸς Δαυίδ·		
ἧς εἶχεν τὸ θυγάτριον	ἡ θυγάτηρ		
αὐτῆς πνεῦμα ἀκάθαρτον,	μου κακῶς δαιμονίζεται.		
	15:23a ὁ δὲ οὐκ ἀπεκρίθη		
	αὐτῇ λόγον.		
ἐλθοῦσα	**15:25** ἡ δὲ ἐλθοῦσα	(προσῆλθεν)[3]	(<>[3]ἦλθεν)[3]
προσέπεσεν	προσεκύνει		
πρὸς τοὺς πόδας αὐτοῦ·	αὐτῷ	[ ][4] αὐτ(ῷ)[4]	[][4] αὐτ(ῷ)[4]
7:26 ἡ δὲ γυνὴ ἦν Ἑλληνίς,		[1]ʃἑκατόνταρχ(ος)[5] ʅ[1]	[1]ʃἑκατόνταρχ⟦(ο)[5]⟧(ς)[5] ʅ[1]
Συροφοινίκισσα τῷ γένει·		[ ][3]	[][3]
καὶ ἠρώτα αὐτὸν		(παρακαλ)[6]ῶν αὐτὸν	(παρακαλ)[6]ῶν αὐτὸν
ἵνα	λέγουσα·	**8:6** (καὶ λέγων·)[7]	⟦(καὶ λέγων·)[7]⟧
	κύριε,	(κύριε,)[8]	()[8]
τὸ δαιμόνιον ἐκβάλῃ	βοήθει μοι.	[1]ʃ (ὁ παῖς)[9] (μου)[7]	[1]ʃ (ὁ παῖς)[9] ⟦(μου)[7]
ἐκ τῆς θυγατρὸς αὐτῆς.		(βέβληται ἐν τῇ οἰκίᾳ	[κακῶς ἔχ][10]<ει>[10]
		παραλυτικός)[10],	
		(δεινῶς βασανιζόμενος)[11]. ʅ[1]	[()][11]. ʅ[1]

[1] Does the sequence of the pericope present the situation of the Centurion, the sick person, and the illness in an introductory narration (Luke), or in a brief introduction to the opening dialogue (Matthew)?

[2] Luke's ἀκούσας δὲ περὶ τοῦ Ἰησοῦ.

[3] Luke's ἀπέστειλεν … πρεσβυτέρους τῶν Ἰουδαίων or Matthew's προσῆλθεν.

[4] Luke's πρὸς αὐτόν or Matthew's αὐτῷ.

[5] Luke's ἑκατοντάρχου δέ τινος or Matthew's ἑκατόνταρχος.

Q 7:~~2~~, 3, ~~4-6a~~

Luke 7:2-6a	Luke 8:41-42a	Mark 5:22-23	John 4:46b-48
7:2 [1]⸂Ἑκατοντάρχ[ου δέ			**4:46b** Καὶ ἦν
τινος][5]			τις βασιλικὸς
[δοῦλος][9]			οὗ ὁ υἱὸς
[κακῶς ἔχων][10]			ἠσθένει
[ἤμελλεν τελευτᾶν][11],			ἐν Καφαρναούμ.
[ὃς ἦν αὐτῷ ἔντιμος][9]. ⸃[1]			
7:3 [ἀκούσας δὲ			**4:47** οὗτος ἀκούσας
περὶ τοῦ Ἰησοῦ][2]			ὅτι Ἰησοῦς ἥκει
			ἐκ τῆς Ἰουδαίας
			εἰς τὴν Γαλιλαίαν
[ἀπέστειλεν][3]	**8:41** καὶ ἰδοὺ ἦλθεν ἀνὴρ	**5:22** Καὶ ἔρχεται	ἀπῆλθεν
	ᾧ ὄνομα Ἰάϊρος καὶ οὗτος	εἷς τῶν ἀρχισυναγώγων,	
[πρὸς][4] αὐτ[ὸν][4]	ἄρχων τῆς συναγωγῆς	ὀνόματι Ἰάϊρος,	πρὸς αὐτὸν
⸂ ⸃[1]	ὑπῆρχεν, καὶ πεσὼν	καὶ ἰδὼν αὐτὸν πίπτει	
[πρεσβυτέρους	παρὰ τοὺς πόδας τοῦ Ἰησοῦ	πρὸς τοὺς πόδας αὐτοῦ	
τῶν Ἰουδαίων][3]			
[ἐρωτ][6]ῶν αὐτὸν	παρεκάλει αὐτὸν εἰσελθεῖν	**5:23** καὶ παρακαλεῖ αὐτὸν	καὶ ἠρώτα
[ὅπως][7]	εἰς τὸ οἶκον αὐτοῦ,	πολλὰ λέγων	ἵνα
( )[8]	**8:42a** ὅτι	ὅτι	
⸂ ⸃[1]	θυγάτηρ μονογενὴς ἦν αὐτῷ	τὸ θυγάτριόν μου	
	ὡς ἐτῶν δώδεκα		
	καὶ αὐτὴ ἀπέθνῃσκεν.	ἐσχάτως ἔχει,	

6 Luke's ἐρωτῶν αὐτόν or Matthew's παρακαλῶν αὐτὸν. (See also Luke 7:4 παρεκάλουν αὐτόν).

7 Luke's ὅπως with indirect discourse or Matthew's direct discourse: καὶ λέγων· … μου … καὶ λέγει αὐτῷ· ἐγὼ … -ω.

8 Matthew's κύριε.

9 Luke's δοῦλος … , ὃς ἦν αὐτῷ ἔντιμος or Matthew's ὁ παῖς.

10 Luke's κακῶς ἔχων or Matthew's βέβληται ἐν τῇ οἰκίᾳ παραλυτικός. (See also Luke 7:6b ἀπὸ τῆς οἰκίας).

11 Luke's ἤμελλεν τελευτᾶν or Matthew's δεινῶς βασανιζόμενος.

Q 7:~~2~~, 3, ~~4-6a~~

Mark 7:25-27	Matt 15:22-23a, 25-26	Matt 8:5b-7	Q 7:~~2~~, 3, ~~4-6a~~
7:27 καὶ ἔλεγεν αὐτῇ· ἄφες πρῶτον χορτασθῆναι τὰ τέκνα, οὐ γάρ ἐστιν καλὸν λαβεῖν	**15:26** ὁ δὲ ἀποκριθεὶς εἶπεν· οὐκ ἔστιν καλὸν λαβεῖν	**8:7** (καὶ λέγει αὐτῷ· ἐγὼ)[7] ἐλθὼν (θεραπεύσ)[12](ω)[7] (αὐτόν;)[12]	(καὶ λέγει αὐτῷ· ἐγὼ)[7]⟧ ἐλθὼν (θεραπεύσ)[12]⟦(ω)[7]⟧ (αὐτόν;)[12]
		[ ][13]	**7:~~4~~** [][13]
τὸν ἄρτον τῶν τέκνων καὶ τοῖς κυναρίοις βαλεῖν.	τὸν ἄρτον τῶν τέκνων καὶ βαλεῖν τοῖς κυναρίοις.		
			7:~~5~~
			7:~~6a~~

JSK: ʃ ʅ[1] indeterminate.
IQP 1994: 7:3 [][2] (προσῆλθεν)[3].
JSK: 7:3 [ ][2] Luke = Q {D}.

JSK: 7:3 ⟦[πρὸς][4]⟧ αὐτ⟦[όν][4]⟧.
IQP 7:3 1994: ἑκατόνταρχ( )[5]ς; JSK: ἑκατόνταρχ⟦<η>[5]ς⟧.

Text Critical Note: See the discussion of the punctuation in the front matter.

[12] Luke's διασώσῃ τὸν δοῦλον αὐτοῦ· or Matthew's θεραπεύσ- αὐτόν;.

[13] Is Luke 7:4-6a in Q?

Q

<>ἦλθεν αὐτῷ ἑκατόνταρχ⟦ο⟧ς παρακαλῶν αὐτὸν ⟦καὶ λέγων·⟧ ὁ παῖς ⟦μου κακῶς ἔχ<ει>. καὶ λέγει αὐτῷ· ἐγὼ⟧ ἐλθὼν θεραπεύσ⟦ω⟧ αὐτόν;	There came to him a centurion exhorting him ⟦and saying: My⟧ boy ⟦<is> doing badly. And he said to him: Am I⟧, by coming, to heal him?

Q 7:~~2~~, 3, ~~4-6a~~

Luke 7:2-6a	Luke 8:41-42a	Mark 5:22-23	John 4:46b-48
( )[7]			
ἐλθὼν [διασώσῃ τὸν δοῦλον αὐτοῦ.][12]		ἵνα ἐλθὼν ἐπιθῇς τὰς χεῖρας αὐτῇ ἵνα σωθῇ καὶ ζήσῃ.	καταβῇ καὶ ἰάσηται αὐτοῦ τὸν υἱόν, ἤμελλεν γὰρ ἀποθνῄσκειν.
7:4 [οἱ δὲ παραγενόμενοι πρὸς τὸν Ἰησοῦν παρεκάλουν αὐτὸν σπουδαίως λέγοντες ὅτι ἄξιός ἐστιν ᾧ παρέξῃ τοῦτο· **7:5** ἀγαπᾷ γὰρ τὸ ἔθνος ἡμῶν καὶ τὴν συναγωγὴν αὐτὸς ᾠκοδόμησεν ἡμῖν. **7:6a** ὁ δὲ Ἰησοῦς ἐπορεύετο σὺν αὐτοῖς.][13]			**4:48** εἶπεν οὖν ὁ Ἰησοῦς πρὸς αὐτόν· ἐὰν μὴ σημεῖα καὶ τέρατα ἴδητε, οὐ μὴ πιστεύσητε.

IQP 1994: 7:3 (καὶ λέγων·)[7] ()[8] [1]ʃ (ὁ παῖς)[9] (μου)[7.9] ⟦[κακῶς ἔχων][10]⟧ [ ][11]. ʅ[1] (καὶ λέγει αὐτῷ· ἐγὼ)[7] ἐλθὼν (θεραπεύσ)[12](ω)[7] (αὐτόν)[12] (ending in a period rather than a question mark).

JSK: 7:3 ⟦(μου)[7.9]⟧.
JMR: 7:3 [()][11].

Ein Zenturio kam zu ihm, bat ihn ⟦und sagte: Mein⟧ Bursche ⟦<ist> krank. Und er sagt zu ihm: Soll ich⟧ kommen und ihn heilen?

Un centurion vint à lui, le suppliant ⟦et disant: Mon⟧ fils ⟦<est> malade. Et il lui dit: Moi⟧ vais-je venir le guérir?

Q 7:6b-c

Mark 7:28	Matt 15:27	Matt 8:8a	Q 7:6b-c
ἡ δὲ ἀπεκρίθη	{ἡ δὲ εἶπεν·	(καὶ ἀποκριθεὶς)[1]	(καὶ ἀποκριθεὶς)[1]
		[ ][2]	[][2]
καὶ		ὁ ἑκατόνταρχ(ο)[3]ς	ὁ ἑκατόνταρχ(ο)[3]ς
λέγει		(ἔφη)[4]	(ἔφη)[4]
αὐτῷ·		[ ][5]·	[][5]·
κύριε·	ναὶ κύριε,	κύριε,	κύριε,
		[ ][6]	[][6]
καὶ τὰ κυνάρια	καὶ γὰρ τὰ κυνάρια	οὐ(κ)[7] [ ][7]	οὐ(κ)[7] [][7]
		⸉ ⸊[8] εἰμὶ ⸉ἱκανὸς⸊[8]	⸉⸊[8] εἰμὶ ⸉ἱκανὸς⸊[8]
ὑποκάτω τῆς τραπέζης		ἵνα ⸉μου⸊[9] ὑπὸ τὴν στέγην	ἵνα ⸉μου⸊[9] ὑπὸ τὴν στέγην
ἐσθίουσιν ἀπὸ τῶν ψιχίων	ἐσθίει ἀπὸ τῶν ψιχίων	⸉ ⸊[9] εἰσέλθῃς,	⸉⸊[9] εἰσέλθῃς,
	τῶν πιπτόντων ἀπὸ τῆς		
	τραπέζης		
τῶν παιδίων.	τῶν κυρίων αὐτῶν.		

IQP 1994: ἑκατονταρχ[( )][3]ς; JSK: ἑκατόνταρχ(η)[3]ς.

PH: (< >)[4] indeterminate.

Text Critical Note (see the discussion in the front matter): In Matt 8:8a ἀποκριθεὶς δέ is in ℵ* B 33 *pc* sa, but καὶ ἀποκριθείς is in ℵ[1] C L W Θ 0233 $f^{1.13}$ 𝔐 lat sy^{h} bo.

1 Matthew's καὶ ἀποκριθείς.
2 Luke's ἤδη δὲ αὐτοῦ οὐ μακρὰν ἀπέχοντος ἀπὸ τῆς οἰκίας ἔπεμψεν φίλους.
3 Luke's ἑκατοντάρχης or Matthew's ἑκατόνταρχος.
4 Luke's λέγων or Matthew's ἔφη.
5 Luke's αὐτῷ.

Q

καὶ ἀποκριθεὶς ὁ ἑκατόνταρχος ἔφη· κύριε, οὐκ εἰμὶ ἱκανὸς ἵνα μου ὑπὸ τὴν στέγην εἰσέλθῃς,	And in reply the centurion said: Master, I am not worthy for you to come under my roof;

Q 7:6b-c

Luke 7:6b-c	Lukan Doublet	Markan Parallel	John 4:51a, 49
( )[1] [ἤδη δὲ αὐτοῦ οὐ μακρὰν ἀπέχοντος ἀπὸ τῆς οἰκίας ἔπεμψεν φίλους][2] ὁ ἑκατοντάρχ[η][3]ς [λέγων][4] [αὐτῷ][5]· κύριε, [μὴ σκύλλου][6], οὐ( )[7] [γὰρ][7] ʃἱκανόςʅ[8] εἰμι ʃ ʅ[8] ἵνα ʃ ʅ[9] ὑπὸ τὴν στέγην ʃμουʅ[9] εἰσέλθῃς·			**4:51a** ἤδη δὲ αὐτοῦ καταβαίνοντος ——— **4:49** λέγει πρὸς αὐτὸν ὁ βασιλικός· κύριε, κατάβηθι πρὶν ἀποθανεῖν τὸ παιδίον μου.

IQP 1994, JSK: ʃ ʅ[8].

IQP 1994: ʃ ʅ[9].

[6] Luke's μὴ σκύλλου.
[7] Luke's οὐ γάρ or Matthew's οὐκ.
[8] The position of ἱκανός before (Luke) or after (Matthew) εἰμι.

[9] The position of μου after (Luke) or before (Matthew) ὑπὸ τὴν στέγην.

Und der Zenturio antwortete «und» sprach: Herr, ich bin nicht würdig, dass du unter mein Dach kommst,

Et en réponse, le centurion dit: Seigneur, je ne suis pas digne que tu entres sous mon toit,

Q 7:7

Markan Parallel	Matthean Doublet	Matt 8:8b	Q 7:7
		[ ][1] ἀλλὰ (μόνον)[2] εἰπὲ λόγῳ, καὶ ἰαθή(σεται)[3] ὁ παῖς μου.	[][1] ἀλλὰ ⟦()[2]⟧ εἰπὲ λόγῳ, καὶ ἰαθή⟦[τω][3]⟧ ὁ παῖς μου.

IQP 1994: ()[2].

IQP 1994: ἰαθή⟦(σεται)[3]⟧.

[1] Luke's διὸ οὐδὲ ἐμαυτὸν ἠξίωσα πρὸς σὲ ἐλθεῖν.

[2] Matthew's μόνον.

Q

ἀλλὰ εἰπὲ λόγῳ, καὶ ἰαθή⟦τω⟧ ὁ παῖς μου.	but say a word, and ⟦let⟧ my boy ⟦be⟧ healed.

Q 7:7

Luke 7:7	Lukan Doublet	Markan Parallel	Gospel of Thomas
[διὸ οὐδὲ ἐμαυτὸν ἠξίωσα πρὸς σὲ ἐλθεῖν][1]· ἀλλὰ ( )[2] εἰπὲ λόγῳ, καὶ ἰαθή[τω][3] ὁ παῖς μου.			

[3] Luke's ἰαθήτω or Matthew's ἰαθήσεται.

aber sage ein Wort, und ⟦lass⟧ meinen Burschen gesund ⟦werden⟧.

mais ne dis qu'une parole et ⟦fais que⟧ mon fils ⟦soit⟧ guéri.

Q 7:8

Markan Parallel	Matthean Doublet	Matt 8:9	Q 7:8
		καὶ γὰρ ἐγὼ ἄνθρωπός εἰμι ὑπὸ ἐξουσίαν [ ][1], ἔχων ὑπ' ἐμαυτὸν στρατιώτας, καὶ λέγω τούτῳ· πορεύθητι, καὶ πορεύεται, καὶ ἄλλῳ· ἔρχου, καὶ ἔρχεται, καὶ τῷ δούλῳ μου· ποίησον τοῦτο, καὶ ποιεῖ.	καὶ γὰρ ἐγὼ ἄνθρωπός εἰμι ὑπὸ ἐξουσίαν [][1], ἔχων ὑπ' ἐμαυτὸν στρατιώτας, καὶ λέγω τούτῳ· πορεύθητι, καὶ πορεύεται, καὶ ἄλλῳ· ἔρχου, καὶ ἔρχεται, καὶ τῷ δούλῳ μου· ποίησον τοῦτο, καὶ ποιεῖ.

[1] Luke's τασσόμενος.

Q

καὶ γὰρ ἐγὼ ἄνθρωπός εἰμι ὑπὸ ἐξουσίαν, ἔχων ὑπ' ἐμαυτὸν στρατιώτας, καὶ λέγω τούτῳ· πορεύθητι, καὶ πορεύεται, καὶ ἄλλῳ· ἔρχου, καὶ ἔρχεται, καὶ τῷ δούλῳ μου· ποίησον τοῦτο, καὶ ποιεῖ.

For I too am a person under authority, with soldiers under me, and I say to one: Go, and he goes, and to another: Come, and he comes, and to my slave: Do this, and he does «it».

Q 7:8

Luke 7:8	Lukan Doublet	Markan Parallel	Gospel of Thomas
καὶ γὰρ ἐγὼ ἄνθρωπός εἰμι ὑπὸ ἐξουσίαν [τασσόμενος][1] ἔχων ὑπ᾽ ἐμαυτὸν στρατιώτας, καὶ λέγω τούτῳ· πορεύθητι, καὶ πορεύεται, καὶ ἄλλῳ· ἔρχου, καὶ ἔρχεται, καὶ τῷ δούλῳ μου· ποίησον τοῦτο, καὶ ποιεῖ.			

Denn auch ich bin ein Mensch unter einer Autorität, und ich habe unter mir Soldaten, und ich sage diesem: Geh, und er geht, und einem anderen: Komm, und er kommt, und meinem Sklaven: Tu dies, und er tut «es».

Car je suis aussi une personne soumise à une autorité, avec des soldats sous mes ordres, et je dis à l'un: Va, et il va; et à un autre: Viens, et il vient; et à mon esclave: Fais ceci, et il «le» fait.

Q 7:9

Markan Parallel	Matthean Doublet	Matt 8:10	Q 7:9
		ἀκούσας δὲ [ ][1]	ἀκούσας δὲ [][1]
		ὁ Ἰησοῦς ἐθαύμασεν	ὁ Ἰησοῦς ἐθαύμασεν
		[ ][2]	[][2]
		καὶ [ ][3]	καὶ [][3]
		⌐εἶπεν¬[4]	⌐εἶπεν¬[4]
		τ(οῖς)[5] ἀκολουθοῦ(σιν)[5]	τ(οῖς)[5] ἀκολουθοῦ(σιν)[5]
		⌐ ¬[4].	⌐¬[4].
		(ἀμὴν)[6] λέγω ὑμῖν,	()[6] λέγω ὑμῖν,
		(παρ')[7] οὐδε(νὶ)[7]	()[7] οὐδε()[7]
		⌐ ¬[8]	⌐ἐν τῷ Ἰσραὴλ¬[8]
		τοσαύτην πίστιν	τοσαύτην πίστιν
		⌐ἐν τῷ Ἰσραὴλ¬[8]	⌐¬[8]
		εὗρον.	εὗρον.

IQP 1994: τ⟦(οῖς)[5]⟧ ἀκολουθοῦ⟦(σιν)[5]⟧.

[1] Luke's ταῦτα.

[2] Luke's αὐτόν.

[3] Luke's στραφείς.

[4] The position of εἶπεν after (Luke) or before (Matthew) the reference to the followers.

Q

ἀκούσας δὲ ὁ Ἰησοῦς ἐθαύμασεν καὶ εἶπεν τοῖς ἀκολουθοῦσιν· λέγω ὑμῖν, οὐδὲ ἐν τῷ Ἰσραὴλ τοσαύτην πίστιν εὗρον.	But Jesus, on hearing, was amazed, and said to those who followed: I tell you, not even in Israel have I found such faith.

Q 7:9

Luke 7:9	Lukan Doublet	Markan Parallel	Gospel of Thomas
ἀκούσας δὲ [ταῦτα][1] ὁ Ἰησοῦς ἐθαύμασεν [αὐτὸν][2] καὶ [στραφεὶς][3] ⸉ ⸊[4] τ[ῷ][5] ἀκολουθοῦ[ντι αὐτῷ ὄχλῳ][5] ⸉εἶπεν⸊[4]· ( )[6] λέγω ὑμῖν, ( )[7] οὐδὲ( )[7] ⸉ἐν τῷ Ἰσραὴλ⸊[8] τοσαύτην πίστιν ⸉ ⸊[8] εὗρον.			

[5] Luke's τῷ ἀκολουθοῦντι αὐτῷ ὄχλῳ or Matthew's τοῖς ἀκολουθοῦσιν.
[6] Matthew's ἀμήν.
[7] Luke's οὐδέ or Matthew's παρ' οὐδενί.
[8] The position of ἐν τῷ Ἰσραήλ before (Luke) or after (Matthew) τοσαύτην πίστιν.

Als er aber das hörte, staunte Jesus und sagte zu denen, die ihm nachfolgten: Ich sage euch, nicht einmal in Israel habe ich solchen Glauben gefunden.

En entendant «cela», Jésus s'étonna et dit à ceux qui l'accompagnaient: Je vous «le» dis, même en Israël, je n'ai pas trouvé une si grande foi.

Q 7:?10?

Mark 7:29	Matt 15:28	Matt 8:13	Q 7:?10?
		[0]/	< >[0]
καὶ	τότε ἀποκριθεὶς	(καὶ εἶπεν)[1]	
εἶπεν	ὁ Ἰησοῦς εἶπεν	(ὁ Ἰησοῦς)[2]	
αὐτῇ·	αὐτῇ·	(τῷ ἑκατοντάρχῃ)[3]·	
διὰ τοῦτον τὸν λόγον	ὦ γύναι,		
ὕπαγε,		(ὕπαγε,	
	μεγάλη σου ἡ πίστις·	ὡς ἐπίστευσας	
	γενηθήτω σοι ὡς θέλεις.	γενηθήτω σοι.)[4]	
ἐξελήλυθεν	καὶ ἰάθη	καὶ (ἰάθη	
ἐκ τῆς θυγατρός σου	ἡ θυγάτηρ αὐτῆς	ὁ παῖς αὐτοῦ	
τὸ δαιμόνιον			
.	ἀπὸ τῆς ὥρας ἐκείνης.	ἐν τῇ ὥρᾳ ἐκείνῃ)[4].	.
		\[0]	

IQP 1994: καὶ ⟦⟧ < >; JSK: < >[0] something was in Q {B}; JMR: < >[0] something was in Q {D}; PH: < >[0] indeterminate.

[0] Is there in Q some concluding statement?

[1] Matthew's εἶπεν.

[2] Matthew's ὁ Ἰησοῦς.

[3] Matthew's τῷ ἑκατοντάρχῃ.

Q

<..>	<..>

Q 7:?10?

Luke 7:10	Lukan Doublet	Mark 7:30	John 4:50-53
[0]/			
( )[1]			**4:50** λέγει αὐτῷ
( )[2]			ὁ Ἰησοῦς·
( )[3]			
			πορεύου, ὁ υἱός σου ζῇ.
[Καὶ		καὶ	ἐπίστευσεν ὁ ἄνθρωπος
ὑποστρέψαντες		ἀπελθοῦσα	τῷ λόγῳ ὃν εἶπεν αὐτῷ
εἰς τὸν οἶκον		εἰς τὸν οἶκον αὐτῆς	ὁ Ἰησοῦς καὶ ἐπορεύετο.
			4:51 ἤδη δὲ αὐτοῦ
			καταβαίνοντος
οἱ πεμφθέντες			οἱ δοῦλοι αὐτοῦ
			ὑπήντησαν αὐτῷ
			λέγοντες ὅτι
			ὁ παῖς αὐτοῦ ζῇ.
			4:52 ἐπύθετο οὖν
			τὴν ὥραν παρ' αὐτῶν
			ἐν ᾗ κομψότερον ἔσχεν·
			εἶπαν οὖν αὐτῷ
			ὅτι ἐχθὲς ὥραν ἑβδόμην
εὗρον		εὗρεν	ἀφῆκεν
τὸν δοῦλον		τὸ παιδίον	αὐτὸν
		βεβλημένον ἐπὶ τὴν κλίνην	
		καὶ τὸ δαιμόνιον	ὁ πυρετός.
ὑγιαίνοντα][4]		ἐξεληλυθός	**4:53** ἔγνω οὖν ὁ πατὴρ
.		.	ὅτι ἐν ἐκείνῃ τῇ ὥρᾳ
\[0]			ἐν ᾗ εἶπεν αὐτῷ
			ὁ Ἰησοῦς·
			ὁ υἱός σου ζῇ,
			καὶ ἐπίστευσεν αὐτὸς
			καὶ ἡ οἰκία αὐτοῦ ὅλη.

[4] The form of the statement about the Centurion's or his delegation's departure and the confirmation of the healing, including Matthew's statement about faith.

<..>

<..>

Q 7:18-19

Markan Parallel	Matthean Doublet	Matt 11:2-3	Q 7:18-19
		11:1 (Καὶ ἐγένετο	()[0]
		ὅτε ἐτέλεσεν ὁ Ἰησοῦς	
		διατάσσων τοῖς δώδεκα	
		μαθηταῖς αὐτοῦ,	
		μετέβη ἐκεῖθεν τοῦ	
		διδάσκειν καὶ κηρύσσειν	
		ἐν ταῖς πόλεσιν αὐτῶν.)[0]	
		11:2 ⸂ ⸃[1]	**7:18** ⸂[ ]⸃[1]
		⸂Ὁ⸃[2]	⸂ὁ⸃[2]
		⸂ (δὲ)[1] ⸃[1]	⸂ ( )⸃[1]
		⸂Ἰωάννης⸃[2]	⸂Ἰωάννης⸃[2]
		(ἀκούσας)[3]	⟦(ἀκούσας)[3]⟧
		(ἐν τῷ δεσμωτηρίῳ)[4]	( )[4]
		(τὰ ἔργα τοῦ Χριστοῦ)[5]	⟦[περὶ πάντων τούτων][5]
		[ ][6]	[][6]
		⸂[ ][7]πέμψ(ας)[7] ⸃[7]	⸂[][7]⟧πέμψ⟦(ας)[7]⟧ ⸃[7]
		(διὰ)[8]	(διὰ)[8]
		τῶν μαθητῶν αὐτοῦ	τῶν μαθητῶν αὐτοῦ
		⸂ ⸃[2]	⸂⸃[2]
		⸂ ⸃[7]	**7:19** ⸂ ⸃[7]
		⸂ ⸃[9]	⸂⸃[9]
		11:3 (εἶπεν)[10]	⟦(εἶπεν)[10]⟧
		⸂(αὐτῷ)[9] ⸃[9]·	⸂(αὐτῷ)[9] ⸃[9]·
		σὺ εἶ ὁ ἐρχόμενος	σὺ εἶ ὁ ἐρχόμενος
		ἢ (ἕτερ)[11]ον προσδοκῶμεν;	ἢ ⟦(ἕτερ)[11]⟧ον προσδοκῶμεν;

IQP 1993: **7:18** ⸂[ ][1] ⸃[1] ⸂ὁ⸃[2] ⸂( )[1] ⸃[1] ⸂Ἰωάννης⸃[2] ( )[3] ⟦()[4]⟧ [( )][5] [][6] ⸂[][7]πέμψ( )[7] ⸃[7] (διὰ)[8] τῶν μαθητῶν αὐτοῦ ⸂⸃[2] **7:19** ⸂⸃[7] ⸂⸃[9] [( )][10] ⸂(αὐτῷ)[9] ⸃[9] σὺ εἶ ὁ ἐρχόμενος ἢ [( )][11]ον προσδοκῶμεν.

0 Is Matt 11:1 in Q?
1 Luke's *καί* or Matthew's postpositive δέ.
2 John as subject after (Luke) or before (Matthew) the introduction of his disciples.
3 Luke's ἀπήγγειλαν Ἰωάννῃ οἱ μαθηταὶ αὐτοῦ or Matthew's ἀκούσας.
4 Matthew's ἐν τῷ δεσμωτηρίῳ.
5 Luke's περὶ πάντων τούτων or Matthew's τὰ ἔργα τοῦ Χριστοῦ.

Q

18 .. ὁ .. Ἰωάννης ⟦ἀκούσας περὶ πάντων τούτων⟧ πέμψ⟦ας⟧ διὰ τῶν μαθητῶν αὐτοῦ **19** ⟦εἶπεν⟧ αὐτῷ· σὺ εἶ ὁ ἐρχόμενος ἢ ⟦ἕτερ⟧ον προσδοκῶμεν;

18 And John, ⟦on hearing about all these things⟧, sending through his disciples, **19** ⟦said⟧ to him: Are you the one to come, or are we to expect someone else?

Q 7:18-19

Luke 7:18-19	Lukan Doublet	Markan Parallel	Gospel of Thomas
()[0]			
7:18 ⸀[Καὶ][1] ⸁[1] ⸀ ⸁[2] ⸀ ⸁[1] ⸀ ⸁[2] [ἀπήγγειλαν Ἰωάννῃ οἱ μαθηταὶ αὐτοῦ][3] ( )[4] [περὶ πάντων τούτων.][5] [καὶ προσκαλεσάμενος][6] ⸀ ⸁[7] [δύο τινὰς][8] τῶν μαθητῶν αὐτοῦ ⸀ὁ Ἰωάννης⸁[2] **7:19** ⸀[ἔ][7]πεμψ[εν][7] ⸁[7] ⸀[πρὸς τὸν κύριον][9] ⸁[9] [λέγων][10] ⸀ ⸁[9]· σὺ εἶ ὁ ἐρχόμενος ἢ [ἄλλ][11]ον προσδοκῶμεν;			

JMR, PH, JSK: ( )[4] indeterminate.

[6] Luke's καὶ προσκαλεσάμενος.
[7] Luke's ἔπεμψεν or Matthew's πέμψας and the divergence of position.
[8] Luke's δύο τινάς or Matthew's διά.
[9] Luke's πρὸς τὸν κύριον or Matthew's αὐτῷ and the divergence of position.
[10] Luke's λέγων or Matthew's εἶπεν.
[11] Luke's ἄλλον or Matthew's ἕτερον.

18 Und ⟦als⟧ Johannes ⟦von all dem hörte⟧, schickte er durch seine Jünger **19** «und ließ» ihm ⟦sagen⟧: Bist du es, der kommen soll, oder müssen wir auf einen anderen warten?

18 Et Jean, ⟦ayant entendu parler de toutes ces choses⟧, envoya lui ⟦demander⟧ par ses disciples: **19** Es-tu celui qui doit venir ou devons-nous en attendre un autre?

Q 7:~~20~~

Markan Parallel	Matthean Doublet	Matthew	Q 7:~~20~~
		[ ][1]	[][1]

[1] Is Luke 7:20 in Q?

Q 7:~~20~~

Luke 7:20	Lukan Doublet	Markan Parallel	Gospel of Thomas
[παραγενόμενοι δὲ πρὸς αὐτὸν οἱ ἄνδρες εἶπαν· Ἰωάννης ὁ βαπτιστὴς ἀπέστειλεν ἡμᾶς πρὸς σὲ λέγων· σὺ εἶ ὁ ἐρχόμενος ἢ ἄλλον προσδοκῶμεν;][1]			

Q 7:~~21~~

Markan Parallel	Matthean Doublet	Matthew	Q 7:~~21~~
		[ ][1]	[][1]

[1] Is Luke 7:21 in Q?

Q 7:~~21~~

Luke 7:21	Lukan Doublet	Mark 3:10	Gospel of Thomas
[ἐν ἐκείνῃ τῇ ὥρᾳ ἐθεράπευσεν πολλοὺς ἀπὸ νόσων καὶ μαστίγων καὶ πνευμάτων πονηρῶν καὶ τυφλοῖς πολλοῖς ἐχαρίσατο βλέπειν.][1]		πολλοὺς γὰρ ἐθεράπευσεν, ὥστε ἐπιπίπτειν αὐτῷ ἵνα αὐτοῦ ἅψωνται ὅσοι εἶχον μάστιγας.	

Q 7:22

Markan Parallel	Matthean Doublet	Matt 11:4-5	Q 7:22
		καὶ ἀποκριθεὶς (ὁ Ἰησοῦς)[1]	καὶ ἀποκριθεὶς ⟦()[1]⟧
		εἶπεν αὐτοῖς·	εἶπεν αὐτοῖς·
		πορευθέντες ἀπαγγείλατε	πορευθέντες ἀπαγγείλατε
		Ἰωάννῃ ἃ	Ἰωάννῃ ἃ
		[2]ʃ (ἀ)[3]κού(ε)[3]τεʅ[2] καὶ	[2]ʃ (ἀ)[3]κού(ε)[3]τεʅ[2] καὶ
		[2]ʃ (βλέπ)[3]ετεʅ[2]·	[2]ʃ (βλέπ)[3]ετεʅ[2]·
		11:5 τυφλοὶ ἀναβλέπουσιν	τυφλοὶ ἀναβλέπουσιν
		(καὶ)[4] χωλοὶ	(καὶ)[4] χωλοὶ
		περιπατοῦσιν,	περιπατοῦσιν,
		λεπροὶ καθαρίζονται	λεπροὶ καθαρίζονται
		καὶ κωφοὶ ἀκούουσιν,	καὶ κωφοὶ ἀκούουσιν,
		(καὶ)[4] νεκροὶ ἐγείρονται	(καὶ)[4] νεκροὶ ἐγείρονται
		(καὶ)[4] πτωχοὶ	(καὶ)[4] πτωχοὶ
		εὐαγγελίζονται·	εὐαγγελίζονται·

IQP 1993: ⟦()[1]⟧.

[1] Matthew's ὁ Ἰησοῦς.

[2] The transposition of the verbs for «hear» and «see.»

Q

καὶ ἀποκριθεὶς εἶπεν αὐτοῖς· πορευθέντες ἀπαγγείλατε Ἰωάννῃ ἃ ἀκούετε καὶ βλέπετε· τυφλοὶ ἀναβλέπουσιν καὶ χωλοὶ περιπατοῦσιν, λεπροὶ καθαρίζονται καὶ κωφοὶ ἀκούουσιν, καὶ νεκροὶ ἐγείρονται καὶ πτωχοὶ εὐαγγελίζονται·

And in reply he said to them: Go report to John what you hear and see: The blind regain their sight and the lame walk around, the skin-diseased are cleansed and the deaf hear, and the dead are raised, and the poor are evangelized.

Q 7:22

Luke 7:22	Isa 61:1 LXX	Isa 42:7,18; 26:19a LXX	Isa 35:5-6a; 29:18-19a LXX
καὶ ἀποκριθεὶς ( )[1]			35:5 τότε ἀνοιχθήσονται
εἶπεν αὐτοῖς·			ὀφθαλμοὶ τυφλῶν,
πορευθέντες ἀπαγγείλατε			καὶ ὦτα κωφῶν ἀκούσονται.
Ἰωάννῃ ἃ		42:7 ἀνοῖξαι ὀφθαλμοὺς τυφλῶν,	35:6a τότε ἁλεῖται ὡς ἔλαφος
[2]⸉ [εἴδ][3]ετε⸊[2] καὶ	Πνεῦμα κυρίου ἐπ' ἐμέ,	ἐξαγαγεῖν ἐκ δεσμῶν δεδεμένους	ὁ κωλός, καὶ τρανὴ ἔσται
[2]⸉ [ἠ][3]κού[σα][3]τε⸊[2].	οὗ εἵνεκεν ἔχρισέν με·	καὶ ἐξ οἴκου φυλακῆς	γλῶσσα μογιλάλων,
τυφλοὶ ἀναβλέπουσιν,	εὐαγγελίσασθαι πτωχοῖς	καθημένους ἐν σκότει.	29:18 καὶ ἀκούσονται
( )[4] χωλοὶ	ἀπέσταλκέν με,	42:18 Οἱ κωφοί, ἀκούσατε,	ἐν τῇ ἡμέρᾳ ἐκείνῃ
περιπατοῦσιν,	ἰάσασθαι τοὺς συντετριμμένους	καὶ οἱ τυφλοί,	κωφοὶ λόγους βιβλίου,
λεπροὶ καθαρίζονται	τῇ καρδίᾳ,	ἀναβλέψατε ἰδεῖν.	καὶ οἱ ἐν τῷ σκότει
καὶ κωφοὶ ἀκούουσιν,	κηρύξαι αἰχμαλώτοις ἄφεσιν	26:19a ἀναστήσονται	καὶ οἱ ἐν τῇ ὁμίχλῃ
( )[4] νεκροὶ ἐγείρονται,	καὶ τυφλοῖς ἀνάβλεψιν,	οἱ νεκροί, καὶ ἐγερθήσονται	ὀφθαλυοὶ τυφλῶν βλέψονται·
( )[4] πτωχοὶ		οἱ ἐν τοῖς μνημείοις, καὶ	29:19a καὶ ἀγαλλιάσονται πτωχοὶ
εὐαγγελίζονται·		εὐφρανθήσονται οἱ ἐν τῇ γῇ·	διὰ κύριον ἐν εὐφροσύνῃ,

[3] Luke's aorist or Matthew's present tense, and the divergence of the stem for the verb of seeing.

[4] Matthew's *καί* (*ter*).

Und er antwortete «und» sagte ihnen: Geht «und» berichtet Johannes, was ihr hört und seht: Blinde sehen wieder, und Lahme gehen umher, Aussätzige werden rein, und Taube hören, und Tote werden erweckt, und Arme bekommen eine gute Botschaft.

Et en réponse, il leur dit: Allez rapporter à Jean ce que vous entendez et voyez: Les aveugles voient de nouveau et les boiteux marchent, les lépreux sont purifiés et les sourds entendent, et les morts se relèvent et les pauvres reçoivent de bonnes nouvelles.

Q 7:23

Markan Parallel	Matthean Doublet	Matt 11:6	Q 7:23
		καὶ μακάριός ἐστιν ὃς ἐὰν μὴ σκανδαλισθῇ ἐν ἐμοί.	καὶ μακάριός ἐστιν ὃς ἐὰν μὴ σκανδαλισθῇ ἐν ἐμοί.

Q

καὶ μακάριός ἐστιν ὃς ἐὰν μὴ σκανδαλισθῇ ἐν ἐμοί.	And blessed is whoever is not offended by me.

Q 7:23

Luke 7:23	Lukan Doublet	Markan Parallel	Gospel of Thomas
καὶ μακάριός ἐστιν ὃς ἐὰν μὴ σκανδαλισθῇ ἐν ἐμοί.			

Und selig ist, wer an mir nicht Anstoß nimmt.	Et bienheureux est celui qui ne subira pas d'offense à cause de moi.

Q 7:24

Markan Parallel	Matthean Doublet	Matt 11:7	Q 7:24
		^{1}⸂ (Τούτ)^{2}ων [ ]^{2} ⸃^{1} δὲ ^{1}⸂ (πορευομέν)^{3}ων⸃^{1} ἤρξατο (ὁ Ἰησοῦς)^{4} λέγειν [ ]^{5} το(ῖ)^{5}ς ὄχλο(ι)^{5}ς περὶ Ἰωάννου· τί ἐξήλθατε εἰς τὴν ἔρημον θεάσασθαι; κάλαμον ὑπὸ ἀνέμου σαλευόμενον;	^{1}⸂ (τούτ)^{2}ων []^{2} ⸃^{1} δὲ ^{1}⸂ [ἀπελθόντ]^{3}ων⸃^{1} ἤρξατο ()^{4} λέγειν []^{5} το(ῖ)^{5}ς ὄχλο(ι)^{5}ς περὶ Ἰωάννου· τί ἐξήλθατε εἰς τὴν ἔρημον θεάσασθαι; κάλαμον ὑπὸ ἀνέμου σαλευόμενον;

Text Critical Note: See the discussion of the punctuation in the front matter.

^{1} The relative position of the participle and its subject.

^{2} The subject of the participle: Luke's τῶν ἀγγέλων or Matthew's τούτων.

Q

τούτων δὲ ἀπελθόντων ἤρξατο λέγειν τοῖς ὄχλοις περὶ Ἰωάννου· τί ἐξήλθατε εἰς τὴν ἔρημον θεάσασθαι; κάλαμον ὑπὸ ἀνέμου σαλευόμενον;

And when they had left, he began to talk to the crowds about John: What did you go out into the wilderness to look at? A reed shaken by the wind?

Gos. Thom. 78.1 (Nag Hammadi II 2)

Λέγει Ἰησοῦς· (διὰ) τί ἐξήλθατε εἰς τὸν ἀγρόν; θεάσασθαι[1] κάλαμον σαλευόμενον ὑπὸ τοῦ ἀνέμου;

Jesus says: Why did you go out to the countryside? To look at a reed shaken by the wind,

[1] Or: ἰδεῖν.

Q 7:24

Luke 7:24	Lukan Doublet	Markan Parallel	*Gos. Thom.* 78.1
[1]ʃ [Ἀπελθόντ][3]ων ʅ[1] δὲ [1]ʃ [τῶν ἀγγέλ][2]ων [Ἰωάννου][2] ʅ[1] ἤρξατο ( )[4] λέγειν [πρὸς][5] το[ὺ][5]ς ὄχλο[υ][5]ς περὶ Ἰωάννου· τί ἐξήλθατε εἰς τὴν ἔρημον θεάσασθαι; κάλαμον ὑπὸ ἀνέμου σαλευόμενον;			ⲡⲉϫⲉ ⲓ̅ⲥ̅ ϫⲉ ⲉⲧⲃⲉ ⲟⲩ ⲁⲧⲉⲧⲛ̅ⲉⲓ ⲉⲃⲟⲗ ⲉⲧⲥⲱϣⲉ ⲉⲛⲁⲩ ⲉⲩⲕⲁϣ ⲉϥⲕⲓⲙ ⲉ̣[ⲃⲟⲗ] ϩⲓⲧⲙ̅ ⲡⲧⲏⲩ

[3] Luke's ἀπελθόντων or Matthew's πορευομένων.
[4] Matthew's ὁ Ἰησοῦς.
[5] Luke's πρὸς τοὺς ὄχλους or Matthew's τοῖς ὄχλοις.

Nachdem sie aber weggegangen waren, begann er zu der Volksmenge über Johannes zu reden: Was seid ihr in die Wüste hinausgegangen zu sehen? Ein Schilfrohr, das vom Wind hin- und herbewegt wird?

Après qu'ils furent partis, il commença à dire aux foules à propos de Jean: Qu'êtes-vous sortis voir au désert? Un roseau agité par le vent?

Jesus spricht: Weshalb seid ihr hinausgegangen aufs Land? Um ein Schilfrohr zu sehen, das vom Wind hin- und herbewegt wird,

[1] Oder: ἰδεῖν.

Jésus dit: Pourquoi êtes-vous sortis dans la campagne? Pour voir un roseau agité par le vent,

[1] Ou: ἰδεῖν.

Q 7:25

Markan Parallel	Matthean Doublet	Matt 11:8	Q 7:25
		ἀλλὰ τί ἐξήλθατε ἰδεῖν; ἄνθρωπον ἐν μαλακοῖς [ ][1] ἠμφιεσμένον; ἰδοὺ οἱ (τὰ μαλακὰ φοροῦ)[2]ντες ἐν τοῖς (οἴκοις τῶν)[3] βασιλέ(ων)[3] εἰσίν.	ἀλλὰ τί ἐξήλθατε ἰδεῖν; ἄνθρωπον ἐν μαλακοῖς [][1] ἠμφιεσμένον; ἰδοὺ οἱ (τὰ μαλακὰ φοροῦ)[2]ντες ἐν τοῖς (οἴκοις τῶν)[3] βασιλέ(ων)[3] εἰσίν.

Text Critical Note: See the discussion of the punctuation in the front matter.

[1] Luke's ἱματίοις.

[2] Luke's ἐν ἱματισμῷ ἐνδόξῳ καὶ τρυφῇ ὑπάρχοντες or Matthew's τὰ μαλακὰ φοροῦντες.

Q

ἀλλὰ τί ἐξήλθατε ἰδεῖν; ἄνθρωπον ἐν μαλακοῖς ἠμφιεσμένον; ἰδοὺ οἱ τὰ μαλακὰ φοροῦντες ἐν τοῖς οἴκοις τῶν βασιλέων εἰσίν.

If not, what *did* you go out to see? A person arrayed in finery? Look, those wearing finery are in kings' houses.

Gos. Thom. 78.2-3 (Nag Hammadi II 2)

(2) καὶ θεάσασθαι ἄνθρωπον μαλακὰ ἱμάτια ἔχοντα[1] [ὡς οἱ] βασιλεῖς [ὑμῶν] καὶ οἱ μεγιστᾶνοι ὑμῶν; (3) οὗτοι ἔχουσιν τὰ ἱμάτια τὰ μαλακὰ καὶ οὐ δυνήσονται γνῶναι τὴν ἀλήθειαν.

(2) and to see a person dressed in soft clothing [like your] kings and your great persons[2]? (3) They are dressed in soft clothing and will not be able to recognize the truth.

[1] Regarding the translation of a present active participle of ἔχειν with ⲉⲟⲩⲛ- … ϩⲓⲱⲱ⸗ compare Luke 8:27 sa.

[1] Zur Wiedergabe eines griechischen Partizip Präsens Aktiv von ἔχειν mit ⲉⲟⲩⲛ- … ϩⲓⲱⲱ⸗ siehe Lukas 8,27 sa.

[1] Pour la traduction du participe présent actif de ἔχειν par ⲉⲟⲩⲛ- … ϩⲓⲱⲱ⸗, voir Luc 8:27 sa.

[2] Or: powerful persons.

Q 7:25

Luke 7:25	Lukan Doublet	Markan Parallel	*Gos. Thom.* 78.2-3
ἀλλὰ τί ἐξήλθατε ἰδεῖν; ἄνθρωπον ἐν μαλακοῖς [ἱματίοις][1] ἠμφιεσμένον; ἰδοὺ οἱ [ἐν ἱματισμῷ ἐνδόξῳ καὶ τρυφῇ ὑπάρχο][2]ντες ἐν τοῖς ( )[3] βασιλε[ίοις][3] εἰσίν.			78.2 ⲁⲩⲱ ⲉⲛⲁⲩ ⲉⲩⲣⲱ̣ⲙ̣[ⲉ ⲉ]ⲩ̣ⲛ̄ϣⲧⲏⲛ ⲉⲩϭⲏⲛ ϩⲓⲱⲱⲃʼ ⲛ̣̄[ⲑⲉ ⲛ̄ⲛⲉⲧ]ⲛ̣̄ⲣ̄ⲣⲱⲟⲩ ⲙⲛ̄ ⲛⲉⲧⲙ̄ⲙⲉⲅⲓⲥⲧⲁⲛⲟⲥ 78.3 ⲛⲁⲉⲓ ⲉⲛ[ⲉ]ϣ̣ⲧ̣ⲏ̣ⲛ ⲉ̣[ⲧ]ϭⲏⲛ ϩⲓⲱⲟⲩ ⲁⲩⲱ ⲥⲉⲛ̣[ⲁ]ϣⲥ̄ⲥⲟⲩⲛ ⲧⲙⲉ ⲁⲛ

[3] Luke's βασιλείοις or Matthew's οἴκοις τῶν βασιλέων.

Nein, was seid ihr hinausgegangen zu sehen? Einen Menschen – fein gekleidet? Siehe, die feine «Sachen» tragen, sind in den Palästen der Könige.

Mais alors qu'êtes-vous sortis voir? Une personne vêtue d'«habits» douillets? Or voilà, ceux qui portent des «habits» douillets sont dans les résidences des rois.

(2) und um einen Menschen zu sehen, der weiche Kleidung trägt [wie eure] Könige und eure Vornehmen[3]? (3) Sie tragen feine[4] Kleidung und werden die Wahrheit nicht erkennen können.

[3] Oder: Mächtigen.
[4] Wörtlich: weiche.

(2) et pour voir une personne portant des habits douillets [comme vos] rois et vos grands[5] (personnages)? (3) Ceux-ci portent les habits douillets et ils ne pourront connaître la vérité.

[5] Ou: puissants.

Q 7:26

Markan Parallel	Matthean Doublet	Matt 11:9	Q 7:26
		ἀλλὰ τί ἐξήλθατε ἰδεῖν; προφήτην; ναὶ λέγω ὑμῖν, καὶ περισσότερον προφήτου.	ἀλλὰ τί ἐξήλθατε ἰδεῖν; προφήτην; ναὶ λέγω ὑμῖν, καὶ περισσότερον προφήτου.

IQP 1994: ἀλλὰ τί ἐξήλθατε; ἰδεῖν προφήτην;

Text Critical Note (see the discussion of the punctuation and of the textual variant in the front matter): In Matt 11:9;προφήτην ἰδεῖν; is in א* B[1] W Z 0281[vid] 892 *pc* and ἰδεῖν; προφήτην; is in א[1] B*.[2] C D L Θ 0233 *f*[1.13] 33 𝔐 latt sy sa.

Q

ἀλλὰ τί ἐξήλθατε ἰδεῖν; προφήτην; ναὶ λέγω ὑμῖν, καὶ περισσότερον προφήτου.	But «then» what did you go out to see? A prophet? Yes, I tell you, even more than a prophet!

Q 7:26

Luke 7:26	Lukan Doublet	Markan Parallel	Gospel of Thomas
ἀλλὰ τί ἐξήλθατε ἰδεῖν; προφήτην; ναὶ λέγω ὑμῖν, καὶ περισσότερον προφήτου.			

Was aber seid ihr «dann» hinausgegangen zu sehen? Einen Propheten? Ja, ich sage euch, mehr noch als einen Propheten.

Mais «alors» qu'êtes-vous sortis voir? Un prophète? Oui, je vous «le» dis, et plus qu'un prophète.

Q 7:27

Exod 23:20a-b LXX	Mal 3:1a LXX	Matt 11:10	Q 7:27
		οὗτός ἐστιν περὶ	οὗτός ἐστιν περὶ
		οὗ {γέγραπται}·	οὗ {γέγραπται}·
Καὶ ἰδοὺ ἐγὼ ἀποστέλλω	ἰδοὺ ἐγὼ ἐξαποστέλλω	{ἰδοὺ} (ἐγὼ)[1] {ἀποστέλλω	{ἰδοὺ} ⟦(ἐγὼ)[1]⟧ {ἀποστέλλω
τὸν ἄγγελόν μου	τὸν ἄγγελόν μου,	τὸν ἄγγελόν μου	τὸν ἄγγελόν μου
πρὸ προσώπου σου,		πρὸ προσώπου σου,	πρὸ προσώπου σου,
ἵνα φυλάξῃ σε	καὶ ἐπιβλέψεται	ὃς κατασκευάσει	ὃς κατασκευάσει
ἐν τῇ ὁδῷ.	ὁδὸν	τὴν ὁδόν σου}	τὴν ὁδόν σου}
	πρὸ προσώπου μου,	ἔμπροσθέν σου.	ἔμπροσθέν σου.

IQP 1994, JSK: ⟦()[1]⟧.

[1] Matthew's ἐγώ.

Q

οὗτός ἐστιν περὶ οὗ γέγραπται· ἰδοὺ ⟦ἐγὼ⟧ ἀποστέλλω τὸν ἄγγελόν μου πρὸ προσώπου σου, ὃς κατασκευάσει τὴν ὁδόν σου ἔμπροσθέν σου.	This is the one about whom it has been written: Look, I am sending my messenger ahead of you, who will prepare your path in front of you.

Q 7:27

Luke 7:27	Lukan Doublet	Mark 1:2	Gospel of Thomas
οὗτός ἐστιν περὶ οὗ {γέγραπται}· {ἰδοὺ ( )[1] ἀποστέλλω τὸν ἄγγελόν μου πρὸ προσώπου σου, ὃς κατασκευάσει τὴν ὁδόν σου} ἔμπροσθέν σου.		Καθὼς γέγραπται ἐν τῷ Ἠσαΐᾳ τῷ προφήτῃ· ἰδοὺ ἀποστέλλω τὸν ἄγγελόν μου πρὸ προσώπου σου, ὃς κατασκευάσει τὴν ὁδόν σου.	

Dieser ist es, über den geschrieben steht: Siehe, ich sende meinen Boten dir voraus, der deinen Weg vor dir bereiten wird.

C'est celui dont il est écrit: Voici ⟦moi⟧ j'envoie mon messager au devant de ta face, c'est lui qui préparera ton chemin devant toi.

Q 7:28

Markan Parallel	Matthean Doublet	Matt 11:11	Q 7:28
		(Ἀμὴν)¹ λέγω ὑμῖν· ²ʃ οὐ(κ ἐγήγερται)³ ʅ²	⟦()¹⟧ λέγω ὑμῖν· ²ʃ οὐ(κ ἐγήγερται)³ ʅ²
		ʃ ʅ⁴ ἐν γεννητοῖς γυναικῶν ʃμείζωνʅ⁴ Ἰωάννου (τοῦ βαπτιστοῦ)⁵	ʃʅ⁴ ἐν γεννητοῖς γυναικῶν ʃμείζωνʅ⁴ Ἰωάννου ()⁵
		ʃ ʅ².	ʃʅ².
		ὁ δὲ μικρότερος ἐν	ὁ δὲ μικρότερος ἐν
		τῇ βασιλείᾳ τ(ῶν οὐρανῶν)⁶ μείζων αὐτοῦ ἐστιν.	τῇ βασιλείᾳ τ[οῦ θεοῦ]⁶ μείζων αὐτοῦ ἐστιν.

JSK: ()¹.

IQP 1994: ʃ ʅ⁴ ἐν γεννητοῖς γυναικῶν ʃμείζωνʅ⁴ Ἰωάννου ()⁵ ʃ ʅ².

¹ Matthew's ἀμήν.

² The position of the negative and the verb at the end (Luke) or at the beginning (Matthew) of the clause.

Q

λέγω ὑμῖν· οὐκ ἐγήγερται ἐν γεννητοῖς γυναικῶν μείζων Ἰωάννου· ὁ δὲ μικρότερος ἐν τῇ βασιλείᾳ τοῦ θεοῦ μείζων αὐτοῦ ἐστιν.

I tell you: There has not arisen among women's offspring «anyone» who surpasses John. Yet the least significant in God's kingdom is more than he.

Gos. Thom. 46 (Nag Hammadi II 2)

(1) Λέγει Ἰησοῦς· ἀπὸ Ἀδὰμ μέχρι Ἰωάννου τοῦ βαπτιστοῦ ἐν γεννητοῖς γυναικῶν μείζων Ἰωάννου τοῦ βαπτιστοῦ οὐδείς ἐστιν, ἵνα μὴ (...)¹ οἱ ὀφθαλμοὶ αὐτοῦ. (2) εἶπον δέ· ὅστις μικρὸς γενήσεται ἐν ὑμῖν τὴν βασιλείαν γνώσεται καὶ μείζων Ἰωάννου ἔσται.

(1) Jesus says: From Adam to John the Baptist, among women's offspring there is no one who surpasses John the Baptist so that his (i.e. John's) eyes need not be downcast[2]. (2) But I have (also) said: Whoever among you becomes little will know the kingdom and will surpass John.

¹ The Coptic text is possibly corrupt; a retranslation is extremely uncertain.

¹ Der koptische Text ist möglicherweise korrupt und kaum rückübersetzbar.

¹ Le texte copte est probablement corrompu; la rétroversion demeure très incertaine.

² It is possible that the text is corrupt. Instead of the consecutive understanding of ϣⲓⲛⲁ, a final (but hardly a causal) understanding is also possible. The literal translation with this second alternative would be: so that his eyes do not get broken, or: so that his eyes do not fail.

Q 7:28

Luke 7:28	Lukan Doublet	Markan Parallel	*Gos. Thom.* 46
( )[1] λέγω ὑμῖν, ⸀ ⸁[2] ⸀μείζων⸁[4] ἐν γεννητοῖς γυναικῶν ⸀ ⸁[4] Ἰωάννου ( )[5] [2]⸀ οὐ[δείς ἐστιν][3] ⸁[2]. ὁ δὲ μικρότερος ἐν τῇ βασιλείᾳ τ[οῦ θεοῦ][6] μείζων αὐτοῦ ἐστιν.			46.1 ⲡⲉϫⲉ ⲓ̅ⲥ̅ ϫⲉ ϫⲓⲛ' ⲁⲇⲁⲙ ϣⲁ ⲓ̈ⲱϩⲁⲛⲛⲏⲥ ⲡⲃⲁⲡⲧⲓⲥⲧⲏⲥ ϩⲛ̅ ⲛ̅ϫⲡⲟ ⲛ̅ⲛ̅ϩⲓⲟⲙⲉ ⲙⲛ̅ ⲡⲉⲧϫⲟⲥⲉ ⲁⲓ̈ⲱϩⲁⲛⲛⲏⲥ ⲡⲃⲁⲡⲧⲓⲥ- ⲧⲏⲥ ϣⲓⲛⲁ ϫⲉ ⲛⲟⲩⲱϭⲡ' ⲛ̅ϭⲓ ⲛⲉϥⲃⲁⲗ 46.2 ⲁⲉⲓϫⲟⲟⲥ ⲇⲉ ϫⲉ ⲡⲉⲧⲛⲁϣⲱⲡⲉ ϩⲛ̅ ⲧⲏⲩⲧⲛ̅ ⲉϥⲟ ⲛ̅ⲕⲟⲩⲉⲓ ϥⲛⲁⲥⲟⲩⲱⲛ ⲧⲙⲛ̅ⲧⲉⲣⲟ ⲁⲩⲱ ϥⲛⲁϫⲓⲥⲉ ⲁⲓ̈ⲱϩⲁⲛ- ⲛⲏⲥ

[3] Luke's οὐδείς ἐστιν or Matthew's οὐκ ἐγήγερται.
[4] The position of μείζων before (Luke) or after (Matthew) ἐν γεννητοῖς γυναικῶν.
[5] Matthew's τοῦ βαπτιστοῦ.
[6] Luke's τοῦ θεοῦ or Matthew's τῶν οὐρανῶν.

Ich sage euch: Unter den von Frauen Geborenen ist kein größerer als Johannes aufgetreten. Doch ist der Kleinste im Reich Gottes größer als er.

Je vous «le» dis: Parmi les rejetons des femmes, il ne s'en est pas levé de plus grand que Jean. Mais le plus petit dans le royaume de Dieu est plus grand que lui.

(1) Jesus spricht: Von Adam bis zu Johannes dem Täufer gibt es unter den von Frauen Geborenen keinen Größeren als Johannes den Täufer, so dass sich seine Augen nicht senken müssen[3]. (2) Ich habe aber (auch) gesagt: Wer unter euch klein werden wird, wird das Königreich erkennen und wird größer als Johannes sein.

[3] Möglicherweise ist der Text korrupt. Statt des konsekutiven Verständnisses des ϣⲓⲛⲁ ist auch ein finales (jedoch kaum ein kausales) möglich, woraus sich als wörtliche Übersetzung ergeben würde: damit seine Augen nicht (zer)brechen bzw. damit seine Augen nicht versagen.

(1) Jésus dit: Depuis Adam jusqu'à Jean le Baptiste, parmi les rejetons des femmes, il n'en est pas de plus grand que Jean le Baptiste, si bien que ses yeux ne seront pas abattus[4]. (2) Mais j'ai dit (aussi): Celui qui, parmi vous, deviendra petit, connaîtra le royaume et il sera plus grand que Jean.

[4] Le texte est peut-être corrompu. Au lieu d'un sens consécutif, il est également possible de comprendre ϣⲓⲛⲁ dans un sens final (le sens causal est moins envisageable). Dans ce cas, la traduction serait: afin que ses yeux ne soient pas abattus.

Q 7:⟦29-30⟧

Markan Parallel	Matt 21:25e, 29	Matt 21:32	Q 7:⟦29-30⟧
		^{0}/ ^{1}⸂	⟦^{0}/ ^{1}⸂
	21:25e διὰ τί οὖν (οὐκ ἐπιστεύσατε αὐτῷ);	(ἦλθεν γὰρ Ἰωάννης πρὸς ὑμᾶς)^{2} (ἐν ὁδῷ δικαιοσύνης)^{3}, (καὶ οὐκ ἐπιστεύσατε αὐτῷ,)^{4} ⸂οἱ⸃^{5} (δὲ)^{4} ⸂τελῶναι⸃^{5} καὶ ^{5}⸂ (αἱ πόρναι)^{6} ⸃^{5} ἐ(πίστευ)^{7}σαν (αὐτῷ)^{7}·	**7:⟦29⟧** («ἦλθεν γὰρ Ἰωάννης πρὸς ὑμᾶς»)^{2} ()^{3}, ( )^{4} ⸂οἱ⸃^{5} ( )^{4} ⸂τελῶναι⸃^{5} καὶ ^{5}⸂ [( )]^{6} ⸃^{5} ἐ[ ]^{7}σαν [ ]^{7}· [( )]^{4}⟧
	21:29 ὁ δὲ ἀποκριθεὶς εἶπεν· οὐ θέλω, (ὕστερον) (δὲ) (μετ)α(μεληθ)εὶς ἀπῆλθεν.	(ὑμεῖς)^{4} δὲ (ἰδόντες οὐδὲ μετεμελήθητε ὕστερον τοῦ πιστεῦσαι)^{4} αὐτ(ῷ)^{4}. ⸃^{1} \\$^{0}$	**7:⟦30⟧** ⟦[( )]^{4} δὲ [( )]^{4} αὐτ[( )]^{4}. ⸃^{1} \\$^{0}$⟧

IQP 1994: Q 7:~~29-30~~ not in Q {D}; IQP 1996: Indeterminate.

PH: Q 7:⟦~~29-30~~⟧.

^{0} Is Luke 7:29-30 par. Matt 21:32 in Q?

^{1} The position of Q 7:29-30 in Q: After Q 7:28 and before Q 7:31 (Lukan order); or after Q 13:30 (Matt 20:16) and before Q 14:16 (Matt 22:1) (Matthean order).

^{2} Is Matthew's ἦλθεν γὰρ Ἰωάννης πρὸς ὑμᾶς in Q?

^{3} Is Matthew's ἐν ὁδῷ δικαιοσύνης in Q?

^{4} Luke's βαπτισθέντες τὸ βάπτισμα Ἰωάννου. οἱ … Φαρισαῖοι καὶ οἱ νομικοὶ τὴν βουλὴν τοῦ θεοῦ ἠθέτησαν εἰς ἑαυτούς μὴ

Q

⟦29⟧ ⟦«ἦλθεν γὰρ Ἰωάννης πρὸς ὑμᾶς» .. οἱ .. τελῶναι καὶ … ἐ…σαν …⟧ ⟦30⟧ ⟦.. δὲ … αὐτ… .⟧

⟦29⟧ ⟦«For John came to you» .., … the tax collectors and … «responded positively»,⟧ ⟦30⟧ ⟦but «the religious authorities rejected» him.⟧

Q 7:⟦29-30⟧

Luke 7:29-30	Lukan Doublet	Markan Parallel	Gospel of Thomas
⁰/ ¹ʃ **7:29** ( )² ( )³ ( )⁴ ⁵ʃ [Καὶ πᾶς ὁ λαὸς ἀκούσας]⁶ ꞉⁵ καὶ ʃοἱ τελῶναι꞉⁵ ἐ[δικαίω]⁷σαν [τὸν θεὸν]⁷ [βαπτισθέντες τὸ βάπτισμα Ἰωάννου· **7:30** οἱ]⁴ δὲ [Φαρισαῖοι καὶ οἱ νομικοὶ τὴν βουλὴν τοῦ θεοῦ ἠθέτησαν εἰς ἑαυτοὺς μὴ βαπτισθέντες ὑπ']⁴ αὐτ[οῦ]⁴. ꞉¹ \⁰			

βαπτισθέντες ὑπ' …οῦ or Matthew's καὶ οὐκ ἐπιστεύσατε αὐτῷ, … δέ … ὑμεῖς … ἰδόντες οὐδὲ μετεμελήθητε ὕστερον τοῦ πιστεῦσαι …ῷ.

5 οἱ τελῶναι in second (Luke) or first (Matthew) position.

6 Luke's καὶ πᾶς ὁ λαὸς ἀκούσας or Matthew's αἱ πόρναι,

7 Luke's ἐδικαίωσαν τὸν θεόν or Matthew's ἐπίστευσαν αὐτῷ.

⟦29⟧ ⟦«Denn Johannes kam zu euch» .., … die Zöllner und … «reagierten positiv»,⟧ ⟦30⟧ ⟦aber «die religiösen Autoritäten lehnten» ihn «ab».⟧

⟦29⟧ ⟦«Car Jean est venu à vous» .., … les collecteurs d'impôts et … «ont acquiescé».⟧ ⟦30⟧ ⟦Mais «les autorités religieuses» l'«ont rejeté».⟧

Q 7:31

Markan Parallel	Matthean Doublet	Matt 11:16a	Q 7:31
		Τίνι (δὲ)¹ ὁμοιώσω [ ]² τῆ(ν)² γενεᾶ(ν)² ταύτη(ν)² [ ]³;	τίνι [( )]¹ ὁμοιώσω []² τῆ(ν)² γενεᾶ(ν)² ταύτη(ν)² [καὶ τίνι ἐ<στ>ὶν ὁμοί<α>]³;

IQP 1994: ( )[1].

[1] Luke's οὖν or Matthew's δέ.

[2] Luke's τοὺς ἀνθρώπους τῆς γενεᾶς ταύτης or Matthew's τὴν γενεὰν ταύτην (see also Q 7:32[1]).

Q

τίνι .. ὁμοιώσω τὴν γενεὰν ταύτην καὶ τίνι ἐ<στ>ὶν ὁμοί<α>;	.. To what am I to compare this generation and what <is it> like?

Q 7:31

Luke 7:31	Lukan Doublet	Markan Parallel	Gospel of Thomas
Τίνι [οὖν][1] ὁμοιώσω [τοὺς ἀνθρώπους][2] τῆ[ς][2] γενεᾶ[ς][2] ταύτη[ς][2] [καὶ τίνι εἰσὶν ὅμοιοι][3];			

[3] Luke's καὶ τίνι εἰσὶν ὅμοιοι.

.. Wem soll ich diese Generation vergleichen, und wem <ist sie> gleich?

.. A quoi vais-je comparer cette génération? Et à quoi <est-elle> comparable?

Q 7:32

Markan Parallel	Matthean Doublet	Matt 11:16b-17	Q 7:32
		11:16b ὁμοί(α)[1] ἐ(στ)[1]ὶν	ὁμοί(α)[1] ἐ(στ)[1]ὶν
		παιδίοις [ ][2]	παιδίοις [][2]
		⸂καθημένοις⸃[3]	⸂καθημένοις⸃[3]
		ἐν (ταῖς)[4]	ἐν ⟦(ταῖς)[4]⟧
		ἀγορ(αῖς)[5]	ἀγορ⟦(αῖς)[5]⟧
		⸂ἃ⸃[6]	⸂ἃ⸃[6]
		⸂ ⸃[3]	⸂⸃[3]
		[ ][7]	[][7]
		προσφωνοῦ(ντα)[8]	προσφωνοῦ(ντα)[8]
		(τοῖς ἑτέρ)[9]οις	⟦(τοῖς ἑτέρ)[9]⟧οις
		⸂ ⸃[6]	⸂⸃[6]
		11:17 λέγ(ουσιν)[10]·	λέγ(ουσιν)[10]·
		ηὐλήσαμεν ὑμῖν	ηὐλήσαμεν ὑμῖν
		καὶ οὐκ ὠρχήσασθε,	καὶ οὐκ ὠρχήσασθε,
		ἐθρηνήσαμεν καὶ οὐκ	ἐθρηνήσαμεν καὶ οὐκ
		ἐ(κόψασθε)[11].	ἐ[κλαύσατε][11].

IQP 1994: ()[4] ἀγορ[()][5]; JSK: ()[4] ἀγορ[ᾶ][5].

IQP 1994: [ ][9]οις … ἐ[ ][11].

1 Luke's ὅμοιοί εἰσιν or Matthew's ὁμοία ἐστίν (see also Q 7:31[2]).

2 Luke's τοῖς.

3 The position of καθημένοις after (Luke) or before (Matthew) the market-place(s).

4 Matthew's ταῖς.

5 Luke's ἀγορᾷ or Matthew's ἀγοραῖς.

Q

ὁμοία ἐστὶν παιδίοις καθημένοις ἐν ⟦ταῖς⟧ ἀγορ⟦αῖς⟧ ἃ προσφωνοῦντα ⟦τοῖς ἑτέρ⟧οις λέγουσιν· ηὐλήσαμεν ὑμῖν καὶ οὐκ ὠρχήσασθε, ἐθρηνήσαμεν καὶ οὐκ ἐκλαύσατε.

It is like children seated in ⟦the⟧ market-place⟦s⟧, who, addressing ⟦the others⟧, say: We fluted for you, but you would not dance; we wailed, but you would not cry.

Q 7:32

Luke 7:32	Lukan Doublet	Markan Parallel	Gospel of Thomas
ὅμοι[οί][1] ε[ἰσ][1]ιν παιδίοις [τοῖς][2] ⸂ ⸃[3] ἐν ( )[4] ἀγορ[ᾷ][5] ⸂ ⸃[6] ⸂καθημένοις⸃[3] [καὶ][7] προσφωνοῦ[σιν][8] [ἀλλήλ][9]οις ⸂ἃ⸃[6] λέγ[ει][10]. ηὐλήσαμεν ὑμῖν καὶ οὐκ ὠρχήσασθε, ἐθρηνήσαμεν καὶ οὐκ ἐ[κλαύσατε][11].			

6 The position of ἅ after (Luke) or before (Matthew) the participle(s).

7 Luke's καί.

8 Luke's προσφωνοῦσιν or Matthew's προσφωνοῦντα.

9 Luke's ἀλλήλοις or Matthew's τοῖς ἑτέροις.

10 Luke's λέγει or Matthew's λέγουσιν.

11 Luke's ἐκλαύσατε or Matthew's ἐκόψασθε.

Sie ist Kindern gleich, die auf ⟦den⟧ Dorfplätz⟦en⟧ sitzen. Sie rufen den ⟦andern⟧ zu und sagen: Wir spielten euch mit der Flöte auf, und ihr habt nicht getanzt, wir stimmten Klagelieder an, und ihr habt nicht geweint.

Elle est comparable à des enfants, assis sur ⟦des⟧ place⟦s⟧ publique⟦s⟧, qui «en» interpellent ⟦d'autres⟧ en disant: Nous avons joué pour vous de la flûte et vous n'avez pas dansé, nous avons fait entendre des plaintes et vous n'avez pas pleuré.

Q 7:33

Markan Parallel	Matthean Doublet	Matt 11:18	Q 7:33
		[ ][1]ἦλ[ ][1]θεν γὰρ Ἰωάννης [ ][2] μή(τε)[3] ἐσθίων [ ][4] μήτε πίνων [ ][4], καὶ λέγ(ουσιν)[5]· δαιμόνιον ἔχει.	[][1]ἦλ[][1]θεν γὰρ Ἰωάννης [][2] μὴ( )[3] ἐσθίων [][4] μήτε πίνων [][4], καὶ λέγ[ετε][5]· δαιμόνιον ἔχει.

IQP 1994: ⟦[][1]⟧ἦλ⟦[][1]⟧θεν.

IQP 1994: μὴ()[3]; JMR, PH, JSK: Indeterminate.

[1] Luke's ἐλήλυθεν or Matthew's ἦλθεν.
[2] Luke's ὁ βαπτιστής.

[3] Luke's μή or Matthew's μήτε.

Q

ἦλθεν γὰρ Ἰωάννης μὴ.. ἐσθίων μήτε πίνων, καὶ λέγετε· δαιμόνιον ἔχει.

For John came, neither eating nor drinking, and you say: He has a demon!

Q 7:33

Luke 7:33	Lukan Doublet	Markan Parallel	Gospel of Thomas
[ἐλ]¹ἠλ[υ]¹θεν γὰρ Ἰωάννης [ὁ βαπτιστὴς]² μὴ( )³ ἐσθίων [ἄρτον]⁴ μήτε πίνων [οἶνον]⁴, καὶ λέγ[ετε]⁵· δαιμόνιον ἔχει.			

4 Luke's ἄρτον ... οἶνον.

5 Luke's λέγετε or Matthew's λέγουσιν.

Denn Johannes kam, er aß nicht und trank nicht, und ihr sagt: Er hat einen Dämon.

Jean est venu en effet, ne mangeant ni ne buvant, et vous dites: Il a un démon.

Q 7:34

Markan Parallel	Matthean Doublet	Matt 11:19a-b	Q 7:34
		[ ][1]ἦλ[ ][1]θεν ὁ υἱὸς τοῦ ἀνθρώπου ἐσθίων καὶ πίνων, καὶ λέγ(ουσιν)[2]· ἰδοὺ ἄνθρωπος φάγος καὶ οἰνοπότης, ⸉ ⸊[3] τελωνῶν ⸉φίλος⸊[3] καὶ ἁμαρτωλῶν.	[][1]ἦλ[][1]θεν ὁ υἱὸς τοῦ ἀνθρώπου ἐσθίων καὶ πίνων, καὶ λέγ[ετε][2]· ἰδοὺ ἄνθρωπος φάγος καὶ οἰνοπότης, ⸉⸊[3] τελωνῶν ⸉φίλος⸊[3] καὶ ἁμαρτωλῶν.

IQP 1994: ⟦[][1]⟧ἦλ⟦[][1]⟧θεν.

[1] Luke's ἐλήλυθεν or Matthew's ἦλθεν.

[2] Luke's λέγετε or Matthew's λέγουσιν.

Q

ἦλθεν ὁ υἱὸς τοῦ ἀνθρώπου ἐσθίων καὶ πίνων, καὶ λέγετε· ἰδοὺ ἄνθρωπος φάγος καὶ οἰνοπότης, τελωνῶν φίλος καὶ ἁμαρτωλῶν.

The son of humanity came, eating and drinking, and you say: Look! A person «who is» a glutton and drunkard, a chum of tax collectors and sinners!

Q 7:34

Luke 7:34	Lukan Doublet	Markan Parallel	Gospel of Thomas
[ἐλ][1]ήλ[υ][1]θεν ὁ υἱὸς τοῦ ἀνθρώπου ἐσθίων καὶ πίνων, καὶ λέγ[ετε][2]· ἰδοὺ ἄνθρωπος φάγος καὶ οἰνοπότης, ⸉φίλος⸊[3] τελωνῶν ⸉ ⸊[3] καὶ ἁμαρτωλῶν.			

[3] The position of φίλος before (Luke) or after (Matthew) τελωνῶν.

Der Menschensohn kam, er aß und trank, und ihr sagt: Siehe «was für ein» Mensch, ein Fresser und Säufer, Freund der Zöllner und Sünder.

Le fils de l'homme est venu, mangeant et buvant, et vous dites: Voici une personne gloutonne et ivrogne, amie des collecteurs d'impôts et des pécheurs.

Q 7:35

Markan Parallel	Matthean Doublet	Matt 11:19c	Q 7:35
		καὶ ἐδικαιώθη ἡ σοφία ἀπὸ [ ][1] τῶν (ἔργ)[2]ων αὐτῆς.	καὶ ἐδικαιώθη ἡ σοφία ἀπὸ [][1] τῶν [τέκν][2]ων αὐτῆς.

[1] Luke's πάντων.

[2] Luke's τέκνων or Matthew's ἔργων.

Q

καὶ ἐδικαιώθη ἡ σοφία ἀπὸ τῶν τέκνων αὐτῆς.	But Wisdom was vindicated by her children.

Q 7:35

Luke 7:35	Lukan Doublet	Markan Parallel	Gospel of Thomas
καὶ ἐδικαιώθη ἡ σοφία ἀπὸ [πάντων][1] τῶν [τέκν][2]ων αὐτῆς.			

Recht bekam aber die Weisheit von ihren Kindern.

Même la Sagesse a été reconnue juste par ses enfants.

Q 9:57

Mark 4:35	Matthean Doublet	Matt 8:18-19	Q 9:57
Καὶ λέγει αὐτοῖς ἐν ἐκείνῃ τῇ ἡμέρᾳ ὀψίας γενομένης· διέλθωμεν εἰς τὸ πέραν.		**8:18** (Ἰδὼν δὲ ὁ Ἰησοῦς ὄχλον περὶ αὐτὸν ἐκέλευσεν ἀπ{ελθ}εῖν {εἰς τὸ πέραν}.)^{0}	()^{0}
		8:19 ^{1}⸉καὶ	^{1}⸉καὶ
		(προσελθὼν)^{2}	[()]^{2}
		⸉ ⸊^{3}	⸉εἶπέν⸊^{3}
		(εἷς γραμματεὺς)^{4}	[τις]^{4}
		⸉εἶπεν⸊^{3}	⸉ ⸊^{3}
		[ ]^{5} αὐτ(ῷ)^{5}·	[]^{5} αὐτ(ῷ)^{5}·
		(διδάσκαλε,)^{6} ἀκολουθήσω	()^{6} ἀκολουθήσω
		σοι ὅπου ἐὰν ἀπέρχῃ.	σοι ὅπου ἐὰν ἀπέρχῃ.
		⸊^{1}⇒ Matt 8:21-22	⸊^{1}⇒ Q 9:60

PH: εἶπεν after the subject {C}; JMR, JSK: Indeterminate.

IQP 1992: ⟦()^{6}⟧.

^{0} Is Matt 8:18 in Q or from Mark?

^{1} The position of Q 9:57-60 (-62) in Q: After Q 7:35 and before Q 10:2 (Lukan order); or after Q 7:10 (Matt 8:13) and before Q 10:2 (Matt 9:37) (Matthean order).

Q

καὶ εἶπέν τις αὐτῷ· ἀκολουθήσω σοι ὅπου ἐὰν ἀπέρχῃ.	And someone said to him: I will follow you wherever you go.

Q 9:57

Luke 9:57	Lukan Doublet	Markan Parallel	Gospel of Thomas
( )⁰ ¹ʃΚαὶ [πορευομένων αὐτῶν ἐν τῇ ὁδῷ]² ʃεἶπένʅ³ [τις]⁴ ʃ ʅ³ [πρὸς]⁵ αὐτ[όν]⁵· ( )⁶ ἀκολουθήσω σοι ὅπου ἐὰν ἀπέρχῃ. ʅ¹⇒ Luke 9:59-60			

[2] Luke's πορευομένων αὐτῶν ἐν τῇ ὁδῷ or Matthew's προσελθών.

[3] The position of εἶπεν before (Luke) or after (Matthew) the subject.

[4] Luke's τις or Matthew's εἷς γραμματεύς.

[5] Luke's πρὸς αὐτόν or Matthew's αὐτῷ.

[6] Matthew's διδάσκαλε.

Und einer sagte ihm: Ich will dir folgen, wohin du auch gehst.

Et quelqu'un lui dit: Je te suivrai partout où tu iras.

Q 9:58

Markan Parallel	Matthean Doublet	Matt 8:20	Q 9:58
		καὶ (λέγει)[1] αὐτῷ ὁ Ἰησοῦς·	καὶ [εἶπεν][1] αὐτῷ ὁ Ἰησοῦς·
		αἱ ἀλώπεκες φωλεοὺς	αἱ ἀλώπεκες φωλεοὺς
		ἔχουσιν	ἔχουσιν
		καὶ τὰ πετεινὰ τοῦ	καὶ τὰ πετεινὰ τοῦ
		οὐρανοῦ	οὐρανοῦ
		κατασκηνώσεις,	κατασκηνώσεις,
		ὁ δὲ υἱὸς	ὁ δὲ υἱὸς
		τοῦ ἀνθρώπου	τοῦ ἀνθρώπου
		οὐκ ἔχει	οὐκ ἔχει
		ποῦ τὴν κεφαλὴν κλίνῃ.	ποῦ τὴν κεφαλὴν κλίνῃ.

IQP 1992: ⟦[εἶπεν][1]⟧.

[1] Luke's εἶπεν or Matthew's λέγει.

Q

καὶ εἶπεν αὐτῷ ὁ Ἰησοῦς· αἱ ἀλώπεκες φωλεοὺς ἔχουσιν καὶ τὰ πετεινὰ τοῦ οὐρανοῦ κατασκηνώσεις, ὁ δὲ υἱὸς τοῦ ἀνθρώπου οὐκ ἔχει ποῦ τὴν κεφαλὴν κλίνῃ.

And Jesus said to him: Foxes have holes, and birds of the sky have nests; but the son of humanity does not have anywhere he can lay his head.

Gos. Thom. 86 (Nag Hammadi II 2)

(1) Λέγει Ἰησοῦς· [αἱ ἀλώπεκες ἔχου]σιν τοὺς [φωλεοὺς αὐτῶν] καὶ τὰ πετεινὰ ἔχει [τὴν] κατασκήνωσιν αὐτῶν, (2) ὁ δὲ υἱὸς τοῦ ἀνθρώπου οὐκ ἔχει ποῦ τὴν κεφαλὴν αὐτοῦ κλίνῃ καὶ ἀναπαύσηται.[1]

(1) Jesus says: [Foxes have their holes] and birds have their nest. (2) But the son of humanity does not have anywhere he can lay down his head (and) rest.

[1] The Coptic text has a direct infinitive connection.
[1] Im koptischen Text liegt ein Infinitivanschluss der Verben vor.
[1] Dans le texte copte, on trouve une proposition infinitive introduite par ⲉ-.

Q 9:58

Luke 9:58	Lukan Doublet	Markan Parallel	*Gos. Thom.* 86
καὶ [εἶπεν][1] αὐτῷ ὁ Ἰησοῦς· αἱ ἀλώπεκες φωλεοὺς ἔχουσιν καὶ τὰ πετεινὰ τοῦ οὐρανοῦ κατασκηνώσεις, ὁ δὲ υἱὸς τοῦ ἀνθρώπου οὐκ ἔχει ποῦ τὴν κεφαλὴν κλίνῃ.			86.1 ⲡⲉϫⲉ ⲓ̅ⲥ̅ ϫⲉ [ⲛ̅ⲃⲁϣⲟⲣ ⲟⲩⲛ̅ⲧ]ⲁ̣ⲩ ⲛⲟ̣ⲩ[ⲃ]ⲏ̣ⲃ̣ ⲁⲩⲱ ⲛ̣̅ϩⲁⲗⲁⲧⲉ ⲟⲩⲛ̅ⲧⲁⲩ ⲙ̣̅ⲙⲁⲩ ⲙ̅ⲡⲉ̣ⲩⲙⲁϩ 86.2 ⲡϣⲏⲣⲉ ⲇⲉ ⲙ̅ⲡⲣⲱⲙⲉ ⲙⲛ̅ⲧⲁϥ' ⲛ̅ⲛ[ⲟ]ⲩⲙⲁ ⲉⲣⲓⲕⲉ ⲛ̅ⲧⲉϥ'ⲁⲡⲉ ⲛ̅ϥ'ⲙ̅ⲧⲟⲛ' ⲙ̅ⲙ̣[ⲟ]ϥ̣'

Und Jesus sagte ihm: Die Füchse haben Höhlen und die Vögel des Himmels Nester, der Menschensohn aber hat keinen Platz, wohin er seinen Kopf legen kann.

Et Jésus lui dit: Les renards ont des terriers et les oiseaux du ciel des nids, mais le fils de l'homme n'a pas où poser sa tête.

(1) Jesus spricht: [Die Füchse haben ihre Höhlen], und die Vögel haben ihr Nest. (2) Aber der Menschensohn hat keinen Platz, wohin er seinen Kopf legen (und) ausruhen kann.

(1) Jésus dit: [Les renards ont leurs terriers] et les oiseaux ont leur nid. (2) Mais le fils de l'homme, il n'a pas où poser sa tête (et) se reposer.

Q 9:59-60

Markan Parallel	Matthean Doublet	Matt 8:21-22	Q 9:59-60
		8:21 [ ]^{1} ἕτερο(ς)^{1}	**9:59** []^{1} ἕτερο(ς)^{1}
		ʃ ʅ^{1}	ʃʅ^{1}
		[ ]^{1} δὲ	[]^{1} δὲ
		(τῶν μαθητῶν αὐτοῦ)^{2}	()^{2}
		εἶπεν (αὐτῷ)^{3}·	εἶπεν (αὐτῷ)^{3}·
		κύριε, ἐπίτρεψόν μοι	κύριε, ἐπίτρεψόν μοι
		ʃπρῶτονʅ^{4}	ʃπρῶτονʅ^{4}
		ἀπελθ(εῖν)^{5}	ἀπελθ(εῖν)^{5}
		ʃ ʅ^{4}	ʃ ʅ^{4}
		(καὶ)^{5} θάψαι	(καὶ)^{5} θάψαι
		τὸν πατέρα μου.	τὸν πατέρα μου.
		8:22 ʃ ʅ^{6}	**9:60** ^{6}ʃ [εἶπεν]^{7} ʅ^{6}
		(ὁ)^{6} δὲ (Ἰησοῦς)^{6}	()^{6} δὲ ()^{6}
		^{6}ʃ (λέγει)^{7} ʅ^{6}	ʃʅ^{6}
		αὐτῷ·	αὐτῷ·
		ʃἀκολούθει μοιʅ^{1}	ʃἀκολούθει μοιʅ^{1}
		(καὶ)^{1} ἄφες τοὺς νεκροὺς	(καὶ)^{1} ἄφες τοὺς νεκροὺς
		θάψαι	θάψαι
		τοὺς ἑαυτῶν νεκρούς	τοὺς ἑαυτῶν νεκρούς
		[ ]^{8}	[]^{8}
		ʅMatt 8:18-19^{1}	ʅQ 9:57^{1}

IQP 1992, JSK: ⟦[]^{1}⟧ ἕτερο⟦(ς)^{1}⟧ ʃ ʅ^{1} ⟦[]^{1}⟧ δὲ ... ⟦(καὶ)^{1}⟧.

IQP 1992, JMR, PH, JSK: ʃπρῶτονʅ^{4} ἀπελθ(εῖν)^{5} ʃ ʅ^{4} {C}.

Text Critical Note (see the discussion in the front matter): In Luke 9:59 κύριε is absent from B* D *pc* sy^{s}, but present in 𝔓$^{45.75}$ ℵ A B^{2} C L W Θ Ξ Ψ 0181 *f*$^{1.13}$ 33 𝔐 lat sy$^{c.p.h}$ co.

Text Critical Note (see the discussion in the front matter): In Luke 9:59 πρῶτον ἀπελθόντι is in ℵ B (D: -θόντα) Ψ 33 892 *al*, ἀπελθόντι alone is in W, ἀπελθεῖν πρῶτον is in A K 2542 *al*, πρῶτον ἀπελθεῖν is in *f*$^{1.13}$ 579 1424, and ἀπελθόντι πρῶτον is in 𝔓$^{45.75vid}$ C L (Θ: -θόντα) Ξ 0181 𝔐.

^{1} Whether there is an opening call by Jesus (Luke) or not (Matthew), and the resultant positioning of ἀκολούθει μοι (which Matthew implements by adding καί).

^{2} Matthew's τῶν μαθητῶν αὐτοῦ.

^{3} Matthew's αὐτῷ.

^{4} The position of πρῶτον after ἀπελθόντι (Luke) or before

Q

59 ἕτερος δὲ εἶπεν αὐτῷ· κύριε, ἐπίτρεψόν μοι πρῶτον ἀπελθεῖν καὶ θάψαι τὸν πατέρα μου. **60** εἶπεν δὲ αὐτῷ· ἀκολούθει μοι καὶ ἄφες τοὺς νεκροὺς θάψαι τοὺς ἑαυτῶν νεκρούς.

59 But another said to him: Master, permit me first to go and bury my father. **60** But he said to him: Follow me, and leave the dead to bury their own dead.

Q 9:59-60

Luke 9:59-60	Lukan Doublet	Markan Parallel	Gospel of Thomas
9:59 [Εἶπεν δὲ πρὸς]¹ ἕτερο[ν]¹· ⸉ἀκολούθει μοι.⸊¹ [ὁ]¹ δὲ ( )² εἶπεν ( )³· κύριε, ἐπίτρεψόν μοι ⸉ ⸊⁴ ἀπελθ[όντι]⁵ ⸉πρῶτον⸊⁴ ( )⁵ θάψαι τὸν πατέρα μου. **9:60** ⁶⸉ [εἶπεν]⁷ ⸊⁶ ( )⁶ δὲ ( )⁶ ⸉ ⸊⁶ αὐτῷ· ⸉ ⸊¹ ( )¹ ἄφες τοὺς νεκροὺς θάψαι τοὺς ἑαυτῶν νεκρούς, [σὺ δὲ ἀπελθὼν διάγγελλε τὴν βασιλείαν τοῦ θεοῦ]⁸. ⸊Luke 9:57¹			

IQP 1992, JSK: ⟦[εἶπεν]⁷⟧.

Text Critical Note (see the discussion in the front matter): In Matt 8:21 αὐτοῦ is absent from א B 33 *pc* it sa, but present in C L W Θ 0250 *f* [1.13] *𝔐* lat sy mae bo.

ἀπελθεῖν (Matthew).

5 Luke's ἀπελθόντι or Matthew's ἀπελθεῖν καί.

6 Luke's lack of an explicit subject or Matthew's ὁ ... Ἰησοῦς, and the resultant shift in the position of the verb.

7 Luke's εἶπεν or Matthew's λέγει.

8 Luke's σὺ δὲ ἀπελθὼν διάγγελλε τὴν βασιλείαν τοῦ θεοῦ.

59 Ein anderer aber sagte ihm: Herr, gestatte mir, zuvor fortzugehen und meinen Vater zu begraben. **60** Er aber sagte ihm: Folge mir, und lass die Toten ihre Toten begraben.

59 Puis un autre lui dit: Seigneur, laisse-moi d'abord partir et enterrer mon père. **60** Mais il lui dit: Suis-moi et laisse les morts enterrer leurs morts.

Q 9:⟦~~61-62~~⟧

Markan Parallel	Matthean Doublet	Matthew	Q 9:⟦~~61-62~~⟧
		[ ][0]	[][0]

JSK: Luke 9:61-62 in Q {B}.

[0] Is Luke 9:61-62 in Q?

Q 9:⟦~~61-62~~⟧

Luke 9:61-62	Lukan Doublet	Markan Parallel	3 Kgdms 19:19a, 20 LXX
9:61 [Εἶπεν δὲ καὶ ἕτερος· ἀκολουθήσω σοι, κύριε· πρῶτον δὲ ἐπίτρεψόν μοι ἀποτάξασθαι τοῖς εἰς τὸν οἶκόν μου. **9:62** εἶπεν δὲ πρὸς αὐτὸν ὁ Ἰησοῦς· οὐδεὶς ἐπιβαλὼν τὴν χεῖρα ἐπ' ἄροτρον καὶ βλέπων εἰς τὰ ὀπίσω εὔθετός ἐστιν τῇ βασιλείᾳ τοῦ θεοῦ.]^{0}			**19:19a** Καὶ ἀπῆλθεν ἐκεῖθεν καὶ εὑρίσκει τὸν Ελισαιε υἱὸν Σαφατ, καὶ αὐτὸς ἠροτρία ἐν βουσίν **19:20** καὶ κατέλιπεν Ελισαιε τὰς βόας καὶ κατέδραμεν ὀπίσω Ηλιου καὶ εἶπεν Καταφιλήσω τὸν πατέρα μου καὶ ἀκολουθήσω ὀπίσω σου· καὶ εἶπεν Ηλιου Ἀνάστρεφε, ὅτι πεποίηκά σοι.

Q 10:~~1~~

Mark 6:7a,c,b, 8a	Matt 10:1	Matt 10:5-6	Q 10:~~1~~
	[0]{	[0]{	[({})][0]
		10:5 [1]ʃ	
6:7a Καὶ προσκαλεῖται	{Καὶ προσκαλε}σάμενος	[ ][2]	
τοὺς δώδεκα	{(τοὺς δώδεκα)}		
	μαθητὰς αὐτοῦ		
6:7c καὶ ἐδίδου αὐτοῖς	{ἔδ}ωκεν {αὐτοῖς}		
ἐξουσίαν	{ἐξουσίαν}		
τῶν πνευμάτων	{πνευμάτων}		
τῶν ἀκαθάρτων,	{ἀκαθάρτων}		
	ὥστε ἐκβάλλειν αὐτὰ		
	καὶ		
	θεραπεύειν		
	πᾶσαν νόσον		
	καὶ πᾶσαν μαλακίαν.		
6:7b καὶ ἤρξατο		{[ ]}[3]	{[]}[3]
αὐτοὺς		[4]ʃ (Τούτους)[7]	[4]ʃ ()[7]
		{(τοὺς δώδεκα)}[4] ʅ[4]	{()}[4] ʅ[4]
ἀποστέλλειν		{ἀπ}[5]έ{στε}[5]ι{λε}[5]ν	{~~ἀπ~~}[5]~~έ~~{~~στε~~}[5]~~ι~~{~~λε~~}[5]~~ν~~
		(ὁ Ἰησοῦς)[6]	()[6]
		ʃ ʅ[4]	[4]ʃ {[]}[7] ʅ[4]
		[ ][8]	[][8]
δύο δύο		[ ][9]	{[]}[9]
6:8a καὶ παρήγγειλεν αὐτοῖς		({παρ}α{γγείλ}ας {αὐτοῖς}	[({})][10]
		λέγων· εἰς ὁδὸν ἐθνῶν	
		μὴ ἀπέλθητε	
		καὶ εἰς πόλιν Σαμαριτῶν	
		μὴ εἰσέλθητε·	
		10:6 πορεύεσθε δὲ μᾶλλον	
		πρὸς τὰ πρόβατα	
		τὰ ἀπολωλότα οἴκου	
		Ἰσραήλ.)[10]	
		ʅ[1]	ʅ[1]
	}[0]	}[0]	

[0] Is Luke 9:1-2a, Luke 10:1, Matt 10:1, or Matt 10:5-6 in Q?

[1] The position of Q 10:1 in Q: After Q 9:57-60, ⟦~~61-62~~⟧ and before Q 10:2 (Lukan order), or after Q 10:2 (Matt 9:37-38) and before Q 10:9 (Matt 10:7) (Matthean order).

[2] Is Luke's μετὰ δὲ ταῦτα ἀνέδειξεν ὁ κύριος ἑτέρους ἑβδομήκοντα δύο in Q?

[3] Is Luke's καί in Q or from Mark?

[4] Is the object after (Luke) or before (Matthew) the verb?

Q 10:~~1~~

Luke 10:1	Luke 9:1-2a	Mark 6:7a,c,b	Gospel of Thomas
[0]{ [1]ʃ	[0]{		
[Μετὰ δὲ ταῦτα ἀνέδειξεν ὁ κύριος ἑτέρους ἑβδομήκοντα δύο][2]	**9:1** Συγ{καλε}σάμενος δὲ ({τοὺς δώδεκα})	**6:7a** Καὶ προσκαλεῖται τοὺς δώδεκα	
	{ἔδ}ωκεν {αὐτοῖς} δύναμιν καὶ {ἐξουσίαν} ἐπὶ πάντα τὰ δαιμόνια	**6:7c** καὶ ἐδίδου αὐτοῖς ἐξουσίαν τῶν πνευμάτων τῶν ἀκαθάρτων,	
	καὶ νόσους θεραπεύειν		
{[καὶ]}[3] ʃ ʅ[4]	**9:2a** {[καὶ]}	**6:7b** καὶ ἤρξατο αὐτοὺς	
{ἀπ}[5]έ{στε}[5]ι{λε}[5]ν ( )[6]	[({ἀπ}έ{στε}ι{λ}εν)	ἀποστέλλειν	
[4]ʃ {[αὐτοὺς]}[7] ʅ[4]	{αὐτούς}]		
[ἀνὰ][8]			
{[δύο δύο]}[9]		δύο δύο	
[πρὸ προσώπου αὐτοῦ εἰς πᾶσαν πόλιν καὶ τόπον οὗ ἤμελλεν αὐτὸς ἔρχεσθαι.][10]			
ʅ[1] }[0]	}[0]		

[5] Is ἀπέστειλεν in Q or from Mark?
[6] Is Matthew's ὁ Ἰησοῦς in Q?
[7] Is Luke's αὐτούς or Matthew's τούτους in Q?
[8] Is Luke's ἀνά in Q?
[9] Is Luke's δύο δύο in Q or from Mark?
[10] Is either formulation in Q?

Q 10:2

Markan Parallel	Matthean Doublet	Matt 9:37-38	Q 10:2
		¹⸀	¹⸀
		(τότε)²	()²
		[ ]³λέγε(ι)³	[ ]³λεγε[( )]³
		[ ]²	[]²
		(τοῖς μαθηταῖς αὐτοῦ)⁴·	(τοῖς μαθηταῖς αὐτοῦ)⁴·
		ὁ μὲν θερισμὸς πολύς,	ὁ μὲν θερισμὸς πολύς,
		οἱ δὲ ἐργάται ὀλίγοι·	οἱ δὲ ἐργάται ὀλίγοι·
		9:38 δεήθητε οὖν τοῦ κυρίου	δεήθητε οὖν τοῦ κυρίου
		τοῦ θερισμοῦ ὅπως	τοῦ θερισμοῦ ὅπως
		⸀ ⸁⁵ ἐκβάλῃ ⸀ἐργάτας⸁⁵	⸀ ⸁⁵ ἐκβάλῃ ⸀ἐργάτας⸁⁵
		εἰς τὸν θερισμὸν αὐτοῦ.	εἰς τὸν θερισμὸν αὐτοῦ.
		⸁¹	⸁¹

IQP 1990: (< >)² ⟦<εἶπεν>³⟧ [( )]⁴.

JSK: []³ λέγε(ι)³; PH: [ἔ]³ λεγε[ν]³; JMR: [ ]³λεγε[( )]³, indeterminate.

¹ The position of Q 10:2 in Q: After Q 9:60 and before Q 10:3 (Lukan order); or after Q 11:14 (Matt 9:32-33) and before Q 10:9b (Matt 10:7) (Matthean order).

² Luke's postpositive δέ or Matthew's initial τότε.

³ Luke's ἔλεγεν or Matthew's λέγει.

Q

..λεγε... τοῖς μαθηταῖς αὐτοῦ· ὁ μὲν θερισμὸς πολύς, οἱ δὲ ἐργάται ὀλίγοι· δεήθητε οὖν τοῦ κυρίου τοῦ θερισμοῦ ὅπως ἐκβάλῃ ἐργάτας εἰς τὸν θερισμὸν αὐτοῦ.

He said to his disciples: The harvest is plentiful, but the workers are few. So ask the Lord of the harvest to dispatch workers into his harvest.

Gos. Thom. 73 (Nag Hammadi II 2)

Λέγει Ἰησοῦς· ὁ μὲν θερισμὸς πολύς, οἱ δὲ ἐργάται ὀλίγοι· δεήθητε δὲ τοῦ κυρίου ἵνα ἐκβάλῃ ἐργάτας εἰς τὸν θερισμόν.

Jesus says: The harvest is plentiful, but the workers are few. But ask the Lord that he may dispatch workers into the harvest.

Q 10:2

Luke 10:2	Lukan Doublet	John 4:35	*Gos. Thom.* 73
[1]ʃ			
( )[2]			
[ἔ][3]λεγε[ν][3]			ⲡⲉϫⲉ ⲓ̅ⲥ̅ ϫⲉ
[δὲ][2]		οὐχ ὑμεῖς λέγετε ὅτι	
[πρὸς αὐτούς][4]·		ἔτι τετράμηνός ἐστιν	
ὁ μὲν θερισμὸς πολύς,		καὶ ὁ θερισμὸς ἔρχεται;	ⲡⲱϩⲥ ⲙⲉⲛ ⲛⲁϣⲱϥ'
οἱ δὲ ἐργάται ὀλίγοι·		ἰδοὺ λέγω ὑμῖν,	ⲛ̄ⲉⲣⲅⲁⲧⲏⲥ ⲇⲉ ⲥⲟⲃⲕ'
δεήθητε οὖν τοῦ κυρίου		ἐπάρατε τοὺς ὀφθαλμοὺς ὑμῶν	ⲥⲟⲡⲥ̄ ⲇⲉ ⲙ̄ⲡϫⲟⲉⲓⲥ
τοῦ θερισμοῦ ὅπως		καὶ θεάσασθε τὰς χώρας	ϣⲓⲛⲁ
ʃἐργάταςʅ[5] ἐκβάλῃ ʃ ʅ[5]		ὅτι λευκαί εἰσιν	ⲉϥⲛⲁⲛⲉϫ' ⲉⲣⲅⲁⲧⲏⲥ
εἰς τὸν θερισμὸν αὐτοῦ.		πρὸς θερισμόν.	ⲉⲃⲟⲗ' ⲉⲡⲱϩ̄ⲥ̄
ʅ[1]			

[4] Luke's πρὸς αὐτούς or Matthew's τοῖς μαθηταῖς αὐτοῦ.
[5] The position of ἐργάτας before (Luke) or after (Matthew) ἐκβάλῃ.

Er sagte zu seinen Jüngern: Die Ernte ist zwar groß, Arbeiter gibt es aber «nur» wenige; bittet daher den Herrn der Ernte, dass er Arbeiter zu seiner Ernte schicke.

Il dit à ses disciples: La moisson est abondante, mais les ouvriers peu nombreux. Priez donc le Seigneur de la moisson d'envoyer des ouvriers pour sa moisson.

Jesus spricht: Die Ernte ist zwar groß, Arbeiter gibt es aber «nur» wenige. Bittet aber den Herrn, dass er Arbeiter zur Ernte schicke.

Jésus dit: La moisson est abondante, mais les ouvriers peu nombreux. Mais priez le Seigneur afin qu'il envoie des ouvriers pour la moisson.

Q 10:3

Markan Parallel	Matthean Doublet	Matt 10:16	Q 10:3
		¹ʃ	¹ʃ
		[ ]²	[ὑπάγετε·]²
		Ἰδοὺ (ἐγὼ)³ ἀποστέλλω	ἰδοὺ ⟦()³⟧ ἀποστέλλω
		ὑμᾶς ὡς (πρόβατα)⁴	ὑμᾶς ὡς (πρόβατα)⁴
		ἐν μέσῳ λύκων·	ἐν μέσῳ λύκων
		(γίνεσθε οὖν	()⁵
		φρόνιμοι	
		ὡς οἱ ὄφεις	
		καὶ ἀκέραιοι	
		ὡς αἱ περιστεραί)⁵.	.
		²¹	²¹

PH: ⟦[]²⟧ ἰδοὺ ⟦(ἐγώ)³⟧.

IQP 1990: ⟦[ὑπάγετε·]²⟧ ἰδοὺ ()³ ἀποστέλλω ὑμᾶς ὡς [ ]⁴.

¹ The position of Q 10:3 in Q: After Q 10:2 and before Q 10:4 (Lukan order); or after Q 10:12 (Matt 10:15) and before Q 12:11 (Matt 10:17-19a) (Matthean order).

² Luke's ὑπάγετε.

³ Matthew's ἐγώ.

Q

ὑπάγετε· ἰδοὺ ἀποστέλλω ὑμᾶς ὡς πρόβατα ἐν μέσῳ λύκων.	Be on your way! Look, I send you like sheep in the midst of wolves.

Gos. Thom. 39.3 (Nag Hammadi II 2)

ὑμεῖς δὲ γίνεσθε φρόνιμοι ὡς οἱ ὄφεις καὶ ἀκέραιοι ὡς αἱ περιστεραί.

You, however, be as shrewd as the serpents and as innocent as the doves!

Gos. Thom. 39.3 (*P. Oxy.* 655)

[ὑμεῖς] δὲ γεί[νεσθε φρόνι]μοι ὡ[ς ὄφεις καὶ ἀ]κέραι[οι ὡς περιστε]ρα[ί].

[You], however, [be as shrewd as serpents and as] innocent [as doves]!

Q 10:3

Luke 10:3	Lukan Doublet	Markan Parallel	*Gos. Thom.* 39.3
¹⸢ [ὑπάγετε·]² ἰδοὺ ( )³ ἀποστέλλω ὑμᾶς ὡς [ἄρνας]⁴ ἐν μέσῳ λύκων ( )⁵ . ⸣¹			ⲛ̄ⲧⲱⲧⲛ̄ ⲇⲉ ϣⲱⲡⲉ ⲙ̄ⲫⲣⲟⲛⲓⲙⲟⲥ ⲛ̄ⲑⲉ ⲛ̄ⲛ̄ϩⲟϥ' ⲁⲩⲱ ⲛ̄ⲁⲕⲉⲣⲁⲓⲟⲥ ⲛ̄ⲑⲉ ⲛ̄ⲛ̄ϭⲣⲟⲙ'ⲡⲉ

⁴ Luke's ἄρνας or Matthew's πρόβατα.
⁵ Matthew's γίνεσθε οὖν φρόνιμοι ὡς οἱ ὄφεις καὶ ἀκέραιοι ὡς αἱ περιστεραί.

Geht! Siehe, ich sende euch wie Schafe mitten unter Wölfe.

Allez! Voici, je vous envoie comme des brebis au milieu des loups.

Ihr aber seid klug wie die Schlangen und lauter wie die Tauben!

Mais vous, soyez prudents comme les serpents et innocents comme les colombes!

[Ihr], aber, [seid klug wie die Schlangen und] lauter [wie die Tauben]!

Mais [vous, soyez prudents comme des serpents et] innocents [comme des colombes]!

Q 10:4

Mark 6:8-9	Matthean Doublet	Matt 10:9-10a	Q 10:4
6:8 καὶ παρήγγειλεν αὐτοῖς		**10:9** [1]ʃ	[1]ʃ
ἵνα μηδὲν αἴρωσιν		{Μὴ} (κτήσησθε)[2]	{μὴ} [βαστάζετε][2]
εἰς ὁδὸν			
εἰ μὴ ῥάβδον μόνον,			
μὴ ἄρτον,		(χρυσὸν μηδὲ ἄργυρον	⟦[βαλλάντιον][3]⟧
		{μη}δὲ {χαλκὸν})[3]	
		({εἰς τ}ὰς {ζών}ας ὑμῶν)[4],	()[4],
μὴ πήραν,		**10:10a** {μὴ πήραν}[5]	{μὴ πήραν}[5],
μὴ εἰς τὴν ζώνην χαλκόν,		({εἰς ὁδὸν})[6]	({})[6]
6:9 ἀλλὰ ὑποδεδεμένους			
σανδάλια,			
καὶ			
μὴ ἐνδύσησθε		({μη}δὲ	({})[7]
δύο χιτῶνας.		{δύο χιτῶνας})[7]	
		μη(δὲ)[8]	μὴ()[8]
		{ὑποδ}ή{μ}ατα	{ὑποδ}ή{μ}ατα,
		({μη}δὲ {ῥάβδον})[9]·	({μη}δὲ {ῥάβδον})[9]·
		[ ][10]	[καὶ μηδένα
			κατὰ τὴν ὁδὸν
			ἀσπάσησθε.][10]
		ʅ[1]	ʅ[1]

IQP 1990, PH: ⟦[βαστάζετε][2]⟧.

IQP 1990: ⟦(ἄργυρ)[3]< >[3](ον)[3]⟧ ()[4], ⟦{μὴ πήραν}[5]⟧ μη( )[8] {ὑποδ}ή{μ}ατα ⟦({μη}δὲ {ῥάβδον})[9]·⟧ [ ][10] ⟦[μηδένα][10]⟧ [ ][10] ⟦[ἀσπάσησθε.][10]⟧.

[1] The position of Q 10:4 in Q: After Q 10:3 and before Q 10:5 (Lukan order); or after Q 10:9 (Matt 10:7-8) and before Q 10:7b (Matt 10:10b) (Matthean order).

[2] Is Luke's μὴ βαστάζετε or Matthew's μὴ κτήσησθε in Q?

[3] Is the money referred to as βαλλάντιον (Luke) or χρυσὸν μηδὲ ἄργυρον μηδὲ χαλκόν (Matthew)? (See also ἀργύριον, Luke 9:3.)

[4] Is Matthew's εἰς τὰς ζώνας ὑμῶν in Q or from Mark?

Q

μὴ βαστάζετε ⟦βαλλάντιον⟧, μὴ πήραν, μὴ ὑποδήματα, μηδὲ ῥάβδον· καὶ μηδένα κατὰ τὴν ὁδὸν ἀσπάσησθε.	Carry no ⟦purse⟧, nor knapsack, nor sandals, nor stick, and greet no one on the road.

Q 10:4

Luke 10:4	Luke 9:3	Mark 6:8-9	4 Kgdms 4:29 LXX
[1]⸂	{καὶ} εἶπ{εν} πρὸς {αὐτο}ύ{ς}·	**6:8** καὶ παρήγγειλεν αὐτοῖς	καὶ εἶπεν Ελισαιε τῷ Γιεζι
{μὴ} [βαστάζετε][2]	{([μη])δὲν αἴρ}[ετε]	ἵνα μηδὲν αἴρωσιν	
	({εἰς}) [τὴν ({ὁδόν})],	εἰς ὁδὸν	
	({μή})τε ({ῥάβδον})	εἰ μὴ ῥάβδον μόνον,	
[βαλλάντιον][3]		μὴ ἄρτον,	
( )[4],			
{μὴ πήραν}[5],	([{μή}])τε ([{πήραν}])	μὴ πήραν,	
({ })[6]		μὴ εἰς τὴν ζώνην χαλκόν,	
	{μή}τε {ἄρτον}	**6:9** ἀλλὰ ὑποδεδεμένους	
	{μή}τε	σανδάλια,	
	(ἀργύρ)ι(ον)	καὶ	
({ })[7]	({μή})τε ἀνὰ	μὴ ἐνδύσησθε	
	({δύο χιτῶνας}) ἔχειν	δύο χιτῶνας.	Ζῶσαι τὴν ὀσφύν σου
μή( )[8]			καὶ λαβὲ τὴν βακτηρίαν
{ὑποδ}ή{μ}ατα,	.		μου ἐν τῇ χειρί σου
( )[9]			καὶ δεῦρο·
[καὶ μηδένα			ὅτι ἐὰν εὕρῃς ἄνδρα,
κατὰ τὴν ὁδὸν			οὐκ εὐλογήσεις αὐτόν,
ἀσπάσησθε.][10]			καὶ ἐὰν εὐλογήσῃ σε ἀνήρ,
⸃[1]			οὐκ ἀποκριθήσῃ αὐτῷ·
			καὶ ἐπιθήσεις
			τὴν βακτηρίαν μου ἐπὶ
			πρόσωπον τοῦ παιδαρίου.

5 Is μὴ πήραν in Q or from Mark?

6 Is Matthew's εἰς ὁδόν in Q or from Mark? (See also variation unit [10]).

7 Is Matthew's μηδὲ δύο χιτῶνας in Q or from Mark?

8 Is Luke's μή or Matthew's μηδέ in Q?

9 Is Matthew's μηδὲ ῥάβδον in Q? (See also μήτε ῥάβδον, Luke 9:3, but εἰ μὴ ῥάβδον in Mark 6:8a.)

10 Is Luke's καὶ μηδένα κατὰ τὴν ὁδὸν ἀσπάσησθε in Q? (See also variation unit [6] and Q 10:5[4].)

Tragt keinen ⟦Geldbeutel⟧, keinen Proviantsack, keine Sandalen und auch keinen Stock, und grüßt niemanden unterwegs.

Ne portez ni ⟦bourse⟧, ni besace, ni sandales, ni bâton; et n'échangez de salutations avec personne en chemin.

Q 10:5

Mark 6:10a-b	Matt 10:11a-b	Matt 10:12	Q 10:5
καὶ ἔλεγεν αὐτοῖς· ὅπου ἐὰν εἰσέλθητε εἰς οἰκίαν,	 [(εἰς) ἣν (δ') {ἂν}] πόλιν ἢ κώμην [{(εἰσ)έλθητε}], ἐξετάσατε τίς ἐν (αὐτῇ) ἄξιός ἐστιν·	₁ʃ {εἰσ}(ερχόμενοι)² δ(ὲ)² {εἰς} (τὴν)² {οἰκίαν} [ ]³ (ἀσπάσασθε)⁴ (αὐτήν)⁵· ʅ¹⇒ Matt Q 10:13	₁ʃ {εἰς} [ἣν]² δ' {[ἂν]² εἰσ[έλθη- τε]}² {οἰκίαν}, ⟦[πρῶτον]³⟧ [λέγετε· εἰρήνη]⁴ ⟦[τῷ οἴκῳ τούτῳ]⁵⟧. ʅ¹⇒ Q 10:6

IQP 1992: ⟦[]³ [λέγετε· εἰρήνη]⁴⟧ [( )]⁵.

[1] The position of Q 10:5-6 in Q: After Q 10:4 and before Q 10:7-8 (Lukan order: οἰκία, then πόλις); or after Q 10:8 (Matt 10:11) and before Q 10:10-11 (Matt 10:14) (Matthean order: πόλις/κώμη, then οἰκία).

[2] Luke's εἰς ἣν δ' ἂν εἰσέλθητε or Matthew's εἰσερχόμενοι δὲ εἰς τήν. (See also Q 10:8.)

Q

εἰς ἣν δ' ἂν εἰσέλθητε οἰκίαν, ⟦πρῶτον⟧ λέγετε· εἰρήνη ⟦τῷ οἴκῳ τούτῳ⟧.	Into whatever house you enter, ⟦first⟧ say: Peace ⟦to this house⟧!

Q 10:5

Luke 10:5	Luke 9:4a	Mark 6:10a-b	Gospel of Thomas
⸀1ʃ		καὶ ἔλεγεν αὐτοῖς·	
{εἰς} [ἣν]² δ' {[ἂν]² εἰσ[έλθη-τε]}²	καὶ [({εἰς}) ἣν] [{ἂν}]	ὅπου ἐὰν εἰσέλθητε	
{οἰκίαν}, [πρῶτον]³ [λέγετε· εἰρήνη]⁴ [τῷ οἴκῳ τούτῳ]⁵. ⸂1⇒ Luke 10:6	[({οἰκίαν})] [({εἰσ)έλθητε}],	εἰς οἰκίαν,	

³ Luke's πρῶτον.
⁴ Luke's λέγετε· εἰρήνη or Matthew's ἀσπάσασθε.
⁵ Luke's τῷ οἴκῳ τούτῳ or Matthew's αὐτήν.

Wenn ihr in ein Haus kommt, sagt ⟦als erstes⟧: Friede ⟦diesem Haus⟧.

Dans quelque maison que vous entriez, dites ⟦d'abord⟧: Paix ⟦à cette maisonnée⟧!

Q 10:6

Markan Parallel	Matt 10:11b	Matt 10:13	Q 10:6
	ἐξετάσατε τίς ἐν αὐτῇ ἄξιός ἐστιν·	καὶ ἐὰν (μὲν)[1] [ ][2] ᾖ (ἡ οἰκία ἀξία)[3], (ἐλθάτω)[4] ʃ ʅ[5] ἡ εἰρήνη ὑμῶν [5]ʃἐπ᾽ αὐτ(ή)[3]νʅ[5], ἐ(ὰν)[6] δὲ μὴ [ ][7] (ᾖ ἀξία)[8], (ἡ εἰρήνη ὑμῶν)[9] (πρὸς)[10] ὑμᾶς (ἐπιστραφήτω)[11]. ʅMatt 10:12[1]	καὶ ἐὰν (μὲν)[1] [ἐκεῖ][2] ᾖ [υἱὸς εἰρήνης][3], (ἐλθάτω)[4] ʃ ʅ[5] ἡ εἰρήνη ὑμῶν [5]ʃἐπ᾽ αὐτ[ό][3]νʅ[5]. ε⟦[ἰ][6]⟧ δὲ μή [][7] ()[8], (ἡ εἰρήνη ὑμῶν)[9] ⟦[ἐφ᾽][10]⟧ ὑμᾶς ⟦(ἐπιστραφήτω)[11]⟧. ʅQ 10:5[1]

IQP 1992: ()[1].

IQP 1992: ⟦(ἐλθάτω)[4]⟧ [5]ʃἐπ᾽ αὐτ[ὸ][3]νʅ[5] ἡ εἰρήνη ὑμῶν ʃ ʅ[5].

[1] Matthew's μέν.

[2] Luke's ἐκεῖ. (See also at Q 10:7-8[0] Mark 6:10c parr.)

[3] Luke's υἱὸς εἰρήνης … αὐτόν or Matthew's ἡ οἰκία ἀξία … αὐτήν.

[4] Luke's ἐπαναπαήσεται or Matthew's ἐλθάτω.

[5] The position of ἐπ᾽ αὐτ…ν between (Luke) or after (Matthew) the verb and ἡ εἰρήνη ὑμῶν.

Q

καὶ ἐὰν μὲν ἐκεῖ ᾖ υἱὸς εἰρήνης, ἐλθάτω ἡ εἰρήνη ὑμῶν ἐπ᾽ αὐτόν· ε⟦ἰ⟧ δὲ μή, ἡ εἰρήνη ὑμῶν ⟦ἐφ᾽⟧ ὑμᾶς ⟦ἐπιστραφήτω⟧.	And if a son of peace be there, let your peace come upon him; but if not, ⟦let⟧ your peace ⟦return upon⟧ you.

Q 10:6

Luke 10:6	Lukan Doublet	Markan Parallel	Gospel of Thomas
καὶ ἐὰν ( )[1] [ἐκεῖ][2] ᾖ [υἱὸς εἰρήνης][3], [ἐπαναπαήσεται][4] [5]ʃἐπ' αὐτ[ὸ][3]ν↑[5] ἡ εἰρήνη ὑμῶν ʃ ↑[5]. ε[ἰ][6] δὲ μή [γε][7], ( )[8] ( )[9] [ἐφ'][10] ὑμᾶς [ἀνακάμψει][11]. ↑Luke 10:5[1]			

IQP 1992: ⟦[][7] ()[8] ()[9]⟧ [( )][10].

[6] Luke's εἰ or Matthew's ἐάν.
[7] Luke's γε.
[8] Matthew's ᾖ ἀξία.
[9] Matthew's ἡ εἰρήνη ὑμῶν.
[10] Luke's ἐφ' or Matthew's πρός.
[11] Luke's ἀνακάμψει or Matthew's ἐπιστραφήτω.

Und wenn dort ein Sohn des Friedens ist, soll euer Friede auf ihn kommen; wenn aber nicht, ⟦soll⟧ euer Friede ⟦auf⟧ euch ⟦zurückkehren⟧.

Et s'il y a là un fils de paix, que votre paix vienne sur lui. Mais si ce n'est pas le cas, ⟦que⟧ votre paix ⟦revienne sur⟧ vous.

Q 10:7-8

1 Tim 5:18b; Mark 6:10b-c	Matt 10:12	Matt 10:10b-11	Q 10:7-8
		10:10b	**10:7**
		/ $\backslash^{0}$	^{0}/
			⟦[ἐν αὐτῇ δὲ τῇ οἰκίᾳ]^{1}⟧
			{μέ⟦()^{2}⟧ν⟦[ε]^{2}⟧τε}
			()^{3}
			[«ἐσθίοντες καὶ πίνοντες
1 Tim 5:18b			τὰ παρ' αὐτῶν»]^{4} $\backslash^{0}$.
ἄξιος ὁ ἐργάτης		ἄξιος γὰρ ὁ ἐργάτης	ἄξιος γὰρ ὁ ἐργάτης
τοῦ μισθοῦ αὐτοῦ.		τ(ῆς τροφῆς)^{5} αὐτοῦ.	τ[οῦ μισθοῦ]^{5} αὐτοῦ.
		[ ]^{6}	⟦[μὴ μεταβαίνετε
			ἐξ οἰκίας εἰς οἰκίαν.]^{6}⟧
Mark 6:10b-c		**10:11** ^{7}/	**10:8** ^{7}/
ὅπου ἐὰν	[({εἰσ})ερχ]όμενοι) (δ)ὲ	[ ]^{8} {εἰς} ἣν (δ')^{8} {ἂν}	[καὶ]^{8} {εἰς} ἣν ()^{8} ἂν
	[({εἰς})] τὴν		
εἰσέλθητε	{οἰκίαν}	πόλιν (ἢ κώμην)^{9}	πόλιν ()^{9}
εἰς οἰκίαν,	ἀσπάσασθε [(αὐτή)]ν·	{εἰσ(έλθητε)}^{10},	{εἰσ}⟦[έρχησθε]^{10}⟧
		(ἐξετάσατε τίς ἐν αὐτῇ	[καὶ δέχωνται ὑμᾶς]^{11},
		ἄξιός ἐστιν·)^{11}	
		[ ]^{12}	⟦[«ἐσθίετε τὰ παρατιθέμενα
			ὑμῖν»]^{12}⟧
		$\backslash^{7}$	$\backslash^{7}$
ἐκεῖ		^{0}/ (κἀ{κεῖ})^{1}	/ $\backslash^{0}$
μένετε		με}(ί)^{2}{ν}(α)^{2}{τε	
ἕως ἂν ἐξέλθητε		(ἕως ἂν ἐξέλθητε)^{3}}.	
ἐκεῖθεν.			

0 Is Luke 10:7a par. Matt 10:11c in Q, and if so, in Q 10:7 (Luke) or in Q 10:8 (Matthew)?

1 Luke's ἐν αὐτῇ δὲ τῇ οἰκίᾳ or Matthew's κἀκεῖ. (See also Q 10:6[2] ἐκεῖ.)

2 Luke's μένετε or Matthew's μείνατε.

3 Matthew's ἕως ἂν ἐξέλθητε. (See also variation unit [6])

4 Luke's ἐσθίοντες καὶ πίνοντες τὰ παρ' αὐτῶν.

5 Luke's τοῦ μισθοῦ or Matthew's τῆς τροφῆς.

Q 10:7-8

Luke 10:7-8	Luke 9:4	Mark 6:10b-c	*Gos. Thom.* 14.4a-b
10:7	καὶ {(εἰς)} ἣν ἂν	ὅπου ἐὰν εἰσέλθητε	
[0]/	{(οἰκίαν)} {εἰσέλθητε},	εἰς οἰκίαν,	
[ἐν αὐτῇ δὲ τῇ οἰκίᾳ][1]	{ἐ(κεῖ	ἐκεῖ	
{μέ( )[2]ν[ε][2]τε}	[μέ)(ν)ε(τε)]}	μένετε	
( )[3]	καὶ {ἐκεῖθεν}	ἕως ἂν ἐξέλθητε	
[ἐσθίοντες καὶ πίνοντες	{ἐξ}έρχεσθε.	ἐκεῖθεν.	
τὰ παρ' αὐτῶν·][4] \[0]			
ἄξιος γὰρ ὁ ἐργάτης			
τ[οῦ μισθοῦ][5] αὐτοῦ.			
[μὴ μεταβαίνετε			
ἐξ οἰκίας εἰς οἰκίαν][6].			
10:8 [7]/			
[καὶ][8] {εἰς} ἣν ( )[8] ἂν			14.4a ⲁⲩⲱ ⲉⲧⲉⲧⲛ̄-ϣⲁⲛⲃⲱⲕ'
πόλιν ( )[9]			ⲉϩⲟⲩⲛ ⲉⲕⲁϩ ⲛⲓⲙ ⲁⲩⲱ
{εἰσ}[έρχησθε][10]			ⲛ̄ⲧⲉⲧⲙ̄ⲙⲟⲟϣⲉ ϩⲛ̄ ⲛ̄ⲭⲱⲣⲁ
[καὶ δέχωνται ὑμᾶς][11],			14.4b ⲉⲩϣⲁⲣ̄ⲡⲁⲣⲁ-ⲇⲉⲭⲉ ⲙ̄ⲙⲱⲧⲛ̄
[ἐσθίετε τὰ παρατιθέμενα ὑμῖν][12]			ⲡⲉⲧⲟⲩⲛⲁⲕⲁⲁϥ ϩⲁⲣⲱⲧⲛ̄ ⲟⲩⲟⲙϥ̄
\[7]			
/ \[0]			

[6] Luke's μὴ μεταβαίνετε ἐξ οἰκίας εἰς οἰκίαν. (See also variation unit [3])

[7] Is Luke 10:8 par. Matt 10:11a-b in Q?

[8] Luke's καὶ or Matthew's δ'.

[9] Matthew's ἢ κώμην.

[10] Luke's εἰσέρχησθε or Matthew's εἰσέλθητε.

[11] Luke's καὶ δέχωνται ὑμᾶς or Matthew's ἐξετάσατε τίς ἐν αὐτῇ ἄξιός ἐστιν.

[12] Luke's ἐσθίετε τὰ παρατιθέμενα ὑμῖν.

Q 10:7-8

1 Tim 5:18b; Mark 6:10b-c	Matt 10:12	Matt 10:10b-11	Q 10:7-8
ἐκεῖθεν.		[ ]^{4} \\$^{0}$	

IQP 1994: Q 10:⟦7-8⟧.

IQP 1994: ^{0}/ [ ]^{1} {μ̶έ̶( )^{2}ν̶[( )]^{2}τ̶ε̶} ⟦()^{3}⟧, [< >]^{4} [ ]^{4} ⟦[τὰ παρ' αὐτῶν]^{4}⟧\\$^{0}$.

Q

7 ⟦ἐν αὐτῇ δὲ τῇ οἰκίᾳ⟧ μέν⟦ε⟧τε «ἐσθίοντες καὶ πίνοντες τὰ παρ' αὐτῶν»· ἄξιος γὰρ ὁ ἐργάτης τοῦ μισθοῦ αὐτοῦ. ⟦μὴ μεταβαίνετε ἐξ οἰκίας εἰς οἰκίαν.⟧ **8** καὶ εἰς ἣν ἂν πόλιν εἰσ⟦έρχησθε⟧ καὶ δέχωνται ὑμᾶς, ⟦«ἐσθίετε τὰ παρατιθέμενα ὑμῖν»⟧

7 ⟦And at that house⟧ remain, «eating and drinking whatever they provide», for the worker is worthy of one's reward. ⟦Do not move around from house to house.⟧ **8** And whatever town you enter and they take you in, ⟦«eat what is set before you»⟧.

Gos. Thom. 14.4a-b (Nag Hammadi II 2)

(4a) καὶ ὅταν εἰσέρχησθε εἰς πᾶσαν γῆν καὶ περιπατῆτε ἐν ταῖς χώραις, (4b) ὅταν παραδέχωνται ὑμᾶς, ἐσθίετε τὸ παρατιθέμενον ὑμῖν

(4a) And if you enter into any land and wander from place to place[1], (4b) (and) if they take you in, (then) eat what is set before you.

[1] Literally: in the countryside.

Q 10:7-8

Luke 10:7-8	**Luke 9:4**	**Mark 6:10b-c**	***Gos. Thom.* 14.4a-b**

IQP 1994: [ ]^{6}; PH: ⟦[]^{6}⟧.
PH: Variation unit ^{7} not in Q {C}.

IQP 1994: **10:8** [ ]^{8} {εἰς} ἣν ( )^{8} ἂν πόλιν ()^{9} {εἰσ}[ερχ]^{10} [ ]^{10}, [ ]^{11} ⟦[]^{12}⟧.

7 Bleibt ⟦in diesem Haus⟧, «esst und trinkt, was sie euch geben», denn der Arbeiter ist seines Lohnes wert. ⟦Wechselt nicht von Haus zu Haus.⟧ **8** Und wenn ihr in eine Stadt kommt und sie nehmen euch auf, ⟦«esst, was euch vorgesetzt wird»⟧.

7 Demeurez ⟦dans cette maison⟧, «mangeant et buvant ce qu'on vous donnera», car l'ouvrier est digne de son salaire. ⟦Ne passez pas de maison en maison.⟧ **8** Dans quelque ville que vous entriez et qu'on vous reçoive, ⟦«mangez ce qu'on placera devant vous»⟧.

(4a) Und wenn ihr in irgendein Land kommt und wandert von Ort zu Ort[2] (4b) (und) wenn sie euch aufnehmen, (dann) esst, was euch vorgesetzt wird.

(4a) Et si vous entrez en quelque contrée et que vous marchez dans les campagnes, (4b) si l'on vous reçoit, mangez ce que l'on placera devant vous.

[2] Wörtlich: in den Gebieten.

Q 10:9

Mark 1:14b-15	Matt 4:17	Matt 10:7-8	Q 10:9
		[1]⸂ [ ][2] ⸂ ⸃[3]	[1]⸂ [καὶ][2] [3]⸂ ⸂{θεραπεύ}ετε⸃[4] [τοὺς ἐν αὐτῇ][5] ἀσθεν⟦(οῦντας)[6]⟧ ⸂⸃[4] ()[7] ⸃[3]
1:14b κηρύσσειν τὸ εὐαγγέλιον τοῦ θεοῦ **1:15** καὶ λέγων ὅτι πεπλήρωται ὁ καιρὸς καὶ ἤγγικεν ἡ βασιλεία τοῦ θεοῦ· μετανοεῖτε καὶ πιστεύετε ἐν τῷ εὐαγγελίῳ	Ἀπὸ τότε ἤρξατο ὁ Ἰησοῦς {(κηρύσσ)ειν} {[καὶ (λέγ)]}ειν· {μετανοεῖτε}· {[(ἤγγικεν)]} γὰρ [{(ἡ βασιλεία}] τῶν οὐρανῶν).	**10:7** (πορευόμενοι δὲ)[8] ({κηρύ}σσετε)[9] λέγ(οντες)[9] [ ][10] (ὅτι)[11] ἤγγικεν [ ][12] ἡ βασιλεία τ(ῶν οὐρανῶν)[13]. **10:8** [3]⸂ ⸂ ⸃[4] [ ][5] ἀσθεν(οῦντας)[6] ⸂{θεραπεύ}ετε⸃[4], (νεκροὺς ἐγείρετε, λεπροὺς καθαρίζετε, {δαιμόνια} {ἐ}κ{βάλλ}ετε· δωρεὰν ἐλάβετε, δωρεὰν δότε)[7] ⸃[3]. ⸃[1]	[καὶ][8] λέγ[ετε][9] ⟦[αὐτοῖς·][10]⟧ ( )[11] ἤγγικεν [ἐφ᾽ ὑμᾶς][12] ἡ βασιλεία τ[οῦ θεοῦ][13]. ⸂⸃[3] ⸃[1]

IQP 1994: [ ][2].

IQP 1994: ⟦[τοὺς ἐν αὐτῇ][5]⟧; PH: ⟦[][5]⟧.

[1] The position of Q 10:9 in Q: After Q 10:7-8 and before Q 10:10 (Lukan order); or after Q 10:2 (Matt 9:37-38) and before Q 10:4 (Matt 10:9) (Matthean order).

[2] Luke's καί.

[3] The instruction to heal prior to (Luke) or after (Matthew) the message.

[4] The position of θεραπεύετε before (Luke) or after (Matthew) ἀσθεν-.

[5] Luke's τοὺς ἐν αὐτῇ.

Q

καὶ θεραπεύετε τοὺς ἐν αὐτῇ ἀσθεν⟦οῦντας⟧ καὶ λέγετε ⟦αὐτοῖς⟧· .. ἤγγικεν ἐφ᾽ ὑμᾶς ἡ βασιλεία τοῦ θεοῦ.

And cure the sick there, and say ⟦to them⟧: The kingdom of God has reached unto you.

Gos. Thom. 14.4c (Nag Hammadi II 2)

(καὶ) θεραπεύετε τοὺς ἀσθενεῖς ἐν αὐτοῖς[1].

Cure the sick among them[2]!

[1] The Coptic term could relate to χῶραι as well. In this case the corresponding Greek term would be ἐν αὐταῖς.

[2] Or: there (in the countryside).

Q 10:9

Luke 10:9	Luke 9:2b	Mark 6:12-13	*Gos. Thom.* 14.4c
[1]⸂			
[καὶ][2]			
[3]⸂			
⸂{θεραπεύ}ετε⸃[4]			ⲛⲉⲧϣⲱⲛⲉ
[τοὺς ἐν αὐτῇ][5]			ⲛ̄ϩⲏⲧⲟⲩ
ἀσθεν[εῖ][6]ς			ⲉⲣⲓⲑⲉⲣⲁⲡⲉⲩⲉ ⲙ̄ⲙⲟⲟⲩ
⸂ ⸃[4]			
( )[7]			
⸃[3]			
[καὶ][8]		**6:12** Καὶ ἐξελθόντες	
λέγ[ετε][9]	{κηρύ}σσειν	ἐκήρυξαν	
[αὐτοῖς·][10]			
( )[11]		ἵνα μετανοῶσιν,	
ἤγγικεν [ἐφ' ὑμᾶς][12]			
ἡ βασιλεία	τ[(ὴ)]ν [(βασιλεία)]ν		
τ[οῦ θεοῦ][13].	[(τ)οῦ θεοῦ]		
⸂ ⸃[3]		**6:13** καὶ	
		δαιμόνια πολλὰ ἐξέβαλλον,	
		καὶ ἤλειφον ἐλαίῳ πολλοὺς	
	καὶ ἰᾶσθαι τοὺς [(ἀσθεν)εῖς],	ἀρρώστους καὶ	
		ἐθεράπευον.	
⸃[1]			

IQP 1994: ἀσθεν(οῦντας)[6].

[6] Luke's ἀσθενεῖς or Matthew's ἀσθενοῦντας.
[7] Matthew's other commands.
[8] Luke's καὶ or Matthew's πορευόμενοι δέ. (See πορεύεσθε δέ in Matt 10:6a and at Q 10:10 ἐκπορευόμενοι in Mark 6:11.)

IQP 1994: ⟦()[11]⟧.

[9] Luke's λέγετε or Matthew's κηρύσσετε λέγοντες.
[10] Luke's αὐτοῖς.
[11] Matthew's ὅτι.
[12] Luke's ἐφ' ὑμᾶς.
[13] Luke's τοῦ θεοῦ or Matthew's τῶν οὐρανῶν.

Heilt die Kranken in ihr und sagt ⟦ihnen⟧: Nahegekommen ist zu auch das Reich Gottes.

Et guérissez les malades qui s'y trouvent et dites⟦-leur⟧: Le royaume de Dieu s'est approché de vous.

Die Kranken unter ihnen[3] heilt!

[1] Der koptische Ausdruck könnte sich auch auf die χῶραι beziehen, dann müsste er griechisch ἐν αὐταῖς lauten.
[3] Oder: in ihnen (den Gebieten).

Guérissez ceux qui, parmi eux,[4] sont malades.

[1] L'expression copte pourrait tout aussi bien se rapporter à χῶραι, auquel cas il faudrait la rendre en grec par ἐν αὐταῖς.
[4] Ou: en elles (les campagnes).

Q 10:10

Mark 6:11a	Matthean Doublet	Matt 10:14a	Q 10:10
		[1]ʃ	[1]ʃ
καὶ ὃς ἂν		{καὶ (ὃς)[2] ἂν}	[εἰς ἣν δ'][2] {ἂν}
τόπος		[ ][2]	[πόλιν εἰσέλθητε][2] {καὶ}
μὴ δέξηται ὑμᾶς		{μὴ δέ(ξη)[3]ται ὑμᾶς	{μὴ δέ}[χων][3]{ται ὑμᾶς}
μηδὲ ἀκούσωσιν		(μηδὲ ἀκούσ}η	()[4]
ὑμῶν,		τοὺς λόγους {ὑμῶν)[4],	,
ἐκπορευόμενοι		ἐ}ξ(ερχ{όμενοι})[5]	{ἐ}ξ⟦(ερχ{όμενοι})[5]
		(ἔξω)[6]	(ἔξω)[6]⟧
		(τῆς οἰκίας ἢ)[7]	()[7]
ἐκεῖθεν		τ(ῆς πόλεως {ἐκεί}νης)[6.8]	τ⟦(ῆς πόλεως {ἐκεί}νης)[6.8]⟧
		[ ][9]	[][9]
		ʅ[1]⇒ Matt 10:15	ʅ[1]⇒ Q 10:12

IQP 1994: ⟦[εἰς ἣν δ'][2]⟧ {ἂν} ⟦[πόλιν εἰσέλθητε {καὶ}][2]⟧ {μὴ δέ}[χων][2.3]{ται ὑμᾶς} ()[4], {ἐ}ξε(ρχ{όμενοι})[5].

PH: (ἔξω)[6] ()[7] τ(ῆς πολέως {ἐκεί}νης)[6.8].

1 The position of Q 10:10-12 in Q: After Q 10:9 and before Q 10:13 (Lukan order); or after Q 10:6 (Matt 10:13) and before Q 12:11 (Matt 10:19) (Matthean order).

2 Luke's εἰς ἣν δ' ἂν πόλιν εἰσέλθητε καί or Matthew's καὶ ὃς ἄν.

3 Luke's μὴ δέχωνται ὑμᾶς or Matthew's μὴ δέξηται ὑμᾶς.

4 Matthew's μηδὲ ἀκούσῃ τοὺς λόγους ὑμῶν.

Q

εἰς ἣν δ' ἂν πόλιν εἰσέλθητε καὶ μὴ δέχωνται ὑμᾶς, ἐξε⟦ρχόμενοι ἔξω⟧ τ⟦ῆς πολέως ἐκείνης⟧

But into whatever town you enter and they do not take you in, on going out ⟦from that town⟧,

Q 10:10

Luke 10:10	Luke 9:5a	Mark 6:11a	Gospel of Thomas
ⁱ1ʃ			
[εἰς ἣν δ' {ἂν}	({[καὶ] ὅσ})οι ({[ἂν]}	καὶ ὃς ἂν	
πόλιν εἰσέλθητε][2] {καὶ}		τόπος	
{μὴ δέ}[χων][3]{ται ὑμᾶς	[{μὴ δέ})χων({ται ὑμᾶς}),	μὴ δέξηται ὑμᾶς	
( )[4],		μηδὲ ἀκούσωσιν	
		ὑμῶν,	
{ἐ}ξ[ελθόντες][5]	({ἐ}ξ]ερχ{όμενοι})	ἐκπορευόμενοι	
[εἰς][6]	ἀπὸ		
( )[7]			
τ[ὰς πλατείας αὐτῆς][6.8]	(τῆς πολέως {ἐκεί}νης)	ἐκεῖθεν	
[εἴπατε·][9]			
ⁱ1 ⇒ Luke 10:12			

[5] Luke's ἐξελθόντες or Matthew's ἐξερχόμενοι.

[6] Luke's εἰς or Matthew's ἔξω and the resultant case of the article(s).

[7] Matthew's τῆς οἰκίας ἤ.

[8] Luke's τὰς πλατείας αὐτῆς or Matthew's τῆς πολέως ἐκείνης. (See also Luke 10:11: τῆς πολέως.)

[9] Luke's εἴπατε·.

Wenn ihr aber in eine Stadt kommt und sie nehmen euch nicht auf, dann geht weg ⟦aus jener Stadt⟧,

Dans quelque ville que vous entriez et qui ne vous recevrait pas, lorsque vous sortez ⟦hors de cette ville⟧,

Q 10:11

Mark 6:11b	Matthean Doublet	Matt 10:14b	Q 10:11
ἐκπορευόμενοι		[ ][1]	[][1]
ἐκεῖθεν ἐκτινάξατε		²ʃ ({ἐκτινάξατε)² ʅ²	²ʃ ({ἐκτινάξατε)² ʅ²
τὸν χοῦν		τὸν} κονιορτὸν	τὸν} κονιορτὸν
τὸν ὑποκάτω		[ ][2]	[][2]
τῶν ποδῶν		{τ(ῶν)² ποδ(ῶν	{τ(ῶν)² ποδ(ῶν
ὑμῶν		ὑμῶν)}²	ὑμῶν)}²
		ʃ ʅ²	ʃʅ²
εἰς μαρτύριον		[ ][3]	[][3]
αὐτοῖς.			
		.	.

[1] Luke's adverbial καί.

[2] Luke's τὸν κολληθέντα ἡμῖν ἐκ τῆς πολέως ὑμῶν εἰς τοὺς πόδας ἀπομασσόμεθα ὑμῖν or Matthew's ἐκτινάξατε … τῶν ποδῶν ὑμῶν.

Q

ἐκτινάξατε τὸν κονιορτὸν τῶν ποδῶν ὑμῶν.	shake off the dust from your feet.

Q 10:11

Luke 10:11	Luke 9:5b	Mark 6:11b	Gospel of Thomas
[καὶ][1]		ἐκπορευόμενοι	
⸂ ⸃[2]		ἐκεῖθεν ἐκτινάξατε	
{τὸν} κονιορτὸν	[({τὸν} κονιορτὸν)]	τὸν χοῦν	
[{τὸν} κολληθέντα ἡμῖν		τὸν ὑποκάτω	
ἐκ τῆς πολέως ὑμῶν			
εἰς][2] {τ}[οὺς][2] {πόδ}[ας][2]	ἀπὸ ({[τ]ῶν [ποδ]ῶν	τῶν ποδῶν	
	[ὑμῶν]})	ὑμῶν	
[2]⸂ [ἀπομασσόμεθα ὑμῖν][2] ⸃[2].	[ἀπο]({τινά})σσε{(τε)}		
[πλὴν τοῦτο γινώσκετε	{εἰς μαρτύριον}	εἰς μαρτύριον	
ὅτι ἤγγικεν	ἐπ' {αὐτο}ύς.	αὐτοῖς.	
ἡ βασιλεία τοῦ θεοῦ][3].			

[3] Luke's kingdom saying (see Luke 10:9).

schüttelt den Staub von euren Füßen ab.	secouez la poussière de vos pieds.

Q 10:12

Markan Parallel	Matt 11:24	Matt 10:15	Q 10:12
	πλὴν [(λέγω ὑμῖν)]	(ἀμὴν)[1] λέγω ὑμῖν	⟦()[1]⟧ λέγω ὑμῖν
	[ὅτι]	[ ][2],	⟦[ὅτι][2]⟧
		⸉ἀνεκτότερον ἔσται⸊[3]	⸉ ⸊[3]
	(γῇ [Σοδόμ]ων)	(γῇ)[4] Σοδόμ(ων	()[4] Σοδόμ[οις][4]
		καὶ Γομόρρων)[4]	
	[(ἀνεκτότερον ἔσται)]		⸉ἀνεκτότερον ἔσται⸊[3]
	[(ἐν] [ἡμέρᾳ)]	ἐν [ ][5] ἡμέρᾳ	ἐν [τῇ][5] ἡμέρᾳ
	(κρίσεως)	(κρίσεως)[5]	[ἐκείνῃ][5]
		⸉ ⸊[3]	⸉ ⸊[3]
	[(ἤ)] σοί.	ἢ τῇ πόλει ἐκείνῃ.	ἢ τῇ πόλει ἐκείνῃ.
		⸊Matt 10:14a[1]	⸊Q 10:10[1]

IQP 1994: ()[1] λέγω ὑμῖν ⟦[ὅτι][2]⟧ ⸉ ⸊[3] ()[4] Σοδόμ[οις][4] ἐν ⟦[τῇ][5]⟧ ἡμέρᾳ [ ][5] ⸉ἀνεκτότερον ἔσται⸊[3].

[1] Matthew's ἀμήν.

[2] Luke's ὅτι.

[3] The position of ἀνεκτότερον ἔσται. (See also Q 10:14.)

Q

λέγω ὑμῖν ⟦ὅτι⟧ Σοδόμοις ἀνεκτότερον ἔσται ἐν τῇ ἡμέρᾳ ἐκείνῃ ἢ τῇ πόλει ἐκείνῃ.	I tell you: For Sodom it shall be more bearable on that day than for that town.

Q 10:12

Luke 10:12	Lukan Doublet	Markan Parallel	Gospel of Thomas
( )[1] λέγω ὑμῖν [ὅτι][2] ⸉ ⸊[3] ( )[4] Σοδόμ[οις][4] ἐν [τῇ][5] ἡμέρᾳ [ἐκείνῃ][5] ⸉ἀνεκτότερον ἔσται⸊[3] ἢ τῇ πόλει ἐκείνῃ. ⸊Luke 10:10[1]			

[4] Luke's Σοδόμοις or Matthew's γῇ Σοδόμων καὶ Γομόρρων. [5] Luke's ἐν τῇ ἡμέρᾳ ἐκείνῃ or Matthew's ἐν ἡμέρᾳ κρίσεως.

Ich sage euch: Sodom wird es an jenem Tag erträglicher ergehen als jener Stadt.	Je vous «le» dis: Pour Sodome, en ce jour-là, ce sera plus supportable que pour cette ville.

Q 10:13

Markan Parallel	Matt 11:23b	Matt 11:21	Q 10:13
		[1]ʃ	[1]ʃ
		οὐαί σοι, Χοραζίν·	οὐαί σοι, Χοραζίν·
		οὐαί σοι, Βηθσαϊδά·	οὐαί σοι, Βηθσαϊδά·
	[(ὅτι εἰ ἐν)] Σοδόμοις	ὅτι εἰ ἐν Τύρῳ	ὅτι εἰ ἐν Τύρῳ
	[(ἐγεν)ήθησαν	καὶ Σιδῶνι ἐγέν(οντο)[2]	καὶ Σιδῶνι ἐγεν[ήθησαν][2]
	(αἱ δυνάμεις αἱ γενόμεναι	αἱ δυνάμεις αἱ γενόμεναι	αἱ δυνάμεις αἱ γενόμεναι
	ἐν)] σοί,	ἐν ὑμῖν,	ἐν ὑμῖν,
	ἔμεινεν ἂν	πάλαι ἂν ἐν σάκκῳ	πάλαι ἂν ἐν σάκκῳ
	μέχρι τῆς σήμερον.	καὶ σποδῷ	καὶ σποδῷ
		[ ][3] μετενόησαν.	[][3] μετενόησαν.
		ʅ[1]⇒ Matt 11:23-24	ʅ[1]⇒ Q 10:15

IQP 1994: ⟦[][3]⟧.

[1] The position of Q 10:13-15 in Q: After Q 10:12 and before Q 10:16 (Lukan order); or after Q 7:34-35 (Matt 11:19) and before Q 10:21 (Matt 11:25) (Matthean order).

[2] Luke's ἐγενήθησαν or Matthew's ἐγένοντο.

Q

οὐαί σοι, Χοραζίν· οὐαί σοι, Βηθσαϊδά· ὅτι εἰ ἐν Τύρῳ καὶ Σιδῶνι ἐγενήθησαν αἱ δυνάμεις αἱ γενόμεναι ἐν ὑμῖν, πάλαι ἂν ἐν σάκκῳ καὶ σποδῷ μετενόησαν.

Woe to you, Chorazin! Woe to you, Bethsaida! For if the wonders performed in you had taken place in Tyre and Sidon, they would have repented long ago, in sackcloth and ashes.

Q 10:13

Luke 10:13	Lukan Doublet	Markan Parallel	Gospel of Thomas
[1]ʃ Οὐαί σοι, Χοραζίν, οὐαί σοι, Βηθσαϊδά· ὅτι εἰ ἐν Τύρῳ καὶ Σιδῶνι ἐγεν[ήθησαν][2] αἱ δυνάμεις αἱ γενόμεναι ἐν ὑμῖν, πάλαι ἂν ἐν σάκκῳ καὶ σποδῷ [καθήμενοι][3] μετενόησαν. ʅ[1]⇒ Luke 10:15			

[3] Luke's καθήμενοι.

Wehe dir, Chorazin! Wehe dir, Betsaida! Denn wenn in Tyrus und Sidon die Krafttaten geschehen wären, die bei euch geschehen sind, längst wären sie in Sack und Asche umgekehrt.

Malheur à toi, Chorazin! Malheur à toi, Bethsaïda! Parce que si les actes de puissance qui ont eu lieu chez vous s'étaient produits à Tyr et à Sidon, «ces dernières» se seraient repenties depuis longtemps avec le sac et la cendre.

Q 10:14

Markan Parallel	Matthean Doublet	Matt 11:22	Q 10:14
		πλὴν (λέγω ὑμῖν)[1], Τύρῳ καὶ Σιδῶνι ἀνεκτότερον ἔσται ἐν (ἡμέρᾳ)[2] κρίσε(ως)[2] ἢ ὑμῖν.	πλὴν ⟦()[1]⟧ Τύρῳ καὶ Σιδῶνι ἀνεκτότερον ἔσται ἐν [τῇ][2] κρίσε[ι][2] ἢ ὑμῖν.

IQP 1994: ()[1].

[1] Matthew's λέγω ὑμῖν.

[2] Luke's τῇ κρίσει or Matthew's ἡμέρᾳ κρίσεως.

Q

πλὴν Τύρῳ καὶ Σιδῶνι ἀνεκτότερον ἔσται ἐν τῇ κρίσει ἢ ὑμῖν.	Yet for Tyre and Sidon it shall be more bearable at the judgment than for you.

Q 10:14

Luke 10:14	Lukan Doublet	Markan Parallel	Gospel of Thomas
πλὴν ( )[1] Τύρῳ καὶ Σιδῶνι ἀνεκτότερον ἔσται ἐν [τῇ][2] κρίσε[ι][2] ἢ ὑμῖν.			

Doch Tyrus und Sidon wird es erträglicher ergehen im Gericht als euch.

D'ailleurs au jugement, ce sera plus supportable pour Tyr et pour Sidon que pour vous.

Q 10:15

Isa 14:13a-c, 15 LXX	Matt 11:21b; 10:15	Matt 11:23-24	Q 10:15
13a-c σὺ δὲ εἶπας ἐν τῇ διανοίᾳ σου		**11:23** καὶ σύ, Καφαρναούμ,	καὶ σύ, Καφαρναούμ,
Εἰς τὸν οὐρανὸν ἀναβήσομαι, ἐπάνω τῶν ἄστρων τοῦ οὐρανοῦ θήσω τὸν θρόνον μου,		μὴ ἕως οὐρανοῦ ὑψωθήσῃ;	μὴ ἕως οὐρανοῦ ὑψωθήσῃ;
15 νῦν δὲ εἰς ᾅδου καταβήσῃ καὶ εἰς τὰ θεμέλια τῆς γῆς.		ἕως [ ][1] ᾅδου καταβήσῃ·	ἕως [τοῦ][1] ᾅδου καταβήσῃ.
	11:21b (ὅτι εἰ ἐν) Τύρῳ καὶ Σιδῶνι (ἐγέν)οντο (αἱ δυνάμεις αἱ γενόμεναι ἐν) ὑμῖν, πάλαι (ἂν) ἐν σάκκῳ καὶ σποδῷ μετενόησαν.	(ὅτι εἰ ἐν Σοδόμοις ἐγενήθησαν αἱ δυνάμεις αἱ γενόμεναι ἐν σοί, ἔμεινεν ἂν μέχρι τῆς σήμερον.	⟦()[2]⟧
	10:15 ἀμὴν (λέγω ὑμῖν), (ἀνεκτότερον ἔσται) Σοδόμων καὶ Γομόρρων (ἐν ἡμέρᾳ κρίσεως ἢ) τῇ πόλει ἐκείνῃ.	**11:24** πλὴν λέγω ὑμῖν ὅτι γῇ Σοδόμων ἀνεκτότερον ἔσται ἐν ἡμέρᾳ κρίσεως ἢ σοί.)[2] ʅMatt 11:21[1]	ʅQ 10:13[1]

IQP 1994: ⟦[τοῦ][1]⟧ ᾅδου καταβήσῃ. ()[2].

Text Critical Note (see the discussion in the front matter): In Luke 10:15 ἢ ἕως τοῦ (- C *pc*) οὐρανοῦ ὑψωθεῖσα; (-θήσῃ B^2 *f*^{1}) is in A B^2 C W Θ Ψ 0115 *f*$^{1.13}$ 33 𝔐 lat sy$^{p.h}$, but μὴ ἕως οὐρανοῦ ὑψωθήσῃ; is in 𝔓$^{45.75}$ ℵ B* D *pc* it sy$^{s.c}$ sa^{mss} bo (L Ξ 579 700: τοῦ οὐρανοῦ). In

Text Critical Note (see the discussion in the front matter): In Luke 10:15 τοῦ is omitted before ᾅδου in 𝔓^{45} ℵ A C D W Θ Ξ Ψ *f*$^{1.13}$ 33 𝔐, but is present in 𝔓^{75} B L 0115 *pc*.

[1] Luke's τοῦ.

[2] Is Matthew 11:23b-24 in Q?

Q

καὶ σύ, Καφαρναούμ, μὴ ἕως οὐρανοῦ ὑψωθήσῃ; ἕως τοῦ ᾅδου καταβήσῃ.

And you, Capernaum, up to heaven will you be exalted? Into Hades shall you come down!

Q 10:15

Luke 10:15	Lukan Doublet	Markan Parallel	Isa 14:13a-c, 15 LXX
καὶ σύ, Καφαρναούμ,			**13a-c** σὺ δὲ εἶπας
			ἐν τῇ διανοίᾳ σου
μὴ ἕως οὐρανοῦ			Εἰς τὸν οὐρανὸν
ὑψωθήσῃ;			ἀναβήσομαι,
			ἐπάνω τῶν ἄστρων
			τοῦ οὐρανοῦ
			θήσω τὸν θρόνον μου,
ἕως [τοῦ][1] ᾄδου			**15** νῦν δὲ εἰς ᾄδου
καταβήσῃ.			καταβήσῃ
			καὶ εἰς τὰ θεμέλια τῆς γῆς.
( )[2]			
↲Luke 10:13[1]			

Matt 11:23 ἢ ἕως τοῦ (- Δ f^{13} *pc*) οὐρανοῦ ὑψωθεῖσα; (-θης is in Γ f^{13} 700 *al* f g^1 q) is in f^{13} 33 𝔐 f h q $sy^{s.p.h}$; $Hier^{ms}$, but μὴ ἕως οὐρανοῦ ὑψωθήσῃ; is in ℵ B* D W Θ lat sy^c co (B^2 L ἥ, C f^1 τοῦ οὐρανοῦ); Ir^{lat}.

Text Critical Note (see the discussion in the front matter): In Luke 10:15 καταβιβασθήσῃ is in $𝔓^{45}$ ℵ A C L W Θ Ξ Ψ 0115 $f^{1.13}$ 33 𝔐 lat $sy^{p.h}$co, but καταβήσῃ is in $𝔓^{75}$ B D 579 *pc* $sy^{s.c}$. In Matt 11:23 καταβιβασθήσῃ is in ℵ C L Θ $f^{1.13}$ 33 𝔐 $sy^{p.h}$ mae bo, but καταβήσῃ is in B D W *pc* latt $sy^{s.c}$ sa; Ir^{lat}.

Und du, Kafarnaum, wirst du etwa zum Himmel erhöht werden? Bis zum Totenreich wirst du hinabsteigen.	Et toi, Capharnaüm, seras-tu élevée jusqu'au ciel? Tu descendras jusqu'au séjour des morts.

Q 10:16

Mark 9:37	Matt 18:5	Matt 10:40	Q 10:16
	καὶ	¹⌐	¹⌐
ὃς ἂν ἓν τῶν τοιούτων παιδίων δέξηται ἐπὶ τῷ ὀνόματί μου, ἐμὲ δέχεται·	{ὃς} ἐ{ὰν} {(δέ)ξηται} {ἓν} {παιδί}ον {τοιοῦτ}ο {ἐπὶ τῷ ὀνόματί μου, ([ἐμ]ὲ δέχεται)}.	Ὁ ({δε}χόμενος)² ὑμ(ᾶς)² {ἐμ(ὲ δέχεται})², [ ]³	ὁ ({δε}χόμενος)² ὑμ(ᾶς)² {ἐμ(ὲ δέχεται})², []³
καὶ ὃς ἂν ἐμὲ δέχηται, οὐκ ἐμὲ δέχεται ἀλλὰ τὸν ἀποστείλαντά με.		{(καὶ)}⁴ ὁ {ἐμὲ (δεχ}όμενος {δέχεται})³ {τὸν ἀποστείλαντά με}. ⌐¹	⟦{(καὶ)}⁴⟧ ὁ {ἐμὲ (δεχ}όμενος {δέχεται})³ {τὸν ἀποστείλαντά με}. ⌐¹

¹ The position of Q 10:16 in Q: After Q 10:15 and before Q 10:21 (Lukan order); or after Q 17:33 (Matt 10:39) and before Q 7:18 (Matt 11:2) (Matthean order).

² Luke's ἀκούων …ῶν …οῦ ἀκούει or Matthew's δεχόμενος …ᾶς …ὲ δέχεται.

Q

ὁ δεχόμενος ὑμᾶς ἐμὲ δέχεται, ⟦καὶ⟧ ὁ ἐμὲ δεχόμενος δέχεται τὸν ἀποστείλαντά με.

Whoever takes you in takes me in, ⟦and⟧ whoever takes me in takes in the one who sent me.

Q 10:16

Luke 10:16	Luke 9:48a-b	Mark 9:37	John 13:20
⸆1	καὶ εἶπεν αὐτοῖς·		ἀμὴν ἀμὴν λέγω ὑμῖν,
Ὁ [ἀκούων][2] ὑμ[ῶν][2]	{ὃς} ἐ{ὰν} {(δέ)ξηται}	ὃς ἂν ἓν τῶν τοιούτων	ὁ λαμβάνων ἄν
	τοῦτο τὸ {παιδί}ον	παιδίων δέξηται	τινα πέμψω
	{ἐπὶ τῷ ὀνόματί μου,	ἐπὶ τῷ ὀνόματί μου,	
{ἐμ}[οῦ ἀκούει][2],	([ἐμ]ὲ δέχεται·	ἐμὲ δέχεται·	ἐμὲ λαμβάνει,
[καὶ ὁ ἀθετῶν ὑμᾶς			
ἐμὲ ἀθετεῖ·][3]			
ὁ [δὲ][4]	καὶ) ὃς ἂν	καὶ ὃς ἂν	ὁ δὲ
{ἐμὲ} [ἀθετῶν	([ἐμὲ] δέ)}ξ{ηται,}	ἐμὲ δέχηται,	ἐμὲ λαμβάνων
ἀθετεῖ][3]	({δέχεται}	οὐκ ἐμὲ δέχεται	λαμβάνει
{τὸν ἀποστείλαντά με}.	[{τὸν ἀποστείλαντά με}])·	ἀλλὰ τὸν ἀποστείλαντά με.	τὸν πέμψαντά με.
⸆1			

[3] Luke's καὶ ὁ ἀθετῶν ὑμᾶς ἐμὲ ἀθετεῖ· … ἀθετῶν ἀθετεῖ or Matthew's lack of a negative formulation but resumption of δεχόμενος δέχεται.

[4] Luke's δέ or Matthew's καί.

Wer euch aufnimmt, nimmt mich auf, ⟦und⟧ wer mich aufnimmt, nimmt den auf, der mich gesandt hat.

Qui vous accueille m'accueille ⟦et⟧ qui m'accueille accueille celui qui m'a envoyé.

Q 10:21

Sir 51:1a, 2a-b	Matthean Doublet	Matt 11:25-26	Q 10:21
		[1]ʃ	[1]ʃ
		11:25 Ἐν (ἐκείνῳ τῷ καιρῷ)[2]	ἐν [( )][2]
		(ἀποκριθεὶς ὁ Ἰησοῦς)[3]	[()][3]
		εἶπεν·	εἶπεν·
51:1a Ἐξομολογήσομαί σοι,		ἐξομολογοῦμαί σοι, πάτερ,	ἐξομολογοῦμαί σοι, πάτερ,
κύριε βασιλεῦ, …		κύριε τοῦ οὐρανοῦ	κύριε τοῦ οὐρανοῦ
		καὶ τῆς γῆς,	καὶ τῆς γῆς,
51:2a-b ὅτι σκεπαστὴς		ὅτι [ ][4]ἔκρυψας	ὅτι [][4]ἔκρυψας
καὶ βοηθὸς		ταῦτα ἀπὸ σοφῶν	ταῦτα ἀπὸ σοφῶν
ἐγένου μοι		καὶ συνετῶν	καὶ συνετῶν
καὶ ἐλυτρώσω		καὶ ἀπεκάλυψας αὐτὰ	καὶ ἀπεκάλυψας αὐτὰ
τὸ σῶμά μου ἐξ ἀπωλείας		νηπίοις·	νηπίοις·
		11:26 ναὶ ὁ πατήρ,	ναὶ ὁ πατήρ,
		ὅτι οὕτως εὐδοκία	ὅτι οὕτως εὐδοκία
		ἐγένετο ἔμπροσθέν σου.	ἐγένετο ἔμπροσθέν σου.
		ʅ[1]⇒ Matt 11:27	ʅ[1]⇒ Q 10:22

JSK: < >[3].

[1] The position of Q 10:21-22 in Q: After Q 10:16 and before Q 10:23 (Lukan order); or after Q 10:15 (Matt 11:23) and before Q 11:17 (Matt 12:25) (Matthean order).

[2] Luke's αὐτῇ τῇ ὥρᾳ or Matthew's ἐκείνῳ τῷ καιρῷ.

Q

ἐν … εἶπεν· ἐξομολογοῦμαί σοι, πάτερ, κύριε τοῦ οὐρανοῦ καὶ τῆς γῆς, ὅτι ἔκρυψας ταῦτα ἀπὸ σοφῶν καὶ συνετῶν καὶ ἀπεκάλυψας αὐτὰ νηπίοις· ναὶ ὁ πατήρ, ὅτι οὕτως εὐδοκία ἐγένετο ἔμπροσθέν σου.

At «that time» he said: I thank you, Father, Lord of heaven and earth, for you hid these things from sages and the learned, and disclosed them to children. Yes, Father, for that is what it has pleased you to do.

Q 10:21

Luke 10:21	Lukan Doublet	Markan Parallel	Gospel of Thomas
¹⟆ Ἐν [αὐτῇ τῇ ὥρᾳ]² [ἠγαλλιάσατο ἐν τῷ πνεύματι τῷ ἁγίῳ καὶ]³ εἶπεν· ἐξομολογοῦμαί σοι, πάτερ, κύριε τοῦ οὐρανοῦ καὶ τῆς γῆς, ὅτι [ἀπ]⁴έκρυψας ταῦτα ἀπὸ σοφῶν καὶ συνετῶν καὶ ἀπεκάλυψας αὐτὰ νηπίοις· ναὶ ὁ πατήρ, ὅτι οὕτως εὐδοκία ἐγένετο ἔμπροσθέν σου. ⟅¹⇒ Luke 10:22			

³ Luke's ἠγαλλιάσατο ἐν τῷ πνεύματι τῷ ἁγίῳ καί or Matthew's ἀποκριθεὶς ὁ Ἰησοῦς.

⁴ Luke's ἀπέκρυψας or Matthew's ἔκρυψας.

In «diesem Augenblick» sagte er: Ich preise dich, Vater, Herr des Himmels und der Erde, denn du hast dies vor Weisen und Gebildeten verborgen und es Unmündigen enthüllt. Ja, Vater, denn so hat es dir gefallen.

En «cet instant» il dit: Je te remercie, Père, Seigneur du ciel et de la terre, de ce que tu as caché ces choses aux sages et aux érudits et que tu les as révélées aux tout petits. Oui, Père, parce que tu as bien voulu qu'il en soit ainsi.

Q 10:22

Markan Parallel	Matthean Doublet	Matt 11:27	Q 10:22
		Πάντα μοι παρεδόθη	πάντα μοι παρεδόθη
		ὑπὸ τοῦ πατρός μου,	ὑπὸ τοῦ πατρός μου,
		καὶ οὐδεὶς (ἐπι)[1]γινώσκει	καὶ οὐδεὶς ()[1]γινώσκει
		[ ][2] (τ)[2]ὸ(ν)[2] υἱὸ(ν)[2]	[][2] (τ)[2]ὸ(ν)[2] υἱὸ(ν)[2]
		εἰ μὴ ὁ πατήρ, (οὐδὲ)[3]	εἰ μὴ ὁ πατήρ, (οὐδὲ)[3]
		[ ][2]	[][2]
		(τ)[2]ὸ(ν)[2] πατ(έ)[2]ρ(α)[2]	(τ)[2]ὸ(ν)[2] πατ(έ)[2]ρ(α)[2]
		(τις)[4] (ἐπι)[1](γινώσκει)[4]	⟦(τις)[4]⟧ ()[1]⟦(γινώσκει)[4]⟧
		εἰ μὴ ὁ υἱὸς	εἰ μὴ ὁ υἱὸς
		καὶ ᾧ ἐὰν βούληται	καὶ ᾧ ἐὰν βούληται
		ὁ υἱὸς ἀποκαλύψαι.	ὁ υἱὸς ἀποκαλύψαι.
		≀Matt 11:25-26[1]	≀Q 10:21[1]

PH: ⟦(ἐπι)[1]⟧γινώσκει ... ⟦(ἐπι)[1](γινώσκει)[4]⟧.

IQP 1991: ⟦(οὐδὲ)[3]⟧ ... ⟦()[4]⟧ ()[1]⟦()[4]⟧.

[1] Luke's γινώσκει or Matthew's ἐπιγινώσκει (*bis*).

[2] Luke's indirect questions or Matthew's nouns as direct objects.

Q

πάντα μοι παρεδόθη ὑπὸ τοῦ πατρός μου, καὶ οὐδεὶς γινώσκει τὸν υἱὸν εἰ μὴ ὁ πατήρ, οὐδὲ τὸν πατέρα ⟦τις γινώσκει⟧ εἰ μὴ ὁ υἱὸς καὶ ᾧ ἐὰν βούληται ὁ υἱὸς ἀποκαλύψαι.

Everything has been entrusted to me by my Father, and no one knows the Son except the Father, nor ⟦does anyone know⟧ the Father except the Son, and to whomever the Son chooses to reveal him.

Gos. Thom. 61.3b (Nag Hammadi II 2)

παρεδόθη μοι ἐκ τῶν τοῦ πατρός μου.

I was given some of that which is my Father's.

Q 10:23 is to be found below, between Q 10:~~22‹ ›23 / Matt 11:28-30~~ and Q 10:24.

Q 10:22

Luke 10:22	Lukan Doublet	John 13:3a; 10:15	*Gos. Thom.* 61.3b
πάντα μοι παρεδόθη ὑπὸ τοῦ πατρός μου, καὶ οὐδεὶς ( )¹γινώσκει [τίς ἐστιν]² ὁ( )² υἱὸ[ς]² εἰ μὴ ὁ πατήρ, [καὶ]³ [τίς ἐστιν]² ( )²ὁ( )² πατ[ὴ]²ρ( )² ( )⁴ ( )¹( )⁴ εἰ μὴ ὁ υἱὸς καὶ ᾧ ἐὰν βούληται ὁ υἱὸς ἀποκαλύψαι. ꝆLuke 10:21¹		13:3a ... πάντα ἔδωκεν αὐτῷ ὁ πατήρ ... 10:15 καθὼς γινώσκει με ὁ πατὴρ κἀγὼ γινώσκω τὸν πατέρα,	ⲁⲩϯ ⲛⲁⲉⲓ ⲉⲃⲟⲗ ϩⲛ̄ ⲛⲁ ⲡⲁⲉⲓⲱⲧ’

³ Luke's καί or Matthew's οὐδέ.

⁴ Is Matthew's τις ..γινώσκει in Q?

Alles wurde mir von meinem Vater übergeben, und keiner kennt den Sohn, nur der Vater, und ⟦keiner kennt⟧ den Vater, nur der Sohn und der, dem es der Sohn enthüllen will.

Tout m'a été remis par mon Père et personne ne connaît le Fils sinon le Père ni ⟦personne⟧ ne ⟦connaît⟧ le Père sinon le Fils et celui à qui le Fils veut bien le révéler.

Mir ist gegeben worden von dem, was meines Vaters ist.

On m'a donné des choses qui venaient de celles de mon Père.

Q 10:23 is to be found below, between Q 10:~~22←→23 / Matt 11:28-30~~ and Q 10:24.

Q 10:~~22‹ ›23/Matt 11:28-30~~

Sir 51:23a, 26a-b, 27b	Matthean Doublet	Matt 11:28-30	Q 10:~~22‹ ›23/Matt 11:28-30~~
51:23a ἐγγίσατε πρός με, ἀπαίδευτοι, **51:26a-b** τὸν τράχηλον ὑμῶν ὑπόθετε ὑπὸ ζυγόν, καὶ ἐπιδεξάσθω ἡ ψυχὴ ὑμῶν παιδείαν. **51:27b** καὶ εὗρον ἐμαυτῷ ἀνάπαυσιν.		(**11:28** Δεῦτε πρός με πάντες οἱ κοπιῶντες καὶ πεφορτισμένοι, κἀγὼ ἀναπαύσω ὑμᾶς. **11:29** ἄρατε τὸν ζυγόν μου ἐφ' ὑμᾶς καὶ μάθετε ἀπ' ἐμοῦ, ὅτι πραΰς εἰμι καὶ ταπεινὸς τῇ καρδίᾳ, καὶ εὑρήσετε ἀνάπαυσιν ταῖς ψυχαῖς ὑμῶν· **11:30** ὁ γὰρ ζυγός μου χρηστὸς καὶ τὸ φορτίον μου ἐλαφρόν ἐστιν.)^0	()^0

Is Matt 11:28-30 in Q?

Gos. Thom. 90 (Nag Hammadi II 2)

(1) Λέγει Ἰησοῦς· δεῦτε πρός με ὅτι χρηστὸς ὁ ζυγός μου καὶ ἡ κυριότης μου πραεῖά ἐστιν (2) καὶ εὑρήσετε ἀνάπαυσιν ὑμῖν.

(1) Jesus says: Come to me, for my yoke is gentle and my lordship is mild. (2) And you will find repose for yourselves.

Q 10:~~22‹ ›23/Matt 11:28-30~~

Luke	Lukan Doublet	Markan Parallel	*Gos. Thom.* 90
( )[0]			90.1 ⲡⲉϫⲉ ⲓ̅ⲏ̅ⲥ̅ ϫⲉ ⲁⲙⲏⲉⲓⲧⲛ̅ ϣⲁⲣⲟⲉⲓ'
			ϫⲉ ⲟⲩⲭⲣⲏⲥⲧⲟⲥ ⲡⲉ ⲡⲁⲛⲁϩⲃ' ⲁⲩⲱ ⲧⲁⲙⲛ̅ⲧ̅ϫⲟⲉⲓⲥ ⲟⲩⲣⲙ̅ⲣⲁϣ ⲧⲉ 90.2 ⲁⲩⲱ ⲧⲉⲧⲛⲁϩⲉ ⲁⲩⲁⲛⲁ<ⲡⲁⲩ>ⲥⲓⲥ[1] ⲛⲏⲧⲛ̅

[1] The codex reads ⲁⲩⲁⲛⲁⲩⲡⲁⲥⲓⲥ.

(1) Jesus spricht: Kommt zu mir, denn mein Joch ist sanft, und meine Herrschaft ist mild. (2) Und ihr werdet Ruhe finden für euch.

(1) Jésus dit: Venez à moi car mon joug est léger et ma domination est douce. (2) Et vous trouverez le repos pour vous.

Q 10:23

Markan Parallel	Matthean Doublet	Matt 13:16	Q 10:23
		¹ʃ [ ]² (ὑμῶν δὲ)³ μακάριοι οἱ ὀφθαλμοὶ (ὅτι)³ βλέπο(υσιν)³ [ ]³ (καὶ τὰ ὦτα ὑμῶν ὅτι ἀκούουσιν)⁴. ʅ¹⇒ Matt 13:17	¹ʃ []² ()³ μακάριοι οἱ ὀφθαλμοὶ [οἱ]³ βλέπο[ντες ἃ βλέπετε]³ ( )⁴. ʅ¹⇒ Q 10:24

IQP 1991: ( )⁴ indeterminate; JMR, JSK: ( )⁴ {D}.

PH: ⟦(καὶ τὰ ὦτα)⁴ ( )⁴ <τὰ>⁴ (ἀκού)⁴ <οντα ἃ ἀκούετε>⁴⟧.

Text Critical Note (see the discussion in the front matter): In Luke 10:23 καὶ ἀκούοντες ἃ ἀκούετε is in D (c e f).

¹ The position of Q 10:23-24 in Q: After Q 10:22 and before Q 11:2b (Lukan order); or after Q 11:26 (Matt 12:45) and before Q 13:18-19 (Matt 13:31-32) (Matthean order).

² Is Luke's καὶ στραφεὶς πρὸς τοὺς μαθητὰς κατ' ἰδίαν εἶπεν in Q?

Q

μακάριοι οἱ ὀφθαλμοὶ οἱ βλέποντες ἃ βλέπετε .. .	Blessed are the eyes that see what you see .. .

Q 10:23

Luke 10:23	Lukan Doublet	Markan Parallel	Gospel of Thomas
¹ʃ [Καὶ στραφεὶς πρὸς τοὺς μαθητὰς κατ' ἰδίαν εἶπεν]². ( )³ μακάριοι οἱ ὀφθαλμοὶ [οἱ]³ βλέπο[ντες ἃ βλέπετε]³ ( )⁴. ʅ¹⇒ Luke 10:24			

³ Luke's οἱ βλέποντες ἃ βλέπετε or Matthew's ὑμῶν δὲ ... ὅτι βλέπουσιν.

⁴ Matthew's καὶ τὰ ὦτα ὑμῶν ὅτι ἀκούουσιν.

Selig die Augen, die sehen, was ihr seht .. .

Bienheureux les yeux qui voient ce que vous voyez .. .

Q 10:24

Markan Parallel	Matthean Doublet	Matt 13:17	Q 10:24
		(ἀμὴν)[1] ⸉γὰρ⸊[1] λέγω ⸉ ⸊[1] ὑμῖν ὅτι πολλοὶ προφῆται καὶ (δίκαιοι)[2] (ἐπεθύμ)[3]ησαν ἰδεῖν ἃ [ ][4] βλέπετε καὶ οὐκ εἶδαν, καὶ ἀκοῦσαι ἃ ἀκούετε καὶ οὐκ ἤκουσαν. ⸊Matt 13:16[1]	⟦()[1]⟧ ⸉ ⸊[1] λέγω ⸉γὰρ⸊[1] ὑμῖν ὅτι πολλοὶ προφῆται καὶ [βασιλεῖς][2] [( )][3]ησαν ἰδεῖν ἃ ⟦[][4]⟧ βλέπετε καὶ οὐκ εἶδαν, καὶ ἀκοῦσαι ἃ ἀκούετε καὶ οὐκ ἤκουσαν. ⸊Q 10:23[1]

IQP 1991: (ἀμὴν)[1].

IQP 1991: ⟦(ἐπεθύμ)[3]⟧ησαν ἰδεῖν ἃ [ὑμεῖς][4].

[1] Matthew's ἀμήν and the resultant positioning of the post-positive γάρ.

[2] Luke's βασιλεῖς or Matthew's δίκαιοι.

Q

λέγω γὰρ ὑμῖν ὅτι πολλοὶ προφῆται καὶ βασιλεῖς ...ησαν ἰδεῖν ἃ βλέπετε καὶ οὐκ εἶδαν, καὶ ἀκοῦσαι ἃ ἀκούετε καὶ οὐκ ἤκουσαν.

For I tell you: Many prophets and kings wanted to see what you see, but never saw it, and to hear what you hear, but never heard it.

Q 10:24

Luke 10:24	Lukan Doublet	Markan Parallel	Gospel of Thomas
( )[1] ⸉ ⸆[1] λέγω ⸉γὰρ⸆[1] ὑμῖν ὅτι πολλοὶ προφῆται καὶ [βασιλεῖς][2] [ἠθέλ][3]ησαν ἰδεῖν ἃ [ὑμεῖς][4] βλέπετε καὶ οὐκ εἶδαν, καὶ ἀκοῦσαι ἃ ἀκούετε καὶ οὐκ ἤκουσαν. ⸆Luke 10:23[1]			

[3] Luke's ἠθέλησαν or Matthew's ἐπεθύμησαν.

[4] Luke's ὑμεῖς.

Denn ich sage euch: Viele Propheten und Könige wünschten zu sehen, was ihr seht, und sahen es nicht, und zu hören, was ihr hört, und hörten es nicht.

Car je vous «le» dis: Nombre de prophètes et de rois ont désiré voir ce que vous voyez et ne l'ont pas vu, et entendre ce que vous entendez et ne l'ont pas entendu.

Q 10:~~25-26~~

Mark 12:28-29a	Matt 19:16	Matt 22:34-37a	Q 10:~~25-26~~
		[0]{	[0]{
		[1]ʃ	[1]ʃ
		22:34 (Οἱ δὲ Φαρισαῖοι {ἀκούσα}ντες {ὅτι} ἐφίμωσεν τοὺς Σαδδουκαίους συνήχθησαν ἐπὶ τὸ αὐτό,)[2]	()[2]
12:28 Καὶ	[({Καὶ}) ἰδοὺ]	**22:35** {καὶ} [ ][3]	**10:25** ~~καὶ~~ [ ][3]
προσελθὼν εἷς τῶν γραμματέων ἀκούσας αὐτῶν συζητούντων, ἰδὼν ὅτι καλῶς ἀπεκρίθη	({εἷς}) {προσελθὼν}		
αὐτοῖς ἐπηρώτησεν	[({αὐτ})]ῷ εἶπεν·	ʃ ({ἐπηρώτησεν} {εἷς} ἐξ αὐτῶν)[4] ≀4	ʃ ( )[4] ≀4
		νομικὸς ʃ [ ][4] ≀4	~~νομικὸς~~ ʃ [ ][4] ≀4
αὐτόν·		[ ][5]πειράζων {αὐτόν}	[][5]~~πειράζων~~ {~~αὐτόν~~}
		ʃ [ ][4] ≀4.	ʃ [ ][4] ≀4.
	[({διδάσκαλε,})	**22:36** {διδάσκαλε,}	{~~διδάσκαλε,~~}
ποία ἐστὶν ἐντολὴ πρώτη	{τί}] {ἀγαθ}ὸν {[ποιήσ]ω ἵνα} σχῶ {[ζωὴν αἰώνιον];}	({ποία} {ἐντολὴ} μεγάλη)[6]	[( )][6]
πάντων;		ʃἐν τῷ νόμῳ;≀7	ʃ~~ἐν τῷ νόμῳ~~;≀7
12:29 ἀπεκρίθη ὁ Ἰησοῦς		**22:37a** {ὁ} δὲ (ἔφη)[8]	**10:26** ~~ὁ δὲ~~ [( )][8]
ὅτι πρώτη ἐστίν·		αὐτ(ῷ)[9]	[][9] ~~αὐτ~~( )[9]
		ʃ ≀7.	ʃ ≀7.
		[ ][10]	[][10]
		}[0]⇒ Matt 22:40	}[0]⇒ Q 10:~~27~~
		≀1⇒ Matt 22:46	≀1⇒ Q 10:~~28~~

IQP 1995, JSK: Q 10:~~25-26~~ not in Q {D}; PH: {C}; JMR: Indeterminate.

Text Critical Note (see the discussion in the front matter): In Matt 22:35 νομικός τις is in F G H *pc*, but both are absent in f^1 e sy^s; νομικός is in

[0] Is Luke 10:25-27 par. Matt 22:34-40 in Q?

[1] The position of Q 10:25-28 in Q: After Q 10:24 and before Q 11:2b (Lukan order); or after Q 14:23 (Matt 22:10) and before Q 11:39a, 42 (Matt 23:1, 23) (Matthean order).

[2] Is Matt 22:34 in Q?

[3] Is Luke's ἰδού in Q?

[4] Is Luke's τις ἀνέστη … λέγων or Matthew's ἐπηρώτησεν εἷς ἐξ αὐτῶν in Q, and which is the position relative to νομικός -πειράζων αὐτόν?

Q

..

..

Q 10:~~25-26~~

Luke 10:25-26	Luke 18:18	Mark 10:17	Gospel of Thomas
0{ 1⸀ ( )2			
10:25 {Καὶ} [ἰδοὺ]3	[({Καὶ}]	Καὶ ἐκπορευομένου αὐτοῦ εἰς ὁδὸν προσδραμὼν εἷς καὶ γονυπετήσας αὐτὸν	
⸀ ( )4 ⸁4	{ἐπηρώτ}ησέν) [τις] [{αὐτὸν}] ἄρχων	ἐπηρώτα αὐτόν·	
νομικός ⸀ [τις ἀνέστη]4 ⸁4 [ἐκ]5πειράζων {αὐτὸν} ⸀ [λέγων·]4 ⸁4 {διδάσκαλε,} [{τί ποιήσ}ας {ζωὴν αἰώνιον κληρονομήσω;}]6 ⸀ ⸁7	[λέγων· {(διδάσκαλε)] ἀγαθέ, [τί ποιήσ}ας {ζωὴν αἰώνιον κληρονομήσω;}]	διδάσκαλε ἀγαθέ, τί ποιήσω ἵνα ζωὴν αἰώνιον κληρονομήσω;	
10:26 {ὁ} δὲ [εἶπεν]8 [πρὸς]9 αὐτ[όν]9· ⸀ἐν τῷ νόμῳ⸁7 [τί γέγραπται; πῶς ἀναγινώσκεις;]10 }0⇒ Luke 10:27 ⸁1⇒ Luke 10:28			

the rest of the manuscript evidence.

5 Is Luke's ἐκ- in Q?

6 Is Luke's τί ποιήσας ζωὴν αἰώνιον κληρονομήσω; or Matthew's ποία ἐντολὴ μεγάλη in Q or from Mark?

7 Is ἐν τῷ νόμῳ in Jesus' question (Luke) or in the lawyer's question (Matthew)?

8 Luke's εἶπεν or Matthew's ἔφη.

9 Luke's πρὸς αὐτόν or Matthew's αὐτῷ.

10 Is Luke's τί γέγραπται; πῶς ἀναγινώσκεις; in Q?

..

..

Q 10:~~27~~

Mark 12:29b-30, 28c,31	Matthean Doublet	Matt 22:37b-40	Q 10:~~27~~
		[ ][1]	[][1]
12:29b ἄκουε, Ἰσραήλ, κύριος ὁ θεὸς ἡμῶν κύριος εἷς ἐστιν,			
12:30 καὶ ἀγαπήσεις κύριον τὸν θεόν σου ἐξ ὅλης τῆς καρδίας σου καὶ ἐξ ὅλης τῆς ψυχῆς σου		**22:37b** {ἀγαπήσεις κύριον τὸν θεόν σου} (ἐν)[2] {ὅλ}ῃ[ ][2] {τ}ῇ[ ][2] {καρδί}ᾳ[ ][2] {σου καὶ} ἐν {ὅλ}ῃ {τ}ῇ {ψυχ}ῇ {σου} [ ][3]	{~~ἀγαπήσεις~~ ~~κύριον τὸν θεόν σου~~} [()][2] {~~ὅλ~~}~~ῃ~~[][2] {~~τ~~}~~ῇ~~[][2] {~~καρδί~~}~~ᾳ~~[][2] {~~σου~~ ~~καὶ~~} ~~ἐν~~ {~~ὅλ~~}~~ῃ~~ {~~τ~~}~~ῇ~~ {~~ψυχ~~}~~ῇ~~ {~~σου~~} [][3]
καὶ ἐξ ὅλης τῆς διανοίας σου καὶ ἐξ ὅλης τῆς ἰσχύος σου.		{καὶ} ἐν {ὅλ}ῃ {τ}ῇ {διανοί}ᾳ {σου}·	{~~καὶ~~} ~~ἐν~~ {~~ὅλ~~}~~ῃ~~ {~~τ~~}~~ῇ~~ {~~διανοί~~}~~ᾳ~~ {~~σου~~},
12:28c ποία ἐστὶν ἐντολὴ πρώτη πάντων; **12:31** δευτέρα αὕτη· ἀγαπήσεις		**22:38** (αὕτη {ἐστὶν} ἡ μεγάλη καὶ {πρώτη} {ἐντολή}. **22:39** {δευτέρα} δὲ ὁμοία {αὐτ}ῇ· {ἀγαπήσεις)[4]	[( )][4]
τὸν πλησίον σου ὡς σεαυτόν. μείζων τούτων ἄλλη ἐντολὴ οὐκ ἔστιν.		τὸν πλησίον σου ὡς σεαυτόν.} **22:40** (ἐν {ταύτ}αις ταῖς δυσὶν {ἐντολ}αῖς ὅλος ὁ νόμος κρέμαται καὶ οἱ προφῆται.)[5] } Matt 22:34-37a[0]	{~~τὸν πλησίον σου~~ ~~ὡς σεαυτόν~~} ()[5] . } Q 10:~~25-26~~[0]

IQP 1995, JSK: Q **10:~~27~~** not in Q {D}; PH: {C}; JMR: Indeterminate.

[1] Is Luke's ὁ δὲ ἀποκριθεὶς εἶπεν· in Q?

[2] Luke's ἐξ with the genitive or Matthew's ἐν with the dative.

[3] Is Luke's καὶ ἐν ὅλῃ τῇ ἰσχύϊ σου in Q?

Q

..	..

Q 10:~~27~~

Luke 10:27	*Did* 1.2b-c	Mark 12:29b-31	Deut 6:4b-5; Lev 19:18c LXX = Gal 5:14b = Rom 13:9c
[ὁ δὲ ἀποκριθεὶς εἶπεν·][1]			
		12:29b ἄκουε, Ἰσραήλ,	**Deut 6:4b** Ἄκουε, Ισραηλ·
		κύριος ὁ θεὸς ἡμῶν	κύριος ὁ θεὸς ἡμῶν
		κύριος εἷς ἐστιν,	κύριος εἷς ἐστιν·
{ἀγαπήσεις	πρῶτον ἀγαπήσεις	**12:30** καὶ ἀγαπήσεις	**6:5** καὶ ἀγαπήσεις
κύριον τὸν θεόν σου	τὸν θεὸν τὸν ποιήσαντά σε	κύριον τὸν θεόν σου	κύριον τὸν θεόν σου
[ἐξ][2] ὅλη[ς][2]		ἐξ ὅλης	ἐξ ὅλης
τῆ[ς][2] καρδία[ς][2] σου		τῆς καρδίας σου	τῆς καρδίας σου
καὶ} ἐν {ὅλ}ῃ {τ}ῇ {ψυχ}ῇ		καὶ ἐξ ὅλης τῆς ψυχῆς	καὶ ἐξ ὅλης τῆς ψυχῆς
{σου [καὶ} ἐν {ὅλ}ῃ		σου	σου
{τ}ῇ {ἰσχύ}ϊ {σου}][3]			
{καὶ} ἐν {ὅλ}ῃ		καὶ ἐξ ὅλης	καὶ ἐξ ὅλης
{τ}ῇ {διανοί}ᾳ {σου},		τῆς διανοίας σου	τῆς δύναμεώς σου.
		καὶ ἐξ ὅλης	
		τῆς ἰσχύος σου.	
[καὶ][4]			**Lev 19:18c =**
			Gal 5:14b = Rom 13:9c
	δεύτερον	**12:31** δευτέρα	καὶ
		αὕτη·	
		ἀγαπήσεις	ἀγαπήσεις
{τὸν πλησίον σου	τὸν πλησίον σου	τὸν πλησίον σου	τὸν πλησίον σου
ὡς σεαυτόν}	ὡς σεαυτόν·	ὡς σεαυτόν.	ὡς σεαυτόν·
( )[5]		μείζων τούτων	
		ἄλλη ἐντολὴ οὐκ ἔστιν.	
.			
} Luke 10:25-26[0]			

[4] Is Matt 22:38-39a in Q?

[5] Is Matt 22:40 in Q?

..

..

Q 10:~~28~~

Mark 12:34c	Matthean Doublet	Matt 22:46	Q 10:~~28~~
		[ ][0]	[][0]
καὶ οὐδεὶς οὐκέτι		{καὶ οὐδεὶς} ἐδύνατο {ἀποκριθ}ῆναι αὐτῷ λόγον	
ἐτόλμα		οὐδὲ {ἐτόλμ}ησέν τις ἀπ' ἐκείνης τῆς ἡμέρας	
αὐτὸν ἐπερωτῆσαι.		{ἐπερωτῆσαι} {αὐτὸν} {οὐκέτι}.	
		≀ Matt 22:34-37a[1]	≀ Q 10:~~25-26~~[1]

IQP 1995: Q **10:~~28~~** not in Q {D}.
JMR, PH, JSK: Q **10:~~28~~** not in Q {B}.

[0] Is Luke 10:28 in Q?

Q 10:~~28~~

Luke 10:28	Luke 20:39; 10:37b; 20:40	Mark 12:32-34	Gospel of Thomas
	20:39 Ἀποκριθέντες δέ τινες τῶν {γραμματέ}ων {εἶπ}α{ν}· {διδάσκαλε,} {καλῶς} {εἶπ}α{ς}.	**12:32** καὶ εἶπεν αὐτῷ ὁ γραμματεύς· καλῶς, διδάσκαλε, ἐπ’ ἀληθείας εἶπες ὅτι εἷς ἐστιν καὶ οὐκ ἔστιν ἄλλος πλὴν αὐτοῦ· **12:33** καὶ τὸ ἀγαπᾶν αὐτὸν ἐξ ὅλης τῆς καρδίας καὶ ἐξ ὅλης τῆς συνέσεως καὶ ἐξ ὅλης τῆς ἰσχύος καὶ τὸ ἀγαπᾶν τὸν πλησίον ὡς ἑαυτὸν περισσότερόν ἐστιν πάντων τῶν ὁλοκαυτωμάτων καὶ θυσιῶν. **12:34** καὶ ὁ Ἰησοῦς ἰδὼν αὐτὸν ὅτι νουνεχῶς ἀπεκρίθη	
[{εἶπεν} δὲ {αὐτῷ·} ὀρθῶς {ἀπεκρίθη}ς· τοῦτο ποίει καὶ ζήσῃ.][0]	**10:37b** [{εἶπεν} δὲ {αὐτῷ}] ὁ Ἰησοῦς· πορεύου καὶ σὺ [ποίει] ὁμοίως.	εἶπεν αὐτῷ· οὐ μακρὰν εἶ ἀπὸ τῆς βασιλείας τοῦ θεοῦ.	
	20:40 {οὐκέτι} γὰρ {ἐτόλμ}ων {ἐπερωτ}ᾶν {αὐτὸν} οὐδέν.	καὶ οὐδεὶς οὐκέτι ἐτόλμα αὐτὸν ἐπερωτῆσαι.	
ʅ Luke 10:25-26[1]			

Q 11:~~1-2a~~, 2b

Did 8.2a	Matthean Doublet	Matt 6:7-10	Q 11:~~1-2a~~, 2b
		0/	0/
		1ʃ	1ʃ
μηδὲ προσεύχεσθε ὡς οἱ ὑποκριταί, ἀλλ' ὡς ἐκέλευσεν ὁ κύριος ἐν τῷ εὐαγγελίῳ αὐτοῦ,		**6:7** (Προσευχόμενοι δὲ μὴ βατταλογήσητε ὥσπερ οἱ ἐθνικοί, δοκοῦσιν γὰρ ὅτι ἐν τῇ πολυλογίᾳ αὐτῶν εἰσακουσθήσονται. **6:8** μὴ οὖν ὁμοιωθῆτε αὐτοῖς· οἶδεν γὰρ ὁ πατὴρ ὑμῶν ὧν χρείαν ἔχετε πρὸ τοῦ ὑμᾶς αἰτῆσαι αὐτόν.)[2]	**11:~~1~~** [()][2]
			11:~~2a~~
οὕτω προσεύχεσθε·		**6:9** (Οὕτως οὖν)[3] προσεύχ(ε)[3]σθε (ὑμεῖς)[3] [ ][3]·	**11:2b** ⟦[ὅταν][3]⟧ προσεύχ⟦[η][3]⟧σθε ⟦()[3]⟧ ⟦[λέγετε][3]⟧·
Πάτερ ἡμῶν ὁ ἐν τοῖς οὐρανοῖς ἁγιασθήτω τὸ ὄνομά σου, ἐλθέτω ἡ βασιλεία σου, γενηθήτω τὸ θέλημά σου ὡς ἐν οὐρανῷ καὶ ἐπὶ γῆς·		Πάτερ (ἡμῶν)[4] (ὁ ἐν τοῖς οὐρανοῖς)[5]· ἁγιασθήτω τὸ ὄνομά σου· **6:10** ἐλθέτω ἡ βασιλεία σου· (γενηθήτω τὸ θέλημά σου, ὡς ἐν οὐρανῷ καὶ ἐπὶ γῆς·)[6]	πάτερ ()[4] ()[5], ἁγιασθήτω τὸ ὄνομά σου· ἐλθέτω ἡ βασιλεία σου· ()[6]
		ʅ1⇒ Matt 6:12-13	ʅ1⇒ Q 11:4
		\0⇒ Matt 6:12-13	\0⇒ Q 11:4

IQP 1989: **11:2b** <…> προσεύχεσθε· πάτερ,.

Text Critical Note (see the discussion in the front matter): In Luke 11:2b ἐφ' ἡμᾶς ἐλθέτω σου ἡ βασιλεία is in D; ἐλθέτω τὸ πνεῦμά σου τὸ ἅγιον ἐφ' ἡμᾶς καὶ καθαρισάτω ἡμᾶς is in (162) 700 (Mcion[T]) GrNy; the rest of the manuscript evidence reads ἐλθέτω ἡ βασιλεία σου.

0 Is the Lord's Prayer in Q?

1 The position of Q 11:2b-4 in Q: After Q 10:24 and before Q 11:9 (Lukan order); or after Q 6:36 (Matt 5:48) and before Q 12:33 (Matt 6:19-20) (Matthean order).

2 Did Q have an introduction (like Luke 11:1-2a or like Matthew 6:7-8)?

Q

⟦ὅταν⟧ προσεύχ⟦η⟧σθε ⟦λέγετε⟧· πάτερ, ἁγιασθήτω τὸ ὄνομά σου· ἐλθέτω ἡ βασιλεία σου·	⟦When⟧ you pray, ⟦say⟧: Father – may your name be kept holy! – let your reign come:

Q 11:~~1-2a~~, 2b

Luke 11:1-2a, 2b	Lukan Doublet	Markan Parallel	Gospel of Thomas
[0]/ [1]ʃ **11:1** [Καὶ ἐγένετο ἐν τῷ εἶναι αὐτὸν ἐν τόπῳ τινὶ προσευχόμενον, ὡς ἐπαύσατο, εἶπέν τις τῶν μαθητῶν αὐτοῦ πρὸς αὐτόν· κύριε, δίδαξον ἡμᾶς προσεύχεσθαι, καθὼς καὶ Ἰωάννης ἐδίδαξεν τοὺς μαθητὰς αὐτοῦ. **11:2a** εἶπεν δὲ αὐτοῖς·][2] **11:2b** [ὅταν][3] προσεύχ[η][3]σθε ( )[3] [λέγετε][3]· Πάτερ ( )[4] ( )[5], ἁγιασθήτω τὸ ὄνομά σου· ἐλθέτω ἡ βασιλεία σου· ( )[6] ι[1]⇒ Luke 11:4 \[0]⇒ Luke 11:4			

[3] Luke's ὅταν προσεύχησθε λέγετε, or Matthew's οὕτως οὖν προσεύχεσθε ὑμεῖς.

[4] Matthew's ἡμῶν.

[5] Matthew's ὁ ἐν τοῖς οὐρανοῖς.

[6] Matthew's γενηθήτω τὸ θέλημά σου, ὡς ἐν οὐρανῷ καὶ ἐπὶ γῆς.

⟦Wenn ihr⟧ betet, ⟦sagt⟧: Vater, dein Name werde geheiligt. Dein Reich komme.

⟦Lorsque⟧ vous priez, ⟦dites⟧: Père, Que ton nom soit sanctifié; que ton règne vienne;

Q 11:3

Did 8.2b	Matthean Doublet	Matt 6:11	Q 11:3
τὸν ἄρτον ἡμῶν τὸν ἐπιούσιον δὸς ἡμῖν σήμερον·		τὸν ἄρτον ἡμῶν τὸν ἐπιούσιον [ ]¹δ(ὸς)¹ ἡμῖν (σ)²ήμερ(ο)²ν·	τὸν ἄρτον ἡμῶν τὸν ἐπιούσιον []¹δ(ὸς)¹ ἡμῖν (σ)²ήμερ(ο)²ν·

¹ Luke's δίδου or Matthew's δός.

² Luke's τὸ καθ' ἡμέραν or Matthew's σήμερον.

Q

τὸν ἄρτον ἡμῶν τὸν ἐπιούσιον δὸς ἡμῖν σήμερον·	Our day's bread give us today;

Q 11:3

Luke 11:3	Lukan Doublet	Markan Parallel	Gospel of Thomas
τὸν ἄρτον ἡμῶν τὸν ἐπιούσιον [δί][1]δ[ου][1] ἡμῖν [τὸ καθ'][2] ἡμέρ[α][2]ν·			

Unser Brot für den Tag gib uns heute.	Notre pain pour ce jour, donne-le-nous aujourd'hui;

Q 11:4

Did 8.2c	Matthean Doublet	Matt 6:12-13	Q 11:4
καὶ ἄφες ἡμῖν		**6:12** καὶ ἄφες ἡμῖν	καὶ ἄφες ἡμῖν
τὰ ὀφειλήματα ἡμῶν,		τὰ (ὀφειλήματα)[1] ἡμῶν,	τὰ (ὀφειλήματα)[1] ἡμῶν,
ὡς καὶ		(ὡς)[2] καὶ [ ][2]	(ὡς)[2] καὶ [][2]
ἡμεῖς		(ἡμεῖς)[3]	(ἡμεῖς)[3]
ἀφήκαμεν		ἀφ(ήκα)[4]μεν	ἀφ(ήκα)[4]μεν
τοῖς		(τοῖς)[5]	(τοῖς)[5]
ὀφειλέταις ἡμῶν·		ὀφειλ(έταις)[5.6] ἡμ(ῶ)[6]ν·	ὀφειλ(έταις)[5.6] ἡμ(ῶ)[6]ν·
καὶ μὴ εἰσενέγκῃς		**6:13** καὶ μὴ εἰσενέγκῃς	καὶ μὴ εἰσενέγκῃς
ἡμᾶς εἰς πειρασμόν,		ἡμᾶς εἰς πειρασμόν	ἡμᾶς εἰς πειρασμόν
ἀλλὰ ῥῦσαι ἡμᾶς ἀπὸ		(ἀλλὰ ῥῦσαι ἡμᾶς ἀπὸ	()[7].
τοῦ πονηροῦ.		τοῦ πονηροῦ)[7].	
		⸂Matt 6:7-10[1]	⸂Q 11:1[1]
		\Matt 6:7-10[0]	\Q 11:1[0]

[1] Luke's τὰς ἁμαρτίας or Matthew's τὰ ὀφειλήματα.
[2] Luke's γάρ or Matthew's ὡς

[3] Luke's αὐτοί or Matthew's ἡμεῖς.
[4] Luke's ἀφίομεν or Matthew's ἀφήκαμεν.

Q

καὶ ἄφες ἡμῖν τὰ ὀφειλήματα ἡμῶν, ὡς καὶ ἡμεῖς ἀφήκαμεν τοῖς ὀφειλέταις ἡμῶν· καὶ μὴ εἰσενέγκῃς ἡμᾶς εἰς πειρασμόν.	and cancel our debts for us, as we too have cancelled for those in debt to us; and do not put us to the test!

Q 11:4

Luke 11:4	Lukan Doublet	Markan Parallel	Gospel of Thomas
καὶ ἄφες ἡμῖν τὰ[ς ἁμαρτίας][1] ἡμῶν, ( )[2] καὶ [γὰρ][2] [αὐτοὶ][3] ἀφ[ίο][4]μεν [παντὶ][5] ὀφείλ[οντι][5.6] ἡμ[ῖ][6]ν· καὶ μὴ εἰσενέγκῃς ἡμᾶς εἰς πειρασμόν ( )[7]. ʅLuke 11:1[1] \Luke 11:1[0]			

[5] Luke's παντί or Matthew's τοῖς.
[6] Luke's ὀφείλοντι ἡμῖν or Matthew's ὀφειλέταις ἡμῶν.

[7] Matthew's ἀλλὰ ῥῦσαι ἡμᾶς ἀπὸ τοῦ πονηροῦ.

Und erlaß uns unsere Schulden, wie auch wir «sie» unseren Schuldnern erlassen haben. Und führe uns nicht in Versuchung.

et remets-nous nos dettes, comme nous aussi «les» avons remises à nos débiteurs; et ne nous entraîne pas dans l'épreuve.

Q 11:⟦~~5-8~~⟧

Markan Parallel	Matthean Doublet	Matthew	Q 11:⟦~~5-8~~⟧
		[ ][0]	⟦[][0]⟧

PH: [][0].

[0] Is Luke 11:5-8 in Q?

Q 11:⟦~~5-8~~⟧

Luke 11:5-8	Lukan Doublet	Markan Parallel	Gospel of Thomas
11:5 [Καὶ εἶπεν πρὸς αὐτούς· τίς ἐξ ὑμῶν ἕξει φίλον καὶ πορεύσεται πρὸς αὐτὸν μεσονυκτίου καὶ εἴπῃ αὐτῷ· φίλε, χρῆσόν μοι τρεῖς ἄρτους, **11:6** ἐπειδὴ φίλος μου παρεγένετο ἐξ ὁδοῦ πρός με καὶ οὐκ ἔχω ὃ παραθήσω αὐτῷ· **11:7** κἀκεῖνος ἔσωθεν ἀποκριθεὶς εἴπῃ· μή μοι κόπους πάρεχε· ἤδη ἡ θύρα κέκλεισται καὶ τὰ παιδία μου μετ' ἐμοῦ εἰς τὴν κοίτην εἰσίν· οὐ δύναμαι ἀναστὰς δοῦναί σοι. **11:8** λέγω ὑμῖν, εἰ καὶ οὐ δώσει αὐτῷ ἀναστὰς διὰ τὸ εἶναι φίλον αὐτοῦ, διά γε τὴν ἀναίδειαν αὐτοῦ ἐγερθεὶς δώσει αὐτῷ ὅσων χρῄζει.][0]			

Q 11:9

Markan Parallel	Matthean Doublet	Matt 7:7	Q 11:9
		[1]ʃ [ ][2] Αἰτεῖτε καὶ δοθήσεται ὑμῖν, ζητεῖτε καὶ εὑρήσετε, κρούετε καὶ ἀνοιγήσεται ὑμῖν· ʅ[1]⇒ Matt 7:11	[1]ʃ [λέγω ὑμῖν,][2] αἰτεῖτε καὶ δοθήσεται ὑμῖν, ζητεῖτε καὶ εὑρήσετε, κρούετε καὶ ἀνοιγήσεται ὑμῖν· ʅ[1] ⇒ Q 11:13

[1] The position of Q 11:9-13 in Q: After Q 11:4 and before Q 11:14 (Lukan order); or after Q 6:42 (Matt 7:4-5) and before Q 6:31 (Matt 7:12) (Matthean order).

[2] Luke's κἀγὼ ὑμῖν λέγω.

Q

λέγω ὑμῖν, αἰτεῖτε καὶ δοθήσεται ὑμῖν, ζητεῖτε καὶ εὑρήσετε, κρούετε καὶ ἀνοιγήσεται ὑμῖν·

I tell you, ask and it will be given to you, search and you will find, knock and it will be opened to you.

Gos. Thom. 92.1 (Nag Hammadi II 2)

Λέγει Ἰησοῦς· ζητεῖτε καὶ εὑρήσετε.

Jesus says: Search and you will find.

Q 11:9

Luke 11:9	Lukan Doublet	John 16:24b	*Gos. Thom.* 92.1
¹ʃ [Κἀγὼ ὑμῖν λέγω]², αἰτεῖτε καὶ δοθήσεται ὑμῖν, ζητεῖτε καὶ εὑρήσετε, κρούετε καὶ ἀνοιγήσεται ὑμῖν· ʅ¹⇒ Luke 11:13		αἰτεῖτε καὶ λήμψεσθε,	ⲡⲉϫⲉ ⲓ̅ⲥ̅ ϫⲉ ϣⲓⲛⲉ ⲁⲩⲱ ⲧⲉⲧⲛⲁϭⲓⲛⲉ

Ich sage euch: Bittet, und euch wird gegeben werden, sucht, und ihr werdet finden, klopft an, und euch wird geöffnet werden.

Je vous dis, demandez et on vous donnera, cherchez et vous trouverez, frappez et on vous ouvrira.

Jesus spricht: Sucht, und ihr werdet finden.

Jésus dit: Cherchez et vous trouverez.

Q 11:10

Markan Parallel	Matthean Doublet	Matt 7:8	Q 11:10
		πᾶς γὰρ ὁ αἰτῶν λαμβάνει καὶ ὁ ζητῶν εὑρίσκει καὶ τῷ κρούοντι ἀνοιγήσεται.	πᾶς γὰρ ὁ αἰτῶν λαμβάνει καὶ ὁ ζητῶν εὑρίσκει καὶ τῷ κρούοντι ἀνοιγήσεται.

Text Critical Note (see the discussion in the front matter): Luke 11:10 reads ἀνοίγεται in 𝔓[75] B D; ἀνοιχθήσεται in A K W Γ Δ 565 1424 *pm*; and ἀνοιγήσεται in 𝔓[45] ℵ C L Θ Ψ $f^{1.13}$ 33 579 700 892 1241 2542 *pm*.

Q

πᾶς γὰρ ὁ αἰτῶν λαμβάνει καὶ ὁ ζητῶν εὑρίσκει καὶ τῷ κρούοντι ἀνοιγήσεται.	For everyone who asks receives, and the one who searches finds, and to the one who knocks will it be opened.

Gos. Thom. 94 (Nag Hammadi II 2)

(1) [Λέγε]ι Ἰησοῦς· ὁ ζητῶν εὑρήσει, (2) [τῷ κρούοντι] ἀνοιγήσεται.	(1) Jesus [says]: The one who searches will find, (2) [to the one who knocks] will it be opened.

Q 11:10

Luke 11:10	Lukan Doublet	Markan Parallel	*Gos. Thom.* 94
πᾶς γὰρ ὁ αἰτῶν λαμβάνει καὶ ὁ ζητῶν εὑρίσκει καὶ τῷ κρούοντι ἀνοιγήσεται.			94.1 [πεϫ]ẹ ⲓ̅ⲥ̅ πετϣιne qnaϭine 94.2 [πεττωϩⲙ̅ e]ϩ̣ογn cenaογωn naq'

Denn jeder, der bittet, empfängt, und der, der sucht, findet, und dem, der anklopft, wird geöffnet werden.

Car quiconque demande reçoit, et celui qui cherche trouve, et à celui qui frappe on ouvrira.

(1) Jesus [spricht]: Der, der sucht, wird finden, (2) [dem, der anklopft,] wird geöffnet werden.

(1) Jésus [dit]: Celui qui cherche trouvera, (2) [à celui qui frappe] on ouvrira.

Q 11:11-12

Markan Parallel	Matthean Doublet	Matt 7:9-10	Q 11:11-12
		7:9 ⸂(ἤ)^{1} ⸃^{1}	**11:11** ⸂( )^{1} ⸃^{1}
		τί(ς ἐστιν)^{2}	τί(ς ἐστιν)^{2}
		⸂[ ]^{1} ⸃^{1} ἐξ ὑμῶν	⸂ []^{1} ⸃^{1} ἐξ ὑμῶν
		(ἄνθρωπο)^{3}(ς, ὃν)^{2}	(ἄνθρωπο)^{3}(ς, ὃν)^{2}
		αἰτήσει ὁ υἱὸς (αὐτοῦ)^{4}	αἰτήσει ὁ υἱὸς (αὐτοῦ)^{4}
		^{5}⸂ (ἄρτ)^{6}ον⸃^{5},	⸂ (ἄρτ)^{6}ον⸃^{5},
		(μὴ)^{7}	(μὴ)^{7}
		^{5}⸂ (λίθ)^{6}ον⸃^{5}	^{5}⸂ (λίθ)^{6}ον⸃^{5}
		⸂ ⸃^{8} ἐπιδώσει ⸂αὐτῷ⸃^{8};	⸂ ⸃^{8} ἐπιδώσει ⸂αὐτῷ⸃^{8};
		7:10 ἢ καὶ	**11:12** ἢ καὶ
		⸂ ⸃^{9}	⸂⸃^{9}
		⸂ἰχθὺν⸃^{5}	⸂ἰχθὺν⸃^{5}
		⸂αἰτήσει⸃^{9},	⸂αἰτήσει⸃^{9},
		(μὴ)^{7}	(μὴ)^{7}
		⸂ ⸃^{10}	⸂⸃^{10}
		⸂ὄφιν⸃^{5}	⸂ὄφιν⸃^{5}
		⸂ἐπιδώσει αὐτῷ⸃^{10};	⸂ἐπιδώσει αὐτῷ⸃^{10};

Text Critical Note (see the discussion in the front matter): In Luke 11:11, before ἰχθύν, ℵ A C (⸂ D) L W Θ Ψ $f^{1.13}$ 33 𝔐 lat $sy^{c.p.h}$ bo have ἄρτον, μὴ λίθον ἐπιδώσει αὐτῷ; (+ *vs.* 12 C) ἢ καί (- ℵ L 33 *pc*), but this is omitted in $𝔓^{45.75}$ B 1241 *pc* ff^{2} i l sy^{s} sa $Mcion^{E}$.

1 Luke's postpositive δέ or Matthew's ἤ.
2 Luke's τίνα agreeing with a noun in the accusative or Matthew's τίς ἐστιν …, ὅν agreeing with a noun in the nominative.
3 Luke's ὁ πατήρ or Matthew's ἄνθρωπος.
4 Matthew's αὐτοῦ.
5 Luke's first position of ἰχθύς and ὄφις and second position of ᾠόν and σκορπίος, or Matthew's first position of ἄρτος and λίθος and second position of ἰχθύς and ὄφις.

Q

11 .. τίς ἐστιν ἐξ ὑμῶν ἄνθρωπος, ὃν αἰτήσει ὁ υἱὸς αὐτοῦ ἄρτον, μὴ λίθον ἐπιδώσει αὐτῷ; **12** ἢ καὶ ἰχθὺν αἰτήσει, μὴ ὄφιν ἐπιδώσει αὐτῷ;

11 .. What person of you, whose child asks for bread, will give him a stone? **12** Or again when he asks for a fish, will give him a snake?

Q 11:11-12

Luke 11:11-12	Lukan Doublet	Markan Parallel	Gospel of Thomas
11:11 ⸂( )^{1} ⸃^{1} τί[να]^{2} ⸂[δὲ]^{1} ⸃^{1} ἐξ ὑμῶν [τ]^{2}[ὁ]^{3}[ν]^{2} [πατ]^{3}[έ]^{2}[ρ]^{3}[α]^{2} αἰτήσει ὁ υἱὸς ( )^{4} ⸂ἰχθύν⸃^{5}, [καὶ ἀντὶ ἰχθύος]^{7} ⸂ὄφιν⸃^{5} ⸂αὐτῷ⸃^{8} ἐπιδώσει ⸂ ⸃^{8}; **11:12** ἢ καὶ ⸂αἰτήσει⸃^{9} ^{5}⸂ [ᾠ]^{6}όν⸃^{5}, ⸂ ⸃^{9} ( )^{7} ⸂ἐπιδώσει αὐτῷ⸃^{10} ^{5}⸂ [σκορπί]^{6}ον⸃^{5} ⸂ ⸃^{10};			

Text Critical Note (see the discussion in the front matter): In Luke 11:11 μὴ ἀντὶ ἰχθύος is in ℵ A C D L W Θ Ψ $f^{1.13}$ 33 𝔐 latt sa^{ms} bo, but μὴ καὶ ἀντὶ ἰχθύος is in Γ *pc* and καὶ ἀντὶ ἰχθύος in 𝔓$^{45.75}$ B *pc*; Mcion^{E}.

6 Luke's ᾠόν and σκορπίος or Matthew's ἄρτος and λίθος.
7 Luke's καὶ ἀντὶ ἰχθύος or Matthew's μή *bis*.
8 The position of ἐπιδώσει after αὐτῷ (Luke) or before it (Matthew).
9 The position of αἰτήσει before its object (Luke) or after it (Matthew).
10 The position of ἐπιδώσει αὐτῷ before its object (Luke) or after it (Matthew).

11 .. Wer von euch ist ein Mensch, der, wenn sein Sohn ihn um ein Brot bittet, ihm einen Stein gäbe? **12** Oder der ihm, wenn er ihn um einen Fisch bittet, eine Schlange gäbe?

11 .. Quelle personne parmi vous, si son fils lui demande du pain, lui donnera une pierre? **12** Ou encore s'il demande un poisson, lui donnera un serpent?

Q 11:13

Markan Parallel	Matthean Doublet	Matt 7:11	Q 11:13
		εἰ οὖν ὑμεῖς πονηροὶ [ ]¹ὄντες οἴδατε δόματα ἀγαθὰ διδόναι τοῖς τέκνοις ὑμῶν, πόσῳ μᾶλλον ὁ πατὴρ (ὑμῶν)² (ὁ)³ ἐ(ν)⁴ (τοῖς)⁵ οὐρανο(ῖς)⁶ δώσει (ἀγαθὰ)⁷ τοῖς αἰτοῦσιν αὐτόν. ≀Matt 7:7¹	εἰ οὖν ὑμεῖς πονηροὶ []¹ὄντες οἴδατε δόματα ἀγαθὰ διδόναι τοῖς τέκνοις ὑμῶν, πόσῳ μᾶλλον ὁ πατὴρ ()² ⟦()³⟧ ἐ[ξ]⁴ ()⁵ οὐρανο[ῦ]⁶ δώσει (ἀγαθὰ)⁷ τοῖς αἰτοῦσιν αὐτόν. ≀Q 11:9¹

Text Critical Note (see the discussion in the front matter): In Luke 11:13 the ὁ preceding ἐξ οὐρανοῦ is omitted in 𝔓⁷⁵ ℵ L Ψ 33 892 *pc* sa bo^pt; ὑμῶν ὁ οὐράνιος is in 𝔓⁴⁵ (579) 1424 (*pc*) l vg^s; ὑμῶν ὁ ἐξ οὐρανοῦ is in C (*f*¹³) *pc*; ὁ ἐξ οὐρανοῦ is in A B D W Θ *f*¹ 𝔐 sy^h.

1 Luke's ὑπάρχοντες or Matthew's ὄντες.

2 Matthew's ὑμῶν.

3 If ὁ is not in Luke, is it in Q?

4 Luke's ἐξ with the genitive or Matthew's ἐν with the dative.

Q

εἰ οὖν ὑμεῖς πονηροὶ ὄντες οἴδατε δόματα ἀγαθὰ διδόναι τοῖς τέκνοις ὑμῶν, πόσῳ μᾶλλον ὁ πατὴρ ἐξ οὐρανοῦ δώσει ἀγαθὰ τοῖς αἰτοῦσιν αὐτόν.

So if you, though evil, know how to give good gifts to your children, by how much more will the Father from heaven give good things to those who ask him!

Q 11:13

Luke 11:13	Lukan Doublet	Markan Parallel	Gospel of Thomas
εἰ οὖν ὑμεῖς πονηροὶ [ὑπάρχ][1]οντες οἴδατε δόματα ἀγαθὰ διδόναι τοῖς τέκνοις ὑμῶν, πόσῳ μᾶλλον ὁ πατὴρ ( )[2] (ὁ)[3] ἐ[ξ][4] ( )[5] οὐρανο[ῦ][6] δώσει [πνεῦμα ἅγιον][7] τοῖς αἰτοῦσιν αὐτόν. ⸆Luke 11:9[1]			

[5] Matthew's τοῖς.

[6] Luke's singular or Matthew's plural for heaven.

[7] Luke's πνεῦμα ἅγιον or Matthew's ἀγαθά.

Wenn nun ihr, die ihr böse seid, euren Kindern gute Gaben zu geben wisst, um wieviel mehr wird der Vater vom Himmel denen Gutes geben, die ihn bitten.

Si donc, vous qui êtes méchants, vous savez offrir de beaux cadeaux à vos enfants, à combien plus forte raison le Père offrira du ciel de bonnes choses à ceux qui «les» lui demandent.

Q 11:14

Markan Parallel	Matt 12:22-23	Matt 9:32-33	Q 11:14
	[1]ʃ	[1]ʃ	[1]ʃ
	12:22	**9:32** (Αὐτῶν)[2]	()[2]
	Τότε	(δὲ)[3]	[καὶ][3]
		(ἐξερχομένων ἰδοὺ)[2]	()[2]
	(προσηνέ)χθη (αὐτῷ)	(προσήνεγκαν αὐτῷ)[4]	⟦[][4]⟧ [ἐ⟦<ξέ>[4]⟧[βαλ][4]⟦<εν>[4]⟧
		(ἄνθρωπον)[5]	()[5]
		[6]ʃκωφὸνʅ[6]	ʃʅ[6]
	([δαιμονι]ζόμενο)ς	δαιμονι(ζόμενον)[4].	δαιμόνι[ον][4]
		[ ][7]	[][7]
	τυφλὸς καὶ [(κωφό)]ς,	ʃ ʅ[6]	[6]ʃκωφόνʅ[6].
	(καὶ)	**9:33** ʃ (καὶ)[8] ʅ[8]	ʃ (καὶ)[8] ʅ[8]
		[ ][9]	[][9]
		ʃ ʅ[8]	ʃʅ[8]
		ʃ ʅ[10]	ʃʅ[10]
	ἐθεράπευσεν	(ἐκβληθέ)[11]ντος	(ἐκβληθέ)[11]ντος
	αὐτόν,	[10]ʃτοῦ δαιμονίουʅ[10]	[10]ʃτοῦ δαιμονίουʅ[10]
	ὥστε τ[(ὸ)]ν [(κωφὸ)]ν	ἐλάλησεν	ἐλάλησεν
	[(λαλ)]εῖν καὶ βλέπειν.	ὁ κωφός.	ὁ κωφὸς
	12:23 [(καὶ)] ἐξίσταντο	καὶ ἐθαύμασαν	καὶ ἐθαύμασαν
	πάντες [(οἱ ὄχλοι)]	οἱ ὄχλοι	οἱ ὄχλοι
	καὶ ἔ(λεγ)ον· μήτι οὗτός	(λέγοντες· οὐδέποτε ἐφάνη	()[12]
	ἐστιν ὁ υἱὸς Δαυίδ;	οὕτως ἐν τῷ Ἰσραήλ)[12].	.
	ʅ[1]⇒Matt 12:24	ʅ[1]⇒Matt 9:34	ʅ[1]⇒Q 11:15

IQP 1991: δαιμόνι⟦[ον][4]⟧.

[1] The position of Q 11:14-15 in Q: After Q 11:13 and before Q 11:16 (Lukan order); or after Q 9:60 (Matt 8:22), and before Q 10:2 (Matt 9:37) (the Matthean order for Matt 9:32-33); or after Q 10:22 (Matt 11:27) and before Q 11:15 (Matt 12:24) (the Matthean order for Matt 12:22-23).

[2] Is Matthew's αὐτῶν ... ἐξερχομένων ἰδού in Q?

[3] Luke's καί or the postpositive δέ in Matt 9:32 (or τότε in Matt 12:22).

[4] ἦν ἐκβάλλων δαιμόνιον (Luke) or προσήνεγκαν αὐτῷ ... δαιμονιζόμενον (Matt 9:32) (or προσηνέχθη αὐτῷ δαιμονιζόμενος in Matt 12:22).

Q

καὶ ἐ⟦<ξέ>⟧βαλ⟦<εν>⟧ δαιμόνιον κωφόν· καὶ ἐκβληθέντος τοῦ δαιμονίου ἐλάλησεν ὁ κωφὸς καὶ ἐθαύμασαν οἱ ὄχλοι.

And he cast out a demon «which made a person» mute. And once the demon was cast out, the mute person spoke. And the crowds were amazed.

Q 11:14

Luke 11:14	Lukan Doublet	Markan Parallel	Gospel of Thomas
[1]⸂ ( )[2] [Καὶ][3] ( )[2] [ἦν ἐκβάλλων][4] ( )[5] ⸂ ⸃[6] δαιμόνι[ον][4] [καὶ αὐτὸ ἦν][7] [6]⸂κωφόν⸃[6]. ⸂ ⸃[8] [ἐγένετο][9] ⸂ [δὲ][8] ⸃[8] [10]⸂τοῦ δαιμονίου⸃[10] [ἐξελθό][11]ντος ⸂ ⸃[10] ἐλάλησεν ὁ κωφὸς καὶ ἐθαύμασαν οἱ ὄχλοι ( )[12] . ⸃[1] ⇒Luke 11:15			

[5] Matthew's ἄνθρωπον.

[6] The position of κωφόν or τυφλὸς καὶ κωφός in Matt 12:22).

[7] Luke's καὶ αὐτὸ ἦν.

[8] Luke's postpositive δέ or Matthew's καί.

[9] Luke's ἐγένετο.

[10] The position of τοῦ δαιμονίου before (Luke) or after (Matthew) the verb of healing.

[11] Luke's ἐξελθόντος or ἐκβληθέντος in Matt 9:33 (or ἐθεράπευσεν in Matt 12:22).

[12] Matthew's λέγοντες· οὐδέποτε ἐφάνη οὕτως ἐν τῷ Ἰσραήλ (or καὶ ἔλεγον· μήτι οὗτός ἐστιν ὁ υἱὸς Δαυίδ; in Matt 12:23).

Und er trieb einen Dämon aus, «der einen Menschen» stumm «machte». Und als der Dämon ausgetrieben war, begann der Stumme zu sprechen. Und die Volksmenge staunte.

Et il expulsa un démon «qui rendait» muet. Et, une fois le démon expulsé, le muet se mit à parler. Et les foules furent dans l'étonnement.

Q 11:15

Mark 3:22	Matt 12:24	Matt 9:34	Q 11:15
	[0]{	[0]{	[0]{
Καὶ οἱ γραμματεῖς	{(οἱ)} δὲ (Φαρισαῖοι)	({οἱ})[1] δὲ (Φαρισαῖοι)[1]	[τινὲς][1] δὲ
οἱ ἀπὸ Ἱεροσολύμων		[ ][2]	[][2]
καταβάντες	ἀκούσ{αντες}		
ἔλεγον ὅτι	[εἶπον]·	{(ἔλεγον)}[3]·	[εἶπον][3]·
Βεελζεβοὺλ ἔχει		{ἐν} [ ][4]	{ἐν} {[Βεελζεβοὺλ]}[4]
καὶ ὅτι ἐν τῷ ἄρχοντι		{τῷ ἄρχοντι	{τῷ ἄρχοντι
τῶν δαιμονίων		τῶν δαιμονίων	τῶν δαιμονίων
	οὗτος οὐκ		
ἐκβάλλει τὰ δαιμόνια.	{ἐκβάλλει τὰ δαιμόνια}	ἐκβάλλει τὰ δαιμόνια}.	ἐκβάλλει τὰ δαιμόνια}.
	εἰ μὴ		
	{[ἐν] ʃ[τῷ]} {[Βεελζεβοὺλ]}		
	{[ἄρχοντι τῶν δαιμονίων]}.		
	}[0]	}[0]	}[0]
	≀ Matt 12:22[1]	≀ Matt 9:32[1]	≀ Q 11:14[1]

IQP 1992, JSK: [τινὲς][1] δὲ ⟦[][2]⟧ [εἶπον][3]

[0] Is Luke 11:15 par. Matt 9:34; (12:24) in Q or from Mark? [2] Luke's ἐξ αὐτῶν.
[1] Luke's τινές or Matthew's οἱ … Φαρισαῖοι.

Q

τινὲς δὲ εἶπον· ἐν Βεελζεβοὺλ τῷ ἄρχοντι τῶν δαιμονίων ἐκβάλλει τὰ δαιμόνια.	But some said: By Beelzebul, the ruler of demons, he casts out demons!

Q 11:16 is to be found below, between Q 11:17-20, ⟦21-22⟧, 23-26,?27-28? and Q 11:29-30.

Q 11:15

Luke 11:15	Lukan Doublet	Mark 3:22	Gospel of Thomas
[0]{			
[τινὲς][1] δὲ		Καὶ οἱ γραμματεῖς	
[ἐξ αὐτῶν][2]		οἱ ἀπὸ Ἱεροσολύμων	
		καταβάντες	
[εἶπον][3]·		ἔλεγον ὅτι	
{ἐν} {[Βεελζεβοὺλ]}[4]		Βεελζεβοὺλ ἔχει	
{τῷ ἄρχοντι		καὶ ὅτι ἐν τῷ ἄρχοντι	
τῶν δαιμονίων		τῶν δαιμονίων	
ἐκβάλλει τὰ δαιμόνια}.		ἐκβάλλει τὰ δαιμόνια.	
}[0]			
₰ Luke 11:14[1]			

[3] Luke's εἶπον or Matthew's ἔλεγον.

[4] Luke's Βεελζεβούλ.

Einige aber sagten: Durch Beelzebul, den Herrscher der Dämonen, treibt er die Dämonen aus!

Mais certains dirent: C'est par Béelzéboul, le chef des démons, qu'il expulse les démons!

Q 11:16 is to be found below, between Q 11:17-20, ⟦21-22⟧, 23-26,?27-28? and Q 11:29-30.

Q 11:17

Mark 3:23-25	Matthean Doublet	Matt 12:25	Q 11:17
		[0]{	[0]{
3:23 Καὶ προσκαλεσάμενος αὐτοὺς ἐν παραβολαῖς			
		[ ][1] ⸂ ⸃[1] εἰδὼς ⸂δὲ⸃[1] ⸂ ⸃[2]	[][1] ⸂⸃[1] εἰδὼς ⸂δὲ⸃[1] ⸂⸃[2]
		τὰ(ς ἐνθυμήσεις)[3] ⸂αὐτῶν⸃[2]	τὰ [διανοήματα] [3] ⸂αὐτῶν⸃[2]
ἔλεγεν αὐτοῖς·		εἶπεν {αὐτοῖς}·	εἶπεν {αὐτοῖς}·
πῶς δύναται σατανᾶς σατανᾶν ἐκβάλλειν;			
3:24 καὶ ἐὰν βασιλεία ἐφ᾽ ἑαυτὴν μερισθῇ,		πᾶσα {βασιλεία} ⸂ ⸃[4] [ ][5]{μερισθ}εῖσα [4]⸂ (καθ᾽)[6] {ἑαυτῇ}(ς)[6] ⸃[4]	πᾶσα {βασιλεία} ⸂⸃[4] [][5]{μερισθ}εῖσα [4]⸂ ⟦(καθ᾽)[6]⟧ {ἑαυτῇ}⟦(ς)[6]⟧ ⸃[4]
οὐ δύναται σταθῆναι ἡ βασιλεία ἐκείνη·		ἐρημοῦται {καὶ}	ἐρημοῦται {καὶ}
3:25 καὶ ἐὰν οἰκία ἐφ᾽ ἑαυτὴν μερισθῇ,		(πᾶσα πόλις ἢ)[7] {οἰκ(ία} {μερισθ}εῖσα καθ᾽ {ἑαυτῆ}ς	(πᾶσα)[7] {οἰκ(ία μερισθ}εῖσα καθ᾽ {ἑαυτῆ}ς
οὐ δυνήσεται ἡ οἰκία ἐκείνη σταθῆναι.		{οὐ} {σταθή}σεται)[8]. }[0]	{οὐ} {σταθή}σεται)[8]. }[0]

IQP 1992: ⸂αὐτῶν⸃[2] τὰ [διανοήματα][3].

IQP 1992: [4]⸂ {[ἐφ᾽][5] ἑαυτή[ν]}[5] ⸃[4] [][6]{μερισθ}εῖσα ⸂ ⸃[4] ἐρημοῦται {καὶ} ()[7] {οἰκ⟦(ία μερισθ}εῖσα καθ᾽ {ἑαυτῆ}ς {οὐ} {σταθή}σεται)[8]⟧.

[0] Is Luke 11:17 par. Matt 12:25 in Q or from Mark?

[1] Luke's inclusion of αὐτός and the resulting position of the postpositive δέ.

[2] The position of αὐτῶν before (Luke) or after (Matthew) the noun it modifies.

[3] Luke's τὰ διανοήματα or Matthew's τὰς ἐνθυμήσεις.

Q

εἰδὼς δὲ τὰ διανοήματα αὐτῶν εἶπεν αὐτοῖς· πᾶσα βασιλεία μερισθεῖσα ⟦καθ᾽⟧ ἑαυτῇ⟦ς⟧ ἐρημοῦται καὶ πᾶσα οἰκία μερισθεῖσα καθ᾽ ἑαυτῆς οὐ σταθήσεται.	But, knowing their thoughts, he said to them: Every kingdom divided against itself is left barren, and every household divided against itself will not stand.

Q 11:17

Luke 11:17	Lukan Doublet	Mark 3:23-25	Gospel of Thomas
[0]{			
		3:23 Καὶ προσκαλεσάμενος αὐτοὺς ἐν παραβολαῖς	
[αὐτὸς][1] ⸂δὲ⸃[1] εἰδὼς ⸂ ⸃[1]			
⸂αὐτῶν⸃[2]			
τὰ [διανοήματα][3]			
⸂ ⸃[2]			
εἶπεν {αὐτοῖς}·		ἔλεγεν αὐτοῖς·	
		πῶς δύναται σατανᾶς σατανᾶν ἐκβάλλειν;	
πᾶσα {βασιλεία}		**3:24** καὶ ἐὰν βασιλεία	
[4]⸂ {[ἐφ']}[6] ἑαυτὴ[ν]}[6] ⸃[4]		ἐφ' ἑαυτὴν	
[δια][5]{μερισθ}εῖσα		μερισθῇ,	
⸂ ⸃[4]			
ἐρημοῦται {καὶ}		οὐ δύναται σταθῆναι ἡ βασιλεία ἐκείνη·	
( )[7]		**3:25** καὶ ἐὰν	
{οἶκ}[ος {ἐ}πὶ οἶκον		οἰκία ἐφ' ἑαυτὴν μερισθῇ,	
		οὐ δυνήσεται ἡ οἰκία ἐκείνη σταθῆναι.	
πίπτει][8].			
}[0]			

[4] The position of ἐφ' ἑαυτήν / καθ' ἑαυτῆς before (Luke) or after (Matthew) (δια)μερισθεῖσα.

[5] Luke's prefix δια-.

[6] Luke's ἐφ' or Matthew's καθ', and the resultant cases.

[7] Matthew's πᾶσα πόλις ἤ.

[8] Luke's οἶκος ἐπὶ οἶκον πίπτει or Matthew's οἰκία μερισθεῖσα καθ' ἑαυτῆς οὐ σταθήσεται.

Er durchschaute aber ihre Gedanken «und» sagte zu ihnen: Jedes Reich, in dem «ein Teil» gegen den andern «steht», wird zur Einöde, und jedes Haus, in dem ein Teil gegen den andern steht, wird nicht Bestand haben.

Mais connaissant leurs pensées, il leur dit: Tout royaume divisé contre lui-même court à sa ruine, et toute maisonnée divisée contre elle-même ne se maintiendra pas.

Q 11:18

Mark 3:26	Matthean Doublet	Matt 12:26	Q 11:18
		^{0}{	^{0}{
καὶ εἰ		ʃ{καὶ}ʅ^{1} εἰ []^{1} ʃ ʅ^{1}	ʃ{καὶ}ʅ^{1} εἰ []^{1} ʃʅ^{1}
ὁ σατανᾶς		ὁ σατανᾶς}	ὁ σατανᾶς}
ἀνέστη		(τὸν σατανᾶν ἐκβάλλει)^{2},	()^{2}
ἐφ᾽ ἑαυτὸν		{ἐφ᾽ ἑαυτὸν}	{ἐφ᾽ ἑαυτὸν}
καὶ ἐμερίσθη,		[ ]^{3}{ἐμερίσθη}·	[]^{3}{ἐμερίσθη},
οὐ δύναται στῆναι		πῶς (οὖν)^{4} {στ}αθήσεται	πῶς ()^{4} {στ}αθήσεται
ἀλλὰ τέλος ἔχει.		ἡ βασιλεία αὐτοῦ;	ἡ βασιλεία αὐτοῦ;
		[ ]^{5}	[]^{5}
		.	.
	d	}^{0}	}^{0}

IQP 1992: [ὅτι λέγετε ἐν Βεελζεβοὺλ ἐκβάλλειν με τὰ δαιμόνια]^{5}. JSK: ⟦[]^{5}⟧.

0 Is Luke 11:18 par. Matt 12:26 in Q or from Mark?

1 The position of καί and Luke's additional δέ.

2 Matthew's τὸν σατανᾶν ἐκβάλλει.

3 Luke's prefix δι-.

Q

καὶ εἰ ὁ σατανᾶς ἐφ᾽ ἑαυτὸν ἐμερίσθη, πῶς σταθήσεται ἡ βασιλεία αὐτοῦ;

And if Satan is divided against himself, how will his kingdom stand?

Q 11:18

Luke 11:18	Lukan Doublet	Mark 3:26	Gospel of Thomas
[0]{			
ʃ ʅ[1] {εἰ} [δὲ][1] ʃ {καὶ} ʅ[1]		καὶ εἰ	
{ὁ σατανᾶς}		ὁ σατανᾶς	
( )[2]		ἀνέστη	
{ἐφ' ἑαυτὸν}		ἐφ' ἑαυτὸν	
[δι][3]{εμερίσθη},		καὶ ἐμερίσθη,	
πῶς ( )[4] {στ}αθήσεται		οὐ δύναται στῆναι	
ἡ βασιλεία αὐτοῦ;		ἀλλὰ τέλος ἔχει.	
[ὅτι λέγετε ἐν Βεελζεβοὺλ			
ἐκβάλλειν με			
τὰ δαιμόνια][5].			
}[0]			

4 Matthew's οὖν.

5 Luke's ὅτι λέγετε ἐν Βεελζεβοὺλ ἐκβάλλειν με τὰ διαμόνια.

Und wenn der Satan in sich selbst geteilt ist, wie wird sein Reich Bestand haben?

Et si Satan est divisé contre lui-même, comment son règne se maintiendra-t-il?

Q 11:19

Markan Parallel	Matthean Doublet	Matt 12:27	Q 11:19
		(καὶ)[1] εἰ [ ][1] ἐγὼ ἐν Βεελζεβοὺλ ἐκβάλλω τὰ δαιμόνια, οἱ υἱοὶ ὑμῶν ἐν τίνι ἐκβάλλουσιν; διὰ τοῦτο αὐτοὶ ⸉ ⸊[2] κριταὶ ἔσονται ⸉ὑμῶν⸊[2].	(καὶ)[1] εἰ [][1] ἐγὼ ἐν Βεελζεβοὺλ ἐκβάλλω τὰ δαιμόνια, οἱ υἱοὶ ὑμῶν ἐν τίνι ἐκβάλλουσιν; διὰ τοῦτο αὐτοὶ ⸉ ⸊[2] κριταὶ ἔσονται ⸉ὑμῶν⸊[2].

IQP 1992: ὑμῶν κριταὶ ἔσονται.

JMR, PH, JSK: ⸉ ⸊[2] κριταὶ ἔσονται ⸉ὑμῶν⸊[2] {C}.

[1] Luke's δέ or Matthew's καί.

[2] The position of ὑμῶν.

Q

καὶ εἰ ἐγὼ ἐν Βεελζεβοὺλ ἐκβάλλω τὰ δαιμόνια, οἱ υἱοὶ ὑμῶν ἐν τίνι ἐκβάλλουσιν; διὰ τοῦτο αὐτοὶ κριταὶ ἔσονται ὑμῶν.	And if I by Beelzebul cast out demons, your sons, by whom do they cast «them» out? This is why they will be your judges.

Q 11:19

Luke 11:19	Lukan Doublet	Markan Parallel	Gospel of Thomas
( )¹ εἰ [δὲ]¹ ἐγὼ ἐν Βεελζεβοὺλ ἐκβάλλω τὰ δαιμόνια, οἱ υἱοὶ ὑμῶν ἐν τίνι ἐκβάλλουσιν; διὰ τοῦτο αὐτοὶ ⸉ὑμῶν⸊² κριταὶ ἔσονται ⸉ ⸊².			

Und wenn ich mit Beelzebul die Dämonen austreibe, mit wem treiben eure Söhne «sie» aus? Darum werden sie eure Richter sein.

Et si moi j'expulse les démons par Béelzéboul, vos fils, par qui «les» expulsent-ils? C'est pourquoi ils seront vos juges.

Q 11:20

Markan Parallel	Matthean Doublet	Matt 12:28	Q 11:20
		εἰ δὲ ἐν (πνεύματι)[1] θεοῦ ἐγὼ ἐκβάλλω τὰ δαιμόνια, ἄρα ἔφθασεν ἐφ' ὑμᾶς ἡ βασιλεία τοῦ θεοῦ.	εἰ δὲ ἐν [δακτύλῳ][1] θεοῦ ἐγὼ ἐκβάλλω τὰ δαιμόνια, ἄρα ἔφθασεν ἐφ' ὑμᾶς ἡ βασιλεία τοῦ θεοῦ.

[1] Luke's δακτύλῳ or Matthew's πνεύματι.

Q

εἰ δὲ ἐν δακτύλῳ θεοῦ ἐγὼ ἐκβάλλω τὰ δαιμόνια, ἄρα ἔφθασεν ἐφ' ὑμᾶς ἡ βασιλεία τοῦ θεοῦ.	But if it is by the finger of God that I cast out demons, then there has come upon you God's reign.

Q 11:20

Luke 11:20	Lukan Doublet	Markan Parallel	Gospel of Thomas
εἰ δὲ ἐν [δακτύλῳ][1] θεοῦ ἐγὼ ἐκβάλλω τὰ δαιμόνια, ἄρα ἔφθασεν ἐφ' ὑμᾶς ἡ βασιλεία τοῦ θεοῦ.			

Wenn ich aber mit dem Finger Gottes die Dämonen austreibe, dann ist das Reich Gottes zu euch «schon» gekommen.

Mais si moi, c'est par le doigt de Dieu que j'expulse les démons, alors le règne de Dieu vient de vous atteindre.

Q 11:⟦21-22⟧

Mark 3:27	Matthean Doublet	Matt 12:29	Q 11:⟦21-22⟧
		0{	0{
ἀλλ᾽ οὐ δύναται οὐδεὶς		(ἢ πῶς {δύναταί}	⟦< >[1]⟧
εἰς τὴν οἰκίαν		τις {εἰσ)[1]ελθ}(εῖν	
τοῦ ἰσχυροῦ		{εἰς)[1] τὴν (οἰκίαν	
εἰσελθὼν		τ)[1]ο(ῦ)[1] ἰσχυρο(ῦ} καὶ)[1]	
τὰ σκεύη αὐτοῦ		{τὰ (σκεύη)[1] αὐτοῦ}	
διαρπάσαι,		({ἁρπάσαι,}	
ἐὰν μὴ πρῶτον		{ἐ)[1]ὰν (μὴ πρῶτον}	
τὸν ἰσχυρὸν δήσῃ,		{δ)[1]ήσῃ} ({τὸν)[1] ἰσχυρό(ν;})[1]	
καὶ τότε τὴν οἰκίαν		{καὶ (τότε)[1] τ(ὴν οἰκίαν)[1]	
αὐτοῦ διαρπάσει.		αὐτοῦ δι(αρπάσει.})[1]	
		}0	}0

IQP 1992: **11:⟦«21»⟧** ⟦«[ὅταν][1] ὁ {ἰσχυρὸ}[ς καθωπλισμένος φυλάσσῃ][1] {τὴν} [ἑαυτοῦ αὐλήν, ἐν εἰρήνῃ ἐστὶν][1] {τὰ} [ὑπάρχοντα][1] {αὐτοῦ}·»⟧ **11:⟦«22»⟧** ⟦«[ἐπ][1]ὰν [δὲ][1] ἰσχυρό[τερος αὐτοῦ][1] [ ][1] [νική][1]-{σῃ} [αὐτόν, τὴν πανοπλίαν αὐτοῦ αἴρει ἐφ᾽ ᾗ ἐπεποίθει][1] καὶ τ[ὰ σκῦλα][1] {αὐτοῦ} δι[( )][1]»⟧.

0 Is Luke 11:21-22 par. Matt 12:29 in Q or from Mark?

1 Is the Q text that of Luke or Matthew?

Q

⟦< >⟧

⟦21⟧ ⟦«A strong person's house cannot be looted,»⟧ ⟦22⟧ ⟦«but if someone still stronger overpowers him, he does get looted.»⟧

Gos. Thom. 35 (Nag Hammadi II 2)

(1) Λέγει Ἰησοῦς· οὐ δύναταί τις εἰσελθεῖν εἰς τὴν οἰκίαν τοῦ ἰσχυροῦ βιάζεσθαι αὐτὸν εἰ μὴ δήσῃ τὰς χεῖρας αὐτοῦ. (2) τότε τὴν οἰκίαν αὐτοῦ μεταθήσει.[1]

(1) Jesus says: It is not possible for someone to enter the house of a strong (person) (and) take it by force unless he binds his hands. (2) Then he will plunder his house.

[1] For the Coptic translation of the Greek verb μετατιθέναι cf Heb 7:12; Jude 4.

Q 11:⟦21-22⟧

Luke 11:⟦21-22⟧	Lukan Doublet	Markan Parallel	*Gos. Thom.* 35
[0]{ **11:21** [ὅταν][1] ὁ {ἰσχυρὸ}[ς καθωπλισμένος φυλάσσῃ][1] {τὴν} [ἑαυτοῦ αὐλήν, ἐν εἰρήνῃ ἐστὶν][1] {τὰ} [ὑπάρχοντα][1]{αὐτοῦ}· **11:22** [ἐπ][1]{ὰν} [δὲ][1] ἰσχυρό[τερος αὐτοῦ ἐπ{ε}][1]λθὼ[ν} νικ][1]{ήσῃ} [αὐτόν, τὴν πανοπλίαν αὐτοῦ αἴρει ἐφ᾽ ᾗ ἐπεποίθει][1] {καὶ} τ[ὰ σκῦλα][1] {αὐτοῦ δι}[αδίδωσιν.][1] }[0]			35.1 ⲡⲉϫⲉ ⲓ̅ⲥ̅ ⲙⲛ̅ ϭⲟⲙʼ ⲛ̅ⲧⲉ ⲟⲩⲁ ⲃⲱⲕʼ ⲉϩⲟⲩⲛ ⲉⲡⲏⲉⲓ ⲙ̅ⲡϫⲱⲱⲣⲉ ⲛ̅ϥϫⲓⲧϥʼ ⲛ̅ϫⲛⲁϩ ⲉⲓ ⲙⲏⲧⲓ ⲛ̅ϥⲙⲟⲩⲣ ⲛ̅ⲛⲉϥϭⲓϫʼ 35.2 ⲧⲟⲧⲉ ϥⲛⲁⲡⲱⲱⲛⲉ ⲉⲃⲟⲗ ⲙ̅ⲡⲉϥⲏⲉⲓ

PH: **11:⟦21⟧** ⟦(ἢ πῶς {δύναταί} τις {εἰσ)[1]ελθ}(εῖν {εἰς)[1] τὴν (οἰκίαν τ)[1]ο(ῦ)[1] ἰσχυρο(ῦ} καὶ)[1] {τὰ (σκεύη)[1] αὐτοῦ <δι>[1]({αρπάσαι,}⟧ **11:⟦22⟧** ⟦({ἐ)[1]ὰν (μὴ πρῶτον} {δ)[1]ήσῃ} ({τὸν)[1] ἰσχυρό(ν;})[1] {καὶ (τότε)[1] τ(ὴν οἰκίαν)[1] αὐτοῦ δι(αρπάσει.})[1]⟧.

⟦21⟧ ⟦«Ein Starker kann nicht beraubt werden,»⟧ ⟦22⟧ ⟦«wenn aber ein Stärkerer ihn besiegt, wird er beraubt.»⟧

⟦21⟧ ⟦«La maison d'une personne puissante ne peut pas être forcée,»⟧ ⟦22⟧ ⟦«mais si un plus puissant que lui a le dessus, il sera pillé.»⟧

(1) Jesus spricht: Es ist nicht möglich, dass jemand in das Haus des Starken hineingeht (und) es gewaltsam nimmt, es sei denn, er fesselt dessen Hände. (2) Dann wird er sein Haus ausplündern.

(1) Jésus dit: Il n'est pas possible que quelqu'un entre dans la maison d'une personne puissante (et) qu'il la prenne de force à moins qu'il ne lui lie les mains. (2) Alors, il mettra sa maison sens dessus dessous.

[1] Zum Verb μετατιθέναι und seiner koptischen Wiedergabe siehe Heb 7,12 und Jd 4.

[1] Pour la traduction copte du verbe grec μετατιθέναι, voir Heb 7:12; Jude 4.

Q 11:23

Markan Parallel	Matthean Doublet	Matt 12:30	Q 11:23
		ὁ μὴ ὢν μετ' ἐμοῦ {κα}τ' ἐμοῦ {ἐστιν}, καὶ ὁ μὴ συνάγων μετ' ἐμοῦ σκορπίζει.	ὁ μὴ ὢν μετ' ἐμοῦ {κα}τ' ἐμοῦ {ἐστιν}, καὶ ὁ μὴ συνάγων μετ' ἐμοῦ σκορπίζει.

Q

ὁ μὴ ὢν μετ' ἐμοῦ κατ' ἐμοῦ ἐστιν, καὶ ὁ μὴ συνάγων μετ' ἐμοῦ σκορπίζει.

The one not with me is against me, and the one not gathering with me scatters.

Q 11:23

Luke 11:23	Luke 9:50c	Mark 9:40	Gospel of Thomas
Ὁ μὴ ὢν μετ' ἐμοῦ {κα}τ' ἐμοῦ {ἐστιν}, καὶ ὁ μὴ συνάγων μετ' ἐμοῦ σκορπίζει.	{ὃς γὰρ οὐκ [(ἔστιν)] [(κα)]θ'} ὑ{μῶν, ὑπὲρ} ὑ{μῶν ἐστιν.}	ὃς γὰρ οὐκ ἔστιν καθ' ἡμῶν, ὑπὲρ ἡμῶν ἐστιν.	

Wer nicht mit mir ist, der ist gegen mich, und wer nicht mit mir sammelt, der zerstreut.

Qui n'est pas avec moi est contre moi, et qui ne rassemble pas avec moi disperse.

Q 11:24

Markan Parallel	Matthean Doublet	Matt 12:43-44a	Q 11:24
		[1]⸂	[1]⸂
		12:43 Ὅταν (δὲ)[2]	ὅταν ()[2]
		τὸ ἀκάθαρτον πνεῦμα	τὸ ἀκάθαρτον πνεῦμα
		ἐξέλθῃ ἀπὸ τοῦ ἀνθρώπου,	ἐξέλθῃ ἀπὸ τοῦ ἀνθρώπου,
		διέρχεται δι᾽ ἀνύδρων τόπων	διέρχεται δι᾽ ἀνύδρων τόπων
		ζητοῦν ἀνάπαυσιν	ζητοῦν ἀνάπαυσιν
		καὶ (οὐχ)[3] εὑρίσκ(ει)[3].	καὶ (οὐχ)[3] εὑρίσκ(ει)[3].
		12:44 τότε[4] λέγει·	⟦τότε[4]⟧ λέγει·
		⸂εἰς τὸν οἶκόν μου⸃[5]	⸂εἰς τὸν οἶκόν μου⸃[5]
		(ἐπι)[6]στρέψω	(ἐπι)[6]στρέψω
		⸂ ⸃[5]	⸂⸃[5]
		ὅθεν ἐξῆλθον·	ὅθεν ἐξῆλθον·
		⸃[1]⇒Matt 12:45	⸃[1]⇒Q 11:26

Text Critical Note (see the discussion in the front matter): In Luke 11:24 τότε is absent in 𝔓^{45} ℵ* A C D W Ψ $f^{1.13}$ 𝔐 lat sy$^{s.c.p}$, but present in 𝔓^{75} ℵ^{2} B L Θ Ξ 070 33 579 892 1241 *pc* b l sy^{h} co.

[1] The position of Q 11:24-26 in Q: After Q 11:23 and before Q 11:(?27-28?), 29 (Lukan order); or after Q 11:31 (Matt 12:42) and before Q 10:23 (Matt 13:16) (Matthean order).

[2] Matthew's δέ.

[3] Luke's μὴ εὑρίσκον or Matthew's οὐχ εὑρίσκει.

Q

ὅταν τὸ ἀκάθαρτον πνεῦμα ἐξέλθῃ ἀπὸ τοῦ ἀνθρώπου, διέρχεται δι᾽ ἀνύδρων τόπων ζητοῦν ἀνάπαυσιν καὶ οὐχ εὑρίσκει. ⟦τότε⟧ λέγει· εἰς τὸν οἶκόν μου ἐπιστρέψω ὅθεν ἐξῆλθον·

When the defiling spirit has left the person, it wanders through waterless regions looking for a resting-place, and finds none. ⟦Then⟧ it says, I will return to my house from which I came.

Q 11:24

Luke 11:24	Lukan Doublet	Markan Parallel	Gospel of Thomas
⌐1 ⌐ Ὅταν ( )[2] τὸ ἀκάθαρτον πνεῦμα ἐξέλθῃ ἀπὸ τοῦ ἀνθρώπου, διέρχεται δι' ἀνύδρων τόπων ζητοῦν ἀνάπαυσιν καὶ [μὴ][3] εὑρίσκ[ον][3]· τότε[4] λέγει· ⌐ ⌐5 [ὑπο][6]στρέψω ⌐εἰς τὸν οἶκόν μου⌐5 ὅθεν ἐξῆλθον· ⌐1⇒Luke 11:26			

[4] The inclusion of τότε (uncertain in Luke).

[5] εἰς τὸν οἶκόν μου after (Luke) or before (Matthew) the verb.

[6] Luke's ὑπο- or Matthew's ἐπι-.

Wenn der unreine Geist aus einem Menschen ausfährt, zieht er durch wasserlose Gegenden und sucht einen Ruheplatz, findet ihn aber nicht. ⟦Dann⟧ sagt er: Ich will in mein Haus zurückkehren, aus dem ich hinausgegangen bin.

Lorsque l'esprit impur est sorti de la personne, il parcourt des régions arides à la recherche de repos et n'en trouve pas. ⟦Alors⟧ il dit: Je veux retourner à la maison de laquelle je suis sorti.

Q 11:25

Markan Parallel	Matthean Doublet	Matt 12:44b	Q 11:25
		καὶ ἐλθὸν εὑρίσκει (σχολάζοντα)[1] σεσαρωμένον καὶ κεκοσμημένον.	καὶ ἐλθὸν εὑρίσκει ()[1] σεσαρωμένον καὶ κεκοσμημένον.

[1] Matthew's σχολάζοντα.

Q

καὶ ἐλθὸν εὑρίσκει σεσαρωμένον καὶ κεκοσμημένον.	And on arrival it finds «it» swept and tidied up.

Q 11:25

Luke 11:25	Lukan Doublet	Markan Parallel	Gospel of Thomas
καὶ ἐλθὸν εὑρίσκει ( )[1] σεσαρωμένον καὶ κεκοσμημένον.			

Und wenn er hinkommt, findet er «es» gefegt und geschmückt.

Et à son arrivée, il «la» trouve balayée et rangée.

Q 11:26

Markan Parallel	Matthean Doublet	Matt 12:45	Q 11:26
		τότε πορεύεται	τότε πορεύεται
		καὶ παραλαμβάνει	καὶ παραλαμβάνει
		(μεθ' ἑαυτοῦ)[1]	(μεθ' ἑαυτοῦ)[1]
		⸉ἑπτὰ⸊[2]	⸉ἑπτὰ⸊[2]
		ἕτερα πνεύματα πονηρότερα	ἕτερα πνεύματα πονηρότερα
		ἑαυτοῦ ⸉ ⸊[2]	ἑαυτοῦ ⸉⸊[2]
		καὶ εἰσελθόντα	καὶ εἰσελθόντα
		κατοικεῖ ἐκεῖ·	κατοικεῖ ἐκεῖ·
		καὶ γίνεται	καὶ γίνεται
		τὰ ἔσχατα	τὰ ἔσχατα
		τοῦ ἀνθρώπου ἐκείνου	τοῦ ἀνθρώπου ἐκείνου
		χείρονα τῶν πρώτων.	χείρονα τῶν πρώτων.
		(οὕτως ἔσται καὶ τῇ γενεᾷ	
		ταύτῃ τῇ πονηρᾷ)[3].	()[3]
		⸊Matt 12:43[1]	⸊Q 11:24[1]

[1] Matthew's μεθ' ἑαυτοῦ.

[2] The position of ἑπτά after (Luke) or before (Matthew) ἕτερα πνεύματα πονηρότερα ἑαυτοῦ.

Q

τότε πορεύεται καὶ παραλαμβάνει μεθ' ἑαυτοῦ ἑπτὰ ἕτερα πνεύματα πονηρότερα ἑαυτοῦ καὶ εἰσελθόντα κατοικεῖ ἐκεῖ· καὶ γίνεται τὰ ἔσχατα τοῦ ἀνθρώπου ἐκείνου χείρονα τῶν πρώτων.

Then it goes and brings with it seven other spirits more evil than itself, and, moving in, they settle there. And the last «circumstances» of that person become worse than the first.

Q 11:26

Luke 11:26	Lukan Doublet	Markan Parallel	Gospel of Thomas
τότε πορεύεται καὶ παραλαμβάνει ( )[1] ⸉ ⸊[2] ἕτερα πνεύματα πονηρότερα ἑαυτοῦ ⸉ἑπτὰ⸊[2] καὶ εἰσελθόντα κατοικεῖ ἐκεῖ· καὶ γίνεται τὰ ἔσχατα τοῦ ἀνθρώπου ἐκείνου χείρονα τῶν πρώτων. ( )[3] ⸊Luke 11:24[1]			

[3] Matthew's οὕτως ἔσται καὶ τῇ γενεᾷ ταύτῃ τῇ πονηρᾷ.

Dann geht er und nimmt mit sich sieben andere Geister, böser als er selbst, und sie gehen hinein und wohnen dort. Und der letzte «Zustand» jenes Menschen wird schlimmer als der erste sein.

Alors il va prendre avec lui sept autres esprits encore plus méchants que lui et ils pénètrent là pour s'y installer. Et cette personne se retrouve finalement «dans un état» pire qu'au début.

Q 11:?27-28?

Markan Parallel	Matthean Doublet	Matthew	Q 11:?27-28?
		[ ][0]	[ ][0]

IQP 1994: [ ][0] indeterminate; JSK: **11:**⟦**27**⟧ ⟦< >[2] «γυνὴ ἐκ τοῦ ὄχλου εἶπεν αὐτῷ· μακαρία ἡ κοιλία ἡ βαστάσασά σε καὶ μαστοὶ οὓς ἐθήλασας».⟧ **11:**⟦**28**⟧ ⟦«αὐτὸς δὲ εἶπεν· μενοῦν μακάριοι οἱ ἀκούοντες τὸν λόγον τοῦ θεοῦ καὶ φυλάσσοντες».⟧.

[0] Is Luke 11:27b-28 in Q?

[1] Does Luke preserve the Q position?

Q

..	..

Gos. Thom. 79.1-2 (Nag Hammadi II 2)

(1) Εἶπεν αὐτῷ γυνή τις ἐκ τοῦ ὄχλου· μακαρία ἡ κοιλία ἡ βαστάσασά σε καὶ οἱ μαστοὶ οἱ θρέψαντές σε. (2) Εἶπεν αὐτ[ῇ]· μακάριοι οἱ ἀκούσαντες τὸν λόγον τοῦ πατρὸς (καὶ) ἀληθῶς φυλάξαντες αὐτόν.

(1) A woman in the crowd said to him: Hail to the womb that carried you and to the breasts that fed you. (2) He said to [her]: Hail to those who have heard the word of the Father (and) have truly kept it.

Q 11:29-30 is to be found below, between Q 11:24-26,?27-28?, 16 and Q 11:31-32.

Q 11:?27-28?

Luke 11:?27-28?	Lukan Doublet	Markan Parallel	*Gos. Thom.* 79.1-2
⁰[¹⸢ **11:27** [Ἐγένετο δὲ ἐν τῷ λέγειν αὐτὸν ταῦτα ἐπάρασά τις φωνὴν][2] γυνὴ ἐκ τοῦ ὄχλου εἶπεν αὐτῷ· μακαρία ἡ κοιλία ἡ βαστάσασά σε καὶ μαστοὶ οὓς ἐθήλασας. **11:28** αὐτὸς δὲ εἶπεν· μενοῦν μακάριοι οἱ ἀκούοντες τὸν λόγον τοῦ θεοῦ καὶ φυλάσσοντες. ⸣¹]⁰			79.1 ⲡⲉϫⲉ ⲟⲩⲥϩⲓⲙ[ⲉ] ⲛⲁϥ ϩⲙ̄ ⲡⲙⲏϣⲉ ϫⲉ ⲛⲉⲉⲓⲁⲧⲥ̣ [ⲛ̄]ⲑϩⲏ ⲛ̄ⲧⲁϩϥⲓ ϩⲁⲣⲟⲕ ⲁⲩⲱ ⲛ̄ⲕⲓ̣[ⲃ]ⲉ ⲉⲛⲧⲁϩⲥⲁⲛⲟⲩϣⲕ 79.2 ⲡⲉϫⲁϥ ⲛⲁ[ⲥ] ϫⲉ ⲛⲉⲉⲓⲁⲧⲟⲩ ⲛ̄ⲛⲉⲛⲧⲁϩⲥⲱⲧⲙ̄ ⲁ'ⲡⲗⲟⲅⲟⲥ ⲙ̄ⲡⲉⲓⲱⲧ ⲁⲩⲁⲣⲉϩ ⲉⲣⲟϥ ϩⲛ̄ ⲟⲩⲙⲉ

PH: ()⁰.

[2] Is ἐγένετο δὲ ἐν τῷ λέγειν αὐτὸν ταῦτα ἐπάρασά τις φωνήν in Q?

..

..

(1) Eine Frau in der Menge sprach zu ihm: Selig der Leib, der dich getragen hat, und die Brüste, die dich ernährt haben. (2) Er sprach zu [ihr]: Selig sind die, die das Wort des Vaters gehört haben (und) es wahrhaft beachtet haben.

(1) Une femme dans la foule lui dit: Bienheureux le ventre qui t'a porté et les seins qui t'ont nourri. (2) Il [lui] dit: Bienheureux ceux qui ont entendu la parole du Père (et) l'ont gardée en vérité.

Q 11:29-30 is to be found below, between Q 11:24-26,?27-28?, 16 and Q 11:31-32.

Q 11:16

Mark 8:11	Matt 16:1	Matt 12:38	Q 11:16
		^{0}{	^{0}{
		^{1}⸀	^{1}⸀
Καὶ	{Καὶ}	(Τότε	⟦()^{2}⟧
ἐξῆλθον	προσε{λθ}όντες	ἀπεκρίθησαν αὐτῷ)^{2}	
		(τινες)^{3}	(τινὲς)^{3}
		[ ]^{4}	⟦[δὲ]^{4}⟧
οἱ Φαρισαῖοι	{(οἱ Φαρισαῖ)οι}	(τῶν γραμματέων	( )^{5}
	(καὶ) Σαδδουκαῖοι	καὶ {Φαρισαί}ων)^{5}	
		(λέγ{οντες})^{2}·	⟦()^{2}⟧
καὶ ἤρξαντο			
συζητεῖν αὐτῷ,	[{πειράζοντες}]	[ ]^{6}	⟦[]^{6}⟧
		(διδάσκαλε,)^{7}	()^{7}
		^{8}⸀	^{8}⸀
ζητοῦντες	ἐπηρώτησαν	(θέλομεν)^{9}	[ἐ{ζήτουν}]^{9}
παρ' αὐτοῦ	[{αὐτὸ}]ν	(ἀπὸ σοῦ)^{10}	[{παρ' αὐτοῦ}]^{10}
		⸂^{8}	⸂^{8}
σημεῖον	[({σημεῖον})]	{σημεῖον}	{σημεῖον}
ἀπὸ τοῦ οὐρανοῦ,	[ἐ]κ {τοῦ [οὐρανοῦ]}	[ ]^{11}	⟦[]^{11}⟧
	ἐπιδεῖξαι αὐτοῖς	(ἰδεῖν)^{9}	()^{9}
		⸀ ⸂^{8}	⸀⸂^{8}
πειράζοντες αὐτόν.			
	.	.	.
		⸂^{1}	⸂^{1}
		}^{0}	}^{0}

IQP 1991: Q 11:⟦16⟧.
IQP 1991, JSK: Q 11:16 belongs between Q 11:15 and Q 11:17 {C}.

IQP 1991, JSK: ⟦[ἕτεροι]^{3} [δὲ]^{4} ()^{5} ()^{2}⟧.
IQP 1991: ^{8}⸀ {σημεῖον} ⟦[ἐξ {οὐρανοῦ}]^{11}⟧ ⸂^{8} [ἐ{ζήτουν}]^{9} ⟦[{}]^{10}⟧

^{0} Is Luke 11:16 par. Matt 12:38 in Q or from Mark?

^{1} The position of Q 11:16: After Q 11:15 and before Q 11:17 (Lukan order); or after Q 6:45 (Matt 12:35) and before Q 11:29 (Matt 12:39) (Matthean order).

^{2} Matthew's τότε ἀπεκρίθησαν αὐτῷ ... λέγοντες·.

^{3} Is the pronominal subject of the demand ἕτεροι (Luke) or τινες (Matthew)?

^{4} Luke's δέ.

^{5} Were those making the demand unidentified (Luke), or identified as ... τῶν γραμματέων καὶ Φαρισαίων (Matt 12:38), or ... τῶν Φαρισαίων (Matt 12:38 emended)?

Q

τινὲς ⟦δὲ⟧ .. ἐζήτουν παρ' αὐτοῦ σημεῖον.	⟦But⟧ some .. were demanding from him a sign.

Q 11:17 is to be found above, between Q 11:14-15 and Q 11:18-20.

Q 11:16

Luke 11:16	Lukan Doublet	Mark 8:11	Gospel of Thomas
°{			
¹⸂			
( )²		Καὶ ἐξῆλθον	
[ἕτεροι]³			
[δὲ]⁴			
( )⁵		οἱ Φαρισαῖοι	
( )²		καὶ ἤρξαντο συζητεῖν αὐτῷ	
[{πειράζοντες}]⁶			
( )⁷			
⸂ ⸃⁸		ζητοῦντες παρ' αὐτοῦ	
{σημεῖον}		σημεῖον	
[ἐξ {οὐρανοῦ}]¹¹		ἀπὸ τοῦ οὐρανοῦ,	
( )⁹			
⁸⸂			
[ἐ{ζήτουν}]⁹		πειράζοντες αὐτόν.	
[{παρ' αὐτοῦ}]¹⁰			
⸃⁸.			
⸃¹			
}⁰			

⸂⸃⁸. IQP 1991, JSK: ⟦([{}])¹⁰⟧.

6 Is Luke's πειράζοντες in Q or from Mark?
7 Matthew's διδάσκαλε.
8 Is the position of ἐζήτουν παρ' αὐτοῦ after σημεῖον (Luke), or is the position of the equivalent θέλομεν ἀπὸ σοῦ before σημεῖον (Matthew)?
9 Is the construction of the demand for a sign ἐζήτουν (Luke) or θέλομεν ... ἰδεῖν (Matthew)?
10 Luke's παρ' αὐτοῦ or Matthew's ἀπὸ σοῦ.
11 Luke's ἐξ οὐρανοῦ.

Einige .. ⟦aber⟧ forderten ein Zeichen von ihm.

⟦Mais⟧ certains .. demandaient un signe de sa part.

Q 11:17 is to be found above, between Q 11:14-15 and Q 11:18-20.

Q 11:29

Mark 8:12	Matt 16:2a, 4	Matt 12:39	Q 11:29
	[0]{	[0]{	[0]{
καὶ ἀναστενάξας		[ ][1] ⸉ ⸊[1] [ ][1]	[ ][1] ⸉ ⸊[1] [ ][1]
τῷ πνεύματι αὐτοῦ			
	16:2a (ὁ [δὲ] ἀποκριθεὶς	(ὁ)[1] ⸉δὲ⸊[1] (ἀποκριθεὶς)[1]	⟦(ὁ)[1]⟧ δὲ ( )1[2]
λέγει·	εἶπεν	(εἶπεν)[2]	⟦(εἶπεν)[2]⟧
	αὐτοῖς·	(αὐτοῖς)[3]·	( )[3]·
τί ἡ γενεὰ αὕτη		[{ }][4]	{[ἡ γενεὰ αὕτη]}[4]
	16:4 [{γενεὰ} πονηρὰ]	γενεὰ πονηρὰ	γενεὰ πονηρά
	καὶ μοιχαλὶς	(καὶ μοιχαλὶς)[5]	( )[5]
		[ ][4]	[ἐστιν][4]·
ζητεῖ σημεῖον;	[{σημεῖον}] ἐπι[{ζητεῖ},	{σημεῖον} (ἐπι)[6]{ζητεῖ},	{σημεῖον} ()[6]{ζητεῖ},
	καὶ {σημεῖον}	καὶ {σημεῖον}	καὶ {σημεῖον}
ἀμὴν λέγω ὑμῖν,			
εἰ δοθήσεται	οὐ {δοθήσεται}	οὐ {δοθήσεται}	οὐ {δοθήσεται}
τῇ γενεᾷ ταύτη	{αὐτῇ}	{αὐτῇ}	{αὐτῇ}
σημεῖον.	{εἰ} μὴ τὸ {σημεῖον} Ἰωνᾶ])	{εἰ} μὴ τὸ {σημεῖον} Ἰωνᾶ	{εἰ} μὴ τὸ {σημεῖον} Ἰωνᾶ
	.	(τοῦ προφήτου)[7].	()[7].
		}[0]	}[0]

IQP 1991: ( )[6] Luke = Q {D}.

JMR, PH, JSK: ( )[6] indeterminate.

[0] Is Luke 11:29 par. Matt 12:39 in Q or from Mark?

[1] Luke's τῶν δὲ ὄχλων ἐπαθροιζομένων or Matthew's ὁ δὲ ἀποκριθείς.

[2] Luke's ἤρξατο λέγειν or Matthew's εἶπεν.

[3] Matthew's αὐτοῖς.

Q

⟦ὁ⟧ δὲ .. ⟦εἶπεν⟧ .. · ἡ γενεὰ αὕτη γενεὰ πονηρὰ .. ἐστιν· σημεῖον ζητεῖ, καὶ σημεῖον οὐ δοθήσεται αὐτῇ εἰ μὴ τὸ σημεῖον Ἰωνᾶ.	But .. ⟦he said⟧ ..: This generation is an evil .. generation; it demands a sign, but a sign will not be given to it – except the sign of Jonah!

Q 11:29

Luke 11:29	Lukan Doublet	Mark 8:12	Gospel of Thomas
⁰{		καὶ ἀναστενάξας	
[Τῶν]¹ ˢδὲ˥¹ [ὄχλων		τῷ πνεύματι αὐτοῦ	
ἐπαθροιζομένων]¹			
( )¹ ˢ ˥¹ ( )¹			
[ἤρξατο {λέγ}ειν]²·		λέγει·	
( )³			
{[ἡ γενεὰ αὕτη]}⁴		τί ἡ γενεὰ αὕτη	
γενεὰ πονηρά			
( )⁵			
[ἐστιν]⁴·			
{σημεῖον} ( )⁶{ζητεῖ},		ζητεῖ σημεῖον;	
καὶ {σημεῖον}			
		ἀμὴν λέγω ὑμῖν,	
οὐ {δοθήσεται}		εἰ δοθήσεται	
{αὐτῇ}		τῇ γενεᾷ ταύτῃ	
{εἰ} μὴ τὸ {σημεῖον} Ἰωνᾶ		σημεῖον.	
( )⁷.			
}⁰			

4 Luke's ἡ γενεὰ αὕτη … ἐστιν.
5 Matthew's καὶ μοιχαλίς.
6 Matthew's ἐπι-.
7 Matthew's τοῦ προφήτου.

⟦Er⟧ aber .. ⟦sagte⟧ ..: Diese Generation ist eine böse .. Generation; sie fordert ein Zeichen, aber ein Zeichen wird ihr nicht gegeben werden, außer dem Zeichen des Jona!

Mais .. ⟦il dit⟧ ..: Cette génération est une génération méchante ..; elle demande un signe, mais il ne lui sera pas donné de signe, si ce n'est le signe de Jonas!

Q 11:30

Markan Parallel	Matthean Doublet	Matt 12:40	Q 11:30
		[ ][1]ὥσ(περ)[1] γὰρ	⟦[καθ][1]⟧ὡς⟦()[1]⟧ γὰρ
		(ἦν)[2] Ἰωνᾶς	[ἐγένετο][2] Ἰωνᾶς
		(ἐν τῇ κοιλίᾳ τοῦ κήτους	()[3]
		τρεῖς ἡμέρας	
		καὶ τρεῖς νύκτας)[3],	
		[ ][4]	[τοῖς Νινευίταις σημεῖον][4],
		οὕτως ἔσται [ ][5]	οὕτως ἔσται ⟦[καὶ][5]⟧
		ὁ υἱὸς τοῦ ἀνθρώπου	ὁ υἱὸς τοῦ ἀνθρώπου
		(ἐν τῇ καρδίᾳ τῆς γῆς τρεῖς	()[3]
		ἡμέρας καὶ τρεῖς νύκτας)[3].	
		[ ][6]	[τῇ γενεᾷ ταύτῃ][6].
		⸂11:29[1]	⸂11:29[1]

IQP 1991: [ ][1]ως( )[1].

[1] Luke's καθώς or Matthew's ὥσπερ.

[2] Luke's ἐγένετο or Matthew's ἦν.

[3] Matthew's ἐν τῇ κοιλίᾳ τοῦ κήτους τρεῖς ἡμέρας καὶ τρεῖς νύκτας ... ἐν τῇ καρδίᾳ τῆς γῆς τρεῖς ἡμέρας καὶ τρεῖς νύκτας.

Q

⟦καθ⟧ὼς γὰρ ἐγένετο Ἰωνᾶς τοῖς Νινευίταις σημεῖον, οὕτως ἔσται ⟦καὶ⟧ ὁ υἱὸς τοῦ ἀνθρώπου τῇ γενεᾷ ταύτῃ.

For as Jonah became to the Ninevites a sign, so ⟦also⟧ will the son of humanity be to this generation.

Q 11:30

Luke 11:30	Lukan Doublet	Markan Parallel	Gospel of Thomas
[καθ][1]ὼς( )[1] γὰρ [ἐγένετο][2] Ἰωνᾶς ( )[3] [τοῖς Νινευίταις σημεῖον][4], οὕτως ἔσται [καὶ][5] ὁ υἱὸς τοῦ ἀνθρώπου ( )[3] [τῇ γενεᾷ ταύτῃ][6]. ˀ11:29[1]			

[4] Luke's τοῖς Νινευίταις σημεῖον.

[5] Luke's καί.

[6] Luke's τῇ γενεᾷ ταύτῃ.

Denn wie Jona für die Niniviten zum Zeichen wurde, so wird es ⟦auch⟧ der Menschensohn für diese Generation sein.

Car de même que Jonas devint un signe pour les Ninivites, de même le fils de l'homme le sera ⟦aussi⟧ pour cette génération.

Q 11:31

Markan Parallel	Matthean Doublet	Matt 12:42	Q 11:31
		[1]⸉ [2]⸉βασίλισσα νότου ἐγερθήσεται ἐν τῇ κρίσει μετὰ [ ][3] τῆς γενεᾶς ταύτης καὶ κατακρινεῖ αὐτ(ήν)[3], ὅτι ἦλθεν ἐκ τῶν περάτων τῆς γῆς ἀκοῦσαι τὴν σοφίαν Σολομῶνος, καὶ ἰδοὺ πλεῖον Σολομῶνος ὧδε. ⸊[2]⇒Matt 12:41 ⸊[1]⇒Matt 12:41	[1]⸉ [2]⸉βασίλισσα νότου ἐγερθήσεται ἐν τῇ κρίσει μετὰ [][3] τῆς γενεᾶς ταύτης καὶ κατακρινεῖ αὐτ(ήν)[3], ὅτι ἦλθεν ἐκ τῶν περάτων τῆς γῆς ἀκοῦσαι τὴν σοφίαν Σολομῶνος, καὶ ἰδοὺ πλεῖον Σολομῶνος ὧδε. ⸊[2]⇒Q 11:32 ⸊[1]⇒Q 11:32

[1] The position of Q 11:31-32 in Q: After Q 11:30 and before Q 11:33 (Lukan order); or after Q 11:30 (Matt 12:40) and before Q 11:24 (Matt 12:43) (Matthean order).

[2] Is Q 11:31 before (Luke) or after (Matthew) Q 12:32?

Q

βασίλισσα νότου ἐγερθήσεται ἐν τῇ κρίσει μετὰ τῆς γενεᾶς ταύτης καὶ κατακρινεῖ αὐτήν, ὅτι ἦλθεν ἐκ τῶν περάτων τῆς γῆς ἀκοῦσαι τὴν σοφίαν Σολομῶνος, καὶ ἰδοὺ πλεῖον Σολομῶνος ὧδε.

The queen of the South will be raised at the judgment with this generation and condemn it, for she came from the ends of the earth to listen to the wisdom of Solomon, and look, something more than Solomon is here!

Q 11:31

Luke 11:31	Lukan Doublet	Markan Parallel	Gospel of Thomas
¹∫ ²∫βασίλισσα νότου ἐγερθήσεται ἐν τῇ κρίσει μετὰ [τῶν ἀνδρῶν]³ τῆς γενεᾶς ταύτης καὶ κατακρινεῖ αὐτ[ούς]³, ὅτι ἦλθεν ἐκ τῶν περάτων τῆς γῆς ἀκοῦσαι τὴν σοφίαν Σολομῶνος, καὶ ἰδοὺ πλεῖον Σολομῶνος ὧδε. ι²⇒Luke 11:32 ι¹⇒Luke 11:32			

³ Luke's τῶν ἀνδρῶν τῆς γενεᾶς ταύτης ... αὐτούς or Matthew's τῆς γενεᾶς ταύτης ... αὐτήν.

Die Königin des Südens wird beim Gericht zusammen mit dieser Generation auferweckt werden, und sie wird sie verurteilen; denn sie kam von den Enden der Erde, um die Weisheit Salomos zu hören, und siehe, mehr als Salomo ist hier.

Lors du jugement, la reine du Midi se lèvera avec cette génération et la condamnera, parce qu'elle est venue des confins de la terre pour écouter la sagesse de Salomon, et voilà qu'ici, il y a plus que Salomon.

Q 11:32

Markan Parallel	Matthean Doublet	Matt 12:41	Q 11:32
		ἄνδρες Νινευῖται ἀναστήσονται ἐν τῇ κρίσει μετὰ τῆς γενεᾶς ταύτης καὶ κατακρινοῦσιν αὐτήν, ὅτι μετενόησαν εἰς τὸ κήρυγμα Ἰωνᾶ, καὶ ἰδοὺ πλεῖον Ἰωνᾶ ὧδε. ≀ Matt 12:42² ≀ Matt 12:42¹	ἄνδρες Νινευῖται ἀναστήσονται ἐν τῇ κρίσει μετὰ τῆς γενεᾶς ταύτης καὶ κατακρινοῦσιν αὐτήν, ὅτι μετενόησαν εἰς τὸ κήρυγμα Ἰωνᾶ, καὶ ἰδοὺ πλεῖον Ἰωνᾶ ὧδε. ≀ Q 11:31² ≀ Q 11:31¹

Q

ἄνδρες Νινευῖται ἀναστήσονται ἐν τῇ κρίσει μετὰ τῆς γενεᾶς ταύτης καὶ κατακρινοῦσιν αὐτήν, ὅτι μετενόησαν εἰς τὸ κήρυγμα Ἰωνᾶ, καὶ ἰδοὺ πλεῖον Ἰωνᾶ ὧδε.

Ninevite men will arise at the judgment with this generation and condemn it. For they repented at the announcement of Jonah, and look, something more than Jonah is here!

Q 11:32

Luke 11:32	Lukan Doublet	Markan Parallel	Gospel of Thomas
ἄνδρες Νινευῖται ἀναστήσονται ἐν τῇ κρίσει μετὰ τῆς γενεᾶς ταύτης καὶ κατακρινοῦσιν αὐτήν· ὅτι μετενόησαν εἰς τὸ κήρυγμα Ἰωνᾶ, καὶ ἰδοὺ πλεῖον Ἰωνᾶ ὧδε. ꞁ Luke 11:32² ꞁ Luke 11:32¹			

Die Männer von Ninive werden beim Gericht zusammen mit dieser Generation auferstehen, und sie werden sie verurteilen; denn sie sind auf die Predigt des Jona hin umgekehrt, und siehe, mehr als Jona ist hier.

Lors du jugement, les Ninivites se relèveront avec cette génération et la condamneront, parce qu'ils se sont convertis à la prédication de Jonas, et voilà qu'ici, il y a plus que Jonas.

Q 11:33

Mark 4:21	Matthean Doublet	Matt 5:15	Q 11:33
Καὶ ἔλεγεν αὐτοῖς·		0{	0{
μήτι ἔρχεται		1⸂οὐδὲ[ ]2	1⸂οὐδε[ὶς]2
ὁ λύχνος		⸂ ⸃3	⸂⸃3
		(καίουσιν)2.4.5	(καί)4<ει>2.5
ἵνα		⸂{λύχνο}ν⸃3	⸂{λύχνο}ν⸃3
		(καὶ)5	(καὶ)5
		⸂ ⸃6	⸂ ⸃6
ὑπὸ τὸν μόδιον			
τεθῇ		{τ}ι{θ}(έα)2σιν	{τ}ί{θ[η]2}σιν
		(αὐτὸν)7	(αὐτὸν)7
ἢ ὑπὸ τὴν κλίνην;		6⸂ ({ὑπὸ τὸν μόδιον})8 ⸃6	6⸂ ⟦[εἰς κρύπτην]8⟧ ⸃6
οὐχ ἵνα ἐπὶ		ἀλλ' {ἐπὶ	ἀλλ' {ἐπὶ
τὴν λυχνίαν τεθῇ;		τὴν λυχνίαν},	τὴν λυχνίαν},
		(καὶ λάμπει πᾶσιν τοῖς	⟦(καὶ λάμπει πᾶσιν τοῖς
		ἐν τῇ οἰκίᾳ)9. ⸃1	ἐν τῇ οἰκίᾳ)9⟧. ⸃1
		}0	}0

Text Critical Note (see the discussion in the front matter): In Luke 11:33 οὐδὲ ὑπὸ τὸν μόδιον is absent in 𝔓45.75 L Γ Ξ 070 *f*1 700* 1241 2542 *pc* sy[s] sa, but is present in ℵ A B C D W Θ Ψ *f*13 𝔐 latt sy(c.p).h (Cl).

IQP 1991: [ ]8; PH: ⟦({ὑπὸ τὸν μόδιον})8⟧.

IQP 1991: [( )]9.

0 Is Luke 11:33 par. Matt 5:15 in Q or from Mark?

1 The position of Q 11:33 in Q: After Q 11:32 and before Q 11:34 (Luke 11:33); or after Q 14:33-35 (Matt 5:13) and before Q 16:17 (Matt 5:18) (Matthean order).

2 οὐδεὶς … ἅψας … τίθησιν (Luke) or οὐδὲ καίουσιν… τιθέασιν (Matthew).

3 The position of λύχνον before (Luke) or after (Matthew) the verb of alluminating.

Q

οὐδεὶς καί<ει> λύχνον καὶ τίθησιν αὐτὸν ⟦εἰς κρύπτην⟧ ἀλλ' ἐπὶ τὴν λυχνίαν, ⟦καὶ λάμπει πᾶσιν τοῖς ἐν τῇ οἰκίᾳ⟧.

No one light<s> a lamp and puts it ⟦in a hidden place⟧, but on the lampstand, ⟦and it gives light for everyone in the house⟧.

Gos. Thom. 33.2-3 (Nag Hammadi II 2)

(2) Οὐδεὶς γὰρ λύχνον ἅψας τίθησιν ὑπὸ τὸν μόδιον οὐδὲ εἰς κρύπτην, (3) ἀλλ' ἐπὶ τὴν λυχνίαν τίθησιν, ἵνα πάντες οἱ εἰσπορευόμενοι καὶ οἱ ἐκπορευόμενοι βλέπωσιν τὸ φῶς αὐτοῦ.

(2) For no one, kindling a lamp, puts it under a bushel, nor does one put it in a hidden place. (3) Rather, one puts it on the lampstand, so that everyone who comes in and goes out will see its light.

Q 11:33

Luke 11:33	**Luke 8:16**	**Mark 4:21**	***Gos. Thom.* 33.2-3**
[0]{		Καὶ ἔλεγεν αὐτοῖς·	
[1]⸀Οὐδε[ὶς][2]	[(Οὐδε)ὶς] δὲ	μήτι ἔρχεται	33.2 ⲙⲁⲣⲉ ⲗⲁⲁⲩ'
⸀{λύχνο}ν⸆[3]	[({λύχνο}ν)]	ὁ λύχνος	ⲅⲁⲣ ϫⲉⲣⲉ
[ἅψας][2.4.5]	[ἅψας]		ϩⲏⲃⲥ
⸀ ⸆[3]			
( )[5]		ἵνα	
[6]⸀ [εἰς κρύπτην][8] ⸆[6]			
	καλύπτει (αὐτὸν) σκεύει		ⲛ̄ϥ'ⲕⲁⲁϥ' ϩⲁ ⲙⲁⲁϫⲉ
{τ}ί{θ[η][2]}σιν			
( )[7]	{ἢ ὑπο}κάτω {κλίνη}ς	ὑπὸ τὸν μόδιον	
⸀οὐδὲ ὑπὸ τὸν μόδιον⸆[6]	{τ}ί{θ[η]}σιν,	τεθῇ	ⲟⲩⲇⲉ
ἀλλ' {ἐπὶ			ⲙⲁϥⲕⲁⲁϥ'
τὴν λυχνίαν},		ἢ ὑπὸ τὴν κλίνην;	ϩⲙ̄ ⲙⲁ ⲉϥϩⲏⲡ'
[ἵνα οἱ εἰσπορευόμενοι	[(ἀλλ'	οὐχ ἵνα	33.3 ⲁⲗⲗⲁ
	{ἐπὶ})]	ἐπὶ	ⲉϣⲁⲣⲉϥⲕⲁⲁϥ' ϩⲓϫⲛ̄
	[({λυχνία})]ς [{τ}ί{θη}σιν],	τὴν λυχνίαν τεθῇ;	ⲧⲗⲩⲭⲛⲓⲁ
	[ἵνα		ϫⲉⲕⲁⲁⲥ ⲟⲩⲟⲛ ⲛⲓⲙ'
	οἱ εἰσπορευόμενοι		ⲉⲧⲃⲏⲕ' ⲉϩⲟⲩⲛ
			ⲁⲩⲱ ⲉⲧⲛ̄ⲛⲏⲩ ⲉⲃⲟⲗ
τὸ φῶς βλέπωσιν][9]. ⸆[1]	βλέπωσιν] [τὸ φῶς].		ⲉⲩⲛⲁⲛⲁⲩ ⲁⲡⲉϥⲟⲩⲟⲉⲓⲛ
}[0]			

Text Critical Note (see the discussion in the front matter): In Luke 11:33 φέγγος is present in 𝔓[45] A K L W Γ Δ Ψ 565 700 *pm*, but φῶς in 𝔓[75] ℵ B C D Θ 070 $f^{1.13}$ 33 892 1241 1424 2542 *pm*.

[4] The choice of verbs for illuminating, ἅπτω (Luke) or καίω (Matthew).

[5] Luke's hypotactic form of the verb ἅψας or Matthew's paratactic form καίουσιν (or: καί<ει>)… καί.

[6] The reference to the false location of the light before (Luke) or after (Matthew) τίθημι. (Luke 11:13 does not include οὐδὲ ὑπὸ τὸν μόδιον. See the Text Critical Note.)

[7] Matthew's αὐτόν.

[8] Luke's εἰς κρύπτην or Matthew's ὑπὸ τὸν μόδιον.

[9] Luke's ἵνα οἱ εἰσπορευόμενοι τὸ φῶς/φέγγος βλέπωσιν or Matthew's καὶ λάμπει πᾶσιν τοῖς ἐν τῇ οἰκίᾳ.

Keiner zünde<t> eine Lampe an und stellt sie ⟦an einen verborgenen Platz⟧, sondern auf den Leuchter, ⟦und sie leuchtet allen im Haus⟧.

Personne n'allum<e> une lampe et la place ⟦dans une cachette⟧, mais sur le lampadaire, ⟦et elle brille pour tous ceux qui sont dans la maison⟧.

(2) Denn keiner zündet eine Lampe an (und) stellt sie unter ein Getreidemaß, auch stellt er sie nicht an einen verborgenen Platz. (3) Vielmehr stellt er sie auf den Leuchter, damit ein jeder, der hereinkommt und herausgeht, ihr Licht sieht.

(2) Car personne n'allume une lampe (et) la place sous le boisseau, ni ne la place dans une cachette. (3) Mais c'est sur le lampadaire qu'il la place, si bien que quiconque entre et sort voit sa lumière.

Q 11:34

Markan Parallel	Matthean Doublet	Matt 6:22-23a	Q 11:34
		6:22 [1]⸀ Ὁ λύχνος τοῦ σώματός ἐστιν ὁ ὀφθαλμός [ ][2]. (ἐ)[3]ὰν (οὖν)[4] ⸀ᾖ⸁[5] ὁ ὀφθαλμός σου ἁπλοῦς ⸀ ⸁[5], [ ][6] ὅλον τὸ σῶμά σου φωτεινὸν ἔστ(αι)[7]· **6:23a** (ἐ)[3]ὰν δὲ (ὁ ὀφθαλμός σου)[8] πονηρὸς ᾖ, [ ][6] (ὅλον)[8] τὸ σῶμά σου σκοτεινὸν (ἔσται)[7]. ⸁[1]⇒Matt 6:23b	[1]⸀ ὁ λύχνος τοῦ σώματός ἐστιν ὁ ὀφθαλμός [][2]. [( )][3]αν ()[4] ⸀ ⸁[5] ὁ ὀφθαλμός σου ἁπλοῦς ⸀ᾖ⸁[5] [][6] ὅλον τὸ σῶμά σου φωτεινόν ἐστ⟦[ιν][7]⟧· [( )][3]ὰν δὲ (ὁ ὀφθαλμός σου)[8] πονηρὸς ᾖ, [][6] (ὅλον)[8] τὸ σῶμά σου σκοτεινόν ⟦()[7]⟧. ⸁[1]⇒Q 11:35

IQP 1991: [ ][2], not in Q {D}.

IQP 1991: [ὅτ][3]αν … [ἐπ][3]άν.

[1] The position of Q 11:34-35 in Q: After Q 11:33 and before Q 11:?39a?, 42 (Lukan order); or after Q 12:34 (Matt 6:21) and before Q 16:13 (Matt 6:24) (Matthean order).

[2] Luke's σού.

[3] Luke's ὅταν … ἐπάν or Matthew's ἐὰν … ἐάν.

Q

ὁ λύχνος τοῦ σώματός ἐστιν ὁ ὀφθαλμός. …αν ὁ ὀφθαλμός σου ἁπλοῦς ᾖ, ὅλον τὸ σῶμά σου φωτεινόν ἐστ⟦ιν⟧· …ὰν δὲ ὁ ὀφθαλμός σου πονηρὸς ᾖ, ὅλον τὸ σῶμά σου σκοτεινόν.

The lamp of the body is the eye. If your eye is generous, your whole body ⟦is⟧ radiant; but if your eye is jaundiced, your whole body «is» dark.

Gos. Thom. 24.3 (Nag Hammadi II 2)

φῶς ἐστιν ἐν ἀνθρώπῳ φωτεινῷ, καὶ φωτίζει τῷ κόσμῳ ὅλῳ· ἐὰν μὴ φωτίζῃ, σκοτεινός ἐστιν.

Light exists inside a person of light, and he[1] shines on the whole world. If he does not shine, there is darkness.

[1] Also possible is the translation: it shines … . If it does not shine… .

Gos. Thom. 24.3 (P. Oxy. 655)

[φῶς ἐσ]τιν [ἐν ἀνθρώπῳ φ]ωτεινῷ, [καὶ φωτίζει τῷ κ]όσμῳ [ὅλῳ· ἐὰν μὴ φωτίζ]ῃ, [τότε σκοτεινός ἐ]στιν.

[Light] exists [inside a person] of light, [and he shines on the whole] world. [If he does not shine, then] there is [darkness].

Q 11:34

Luke 11:34	Lukan Doublet	Markan Parallel	*Gos. Thom.* 24.3
[1]⸂			
Ὁ λύχνος τοῦ σώματός			ⲟⲩⲛ̄ ⲟⲩⲟⲉⲓⲛ' ϣⲟⲟⲡ'
ἐστιν ὁ ὀφθαλμός [σου][2].			ⲙ̄ⲫⲟⲩⲛ ⲛ̄ⲛⲟⲩⲣⲙ̄ⲟⲩⲟⲉⲓⲛ
[ὅτ][3]αν			
( )[4]			
⸂ ⸃[5] ὁ ὀφθαλμός σου			
ἁπλοῦς ⸂ᾖ⸃[5],			
[καὶ][6] ὅλον τὸ σῶμά σου			ⲁⲩⲱ ϥⲣ̄ ⲟⲩⲟⲉⲓⲛ
φωτεινὸν ἐστ[ιν][7]·			ⲉⲡⲕⲟⲥⲙⲟⲥ ⲧⲏⲣϥ'
[ἐπ][3]ὰν δὲ			ⲉϥⲧⲙ̄ⲣ ⲟⲩⲟⲉⲓⲛ'
( )[8]			
πονηρὸς ᾖ, [καὶ][6]			
( )[8] τὸ σῶμά σου			
σκοτεινόν ( )[7].			ⲟⲩⲕⲁⲕⲉ ⲡⲉ
⸃[1]⇒Luke 11:35			

JMR, PH, JSK: ⸂ ⸃[5] indeterminate.

[4] Matthew's οὖν.

[5] The position of ᾖ after (Luke) or before (Matthew) ὁ ὀφθαλμός σου ἁπλοῦς.

[6] Luke's καὶ … καί.

[7] Luke's ἐστιν or Matthew's ἔσται *bis*.

[8] Matthew's ὁ ὀφθαλμός σου … ὅλον.

Die Lampe des Leibes ist das Auge. Wenn dein Auge lauter ist, ⟦ist⟧ dein ganzer Leib licht; wenn aber dein Auge böse ist, «ist» dein ganzer Leib finster.

La lampe du corps, c'est l'oeil. Si ton œil est sain, ton corps tout entier ⟦est⟧ lumineux; mais si ton œil est malade, ton corps tout entier «est» ténébreux.

Es existiert Licht im Inneren eines Lichtmenschen, und er[2] erleuchtet die ganze Welt. Wenn er nicht leuchtet, ist er finster.

[2] Möglich ist auch die Übersetzung: es erleuchtet … . Wenn es nicht leuchtet… .

Il y a de la lumière à l'intérieur d'un homme de lumière et il[3] illumine le monde entier. S'il n'illumine pas, ce sont les ténèbres.

[3] Autre traduction possible: elle illumine … . Si elle n'illumine pas … .

Es existiert [Licht im Inneren eines] Licht[menschen, und er erleuchtet die ganze] Welt. [Wenn er nicht leuchtet, dann] ist [er finster].

Il y a [de la lumière à l'intérieur d'un homme] de lumière [et il brille pour le] monde [entier. Si] elle [ne brille pas, alors] ce sont [les ténèbres].

Q 11:35

Markan Parallel	Matthean Doublet	Matt 6:23b	Q 11:35
		(εἰ)[1] οὖν [ ][1] τὸ φῶς τὸ ἐν σοὶ σκότος ἐστίν, (τὸ σκότος πόσον)[1]. ↱Matt 6:22-23a[1]	(εἰ)[1] οὖν [][1] τὸ φῶς τὸ ἐν σοὶ σκότος ἐστίν, (τὸ σκότος πόσον)[1]. ↱Q 11:34[1]

[1] Luke's σκόπει … μή or Matthew's εἰ …, τὸ σκότος πόσον.

Q

εἰ οὖν τὸ φῶς τὸ ἐν σοὶ σκότος ἐστίν, τὸ σκότος πόσον.	So if the light within you is dark, how great «must» the darkness «be»!

Q 11:35

Luke 11:35	Lukan Doublet	Markan Parallel	Gospel of Thomas
[σκόπει][1] οὖν [μὴ][1] τὸ φῶς τὸ ἐν σοὶ σκότος ἐστίν ( )[1]. ⸀Luke 11:34[1]			

Wenn also das Licht in dir Finsternis ist, wie groß «ist» die Finsternis!

Si donc la lumière qui est en toi est ténèbres, combien grandes «sont» les ténèbres!

Q 11:⟦~~36~~⟧

Markan Parallel	Matthean Doublet	Matthew	Q 11:⟦~~36~~⟧
		[ ]⁰	⟦[]⁰⟧

IQP 1991: ⟦[«»]⁰⟧.

PH: []⁰.

⁰ Is Luke 11:36 in Q?

Q 11:⟦~~36~~⟧

Luke 11:36	Lukan Doublet	Markan Parallel	Gospel of Thomas
[εἰ οὖν τὸ σῶμά σου ὅλον φωτεινόν, μὴ ἔχον μέρος τι σκοτεινόν, ἔσται φωτεινὸν ὅλον ὡς ὅταν ὁ λύχνος τῇ ἀστραπῇ φωτίζῃ σε.]⁰			

Q 11:?39a?

Mark 12:37b-38a	Matthean Doublet	Matt 23:1-2a	Q 11:?39a?
		0/	0/
		1ʃ	1ʃ
12:37b Καὶ ὁ πολὺς ὄχλος ἤκουεν αὐτοῦ ἡδέως.		**23:1** ʃ ʅ2	2ʃ [( )]3 ʅ2
12:38a Καὶ ἐν τῇ διδαχῇ αὐτοῦ		(Τότε)4	[( )]4
		ὁ (Ἰησοῦς)5	~~ὁ~~ [( )]5
		2ʃ (ἐλάλησεν)3 ʅ2	ʃ ʅ2
		(τοῖς {ὄχλο}ις καὶ τοῖς μαθηταῖς αὐτοῦ	[( )]6
ἔλεγεν·		**23:2a** {λέγ}ων)6.	
		ʅ1⇒Matt 23:29-32	ʅ1⇒Q 11:47-48
		\0	\0

IQP 1991: ὁ δὲ ε⟦ἶπ⟧εν·. (This reading is based on Luke 11:46a.)

0 Is some quotation formula in Q?
1 The position of the Woes in Q: After Q 11:35, ⟦~~36~~⟧ and before Q 12:2 (Lukan order); or after Q 14:15-24 (Matt 22:1-14) and before Q 13:34-35 (Matt 23:37-39) (Matthean order).
2 The position of the verb before (Luke) or after (Matthew) the subject.

Q

..	..

Q 11:39b, ⟦~~40~~⟧, 41 is to be found below, between Q 11:?39a?, 42 and Q 11:43-44.

Q 11:?39a?

Luke 11:39a	Luke 20:45	Mark 7:6a	Gospel of Thomas
⁰/	Ἀκούοντος [δὲ]		
¹∫	παντὸς τοῦ λαοῦ		
²∫ [{εἶπεν}]³ ⸂²	[{εἶπεν}]	Ὁ δὲ εἶπεν	
∫ [δὲ]⁴ ⸂³			
ὁ [κύριος]⁵			
∫ ⸂²			
[πρὸς {αὐτό}ν]⁶·	(τοῖς μαθηταῖς {αὐτο}ῦ)·	αὐτοῖς·	
⸂¹⇒Luke 11:47-48			
\⁰			

³ Luke's εἶπεν or Matthew's ἐλάλησεν.
⁴ Luke's postpositive δέ or Matthew's τότε.
⁵ Luke's κύριος or Matthew's Ἰησοῦς.
⁶ Luke's πρὸς αὐτόν or Matthew's τοῖς ὄχλοις καὶ τοῖς μαθηταῖς αὐτοῦ λέγων.

..

..

Q 11:39b, ⟦~~40~~⟧, 41 is to be found below, between Q 11:?39a?, 42 and Q 11:43-44.

Q 11:42

Markan Parallel	Matthean Doublet	Matt 23:23	Q 11:42
		1⸀	1⸀
		[ ]² Οὐαὶ ὑμῖν,	[]² οὐαὶ ὑμῖν
		(γραμματεῖς καὶ)³	()³
		[ ]⁴ Φαρισαῖοι[ ]⁴	⟦[τοῖς]⁴⟧ Φαρισαίοι⟦[ς]⁴⟧
		(ὑποκριταί)⁵,	()⁵,
		ὅτι ἀποδεκατοῦτε	ὅτι ἀποδεκατοῦτε
		τὸ ἡδύοσμον	τὸ ἡδύοσμον
		καὶ τὸ (ἄνηθ)⁶ον	καὶ τὸ (ἄνηθ)⁶ον
		καὶ (τὸ κύμι)⁷νον	καὶ (τὸ κύμι)⁷νον
		καὶ (ἀφήκατε)⁸	καὶ ⟦(ἀφήκατε)⁸⟧
		(τὰ βαρύτερα τοῦ νόμου)⁹,	()⁹
		τὴν κρίσιν καὶ	τὴν κρίσιν καὶ
		τ(ὸ ἔλεος καὶ τὴν πίστιν)¹⁰.	τ(ὸ ἔλεος καὶ τὴν πίστιν)¹⁰.
		ταῦτα δὲ ἔδει ποιῆσαι	ταῦτα δὲ ἔδει ποιῆσαι
		κἀκεῖνα μὴ (ἀφιέ)¹¹ναι.	κἀκεῖνα μὴ ⟦(ἀφιέ)¹¹⟧ναι.
		⸃1	⸃1

Text Critical Note (see the discussion in the front matter): In Luke 11:42 ταῦτα δὲ ἔδει ποιῆσαι κἀκεῖνα μὴ παρεῖναι is absent in D (b [but placed after verse 41]); ταῦτα ἔδει ποιῆσαι κἀκεῖνα μὴ παρεῖναι is present in ℵ* A W f^1 𝔐 sy^s bo^mss; ταῦτα δὲ ἔδει ποιῆσαι κἀκεῖνα μὴ ἀφιέ-

IQP 1991: [ἀλλὰ]² οὐαὶ ὑμῖν ()³ [τοῖς]⁴ Φαρισαίοι[ς]⁴.
IQP 1991: τὸ ⟦(ἄνηθ)⁶⟧ον καὶ ⟦(τὸ κύμι)⁷⟧νον καὶ [παρέρχεσθε]⁸.
PH: (ἀφήκατε)⁸; JMR, JSK: ⟦(ἀφήκατε)⁸⟧.
IQP 1991: τ[ὴν ἀγάπην τοῦ θεοῦ]¹⁰.

¹ The position of Q 11:42 in Q: After Q 11:39b, 41 and before Q 11:43 (Lukan order); or after Q 11:52 (Matt 23:13) and before Q 11:39b, 41 (Matt 23:25-26) (Matthean order).

² Luke's ἀλλά.

³ Matthew's γραμματεῖς καί.

⁴ Luke's τοῖς Φαρισαίοις or Matthew's Φαρισαῖοι.

⁵ Matthew's ὑποκριταί.

Q

οὐαὶ ὑμῖν ⟦τοῖς⟧ Φαρισαίοι⟦ς⟧, ὅτι ἀποδεκατοῦτε τὸ ἡδύοσμον καὶ τὸ ἄνηθον καὶ τὸ κύμινον καὶ ⟦ἀφήκατε⟧ τὴν κρίσιν καὶ τὸ ἔλεος καὶ τὴν πίστιν· ταῦτα δὲ ἔδει ποιῆσαι κἀκεῖνα μὴ ⟦ἀφιέ⟧ναι.

Woe to you, Pharisees, for you tithe mint and dill and cumin, and ⟦give up⟧ justice and mercy and faithfulness. But these one had to do, without giving up those.

Q 11:43-44 is to be found below, between Q 11:?39a?, 42, 39b, ⟦~~40~~⟧, 41 and Q 11:46b, 52, 47-51.

Q 11:42

Luke 11:42	Lukan Doublet	Markan Parallel	Gospel of Thomas
¹ʃ [ἀλλὰ]² οὐαὶ ὑμῖν ( )³ [τοῖς]⁴ Φαρισαίοι[ς]⁴ ( )⁵, ὅτι ἀποδεκατοῦτε τὸ ἡδύοσμον καὶ τὸ [πήγαν]⁶ον καὶ [πᾶν λάχα]⁷νον καὶ [παρέρχεσθε]⁸ ( )⁹ τὴν κρίσιν καὶ τ[ὴν ἀγάπην τοῦ θεοῦ]¹⁰. ταῦτα δὲ ἔδει ποιῆσαι κἀκεῖνα μὴ [παρεῖ]¹¹ναι. ʅ¹			

ναι is in B[2] C W Θ Ψ 0108 *f*[1] 33 𝔐; ταῦτα δὲ ἔδει ποιῆσαι κἀκεῖνα μὴ ἀφεῖναι is in 𝔓[45] א* 892 *pc*; ταῦτα δὲ ἔδει ποιῆσαι κἀκεῖνα μὴ παραφιέναι is in A; and ταῦτα δὲ ἔδει ποιῆσαι κἀκεῖνα μὴ παρεῖναι is in 𝔓[75] א[1] B* L *f*[13] *pc* lat sy[(c).p.h].

JSK: τ⟦(ὸ ἔλεος καὶ τὴν πίστιν)¹⁰⟧.
IQP 1991: [παρεῖ]¹¹ναι.

JSK: ⟦[παρεῖ]¹¹⟧ναι.

⁶ Luke's πήγανον or Matthew's ἄνηθον.
⁷ Luke's πᾶν λάχανον or Matthew's τὸ κύμινον.
⁸ Luke's παρέρχεσθε or Matthew's ἀφήκατε.

⁹ Matthew's τὰ βαρύτερα τοῦ νόμου.
¹⁰ Luke's τὴν ἀγάπην τοῦ θεοῦ or Matthew's τὸ ἔλεος καὶ τὴν πίστιν.

Wehe euch, ⟦den⟧ Pharisäern, denn ihr gebt den Zehnten von der Minze und vom Dill und vom Kümmel und ⟦lässt⟧ das Recht und die Barmherzigkeit und die Treue ⟦außer Acht⟧. Dies aber wäre zu tun und jenes nicht außer Acht zu lassen.

Malheur à vous, Pharisiens, parce que vous offrez la dîme de la menthe, de l'aneth et du cumin et vous ⟦négligez⟧ la justice, la miséricorde et la fidélité. Mais il fallait mettre en pratique celles-ci, sans négliger pour autant ceux-là.

Q 11:43-44 is to be found below, between Q 11:?39a?, 42, 39b, ⟦~~40~~⟧, 41 and Q 11:46b, 52, 47-51.

Q 11:?39a?, 42, 39b, ⟦~~40~~⟧, 41, 43-44

Q 11:39b

Markan Parallel	Matthean Doublet	Matt 23:25	Q 11:39b
		^{1}ʃ	^{1}ʃ
		(Οὐαὶ)^{2} ὑμ(ῖν,)^{2}	(οὐαὶ)^{2} ὑμ(ῖν,)^{2}
		(γραμματεῖς καὶ)^{3}	()^{3}
		[ ]^{5}	⟦<τ>^{4}[οἱ]^{4}<ς>^{4}⟧
		Φαρισαῖοι^{4}	Φαρισαίοι⟦<ς>^{4}⟧
		(ὑποκριταί)^{5},	()^{5},
		(ὅτι)^{2}	(ὅτι)^{2}
		ʃκαθαρίζετεʅ^{2}	ʃκαθαρίζετεʅ^{2}
		τὸ ἔξωθεν τοῦ ποτηρίου	τὸ ἔξωθεν τοῦ ποτηρίου
		καὶ τ(ῆς)^{6} π(αροψίδ)^{6}ος	καὶ τ(ῆς)^{6} π(αροψίδ)^{6}ος
		ʃ ʅ^{2},	ʃʅ^{2},
		ʃ [ ]^{7} ʅ^{7}	ʃ ⟦[]^{7}⟧ ʅ^{7}
		ἔσωθεν	ἔσωθεν
		ʃδὲʅ^{7}	ʃδὲʅ^{7}
		[ ]^{7} γέμ(ουσιν)^{7}	⟦[]^{7}⟧ γέμ⟦(ουσιν)^{7}⟧
		(ἐξ)^{8} ἁρπαγῆς	(ἐξ)^{8} ἁρπαγῆς
		καὶ (ἀκρασ)^{9}ίας.	καὶ (ἀκρασ)^{9}ίας.
		ʅ^{1}⇒ Matt 23:26b	ʅ^{1}⇒ Q 11:41

IQP 1991: <τ>^{4}[οἱ]^{4}<ς>^{4} Φαρισαίοι<ς>^{4}.

IQP 1991: ʃ [τὸ]^{7} δὲʅ^{7} ἔσωθεν ʃʅ^{7} []^{7} γέμ[ει]^{7}.

1 The position of Q 11:39b-41 in Q: After Q 11:35, ⟦~~36~~⟧,?39a? and before Q 11:42 (Lukan order); or after Q 11:42 (Matt 23:23) and before Q 11:44 (Matt 23:27) (Matthean order).

2 Luke's νῦν ὑμεῖς or Matthew's οὐαὶ ὑμῖν and the ὅτι clause with the resultant earlier position of καθαρίζετε.

3 Matthew's γραμματεῖς καί.

Q

οὐαὶ ὑμῖν, ⟦<τ>οἱ<ς>⟧ Φαρισαίοι⟦<ς>⟧, ὅτι καθαρίζετε τὸ ἔξωθεν τοῦ ποτηρίου καὶ τῆς παροψίδος, ἔσωθεν δὲ γέμ⟦ουσιν⟧ ἐξ ἁρπαγῆς καὶ ἀκρασίας.

Woe to you, Pharisees, for you purify the outside of the cup and dish, but inside ⟦they are⟧ full of plunder and dissipation.

Gos. Thom. 89.1 (Nag Hammadi II 2)

Λέγει Ἰησοῦς· (διὰ) τί νίπτετε τὸ ἔξωθεν τοῦ ποτηρίου;

(1) Jesus says: Why do you wash the outside of the cup?

Q 11:39b

Luke 11:39b	Lukan Doublet	Markan Parallel	*Gos. Thom.* 89.1
[1]ʃ [νῦν][2] ὑμ[εῖς][2] ( )[3] [οἱ][5] Φαρισαῖοι[4] ( )[5] ( )[2] ʃ ʅ[2] τὸ ἔξωθεν τοῦ ποτηρίου καὶ τ[οῦ][6] π[ίνακ][6]ος ʃκαθαρίζετεʅ[2], ʃ [τὸ][7] δὲʅ[7] ἔσωθεν ʃ ʅ[7] [ὑμῶν][7] γέμ[ει][7] ( )[8] ἁρπαγῆς καὶ [πονηρ][9]ίας. ʅ[1]⇒ Luke 11:41			89.1 ⲡⲉϫⲉ ⲓ̅ⲥ̅ ϫⲉ ⲉⲧⲃⲉ ⲟⲩ ⲧⲉⲧⲛ̅ⲉⲓⲱⲉ ⲙ̅ⲡⲥⲁ ⲛⲃⲟⲗʼ ⲙ̅ⲡⲡⲟⲧⲏⲣⲓⲟⲛ

PH: ʃ ʅ[7] ἔσωθεν ʃ [][7] δὲʅ[7] [][7] γέμ(ουσιν)[7].

JSK: ʃ ʅ[7] ἔσωθεν ʃ [ ][7] δὲʅ[7] [ ][7] γέμ( )[7].

[4] The noun(s) in the vocative (Matthew and Luke), or in a conjectured dative, as in Q 11:42, 43, <44>, 46b, 52.

[5] Luke's οἱ or Matthew's ὑποκριταί.

[6] Luke's τοῦ πίνακος or Matthew's τῆς παροψίδος.

[7] Luke's τὸ δὲ ἔσωθεν ὑμῶν γέμει or Matthew's ἔσωθεν δὲ γέμουσιν.

[8] Matthew's ἐξ.

[9] Luke's πονηρίας or Matthew's ἀκρασίας.

Wehe euch, ⟦<den>⟧ Pharisäern, denn ihr reinigt die Außenseite des Bechers und der Schüssel, innen aber ⟦sind sie⟧ voll von Raub und Gier.

Malheur à vous, Pharisiens, parce que vous purifiez l'extérieur de la coupe et du plat, mais à l'intérieur, ⟦ils sont⟧ pleins de rapacité et d'avidité.

(1) Jesus spricht: Weshalb wascht ihr die Außenseite des Bechers?

(1) Jésus dit: Pourquoi lavez-vous l'extérieur de la coupe?

Q 11:⟦~~40~~⟧

Markan Parallel	Matthean Doublet	Matt 23:26a	Q 11:⟦~~40~~⟧
		(Φαρισαῖε τυφλέ)[1], [ ][2]	⟦[][1] [][2]⟧

IQP 1991: [ ][1] [οὐχ ὁ ποιήσας τὸ ἔξωθεν καὶ τὸ ἔσωθεν ἐποίησεν;][2]. JSK: [ ][1], [ ][2].

[1] Luke's ἄφρονες or Matthew's Φαρισαῖε τυφλέ.

[2] Luke's οὐχ ὁ ποιήσας τὸ ἔξωθεν καὶ τὸ ἔσωθεν ἐποίησεν;.

Gos. Thom. 89.2 (Nag Hammadi II 2)

οὐ νοεῖτε ὅτι ὁ ποιήσας τὸ ἔσωθεν οὗτος καὶ τὸ ἔξωθεν ἐποίησεν;

Do you not understand that the one who created the inside is also the one who created the outside?

Q 11:⟦~~40~~⟧

Luke 11:40	Lukan Doublet	Markan Parallel	*Gos. Thom.* 89.2
[ἄφρονες][1], [οὐχ ὁ ποιήσας τὸ ἔξωθεν καὶ τὸ ἔσωθεν ἐποίησεν;][2]			ⲧⲉⲧⲛ̄ⲣ̄ⲛⲟⲉⲓ ⲁⲛ ϫⲉ ⲡⲉⲛⲧⲁϩⲧⲁⲙⲓⲟ ⲙ̄ⲡⲥⲁ ⲛ̄ϩⲟⲩⲛ ⲛ̄ⲧⲟϥ ⲟⲛ' ⲡⲉⲛⲧⲁϥⲧⲁⲙⲓⲟ ⲙ̄ⲡⲥⲁ ⲛⲃⲟⲗ'

Versteht ihr nicht, daß der, der die Innenseite geschaffen hat, auch der ist, der die Außenseite geschaffen hat?

Ne comprenez-vous pas que celui qui a fait l'intérieur, c'est lui aussi qui a fait l'extérieur?

Q 11:41

Markan Parallel	Matthean Doublet	Matt 23:26b	Q 11:41
		[0]/	[0]/
		[ ][1]	[][1]
		[2]ʃ (καθάρισον)[3] ʅ[2]	[2]ʃ ⟦(καθαρίσ<ατε>)[3]⟧ ʅ[2]
		(πρῶτον)[4]	( )[4]
		τ(ὸ)[5] ἐν(τὸς τοῦ ποτηρίου)[5]	τ(ὸ)[5] ἐν(τὸς τοῦ ποτηρίου)[5]
		ʃ ʅ[2],	ʃʅ[2],
		(ἵνα γένηται)[6] καὶ	( )[6] καὶ [ ][6]
		(τὸ ἐκτὸς αὐτοῦ)[7]	(τὸ ἐκτὸς αὐτοῦ)[7]
		καθαρ(όν)[7].	καθαρ(όν)[7] [ ][6].
		\[0]	\[0]
		ʅMatt 23:25[1]	ʅQ 11:39b[1]

JMR, PH, JSK: ( )[4] indeterminate.

[0] Is Luke 11:41 par. Matt 23:26b in Q?
[1] Luke's πλήν.

[2] The position of the verb after (Luke) or before (Matthew) the object.
[3] Luke's δότε ἐλεημοσύνην or Matthew's καθάρισον.

Q

⟦καθαρίσ<ατε>⟧ .. τὸ ἐντὸς τοῦ ποτηρίου, .. καὶ .. τὸ ἐκτὸς αὐτοῦ καθαρόν .. .	⟦Purify⟧ .. the inside of the cup, … its outside … pure.

Q 11:42 is to be found above, between Q 11:?39a? and Q 11:39b, ⟦~~40~~⟧, 41, 43-44.

Q 11:41

Luke 11:41	Lukan Doublet	Markan Parallel	Gospel of Thomas
[0]/ [πλὴν][1] ʃ ʅ[2] ( )[4] τ[ὰ][5] ἐν[όντα][5] [2]ʃ [δότε ἐλεημοσύνην][3] ʅ[2], καὶ [ἰδοὺ][6] [πάντα][7] καθαρ[ὰ ὑμῖν][7] [ἐστιν][6]. \[0] ʅLuke 11:39b[1]			

[4] Matthew's πρῶτον.
[5] Luke's τὰ ἐνόντα or Matthew's τὸ ἐντὸς τοῦ ποτηρίου.
[6] Luke's καὶ ἰδοὺ … ἐστιν or Matthew's ἵνα γένηται.
[7] Luke's πάντα καθαρὰ ὑμῖν or Matthew's τὸ ἐκτὸς αὐτοῦ καθαρόν.

⟦Reinigt⟧ .. den Inhalt des Bechers, … sein Äußeres … rein … .

⟦Purifiez⟧ .. l'intérieur de la coupe, … son extérieur … pur.

Q 11:42 is to be found above, between Q 11:?39a? and Q 11:39b, ⟦~~40~~⟧, 41, 43-44.

Q 11:43

Mark 12:39b,a, 38c	Matthean Doublet	Matt 23:5-7	Q 11:43
		^{0}{	^{0}{
		^{1}ʃ	^{1}ʃ
		23:5 (πάντα δὲ τὰ ἔργα αὐτῶν ποιοῦσιν πρὸς τὸ θεαθῆναι τοῖς ἀνθρώποις· πλατύνουσιν γὰρ τὰ φυλακτήρια αὐτῶν καὶ μεγαλύνουσιν τὰ κράσπεδα,)^{2}	[οὐαὶ ὑμῖν τοῖς Φαρισαίοις, ὅτι]^{2}
		23:6 (φιλοῦσιν δὲ)^{3}	(φιλ)^{3}<εῖτε>^{3} ()^{3}
12:39b καὶ πρωτοκλισίας ἐν τοῖς δείπνοις,		(τὴν {πρωτοκλισία}ν {ἐν τοῖς δείπνοις} καὶ)^{4}	⟦(τὴν {πρωτοκλισία}ν {ἐν τοῖς δείπνοις} καὶ)^{4}⟧
12:39a καὶ πρωτοκαθεδρίας ἐν ταῖς συναγωγαῖς		τ(ὰς)^{5} {πρωτοκαθεδρία(ς)^{5} ἐν ταῖς συναγωγαῖς}	τ[ὴν]^{5} {πρωτοκαθεδρία}[ν]^{5} {ἐν ταῖς συναγωγαῖς}
12:38c καὶ ἀσπασμοὺς ἐν ταῖς ἀγοραῖς		**23:7** {καὶ} τοὺς {ἀσπασμοὺς ἐν ταῖς ἀγοραῖς}	{καὶ} τοὺς {ἀσπασμοὺς ἐν ταῖς ἀγοραῖς}
		(καὶ καλεῖσθαι ὑπὸ τῶν ἀνθρώπων ῥαββί)^{6}.	()^{6}.
		ʅ^{1}	ʅ^{1}
		}^{0}	}^{0}

IQP 1991: ⟦(φιλ)^{2}<εῖτε>^{2}⟧ ()^{3} ({ })^{4}.

^{0} Is Luke 11:43 par. Matt 23:5-7 in Q or from Mark?

^{1} The position of Q 11:43 in Q: After Q 11:42 and before Q 11:44 (Lukan order); or after Q 11:46b (Matt 23:4) and before Q 14:⟦11⟧ (Matt 23:12) (Matthean order).

^{2} Luke's οὐαὶ ὑμῖν τοῖς Φαρισαίοις, ὅτι or Matthew's πάντα δὲ τὰ ἔργα αὐτῶν ... τὰ κράσπεδα.

^{3} Luke's ἀγαπᾶτε or Matthew's φιλοῦσιν δέ.

Q

οὐαὶ ὑμῖν τοῖς Φαρισαίοις, ὅτι φιλ<εῖτε> ⟦τὴν πρωτοκλισίαν ἐν τοῖς δείπνοις καὶ⟧ τὴν πρωτοκαθεδρίαν ἐν ταῖς συναγωγαῖς καὶ τοὺς ἀσπασμοὺς ἐν ταῖς ἀγοραῖς.

Woe to you, Pharisees, for <you> love ⟦the place of honor at banquets and⟧ the front seat in the synagogues and accolades in the markets.

Q 11:43

Luke 11:43	Luke 20:46	Mark 12:38b-39	Gospel of Thomas
[0]{			
[1]⸂			
[Οὐαὶ ὑμῖν τοῖς Φαρισαίοις, ὅτι][2]	προσέχ{ετε ἀπὸ τῶν γραμματέων τῶν θελόντων} {περιπατεῖν} {ἐν στολαῖς}	**12:38b** βλέπετε ἀπὸ τῶν γραμματέων τῶν θελόντων ἐν στολαῖς περιπατεῖν	
[ἀγαπᾶτε][3] ( )[3] ( )[4]	{καὶ} (φιλού)ντων	καὶ	
τ[ὴν][5] {πρωτοκαθεδρία}[ν][5] {ἐν ταῖς συναγωγαῖς} {καὶ} τοὺς {ἀσπασμοὺς ἐν ταῖς ἀγοραῖς}	{ἀσπασμοὺς ἐν ταῖς ἀγοραῖς καὶ ([πρωτοκαθεδρία]ς [ἐν ταῖς συναγωγαῖς] καὶ) (πρωτοκλισία)ς (ἐν τοῖς δείπνοις,)}	ἀσπασμοὺς ἐν ταῖς ἀγοραῖς **12:39** καὶ πρωτοκαθεδρίας ἐν ταῖς συναγωγαῖς καὶ πρωτοκλισίας ἐν τοῖς δείπνοις,	
( )[6].			
⸃[1]			
}[0]			

[4] Matthew's τὴν πρωτοκλισίαν ἐν τοῖς δείπνοις καί.

[5] Luke's τὴν πρωτοκαθεδρίαν or Matthew's τὰς πρωτοκαθεδρίας.

[6] Matthew's καὶ καλεῖσθαι ὑπὸ τῶν ἀνθρώπων ῥαββί.

Wehe euch, den Pharisäern, denn <ihr> liebt ⟦den Ehrenplatz bei den Gastmählern und⟧ den Ehrensitz in den Synagogen und die «ehrerbietigen» Grüße auf den Marktplätzen.

Malheur à vous, Pharisiens, parce que <vous> aimez ⟦le lit d'honneur dans les banquets et⟧ le siège d'honneur dans les synagogues et les révérences sur les places publiques.

Q 11:44

Markan Parallel	Matthean Doublet	Matt 23:27-28	Q 11:44
		23:27 [1]⸉	[1]⸉
		Οὐαὶ ὑμῖν,	οὐαὶ ὑμῖν,
		(γραμματεῖς καὶ)[2]	()[2]
		(Φαρισαῖοι)[3]	⟦<τοῖς>[3] (Φαρισαίοι<ς>,)[3]⟧
		(ὑποκριταί,)[4]	()[4]
		ὅτι (παρομοιάζε)[5]τε [ ][5]	ὅτι ⟦[ἐσ][5]⟧τὲ ⟦[ὡς][5]⟧
		(τάφοις)[6]	[τὰ μνημεῖα][6]
		(κεκονιαμένοις,)[7]	[τὰ ἄδηλα][7],
		(οἵτινες ἔξωθεν	[καὶ οἱ ἄνθρωποι οἱ
		μὲν φαίνονται ὡραῖοι,	περιπατοῦντες ἐπάνω
		ἔσωθεν δὲ γέμουσιν	οὐκ οἴδασιν][8].
		ὀστέων νεκρῶν καὶ πάσης	
		ἀκαθαρσίας)[8].	
		23:28 (οὕτως καὶ ὑμεῖς	()[9]
		ἔξωθεν μὲν φαίνεσθε	
		τοῖς ἀνθρώποις δίκαιοι,	
		ἔσωθεν δέ ἐστε μεστοὶ	
		ὑποκρίσεως καὶ ἀνομίας)[9].	
		⸊[1]	⸊[1]

IQP 1991: ()[3].

IQP 1991: ⟦[τὰ μνημεῖα][6] [τὰ ἄδηλα][7]⟧.

[1] The position of 11:44 in Q: After Q 11:43 and before Q 11:46b (Lukan order); or after Q 11:39b-41 (Matt 23:25-26) and before Q 11:47-48 (Matt 23:29-31) (Matthean order).

[2] Matthew's γραμματεῖς καί.

[3] Luke's omission of the addressees, or Luke's standard τοῖς Φαρισαίοις as an emendation, or Matthew's Φαρισαῖοι.

[4] Matthew's ὑποκριταί.

Q

οὐαὶ ὑμῖν, ⟦<τοῖς> Φαρισαίοι<ς>,⟧ ὅτι ⟦ἐσ⟧τὲ ⟦ὡς⟧ τὰ μνημεῖα τὰ ἄδηλα, καὶ οἱ ἄνθρωποι οἱ περιπατοῦντες ἐπάνω οὐκ οἴδασιν.

Woe to you, ⟦Pharisees,⟧ for you ⟦are like⟧ indistinct tombs, and people walking on top are unaware.

Q 11:44

Luke 11:44	Lukan Doublet	Markan Parallel	Gospel of Thomas
¹⸢ Οὐαὶ ὑμῖν, ( )² ( )³ ( )⁴ ὅτι [ἐσ]⁵τὲ [ὡς]⁵ [τὰ μνημεῖα]⁶ [τὰ ἄδηλα]⁷, [καὶ οἱ ἄνθρωποι οἱ περιπατοῦντες ἐπάνω οὐκ οἴδασιν]⁸. ( )⁹ ⸣¹			

[5] Luke's ἐστὲ ὡς or Matthew's παρομοιάζετε.
[6] Luke's τὰ μνημεῖα or Matthew's τάφοις.
[7] Luke's τὰ ἄδηλα or Matthew's κεκονιαμένοις.
[8] Luke's καὶ οἱ ἄνθρωποι οἱ περιπατοῦντες ἐπάνω οὐκ οἴδασιν or Matthew's οἵτινες ἔξωθεν μὲν φαίνονται ὡραῖοι, ἔσωθεν δὲ γέμουσιν ὀστέων νεκρῶν καὶ πάσης ἀκαθαρσίας.
[9] Is Matt 23:28 in Q?

Wehe euch, ⟦<den> Pharisäern,⟧ denn ihr ⟦seid wie⟧ unkenntliche Gräber, und die Menschen, die darübergehen, merken es nicht.

Malheur à vous, ⟦Pharisiens,⟧ parce que vous ⟦êtes comme⟧ des tombes non signalées, et les gens marchent dessus sans le savoir.

Q 11:46b, 52, 47-48

Q 11:46b

Markan Parallel	Matthean Doublet	Matt 23:4	Q 11:46b
		^{1}ʃ ʃ ʅ^{2} ʃ ʅ^{3} [ ]^{3} [ ]^{4} [ ]^{5}[ ]^{4} ʃ [ ]^{3} ʅ^{3} [ ]^{6} (δεσμεύ)^{7}(ουσιν)^{3} ʃ (δὲ)^{2} ʅ^{2} ʃ ʅ^{7} φορτία (βαρέα καὶ δυσβάστακτα)^{8} (καὶ ἐπιτιθ)^{7}(έασιν)^{3} (ἐπὶ τοὺς ὤμους)^{7} ʃτ(ῶν)^{7} ἀνθρώπ(ων)^{7} ʅ^{7}, ʃ ʅ^{9} αὐτοὶ ʃ (δὲ)^{9} ʅ^{9} [ ]^{10} τῷ[ ]^{10} δακτύλῳ[ ]^{10} (αὐτ)^{3}ῶν οὐ (θέλ)^{11}(ουσιν)^{3} (κινῆσαι)^{11} (αὐτά)^{12}. ʅ^{1}	^{1}ʃ ʃ ⟦[καὶ]^{2}⟧ ʅ^{2} ʃοὐαὶʅ^{3} [ὑμῖν]^{3} [τοῖς]^{4} ⟦[νομικ]^{5}⟧[οῖς]^{4} ʃʅ^{3}, [ὅτι]^{6} ⟦(δεσμεύ)^{7}⟧<ετε>)^{3} ʃ ʅ^{2} ʃ ʅ^{7} φορτία [( )]^{8} ^{8}ʃ ⟦(καὶ ἐπιτίθ)^{7}⟧<ετε>^{3} ⟦(ἐπὶ τοὺς ὤμους)^{7} ʃτ(ῶν)^{7} ἀνθρώπ(ων)^{7}⟧ ʅ^{7}, ʃ ʅ^{9} αὐτοὶ ʃ ⟦(δὲ)^{9}⟧ ʅ^{9} []^{10} τῷ[]^{10} δακτύλῳ[]^{10} [ὑμ]^{3}ῶν οὐ ⟦(θέλ)^{11}⟧<ετε>^{3} ⟦(κινῆσαι)^{11}⟧ (αὐτά)^{12}. ʅ^{1}

Text Critical Note (see the discussion in the front matter): In Matt 23:4 βαρέα only is in L *f* ^{1} 892 *pc* it sy$^{s.c.p}$ bo Ir^{lat}; δυσβάστακτα only

IQP 1991: ʃ []^{2} ʅ^{2}.
PH: ʃ ⟦[]^{2}⟧ ʅ^{2}.

IQP 1991: ⟦[τοῖς]^{4} <φαρισαί>^{5}[οις]^{4}⟧ ʃʅ^{3}, [ὅτι]^{6} ⟦[φορτίζετε]^{7}⟧ ʃʅ^{2} ʃ τ[οὺς]^{7} ἀνθρώπ[ους]^{7} ʅ^{7} φορτία ()^{8} δυσβάστακτα ( )^{7}( )^{3} ( )^{7} ʃʅ^{7}.

1 The position of 11:46b in Q: After Q 11:44 and before Q 11:47 (Lukan order); or after Q 14:~~15~~, ⟦16-21⟧, ~~22~~, ⟦23⟧, ~~24~~ (Matt 22:1-10) and before Q 11:43 (Matt 23:5-7) (Matthean order).

2 Luke's καί or Matthew's postpositive δέ.

3 Luke's irregular sequence (ὑμῖν … οὐαί) or emended to the standard Lukan sequence (οὐαὶ ὑμῖν …) and the use of the second person throughout or the omission of the Woe formula altogether and the use of the third person throughout (Matthew).

4 Luke's dative construction, or a conjectured vocative from Matthew's standard construction.

5 Luke's noun νομικοί or, conjectured, the standard Lukan noun Φαρισαῖοι or no noun (Matthew) or, conjectured,

Q

⟦καὶ⟧ οὐαὶ ὑμῖν τοῖς ⟦νομικ⟧οῖς, ὅτι ⟦δεσμεύ⟧<ετε> φορτία … ⟦καὶ ἐπιτίθ⟧<ετε> ⟦ἐπὶ τοὺς ὤμους τῶν ἀνθρώπων⟧, αὐτοὶ ⟦δὲ⟧ τῷ δακτύλῳ ὑμῶν οὐ ⟦θέλ⟧<ετε> ⟦κινῆσαι⟧ αὐτά.	⟦And⟧ woe to you, ⟦exegetes of the Law,⟧ for <you> ⟦bind⟧ … burdens, ⟦and load on the backs of people, but⟧ <you your>selves do not ⟦want «to lift»⟧ your finger ⟦to move⟧ them.

Q 11:47-51 is to be found below, between Q 11:52 and Q 12:2-3.

Q 11:46b

Luke 11:46b	Lukan Doublet	Markan Parallel	Gospel of Thomas
[1]ʃ ʃ [καὶ][2] ʅ[2] ʃ ʅ[3] [ὑμῖν][3] [τοῖς][4] [νομικ][5][οῖς][4] ʃ [οὐαί][3] ʅ[3], [ὅτι][6] [φορτίζ][7][ετε][3] ʃ ʅ[2] ʃτ[οὺς][7] ἀνθρώπ[ους][7] ʅ[7] φορτία [δυσβάστακτα][8] ( )[7]( )[3] ( )[7] ʃ ʅ[7], ʃ [καὶ][9] ʅ[9] αὐτοὶ ʃ ʅ[9] [ἑνὶ][10] τῶ[ν][10] δακτύλω[ν][10] [ὑμ][3]ῶν οὐ [προσψαύ][11][ετε][3] [τοῖς φορτίοις][12]. ʅ[1]			

is in 700 *pc*; μεγάλα βαρέα is in ℵ; and βαρέα καὶ δυσβάστακτα is in B D(*) W Θ 0102 0107 *f* 13 33 𝔐 lat syh sa (mae).

JMR, PH, JSK: [( )][8] indeterminate, since it is indeterminate whether καὶ δυσβάστακτα is in Matthew.

IQP 1991: ʃ [καὶ][9] ʅ[9] αὐτοὶ ʃʅ[9] ⟦[][10]⟧ τῷ⟦[][10]⟧ δακτύλῳ⟦[][10]⟧ [ὑμ][3]ῶν οὐ [( )][11.3] (αὐτά)[12].

the standard Matthaean formulation γραμματεῖς καὶ Φαρισαῖοι.

6 Luke's ὅτι.

7 Luke's φορτίζ- … τοὺς ἀνθρώπους or Matthew's δεσμεύ- … καὶ ἐπιτιθέασιν ἐπὶ τοὺς ὤμους τῶν ἀνθρώπων, with the resultant divergence of position for the reference to the people.

8 Luke's δυσβάστακτα or Matthew's βαρέα and the textually uncertain καὶ δυσβάστακτα.

9 Luke's καί or Matthew's postpositive δέ.

10 Luke's ἑνὶ τῶν δακτύλων or Matthew's τῷ δακτύλῳ.

11 Luke's προσψαύετε or Matthew's θέλουσιν κινῆσαι.

12 Luke's τοῖς φορτίοις or Matthew's αὐτά.

Wehe ⟦auch⟧ euch, den ⟦Gesetzeslehrern⟧, denn <ihr> ⟦schnür⟧<t> … Lasten ⟦zusammen und leg⟧<t> ⟦«sie» auf die Schultern der Menschen⟧, selbst ⟦aber woll⟧<t ihr> sie nicht «einmal» mit eurem Finger ⟦bewegen⟧.

⟦Et⟧ malheur à vous ⟦exégètes de la Loi⟧, parce que <vous> ⟦fabriqu⟧<ez> des fardeaux …, ⟦et⟧ <vous> ⟦«les» charg⟧<ez> ⟦sur les épaules des gens, mais⟧ <vous->mêmes, <vous> ⟦ne voul⟧<ez> pas «lever» le «petit» doigt ⟦pour⟧ les ⟦déplacer⟧.

Q 11:47-51 is to be found below, between Q 11:52 and Q 12:2-3.

Q 11:52

Markan Parallel	Matthean Doublet	Matt 23:13	Q 11:52
		[1]ʃ	[1]ʃ
		Οὐαὶ	οὐαὶ
		(δὲ)[2] ὑμῖν,	()[2] ὑμῖν
		(γραμματεῖς καὶ Φαρισαῖοι)[3.4]	[τοῖς][3] ⟦[νομικ][4]⟧[οῖς][3]
		(ὑποκριταί)[5],	()[5],
		ὅτι [ ][6] κλεί(ετε)[6]	ὅτι ⟦[][6]⟧ κλεί ⟦(ετε)[6]⟧
		τ(ὴν βασιλείαν	τ⟦(ὴν βασιλείαν
		τῶν οὐρανῶν)[7]	τ)[7]<οῦ θεοῦ>[7]
		(ἔμπροσθεν τῶν ἀνθρώπων)[8]·	(ἔμπροσθεν τῶν ἀνθρώπων)[8]⟧·
		(ὑμεῖς)[9]	(ὑμεῖς)[9]
		(γὰρ)[10]	⟦()[10]⟧
		οὐκ εἰσ(έρχεσθε)[11]	οὐκ εἰσ[ήλθατε][11]
		(οὐδὲ)[12]	⟦(οὐδὲ)[12]⟧
		τοὺς εἰσερχομένους	τοὺς εἰσερχομένους
		(ἀφίετε εἰσελθεῖν)[13].	(ἀφίετε εἰσελθεῖν)[13].
		ʅ[1]	ʅ[1]

JSK: The order is Q 11:46b, 47-51, 52 {B}.
IQP 1991: ⟦(φαρισαί)[4]⟧οι<ς >, ὅτι ⟦[ἤρατε τὴν][6] κλεῖ⟦[δα][6] τ[ῆς γνώσεως][7] ()[8]· ()[9] ()[10]⟧ οὐκ εἰσ⟦[ήλθατε][11] (οὐδὲ)[12]⟧ … ⟦(ἀφ)[13]<ήκατε>[13] (εἰσελθεῖν)[13]⟧.

[1] The position of 11:52 in Q: After Q 11:51 and before Q 12:2 (Lukan order); or after Q 11:43 (Matt 23:5-7) and before Q 11:42 (Matt 23:23) (Matthean order).
[2] Matthew's δέ.
[3] Luke's dative or Matthew's vocative.
[4] Luke's νομικοί or Matthew's γραμματεῖς καὶ Φαρισαῖοι.
[5] Matthew's ὑποκριταί.
[6] Luke's ἤρατε τὴν κλεῖδα or Matthew's κλείετε.

Q

οὐαὶ ὑμῖν τοῖς ⟦νομικ⟧οῖς, ὅτι κλείετε ⟦τὴν βασιλείαν⟧ τ⟦<οῦ θεοῦ> ἔμπροσθεν τῶν ἀνθρώπων⟧· ὑμεῖς οὐκ εἰσήλθατε ⟦οὐδὲ⟧ τοὺς εἰσερχομένους ἀφίετε εἰσελθεῖν.

Woe to you, ⟦exegetes of the Law,⟧ for you shut the ⟦kingdom of <God> from people⟧; you did not go in, ⟦nor⟧ let in those «trying to» get in.

Gos. Thom. 39.1-2 (Nag Hammadi II 2)

(1) Λέγει Ἰησοῦς· οἱ Φαρισαῖοι καὶ οἱ γραμματεῖς ἔλαβον τὰς κλεῖδας τῆς γνώσεως, ἔκρυψαν αὐτάς. (2) οὔτε εἰσῆλθον καὶ τοὺς θέλοντας εἰσελθεῖν ἀφῆκαν.

(1) Jesus says: The Pharisees and the scribes have received the keys of knowledge, (but) they have hidden them[1]. (2) Neither have they gone in, nor have they let in those who wanted in.

[1] Or: took away the keys of knowledge and have hidden them.

Gos. Thom. 39.1-2 (P. Oxy. 655)

(1) [λέγει Ἰ(ησοῦ)ς· οἱ Φαρισαῖοι καὶ οἱ γραμματεῖς] ἔλ[αβον τὰς κλεῖδας] τῆς [γνώσεως. αὐτοὶ ἔ]κρυψ[αν αὐτάς. (2) οὔτε] εἰσῆλ[θον, οὔτε τοὺς] εἰσερ[χομένους ἀφῆ]καν [εἰσελθεῖν].

(1) [Jesus says: The Pharisees and the scribes have received the keys] of [knowledge. They] have hidden [them]. (2) [Neither have they] entered, [nor] let [in those (trying to) get] in.

Q 12:2 is to be found below, between Q 11:46b, 52, 47-51 and Q 12:3.

Q 11:52

Luke 11:52	Lukan Doublet	Markan Parallel	*Gos. Thom.* 39.1-2
[1]⸂ Οὐαὶ ( )[2] ὑμῖν [τοῖς][3] [νομικ][4][οῖς][3] ( )[5], ὅτι [ἤρατε τὴν][6] κλεῖ[δα][6] τ[ῆς γνώσεως][7] ( )[8]. [αὐτοὶ][9] ( )[10] οὐκ εἰσ[ήλθατε][11] [καὶ][12] τοὺς εἰσερχομένους [ἐκωλύσατε][13]. ⸃[1]			39.1 πεχε ⲓ̄ⲥ̄ χε ⲙ̄ⲫⲁⲣⲓⲥⲁⲓⲟⲥ ⲙⲛ̄ ⲛ̄ⲅⲣⲁⲙⲙⲁⲧⲉⲩⲥ ⲁⲩϫⲓ ⲛ̄ϣⲁϣⲧʼ ⲛ̄ⲧⲅⲛⲱⲥⲓⲥ ⲁⲩϩⲟⲡⲟⲩ 39.2 ⲟⲩⲧⲉ ⲙ̄ⲡⲟⲩⲃⲱⲕʼ ⲉϩⲟⲩⲛ ⲁⲩⲱ ⲛⲉⲧⲟⲩⲱϣ ⲉⲃⲱⲕʼ ⲉϩⲟⲩⲛ ⲙ̄ⲡⲟⲩⲕⲁⲁⲩ

PH: [][6] κλεί(ετε)[6] τ(ὴν βασιλείαν τ)[7]<οῦ θεοῦ>[7] (ἔμπροσθεν τῶν ἀνθρώπων)[8].

[7] Luke's τῆς γνώσεως or Matthew's τὴν βασιλείαν τῶν οὐρανῶν (or a conjectured τὴν βασιλείαν τ<οῦ θεοῦ>).
[8] Matthew's ἔμπροσθεν τῶν ἀνθρώπων.
[9] Luke's αὐτοί or Matthew's ὑμεῖς.
[10] Matthew's γάρ.
[11] Luke's εἰσήλθατε or Matthew's εἰσέρχεσθε.
[12] Luke's καί or Matthew's οὐδέ.
[13] Luke's ἐκωλύσατε or Matthew's ἀφίετε εἰσελθεῖν.

Wehe euch, den ⟦Gesetzeslehrern⟧, denn ihr verschließt das ⟦Reich <Gottes> vor den Menschen⟧; selbst seid ihr nicht hineingegangen, ⟦noch⟧ lasst ihr die hineingehen, die hineingehen «wollen».

Malheur à vous, ⟦exégètes de la Loi,⟧ parce que vous enfermez ⟦les gens hors⟧ du ⟦royaume de <Dieu>⟧; vous-mêmes, vous n'«y» êtes pas entrés ⟦et⟧ vous ⟦ne⟧ laissez ⟦pas⟧ entrer ceux qui «voudraient y» entrer.

(1) Jesus spricht: Die Pharisäer und die Schriftgelehrten haben die Schlüssel der Erkenntnis empfangen, (doch) sie haben sie versteckt[2]. (2) Weder sind sie hineingegangen, noch haben sie die gelassen, die hineingehen wollten.

[2] Oder: weggenommen und haben sie versteckt.

(1) Jésus dit: Les pharisiens et les scribes ont reçu les clefs de la connaissance (mais) les ont cachées[3]. (2) Ils ne sont ni entrés, ni n'ont laissé entrer ceux qui voulaient.

[3] Ou: ont enlevé les clefs de la connaissance et les ont cachées.

(1) [Jesus spricht: Die Pharisäer und die Schriftgelehrten haben die Schlüssel] der [Erkenntnis empfangen. Sie] haben sie versteckt. (2) [Weder sind sie] hineingegangen, [noch] haben sie [die hineingehen] lassen, [die] hinein[gehen (wollten)].

(1) [Jésus dit: Les pharisiens et les scribes] ont reçu [les clefs] de la [connaissance. Ils les] ont cachées. (2) [Ils ne sont ni] entrés, [ni n'] ont laissé [entrer ceux qui (voudraient y) entrer].

Q 12:2 is to be found below, between Q 11:46b, 52, 47-51 and Q 12:3.

Q 11:47-48

Markan Parallel	Matthean Doublet	Matt 23:29-32	Q 11:47-48
		23:29 Οὐαὶ ὑμῖν,	**11:47** οὐαὶ ὑμῖν,
		(γραμματεῖς καὶ Φαρισαῖοι	()[1]
		ὑποκριταί,)[1]	
		ὅτι οἰκοδομεῖτε	ὅτι οἰκοδομεῖτε
		⸂ (τοὺς τάφους)[2] ⸃[2]	⸂τὰ μνημεῖα⸃[2]
		τῶν προφητῶν	τῶν προφητῶν
		(καὶ κοσμεῖτε)[2]	()[2]
		⸂τὰ μνημεῖα⸃[2]	⸂⸃[2]
		(τῶν δικαίων)[2],	()[2],
		23:30 (καὶ λέγετε·	()[3]
		εἰ ἤμεθα ἐν ταῖς ἡμέραις	
		τῶν)[3] πατέρ(ων ἡ)[3]μῶν,	[οἱ δὲ][3] πατέρ[ες ὑ][3]μῶν
		(οὐκ ἂν ἤμεθα αὐτῶν κοινωνοὶ	
		ἐν τῷ αἵματι τῶν προφητῶν.)[3]	[ἀπέκτειναν αὐτούς.][3]
		23:31 (ὥστε)[4]	**11:48** [( )][4]
		μαρτυρ(εῖτε ἑαυτοῖς ὅτι)[5]	μαρτυρ⟦(εῖτε ἑαυτοῖς ὅτι)[5]
		(υἱοί)[6] ἐστε	(υἱοί)[6]⟧ ἐστε
		(τῶν φονευσάντων	⟦()[7]⟧
		τοὺς προφήτας.)[7]	
		23:32 καὶ	⟦~~καὶ~~⟧
		(ὑμεῖς πληρώσατε	⟦[()][8]⟧
		τὸ μέτρον)[8]	
		τῶν πατέρων ὑμῶν	τῶν πατέρων ὑμῶν
		[ ][9]	[ ][9]
		.	.
		⸃ Matt 23:1-2a[0]	⸃ Q 11:?39a?[0]

IQP 1991: **11:48** ⟦[ἄρα][4]⟧ μάρτυρ⟦[ές][5] ()[6] ἐστε⟧ ()[7] καὶ [( )][8] τῶν πατέρων ὑμῶν, [ὅτι ⟦αὐτοὶ μὲν ἀπέκτειναν αὐτούς,⟧ ὑμεῖς ⟦δὲ οἰ-

1 Luke's omission of the addressees or Matthew's γραμματεῖς καὶ Φαρισαῖοι ὑποκριταί.

2 Luke's single clause including τὰ μνημεῖα or Matthew's two parallel clauses with τοὺς τάφους in the first and τὰ μνημεῖα in the second.

3 Luke's οἱ δὲ πατέρες ὑμῶν ἀπέκτειναν αὐτούς or Matthew's καὶ λέγετε· εἰ ἤμεθα ἐν ταῖς ἡμέραις τῶν πατέρων ἡμῶν, οὐκ ἂν ἤμεθα αὐτῶν κοινωνοὶ ἐν τῷ αἵματι τῶν προφητῶν.

4 Luke's ἄρα or Matthew's ὥστε.

Q

47 οὐαὶ ὑμῖν, ὅτι οἰκοδομεῖτε τὰ μνημεῖα τῶν προφητῶν, οἱ δὲ πατέρες ὑμῶν ἀπέκτειναν αὐτούς. **48** … μαρτυρ⟦εῖτε ἑαυτοῖς ὅτι υἱοί⟧ ἐστε τῶν πατέρων ὑμῶν. ..

47 Woe to you, for you build the tombs of the prophets, but your «fore»fathers killed them. **48** «Thus» ⟦you⟧ witness ⟦against yourselves that⟧ you are ⟦the sons⟧ of your «fore»fathers. ..

Q 11:47-48

Luke 11:47-48	Lukan Doublet	Markan Parallel	Gospel of Thomas
11:47 Οὐαὶ ὑμῖν, ( )[1] ὅτι οἰκοδομεῖτε ʃτὰ μνημεῖα≀[2] τῶν προφητῶν ( )[2] ʃ ≀[2] ( )[2], ( )[3] [οἱ δὲ][3] πατέρ[ες ὑ][3]μῶν [ἀπέκτειναν αὐτούς.][3] **11:48** [ἄρα][4] μάρτυρ[ές][5] ( )[6] ἐστε ( )[7] καὶ [συνευδοκεῖτε τοῖς ἔργοις][8] τῶν πατέρων ὑμῶν, [ὅτι αὐτοὶ μὲν ἀπέκτειναν αὐτούς, ὑμεῖς δὲ οἰκοδομεῖτε][9]. ≀ Luke 11:39a[0]			

κοδομεῖτε][9]⟧.

JMR, PH, JSK: [ ][3] indeterminate.

[5] Luke's μάρτυρες or Matthew's μαρτυρεῖτε ἑαυτοῖς ὅτι.

[6] Matthew's υἱοί.

[7] Matthew's τῶν φονευσάντων τοὺς προφήτας.

[8] Luke's συνευδοκεῖτε τοῖς ἔργοις or Matthew's ὑμεῖς πληρώσατε τὸ μέτρον.

[9] Luke's ὅτι αὐτοὶ μὲν ἀπέκτειναν αὐτούς, ὑμεῖς δὲ οἰκοδομεῖτε.

47 Wehe euch, denn ihr baut die Grabdenkmäler für die Propheten, eure Väter aber haben sie getötet. **48** «So» ⟦gebt ihr⟧ Zeugnis ⟦gegen euch selbst, dass⟧ ihr ⟦die Söhne⟧ eurer Väter seid. ..

47 Malheur à vous, parce que vous bâtissez les tombeaux des prophètes, mais vos pères les ont tués. **48** «Ainsi» ⟦vous⟧ témoign⟦ez contre vous-mêmes, que⟧ vous êtes ⟦les fils⟧ de vos pères. ..

Q 11:49

Markan Parallel	Matthean Doublet	Matt 23:34	Q 11:49
		1ʃ	1ʃ
		Διὰ τοῦτο	διὰ τοῦτο
		(ἰδοὺ ἐγὼ)[2]	[καὶ ἡ σοφία][2]
		[ ][3]	[ ][3]
		[ ][4]	[εἶπεν][4]·
		ἀποστέλ(λ)[5]ω	ἀποστελ()[5]ῶ
		(πρὸς)[6]	⟦(πρὸς)[6]⟧
		(ὑμᾶς)[7] προφήτας	[αὐτοὺς][7] προφήτας
		καὶ (σοφ)[8]οὺς	καὶ (σοφ)[8]ούς
		(καὶ γραμματεῖς)[9]·	()[9],
		[ ][10] ἐξ αὐτῶν	[καὶ][10] ἐξ αὐτῶν
		ἀποκτεν(εῖτε)[7] καὶ	ἀποκτεν[οῦσιν][7] καὶ
		(σταυρώσετε	()[11]
		καὶ ἐξ αὐτῶν μαστιγώσετε	
		ἐν ταῖς συναγωγαῖς ὑμῶν	
		καὶ)[11] διώξ(ετε)[7]	διώξ[ουσιν][7]
		(ἀπὸ πόλεως εἰς πόλιν)[12]·	()[12],
		ʅ1⇒Matt 23:36	ʅ1⇒Q 11:51

IQP 1993: [ ][3] Matt=Q {D}.

JMR, PH, JSK: [ ][3] indeterminate.

1 The position of Q 11:49-51 in relation to the Woes: Before the last Lukan woe (Luke 12:52) or after the last Matthean woe (Matt 23:29-32).

2 Luke's καὶ ἡ σοφία or Matthew's ἰδοὺ ἐγώ.

3 Luke's τοῦ θεοῦ.

4 Luke's εἶπεν.

5 Luke's ἀποστελῶ or Matthew's ἀποστέλλω.

6 Luke's εἰς or Matthew's πρός.

Q

διὰ τοῦτο καὶ ἡ σοφία .. εἶπεν· ἀποστελῶ ⟦πρὸς⟧ αὐτοὺς προφήτας καὶ σοφούς, καὶ ἐξ αὐτῶν ἀποκτενοῦσιν καὶ διώξουσιν,

Therefore also .. Wisdom said: I will send them prophets and sages, and «some» of them they will kill and persecute,

Q 11:49

Luke 11:49	Lukan Doublet	Markan Parallel	Gospel of Thomas
1ʃ διὰ τοῦτο [καὶ ἡ σοφία][2] [τοῦ θεοῦ][3] [εἶπεν][4]· ἀποστελ( )[5]ῶ [εἰς][6] [αὐτοὺς][7] προφήτας καὶ [ἀποστόλ][8]ους ( )[9], [καὶ][10] ἐξ αὐτῶν ἀποκτεν[οῦσιν][7] καὶ ( )[11] διώξ[ουσιν][7] ( )[12], ʅ1⇒Luke 11:51			

IQP 1993: ( )[6].

IQP 1993: [ἀποστόλ][8]ους.

7 Luke's αὐτούς or Matthew's ὑμᾶς and the resultant persons of the verbs.

8 Luke's ἀποστόλους or Matthew's σοφούς.

9 Matthew's γραμματεῖς.

10 Luke's καί.

11 Matthew's σταυρώσετε καὶ ἐξ αὐτῶν μαστιγώσετε ἐν ταῖς συναγωγαῖς ὑμῶν καί.

12 Matthew's ἀπὸ πόλεως εἰς πόλιν.

Darum sagte auch die Weisheit ..: Ich werde ⟦zu⟧ ihnen Propheten und Weise senden, und «einige» von ihnen werden sie töten und verfolgen,

C'est pourquoi aussi la Sagesse .. dit: J'enverrai ⟦auprès⟧ d'eux des prophètes et des sages, et, parmi eux, ils en tueront et en persécuteront,

Q 11:50

Markan Parallel	Matthean Doublet	Matt 23:35a	Q 11:50
		(ὅπως)[1]	⟦[ἵνα][1]⟧
		(ἔλθῃ)[2]	[ἐκζητηθῇ][2]
		[3]⸂ (ἐφ')[2]	⸂⸃[3]
		(ὑμᾶς)[8] ⸃[3]	
		[ ][4] [4]⸂πᾶν[ ][4]⸃[4] αἷμα ⸂ ⸃[4]	[τὸ][4] ⸂⸃[4] αἷμα [4]⸂πάν[των][4]⸃[4]
		(δίκαιον)[5]	[τῶν προφητῶν][5]
		[ ][4]	[τὸ][4]
		ἐκ[ ][6]χυ(ννό)[6]μενον	ἐκ[κε][6]χυ()[6]μένον
		(ἐπὶ τῆς γῆς)[7]	[ἀπὸ καταβολῆς κόσμου][7]
		⸂ ⸃[3]	[3]⸂ [ἀπὸ][2]
			[τῆς γενεᾶς ταύτης][8] ⸃[3],

1 Luke's ἵνα or Matthew's ὅπως.

2 Luke's ἐκζητηθῃ … ἀπό or Matthew's ἔλθῇ ἐφ'.

3 The position of the prepositional phrases modifying the verb: At the end (Luke) or immediately following the verb (Matthew).

Q

⟦ἵνα⟧ ἐκζητηθῇ τὸ αἷμα πάντων τῶν προφητῶν τὸ ἐκκεχυμένον ἀπὸ καταβολῆς κόσμου ἀπὸ τῆς γενεᾶς ταύτης,

so that «a settling of accounts for» the blood of all the prophets poured out from the founding of the world may be required of this generation,

Q 11:50

Luke 11:50	Lukan Doublet	Markan Parallel	Gospel of Thomas
[ἵνα][1] [ἐκζητηθῇ][2] ⸀ ⸁[3] [τὸ][4] ⸀ ⸁[4] αἷμα [4]⸀πάν[των][4] ⸁[4] [τῶν προφητῶν][5] [τὸ][4] ἐκ[κε][6]χυ( )[6]μένον [ἀπὸ καταβολῆς κόσμου][7] [3]⸀ [ἀπὸ][2] [τῆς γενεᾶς ταύτης][8] ⸁[3],			

[4] Luke's τὸ αἷμα πάντων ... τό or Matthew's πᾶν αἷμα.
[5] Luke's τῶν προφητῶν or Matthew's δίκαιον.
[6] Luke's ἐκκεχυμένον or Matthew's ἐκχυννόμενον.
[7] Luke's ἀπὸ καταβολῆς κόσμου or Matthew's ἐπὶ τῆς γῆς.
[8] Luke's τῆς γενεᾶς ταύτης or Matthew's ὑμᾶς.

damit das Blut aller Propheten, das von Anfang der Welt an vergossen wurde, von dieser Generation eingefordert wird,

de sorte qu'il soit demandé compte à cette génération du sang versé de tous les prophètes depuis la fondation du monde,

Q 11:51

Markan Parallel	Matthean Doublet	Matt 23:35b-36	Q 11:51
		23:35b ἀπὸ (τοῦ)[1] αἵματος	ἀπὸ ⟦()[1]⟧ αἵματος
		Ἅβελ	Ἅβελ
		(τοῦ δικαίου)[2]	()[2]
		ἕως (τοῦ)[1] αἵματος	ἕως ⟦()[1]⟧ αἵματος
		Ζαχαρίου	Ζαχαρίου
		(υἱοῦ Βαραχίου)[3],	()[3]
		(ὃν ἐφονεύσατε)[4]	[τοῦ ἀπολομένου][4]
		μεταξὺ [5]⸉τοῦ (να)[6]οῦ⸊[5]	μεταξὺ ⸉τοῦ θυσιαστηρίου⸊[5]
		καὶ [5]⸉τοῦ θυσιαστηρίου⸊[5].	καὶ [5]⸉τοῦ [οἴκ][6]ου⸊[5].
		23:36 (ἀμὴν)[7] λέγω ὑμῖν,	[ναὶ][7] λέγω ὑμῖν,
		(ἥξει)[8]	[ἐκζητηθήσεται][8]
		(ταῦτα πάντα)[9]	()[9]
		(ἐπὶ)[8] τὴ(ν)[8] γενεὰ(ν)[8]	[ἀπὸ][8] τῆ[ς][8] γενεᾶ[ς][8]
		ταύτη(ν)[8].	ταύτη[ς][8].
		⸊Matt 23:34[1]	⸊Q 11:49[1]

IQP 1993: ⟦[ἐκζητηθήσεται ()[9] ἀπὸ][8]⟧ τῆ⟦[ς][8]⟧ γενεᾶ⟦[ς][8]⟧ ταύτη⟦[ς][8]⟧.

[1] Matthew's τοῦ … τοῦ.
[2] Matthew's τοῦ δικαίου.
[3] Matthew's υἱοῦ Βαραχίου.
[4] Luke's τοῦ ἀπολομένου or Matthew's ὃν ἐφονεύσατε.
[5] Luke's position of τοῦ θυσιαστηρίου before καί with τοῦ …ου coming after καί, or Matthew's reverse sequence.

Q

ἀπὸ αἵματος Ἅβελ ἕως αἵματος Ζαχαρίου τοῦ ἀπολομένου μεταξὺ τοῦ θυσιαστηρίου καὶ τοῦ οἴκου· ναὶ λέγω ὑμῖν, ἐκζητηθήσεται ἀπὸ τῆς γενεᾶς ταύτης.

from «the» blood of Abel to «the» blood of Zechariah, murdered between the sacrificial altar and the House. Yes, I tell you, «an accounting» will be required of this generation!

Q 11:52 is to be found above, between Q 11:46b and Q 11:47-51.

Q 11:51

Luke 11:51	Lukan Doublet	Markan Parallel	Gospel of Thomas
ἀπὸ ( )[1] αἵματος Ἅβελ ( )[2] ἕως ( )[1] αἵματος Ζαχαρίου ( )[3] [τοῦ ἀπολομένου][4] μεταξὺ ⸂τοῦ θυσιαστηρίου⸃[5] καὶ [5]⸂τοῦ [οἴκ][6]ου⸃[5]. [ναὶ][7] λέγω ὑμῖν, [ἐκζητηθήσεται][8] ( )[9] [ἀπὸ][8] τῆ[ς][8] γενεᾶ[ς][8] ταύτη[ς][8]. ⸃Luke 11:49[1]			

6 Luke's οἴκου or Matthew's ναοῦ.

7 Luke's ναί or Matthew's ἀμήν.

8 Luke's verb, corresponding preposition, and resultant case, or Matthew's.

9 Matthew's ταῦτα πάντα.

vom Blut Abels bis zum Blut des Zacharias, der zwischen dem Altar und dem Tempel umgebracht wurde. Ja, ich sage euch, von dieser Generation wird es eingefordert werden.

depuis «le» sang d'Abel jusqu'«au» sang de Zacharie, qui a péri entre l'autel et la Demeure. Oui, je vous «le» dis, il sera demandé compte à cette génération.

Q 11:52 is to be found above, between Q 11:46b and Q 11:47-51.

Q 12:2

Mark 4:22	Matthean Doublet	Matt 10:26	Q 12:2
		^{0}{	^{0}{
		^{1}⸂	^{1}⸂
		(Μὴ οὖν	()^{2}
		φοβηθῆτε αὐτούς)^{2}·	
οὐ		{οὐ}δὲν	{οὐ}δὲν
γάρ		{(γάρ)^{3}	[()]^{3}
		⸂ ⸃^{4}	^{4}⸂[]^{5}κεκαλυμμένον⸃^{4}
ἐστιν		ἐστιν}	{ἐστὶν}
κρυπτὸν		^{4}⸂ [ ]^{5}κεκαλυμμένον⸃^{4}	⸂ ⸃^{4}
ἐὰν μὴ ἵνα φανερωθῇ,		ὃ οὐκ ἀποκαλυφθήσεται	ὃ οὐκ ἀποκαλυφθήσεται
οὐδὲ ἐγένετο ἀπόκρυφον		καὶ {κρυπτὸν}	καὶ {κρυπτὸν}
		ὃ οὐ γνωσθήσεται.	ὃ οὐ γνωσθήσεται.
ἀλλ' ἵνα ἔλθῃ εἰς φανερόν.		⸃^{1}⇒ Matt 10:33	⸃^{1}⇒ Q 12:9
		}^{0}	}^{0}

JMR: ( )^{3}.

JMR, PH, JSK: ⸂ ⸃^{4} indeterminate.

^{0} Is Luke 12:2 par. Matt 10:26 in Q or from Mark?

^{1} The position of Q 12:2-9 in Q: After Q 11:52 and before Q 12:10 (Lukan order); or after Q 6:40 (Matt 10:24) and before Q 12:51 (Matt 10:34) (Matthean order).

Q

οὐδὲν κεκαλυμμένον ἐστὶν ὃ οὐκ ἀποκαλυφθήσεται καὶ κρυπτὸν ὃ οὐ γνωσθήσεται.

Nothing is covered up that will not be exposed, and hidden that will not be known.

Gos. Thom. (Nag Hammadi II 2)

5.2=6.5 οὐ γάρ ἐστιν κρυπτὸν ὃ οὐ φανερὸν γενήσεται.

5.2=6.5 For there is nothing hidden that will not become manifest.

Gos. Thom. 5.2 (P. Oxy. 654)

[οὐ γάρ ἐσ]τιν κρυπτὸν ὃ οὐ φανε[ρὸν γενήσεται], καὶ τεθαμμένον ὃ ο[ὐκ ἐγερθήσεται].

[For there is nothing] hidden that [will] not [become] manifest, nor buried that [will not be raised].

Gos. Thom. 6.5 (P. Oxy. 654)

[οὐδὲν γάρ ἐστι]ν ἀ[π]οκεκρ[υμμένον ὃ οὐ φανερὸν ἔσται].

[For nothing is] concealed [that will not be manifest].

Q 12:2

Luke 12:2	Luke 8:17	Mark 4:22	*Gos. Thom.* 5.2 = 6.5
⁰{			
¹ʃ			
( )²			
{Οὐ}δὲν	{[(οὐ)]	οὐ	5.2=6.5 ⲘⲚ̄ ⲖⲀⲀⲨ
[δὲ]³	(γάρ)	γάρ	ⲄⲀⲢ
⁴ʃ[συγ]⁵κεκαλυμμένονʅ⁴			
{ἐστὶν}	[(ἐστιν)]	ἐστιν	
ʃ ʅ⁴	κρυπτὸν}	κρυπτὸν	ⲈϤϨⲎⲠ'
ὃ οὐκ ἀποκαλυφθήσεται	[(ὃ οὐ)] {φανερ}ὸν γενήσεται	ἐὰν μὴ ἵνα φανερωθῇ,	ⲈϤⲚⲀⲞⲨⲰⲚϨ ⲈⲂⲞⲖ ⲀⲚ
καὶ {κρυπτὸν}	{οὐδὲ} {ἀπόκρυφον}	οὐδὲ ἐγένετο ἀπόκρυφον	
ὃ οὐ γνωσθήσεται.	[(ὃ οὐ)] μὴ [(γνωσθῇ)]		
ʅ¹⇒ Luke 12:9	καὶ {εἰς φανερὸν} {ἔλθῃ}.	ἀλλ' ἵνα ἔλθῃ εἰς φανερόν.	
}⁰			

² Matthew's μὴ οὖν φοβηθῆτε αὐτούς. See also Luke 12:5 φοβηθῆτε (*bis*).

³ Luke's δέ or Matthew's γάρ.

⁴ The position of -κεκαλυμμένον before (Luke) or after (Matthew) ἐστιν.

⁵ Luke's compound verbal form συγκεκαλυμμένον.

Nichts ist verhüllt, das nicht enthüllt werden wird, und verborgen, das nicht erkannt werden wird.

Il n'y a rien de voilé qui ne sera pas dévoilé ni de caché qui ne sera pas connu.

5.2=6.5 Denn es gibt nichts Verborgenes, das nicht offenbar werden wird.

5.2=6.5 Car il n'est rien de caché qui ne sera manifesté.

[Denn es gibt nichts] Verborgenes, das nicht offenbar [werden wird], und (nichts) Begrabenes, das [nicht auferweckt werden wird].

[Car il n']est rien de caché qui ne [sera] manifesté et (rien d')enseveli qui [ne sera ressuscité].

[Denn nichts ist] verborgen, [das nicht offenbar sein wird].

[Car il n'y a rien de] dissimulé [qui ne sera manifesté].

Q 12:3

Markan Parallel	Matthean Doublet	Matt 10:27	Q 12:3
		[ ][1]	[][1]
		(ὃ)[2][ ][2]	(ὃ)[2][][2]
		(λέγω ὑμῖν)[3]	(λέγω ὑμῖν)[3]
		ἐν τῇ σκοτίᾳ	ἐν τῇ σκοτίᾳ
		εἴπατε ἐν τῷ φωτί,	εἴπατε ἐν τῷ φωτί,
		[ ][4]	[][4]
		καὶ ὃ (εἰς)[5] τὸ οὖς	καὶ ὃ (εἰς)[5] τὸ οὖς
		(ἀκούετε)[6]	(ἀκούετε)[6]
		[ ][7]	[ ][7]
		κηρύ(ξατε)[4]	κηρύ(ξατε)[4]
		ἐπὶ τῶν δωμάτων.	ἐπὶ τῶν δωμάτων.

PH: ()[3]… [ἀκουσθήσεται][4]… [ἐλαλήσατε][6]… κηρυ[χθήσεται][4].

IQP 1989, JMR, PH, JSK: [ ][7] {D}, not in Q.

1 Luke's ἀνθ 'ὧν.
2 Luke's ὅσα or Matthew's ὅ.
3 Matthew's λέγω ὑμῖν and the resultant divergences of syntax.

4 Luke's future passive indicatives (including ἀκουσθήσεται) or Matthew's aorist active imperatives (including ἀκούετε), one of which, εἴπατε, is in Luke in the indicative.

Q

ὃ λέγω ὑμῖν ἐν τῇ σκοτίᾳ εἴπατε ἐν τῷ φωτί, καὶ ὃ εἰς τὸ οὖς ἀκούετε κηρύξατε ἐπὶ τῶν δωμάτων.

What I say to you in the dark, speak in the light; and what you hear «whispered» in the ear, proclaim on the housetops.

Gos. Thom. 33.1 (Nag Hammadi II 2)

Λέγει Ἰησοῦς· ὃ ἀκούσεις εἰς τὸ οὖς σου, εἰς τὸ ἄλλο οὖς[1] κήρυξον ἐπὶ τῶν δωμάτων ὑμῶν.

Jesus says: What you will hear (whispered) in your ear, proclaim on your rooftops in (someone) else's ear.[2]

1 The passage may be corrupt due to dittography in the Coptic text.
1 Dieses Stück kann eine im koptischen Text durch Dittographie entstandene Textverderbnis sein.
1 Le texte est peut-être corrompu en raison d'une dittographie dans le texte copte.

2 The text is perhaps to be considered corrupt. There is however – on the assumption that the Coptic ϩⲙ̄ is the equivalent of a Greek εἰς – still another possibility for understanding the given text as meaningful: "… will hear (whispered) in your (one) ear (and) in (your) other ear, proclaim …" (as a play on words, a circumlocation for: "with both ears"). If the Coptic ϩⲙ̄ reproduces a Greek ἐν, one could – on the assumption that the text is to be considered as corrupt as the result of dittography – translate as follows: "… What you will hear with your ear ~~with the other ear~~, proclaim on your roofs." Otherwise one could seek to understand the given text as meaningful as follows: Either: "… with your ear, proclaim

Q 12:3

Luke 12:3	Lukan Doublet	Markan Parallel	*Gos. Thom.* 33.1
[ἀνθ' ὧν][1]			
(ὅ)[2][σα][2]			
( )[3]			ⲡⲉϫⲉ ⲓ̅ⲥ̅
ἐν τῇ σκοτίᾳ			
εἴπατε ἐν τῷ φωτὶ			
[ἀκουσθήσεται][4],			
καὶ ὃ [πρὸς][5] τὸ οὖς			ⲡⲉⲧ'ⲕⲛⲁⲥⲱⲧⲙ̅ ⲉⲣⲟϥ ϩⲙ̅
[ἐλαλήσατε][6]			ⲡⲉⲕ'ⲙⲁⲁϫⲉ
[ἐν τοῖς ταμείοις][7]			{ϩⲙ̅ ⲡⲕⲉⲙⲁⲁϫⲉ}
κηρυ[χθήσεται][4]			ⲧⲁϣⲉ ⲟⲉⲓϣ' ⲙ̅ⲙⲟϥ'
ἐπὶ τῶν δωμάτων.			ϩⲓϫⲛ̅ ⲛⲉⲧⲛ̅ϫⲉⲛⲉⲡⲱⲣ'

5 Luke's πρός or Matthew's εἰς.

6 Luke's ἐλαλήσατε or Matthew's ἀκούετε. (See also ἀκουσθήσεται in Luke 12:3a).

7 Luke's ἐν τοῖς ταμείοις.

Was ich «zu» euch im Dunkeln sage, sagt im Licht, und was ihr ins Ohr «geflüstert» hört, verkündet auf den Dächern.

Ce que je vous dis dans l'obscurité, dites-«le» en «pleine» lumière, et ce que vous entendez à l'oreille, proclamez«-le» sur les toits.

Jesus spricht: Was du in dein Ohr (geflüstert) hören wirst, verkündige es von euren Dächern in (jemand) anderes Ohr.[3]

Jésus dit: Ce que tu entendras (chuchoté) à ton oreille, proclame-le sur vos toits à l'oreille de (quelqu'un)[4] d'autre.

3 Der Text ist vielleicht als korrupt anzusehen; es gibt jedoch – unter der Voraussetzung, dass das koptische ϩⲙ̅ das Äquivalent eines griechischen εἰς ist – noch eine andere Möglichkeit, den vorliegenden Text als sinnvoll zu verstehen: "… in dein (eines) Ohr (geflüstert) hören wirst (und) in (dein) anderes Ohr, verkündige …" (als wortspielerische Umschreibung für: "mit beiden Ohren"). Wenn das koptische ϩⲙ̅ ein griechisches ἐν wiedergibt, könnte man – unter der Annahme, dass der Text auf Grund von Dittographie als korrupt anzusehen ist – folgendermaßen übersetzen: "… Was du hörst mit deinem Ohr ~~mit dem anderen Ohr~~, verkündige es auf euren Dächern." Ansonsten könnte man den vorlie-

4 Le passage est peut-être corrompu. Toutefois, dans l'hypothèse où le copte ϩⲙ̅ serait l'équivalent du grec εἰς, il serait encore possible de comprendre, d'une manière satisfaisante, le texte tel que transmis: "… (chuchoté) à ton oreille (et) à (ton) autre oreille, proclame-le …" (une manière imagée de dire "ce que tu entendras de tes deux oreilles"). Si le copte ϩⲙ̅ rend le grec ἐν et dans l'hypothèse que le texte soit corrompu du fait d'une dittographie, on pourrait traduire ainsi: "… Ce que tu entendras de ton oreille ~~de l'autre oreille~~, proclame-le sur vos toits". On pourrait aussi chercher à comprendre le texte tel que transmis de la manière suivante, soit: "… de ton oreille, proclame-le sur vos toits à l'oreille de

Q 12:3

Markan Parallel	Matthean Doublet	Matt 10:27	Q 12:3
		it on your roofs into (somebody) else's ear"; or: "... with your (one) ear (and) with (your) other ear, proclaim...".	

Gos. Thom. 33.1 (P. Oxy. 1)

λέγει Ἰ(ησοῦ)ς· ὃ ἀκούεις [ε]ἰς τ̣ὸ ἓ̣ν̣ ὠ̣τ̣ίον σ̣ο̣υ, τ̣ο̣[ῦτο κήρυξον ...]

Jesus says: <What> you (sg.) hear (whispered) in one of your (sg.) ears, [proclaim ...]

Q 12:3

Luke 12:3	Lukan Doublet	Markan Parallel	*Gos. Thom.* 33.1

genden Text in folgender Weise als sinnvoll zu verstehen versuchen: Entweder: "… mit deinem Ohr, verkündige es auf euren Dächern in (jemand) anderes Ohr"; oder: "… mit deinem (einen) Ohr (und) mit (deinem) anderen Ohr, verkündige…."

(quelqu'un) d'autre", ou: "… de ton oreille (et) de (ton) autre oreille, proclame-le…".

Jesus spricht: <Was> du hörst (geflüstert) in dein eines Ohr, [verkündige] es […]

Jésus dit: <Ce que> tu entends (chuchoté) à une de tes oreilles, [proclame]-le […]

Q 12:4

Markan Parallel	Matt 10:28b	Matt 10:28a	Q 12:4
		(καὶ)[1]	(καὶ)[1]
	([φοβ]εῖσθε) δὲ μᾶλλον	μὴ φοβ(εῖσθε)[2]	μὴ φοβ(εῖσθε)[2]
	τὸν	ἀπὸ τῶν	ἀπὸ τῶν
	(δυνάμεν)ον	ἀποκτε(ν)[3]νόντων	ἀποκτε⟦(ν)[3]⟧νόντων
	καὶ (ψυχὴν)	τὸ σῶμα,	τὸ σῶμα,
		∫(τὴν)[4] ≀4	∫(τὴν)[4] ≀4
	καὶ	(δὲ)[5]	(δὲ)[5]
	([σῶμα])	∫(ψυχὴν)[4] ≀4	∫(ψυχὴν)[4] ≀4
	ἀπολέσαι	μὴ (δυναμένων)[6] ∫≀4	μὴ (δυναμένων)[6] ∫ ≀4
	ἐν γεέννῃ.	(ἀποκτεῖναι)[6].	(ἀποκτεῖναι)[6].

PH: ἀποκτε(ν)[3]νόντων.

IQP 1989: ⟦∫(τὴν)[4] ≀4 (δὲ)[5] ∫(ψυχὴν)[4] ≀4⟧ μὴ (δυναμένων) ⟦∫≀4 (ἀποκτεῖναι)[6]⟧.

Text Critical Note: See the discussion of the orthography in the front matter.

[1] Luke's λέγω δὲ ὑμῖν τοῖς φίλοις μου or Matthew's καί.
[2] Luke's φοβηθῆτε or Matthew's φοβεῖσθε.
[3] Orthography: Luke's ἀποκτεινόντων or Matthew's ἀποκτεννόντων.

Q

καὶ μὴ φοβεῖσθε ἀπὸ τῶν ἀποκτε⟦ν⟧νόντων τὸ σῶμα, τὴν δὲ ψυχὴν μὴ δυναμένων ἀποκτεῖναι·	And do not be afraid of those who kill the body, but cannot kill the soul.

Q 12:4

Luke 12:4	Luke 12:5a-b	Markan Parallel	Gospel of Thomas
[Λέγω δὲ ὑμῖν τοῖς φίλοις μου,][1] μὴ φοβ[ηθῆτε][2] ἀπὸ τῶν ἀποκτε[ι][3]νόντων τὸ σῶμα [καὶ μετὰ ταῦτα][5] ʃ ʅ[4] μὴ [ἐχόντων][6] ʃ[περισσότερόν τι][4] ʅ[4] [ποιῆσαι][6].	ὑποδείξω [δὲ ὑμῖν] τίνα φοβηθῆτε· [(φοβ)ήθητε] τὸν [μετὰ] τὸ [(ἀποκτ)εῖν]αι [ἔχοντ]α ἐξουσίαν ἐμβαλεῖν εἰς τὴν γέενναν.		

[4] Luke's περισσότερόν τι or Matthew's τὴν … ψυχήν, and the divergence in the positions.
[5] Luke's καὶ μετὰ ταῦτα or Matthew's postpositive δέ.
[6] Luke's ἐχόντων … ποιῆσαι or Matthew's δυναμένων ἀποκτεῖναι. (See also Luke 12:5 ἀποκτεῖναι.)

Und fürchtet euch nicht vor denen, die den Leib töten, die Seele aber nicht töten können.

Et ne craignez pas ceux qui tuent le corps, mais ne peuvent pas tuer l'âme.

Q 12:5

Markan Parallel	Matt 10:28a	Matt 10:28b	Q 12:5
	καὶ	[ ][1] ʃ ʅ[1]	[][1] ʃʅ[1]
		[ ][1]	[][1]
	μὴ ([φοβ]εῖσθε)	φοβ(εῖσθε)[2] ʃδὲʅ[1]	φοβ(εῖσθε)[2] ʃδὲʅ[1]
	ἀπὸ τῶν [ἀποκτ]ε[ν]νόντων	(μᾶλλον)[3] τὸν [ ][3]	( )[3] τὸν [][3]
		(δυνάμενον)[4]	(δυνάμενον)[4]
	τὸ (σῶμα), τὴν δὲ (ψυχὴν)	(καὶ ψυχὴν καὶ σῶμα	(καὶ ψυχὴν καὶ σῶμα
	μὴ (δυναμέν)ων ἀποκτεῖναι·	ἀπολέσαι ἐν)[5]	ἀπολέσαι ἐν)[5]
		[ ][6]	[τ<ῇ>][6]
		γεένν(ῃ)[5].	γεένν(ῃ)[5].
		[ ][7]	[][7]

JMR: ( )[3] not in Q {D}; PH: ⟦(μᾶλλον)[3]⟧; JSK: ( )[3] indeterminate. JSK, IQP 1989: [ ][3] [ ][4] [ ][5].

[1] Luke's ὑποδείξω δὲ ὑμῖν τίνα φοβηθῆτε, which moves forward the postpositive δέ.

[2] Luke's φοβήθητε or Matthew's φοβεῖσθε. (See variation unit [7] and Matt 10:26 at Q 12:2 φοβηθῆτε.)

[3] Luke's τὸν μετὰ τὸ ἀποκτεῖναι or Matthew's μᾶλλον τόν.

Q

φοβεῖσθε δὲ .. τὸν δυνάμενον καὶ ψυχὴν καὶ σῶμα ἀπολέσαι ἐν τ<ῇ> γεέννῃ.	But fear .. the one who is able to destroy both the soul and body in Gehenna.

Q 12:5

Luke 12:5	Luke 12:4	Markan Parallel	Gospel of Thomas
[ὑποδείξω][1] ʃδὲʅ[1] [ὑμῖν τίνα φοβηθῆτε·][1] φοβ[ήθητε][2] ʃ ʅ[1] ( )[3] τὸν [μετὰ τὸ ἀποκτεῖναι][3] [ἔχοντα ἐξουσίαν][4] [ἐμβαλεῖν εἰς][5] [τὴν][6] γέενν[αν][5]. [ναὶ λέγω ὑμῖν, τοῦτον φοβήθητε.][7]	Λέγω [δὲ ὑμῖν] τοῖς φίλοις μου, μὴ [(φοβ)ηθῆτε] ἀπὸ τῶν [ἀποκτειν]όντων τὸ σῶμα καὶ [μετὰ] ταῦτα μὴ [ἐχόντ]ων περισσότερόν τι ποιῆσαι.		

PH: [][7].

[4] Luke's ἔχοντα ἐξουσίαν or Matthew's δυνάμενον.

[5] Luke's ἐμβαλεῖν εἰς or Matthew's καὶ ψυχὴν καὶ σῶμα ἀπολέσαι ἐν and the resultant case.

[6] Luke's τήν.

[7] Luke's ναὶ λέγω ὑμῖν, τοῦτον φοβήθητε.

Fürchtet aber .. den, der auch Seele und Leib in <der> Gehenna vernichten kann.

Craignez en revanche .. celui qui peut détruire l'âme et le corps dans <la> Géhenne.

Q 12:6

Markan Parallel	Matthean Doublet	Matt 10:29	Q 12:6
		οὐχὶ (δύο)[1] στρουθία ⸉ ⸊[2] ἀσσαρί(ου)[1] [ ][1] [2]⸉πωλ(εῖ)[3]ται⸊[2]; καὶ ἓν ἐξ αὐτῶν οὐ (πεσεῖται)[4] (ἐπὶ τὴν γῆν)[5] (ἄνευ)[6] τοῦ (πατρὸς ὑμῶν)[7].	οὐχὶ ⟦[πέντε][1]⟧ στρουθία [2]⸉πωλ[οῦν][3]ται⸊[2] ἀσσαρί⟦[ων][1] [δύο][1]⟧ ⸉ ⸊[2]; καὶ ἓν ἐξ αὐτῶν οὐ (πεσεῖται)[4] (ἐπὶ τὴν γῆν)[5] (ἄνευ)[6] τοῦ ⟦(πατρὸς ὑμῶν)[7]⟧.

JSK: [πέντε][1].

IQP 1989: ἀσσαρί[ων][1] [δύο][1].

[1] Luke's πέντε ... ἀσσαρίων δύο or Matthew's δύο ... ἀσσαρίου.

[2] The position of πωλ...ται before (Luke) or after (Matthew) the price.

[3] Luke's πωλοῦνται or Matthew's πωλεῖται.

Q

οὐχὶ ⟦πέντε⟧ στρουθία πωλοῦνται ἀσσαρί⟦ων δύο⟧; καὶ ἓν ἐξ αὐτῶν οὐ πεσεῖται ἐπὶ τὴν γῆν ἄνευ τοῦ ⟦πατρὸς ὑμῶν⟧.

Are not ⟦five⟧ sparrows sold for ⟦two⟧ cents? And yet not one of them will fall to earth without ⟦your Father's⟧ «consent».

Q 12:6

Luke 12:6	Lukan Doublet	Markan Parallel	Gospel of Thomas
οὐχὶ [πέντε][1] στρουθία ²⸉πωλ[οῦν]³ται⸊² ἀσσαρί[ων][1] [δύο][1] ⸉ ⸊²; καὶ ἓν ἐξ αὐτῶν οὐ[κ ἔστιν ἐπιλελησμένον][4] ( )[5] [ἐνώπιον][6] τοῦ [θεοῦ][7].			

IQP 1989, JSK: [θεοῦ][7].

[4] Luke's οὐκ ἔστιν ἐπιλελησμένον or Matthew's οὐ πεσεῖται.
[5] Matthew's ἐπὶ τὴν γῆν.
[6] Luke's ἐνώπιον or Matthew's ἄνευ.
[7] Luke's θεοῦ or Matthew's πατρὸς ὑμῶν.

Werden nicht ⟦fünf⟧ Spatzen für ⟦zwei⟧ Asse verkauft? Und doch wird nicht einer von ihnen auf die Erde fallen ohne ⟦euren Vater⟧.

Ne vend-on pas ⟦cinq⟧ moineaux pour ⟦deux⟧ sous? Et pas un d'entre eux ne tombera à terre sans «la volonté de» ⟦votre Père⟧.

Q 12:7

Markan Parallel	Matthean Doublet	Matt 10:30-31	Q 12:7
		10:30 ⸉ὑμῶν⸊¹ (δὲ)² καὶ αἱ τρίχες τῆς κεφαλῆς ⸉ ⸊¹ πᾶσαι ἠριθμη(μέναι εἰσίν)³. **10:31** μὴ (οὖν)⁴ φοβεῖσθε· πολλῶν στρουθίων διαφέρετε (ὑμεῖς)⁵.	⸉ὑμῶν⸊¹ ⟦(δὲ)²⟧ καὶ αἱ τρίχες τῆς κεφαλῆς ⸉ ⸊¹ πᾶσαι ἠριθμη⟦(μέναι εἰσίν)³⟧. μὴ ()⁴ φοβεῖσθε· πολλῶν στρουθίων διαφέρετε (ὑμεῖς)⁵.

IQP 1989: ⸉ ⸊¹ [ ]²... ⸉ὑμῶν⸊¹.

JSK: ⸉ ⸊¹ [ἀλλὰ]²... ⸉ὑμῶν⸊¹.

¹ The position of ὑμῶν after (Luke) or before (Matthew) καὶ αἱ τρίχες τῆς κεφαλῆς.

² Luke's ἀλλά or Matthew's postpositive δέ.

³ Luke's ἠρίθμηνται or Matthew's ἠριθμημέναι εἰσίν.

Q

ὑμῶν ⟦δὲ⟧ καὶ αἱ τρίχες τῆς κεφαλῆς πᾶσαι ἠρίθμη⟦μέναι εἰσίν⟧. μὴ φοβεῖσθε· πολλῶν στρουθίων διαφέρετε ὑμεῖς.	But even the hairs of your head all are numbered. Do not be afraid, you are worth more than many sparrows.

Q 12:7

Luke 12:7	Luke 21:18	Markan Parallel	Gospel of Thomas
⸀ ⸁[1] [ἀλλὰ][2] καὶ αἱ τρίχες τῆς κεφαλῆς ⸀ὑμῶν⸁[1] πᾶσαι ἠρίθμη[νται][3]. μὴ ( )[4] φοβεῖσθε· πολλῶν στρουθίων διαφέρετε ( )[5].	 καὶ θ[(ρὶ)]ξ ἐκ [(τῆς κεφαλῆς) (ὑμῶν)] οὐ μὴ ἀπόληται.		

IQP 1989, JSK: ἠρίθμη[νται][3].

[4] Matthew's οὖν.
[5] Matthew's ὑμεῖς.

Aber selbst die Haare auf eurem Kopf sind alle gezählt. Fürchtet euch nicht: Ihr seid mehr wert als viele Spatzen.

Mais même les cheveux de votre tête sont tous comptés. Soyez sans crainte. Vous valez mieux, vous, que d'innombrables moineaux.

Q 12:8

Markan Parallel	Matthean Doublet	Matt 10:32	Q 12:8
		[ ][1] Πᾶς (οὖν)[1] ὅσ(τις)[2] [ ][3] ὁμολογήσ(ει)[3] ἐν ἐμοὶ ἔμπροσθεν τῶν ἀνθρώπων, [4]⸉ὁμολογήσ(ω)[5] ⸊[4] κἀ(γὼ)[5] ⸉ ⸊[4] ἐν αὐτῷ ἔμπροσθεν [ ][6] τοῦ (πατρός μου τοῦ ἐν τοῖς οὐρανοῖς)[7]·	[][1] πᾶς ()[1] ὃς()[2] ⟦[ἂν][3]⟧ ὁμολογήσ⟦[ῃ][3]⟧ ἐν ἐμοὶ ἔμπροσθεν τῶν ἀνθρώπων, ⸉⸊[4] κα⟦[ὶ ὁ υἱὸς τοῦ ἀνθρώπου][5]⟧ [4]⸉ὁμολογήσ⟦[ει][5]⟧ ⸊[4] ἐν αὐτῷ ἔμπροσθεν [τῶν ἀγγέλων][6] τοῦ [ ][7]·

IQP 1993: [ἂν][3] ὁμολογήσ[ῃ][3].
PH: ⸉ ⸊[4] Luke = Q {C}.

IQP 1993: κα[ ][5] [4]⸉ὁμολογήσ[ ][5] ⸊[4].
PH: κα⟦[ὶ][5] <ἐ>[5](γὼ)[5]⟧ [4]⸉ὁμολογήσ⟦(ω)[5]⟧ ⸊[4].

[1] Luke's λέγω δὲ ὑμῖν or Matthew's οὖν.
[2] Matthew's -τις.
[3] Luke's ἂν ὁμολογήσῃ or Matthew's ὁμολογήσει.

[4] The position of the second ὁμολογήσ- after (Luke) or before (Matthew) the subject.

Q

πᾶς ὃς ⟦ἂν⟧ ὁμολογήσ⟦ῃ⟧ ἐν ἐμοὶ ἔμπροσθεν τῶν ἀνθρώπων, κα⟦ὶ ὁ υἱὸς τοῦ ἀνθρώπου⟧ ὁμολογήσ⟦ει⟧ ἐν αὐτῷ ἔμπροσθεν τῶν ἀγγέλων ..·	Anyone who ⟦may⟧ speak out for me in public, ⟦the son of humanity⟧ will also speak out for him before the angels .. .

Q 12:8

Luke 12:8	Lukan Doublet	Markan Parallel	Gospel of Thomas
[Λέγω δὲ ὑμῖν][1], πᾶς ( )[1] ὅς( )[2] [ἂν][3] ὁμολογήσ[η][3] ἐν ἐμοὶ ἔμπροσθεν τῶν ἀνθρώπων, ʃ ʅ[4] κα[ὶ ὁ υἱὸς τοῦ ἀνθρώπου][5] [4]ʃὁμολογήσ[ει][5] ʅ[4] ἐν αὐτῷ ἔμπροσθεν [τῶν ἀγγέλων][6] τοῦ [θεοῦ][7].			

IQP 1993: τ[ ][6] τοῦ [( )][7].
JSK: ⟦[θεοῦ][7]⟧.

[5] Luke's καὶ ὁ υἱὸς τοῦ ἀνθρώπου or Matthew's κἀγώ and in each case the corresponding verb form.

[6] Luke's τῶν ἀγγέλων.

[7] Luke's θεοῦ or Matthew's πατρός μου τοῦ ἐν τοῖς οὐρανοῖς.

Jeder, der sich zu mir vor den Menschen bekennt, zu dem wird ⟦sich⟧ auch ⟦der Menschensohn⟧ vor den Engeln .. bekennen.

Quiconque ⟦viendrait à⟧ se déclarer pour moi devant les hommes, ⟦le fils de l'homme⟧ aussi se déclarera pour lui devant les anges .. .

Q 12:9

Mark 8:38	Matt 16:27	Matt 10:33	Q 12:9
ὃς γὰρ ἐὰν		({ὅσ}τις)^{1} δ' ({ἂν})^{1}	({ὃς}<>)^{1} δ' ({ἂν})^{1}
ἐπαισχυνθῇ με		ἀρνήσ(ηταί)^{1} {με}	ἀρνή(σηταί)^{1} {με}
καὶ τοὺς ἐμοὺς λόγους			
ἐν τῇ γενεᾷ ταύτῃ			
τῇ μοιχαλίδι καὶ ἁμαρτωλῷ,			
		(ἔμπροσθεν)^{2}	(ἔμπροσθεν)^{2}
		τῶν ἀνθρώπων,	τῶν ἀνθρώπων,
καὶ	μέλλει γὰρ		
ὁ υἱὸς τοῦ ἀνθρώπου	{ὁ υἱὸς τοῦ ἀνθρώπου}		
ἐπαισχυνθήσεται		[ ]^{3}ἀρνή(σομαι)^{4}	[]^{3}ἀρνη⟦[{θήσεται}]^{4}⟧
αὐτόν,		(κἀγὼ {αὐτὸν})^{4}	⟦()^{4}⟧
ὅταν ἔλθῃ	ἔρχεσθαι		
ἐν τῇ δόξῃ	{ἐν τῇ δόξῃ	(ἔμπροσθεν)^{2}	(ἔμπροσθεν)^{2}
		{[ ]}^{5}	{[τῶν ἀγγέλων]}^{5}
τοῦ πατρὸς αὐτοῦ	(τοῦ πατρὸς) αὐτοῦ	({τοῦ πατρός} μου	[ ]^{6}
μετὰ τῶν ἀγγέλων	μετὰ [τῶν ἀγγέλων]}	τοῦ ἐν τοῖς οὐρανοῖς)^{6}	
τῶν ἁγίων.	αὐτοῦ,	.	.
		ʅ Matt 10:26^{1}	ʅ Q 12:2^{1}
	καὶ τότε ἀποδώσει ἑκάστῳ		
	κατὰ τὴν πρᾶξιν αὐτοῦ.		

IQP 1993: []^{3}ἀρνη[ ]^{4} ()^{4}.

PH: ⟦ ʃ ʅ^{4} {(κα)^{4}<ὶ} ἐ>^{4}(γὼ)^{4}⟧ ^{4}ʃ []^{3}ἀρνή⟦(σομαι)^{4} ʅ^{4} ({αὐτόν})^{4}⟧.

1 Luke's ὁ δὲ ἀρνησάμενός με or Matthew's ὅστις δ' ἂν ἀρνήσηταί με.

2 Luke's ἐνώπιον … ἐνώπιον or Matthew's ἔμπροσθεν … ἔμπροσθεν.

3 Luke's prefix ἀπ-.

Q

ὃς δ' ἂν ἀρνήσηταί με ἔμπροσθεν τῶν ἀνθρώπων, ἀρνη⟦θήσεται⟧ ἔμπροσθεν τῶν ἀγγέλων .. .

But whoever may deny me in public ⟦will be⟧ den⟦ied⟧ before the angels .. .

Q 12:9

Luke 12:9	Luke 9:26	Mark 8:38	Gospel of Thomas
[ὁ][1] δ[ὲ][1] ({ })[1] ἀρνησ[άμενός][1] {με}	{(ὃς) γὰρ} {(ἂν) ἐπαισχυνθῇ με καὶ τοὺς ἐμοὺς λόγους},	ὃς γὰρ ἐὰν ἐπαισχυνθῇ με καὶ τοὺς ἐμοὺς λόγους ἐν τῇ γενεᾷ ταύτῃ τῇ μοιχαλίδι καὶ ἁμαρτωλῷ,	
[ἐνώπιον][2] τῶν ἀνθρώπων			
[ἀπ][3]αρνη[{θήσεται}][4] ( )[4]	τοῦτον {ὁ υἱὸς τοῦ ἀνθρώπου ἐπαισχυν[θήσεται]},	καὶ ὁ υἱὸς τοῦ ἀνθρώπου ἐπαισχυνθήσεται αὐτόν,	
	{ὅταν ἔλθῃ ἐν τῇ δόξῃ} αὐτοῦ	ὅταν ἔλθῃ ἐν τῇ δόξῃ	
[ἐνώπιον][2] {[τῶν ἀγγέλων]}[5] [τοῦ θεοῦ][6]	καὶ {(τοῦ πατρὸς)} καὶ {[τῶν]} {ἁγίων} {[ἀγγέλων]}.	τοῦ πατρὸς αὐτοῦ μετὰ τῶν ἀγγέλων τῶν ἁγίων.	
. ≀ Luke 12:2[1]			

IQP 1993: τ[ ][5] [( )][6].

JSK: ⟦[τοῦ θεοῦ][6]⟧.

[4] Luke's -αρνηθήσεται or Matthew's ἀρνήσομαι κἀγὼ αὐτόν.
[5] Luke's τῶν ἀγγέλων.

[6] Luke's τοῦ θεοῦ or Matthew's τοῦ πατρός μου τοῦ ἐν τοῖς οὐρανοῖς.

Wer mich aber vor den Menschen verleugnet, ⟦wird⟧ vor den Engeln .. verleugne⟦t werden⟧.

Mais celui qui me renierait devant les hommes, ⟦sera⟧ reni⟦é⟧ devant les anges .. .

Q 12:10

Mark 3:28-29	Matt 12:31, 32c	Matt 12:32a-b	Q 12:10
		[0]/	[0]/
		[1]ʃ	[1]ʃ
3:28 Ἀμὴν λέγω ὑμῖν ὅτι	**12:31** Διὰ τοῦτο {λέγω ὑμῖν},	καὶ [ ][2]	καὶ [][2]
πάντα	[{πᾶ}σ]α {ἁμαρτ}ία {καὶ}	ὃς (ἐὰν εἴπῃ)[3] λόγον	ὃς (ἐὰν εἴπῃ)[3] λόγον
ἀφεθήσεται	{βλασφημία} [{ἀφεθήσεται}]	(κατὰ)[4]	[εἰς][4]
τοῖς υἱοῖς	[({το)]ῖς}	{το}(ῦ)[4] {υἱο}(ῦ)[4]	{τὸ}[ν][4] {υἱὸ}[ν][4]
τῶν ἀνθρώπων	[({ἀνθρώπ}ο)]ις},	{τ}οῦ {ἀνθρώπ}ου,	{τ}οῦ {ἀνθρώπ}ου,
τὰ ἁμαρτήματα		{ἀφεθήσεται} αὐτῷ·	{ἀφεθήσεται} αὐτῷ·
καὶ αἱ βλασφημίαι			
ὅσα ἐὰν βλασφημήσωσιν·			
3:29 ὃς δ᾽ ἂν	ἢ [({δ})ὲ] ([{το}]ῦ [{πνεύμα}]τος)	{(ὃς)[5] δ᾽ (ἂν)[5]}	{(ὃς)[5] δ᾽ (ἂν)}[5]
βλασφημήσῃ	[{βλασφημ}]ία	[6]ʃ (εἴπ)[7]{(ῃ)}[5] ʅ[6]	[6]ʃ ⟦[εἴπ][7]⟧{(ῃ)}[5] ʅ[6]
εἰς		(κατὰ)[4]	[εἰς][4]
		ʃ ʅ[8]	[8]ʃτὸ}()[4] {ἅγιο[ν]}[4] ʅ[8]
τὸ πνεῦμα		({το}ῦ)[4] {πνεύμα}(τος)[4]	()[4] {πνεῦμα}()[4]
τὸ ἅγιον,		[8]ʃ{το}(ῦ)[4] {ἁγίο}(υ)[4] ʅ[8],	ʃ ʅ[8]
		ʃ ʅ[6]	ʃʅ[6]
οὐκ ἔχει ἄφεσιν	[({οὐκ} {ἀφ}εθήσεται).]	{οὐκ} {ἀφ}εθήσεται	{οὐκ} {ἀφ}εθήσεται
		(αὐτῷ)[5]	(αὐτῷ)[5].
		ʅ[1]	ʅ[1]
εἰς	**12:32c** οὔτε ἐν τούτῳ		
τὸν αἰῶνα,	{τ}ῷ {αἰῶν}ι		
ἀλλὰ ἔνοχός ἐστιν	οὔτε ἐν τῷ μέλλοντι.		
αἰωνίου ἁμαρτήματος.		\[0]	\[0]

IQP 1990, JMR: ⟦[εἰς][4]⟧ {τὸ}⟦[ν][4]⟧ {υἱὸ}⟦[ν][4]⟧ … ⟦{[εἰς]}[4]⟧ [8]ʃ {τὸ}⟦()[4]⟧ {ἅγιο⟦[ν]}[4]⟧ ʅ[8] ⟦()[4]⟧ {πνεῦμα}⟦()[4]⟧.

[0] Is Luke 12:10 par. Matt 12:32a-b in Q or from Mark?

[1] The position of Q 12:10 in Q: After Q 12:9 and before Q 12:11 (Lukan order); or after Q 11:23 (Matt 12:30) and before Q 6:43-44 (Matt 12:33) (Matthean order).

[2] Luke's πᾶς.

[3] Luke's ὃς ἐρεῖ or Matthew's ὃ ἐὰν εἴπῃ.

[4] Luke's εἰς (see Mark 3:29) or Matthew's κατά and the resultant case.

Q 12:10

Luke 12:10	Lukan Doublet	Mark 3:29a	*Gos. Thom.* 44
[0]/			44.1 ⲡⲉϫⲉ ⲓ̅ⲥ̅ ϫⲉ
			ⲡⲉⲧⲁϫⲉ ⲟⲩⲁ ⲁⲡⲉⲓⲱⲧ’
[1]⸢			ⲥⲉⲛⲁⲕⲱ ⲉⲃⲟⲗ ⲛⲁϥ’
Καὶ [{πᾶ}ς][2]			44.2 ⲁⲩⲱ
ὃς [ἐρεῖ][3] λόγον			ⲡⲉⲧⲁϫⲉ ⲟⲩⲁ
[εἰς][4]			
{τὸ}[ν][4] {υἱὸ}[ν][4]			ⲉⲡϣⲏⲣⲉ
{τ}οῦ {ἀνθρώπ}ου,			
{ἀφεθήσεται} αὐτῷ·			ⲥⲉⲛⲁⲕⲱ ⲉⲃⲟⲗ ⲛⲁϥ’
[τῷ][5] {δ}ὲ		**3:29a** ὃς δ’ ἂν	44.3 ⲡⲉⲧⲁϫⲉ
⸢ ⸣[6]		βλασφημήσῃ	ⲟⲩⲁ ⲇⲉ
{[εἰς][4]		εἰς	
[8]⸢τὸ}( )[4] {ἅγιο[ν]}[4] ⸣[8]			
( )[4] {πνεῦμα}( )[4]		τὸ πνεῦμα	ⲁⲡⲡ̅ⲛ̅ⲁ̅
⸢ ⸣[8]		τὸ ἅγιον,	ⲉⲧⲟⲩⲁⲁⲃ
[6]⸢ {[βλασφημήσ]}[7][αντι][5] ⸣[6]			
{οὐκ} {ἀφ}εθήσεται		οὐκ ἔχει ἄφεσιν	ⲥⲉⲛⲁⲕⲱ ⲁⲛ ⲉⲃⲟⲗ
( )[5].			ⲛⲁϥ’
⸣[1]			
			ⲟⲩⲧⲉ ϩⲙ̅ ⲡⲕⲁϩ
			ⲟⲩⲧⲉ ϩⲛ̅ ⲧⲡⲉ
\[0]			

IQP 1990: ⟦{[βλασφημήσ][7](η)[5].

[5] Luke's τῷ ...-αντι or Matthew's ὅς ... ἂν ...-η ...αὐτῷ. (See also the relative construction at variation unit [3].)

[6] The position of the verb.

[7] Luke's βλασφημήσ- or Matthew's εἴπ-.

[8] The position of the article and the adjective ἅγιος in relation to the noun πνεῦμα.

Q 12:10

Mark 3:28-29	Matt 12:31, 32c	Matt 12:32a-b	Q 12:10

Q

καὶ ὃς ἐὰν εἴπῃ λόγον εἰς τὸν υἱὸν τοῦ ἀνθρώπου ἀφεθήσεται αὐτῷ· ὃς δ' ἂν ⟦εἴπ⟧ῃ εἰς τὸ ἅγιον πνεῦμα οὐκ ἀφεθήσεται αὐτῷ.

And whoever says a word against the son of humanity, it will be forgiven him; but whoever ⟦speaks⟧ against the holy Spirit, it will not be forgiven him.

Gos. Thom. 44 (Nag Hammadi II 2)

(1) Λέγει Ἰησοῦς· ὃς ἂν βλασφημήσῃ εἰς[1] τὸν πατέρα, ἀφεθήσεται αὐτῷ. (2) καὶ ὃς ἂν βλασφημήσῃ εἰς τὸν υἱόν, ἀφεθήσεται αὐτῷ. (3) ὃς δ' ἂν βλασφημήσῃ εἰς τὸ πνεῦμα τὸ ἅγιον, οὐκ ἀφεθήσεται αὐτῷ οὔτε ἐπὶ τῆς γῆς οὔτε ἐν τῷ οὐρανῷ.

(1) Jesus says: Whoever blasphemes against the Father, it will be forgiven him. (2) And whoever blasphemes against the Son, it will be forgiven him. (3) But whoever blasphemes against the Holy Spirit, it will not be forgiven him, neither on earth nor in heaven.

[1] Instead of εἰς it is also possible to use the direct object or κατά with the accusative.

[1] Statt εἰς ist auch unmittelbar Objektanschluss oder κατά mit Akkusativ möglich.

[1] Au lieu de εἰς, on pourrait avoir un complément d'objet direct ou κατά avec l'accusatif.

Q 12:10

Luke 12:10	Lukan Doublet	Mark 3:29a	*Gos. Thom.* 44

Und wer ein Wort gegen den Menschensohn spricht, dem wird vergeben werden; wer aber gegen den heiligen Geist ⟦spricht⟧, dem wird nicht vergeben werden.

Et si quelqu'un dit une parole contre le fils de l'homme, il lui sera remis; mais si quelqu'un ⟦parle⟧ contre l'Esprit saint, il ne lui sera pas remis.

(1) Jesus spricht: Wer den Vater lästern wird, dem wird vergeben werden. (2) Und wer den Sohn lästern wird, dem wird vergeben werden. (3) Wer aber den Heiligen Geist lästern wird, dem wird nicht vergeben werden, weder auf der Erde noch im Himmel.

(1) Jésus dit: Celui qui blasphème contre le Père, il lui sera remis. (2) Et celui qui blasphème contre le Fils, il lui sera remis. (3) Mais celui qui blasphème contre l'Esprit Saint, il ne lui sera pas remis, ni sur la terre ni dans le ciel.

Q 12:11

Mark 13:9-11a	Matthean Doublet	Matt 10:17-19a	Q 12:11
		^{0}{	^{0}{
13:9 βλέπετε δὲ ὑμεῖς		**10:17** Προσέχ{ετε [(δὲ})] ἀπὸ	
ἑαυτούς·		τῶν ἀνθρώπων·	
παραδώσουσιν		{(παραδώσ)ου[(σιν)]} γὰρ	
ὑμᾶς εἰς συνέδρια		{[(ὑμᾶς)] εἰς συνέδρια	
καὶ εἰς		καὶ} ἐν	
συναγωγὰς δαρήσεσθε		ταῖς {[συναγωγα]}ῖς αὐτῶν	
		μαστιγώσουσιν ὑμᾶς·	
καὶ ἐπὶ ἡγεμόνων καὶ		**10:18** {[καὶ] ἐπὶ ἡγεμόν}ας	
βασιλέων σταθήσεσθε		δὲ {καὶ βασιλε}ῖς	
ἕνεκεν ἐμοῦ		{ἀ}χθή{σεσθε ἕνεκεν ἐμοῦ	
εἰς μαρτύριον αὐτοῖς.		εἰς μαρτύριον αὐτοῖς	
13:10 καὶ εἰς πάντα τὰ ἔθνη		καὶ} {τ}οῖς {ἔθν}εσιν.	
πρῶτον δεῖ κηρυχθῆναι			
τὸ εὐαγγέλιον.			
		≀^{1}	≀^{1}
13:11a καὶ ὅταν		**10:19a** {ὅταν} δὲ	{ὅταν} δὲ
ἄγωσιν ὑμᾶς παραδιδόντες,		({παραδ})^{2}{ῶσιν ὑμᾶς}	[εἰσφέρ]^{2}{ωσιν ὑμᾶς}
		[ ]^{3}	⟦<εἰς>^{3}⟧
		[ ]^{4}	[τὰς {συναγωγάς}]^{4}
		[ ]^{5}	[]^{5}
		,	,
μὴ προμεριμνᾶτε		{μὴ} {μεριμν}ήση{τε}	{μὴ} {μεριμν}ήση{τε}
τί		πῶς ἢ {τί	πῶς ἢ {τί}
		[ ]^{6}	[]^{6}
λαλήσητε,		(λαλήσ)^{7}ητε}·	[εἴπ]^{7}{ητε}·
		≀^{1} ⇒ Matt 10:19b-20	≀^{1} ⇒ Q 12:12
		}^{0} ⇒ Matt 10:19b-20	}^{0}⇒ Q 12:12

0 Are the agreements in Luke 12:11-12 (21:12-15) par. Matt 10:19 (10:17-18, 20) in Q or from Mark?

1 The position of Q 12:11-12 in Q: After Q 12:10 and before Q 12:22b (Lukan order); or after Q 10:3 (Matt 10:16) and before Q 6:40 (Matt 10:24) (Matthean order).

2 Luke's εἰσφέρωσιν or Matthew's παραδῶσιν.

Q 12:11

Luke 12:11	Luke 21:12-14	Mark 13:9-11a	Gospel of Thomas
[0]{	**21:12** Πρὸ [({δὲ})] τούτων		
	πάντων ἐπιβαλοῦ[(σιν)]		
	ἐφ' {[(ὑμᾶς)]} τὰς χεῖρας	**13:9** βλέπετε δὲ ὑμεῖς	
	αὐτῶν {καὶ} διώξουσιν,	ἑαυτούς·	
	{(παραδ)ιδόντες}	παραδώσουσιν	
		ὑμᾶς εἰς συνέδρια	
	{εἰς}	καὶ εἰς	
	[τὰς {συναγωγὰς} καὶ]	συναγωγὰς δαρήσεσθε	
	φυλακάς, ἀπ{αγ}ομένους		
	{ἐπὶ} {βασιλε}ῖς	καὶ ἐπὶ ἡγεμόνων καὶ	
	[{καὶ}] {ἡγεμόν}[ας]	βασιλέων σταθήσεσθε	
	{ἕνεκεν} τοῦ ὀνόματός {μου}·	ἕνεκεν ἐμοῦ	
	21:13 ἀποβήσεται ὑμῖν		
	{εἰς μαρτύριον}.	εἰς μαρτύριον αὐτοῖς.	
		13:10 καὶ εἰς πάντα τὰ ἔθνη	
		πρῶτον δεῖ κηρυχθῆναι	
		τὸ εὐαγγέλιον.	
≀1			
{῞Οταν} δὲ	**21:14** θέτε οὖν ἐν	**13:11a** καὶ ὅταν	
[εἰσφέρ][2]{ωσιν ὑμᾶς}	ταῖς καρδίαις {[ὑμ]}ῶν	ἄγωσιν ὑμᾶς παραδιδόντες,	
[{ἐπὶ}][3]			
[τὰς {συναγωγὰς}][4]			
[{καὶ} τὰς ἀρχὰς καὶ			
τὰς ἐξουσίας][5],			
{μὴ} {μεριμν}ήση{τε}	([{μὴ}]) προ}μελετᾶν	μὴ προμεριμνᾶτε	
πῶς ἢ {τί}		τί	
[ἀπολογήσησθε ἢ τί][6]	[ἀπολογηθῆ]ναι·		
[εἴπ][7]{ητε}·		λαλήσητε,	
≀1 ⇒ Luke 12:12			
}[0]⇒ Luke 12:12	}[0]⇒ Luke 21:15		

3 Luke's ἐπί or an emendation εἰς or neither (Matt 10:19a).

4 Luke's τὰς συναγωγάς (reminiscence in Matt 10:17?).

5 Luke's καὶ τὰς ἀρχὰς καὶ τὰς ἐξουσίας. (There are two locations also in Matt 10:17 par. Mark 13:9.)

6 Luke's ἀπολογήσησθε ἢ τί.

7 Luke's εἴπητε or Matthew's λαλήσητε.

Q 12:11

Mark 13:9-11a	Matthean Doublet	Matt 10:17-19a	Q 12:11
IQP 1994: Q 12:⟦11-12⟧.		PH: ⟦({παραδ})²⟧{ῶσιν ὑμᾶς}.	

Q

ὅταν δὲ εἰσφέρωσιν ὑμᾶς ⟦<εἰς>⟧ τὰς συναγωγάς, μὴ μεριμνήσητε πῶς ἢ τί εἴπητε·

When they bring you before synagogues, do not be anxious about how or what you are to say;

Q 12:11

Luke 12:11	Luke 21:12-14	Markan Parallel	Gospel of Thomas
IQP 1994: < >[3].		PH: ⟦[τὰς συναγωγάς][4]⟧.	

Wenn sie euch vor die Synagogen«gerichte» bringen, macht euch keine Sorgen, wie und was ihr sprechen sollt;

Quand on vous fera comparaître devant les Synagogues, ne vous inquiétez pas de comment «vous parlerez», ni de ce que vous direz;

Q 12:12

Mark 13:11b-c	Matt 10:20	Matt 10:19b	Q 12:12
		[ ]^{1}	⟦[τὸ]^{1}⟧
ἀλλ' ὃ ἐὰν δοθῇ		⸉({δοθή}σεται)^{2} ⸊^{2} γὰρ	⸉⸊^{2} γὰρ
		[ ]^{1}	⟦[ἅγιον πνεῦμα]^{1}
ὑμῖν		⸉ ⸊^{2} {ὑμ(ῖν)^{2}}	⸉ [διδάξει]^{2}⟧ ⸊^{2} {ὑμ}⟦[ᾶς]^{2}⟧
ἐν ἐκείνῃ τῇ ὥρᾳ		{ἐν (ἐκείν)^{3}ῃ τῇ ὥρᾳ}	{ἐν} [( )]^{3}{ῃ τῇ ὥρᾳ}
τοῦτο		(τί)^{4}	(τί)^{4}
		[ ]^{5}	[]^{5}
λαλεῖτε·		({λαλ}ήσ)^{6}(η{τε})^{5}·	[εἴπ]^{6}<η{τε}>^{5}.
οὐ γάρ ἐστε ὑμεῖς	{οὐ γὰρ} {ὑμεῖς} {ἐστε}		
οἱ λαλοῦντες	{οἱ λαλοῦντες		
ἀλλὰ τὸ πνεῦμα	ἀλλὰ [τὸ] [πνεῦμα]		
τὸ ἅγιον.	το}ῦ πατρὸς ὑμῶν		
	τὸ λαλοῦν ἐν [ὑμ]ῖν.		
		⸊Matt 10:19a^{1}	⸊Q 12:11^{1}
		}Matt 10:17-19a^{0}	}Q 12:11^{0}

IQP 1994: [ ]^{1} ⸉ ⸊^{2} γὰρ [ ]^{1}.

JMR: ( )^{3}.

^{1} Is Luke's τὸ … ἅγιον πνεῦμα in Q (see Matt 10:20) or a reminiscence from Mark 13:11c par. Matt 10:20?

^{2} Luke's διδάξει ὑμᾶς or Matthew's δοθήσεται … ὑμῖν, and the resultant position after (Luke) or surrounding (Matthew) the postpositive γάρ.

Q

⟦τὸ⟧ γὰρ ⟦ἅγιον πνεῦμα διδάξει⟧ ὑμ⟦ᾶς⟧ ἐν …ῃ τῇ ὥρᾳ τί εἴπ<ητε>.

for ⟦the holy Spirit will teach⟧ you in that .. hour what you are to say.

Q 12:~~13-15~~, ⟦~~16-20~~⟧, ~~21~~, 33-34 is to be found below, between Q 12:2-12, ~~12↔33 / Matt 10:23~~ and Q 12:22b-31, ~~32~~.

Q 12:12

Luke 12:12	Luke 21:15	Mark 13:11b-c	John 14:26
			ὁ δὲ παράκλητος,
[{τὸ}][1]			τὸ
ʃ ʅ[2] γὰρ	ἐγὼ [(γὰρ)] ({δ})ώσω	ἀλλ᾽ ὃ ἐὰν δοθῇ	
[{ἅγιον} {πνεῦμα}][1]			πνεῦμα τὸ ἅγιον,
			ὃ πέμψει ὁ πατὴρ
			ἐν τῷ ὀνόματί μου,
ʃ [διδάξει][2] ʅ[2] {ὑμ}[ᾶς][2]	({[ὑμ]ῖν})	ὑμῖν	ἐκεῖνος ὑμᾶς διδάξει
{ἐν} [αὐτ][3]{ῇ τῇ ὥρᾳ}		ἐν ἐκείνῃ τῇ ὥρᾳ	
[ἃ][4]	στόμα καὶ σοφίαν	τοῦτο	πάντα καὶ
[δεῖ][5]	ᾗ οὐ δυνήσονται ἀντιστῆναι		ὑπομνήσει ὑμᾶς πάντα
[εἰπ][6][εῖν][5].	ἢ ἀντ[ειπεῖν] ἅπαντες	λαλεῖτε·	ἃ εἶπον ὑμῖν ἐγώ.
	οἱ ἀντικείμενοι ὑμῖν.	οὐ γάρ ἐστε ὑμεῖς	
		οἱ λαλοῦντες	
		ἀλλὰ τὸ πνεῦμα	
		τὸ ἅγιον.	
ʅLuke 12:11[1]			
}Luke 12:11[0]	}Luke 21:12-14[0]		

IQP 1994: ⟦[εἴπ][6]⟧<(η{τε})>[5].

[3] Luke's αὐτῇ or Matthew's ἐκείνῃ.
[4] Luke's ἅ or Matthew's τί.

[5] Luke's formulation with δεῖ and the infinitive or Matthew's second person plural.
[6] Luke's verb λέγω or Matthew's λαλέω.

denn ⟦der heilige Geist wird⟧ euch in …er Stunde ⟦lehren⟧, was ihr sprechen sollt.

en effet, ⟦l'Esprit saint⟧ vous ⟦enseignera⟧ à … heure ce que vous aurez à dire.

Q 12:~~13-15~~, ⟦~~16-20~~⟧, ~~21~~, 33-34 is to be found below, between Q 12:2-12, ~~12↔33 / Matt 10:23~~ and Q 12:22b-31, ~~32~~.

Q 12:~~12⟨ ⟩33/Matt 10:23~~

Markan Parallel	Matthean Doublet	Matt 10:23	Q 12:~~12⟨ ⟩33/Matt 10:23~~
		(Ὅταν δὲ διώκωσιν ὑμᾶς ἐν τῇ πόλει ταύτῃ, φεύγετε εἰς τὴν ἑτέραν· ἀμὴν γὰρ λέγω ὑμῖν, οὐ μὴ τελέσητε τὰς πόλεις τοῦ Ἰσραὴλ ἕως ἂν ἔλθῃ ὁ υἱὸς τοῦ ἀνθρώπου.)⁰	()⁰

JMR: ( )⁰ not in Q {D}.

⁰ Is Matt 10:23 in Q?

Q 12:~~12‹ ›33/Matt 10:23~~

Luke	Lukan Doublet	Markan Parallel	Gospel of Thomas
( )[0]			

Q 12:~~13-14~~

Markan Parallel	Matthean Doublet	Matthew	Q 12:~~13-14~~
		[ ]⁰	[]⁰

IQP 1994: 〚[]⁰〛.

JSK: In Q {C}.

⁰ Is Luke 12:13-14 in Q?

Gos. Thom. 72.1-2 (Nag Hammadi II 2)

(1) [Εἶπ]εν ἄν[θρωπ]ός τις αὐτῷ· εἰπὲ τοῖς ἀδελφοῖς μου ἵνα μερίσωνται μετ᾽ ἐμοῦ τὰ σκεύη τοῦ πατρός μου. (2) εἶπεν αὐτῷ· ὦ ἄνθρωπε, τίς με κατέστησεν μεριστήν;

(1) A [person said] to him: Tell my brothers that they have to divide my father's possessions with me. (2) He said to him: Man, who made me a divider?

Q 12:~~13-14~~

Luke 12:13-14	Lukan Doublet	Markan Parallel	*Gos. Thom.* 72.1-2
[**12:13** Εἶπεν δέ τις ἐκ τοῦ ὄχλου αὐτῷ· διδάσκαλε, εἰπὲ τῷ ἀδελφῷ μου μερίσασθαι μετ' ἐμοῦ τὴν κληρονομίαν.			72.1 [ⲡⲉ]ϫ̣ⲉ̣ ⲟ̣ⲩⲣ̣[ⲱⲙ]ⲉ̣ ⲛⲁ̣ϥ ϫⲉ ϫⲟⲟⲥ ⲛ̅ⲛⲁⲥⲛⲏⲩ ϣⲓⲛⲁ ⲉⲩⲛⲁ̣ⲡⲱϣⲉ ⲛ̅ⲛ̅ϩⲛⲁⲁⲩ ⲙ̅ⲡⲁⲉⲓⲱⲧ' ⲛⲙ̅ⲙⲁⲉⲓ
12:14 ὁ δὲ εἶπεν αὐτῷ· ἄνθρωπε, τίς με κατέστησεν κριτὴν ἢ μεριστὴν ἐφ' ὑμᾶς;][0]			72.2 ⲡⲉϫⲁϥ ⲛⲁϥ' ϫⲉ ⲱ ⲡⲣⲱⲙⲉ ⲛⲓⲙ ⲡⲉ ⲛ̅ⲧⲁϩⲁⲁⲧ' ⲛ̅ⲣⲉϥⲡⲱϣⲉ

(1) Ein [Mensch sprach] zu ihm: Sage meinen Brüdern, dass sie den Besitz meines Vaters mit mir teilen sollen. (2) Er sprach zu ihm: O Mensch, wer hat mich zum Teiler gemacht?

(1) Une [personne] lui [dit]: Dis à mes frères qu'ils partagent les biens de mon père avec moi. (2) Il lui dit: Ô homme, qui m'a établi pour faire «vos» partages?

Q 12:~~15~~

Markan Parallel	Matthean Doublet	Matthew	Q 12:~~15~~
		[ ][0]	[][0]

[0] Is Luke 12:15 in Q?

Q 12:~~15~~

Luke 12:15	Lukan Doublet	Markan Parallel	Gospel of Thomas
[12:15 εἶπεν δὲ πρὸς αὐτούς· ὁρᾶτε καὶ φυλάσσεσθε ἀπὸ πάσης πλεονεξίας, ὅτι οὐκ ἐν τῷ περισσεύειν τινὶ ἡ ζωὴ αὐτοῦ ἐστιν ἐκ τῶν ὑπαρχόντων αὐτῷ.][0]			

Q 12:⟦~~16-20~~⟧

Markan Parallel	Matthean Doublet	Matthew	Q 12:⟦~~16-20~~⟧
		[ ]^{0}	⟦[]^{0}⟧

IQP 1994: ⟦[ ]^{0}⟧.

JSK: In Q {C}; PH: []^{0}; JMR: ⟦[]^{0}⟧.

^{0} Is Luke 12:16-20 in Q?

Gos. Thom. 63.1-3 (Nag Hammadi II 2)

(1) Λέγει Ἰησοῦς· ἄνθρωπος πλούσιος (τις) ἦν, ὃς εἶχεν πολλὰ χρήματα. (2) εἶπεν· τοῖς ἐμοῖς χρήμασιν χρήσομαι εἰς τὸ σπεῖραι καὶ θερίσαι καὶ φυτεῦσαι καὶ πληρῶσαι τοὺς θησαυρούς μου καρπῶν, ἵνα μηδενὸς ὑστερήσω. (3) ταῦτα ἐφρόνει ἐν τῇ καρδίᾳ αὐτοῦ. καὶ ἐν ἐκείνῃ τῇ νυκτὶ ἀπέθανεν.

(1) Jesus says: There was a rich person who had many possessions. (2) He said: I will use my possessions so that I might sow, reap, plant (and) fill my storehouses with fruit so that I will not lack anything. (3) This was what he was thinking in his heart. And in that night he died.

Q 12:⟦~~16-20~~⟧

Luke 12:16-20	Lukan Doublet	Markan Parallel	*Gos. Thom.* 63.1-3
[**12:16** Εἶπεν δὲ παραβολὴν πρὸς αὐτοὺς λέγων· ἀνθρώπου τινὸς πλουσίου εὐφόρησεν ἡ χώρα. **12:17** καὶ διελογίζετο ἐν ἑαυτῷ λέγων· τί ποιήσω, ὅτι οὐκ ἔχω ποῦ συνάξω τοὺς καρπούς μου; **12:18** καὶ εἶπεν· τοῦτο ποιήσω, καθελῶ μου τὰς ἀποθήκας καὶ μείζονας οἰκοδομήσω καὶ συνάξω ἐκεῖ πάντα τὸν σῖτον καὶ τὰ ἀγαθά μου **12:19** καὶ ἐρῶ τῇ ψυχῇ μου· ψυχή, ἔχεις πολλὰ ἀγαθὰ κείμενα εἰς ἔτη πολλά· ἀναπαύου, φάγε, πίε, εὐφραίνου. **12:20** εἶπεν δὲ αὐτῷ ὁ θεός· ἄφρων, ταύτῃ τῇ νυκτὶ τὴν ψυχήν σου ἀπαιτοῦσιν ἀπὸ σοῦ· ἃ δὲ ἡτοίμασας, τίνι ἔσται;]⁰			63.1 ⲡⲉϫⲉ ⲓ̅ⲥ̅ ϫⲉ ⲛⲉⲩⲛ̄ ⲟⲩⲣⲱⲙⲉ ⲙ̄ⲡⲗⲟⲩⲥⲓⲟⲥ ⲉⲩⲛ̄ⲧⲁϥ ⲙ̄ⲙⲁⲩ ⲛ̄ϩⲁϩ ⲛ̄ⲭⲣⲏⲙⲁ 63.2 ⲡⲉϫⲁϥ ϫⲉ ϯⲛⲁⲣ̄ⲭⲣⲱ ⲛ̄ⲛⲁⲭⲣⲏⲙⲁ ϫⲉⲕⲁⲁⲥ ⲉⲉⲓⲛⲁϫⲟ ⲛ̄ⲧⲁⲱⲥϩ ⲛ̄ⲧⲁⲧⲱϭⲉ ⲛ̄ⲧⲁⲙⲟⲩϩ ⲛ̄ⲛⲁⲉϩⲱⲣ ⲛ̄ⲕⲁⲣ'ⲡⲟⲥ ϣⲓⲛⲁ ϫⲉ ⲛⲓⲣ̄ ϭⲣⲱϩ ⲗ̄ⲁⲁⲩ 63.3 ⲛⲁⲉⲓ ⲛⲉⲛⲉϥⲙⲉⲉⲩⲉ ⲉⲣⲟⲟⲩ ϩⲙ̄ ⲡⲉϥϩⲏⲧ' ⲁⲩⲱ ϩⲛ̄ ⲧⲟⲩϣⲏ ⲉⲧⲙ̄ⲙⲁⲩ ⲁϥⲙⲟⲩ

(1) Jesus spricht: Es war ein reicher Mann, der viele Güter hatte. (2) Er sprach: Ich werde meine Güter gebrauchen, dass ich säe, ernte, pflanze (und) meine Scheunen mit Frucht fülle, damit ich nicht an etwas Mangel habe. (3) Dies war es, was er in seinem Herzen dachte. Und in jener Nacht starb er.

(1) Jésus dit: Il y avait un riche qui avait de nombreux biens. (2) Il dit: J'utiliserai mes biens pour semer, moissonner, planter (et) remplir mes greniers de fruits afin que je ne manque de rien. (3) Telles sont les choses qu'il pensait dans son cœur et, cette nuit-là, il mourut.

Q 12:~~21~~

Markan Parallel	Matt 6:19-20	Matthew	Q 12:~~21~~
	6:19 [Μὴ] [θησαυρίζ]ετε ὑμῖν θησαυροὺς ἐπὶ τῆς γῆς, ὅπου σὴς καὶ βρῶσις ἀφανίζει καὶ ὅπου κλέπται διορύσσουσιν καὶ κλέπτουσιν· **6:20** θησαυρίζετε δὲ ὑμῖν θησαυροὺς ἐν οὐρανῷ, ὅπου οὔτε σὴς οὔτε βρῶσις ἀφανίζει καὶ ὅπου κλέπται οὐ διορύσσουσιν οὐδὲ κλέπτουσιν·	[ ]⁰	[]⁰

IQP 1994: ⟦[]⁰⟧.

JSK: [ ]⁰ indeterminate.

⁰ Is Luke 12:21 in Q?

Q 12:22b-31, ~~32~~ is to be found below, between Q 12:2-12, ~~12↔33/Matt 10:23,~~ ~~13-15~~, ⟦~~16-20~~⟧, ~~21~~, 33-34 and Q 12:⟦~~35-38~~⟧, 39-40.

Q 12:~~21~~

Luke 12:21	Lukan Doublet	Markan Parallel	Gospel of Thomas
[**12:21** οὕτως ὁ θησαυρίζων ἑαυτῷ καὶ μὴ εἰς θεὸν πλουτῶν.][0]			

Q 12:22b-31, ~~32~~ is to be found below, between Q 12:2-12, ~~12↔33/Matt 10:23,~~ ~~13-15~~, ⟦~~16-20~~⟧, ~~21~~, 33-34 and Q 12:⟦~~35-38~~⟧, 39-40.

Q 12:33

Mark 10:21b	Matt 19:21b	Matt 6:19-20	Q 12:33
		[0]/	[0]/
		[1]⸉	[1]⸉
ἕν σε ὑστερεῖ·	εἰ θέλεις τέλειος εἶναι,	**6:19** (Μὴ θησαυρίζετε	(«μὴ θησαυρίζετε
		ὑμῖν θησαυροὺς	ὑμῖν θησαυροὺς
ὕπαγε,	{ὕπαγε}	ἐπὶ τῆς γῆς, ὅπου σὴς	ἐπὶ τῆς γῆς, ὅπου σὴς
ὅσα ἔχεις		καὶ βρῶσις ἀφανίζει	καὶ βρῶσις ἀφανίζει
πώλησον	{[πώλησ]όν}	καὶ ὅπου κλέπται	καὶ ὅπου κλέπται
	σου [τὰ ὑπάρχοντα]	διορύσσουσιν	διορύσσουσιν
καὶ δὸς τοῖς πτωχοῖς,	{[καὶ δὸ]ς τοῖς πτωχοῖς,	καὶ κλέπτουσιν·)[2]	καὶ κλέπτουσιν·»)[2]
		6:20 (θησαυρίζε)[3]τε	(θησαυρίζε)[3]τε
		(δὲ)[4]	(δὲ)[4]
		(ὑμῖν)[5]	(ὑμῖν)[5]
		[ ][6]	[][6]
καὶ ἕξεις θησαυρὸν	καὶ ἕξεις [(θησαυρὸ)ν]	{θησαυρο}(ὺς)[7]	{θησαυρο}( )[7]
		[ ][8]	[][8]
ἐν	[(ἐν]	{ἐν [ ][9]	{ἐν ⟦[][9]⟧
οὐρανῷ,	[οὐραν)}οῖς],	οὐραν(ῷ)}[10],	οὐραν⟦(ῷ)}[10]⟧,
		ὅπου	ὅπου
		[11]⸉ (οὔτε)[12] σὴς	[11]⸉ (οὔτε)[12] σὴς
		(οὔτε βρῶσις)[12]	(οὔτε βρῶσις)[12]
		(ἀφανίζει)[13]	(ἀφανίζει)[13]
		⸊[11]	⸊[11]
		(καὶ ὅπου)[14]	(καὶ ὅπου)[14]
		[11]⸉κλέπτ(αι)[15]	[11]⸉κλέπτ(αι)[15]
		οὐ (διορύσσ)[16](ουσιν)[15.17]	οὐ (διορύσσ)[16](ουσιν)[15.17]
		(οὐδὲ κλέπτ)[17](ουσιν)[15.17] ⸊[11].	(οὐδὲ κλέπτ)[17](ουσιν)[15.17] ⸊[11].

[0] Is Q 12:33-34 in Q?

[1] The position of Q 12:33-34: After Q 12:22-31, and before Q 12:39 (Lukan order); or after Q 11:4 (Matt 6:13a) and before Q 12:22b-31 (Matt 6:25-34) (Matthean order emended by omitting Matt 6:22-23,24 par. Luke 11:34-35; 16:13).

[2] Is Luke's πωλήσατε τὰ ὑπάρχοντα ὑμῶν καὶ δότε ἐλεημοσύνην· or Matt 6:19 in Q?

[3] Luke's ποιήσατε or Matthew's θησαυρίζετε.

[4] Matthew's δέ.

[5] Luke's ἑαυτοῖς or Matthew's ὑμῖν.

[6] Luke's βαλλάντια μὴ παλαιούμενα.

[7] Luke's θησαυρόν or Matthew's θησαυρούς.

[8] Luke's ἀνέκλειπτον.

Q 12:33

Luke 12:33	Luke 12:21; 18:22b	Mark 10:21b	*Gos. Thom.* 76.3
[0]/			
[1]ʃ	**12:21** οὕτως		
	ὁ (θησαυρίζ)ων ἑαυτῷ		
	καὶ μὴ εἰς θεὸν πλουτῶν.	ἕν σε ὑστερεῖ·	
		ὕπαγε,	
	18:22b πάντα {ὅσα ἔχεις	ὅσα ἔχεις	
[{Πωλήσ}ατε	[πώλησ]ον	πώλησον	
τὰ ὑπάρχοντα ὑμῶν			
{καὶ δό}τε ἐλεημοσύνην·][2]	[καὶ]} διά{[δο]ς} {πτωχοῖς,	καὶ δὸς τοῖς πτωχοῖς,	
[ποιήσα][3]τε			
( )[4]			
[ἑαυτοῖς][5]			ⲚⲦⲰⲦⲚ̄ ϨⲰⲦ'ⲦⲎⲨⲦⲚ̄
[βαλλάντια	καὶ ἕξεις	καὶ ἕξεις	ϢⲒⲚⲈ
μὴ παλαιούμενα][6],			
{θησαυρὸ[ν]}[7]	[(θησαυρὸ)ν]	θησαυρὸν	Ⲛ̄ⲤⲀ ⲠⲈϤⲈϨⲞ
[ἀνέκλειπτον][8]			ⲈⲘⲀϤⲰϪⲚ̄
{ἐν} [τοῖς][9]	[(ἐν)} τοῖς	ἐν	ⲈϤⲘⲎⲚ' ⲈⲂⲞⲖ
{οὐραν}[οῖς][10],	{(οὐραν)}οῖς,]	οὐρανῷ,	
ὅπου			ⲠⲘⲀ
[11]ʃ κλέπτ[ης][15]			ⲈⲘⲀⲢⲈ ϪⲞⲞⲖⲈⲤ
οὐ[κ ἐγγίζ][16][ει][15]			ⲦϨⲚⲞ ⲈϨⲞⲨⲚ' ⲈⲘⲀⲨ
( )[17]( )[15]			ⲈⲞⲨⲰⲘ'
ʅ[11]			
[οὐδὲ][14]			ⲞⲨⲆⲈ
[11]ʃ ( )[12] σὴς ( )[12]			ⲘⲀⲢⲈ ϤϤⲚ̄Ⲧ
[διαφθείρει][13]			ⲦⲀⲔⲞ
ʅ[11].			

[9] Luke's τοῖς.

[10] Luke's οὐρανοῖς or Matthew's οὐρανῷ.

[11] Is the first position given to κλέπτης/-αι (Luke) or to σής (οὔτε βρῶσις) (Matthew)?

[12] Matthew's duplication (see variation unit [17]): οὔτε ... οὔτε βρῶσις.

[13] Luke's διαφθείρει or Matthew's ἀφανίζει.

[14] Luke's οὐδέ or Matthew's καὶ ὅπου.

[15] Luke's κλέπτης or Matthew's κλέπται, and the resultant number of the verb(s).

[16] Luke's οὐκ ἐγγίζ- or Matthew's οὐ διορύσσ-.

[17] Matthew's duplication (see variation unit [12]) οὐδὲ κλέπτουσιν.

Q 12:33

Mark 10:21b	Matt 19:21b	Matt 6:19-20	Q 12:33
καὶ δεῦρο ἀκολούθει μοι.	{καὶ δεῦρο ἀκολούθει μοι.}	ʅ¹⇒ Matt 6:21 \⁰⇒ Matt 6:21	ʅ¹ ⇒ Q 12:34 \⁰ ⇒ Q 12:34

IQP 1994: ʃ ʅ¹ indeterminate; JMR, PH: Matthew = Q (without Matt 6:22-23, 24 intervening); JSK: Luke = Q {C}.

IQP 1994: Luke 12:21 is not in Q {C}; JSK: Indeterminate.
IQP 1994: ⟦(«»)²⟧ in Q.

Q

«μὴ θησαυρίζετε ὑμῖν θησαυροὺς ἐπὶ τῆς γῆς, ὅπου σὴς καὶ βρῶσις ἀφανίζει καὶ ὅπου κλέπται διορύσσουσιν καὶ κλέπτουσιν·» θησαυρίζετε δὲ ὑμῖν θησαυρο... ἐν οὐραν⟦ῷ⟧, ὅπου οὔτε σὴς οὔτε βρῶσις ἀφανίζει καὶ ὅπου κλέπται οὐ διορύσσουσιν οὐδὲ κλέπτουσιν·

«Do not treasure for yourselves treasures on earth, where moth and gnawing deface and where robbers dig through and rob,» but treasure for yourselves treasure«s» in heaven, where neither moth nor gnawing defaces and where robbers do not dig through nor rob.

Gos. Thom. 76.3 (Nag Hammadi II 2)

ζητεῖτε καὶ ὑμεῖς τὸν θησαυρὸν αὐτοῦ τὸν ἀνέκλειπτον (καὶ) μένοντα ὅπου σὴς οὐκ ἐγγίζει εἰς τὸ βιβρῶσκειν οὐδὲ σκώληξ ἀφανίζει.

You too search for his treasure which does not perish, which stays where moth cannot reach (it) to eat (it) nor worm deface (it).

Q 12:33

Luke 12:33	Luke 12:21; 18:22b	Mark 10:21b	*Gos. Thom.* 76.3
₰[1]⇒ Luke 12:34 \[0]⇒ Luke 12:34	{καὶ δεῦρο ἀκολούθει μοι.}	καὶ δεῦρο ἀκολούθει μοι.	

IQP 1994: ⟦(δὲ)[4] (ὑμῖν)[5]⟧.
IQP 1994: {θησαυρο}( )[7] ⟦[][8]⟧ {ἐν [}][9].

IQP 1994: οὐραν}[οῖς][10], ὅπου [11]ʃ ⟦(οὔτε)[12]⟧ σὴς ⟦(οὔτε βρῶσις)[12] (ἀφανίζει)[13] ₰[11] (καὶ ὅπου)[14]⟧ [11]ʃκλέπτ( )[15] οὐ ⟦(διορύσσ)[16]⟧( )[15] ⟦(οὐδὲ κλέπτ)[17]⟧( )[15].

«Sammelt euch nicht Schätze auf der Erde, wo Motte und Rost sie zerstören und wo Diebe einbrechen und sie stehlen;» sammelt euch vielmehr Schätz«e» im Himmel, wo weder Motte noch Rost «sie» zerstören und wo Diebe weder einbrechen noch stehlen.

«N'amassez pas pour vous des trésors sur terre, là où la mite et la rouille font tout disparaître, et là où les voleurs percent les murs et volent.» Mais amassez pour vous de«s» trésor«s» dans le ciel, là où ni la mite ni la rouille font tout disparaître et là où les voleurs ne percent pas les murs ni ne volent.

Sucht auch ihr nach seinem Schatz, der nicht verdirbt, der bleibt, wo keine Motte hinkommt, um zu fressen, und kein Wurm zerstört.

Vous aussi, recherchez son trésor qui ne passe pas, qui demeure, là où la mite ne s'introduit pas pour dévorer et (où) le ver ne fait pas (tout) disparaître.

Q 12:34

Markan Parallel	Matthean Doublet	Matt 6:21	Q 12:34
		ὅπου γάρ ἐστιν ὁ θησαυρός (σου)[1], ἐκεῖ ⸂ἔσται⸃[2] καὶ ἡ καρδία (σου)[1]. ⸂ ⸃[2] ⸃Matt 6:19-20[1] \Matt 6:19-20[0]	ὅπου γάρ ἐστιν ὁ θησαυρός (σου)[1], ἐκεῖ ⸂ἔσται⸃[2] καὶ ἡ καρδία (σου)[1]. ⸂⸃[2] ⸃Q 12:33[1] \Q 12:33[0]

IQP 1994: ⟦(σου)[1]⟧ … ⟦(σου)[1]⟧.

[1] Luke's ὑμῶν … ὑμῶν or Matthew's σου … σου.

[2] The position of ἔσται after (Luke) or before (Matthew) the subject.

Q

ὅπου γάρ ἐστιν ὁ θησαυρός σου, ἐκεῖ ἔσται καὶ ἡ καρδία σου.	For where your treasure is, there will also be your heart.

Q 12:⟦~~35-38~~⟧ is to be found below, between Q 12:33-34, 22b-31, ~~32~~ and Q 12:39-40.

Q 12:34

Luke 12:34	Lukan Doublet	Markan Parallel	Gospel of Thomas
ὅπου γάρ ἐστιν ὁ θησαυρὸς [ὑμῶν][1], ἐκεῖ ʃ ʅ[2] καὶ ἡ καρδία [ὑμῶν][1] ʃἔσταιʅ[2]. ʅLuke 12:33[1] \ʅLuke 12:33[0]			

Denn wo dein Schatz ist, dort wird auch dein Herz sein.	Car là où est ton trésor, là aussi sera ton cœur.

Q 12:⟦~~35-38~~⟧ is to be found below, between Q 12:33-34, 22b-31, ~~32~~ and Q 12:39-40.

Q 12:22b

Markan Parallel	Matthean Doublet	Matt 6:25a	Q 12:22b
		¹ʃ	¹ʃ
		[ ]²	[]²
		Διὰ τοῦτο λέγω ὑμῖν· μὴ μεριμνᾶτε	διὰ τοῦτο λέγω ὑμῖν· μὴ μεριμνᾶτε
		τῇ ψυχῇ (ὑμῶν)³ τί φάγητε (ἢ τί πίητε)⁴, μηδὲ τῷ σώματι (ὑμῶν)³ τί ἐνδύσησθε. ʅ¹⇒ Matt 6:33	τῇ ψυχῇ (ὑμῶν)³ τί φάγητε ()⁴, μηδὲ τῷ σώματι (ὑμῶν)³ τί ἐνδύσησθε. ʅ¹⇒ Q 12:31

IQP 1992: ( )³… ( )³ indeterminate.

Text Critical Note: (see the discussion in the front matter): In Matt 6:25a *καὶ τί πίητε* is in L Θ 0233 𝔐 sy[p.h], but the clause is comple-

[1] The position of Q 12:22b-31 in Q: After Q 12:12 and before Q 12:39 (Lukan order); or after Q 16:13 (Matt 6:24) and before Q 11:34; 6:37 (Matt 6:22; 7:1) (Matthean order).

Q

διὰ τοῦτο λέγω ὑμῖν· μὴ μεριμνᾶτε τῇ ψυχῇ ὑμῶν τί φάγητε, μηδὲ τῷ σώματι ὑμῶν τί ἐνδύσησθε.	Therefore I tell you, do not be anxious about your life, what you are to eat, nor about your body, with what you are to clothe yourself.

Gos. Thom. 36.1 (Nag Hammadi II 2)

ⲡⲉϫⲉ ⲓ̅ⲥ̅ ⲙⲛ̅ϥⲓ ⲣⲟⲟⲩϣ ϫⲓⲛ ϩⲧⲟⲟⲩⲉ ϣⲁ ⲣⲟⲩϩⲉ ⲁⲩⲱ ϫⲓⲛ ϩⲓⲣⲟⲩϩⲉ ϣⲁ ϩⲧⲟⲟⲩⲉ ϫⲉ ⲟⲩ ⲡⲉ<ⲧ>ⲉⲧⲛⲁⲧⲁⲁϥ[1] ϩⲓⲱⲧ' ⲧⲏⲩⲧⲛ̅

Λέγει Ἰησοῦς· μὴ μεριμνᾶτε ἀπὸ πρωῒ ἕως ὀψὲ καὶ ἀφ' ἑσπέρας ἕως πρωῒ τί ἐνδύσεσθε.

Jesus says: Do not be anxious from morning to late and from evening to morning with what you will clothe yourself.

[1] Codex: **ⲡⲉⲉⲧⲛⲁⲧⲁⲁϥ**

Gos. Thom. 36.1 (P. Oxy. 655)

[λέγει Ἰ(ησοῦ)ς· μὴ μεριμνᾶτε ἀ]πὸ πρωῒ ἕ[ως ὀψέ, μήτ]ε ἀφ' ἑσπ[έρας ἕως π]ρωΐ, μήτε [τῇ τροφῇ ὑ]μῶν τί φά[γητε, μήτε] τῇ στ[ολῇ ὑμῶν] τί ἐνδύ[ση]σθε.

(1) [Jesus says, Do not be anxious] from morning [to late nor] from evening [to] morning, either [about] your [food], what [you are to] eat, [or] about [your robe], with what you [are to] clothe yourself.

Q 12:22b

Luke 12:22	Lukan Doublet	Markan Parallel	*Gos. Thom.* 36.1 (P. Oxy. 655)
1ʃ			
[Εἶπεν δὲ πρὸς			[λέγει Ἰ(ησοῦ)ς·
τοὺς μαθητὰς αὐτοῦ·][2]			
διὰ τοῦτο λέγω ὑμῖν·			
μὴ μεριμνᾶτε			μὴ μεριμνᾶτε
			ἀ]πὸ πρωῒ ἕ[ως ὀψέ, μήτ]ε
			ἀφ᾽ ἑσπ[έρας ἕως π]ρωΐ,
τῇ ψυχῇ ( )[3]			μήτε [τῇ τροφῇ ὑ]μῶν
τί φάγητε ( )[4],			τί φά[γητε,
μηδὲ τῷ σώματι ( )[3]			μήτε] τῇ στ[ολῇ ὑμῶν]
τί ἐνδύσησθε.			τί ἐνδύ[ση]σθε.
ʅ1⇒ Luke 12:31			

tely absent in ℵ *f*[1] 892 *l* 2211 *pc* a b ff[1] k l vg sy[c] sa[mss], while ἢ τί πίητε is in B W *f*[13] 33 *al* it sa[mss] mae bo; Or Hier[mss].

[2] Luke's εἶπεν δὲ πρὸς τοὺς μαθητὰς αὐτοῦ.

[3] Matthew's ὑμῶν (*bis*).

[4] Matthew's ἢ τί πίητε.

Daher sage ich euch: Sorgt euch nicht um euer Leben, was ihr essen sollt, und nicht um euren Leib, was ihr anziehen sollt.

C'est pourquoi je vous dis: Ne vous inquiétez pas pour votre vie de ce que vous allez manger, ni pour votre corps de quoi vous allez le vêtir.

Jesus spricht: Sorgt euch nicht vom Morgen bis zum Abend und von der Abendzeit bis zum Morgen, was ihr anziehen werdet.

Jésus dit: Ne vous inquiétez pas du matin au soir et du soir au matin (de) ce dont vous vous vêtirez.

(1) [Jesus spricht: Sorgt euch nicht] vom Morgen [bis zum Abend und] von der Abendzeit [bis] zum Morgen, weder [um] eure [Nahrung], (nämlich) was [ihr] essen [sollt, noch] um [eure Kleidung], (nämlich) was ihr anziehen [sollt].

(1) [Jésus dit: Ne vous inquiétez pas] du matin [au soir et] du soir [au] matin, ni [pour] votre [nourriture], (de) ce que [vous allez] manger, [ni] pour [votre habillement], (de) ce dont vous allez vous vêtir.

Q 12:23

Markan Parallel	Matthean Doublet	Matt 6:25b	Q 12:23
		(οὐχὶ)[1] ἡ [ ][1] ψυχὴ πλεῖόν ἐστιν τῆς τροφῆς καὶ τὸ σῶμα τοῦ ἐνδύματος;	(οὐχὶ)[1] ἡ [][1] ψυχὴ πλεῖόν ἐστιν τῆς τροφῆς καὶ τὸ σῶμα τοῦ ἐνδύματος;

[1] Luke's γάρ and the declarative sentence or Matthew's οὐχί and the interrogative sentence.

Q

οὐχὶ ἡ ψυχὴ πλεῖόν ἐστιν τῆς τροφῆς καὶ τὸ σῶμα τοῦ ἐνδύματος;	Is not life more than food, and the body than clothing?

Q 12:23

Luke 12:23	Lukan Doublet	Markan Parallel	Gospel of Thomas
( )[1] ἡ [γὰρ][1] ψυχὴ πλεῖόν ἐστιν τῆς τροφῆς καὶ τὸ σῶμα τοῦ ἐνδύματος.			

Ist nicht das Leben mehr als Nahrung und der Leib «mehr» als Kleidung?

La vie n'est-elle pas davantage que la nourriture et le corps «davantage» que le vêtement?

Q 12:24

Markan Parallel	Matthean Doublet	Matt 6:26	Q 12:24
		(ἐμβλέψ)[1]ατε (εἰς)[1]	[κατανοήσ][1]ατε ()[1]
		τ(ὰ πετεινὰ τοῦ οὐρανοῦ)[2]	τ[οὺς κόρακας][2]
		ὅτι οὐ σπείρουσιν	ὅτι οὐ σπείρουσιν
		οὐδὲ θερίζουσιν	οὐδὲ θερίζουσιν
		[ ][3] οὐδὲ (συνάγουσιν εἰς)[3]	[][3] οὐδὲ (συνάγουσιν εἰς)[3]
		ἀποθήκ(ας)[3],	ἀποθήκ(ας)[3],
		καὶ ὁ (πατὴρ ὑμῶν	καὶ ὁ [θεὸς][4]
		ὁ οὐράνιος)[4]	
		τρέφει αὐτ(ά)[2]·	τρέφει αὐτ[ούς] [2]·
		(οὐχ)[5]	(οὐχ)[5]
		ʃὑμεῖςʅ[6] μᾶλλον	ʃὑμεῖςʅ[6] μᾶλλον
		ʃ ʅ[6]	ʃʅ[6]
		διαφέρετε (αὐτ)[7]ῶν;	διαφέρετε [τῶν πετειν][7]ῶν;

IQP 1992, PH: ⟦(ἐμβλέψ)[1]⟧ατε ⟦(εἰς)[1]⟧.

IQP 1992: ( )[3] ἀποθήκ( )[3].

[1] Luke's κατανοήσατε or Matthew's ἐμβλέψατε εἰς.

[2] Luke's τοὺς κόρακας or Matthew's τὰ πετεινὰ τοῦ οὐρανοῦ.

[3] Luke's οἷς οὐκ ἔστιν ταμεῖον or Matthew's συνάγουσιν εἰς, and the resultant case, and the number, of "barn."

[4] Luke's θεός or Matthew's πατὴρ ὑμῶν ὁ οὐράνιος.

Q

κατανοήσατε τοὺς κόρακας ὅτι οὐ σπείρουσιν οὐδὲ θερίζουσιν οὐδὲ συνάγουσιν εἰς ἀποθήκας, καὶ ὁ θεὸς τρέφει αὐτούς· οὐχ ὑμεῖς μᾶλλον διαφέρετε τῶν πετεινῶν;

Consider the ravens: They neither sow nor reap nor gather into barns, and yet God feeds them. Are you not better than the birds?

Q 12:24

Luke 12:24	Lukan Doublet	Markan Parallel	Gospel of Thomas
[κατανοήσ][1]ατε ( )[1] τ[οὺς κόρακας][2] ὅτι οὐ σπείρουσιν οὐδὲ θερίζουσιν, [οἷς οὐκ ἔστιν ταμεῖον][3] οὐδὲ ( )[3] ἀποθήκ[η][3], καὶ ὁ [θεὸς][4] τρέφει αὐτ[ούς][2]. [πόσῳ][5] ⸀ ⸃[6] μᾶλλον ⸀ὑμεῖς⸃[6] διαφέρετε [τῶν πετειν][7]ῶν.			

[5] Luke's πόσῳ introducing an exclamation or Matthew's οὐχ introducing a question.

[6] The position of ὑμεῖς after (Luke) or before (Matthew) μᾶλλον.

[7] Luke's τῶν πετεινῶν or Matthew's αὐτῶν.

Beobachtet die Raben: Sie säen nicht und ernten nicht und sammeln nicht in Scheunen, und Gott ernährt sie. Seid ihr nicht mehr wert als die Vögel?

Observez les corbeaux: ils ne sèment pas, ne récoltent pas ni n'amassent dans des greniers, et Dieu les nourrit: vous, ne valez-vous pas mieux que les oiseaux?

Q 12:25

Markan Parallel	Matthean Doublet	Matt 6:27	Q 12:25
		τίς δὲ ἐξ ὑμῶν μεριμνῶν δύναται ⸉προσθεῖναι⸊[1] ἐπὶ τὴν ἡλικίαν αὐτοῦ ⸉ ⸊[1] πῆχυν (ἕνα)[2];	τίς δὲ ἐξ ὑμῶν μεριμνῶν δύναται ⸉προσθεῖναι⸊[1] ἐπὶ τὴν ἡλικίαν αὐτοῦ ⸉⸊[1] πῆχυν ( )[2];

IQP 1992: ⸉ ⸊[1] ἐπὶ τὴν ἡλικίαν αὐτοῦ ⸉προσθεῖναι⸊[1].

Text Critical Note: (see the discussion in the front matter): In Luke 12:25 προσθεῖναι ἐπὶ τὴν ἡλικίαν αὐτοῦ is in 𝔓45 ℵ A D L Q W Θ Ψ 070 $f^{1.13}$ 33 𝔐 latt, but ἐπὶ τῆς ἡλικίαν αὐτοῦ προσθεῖναι in 𝔓75 B 579 *pc*.

[1] The position of προσθεῖναι after (Luke) or before (Matthew) ἐπὶ τὴν ἡλικίαν αὐτοῦ.

[2] Matthew's ἕνα.

Q

τίς δὲ ἐξ ὑμῶν μεριμνῶν δύναται προσθεῖναι ἐπὶ τὴν ἡλικίαν αὐτοῦ πῆχυν ..;

And who of you by being anxious is able to add to one's stature a .. cubit?

Gos. Thom. 36.4 (P. Oxy. 655)

(4) τίς ἂν προσθ<εί>η ἐπὶ τὴν εἰλικίαν ὑμῶν; αὐτὸ[ς δ]ώσει ὑμεῖς τὸ ἔνδυμα ὑμῶν.

(4) Who might add to your stature? He it is who will give you your clothing.

Q 12:25

Luke 12:25	Lukan Doublet	Markan Parallel	*Gos. Thom.* 36.4 (P. Oxy. 655)
τίς δὲ ἐξ ὑμῶν μεριμνῶν δύναται ⸂ ⸃^{1} ἐπὶ τὴν ἡλικίαν αὐτοῦ ⸂προσθεῖναι⸃^{1} πῆχυν ( )^{2};			τίς ἂν προσθ<εἰ>η ἐπὶ τὴν εἰλικίαν ὑμῶν; αὐτὸ[ς δ]ώσει ὑμεῖς τὸ ἔνδυμα ὑμῶν.

Text Critical Note: (see the discussion in the front matter): In Luke 12:25 πῆχυν ἕνα is in ℵ^{1} A L Q W Θ Ψ 070 $f^{1.13}$ 33 𝔐 lat sy, but πῆχυν only in 𝔓$^{45.75}$ B D ff^{2} i l.

Wer von euch vermag mit seiner Sorge seiner Lebenszeit eine Spanne hinzuzufügen?	Et qui d'entre vous peut, par son inquiétude, ajouter une .. coudée à sa taille?

(4) Wer könnte eurer Lebenszeit (etwas) hinzufügen? Er selbst wird euch euer Gewand geben!

(4) Qui pourrait ajouter à votre taille? C'est lui qui vous donnera votre vêtement.

Q 12:26

Markan Parallel	Matthean Doublet	Matt 6:28a	Q 12:26
		(καὶ)[1]	(καὶ)[1]
		ʃ ʅ[2]	ʃʅ[2]
		περὶ (ἐνδύματος)[3]	περὶ (ἐνδύματος)[3]
		ʃτίʅ[2] μεριμνᾶτε;	ʃτίʅ[2] μεριμνᾶτε;

[1] Luke's εἰ οὖν οὐδὲ ἐλάχιστον δύνασθε or Matthew's καί.

[2] The position of τί before (Luke) or after (Matthew) the prepositional phrase.

Q

καὶ περὶ ἐνδύματος τί μεριμνᾶτε;	And why are you anxious about clothing?

Q 12:26

Luke 12:26	Lukan Doublet	Markan Parallel	Gospel of Thomas
[εἰ οὖν οὐδὲ ἐλάχιστον δύνασθε,][1] ⸉τί⸊[2] περὶ [τῶν λοιπῶν][3] ⸉ ⸊[2] μεριμνᾶτε;			

[3] Luke's τῶν λοιπῶν or Matthew's ἐνδύματος.

Und was sorgt ihr euch um Kleidung?	Et pourquoi vous inquiétez-vous de vêtement?

Q 12:27

Markan Parallel	Matthean Doublet	Matt 6:28b-29	Q 12:27
		6:28b κατα(μάθε)[1]τε τὰ κρίνα	κατα⟦(μάθε)[1]⟧τε τὰ κρίνα
		(τοῦ ἀγροῦ)[2] πῶς	()[2] πῶς
		αὐξάν(ουσιν)[3]·	αὐξάν⟦[ει][3]⟧·
		οὐ κοπι(ῶσιν)[3]	οὐ κοπι⟦[ᾷ][3]⟧
		οὐδὲ νήθ(ουσιν)[3]·	οὐδὲ νήθ⟦[ει][3]⟧·
		6:29 λέγω δὲ ὑμῖν	λέγω δὲ ὑμῖν,
		(ὅτι)[4] οὐδὲ Σολομὼν ἐν πάσῃ	⟦()[4]⟧ οὐδὲ Σολομὼν ἐν πάσῃ
		τῇ δόξῃ αὐτοῦ	τῇ δόξῃ αὐτοῦ
		περιεβάλετο ὡς ἓν τούτων.	περιεβάλετο ὡς ἓν τούτων.

IQP 1992: κατα[( )][1]τε τὰ κρίνα ()[2] πῶς αὐξάν(ουσιν)[3]· οὐ κοπι(ῶσιν)[3] οὐδὲ νήθ(ουσιν)[3]·.

PH: αὐξάν⟦(ουσιν)[3]⟧· οὐ κοπι⟦(ῶσιν)[3]⟧ οὐδὲ νήθ⟦(ουσιν)[3]⟧·.

Text Critical Note: The original reading οὐ ξαίνει («do not card») is, already in Q, corrupted by a scribal error into αὐξάνει (see the **Excursus on the Scribal Error in Q 12:27**, above, pp. xcix-ci). In Matt 6:28 αὐξάνουσιν· οὐ κοπιοῦσιν οὐδὲ νήθουσιν is in B (33); οὐ ξαίνουσιν οὐδὲ νήθουσιν οὐδὲ κοπιῶσιν is in א*vid; αὐξάνει· οὐ κοπιᾷ οὐδὲ νήθει is in L W 0233 0281 *f* 13 𝔐; and αὐξάνουσιν· οὐ κοπιῶσιν οὐδὲ νήθου-

[1] Luke's κατανοήσατε or Matthew's καταμάθετε.

[2] Matthew's τοῦ ἀγροῦ.

Q

κατα⟦μάθε⟧τε τὰ κρίνα πῶς αὐξάν⟦ει⟧· οὐ κοπι⟦ᾷ⟧ οὐδὲ νήθ⟦ει⟧· λέγω δὲ ὑμῖν, οὐδὲ Σολομὼν ἐν πάσῃ τῇ δόξῃ αὐτοῦ περιεβάλετο ὡς ἓν τούτων.

⟦Observe⟧ the lilies, how they grow: They do not work nor do they spin. Yet I tell you: Not even Solomon in all his glory was arrayed like one of these.

Gos. Thom. 36.2-3 (P. Oxy. 655)

(2) [πολ]λῷ κρεί[σσον]ές ἐ̣[στε] τῶν [κρί]νων, ἅτι[να ο]ὐ ξα[ί]νει οὐδὲ ν[ήθ]ει. (3) κ̣[αὶ] ἓν ἔχ̣οντ[ες ἔ]νδ[υ]μα, τί ἐν[.....]..αι ὑμεῖς;

(2) [You are far] better than the [lilies] which [do not] card nor [spin]. (3) [And] having *one* clothing, … you …?

Q 12:27

Luke 12:27	Lukan Doublet	Markan Parallel	*Gos. Thom.* 36.2-3 (P. Oxy. 655)
κατα[νοήσα][1]τε τὰ κρίνα ( )[2] πῶς αὐξάν[ει][3]· οὐ κοπι[ᾷ][3] οὐδὲ νήθ[ει][3]· λέγω δὲ ὑμῖν, ( )[4] οὐδὲ Σολομὼν ἐν πάσῃ τῇ δόξῃ αὐτοῦ περιεβάλετο ὡς ἓν τούτων.			**36.2** [πολ]λῷ κρεί[σσον]ές ἐ̣[στε] τῶν [κρί]νων, ἅτι[να ο]ὐ ξα[ί]νει οὐδὲ ν[ήθ]ει. **36.3** κ̣[αὶ] ἓν ἔχ̣ο̣ντ[ες ἔ]νδ[υ]μα, τί ἐν[.....]..αι ὑμεῖς;

σιν is in ℵ[1] (αὐξάνουσιν· οὐ νήθουσιν οὐδὲ κοπιῶσιν in Θ sy[c]) *f*[1] Ath. In Luke 12:27 οὐτὲ νήθει οὐτὲ ὑφαίνει is in D sy[s.c] Cl (in inverse order in a and Mcion[T]), but αὐξάνει· οὐ κοπιᾷ οὐδὲ νήθει is in 𝔓[45.75] *rell.*

[3] Luke's singular verb endings or Matthew's plurals.

[4] Matthew's ὅτι.

⟦Lernt⟧ von den Lilien, wie sie wachsen: Sie mühen sich nicht ab und sie spinnen nicht. Ich sage euch aber: Selbst Salomo in all seiner Pracht war nicht angezogen wie eine von ihnen.

⟦Apprenez⟧ comment croissent les lis: Ils ne peinent ni ne filent. Alors je vous dis: Même Salomon dans toute sa gloire n'a pas été revêtu comme l'un d'eux.

(2) [Ihr seid (doch) viel] besser als die [Lilien], die [keine] «Wolle» krempeln und auch nicht [spinnen]. (3) [Und] wenn ihr *ein* Gewand habt, … ihr …?

(2) [Vous valez bien] mieux que les [lis], qui [ne] cardent ni ne [filent]. (3) [Et] du moment que vous avez *un* vêtement, … vous …?

Q 12:28

Markan Parallel	Matthean Doublet	Matt 6:30	Q 12:28
		εἰ δὲ	εἰ δὲ
		⸂τὸν χόρτον⸃[1]	⸂⸃[1]
		(τοῦ)[2] ἀγρ(οῦ)[2]	[ἐν][2] ἀγρ[ῷ][2]
		⸂ ⸃[1]	⸂τὸν χόρτον⸃[1]
		⸂ ⸃[3] σήμερον ⸂ὄντα⸃[3]	⸂ὄντα⸃[3] σήμερον ⸂⸃[3]
		καὶ αὔριον εἰς κλίβανον	καὶ αὔριον εἰς κλίβανον
		βαλλόμενον	βαλλόμενον
		ὁ θεὸς οὕτως	ὁ θεὸς οὕτως
		ἀμφιέ(ννυσιν)[4],	ἀμφιέ⟦(ννυσιν)[4]⟧,
		(οὐ)[5] πο(λλ)[5]ῷ	(οὐ)[5] πο(λλ)[5]ῷ
		μᾶλλον ὑμᾶς,	μᾶλλον ὑμᾶς,
		ὀλιγόπιστοι;	ὀλιγόπιστοι;

PH: ⸂⸃[3] σήμερον ⸂ὄντα⸃[3].

IQP 1992: ἀμφιέ( )[4], ⟦(οὐ)[5]⟧ πο⟦(λλ)[5]⟧ῷ.

[1] The position of τὸν χόρτον after (Luke) or before (Matthew) the field.

[2] Luke's ἐν ἀγρῷ or Matthew's τοῦ ἀγροῦ.

Q

εἰ δὲ ἐν ἀγρῷ τὸν χόρτον ὄντα σήμερον καὶ αὔριον εἰς κλίβανον βαλλόμενον ὁ θεὸς οὕτως ἀμφιέ⟦ννυσιν⟧, οὐ πολλῷ μᾶλλον ὑμᾶς, ὀλιγόπιστοι;	But if in the field the grass, there today and tomorrow thrown into the oven, God clothes thus, will he not much more clothe you, persons of petty faith!

Gos. Thom. 36.2 (P. Oxy. 655)

(2) [πολ]λῷ κρεί[σσον]ές ἐ̣[στε] τῶν [κρί]νων, ἅτι[να ο]ὐ ξα[ί]νει οὐδὲ ν[ήθ]ει.

(2) [You are far] better than the [lilies], which [do not] card nor [spin].

Q 12:28

Luke 12:28	Lukan Doublet	Markan Parallel	*Gos. Thom.* 36.2 (P. Oxy. 655)
εἰ δὲ			
⸂ ⸃[1]			
[ἐν][2] ἀγρ[ῷ][2]			
⸂τὸν χόρτον⸃[1]			
⸂ὄντα⸃[3] σήμερον ⸂ ⸃[3]			
καὶ αὔριον εἰς κλίβανον			
βαλλόμενον			
ὁ θεὸς οὕτως			
ἀμφιέ[ζει][4],			
( )[5] πό[σ][5]ω			[πολ]λῷ
μᾶλλον ὑμᾶς,			κρεί[σσον]ές ἐ̣[στε]
ὀλιγόπιστοι.			τῶν [κρί]νων,
			ἅτι[να ο]ὐ ξα[ί]νει
			οὐδὲ ν[ήθ]ει.

[3] The position of ὄντα before (Luke) or after (Matthew) σήμερον.

[4] Luke's ἀμφιέζει or Matthew's ἀμφιέννυσιν.

[5] Luke's πόσῳ or Matthew's οὐ πολλῷ ...;

Wenn aber Gott das Gras auf dem Feld, das heute dasteht und morgen in den Ofen geworfen wird, so anzieht, nicht um viel mehr euch, ihr Kleingläubigen?

Mais si, en plein champ, Dieu habille de la sorte l'herbe qui est là aujourd'hui et sera demain jetée dans le four, n'en fera-t-il pas beaucoup plus pour vous, personnes de peu de foi?

(2) [Ihr seid (doch) viel] besser als die [Lilien], die [keine] «Wolle» krempeln und auch nicht [spinnen].

(2) [Vous valez bien] mieux que les [lis], qui [ne] cardent ni ne [filent].

Q 12:29

Markan Parallel	Matthean Doublet	Matt 6:31	Q 12:29
		[ ]¹ μὴ (οὖν)¹ (μεριμνήση)²τε (λέγοντες)³· τί φάγ(ωμεν)³; (ἤ)⁴· τί πί(ωμεν)³; (ἤ)⁴· (τί περιβαλώμεθα)⁵ [ ]⁶;	⟦[]¹⟧ μὴ ⟦(οὖν)¹⟧ (μεριμνήση)²τε (λέγοντες)³· τί φάγ(ωμεν)³; ⟦(ἤ)⁴⟧· τί πί(ωμεν)³; ⟦(ἤ)⁴⟧· (τί περιβαλώμεθα)⁵ []⁶;

IQP 1992: ( )⁴… ( )⁴·.

1 Luke's καὶ ὑμεῖς or Matthew's οὖν.
2 Luke's ζητεῖτε or Matthew's μεριμνήσητε.
3 Luke's indirect discourse or Matthew's λέγοντες and direct discourse.

Q

μὴ ⟦οὖν⟧ μεριμνήσητε λέγοντες· τί φάγωμεν; ⟦ἤ⟧· τί πίωμεν; ⟦ἤ⟧· τί περιβαλώμεθα;

⟦So⟧ do not be anxious, saying: What are we to eat? ⟦Or:⟧ What are we to drink? ⟦Or:⟧ What are we to wear?

Q 12:29

Luke 12:29	Lukan Doublet	Markan Parallel	Gospel of Thomas
[καὶ ὑμεῖς][1] μὴ ( )[1] [ζητεῖ][2]τε ( )[3] τί φάγ[ητε][3] [καὶ][4] τί πί[ητε][3] [καὶ][4] ( )[5] [μὴ μετεωρίζεσθε][6].			

[4] Luke's καί or Matthew's ἤ.
[5] Matthew's τί περιβαλώμεθα.
[6] Luke's μὴ μετεωρίζεσθε.

Sorgt euch ⟦also⟧ nicht, indem ihr sagt: Was sollen wir essen? ⟦Oder:⟧ Was sollen wir trinken? ⟦Oder:⟧ Was sollen wir anziehen?

Ne vous inquiétez ⟦donc⟧ pas en disant: Qu'allons-nous manger? ⟦Ou:⟧ Qu'allons-nous boire? ⟦Ou bien:⟧ Qu'allons-nous revêtir?

Q 12:30

Markan Parallel	Matt 6:7-8	Matt 6:32	Q 12:30
	6:7 Προσευχόμενοι δὲ μὴ		
	βατταλογήσητε	⸂πάντα⸃[1] γὰρ ⸂ταῦτα⸃[1]	⸂πάντα⸃[1] γὰρ ⸂ταῦτα⸃[1]
	ὥσπερ οἱ ([ἐθν])ικοί,	τὰ ἔθνη [ ][2]	τὰ ἔθνη [][2]
	δοκοῦσιν	ἐπιζητοῦσιν·	ἐπιζητοῦσιν·
	γὰρ ὅτι ἐν τῇ πολυλογίᾳ		
	αὐτῶν εἰσακουσθήσονται.		
	6:8 μὴ οὖν ὁμοιωθῆτε		
	αὐτοῖς·		
	([οἶδεν])	⸂οἶδεν⸃[3]	⸂οἶδεν⸃[3]
		⸂ ⸃[4]	⸂ ⸃[4]
	γὰρ	(γὰρ)[5]	⟦(γὰρ)[5]⟧
	ὁ πατὴρ	⸂ὁ πατὴρ⸃[4]	⸂ὁ πατὴρ⸃[4]
		⸂ ⸃[3]	⸂ ⸃[3]
	ὑμῶν	⸂ὑμῶν⸃[4]	⸂ὑμῶν⸃[4]
		(ὁ οὐράνιος)[6]	()[6]
	ὧν ([χρ])είαν ἔχετε πρὸ	ὅτι χρῄζετε τούτων	ὅτι χρῄζετε τούτων
	τοῦ ὑμᾶς αἰτῆσαι αὐτόν.	(ἁπάντων)[7].	⟦(ἁπάντων)[7]⟧.

IQP 1992: ⸂ ⸃[3] ⸂ὑμῶν⸃[4] ⟦(γὰρ)[5]⟧ ⸂ὁ πατὴρ⸃[4] ⸂οἶδεν⸃[3] ⸂ ⸃[4].

IQP 1992: ()[7].

1 The position of ταῦτα before (Luke) or after (Matthew) πάντα.

2 Luke's τοῦ κόσμου.

3 The position of οἶδεν after (Luke) or before (Matthew) the particle and ὁ πατήρ.

Q

πάντα γὰρ ταῦτα τὰ ἔθνη ἐπιζητοῦσιν· οἶδεν ⟦γὰρ⟧ ὁ πατὴρ ὑμῶν ὅτι χρῄζετε τούτων ⟦ἁπάντων⟧.

For all these the Gentiles seek; ⟦for⟧ your Father knows that you need them ⟦all⟧.

Q 12:30

Luke 12:30	Lukan Doublet	Markan Parallel	Gospel of Thomas
⸂ταῦτα⸃[1] γὰρ ⸂πάντα⸃[1] τὰ ἔθνη [τοῦ κόσμου][2] ἐπιζητοῦσιν, ⸂ ⸃[3] ⸂ὑμῶν⸃[4] [δὲ][5] ⸂ὁ πατὴρ⸃[4] ⸂οἶδεν⸃[3] ⸂ ⸃[4] ( )[6] ὅτι χρῄζετε τούτων ( )[7].			

[4] The position of ὁ πατήρ after (Luke) or before (Matthew) ὑμῶν.
[5] Luke's δέ or Matthew's γάρ.
[6] Matthew's ὁ οὐράνιος.
[7] Matthew's ἁπάντων.

Denn all dies suchen die Heidenvölker; ⟦denn⟧ euer Vater weiß, dass ihr das ⟦alles⟧ braucht.

Car toutes ces choses, ce sont les païens qui les recherchent; votre Père sait ⟦en effet⟧ que vous avez besoin ⟦de toutes⟧ ces choses.

Q 12:31

Markan Parallel	Matthean Doublet	Matt 6:33	Q 12:31
		ʃ ͏ʅ[1] ζητεῖτε ʃ (δὲ)[1] ʅ[1] (πρῶτον)[2] τὴν βασιλείαν τοῦ θεοῦ (καὶ τὴν δικαιοσύνην)[3] αὐτοῦ, καὶ ταῦτα (πάντα)[4] προστεθήσεται ὑμῖν. ʅMatt 6:25a[1]	ʃ ʅ[1] ζητεῖτε ʃ (δὲ)[1] ʅ[1] ⟦()[2]⟧ τὴν βασιλείαν ()[3] αὐτοῦ, καὶ ταῦτα ⟦(πάντα)[4]⟧ προστεθήσεται ὑμῖν. ʅQ 12:22[1]

IQP 1992: ()[2]… ()[4].

Text Critical Note (see the discussion in the front matter): In Matt 6:33 τὴν βασιλείαν καὶ τὴν δικαιοσύνην αὐτοῦ is in א (k) l sa bo Eus; τὴν δικαιοσύνην καὶ τὴν βασιλείαν is in B; τὴν βασιλείαν τῶν οὐρανῶν καὶ τὴν δικαιοσύνην αὐτοῦ is in Cl; and τὴν βασιλείαν τοῦ θεοῦ καὶ τὴν

[1] Luke's πλήν or Matthew's δέ.

[2] Matthew's πρῶτον.

Q

ζητεῖτε δὲ τὴν βασιλείαν αὐτοῦ, καὶ ταῦτα ⟦πάντα⟧ προστεθή-σεται ὑμῖν.	But seek his kingdom, and ⟦all⟧ these shall be granted to you.

Q 12:31

Luke 12:31	Lukan Doublet	Markan Parallel	Gospel of Thomas
ʃ [πλὴν][1] ʅ[1] ζητεῖτε ʃ ʅ[1] ( )[2] τὴν βασιλείαν ( )[3] αὐτοῦ, καὶ ταῦτα ( )[4] προστεθήσεται ὑμῖν. ʅLuke 12:22[1]			

δικαιοσύνην αὐτοῦ is in L W Θ 0233 $f^{1.13}$ 33 𝔐 lat sy mae. In Luke 12:31 βασιλείαν τοῦ θεοῦ is in 𝔓[45] A D[1] Q W Θ 070 $f^{1.13}$ 33 𝔐 lat sy Mcion[E]; simply βασιλείαν is in 𝔓[75]; and βασιλείαν αὐτοῦ is in ℵ B D* L Ψ 579 892 *pc* a c co.

[3] Matthew's καὶ τὴν δικαιοσύνην. (It is assumed that τοῦ θεοῦ is not in Matthew.)

[4] Matthew's πάντα.

Sucht hingegen sein Reich, und das ⟦alles⟧ wird euch dazugegeben werden.

Mais cherchez son royaume et ⟦toutes⟧ ces choses vous seront données par surcroît.

Q 12:~~32~~

Markan Parallel	Matthean Doublet	Matt 6:34	Q 12:~~32~~
		μὴ (οὖν μεριμνήσητε εἰς τὴν αὔριον, ἡ γὰρ αὔριον μεριμνήσει ἑαυτῆς· ἀρκετὸν τῇ ἡμέρᾳ ἡ κακία αὐτῆς.)[0]	~~μὴ~~ [()][0]

[0] Is Luke 12:32 par. Matt 6:34 in Q?

Q 12:33-34 is to be found above, between Q 12:2-12, ~~12↔33/Matt 10:23~~, ~~13-15~~, ⟦~~16-20~~⟧, ~~21~~ and Q 12:22b-31.

Q 12:~~32~~

Luke 12:32	Lukan Doublet	Markan Parallel	Gospel of Thomas
Μὴ [φοβοῦ, τὸ μικρὸν ποίμνιον, ὅτι εὐδόκησεν ὁ πατὴρ ὑμῶν δοῦναι ὑμῖν τὴν βασιλείαν.][0]			

Q 12:33-34 is to be found above, between Q 12:2-12, ~~12↔33/Matt 10:23~~, ~~13-15~~, ⟦~~16-20~~⟧, ~~21~~ and Q 12:22b-31.

Q 12:⟦~~35-38~~⟧

Mark 13:37, 35	Matt 24:46, 42	Matt 25:1-13	Q 12:⟦~~35-38~~⟧
		(**25:1** Τότε ὁμοιωθήσεται ἡ βασιλεία τῶν οὐρανῶν δέκα παρθένοις, αἵτινες λαβοῦσαι τὰς λαμπάδας ἑαυτῶν ἐξῆλθον εἰς ὑπάντησιν τοῦ νυμφίου. **25:2** πέντε δὲ ἐξ αὐτῶν ἦσαν μωραὶ καὶ πέντε φρόνιμοι. **25:3** αἱ γὰρ μωραὶ λαβοῦσαι τὰς λαμπάδας αὐτῶν οὐκ ἔλαβον μεθ' ἑαυτῶν ἔλαιον. **25:4** αἱ δὲ φρόνιμοι ἔλαβον ἔλαιον ἐν τοῖς ἀγγείοις μετὰ τῶν λαμπάδων ἑαυτῶν. **25:5** χρονίζοντος δὲ τοῦ νυμφίου ἐνύσταξαν πᾶσαι καὶ ἐκάθευδον. **25:6** μέσης δὲ νυκτὸς κραυγὴ γέγονεν· ἰδοὺ ὁ νυμφίος, ἐξέρχεσθε εἰς ἀπάντησιν αὐτοῦ. **25:7** τότε ἠγέρθησαν πᾶσαι αἱ παρθένοι ἐκεῖναι καὶ ἐκόσμησαν τὰς λαμπάδας ἑαυτῶν. **25:8** αἱ δὲ μωραὶ ταῖς φρονίμοις εἶπαν· δότε ἡμῖν ἐκ τοῦ ἐλαίου ὑμῶν, ὅτι αἱ λαμπάδες ἡμῶν σβέννυνται. **25:9** ἀπεκρίθησαν δὲ αἱ φρόνιμοι λέγουσαι· μήποτε οὐ μὴ ἀρκέσῃ ἡμῖν καὶ ὑμῖν· πορεύεσθε μᾶλλον πρὸς τοὺς πωλοῦντας καὶ ἀγοράσατε ἑαυταῖς.	⟦[()]^0⟧

Q 12:⟦~~35-38~~⟧

Luke 12:35-38	Luke 12:43	Mark 13:33-34, 37, 35-36	*Gos. Thom.* 21.7
[**12:35** Ἔστωσαν ὑμῶν αἱ ὀσφύες περιεζωσμέναι καὶ οἱ λύχνοι καιόμενοι·		**13:33** Βλέπετε, ἀγρυπνεῖτε· οὐκ οἴδατε γὰρ πότε ὁ καιρός ἐστιν.	ⲙⲟⲩⲣ’ ⲙ̄ⲙⲱⲧⲛ̄ ⲉϫⲛ̄ ⲛⲉⲧⲛ̄ϯⲡⲉ ϩⲛ̄ ⲟⲩⲛⲟϭ ⲛ̄ⲇⲩⲛⲁⲙⲓⲥ ϣⲓⲛⲁ ϫⲉ ⲛⲉⲛⲗⲏⲥⲧⲏⲥ ϩⲉ ⲉϩⲓⲏ ⲉⲉⲓ ϣⲁⲣⲱⲧⲛ̄

Q 12:⟦~~35-38~~⟧

Mark 13:37, 35	Matt 24:46, 42	Matt 25:1-13	Q 12:⟦~~35-38~~⟧
		25:10 ἀπερχομένων δὲ αὐτῶν ἀγοράσαι ἦλθεν ὁ νυμφίος, καὶ αἱ ἕτοιμοι εἰσῆ)[0] λθ(ον μετ᾽ αὐτοῦ εἰς τοὺς)[0] γάμ(ους καὶ ἐκλείσθη ἡ θύρα. **25:11** ὕστερον δὲ ἔρχονται καὶ αἱ λοιπαὶ παρθένοι λέγουσαι· κύριε κύριε,)[0] ἄνοιξ(ον ἡμῖν.	 ~~γαμ~~ ~~λθ~~ ~~ἄνοιξ~~
13:37 ὃ δὲ ὑμῖν λέγω πᾶσιν λέγω, γρηγορεῖτε.	**24:46** [μακάριο]ς [ὁ] [δοῦλο]ς [ἐκεῖνο]ς [ὃ]ν [ἐλθὼν {ὁ κύριος}] αὐτοῦ [{εὑρ}ήσει] οὕτως ποιοῦντα·	**25:12** ὁ δὲ ἀποκριθεὶς εἶπεν·)[0] ἀμὴν {λέγω} {ὑμῖν}, (οὐκ οἶδα ὑμᾶς.)[0]	~~ἀμὴν λέγω ὑμῖν,~~
13:35 γρηγορεῖτε οὖν· οὐκ οἴδατε γὰρ πότε ὁ κύριος τῆς οἰκίας ἔρχεται, ἢ ὀψὲ ἢ μεσονύκτιον ἢ ἀλεκτοροφωνίας ἢ πρωΐ, **13:36** μὴ ἐλθὼν ἐξαίφνης εὕρῃ ὑμᾶς καθεύδοντας.	**24:42** {Γρηγορεῖτε οὖν}, ὅτι {οὐκ οἴδατε} ποίᾳ ἡμέρᾳ {ὁ κύριος} ὑμῶν {ἔρχεται}.	**25:13** {γρηγορ(εῖτε οὖν}, ὅτι {οὐκ οἴδατε} τὴν ἡμέραν οὐδὲ τὴν ὥραν.)[0]	{~~γρηγορ~~}

[0] Are γαμ-, -λθ-, ἄνοιξ-, γρηγορ-, ἀμὴν λέγω ὑμῖν vestiges of a Q text behind Luke 12:35-38 and Matt 25:10-13?

Gos. Thom. 21.7 (Nag Hammadi II 2)

περιζώσασθε τὰς ὀσφύας ὑμῶν ἐν δυνάμει μεγάλῃ, ἵνα μὴ εὕρωσιν οἱ λῃσταί, ποίας[1] εἰσέλθωσιν εἰς ὑμᾶς.

Gird your loins with great strength, so that the robbers will not find a way to get to you.

[1] Cf. the sahidic translation of Luke 5:19.
[1] Vgl. die sahidische Übersetzung von Lk 5,19.
[1] Cf. la traduction sahidique de Luc 5:19.

Q 12:⟦~~35-38~~⟧

Luke 12:35-38	Luke 12:43	Mark 13:33-34, 37, 35-36	*Gos. Thom.* 21.7
12:36 καὶ ὑμεῖς ὅμοιοι ἀνθρώποις προσδεχομένοις τὸν κύριον ἑαυτῶν πότε ἀναλύσῃ ἐκ τῶν]^0 γάμ[ων, ἵνα ἐ]^0 λθ[όντος καὶ κρούσαντος εὐθέως]^0 ἀνοίξ[ωσιν αὐτῷ.		**13:34** Ὡς ἄνθρωπος ἀπόδημος ἀφεὶς τὴν οἰκίαν αὐτοῦ καὶ δοὺς τοῖς δούλοις αὐτοῦ τὴν ἐξουσίαν ἑκάστῳ τὸ ἔργον αὐτοῦ καὶ τῷ θυρωρῷ ἐνετείλατο ἵνα γρηγορῇ.	
12:37 μακάριοι οἱ δοῦλοι ἐκεῖνοι, οὓς {ἐλθὼν} {ὁ κύριος} {εὑρ}ήσει]^0	[μακάριο]ς [ὁ] [δοῦλο]ς [ἐκεῖνο]ς, [ὃ]ν [ἐλθὼν {ὁ κύριος}] αὐτοῦ [{εὑρ}ήσει] ποιοῦντα οὕτως.	**13:37** ὃ δὲ ὑμῖν λέγω πᾶσιν λέγω, γρηγορεῖτε.	
{γρηγορ}[οῦντας·]^0 ἀμὴν λέγω ὑμῖν [ὅτι περιζώσεται καὶ ἀνακλινεῖ αὐτοὺς καὶ παρελθὼν διακονήσει αὐτοῖς. **12:38** κἂν ἐν τῇ δευτέρᾳ κἂν ἐν τῇ τρίτῃ φυλακῇ {ἔλθ}ῃ καὶ {εὕρῃ} οὕτως, μακάριοί εἰσιν ἐκεῖνοι.]^0		**13:35** γρηγορεῖτε οὖν· οὐκ οἴδατε γὰρ πότε ὁ κύριος τῆς οἰκίας ἔρχεται, ἢ ὀψὲ ἢ μεσονύκτιον ἢ ἀλεκτοροφωνίας ἢ πρωΐ, **13:36** μὴ ἐλθὼν ἐξαίφνης εὕρῃ ὑμᾶς καθεύδοντας.	

Gürtet eure Lenden mit großer Kraft, damit die Räuber keinen Weg finden, um zu euch zu kommen.

Ceignez-vous les reins d'une grande force, afin que les voleurs ne trouvent pas de chemin pour venir jusqu'à vous.

Q 12:39

Rev 3:3b	Matthean Doublet	Matt 24:43	Q 12:39
		¹ ⸀	¹ ⸀
		(Ἐκεῖνο)² δὲ γινώσκετε	⟦(ἐκεῖνο)⟧² δὲ γινώσκετε
ἐὰν οὖν μὴ γρηγορήσῃς,		ὅτι εἰ ᾔδει ὁ οἰκοδεσπότης	ὅτι εἰ ᾔδει ὁ οἰκοδεσπότης
		ποίᾳ (φυλακῇ)³	ποίᾳ (φυλακῇ)³
ἥξω ὡς κλέπτης,		ὁ κλέπτης ἔρχεται,	ὁ κλέπτης ἔρχεται,
		(ἐγρηγόρησεν ἂν καὶ)⁴	()⁴
καὶ οὐ μὴ γνῷς ποίαν		οὐκ ἂν (εἴασ)⁵εν	οὐκ ἂν ⟦(εἴασ)⁵⟧εν
		διορυχθῆναι	διορυχθῆναι
ὥραν ἥξω ἐπὶ σέ.		τ(ὴ)⁶ν οἰκ(ία)⁶ν αὐτοῦ.	τ[ὸν] ⁶ν οἶκ[ο]⁶ν αὐτοῦ.
		⸂¹⇒ Matt 24:50-51	⸂¹⇒ Q 12:46

PH: ⟦(ἐγρηγόρησεν ἂν καὶ)⁴⟧.

IQP 1992: ⟦[ἀφῆκ]⁵⟧εν διορυχθῆναι τ[( )]⁶ν οἰκ[( )]⁶ν.

Text Critical Note (see the discussion in the front matter): In Luke 12:39, in place of οὐκ ἄν, one finds ἐγρηγόρησεν ἄν (ἄν omitted in א¹) καὶ

¹ The position of Q 12:39-46 in Q: After Q 12:34 and before Q 12:⟦49⟧, 51 (Lukan order); or after Q 17:35 (Matt 24:41) and before Q 13:25 (Matt 25:10-12) (Matthean order).

Q

⟦ἐκεῖν⟧ο δὲ γινώσκετε ὅτι εἰ ᾔδει ὁ οἰκοδεσπότης ποίᾳ φυλακῇ ὁ κλέπτης ἔρχεται, οὐκ ἂν ⟦εἴασ⟧εν διορυχθῆναι τὸν οἶκον αὐτοῦ.

But know this: If the householder had known in which watch the robber was coming, he would not have let his house be dug into.

Gos. Thom. 21.5 (Nag Hammadi II 2)

διὰ τοῦτο λέγω· εἰ μανθάνει¹ ὁ οἰκοδεσπότης ὅτι ἔρχεται ὁ κλέπτης γρηγορήσει πρὶν ἐλθεῖν αὐτὸν καὶ οὐκ ἐάσει αὐτὸν διορύξαι τὴν οἰκίαν αὐτοῦ τῆς βασιλείας αὐτοῦ τοῦ αἴρειν τὰ σκεύη αὐτοῦ.

That is why I say: When the householder learns that the robber is coming, he will be on guard before he comes (and) will not let him dig into his house, his domain², to carry away his possessions.

¹ The verb is translated with ⲉⲓⲙⲉ, for instance Acts 23:27 sa; another possibility: οἶδεν.

¹ Dieses Verb wird z. B. auch Apg 23,27 sa mit ⲉⲓⲙⲉ wiedergegeben; andere Möglichkeit: οἶδεν.

¹ Pour une traduction de ce verbe par ⲉⲓⲙⲉ, voir, par exemple, Actes 23:27 sa; une autre possibilité serait οἶδεν.

² The Coptic genitive here is to be understood as an explicative genitive.

Q 12:39

Luke 12:39	Lukan Doublet	*Gos. Thom.* 21.5	*Gos. Thom.* 103
1⸆			
[τοῦτο][2] δὲ γινώσκετε		ⲇⲓⲁ ⲧⲟⲩⲧⲟ ϯϫⲱ ⲙ̄ⲙⲟⲥ	ⲡⲉϫⲉ ⲓ̅ⲥ̅ ϫⲉ
ὅτι εἰ ᾔδει ὁ οἰκοδεσπότης		ϫⲉ ⲉϥ'ϣⲁⲉⲓⲙⲉ	ⲟⲩⲙⲁ̣[ⲕⲁ]ⲣⲓⲟⲥ ⲡⲉ
		ⲛ̄ϭⲓ ⲡϫⲉⲥϩⲛ̄ⲏⲉⲓ	ⲡⲣⲱⲙⲉ ⲡⲁⲉⲓ ⲉⲧⲥⲟⲟⲩⲛ ϫⲉ
ποίᾳ [ὥρᾳ][3]		ϫⲉ ϥⲛⲏⲩ	ϩ[ⲛ̄ ⲁϣ] ⲙ̄ⲙⲉⲣⲟⲥ
ὁ κλέπτης ἔρχεται,		ⲛ̄ϭⲓ ⲡⲣⲉϥϫⲓⲟⲩⲉ	ⲉⲛⲗⲏⲥⲧⲏⲥ ⲛⲏⲩ ⲉϩⲟⲩⲛ
( )[4]		ϥⲛⲁⲣⲟⲉⲓⲥ ⲉⲙⲡⲁⲧⲉϥ'ⲉⲓ	ϣⲓⲛⲁ̣ [ⲉϥ]ⲛ̣ⲁⲧⲱⲟⲩⲛ'
οὐκ ἂν [ἀφῆκ][5]εν		ⲛ̄ϥⲧⲙ̄ⲕⲁⲁϥ' ⲉϣⲟϫⲧ'	ⲛ̄ϥⲥⲱⲟⲩϩ
διορυχθῆναι		ⲉϩⲟⲩⲛ ⲉⲡⲉϥⲏⲉⲓ	
τ[ὸ][6]ν οἶκ[ο][6]ν αὐτοῦ.		ⲛ̄ⲧⲉ ⲧⲉϥ'ⲙⲛ̄ⲧⲉⲣⲟ	ⲛ̄ⲧⲉϥ'ⲙⲛ̄ⲧⲉ̣[ⲣⲟ]
			ⲁⲩⲱ ⲛ̄ϥⲙⲟⲩⲣ ⲙ̄ⲙⲟϥ
⸉1⇒ Luke 12:46		ⲉⲧⲣⲉϥϥⲓ ⲛ̄ⲛⲉϥ'ⲥⲕⲉⲩⲟⲥ	ⲉϫⲛ̄ ⲧⲉϥ'ϯⲡⲉ
			ϩ̣[ⲁ] ⲧⲉϩⲏ ⲉⲙ'ⲡⲁⲧⲟⲩⲉⲓ
			ⲉ̇ϩⲟⲩⲛ

οὐκ (ἂν added in A Q Θ 070 33 2542 *pm*) in ℵ^{1} A B L Q W Θ Ψ 070 *f*$^{1.13}$ 33 𝔐 lat sy$^{p.h}$ sa^{ms} bo, but οὐκ ἂν in 𝔓^{75} ℵ* (D) e i sy$^{s.c}$ sa^{mss} Mcion^{T}.

[2] Luke's τοῦτο or Matthew's ἐκεῖνο.
[3] Luke's ὥρᾳ or Matthew's φυλακῇ.
[4] Matthew's ἐγρηγόρησεν ἂν καί.
[5] Luke's ἀφῆκεν or Matthew's εἴασεν.
[6] Luke's τὸν οἶκον or Matthew's τὴν οἰκίαν.

⟦Jenes⟧ aber erkennt: Wenn der Hausherr gewusst hätte, zu welcher Nachtwache der Dieb kommt, hätte er nicht zugelassen, dass in sein Haus eingebrochen wird.

Mais sachez ce⟦la⟧: si le maître de maison connaissait «d'avance» le tour de garde au cours duquel viendra le voleur, il ne laisserait pas sa maison être percée.

Deshalb sage ich: Wenn der Hausherr erfährt, dass der Dieb im Begriff ist zu kommen, wird er wachsam sein, bevor er kommt (und) wird ihn nicht eindringen lassen in sein Haus, seinen Herrschaftsbereich[3], dass er seine Habe wegnehme.

[3] Der koptische Genitiv ist explikativ zu verstehen.

C'est pourquoi je dis: Si le maître de maison apprend que le voleur viendra, il veillera avant qu'il vienne (et) il ne le laissera pas percer sa maison, son royaume,[4] pour emporter ses biens.

[4] Le génitif copte a valeur explicative.

Q 12:39

Rev 3:3b	Matthean Doublet	Matt 24:43	Q 12:39

Gos. Thom. 103 (Nag Hammadi II 2)

Λέγει Ἰησοῦς· μακάριος ὁ ἄνθρωπος, ὃς οἶδεν [ποίῳ] μέρει οἱ λησταὶ εἰσέρχονται, ἵνα ἀναστὰς συναγάγῃ τὴν βασιλείαν αὐτοῦ καὶ περιζώσῃ τὴν ὀσφὺν αὐτοῦ πρὶν εἰσπορεύεσθαι αὐτούς.

Jesus says: Blessed is the person who knows at [which] point (of the house)[1] the robbers are going to enter, so that [he] may arise to gather together his [domain] and gird his loins before they enter.

[1] Or: at [what] part (of the night).

Q 12:39

Luke 12:39	**Lukan Doublet**	***Gos. Thom.* 21.5**	***Gos. Thom.* 103**

Jesus spricht: Selig ist der Mensch, der weiß, an [welcher] Stelle[2] die Räuber eindringen werden, damit [er] aufstehe, seinen [Herrschaftsbereich] sammle und seine Lende gürte, bevor sie hereinkommen.

[2] Oder: in [welchem] Teil (der Nacht).

Jésus dit: Bienheureux est l'homme qui sait dans [quelle] partie (de son domaine)[3] les voleurs viendront, pour qu'[il] se lève, rassemble son [domaine] et se ceigne les reins avant qu'ils ne s'introduisent.

[3] Ou: dans [quelle] partie (de la nuit).

Q 12:40

Mark 13:35a-b	Matt 24:42	Matt 24:44	Q 12:40
γρηγορεῖτε οὖν· οὐκ οἴδατε γὰρ πότε ὁ κύριος τῆς οἰκίας ἔρχεται,	{[Γρηγορεῖτε οὖν}, ὅτι {οὐκ οἴδατε} ποίᾳ ἡμέρᾳ {ὁ κύριος} ὑμῶν {ἔρχεται}.	(διὰ τοῦτο)[1] καὶ ὑμεῖς γίνεσθε ἕτοιμοι, ὅτι ᾗ ⸂ ⸃[2] οὐ δοκεῖτε ⸂ὥρᾳ⸃[2] ὁ υἱὸς τοῦ ἀνθρώπου ἔρχεται.	()[1] καὶ ὑμεῖς γίνεσθε ἕτοιμοι, ὅτι ᾗ ⸂⸃[2] οὐ δοκεῖτε ⸂ὥρᾳ⸃[2] ὁ υἱὸς τοῦ ἀνθρώπου ἔρχεται.

[1] Matthew's διὰ τοῦτο.

[2] The position of ὥρᾳ before (Luke) or after (Matthew) οὐ δοκεῖτε.

Q

καὶ ὑμεῖς γίνεσθε ἕτοιμοι, ὅτι ᾗ οὐ δοκεῖτε ὥρᾳ ὁ υἱὸς τοῦ ἀνθρώπου ἔρχεται.

You also must be ready, for the Son of Humanity is coming at an hour you do not expect.

Q 12:40

Luke 12:40	Lukan Doublet	Mark 13:35a-b	Gospel of Thomas
( )[1] καὶ ὑμεῖς γίνεσθε ἕτοιμοι, ὅτι ᾗ ⸉ὥρᾳ⸊[2] οὐ δοκεῖτε ⸉ ⸊[2] ὁ υἱὸς τοῦ ἀνθρώπου ἔρχεται.		γρηγορεῖτε οὖν· οὐκ οἴδατε γὰρ πότε ὁ κύριος τῆς οἰκίας ἔρχεται,	

Haltet euch also bereit, denn der Menschensohn kommt zu einer Stunde, in der ihr nicht «damit» rechnet.

Vous aussi, soyez prêts, parce que le Fils de l'homme vient à une heure où vous ne vous y attendez pas.

Q 12:42

Ps 103:27 LXX	Matt 25:21b	Matt 24:45	Q 12:42
	ἔφη αὐτῷ [ὁ κύριος] αὐτοῦ·	[ ][1]	[][1]
	εὖ,	Τίς ἄρα ἐστὶν	τίς ἄρα ἐστὶν
	(δοῦλ)ε ἀγαθὲ	ὁ πιστὸς (δοῦλ)[2]ος	ὁ πιστὸς (δοῦλ)[2]ος
	(καὶ) ([πιστ])έ,	(καὶ)[3] φρόνιμος	⟦(καὶ)[3]⟧ φρόνιμος
πάντα πρὸς σὲ	ἐπὶ ὀλίγα	ὃν κατ(έ)[4]στησε(ν)[4]	ὃν κατ(έ)[4]στησε(ν)[4]
	ἦς πιστός,	ὁ κύριος	ὁ κύριος
προσδοκῶσιν	([ἐπὶ]) πολλῶν	ἐπὶ τῆς (οἰκετ)[5]είας αὐτοῦ	ἐπὶ τῆς (οἰκετ)[5]είας αὐτοῦ
δοῦναι	σε [(κατ)α(στήσ)]ω·	τοῦ δο(ῦ)[6]ναι	τοῦ δο⟦(ῦ)[6]⟧ναι
	εἴσελθε	(αὐτοῖς)[7]	⟦(αὐτοῖς)[7]⟧
	εἰς τὴν χαρὰν	∫ ≀[8]	∫ἐν καιρῷ≀[8]
τὴν τροφὴν αὐτοῖς	τοῦ ([κυρίο])υ σου.	τ(ὴν τροφὴν)[9]	τ(ὴν τροφήν)[9]
εὔκαιρον.		∫ἐν καιρῷ≀[8];	∫≀[8];

IQP 1991: (καί)[3].

JSK: δι[δό][6]ναι.

[1] Luke's καὶ εἶπεν ὁ κύριος.
[2] Luke's οἰκονόμος or Matthew's δοῦλος.
[3] Luke's ὁ or Matthew's καί.

[4] Luke's καταστήσει or Matthew's κατέστησεν.
[5] Luke's θεραπείας or Matthew's οἰκετείας.

Q

τίς ἄρα ἐστὶν ὁ πιστὸς δοῦλος ⟦καὶ⟧ φρόνιμος ὃν κατέστησεν ὁ κύριος ἐπὶ τῆς οἰκετείας αὐτοῦ τοῦ δο⟦ῦ⟧ναι ⟦αὐτοῖς⟧ ἐν καιρῷ τὴν τροφήν.

Who then is the faithful ⟦and⟧ wise slave whom the master put over his household to give ⟦them⟧ food on time?

Q 12:42

Luke 12:42	Lukan Doublet	Markan Parallel	Gospel of Thomas
[καὶ εἶπεν ὁ κύριος][1]· τίς ἄρα ἐστὶν ὁ πιστὸς [οἰκονόμ][2]ος [ὁ][3] φρόνιμος, ὃν κατ[α][4]στήσε[ι][4] ὁ κύριος ἐπὶ τῆς [θεραπ][5]είας αὐτοῦ τοῦ [δι][6]δόναι ( )[7] ʃἐν καιρῷ ʅ[8] τ[ὸ σιτομέτριον][9] ʃ ʅ[8];			

JSK: ἐν καιρῷ in Lukan position {C}; JMR, PH: Indeterminate.

IQP 1991: τ( )[9].

[6] Luke's διδόναι or Matthew's δοῦναι.
[7] Matthew's αὐτοῖς.

[8] The position of ἐν καιρῷ before (Luke) or after (Matthew) the reference to the food.
[9] Luke's τὸ σιτομέτριον or Matthew's τὴν τροφήν.

Wer also ist der treue ⟦und⟧ kluge Sklave, den der Herr über sein Hausgesinde setzte, um ⟦ihnen⟧ zur rechten Zeit das Essen zu geben?

Quel est donc l'esclave fidèle ⟦et⟧ avisé que le maître a établi sur sa domesticité pour ⟦leur⟧ donner en temps voulu «leur» nourriture?

Q 12:43

Mark 13:36	Matthean Doublet	Matt 24:46	Q 12:43
μὴ ἐλθὼν ἐξαίφνης εὕρῃ ὑμᾶς καθεύδοντας.		μακάριος ὁ δοῦλος ἐκεῖνος ὃν {ἐλθὼν} ὁ κύριος αὐτοῦ {εὑρ}ήσει ʃ ʅ[1] οὕτως ʃποιοῦνταʅ[1].	μακάριος ὁ δοῦλος ἐκεῖνος, ὃν {ἐλθὼν} ὁ κύριος αὐτοῦ {εὑρ}ήσει ʃʅ[1] οὕτως ʃποιοῦνταʅ[1].

[1] The position of ποιοῦντα before (Luke) or after (Matthew) οὕτως.

Q

μακάριος ὁ δοῦλος ἐκεῖνος, ὃν ἐλθὼν ὁ κύριος αὐτοῦ εὑρήσει οὕτως ποιοῦντα·	Blessed is that slave whose master, on coming, will find so doing.

Q 12:43

Luke 12:43	Luke 12:37a	Mark 13:36	Gospel of Thomas
μακάριος ὁ δοῦλος ἐκεῖνος, ὃν {ἐλθὼν} ὁ κύριος αὐτοῦ {εὑρ}ήσει ʃποιοῦνταˀ¹ οὕτως ʃ ˀ¹.	[(μακάριο)]ι [(ο)]ἱ [(δοῦλο)]ι [(ἐκεῖνο)]ι, [(ο)]ὓς [(ἐλθὼν ὁ κύριος)] [(εὑρήσει)] γρηγοροῦντας·	 μὴ ἐλθὼν ἐξαίφνης εὕρῃ ὑμᾶς καθεύδοντας.	

Selig ist jener Sklave, den sein Herr, wenn er kommt, so handelnd finden wird.

Bienheureux cet esclave qu'en arrivant son maître trouvera en train d'agir de la sorte.

Q 12:44

Markan Parallel	Matthean Doublet	Matt 24:47	Q 12:44
		(ἀμὴν)[1] λέγω ὑμῖν ὅτι ἐπὶ πᾶσιν τοῖς ὑπάρχουσιν αὐτοῦ καταστήσει αὐτόν.	⟦(ἀμὴν)[1]⟧ λέγω ὑμῖν ὅτι ἐπὶ πᾶσιν τοῖς ὑπάρχουσιν αὐτοῦ καταστήσει αὐτόν.

Text Critical Note: See the discussion in the front matter as to whether Luke 12:44 is in Luke.

JSK: [ ][1].

[1] Luke's ἀληθῶς or Matthew's ἀμήν.

Q

⟦ἀμὴν⟧ λέγω ὑμῖν ὅτι ἐπὶ πᾶσιν τοῖς ὑπάρχουσιν αὐτοῦ καταστήσει αὐτόν.	⟦Amen⟧, I tell you, he will appoint him over all his possessions.

Q 12:44

Luke 12:44	Luke 12:37b	Markan Parallel	Gospel of Thomas
[ἀληθῶς][1] λέγω ὑμῖν ὅτι ἐπὶ πᾶσιν τοῖς ὑπάρχουσιν αὐτοῦ καταστήσει αὐτόν.	(ἀμὴν [λέγω ὑμῖν ὅτι]) ...		

⟦Amen⟧, ich sage euch: Über seinen ganzen Besitz wird er ihn stellen.

⟦Amen⟧, je vous dis qu'il l'établira sur tous ses biens.

Q 12:45

Markan Parallel	Matthean Doublet	Matt 24:48-49	Q 12:45
		24:48 ἐὰν δὲ εἴπῃ ὁ (κακὸς)[1] δοῦλος ἐκεῖνος ἐν τῇ καρδίᾳ αὐτοῦ· χρονίζει ⸉μου⸊[2] ὁ κύριος ⸉ ⸊[2] [ ][3], **24:49** καὶ ἄρξηται τύπτειν τοὺς (συνδούλους αὐτοῦ)[4], ἐσθί(η)[5] (δ)[6]ὲ καὶ πίν(ῃ)[5] (μετὰ τῶν)[7] μεθυ(όντων)[5.7],	ἐὰν δὲ εἴπῃ ὁ ()[1] δοῦλος ἐκεῖνος ἐν τῇ καρδίᾳ αὐτοῦ· χρονίζει ⸉ ⸊[2] ὁ κύριός ⸉μου⸊[2] ⟦[][3]⟧, καὶ ἄρξηται τύπτειν τοὺς ⟦(συνδούλους αὐτοῦ)[4]⟧, ἐσθί⟦(η)[5]⟧ (δ)[6]ὲ καὶ πίν⟦(ῃ)[5] (μετὰ τῶν)[7]⟧ μεθυ⟦(όντων)[5.7]⟧,

IQP 1991, JMR, PH, JSK: ⸉ ⸊[2] ὁ κύριός ⸉μου⸊[2] indeterminate.

IQP 1991: [( )][4]; JSK: ⟦[παῖδας καὶ τὰς παιδίσκας][4]⟧.

[1] Matthew's κακός.

[2] The position of μου after (Luke) or before (Matthew) ὁ κύριος.

[3] Luke's ἔρχεσθαι.

[4] Luke's παῖδας καὶ τὰς παιδίσκας or Matthew's συνδούλους αὐτοῦ.

Q

ἐὰν δὲ εἴπῃ ὁ δοῦλος ἐκεῖνος ἐν τῇ καρδίᾳ αὐτοῦ· χρονίζει ὁ κύριός μου, καὶ ἄρξηται τύπτειν τοὺς ⟦συνδούλους αὐτοῦ⟧, ἐσθί⟦ῃ⟧ δὲ καὶ πίν⟦ῃ μετὰ τῶν⟧ μεθυ⟦όντων⟧,

But if that slave says in his heart: My master is delayed, and begins to beat ⟦his fellow slaves⟧, and eats and drinks ⟦with the⟧ drunk⟦ards⟧,

Q 12:45

Luke 12:45	Lukan Doublet	Markan Parallel	Gospel of Thomas
ἐὰν δὲ εἴπῃ ὁ ( )[1] δοῦλος ἐκεῖνος ἐν τῇ καρδίᾳ αὐτοῦ· χρονίζει ⸂ ⸃[2] ὁ κύριός ⸂μου⸃[2] [ἔρχεσθαι][3], καὶ ἄρξηται τύπτειν τοὺς [παῖδας καὶ τὰς παιδίσκας][4], ἐσθί[ειν][5] [τ][6]ε καὶ πίν[ειν][5] [καὶ][7] μεθύ[σκεσθαι][5.7],			

IQP 1991, JSK: ἐσθί⟦[ειν][5]⟧ (δ)[6]ὲ καὶ πίν⟦[ειν][5] [καὶ][7]⟧ μεθύ⟦[σκεσθαι][5.7]⟧.

[5] Luke's infinitive forms or Matthew's subjunctives.

[6] Luke's τε or Matthew's δέ.

[7] Luke's καὶ μεθύσκεσθαι or Matthew's μετὰ τῶν μεθυόντων.

Wenn aber jener Sklave in seinem Herzen sagt: Mein Herr lässt sich Zeit, und anfängt, ⟦seine Mitsklaven⟧ zu schlagen, und ⟦mit den⟧ Trunken⟦bolden⟧ isst und trinkt,

Mais si cet esclave se met à dire en son cœur: Mon maître tarde, et qu'il commence à battre ⟦ses compagnons d'esclavage⟧, et qu'il mange, puis qu'il boive ⟦avec les⟧ ivr⟦ognes⟧,

Q 12:46

Markan Parallel	Matthean Doublet	Matt 24:50-51	Q 12:46
		24:50 ἥξει ὁ κύριος τοῦ δούλου ἐκείνου ἐν ἡμέρᾳ ᾗ οὐ προσδοκᾷ καὶ ἐν ὥρᾳ ᾗ οὐ γινώσκει, **24:51** καὶ διχοτομήσει αὐτὸν καὶ τὸ μέρος αὐτοῦ μετὰ τῶν (ὑποκρι)[1]τῶν θήσει· (ἐκεῖ ἔσται ὁ κλαυθμὸς καὶ ὁ βρυγμὸς τῶν ὀδόντων)[2]. ⸂Matt 24:43[1]	ἥξει ὁ κύριος τοῦ δούλου ἐκείνου ἐν ἡμέρᾳ ᾗ οὐ προσδοκᾷ καὶ ἐν ὥρᾳ ᾗ οὐ γινώσκει, καὶ διχοτομήσει αὐτὸν καὶ τὸ μέρος αὐτοῦ μετὰ τῶν [ἀπίσ][1]των θήσει. ()[2] . ⸂ Q 12:39[1]

[1] Luke's ἀπίστων or Matthew's ὑποκριτῶν.

[2] Matthew's ἐκεῖ ἔσται ὁ κλαυθμὸς καὶ ὁ βρυγμὸς τῶν ὀδόντων.

Q

ἥξει ὁ κύριος τοῦ δούλου ἐκείνου ἐν ἡμέρᾳ ᾗ οὐ προσδοκᾷ καὶ ἐν ὥρᾳ ᾗ οὐ γινώσκει, καὶ διχοτομήσει αὐτὸν καὶ τὸ μέρος αὐτοῦ μετὰ τῶν ἀπίστων θήσει.	the master of that slave will come on a day he does not expect and at an hour he does not know, and will cut him to pieces and give him an inheritance with the faithless.

Q 12:46

Luke 12:46	Lukan Doublet	Markan Parallel	Gospel of Thomas
ἥξει ὁ κύριος τοῦ δούλου ἐκείνου ἐν ἡμέρᾳ ᾗ οὐ προσδοκᾷ καὶ ἐν ὥρᾳ ᾗ οὐ γινώσκει, καὶ διχοτομήσει αὐτὸν καὶ τὸ μέρος αὐτοῦ μετὰ τῶν [ἀπίσ][1]των θήσει. ( )[2] . ὶ Luke 12:39[1]			

wird der Herr jenes Sklaven an einem Tag kommen, an dem er es nicht erwartet, und zu einer Stunde, die er nicht kennt, und er wird ihn in Stücke hauen und ihm seinen Platz unter den Treulosen zuweisen.

le maître de cet esclave viendra un jour où il ne l'attend pas et à une heure qu'il ne connaît pas, et il le taillera en pièces et lui assignera sa part parmi les infidèles.

Q 12:⟦49⟧

Markan Parallel	Matt 10:34	Matthew	Q 12:⟦49⟧
	Μὴ νομίσητε ὅτι [ἦλθον βαλεῖν] εἰρήνην [ἐπὶ τὴν γῆν]· οὐκ [ἦλθον βαλεῖν] εἰρήνην ἀλλὰ μάχαιραν.	¹ʃ [ ]⁰ ɩ¹⇒ Matt 10:35-36	¹ʃ ⟦ «[πῦρ ἦλθον βαλεῖν ἐπὶ τὴν γῆν, καὶ τί θέλω εἰ ἤδη ἀνήφθη.]⁰» ⟧ ɩ¹⇒ Q 12:53

IQP 1993: [ ]⁰.

PH: []⁰.

⁰ Is Luke 12:49 in Q?

¹ The position of Q 12:49-53 in Q: After Q 12:46 and before Q 12:⟦54-55⟧, 58 (Lukan order); or after Q 12:9 (Matt 10:33) and before Q 14:26 (Matt 10:37) (Matthean

Q

⟦«πῦρ ἦλθον βαλεῖν ἐπὶ τὴν γῆν, καὶ τί θέλω εἰ ἤδη ἀνήφθη.»⟧

⟦«Fire have I come to hurl on the earth, and how I wish it had already blazed up!»⟧

Gos. Thom. 10 (Nag Hammadi II 2)

Λέγει Ἰησοῦς· ἔβαλον πῦρ εἰς τὸν κόσμον. καὶ ἰδοὺ τηρῶ αὐτό[1], ἕως ἂν πυροῖ.

Jesus says: I have hurled fire on the world, and see, I am guarding it until it blazes up[2].

¹ According to the Coptic text the pronominal object may also refer to τὸν κόσμον. In this case the Greek text should read αὐτόν.

¹ Nach dem koptischen Text kann sich das pronominale Objekt auch auf τὸν κόσμον beziehen. Im griechischen Text müsste dann αὐτόν stehen.

¹ D'après le texte copte, l'objet pronominal pourrait renvoyer tout aussi bien à τὸν κόσμον, auquel cas le texte grec devrait porter αὐτόν.

² Or: I am protecting it (the world) until it blazes up.

Q 12:⟦49⟧

Luke 12:49	Luke 12:51	Markan Parallel	*Gos. Thom.* 10
¹ʃ [Πῦρ ἦλθον βαλεῖν ἐπὶ τὴν γῆν, καὶ τί θέλω εἰ ἤδη ἀνήφθη.]⁰ ʅ¹⇒ Luke 12:53	δοκεῖτε ὅτι εἰρήνην παρεγενόμην δοῦναι ἐν [τῇ] [γῇ]; οὐχί, λέγω ὑμῖν, ἀλλ᾽ ἢ διαμερισμόν.		ⲡⲉϫⲉ ⲓ̅ⲥ̅ ϫⲉ ⲁⲉⲓⲛⲟⲩϫⲉ ⲛ̄ⲟⲩⲕⲱϩ̄ⲧ᾽ ⲉϫⲛ̄ ⲡⲕⲟⲥⲙⲟⲥ ⲁⲩⲱ ⲉⲓⲥϩⲏⲏⲧⲉ ϯⲁⲣⲉϩ ⲉⲣⲟϥ᾽ ϣⲁⲛⲧⲉϥϫⲉⲣⲟ

order).

⟦«Feuer auf die Erde zu werfen, bin ich gekommen, und wie wollte ich, dass es schon brenne.»⟧

⟦«C'est du feu que je suis venu jeter sur la terre, et comme je voudrais qu'il soit déjà allumé!»⟧

Jesus spricht: Ich habe Feuer in die Welt geworfen, und siehe, ich bewahre es, bis es lodert.[3]

[3] Oder: ich bewahre sie (die Welt), bis sie lodert.

Jésus dit: J'ai jeté du feu sur le monde, et voici que je le garde jusqu'à ce qu'il flambe.[4]

[4] Ou: je le (le monde) garde, jusqu'à ce qu'il flambe.

Q 12:~~50~~

Markan Parallel	Matthean Doublet	Matthew	Q 12:~~50~~
		[ ][0]	[][0]

[0] Is Luke 12:50 in Q?

Q 12:~~50~~

Luke 12:50	Lukan Doublet	Mark 10:38b	Gospel of Thomas
[{βάπτισμα} δὲ ἔχω {βαπτισθῆναι}, καὶ πῶς συνέχομαι ἕως ὅτου τελεσθῇ.][0]		δύνασθε πιεῖν τὸ ποτήριον ὃ ἐγὼ πίνω ἢ τὸ βάπτισμα ὃ ἐγὼ βαπτίζομαι βαπτισθῆναι;	

Q 12:51

Markan Parallel	Matthean Doublet	Matt 10:34	Q 12:51
		(Μὴ νομίση)[1]τε ὅτι	⟦[δοκεῖ][1]⟧τε ὅτι
		ʃ ʅ[2]	ʃʅ[2]
		(ἦλθον)[3]	(ἦλθον)[3]
		(βαλεῖν)[4]	(βαλεῖν)[4]
		ʃεἰρήνηνʅ[2]	ʃεἰρήνηνʅ[2]
		(ἐπὶ)[5] τὴ(ν)[5] γῆ(ν)[5]·	(ἐπὶ)[5] τὴ(ν)[5] γῆ(ν)[5]⟦;⟧
		οὐ(κ ἦλθον	οὐ(κ ἦλθον
		βαλεῖν εἰρήνην)[6]	βαλεῖν εἰρήνην)[6]
		ἀλλ(ὰ μάχαιραν)[7].	ἀλλ(ὰ μάχαιραν)[7].

IQP 1993: [( )][1].

PH: (μὴ νομίση)[1]τε.

[1] Luke's interrogative δοκεῖτε or Matthew's imperative μὴ νομίσητε.

[2] The position of εἰρήνην before (Luke) or after (Matthew) the verbs.

[3] Luke's παρεγενόμην or Matthew's ἦλθον.

Q

⟦δοκεῖ⟧τε ὅτι ἦλθον βαλεῖν εἰρήνην ἐπὶ τὴν γῆν; οὐκ ἦλθον βαλεῖν εἰρήνην ἀλλὰ μάχαιραν.

⟦Do you⟧ think that I have come to hurl peace on earth? I did not come to hurl peace, but a sword!

Gos. Thom. 16.1-2 (Nag Hammadi II 2)

(1) Λέγει Ἰησοῦς· τάχα δοκοῦσιν οἱ ἄνθρωποι ὅτι ἦλθον βαλεῖν εἰρήνην ἐπὶ τὸν κόσμον, (2) καὶ οὐκ οἴδασιν ὅτι ἦλθον βαλεῖν διαμερισμούς[1] ἐπὶ τὴν γῆν, πῦρ, μάχαιραν, πόλεμον.

(1) Jesus says: Perhaps people think that I have come to hurl peace on the earth. (2) But they do not know that I have come to hurl dissension on the earth: fire, sword, war.

[1] Other Greek terms can be assumed (σχίσματα, διχοστασίας). The Coptic text is not in accordance with Luke 12:51 sa.

[1] Hier könnten auch andere griechische Wörter vermutet werden (σχίσματα, διχοστασίας); der koptische Text entspricht nicht dem von Lk 12,51 sa.

[1] D'autres équivalents grecs pourraient être envisagés (σχίσματα, διχοστασίας). Le texte copte ne s'accorde pas avec Luc 12:51 sa.

Q 12:51

Luke 12:51	Luke 12:49	Markan Parallel	*Gos. Thom.* 16.1-2
[δοκεῖ][1]τε ὅτι			16.1 πεχε ⲓ̅ⲥ̅ χε ταχα
ʃεἰρήνηνʅ[2]	πῦρ		ευμεευε ⲛ̅ϭι ⲣ̅ⲣⲱⲙⲉ
[παρεγενόμην][3]	(ἦλθον		χε ⲛ̅ταειει
[δοῦναι][4]	βαλεῖν)		ενουχε
ʃ ʅ[2]			ⲛ̅ουειρηνη
[ἐν][5] τῇ( )[5] γῇ( )[5];	(ἐπὶ [τὴ]ν [γῆ]ν),		εχⲙ̅ πκοσμος
			16.2 αυω σεσοουn
οὐ[χί, λέγω ὑμῖν,][6]	καὶ τί θέλω		αν χε ⲛ̅ταειει
	εἰ ἤδη		ανουχε ⲛ̅ϩⲛ̅πωρχ'
			εχⲛ̅ πκαϩ
ἀλλ' [ἢ διαμερισμόν][7].	ἀνήφθη.		ουκωϩτ' ουσηϥε'
			ουπολεμος

[4] Luke's δοῦναι or Matthew's βαλεῖν.

[5] Luke's ἐν or Matthew's ἐπί and the resultant case of the article and noun.

[6] Luke's οὐχί, λέγω ὑμῖν, or Matthew's οὐκ ἦλθον βαλεῖν εἰρήνην.

[7] Luke's ἀλλ' ἢ διαμερισμόν or Matthew's ἀλλὰ μάχαιραν.

Meint ⟦ihr⟧, dass ich gekommen bin, Frieden auf die Erde zu werfen? Ich bin nicht gekommen, Frieden zu werfen, sondern das Schwert.

Pensez-⟦vous⟧ que je sois venu pour jeter la paix sur terre? Je ne suis pas venu pour jeter la paix, mais l'épée.

(1) Jesus spricht: Vielleicht denken die Menschen, dass ich gekommen bin, Frieden in die Welt zu werfen. (2) Doch sie wissen nicht, dass ich gekommen bin, Zwistigkeiten auf die Erde zu werfen: Feuer, Schwert, Krieg.

(1) Jésus dit: Les gens pensent peut-être que je suis venu pour jeter la paix sur le monde. (2) Et ils ne savent pas que je suis venu pour jeter des dissensions sur la terre: le feu, l'épée, la guerre.

Q 12:~~52~~

Markan Parallel	Matt 10:35a, 36b	Matthew	Q 12:~~52~~
	10:35a ἦλθον [γὰρ] ... **10:36b** οἱ [οἰκ]ιακοὶ αὐτοῦ.	[ ]⁰	[]⁰

JSK: ⟦[]⁰⟧.

⁰ Is Luke 12:52 in Q?

Gos. Thom. 16.3a (Nag Hammadi II 2)

πέντε γὰρ ἔσονται ἐν οἴκῳ· τρεῖς ἔσονται ἐπὶ δυσὶ καὶ δύο ἐπὶ τρισίν,

For there will be five in one house: there will be three against two and two against three,

Q 12:~~52~~

Luke 12:52	Lukan Doublet	Markan Parallel	*Gos. Thom.* 16.3a
[ἔσονται γὰρ ἀπὸ τοῦ νῦν πέντε ἐν ἑνὶ οἴκῳ διαμεμερισμένοι, τρεῖς ἐπὶ δυσὶν καὶ δύο ἐπὶ τρισίν,][0]			ⲟⲩⲛ̄ ϯⲟⲩ ⲅⲁⲣ ⲛⲁϣϣ̣ⲱ̣ⲡ̣ⲉ̣ ϩⲛ̄ ⲟⲩⲏⲉⲓ ⲟⲩⲛ̄ ϣⲟⲙⲧ ⲛⲁϣⲱⲡⲉ ⲉϫⲛ̄ ⲥⲛⲁⲩ ⲁⲩⲱ ⲥⲛⲁⲩ ⲉϫⲛ̄ ϣⲟⲙⲧ’

Es werden nämlich fünf in einem Haus sein: Es werden drei gegen zwei sein und zwei gegen drei,

Car ils seront cinq dans une maison: trois seront contre deux et deux contre trois,

Q 12:53

Mic 7:6	Matthean Doublet	Matt 10:35-36	Q 12:53
		(ἦλθον)[1]	(ἦλθον)[1]
διότι		(γὰρ)[2]	(γὰρ)[2]
		(διχάσ)[3](αι)[1]	(διχάσ)[3](αι)[1]
		[ ][4]	[][4]
υἱὸς		(ἄνθρωπο)[5](ν)[1]	[υἱὸ][5](ν)[1]
ἀτιμάζει			
		(κατὰ)[6]	⟦(κατὰ)[6]⟧
		(τοῦ)[5]	()[5]
πατέρα,		πατρ(ὸς)[6]	πατρ⟦(ὸς)[6]⟧
		(αὐτοῦ)[5]	()[5]
		[ ][4]	[][4]
θυγάτηρ ἐπαναστήσεται		(καὶ)[7] θυγατ(έ)[1]ρ(α)[1]	⟦(καὶ)[7]⟧ θυγατ(έ)[1]ρ(α)[1]
ἐπὶ τὴν		(κατὰ)[6] τῆ(ς)[6]	⟦(κατὰ)[6]⟧ τῆ⟦(ς)[6]⟧
μητέρα		μητ[ ][6]ρ(ὸς)[6]	μητ⟦[][6]⟧ρ⟦(ὸς)[6]⟧
αὐτῆς,		(αὐτῆς)[8]	(αὐτῆς)[8],
		[ ][4]	[][4]
		[ ][8]	[][8]
		[ ][4]	[][4]
νύμφη		(καὶ)[7] νύμφη(ν)[1]	⟦(καὶ)[7]⟧ νύμφη(ν)[1]
ἐπὶ τὴν πενθερὰν		(κατὰ)[6] τῆ(ς)[6] πενθερᾶ(ς)[6]	⟦(κατὰ)[6]⟧ τῆ⟦(ς)[6]⟧ πενθερᾶ⟦(ς)[6]⟧
αὐτῆς,		(αὐτῆς)[8],	(αὐτῆς)[8].
ἐχθροὶ		**10:36** (καὶ ἐχθροὶ	⟦()[9]⟧
ἀνδρὸς		τοῦ ἀνθρώπου	
οἱ ἄνδρες			
οἱ ἐν τῷ οἴκῳ αὐτοῦ.		οἱ οἰκιακοὶ αὐτοῦ.)[9]	
		⸂At Q 12:49[1]	⸂Q 12:49[1]

Text Critical Note: See the discussion of Mic 7:6 in the front matter.

JSK: ⟦[][4]⟧ … ⟦[][4]⟧ … ⟦[][4]⟧.
IQP 1993: ⟦[υἱὸ][5]<ν>[1]⟧ … ⟦()[5]⟧ … ⟦()[5]⟧.

IQP 1993, JMR: [ἐπὶ][6]… πατρ[ί][6]… [ἐπὶ][6] τὴ[ν][6] μητ[έ][6]ρ[α][6]… [ἐπὶ][6] τὴ[ν][6] πενθερ[ά][6]ν.

1 Matthew's first person formulation with ἦλθον, plus the infinitive and objects in the accusative case (in distinction to Luke's passive verb with subjects in the nominative).

2 Matthew's γάρ.

3 Luke's διαμερισθήσονται or Matthew's διχάσαι.

4 Luke's insertion, before each negative relationship of the younger generation to the older, of the negative relationship of the older to the younger, connected (*bis*) by καί (in distinction to Matthew's καί between each relationship, see variation unit 7).

Q 12:53

Luke 12:53	Lukan Doublet	Mark 13:12	*Gos. Thom.* 16.3b
( )[1]		καὶ παραδώσει	
( )[2]		ἀδελφὸς ἀδελφὸν	
[διαμερισθήσονται][3]		εἰς θάνατον καὶ	
[πατὴρ ἐπὶ υἱῷ καὶ][4]		πατὴρ τέκνον, καὶ	ⲡⲉⲓⲱⲧ' ⲉϫⲙ̄ ⲡϣⲏⲣⲉ ⲁⲩⲱ
[υἱὸ][5][ς][1]		ἐπαναστήσονται τέκνα	ⲡϣⲏⲣⲉ
[ἐπὶ][6]		ἐπὶ	ⲉϫⲙ̄
( )[5]			
πατρ[ί][6]		γονεῖς	ⲡⲉⲓⲱⲧ'
( )[5],		καὶ θανατώσουσιν αὐτούς·	
[μήτηρ ἐπὶ τὴν θυγατέρα καὶ][4]			
( )[7] θυγάτ[η][1]ρ( )[1]			
[ἐπὶ][6] τή[ν][6]			
μητ[έ][6]ρ[α][6]			
( )[8],			
[πενθερὰ ἐπὶ τὴν νύμφην][4]			
[αὐτῆς][8]			
[καὶ][4]			
( )[7] νύμφη( )[1]			
[ἐπὶ][6] τή[ν][6] πενθερά[ν][6]			
( )[8].			
( )[9]			
ʅLuke 12:49[1]			

IQP 1993: (καὶ)[7]… (καὶ)[7].

[5] Luke's υἱός or Matthew's ἄνθρωπον plus the article with "father" and the clarifying possessive pronoun.

[6] Luke's ἐπί or Matthew's κατά, and the resultant cases of the objects.

[7] Matthew's καί between each relationship (in distinction to Luke's καί within each relationship, see variation unit [4]).

[8] Luke's αὐτῆς referring back to the mother-in-law or Matthew's αὐτῆς … αὐτῆς referring back to the younger generation.

[9] Is Matt 10:36 in Q?

Q 12:53

Mic 7:6	Matthean Doublet	Matt 10:35-36	Q 12:53

Q

ἦλθον γὰρ διχάσαι υἱὸν ⟦κατὰ⟧ πατρ⟦ὸς καὶ⟧ θυγατέρα ⟦κατὰ⟧ τῆ⟦ς⟧ μητρ⟦ὸς⟧ αὐτῆς, ⟦καὶ⟧ νύμφην ⟦κατὰ⟧ τῆ⟦ς⟧ πενθερᾶ⟦ς⟧ αὐτῆς.

For I have come to divide son against father, ⟦and⟧ daughter against her mother, ⟦and⟧ daughter-in-law against her mother-in-law.

Gos. Thom. **16.3b (Nag Hammadi II 2)**

ὁ πατὴρ ἐπὶ τῷ υἱῷ καὶ ὁ υἱὸς ἐπὶ τῷ πατρί.

father against son and son against father.

Q 12:53

Luke 12:53	**Lukan Doublet**	**Mark 13:12**	***Gos. Thom.* 16.3b**

Denn ich bin gekommen zu entzweien: «den» Sohn ⟦gegen⟧ «den» Vater ⟦und⟧ «die» Tochter gegen ihre Mutter ⟦und⟧ «die» Schwiegertochter gegen ihre Schwiegermutter.

Car je suis venu diviser fils contre père ⟦et⟧ fille contre sa mère ⟦et⟧ belle-fille contre sa belle-mère.

der Vater gegen den Sohn und der Sohn gegen den Vater.

le père contre le fils et le fils contre le père.

Q 12:⟦54-55⟧

Markan Parallel	Matthean Doublet	Matt 16:2-3a	Q 12:⟦54-55⟧
		0/	⟦0/
		1ʃ	1ʃ
		ʃ ≀2	2ʃ [( )]3 ≀2
		(ὁ)4 δὲ	()4 ~~δὲ~~
		(ἀποκριθεὶς)4	[()]4
		2ʃ (εἶπεν)3 ≀2	ʃ ≀2
		(αὐτοῖς)5·	[( )]5
		(ὀψίας γενομένης)6	(ὀψίας γενομένης)6
		[ ]7 λέγετε	[]7 λέγετε
		[ ]8·	[]8·
		(εὐδία, πυρράζει γὰρ ὁ οὐρανός·)6	(εὐδία, πυρράζει γὰρ ὁ οὐρανός·)6
		[ ]9	[]9⟧
		16:3a καὶ (πρωΐ)6	**12:55** ⟦καὶ (πρωΐ)6
		[ ]10·	[]10·
		(σήμερον χειμών, πυρράζει γὰρ στυγνάζων ὁ οὐρανός)6.	(σήμερον χειμών, πυρράζει γὰρ στυγνάζων ὁ οὐρανός)6.
		[ ]9	[]9⟧
		≀1⇒ Matt 16:3b	≀1⇒ Q 12:⟦56⟧
		\0⇒ Matt 16:3b	\0 ⇒ Q 12:⟦56⟧

PH: 2ʃ []3 ≀2 ()4 ~~δὲ~~ [()]4 2ʃ ()3 ≀2 [()]5.

JSK: ⟦[ὅταν ἴδητε τὴν νεφέλην ἀνατέλλουσαν ἐπὶ δυσμῶν,]6… [ὄμβρος

Text Critical Note (see the discussion in the front matter): Matt 16:2b-3 is omitted by א B X Γ f^{13} 579 *al* sy^s.c sa mae bo^pt Or Hier^mss, but is included in C D L W Θ f^{1} 33 𝔐 latt sy^p.h bo^pt Eus.

0 Is Luke 12:54-56 par. Matt 16:2b-3 in Q?

1 The position of Q 12:54-56 in Q: After Q 12:53 and before Q 12:58 (Lukan order); or after Q 13:20-21; 6:39 (Matt 13:33; 15:14) and before Q 17:1 (Matt 18:7) (Matthean order).

2 The position of the finite verb for speaking.

3 Luke's imperfect tense or Matthew's aorist.

4 Luke's adverbial καί or Matthew's articular participle ὁ … ἀποκριθείς.

Q

⟦54⟧ ⟦… ὀψίας γενομένης λέγετε· εὐδία, πυρράζει γὰρ ὁ οὐρανός·⟧ ⟦55⟧ ⟦καὶ πρωΐ· σήμερον χειμών, πυρράζει γὰρ στυγνάζων ὁ οὐρανός·⟧

⟦54⟧ ⟦«But he said to them:» When evening has come, you say: Good weather! For the sky is flame red.⟧ ⟦55⟧ ⟦And at dawn: Today «it's» wintry! For the lowering sky is flame red.⟧

Q 12:⟦54-55⟧

Luke 12:⟦54-55⟧	Lukan Doublet	Markan Parallel	Gospel of Thomas
0/ 1⸃ 2⸃ [Ἔλεγεν]3 ⸂2 ( )4 δὲ [καὶ]4 ⸃ ⸂2 [τοῖς ὄχλοις]5· [ὅταν ἴδητε τὴν νεφέλην ἀνατέλλουσαν ἐπὶ δυσμῶν,]6 [εὐθέως]7 λέγετε [ὅτι]8 [ὄμβρος ἔρχεται,]6 [καὶ γίνεται οὕτως·]9 **12:55** καὶ [ὅταν νότον πνέοντα,]6 [λέγετε ὅτι]10 [καύσων ἔσται,]6 [καὶ γίνεται]9. ⸂1⇒ Luke 12:56 \0⇒ Luke 12:56			

ἔρχεται, καὶ γίνεται οὕτως· **12:55** καὶ ὅταν νότον πνέοντα,]6 []9 [καύσων ἔσται, καὶ γίνεται]6⟧.

5 Luke's τοῖς ὄχλοις or Matthew's αὐτοῖς.
6 Luke's forebodings of rain and heat or Matthew's forebodings of fair and stormy weather, and the diverging proverbial formulations.
7 Luke's εὐθέως.
8 Luke's ὅτι.
9 Luke's καὶ γίνεται οὕτως … καὶ γίνεται.
10 Luke's repetition of λέγετε ὅτι.

⟦54⟧ ⟦«Er aber sagte ihnen:» Wenn es Abend geworden ist, sagt ihr: «Es gibt» gutes Wetter, denn der Himmel ist feuerrot,⟧ ⟦55⟧ ⟦und am Morgen: Heute «gibt es» schlechtes Wetter, denn feuerrot ist der trübe Himmel.⟧

⟦54⟧ ⟦«Mais il leur dit:» Le soir venu, vous dites: Il va faire beau, car le ciel rougeoie,⟧ ⟦55⟧ ⟦et au point du jour: Aujourd'hui, «c'est» le mauvais temps! Car le ciel maussade est rouge.⟧

Q 12:⟦56⟧

Markan Parallel	Matthean Doublet	Matt 16:3b	Q 12:⟦56⟧
			⟦
		[ ][1]	[][1]
		τὸ (μὲν)[2] πρόσωπον	τὸ ()[2] πρόσωπον
		[ ][3] τοῦ οὐρανοῦ	[][3] τοῦ οὐρανοῦ
		(γινώσκε)[4]τε	[οἴδα][4]τε
		(διακρίν)[5]ειν,	(διακρίν)[5]ειν,
		ʃ ͺ6	[6]ʃτ[ὸν][7.8] καιρ[ὸν][7.8] ͺ6
		(τὰ)[8] δὲ (σημεῖα)[8]	()[8] δὲ ()[8]
		[6]ʃτ(ῶν)[7.8] καιρ(ῶν)[7.8] ͺ6	ʃͺ6
		[ ][9] οὐ (δύνασθε)[9];	[][9] οὐ (δύνασθε)[9];
			⟧
		ͺMatt 16:2-3a[1]	ͺQ 12:⟦54-55[1]⟧
		\Matt 16:2-3a[0]	\Q 12:⟦54-55[0]⟧

JSK: ⟦[τῆς γῆς καὶ][3]⟧.

1 Luke's ὑποκριταί.
2 Matthew's μέν.
3 Luke's τῆς γῆς καί.
4 Luke's οἴδατε or Matthew's γινώσκετε.
5 Luke's δοκιμάζειν or Matthew's διακρίνειν.
6 The position of the reference to time before (Luke) or after (Matthew) the postpositive δέ.

Q

⟦τὸ πρόσωπον τοῦ οὐρανοῦ οἴδατε διακρίνειν, τὸν καιρὸν δὲ οὐ δύνασθε;⟧	⟦The face of the sky you know to interpret, but the time you are not able to?⟧

Gos. Thom. 91.2 (Nag Hammadi II 2)

λέγει αὐτοῖς· τὸ πρόσωπον τοῦ οὐρανοῦ καὶ τῆς γῆς πειράζετε, τὸν δὲ κατὰ πρόσωπον ὑμῶν οὐκ οἴδατε καὶ τὸν καιρὸν τοῦτον οὐκ οἴδατε πειράζειν.

(2) He said to them: You test the face of sky and earth; but the one who is before you, you have not recognized, and you do not know how to test this opportunity[1].

1 Or: (right) time.

Q 12:⟦56⟧

Luke 12:⟦56⟧	Lukan Doublet	Markan Parallel	*Gos. Thom.* 91.2
[ὑποκριταί]¹, τὸ ( )² πρόσωπον [τῆς γῆς καὶ]³ τοῦ οὐρανοῦ [οἶδα]⁴τε [δοκιμάζ]⁵ειν, ⁶ʃτ[ὸν]⁷·⁸ καιρ[ὸν]⁷·⁸ ≀⁶ ( )⁸ δὲ ( )⁸ ʃ ≀⁶ [τοῦτον πῶς]⁹ οὐ[κ οἴδατε δοκιμάζειν]⁹; ≀Luke 12:54-55¹ \Luke 12:54-55⁰			πεϫαϥ ναγ ϫε τετν̄ρ̄πιραζε м̄πϩο ν̄τπε мн̄ πκαϩ αγω πετν̄πετν̄мто εβολ' м̄πετν̄cογωνϥ' αγω πεєικαιρος τετν̄cοογν αν ν̄ρ̄πιραζε м̄μοϥ'

[7] The number of ὁ καιρός.
[8] Matthew's τὰ … σημεῖα and the resultant case of the reference to time(s).
[9] Luke's τοῦτον πῶς, and the repetition; or Matthew's ellipsis using δύνασθε.

⟦Das Aussehen des Himmels versteht ihr zu beurteilen, die Zeit aber könnt ihr nicht «beurteilen»?⟧

⟦La face du ciel, vous savez l'interpréter, mais le moment opportun, ne le pouvez-vous pas?⟧

(2) Er sprach zu ihnen: Ihr prüft das Aussehen des Himmels und der Erde; doch der, der vor euch ist — ihn habt ihr nicht erkannt, und diese Gelegenheit[2] wisst ihr nicht zu erproben.

[2] Oder: diesen Augenblick.

(2) Il leur dit: Vous évaluez la face du ciel et de la terre, et celui qui est devant vous, vous ne l'avez pas connu. Et le moment opportun[3], vous ne savez pas l'évaluer.

[3] Ou: cette occasion-ci.

Q 12:~~57~~

Markan Parallel	Matthean Doublet	Matthew	Q 12:~~57~~
		[ ][0]	[][0]

[0] Is Luke 12:57 in Q?

Q 12:~~57~~

Luke 12:57	Lukan Doublet	Markan Parallel	Gospel of Thomas
[Τί δὲ καὶ ἀφ' ἑαυτῶν οὐ κρίνετε τὸ δίκαιον;]^{0}			

Q 12:58

Markan Parallel	Matthean Doublet	Matt 5:25	Q 12:58
		[1]ʃ	[1]ʃ
		ʃ ʅ[2a]	[2a]ʃ ⟦(ἕως ὅτου)[3]⟧
			[][4]
			[( )][5]
			μετ[ὰ][2] ʅ[2a]
		ʃ ʅ[2b]	[2b]ʃτ[οῦ][6] ἀντιδίκ[ου][6] σουʅ[2b]
		ʃ ʅ[2c]	[2c]ʃ ⟦[][7]⟧ ʅ[2c]
		ʃ ʅ[8]	ʃἐν τῇ ὁδῷʅ[8],
		(ἴσθι εὐνοῶν)[6]	[δὸς ἐργασίαν
			ἀπηλλάχθαι ἀπ᾽][6]
		[2b]ʃτ(ῷ)[6] ἀντιδίκ(ῳ)[6] σουʅ[2b]	ʃʅ[2b]
		[2d]ʃ (ταχύ)[9] ʅ[2d],	ʃʅ[2d]
		[2a]ʃ (ἕως ὅτου)[3]	ʃʅ[2a]
		[ ][4]	
		(εἶ)[5]	
		μετ᾽[ ][2] ʅ[2a]	
		αὐτοῦ	αὐτοῦ
		[2c]ʃ [ ][7] ʅ[2c]	ʃʅ[2c]
		ʃ ʅ[2d]	[2d]ʃ ⟦()[9]⟧ ʅ[2d]
		ʃἐν τῇ ὁδῷʅ[8],	ʃʅ[8],
		μήποτέ [10]ʃσε	μήποτέ [10]ʃσε
		παραδῷ[ ][11] ʅ[10]	παραδῷ[][11] ʅ[10]
		[ ][12]	[][12]
		(ὁ ἀντίδικος)[13]	⟦(ὁ ἀντίδικος)[13]⟧
		[ ][14] τ(ῷ)[14] κριτῇ[ ][14]	[][14] τ(ῷ)[14] κριτῇ[][14]
		καὶ ὁ κριτής	καὶ ὁ κριτής
		ʃ ʅ[10]	ʃʅ[10]

1 The position of Q 12:58-59 in Q: After Q 12:53, ⟦54-56⟧ and before Q 13:18 (Lukan order); or after Q 16:17 (Matt 5:18) and before Q 16:18 (Matt 5:32) (Matthean order).

2 The order of the main and subordinate clauses and their components.

3 Luke's ὡς or Matthew's ἕως ὅτου.

4 Luke's γάρ.

5 Luke's ὑπάγεις or Matthew's εἶ.

6 The choice of main clauses and hence, for ὁ ἀντίδικος, the choice of Luke's genitive or Matthew's dative case (the decision depends on variant [2].

7 Luke's ἐπ᾽ ἄρχοντα (the position depends on variant [2]).

Q 12:58

Luke 12:58	Lukan Doublet	Markan Parallel	Gospel of Thomas
¹ʃ ²ᵃʃ [ὡς]³ [γὰρ]⁴ [ὑπάγεις]⁵ μετ[ὰ]² ʅ²ᵃ ²ᵇʃτ[οῦ]⁶ ἀντιδίκ[ου]⁶ σουʅ²ᵇ ²ᶜʃ [ἐπ' ἄρχοντα]⁷ ʅ²ᶜ, ʃἐν τῇ ὁδῷʅ⁸ [δὸς ἐργασίαν ἀπηλλάχθαι ἀπ']⁶ ʃ ʅ²ᵇ ʃ ʅ²ᵈ ʃ ʅ²ᵃ αὐτοῦ ʃ ʅ²ᶜ ²ᵈʃ ( )⁹ ʅ²ᵈ ʃ ʅ⁸, μήποτε ʃ ʅ¹⁰ [κατασύρῃ σε]¹² ( )¹³ [πρὸς]¹⁴ τ[ὸν]¹⁴ κριτή[ν]¹⁴, καὶ ὁ κριτής ¹⁰ʃσε παραδώ[σει]¹¹ ʅ¹⁰			

⁸ The position of ἐν τῇ ὁδῷ where the main clause and the subordinate clause meet (Luke), or at the conclusion of the subordinate clause that itself follows the main clause (Matthew).

⁹ Matthew's ταχύ (the position depends on variant ²).

¹⁰ The position of the phrase σε παραδω-.

¹¹ Luke's παραδώσει or Matthew's παραδῷ.

¹² Luke's κατασύρῃ σε.

¹³ Luke's unexpressed subject or Matthew's ὁ ἀντίδικος.

¹⁴ Luke's πρὸς τὸν κριτήν or Matthew's τῷ κριτῇ.

Q 12:58

Markan Parallel	Matthean Doublet	Matt 5:25	Q 12:58
		τῷ (ὑπηρέτῃ)[15] καὶ [ ][16] [ ][17] ⸉ ⸊[18] εἰς φυλακὴν [18]⸉ β[ ][17]λ(ηθήσῃ)[17] ⸊[18]. ⸊[1]⇒ Matt 5:26	τῷ (ὑπηρέτῃ)[15] καὶ ⟦[ὁ][16] <ὑπηρέτης>[16] [σε][17]⟧ [18]⸉ β⟦[α][17]⟧λ⟦[εῖ][17]⟧ ⸊[18] εἰς φυλακὴν ⸉⸊[18]. ⸊[1]⇒ Q 12:59

PH: [2a]⸉ (ἕως ὅτου)[3] [][4].
IQP 1994: (εἶ)[5].

PH: ⸉ ⸊[8].

[15] Luke's πράκτορι or Matthew's ὑπηρέτῃ.

[16] Luke's repetition of the agent.

Q

⟦ἕως ὅτου⟧ ... μετὰ τοῦ ἀντιδίκου σου ἐν τῇ ὁδῷ, δὸς ἐργασίαν ἀπηλλάχθαι ἀπ' αὐτοῦ, μήποτέ σε παραδῷ ⟦ὁ ἀντίδικος⟧ τῷ κριτῇ καὶ ὁ κριτὴς τῷ ὑπηρέτῃ καὶ ⟦ὁ <ὑπηρέτης> σε⟧ β⟦α⟧λ⟦εῖ⟧ εἰς φυλακήν.

⟦While⟧ you «go along» with your opponent on the way, make an effort to get loose from him, lest ⟦the opponent⟧ hand you over to the judge, and the judge to the assistant, and ⟦the <assistant>⟧ throw ⟦you⟧ into prison.

Q 12:58

Luke 12:58	Lukan Doublet	Markan Parallel	Gospel of Thomas
τῷ [πράκτορι][15], καὶ [ὁ πράκτωρ][16] [σε][17] [18]⸂ β[α][17]λ[εῖ][17] ⸃[18] εἰς φυλακήν ⸂ ⸃[18]. ⸃[1]⇒ Luke 12:59			

IQP 1994: [ ][17] [18]⸂ β[ ][17]λ[ ][17] ⸃[18].

[17] Luke's σε βαλεῖ or Matthew's βληθήσῃ.

[18] The position of the verb βάλλω.

⟦Solange⟧ du mit deinem Prozessgegner auf dem Weg «bist», gib dir Mühe, von ihm loszukommen, damit dich ⟦der Prozessgegner⟧ nicht dem Richter übergebe und der Richter dem «Gerichts»diener und ⟦der <«Gerichts»diener> dich⟧ ins Gefängnis werfe.

⟦Tandis que⟧ tu «es» en chemin avec ton adversaire, fais un effort pour te séparer de lui, de peur que ⟦l'adversaire⟧ ne te livre au juge et le juge à son assesseur et que ⟦l'<assesseur>⟧ ne ⟦te⟧ jette en prison.

Q 12:59

Did 1.5-6	Matthean Doublet	Matt 5:26	Q 12:59
καὶ οὐκ ἐξελεύσεται ἐκεῖθεν, μέχρις οὗ ἀποδῷ τὸν ἔσχατον κοδράντην.		(ἀμὴν)[1] λέγω σοι, οὐ μὴ ἐξέλθῃς ἐκεῖθεν, ἕως [ ][2] (ἂν)[3] ⸉ἀποδῷς⸊[4] τὸ(ν)[5] ἔσχατον (κοδράντην)[5] ⸉ ⸊[4]. ⸊Matt 5:25[1]	⟦()[1]⟧ λέγω σοι, οὐ μὴ ἐξέλθῃς ἐκεῖθεν, ἕως ⟦[][2]⟧ ⟦()[3]⟧ ⸉ ⸊[4] τὸ⟦(ν)[5]⟧ ἔσχατον ⟦(κοδράντην)[5]⟧ ⸉ἀποδῷς⸊[4]. ⸊Q 12:58[1]

JMR: ( )[1].

IQP 1994: [ ][2] ()[3].

[1] Matthew's ἀμήν.
[2] Luke's καί.

[3] Matthew's ἄν.

Q

λέγω σοι, οὐ μὴ ἐξέλθῃς ἐκεῖθεν, ἕως τὸ⟦ν⟧ ἔσχατον ⟦κοδράντην⟧ ἀποδῷς.

I say to you: You will not get out of there until you pay the last ⟦penny⟧!

Q 12:59

Luke 12:59	Lukan Doublet	Markan Parallel	Gospel of Thomas
( )¹ λέγω σοι, οὐ μὴ ἐξέλθῃς ἐκεῖθεν, ἕως [καὶ]² ( )³ ⸉ ⸊⁴ τὸ( )⁵ ἔσχατον [λεπτὸν]⁵ ⸉ἀποδῷς⸊⁴. ⸊Luke 12:58¹			

IQP 1994: τὸ(ν)⁵ ... (κοδράντην)⁵.

[4] The position of the verb ἀποδῷς after (Luke) or before (Matthew) its object.

[5] Luke's λεπτόν or Matthew's κοδράντην.

Ich sage dir: Du wirst von dort nicht herauskommen, bis du den letzten ⟦Pfennig⟧ zurückgezahlt hast!

Je te «le» dis: Tu n'en sortiras pas avant que tu n'aies rendu le dernier ⟦centime⟧!

Q 13:18-19

Mark 4:30-32	Matthean Doublet	Matt 13:31-32	Q 13:18-19
		^{0}{	^{0}{
		^{1}ʃ	^{1}ʃ
		13:31 (Ἄλλην {παραβολὴ}ν	({})^{2}
		παρέ{θ}ηκεν αὐτοῖς)^{2}	
4:30 Καὶ ἔλεγεν·		{λέγ}(ων)^{2} [ ]^{2}·	**13:18** {[]^{2}~~λεγ~~[]^{2}}()^{2} []^{2}
πῶς ὁμοιώσωμεν		[ ]^{3}	[τίνι {ὁμοί}α ἐστὶν]^{3}
τὴν βασιλείαν		ʃ ʅ^{3}	^{3}ʃ {ἡ} {βασιλεία}
τοῦ θεοῦ			{τ[οῦ θεοῦ]}^{4} ʅ^{3}
ἢ ἐν τίνι		[ ]^{5}	[καὶ {τίνι}
αὐτὴν παραβολῇ θῶμεν;			{ὁμοιώσω} {αὐτήν;}]^{5}
		ὁμοία ἐστὶν	**13:19** ὁμοία ἐστὶν
		^{3}ʃ {ἡ} {βασιλεία}	ʃʅ^{3}
		{τ}(ῶν οὐρανῶν)^{4} ʅ^{3}	
4:31 ὡς κόκκῳ σινάπεως,		{κόκκῳ σινάπεως,	{κόκκῳ σινάπεως,
ὃς		ὅ}ν	ὅ}ν
ὅταν σπαρῇ		λαβὼν ἄνθρωπος ἔ({σπ}ει{ρ})^{6}εν	λαβὼν ἄνθρωπος ἔ[βαλ]^{6}εν
ἐπὶ τῆς γῆς,		(ἐν)^{6} ({τ}ῷ ἀγρ)^{7}(ῷ)^{6}	[εἰς]^{6} ⟦[κῆπ]^{7}⟧[ον]^{6}
		[ ]^{8}αὐτοῦ·	[]^{8}αὐτοῦ·
μικρότερον ὂν		**13:32** (ὃ {μικρότερον} μέν ἐστιν	({})^{9}
πάντων τῶν σπερμάτων		{πάντων τῶν σπερμάτων},)^{9}	
τῶν ἐπὶ τῆς γῆς,			
4:32 καὶ ὅταν σπαρῇ,		({ὅταν} δὲ	[{καὶ}
ἀναβαίνει καὶ γίνεται		α)^{10}ὐξη(θῇ)^{10}	η]^{10}ὔξη[σεν]^{10}
μεῖζον πάντων τῶν λαχάνων		({μεῖζον} {τῶν λαχάνων} ἐστὶν)^{9}	({})^{9}
καὶ ποιεῖ		{καὶ} [ ]^{11}{γ(ί)^{11}νετ(αι})^{11}	{καὶ} [ἐ]^{11}{γ}[έ]^{11}{νετ}[ο]^{11}
κλάδους μεγάλους,		[ ]^{12} δένδρον,	[εἰς]^{12} δένδρον,
ὥστε δύνασθαι		({ὥστε})^{13}	[καὶ]^{13}
ὑπὸ τὴν σκιὰν αὐτοῦ		(ἐλθεῖν)^{14}	⟦()^{14}⟧
τὰ πετεινὰ τοῦ οὐρανοῦ		{τὰ πετεινὰ τοῦ οὐρανοῦ}	{τὰ πετεινὰ τοῦ οὐρανοῦ
		(καὶ)^{14}	⟦()^{14}⟧

0 Is Luke 13:18-19 par. Matt 13:31-32 in Q or from Mark?

1 The position of Q 13:18-19, 20-21 in Q: After Q 12:59 and before Q 13:24 (Lukan order); or after Q 10:24 (Matt 13:17) and before Q 6:39 (Matt 15:14b) (Matthean order).

2 Luke's ἔλεγεν οὖν or Matthew's ἄλλην παραβολὴν παρέθηκεν αὐτοῖς λέγων.

3 Luke's initial question τίνι ὁμοία ἐστίν and the resultant position of the reference to the kingdom prior to (Luke) or at the beginning of (Matthew) the parable.

4 Luke's τοῦ θεοῦ or Matthew's τῶν οὐρανῶν.

5 Luke's second question, καὶ τίνι ὁμοιώσω αὐτήν;

Q 13:18-19

Luke 13:18-19	Mark 4:30-32	Ps 103:12a LXX	*Gos. Thom.* 20
[0]{			
[1]⸆			
({ })[2]			
13:18 {[΄Ε][2]λεγ[εν][2]} [οὖν][2]	**4:30** Καὶ ἔλεγεν·		**20.1** ⲡⲉϫⲉ ⲙ̅ⲙⲁⲑⲏⲧⲏⲥ
			ⲛ̅ⲓ̅ⲥ̅ ϫⲉ
[τίνι {ὁμοί}α ἐστὶν][3]	πῶς ὁμοιώσωμεν		ϫⲟⲟⲥ ⲉⲣⲟⲛ ϫⲉ
[3]⸆ {ἡ} {βασιλεία}	τὴν βασιλείαν		ⲧⲙⲛ̅ⲧⲉⲣⲟ
{τ[οῦ θεοῦ]}[4] ⸇[3]	τοῦ θεοῦ		ⲛⲙ̅ⲡⲏⲩⲉ
[καὶ {τίνι}	ἢ ἐν τίνι		ⲉⲥⲧⲛ̅ⲧⲱⲛ ⲉⲛⲓⲙ
{ὁμοιώσω} {αὐτήν;}][5]	αὐτὴν παραβολῇ θῶμεν;		**20.2** ⲡⲉϫⲁϥ ⲛⲁⲩ ϫⲉ
13:19 ὁμοία ἐστὶν			ⲉⲥⲧⲛ̅ⲧⲱⲛ
⸆ ⸇[3]			
{κόκκῳ σινάπεως,	**4:31** ὡς κόκκῳ σινάπεως,		ⲁⲩⲃⲗ̅ⲃⲓⲗⲉ ⲛ̅ϣⲗ̅ⲧⲁⲙ
ὃ}ν	ὃς		
λαβὼν ἄνθρωπος ἔ[βαλ][6]εν	ὅταν σπαρῇ		
[εἰς][6] [κῆπ][7][ον][6]	ἐπὶ τῆς γῆς,		
[ἑ][8]αυτοῦ,			
({ })[9]	μικρότερον ὂν		**20.3** <ⲥ>ⲥⲟⲃ̅ⲕ̅[1] ⲡⲁⲣⲁ
	πάντων τῶν σπερμάτων		ⲛ̅ϭⲣⲟϭ ⲧⲏⲣⲟⲩ
	τῶν ἐπὶ τῆς γῆς,		
[{καὶ}	**4:32** καὶ ὅταν σπαρῇ,		**20.4** ϩⲟⲧⲁⲛ ⲇⲉ ⲉⲥϣⲁⲛϩⲉ
η][10]ὔξη[σεν][10]	ἀναβαίνει καὶ γίνεται		ⲉϫⲙ̅ ⲡⲕⲁϩ
({ })[9]	μεῖζον πάντων τῶν λαχάνων		ⲉⲧⲟⲩⲣ̅ ϩⲱⲃ ⲉⲣⲟϥ
{καὶ} [ἐ][11]{γ}[έ][11]{νετ}[ο][11]	καὶ ποιεῖ		ϣⲁϥⲧⲉⲩⲟ ⲉⲃⲟⲗ
[εἰς][12] δένδρον,	κλάδους μεγάλους,		ⲛ̅ⲛⲟⲩⲛⲟϭ ⲛ̅ⲧⲁⲣ
[καὶ][13]	ὥστε δύνασθαι		ⲛ̅ϥϣⲱⲡⲉ
( )[14]	ὑπὸ τὴν σκιὰν αὐτοῦ	ἐπ᾽ αὐτὰ	ⲛ̅ⲥⲕⲉⲡⲏ
{τὰ πετεινὰ τοῦ οὐρανοῦ	τὰ πετεινὰ τοῦ οὐρανοῦ	τὰ πετεινὰ τοῦ οὐρανοῦ	ⲛ̅ϩⲁⲗⲁⲧⲉ ⲛ̅ⲧⲡⲉ
( )[14]			

6 Luke's ἔβαλεν εἰς or Matthew's ἔσπειρεν ἐν, and the resultant case of the object.

7 Luke's κῆπον or Matthew's τῷ ἀγρῷ.

8 Luke's ἑαυτοῦ or Matthew's αὐτοῦ.

9 Matthew's ὃ μικρότερον μέν ἐστιν πάντων τῶν σπερμάτων … μεῖζον τῶν λαχάνων ἐστίν.

10 Luke's καὶ ηὔξησεν or Matthew's ὅταν δὲ αὐξηθῇ.

11 Luke's ἐγένετο or Matthew's γίνεται.

12 Luke's εἰς.

13 Luke's καί … κατεσκήνωσεν or Matthew's ὥστε … κατασκηνοῦν.

14 Matthew's additional verb, ἐλθεῖν, and the resultant καί.

Q 13:18-19

Mark 4:30-32	Matthean Doublet	Matt 13:31-32	Q 13:18-19
κατασκηνοῦν.		{κατ(α)^{13}σκην(οῦν)^{13}} ἐν τοῖς {κλάδο}ις {αὐτοῦ}. ʅ^{1}⇒ Matt 13:33 }^{0}	κατ}[ε]^{13}{σκήν}[ωσεν]^{13} ἐν τοῖς {κλάδο}ις {αὐτοῦ}. ʅ^{1}⇒ Q 13:20-21 }^{0}

IQP 1990: ({ })^{2} {[ ]^{2}~~λεγ~~[ ]^{2}}( )^{2} [ ]^{2}.

IQP 1990: [κῆπ]^{7}[ον]^{6}; PH: ⟦(τ<ὸν> ἀγρ)^{7}⟧<όν>^{6}.

Text Critical Note (see the discussion in the front matter): In Luke 13:19 δένδρον μέγα is in 𝔓^{45} A W Θ Ψ *f* $^{(1).13}$ 33 𝔐 lat sy$^{p.h}$ bo^{pt},

Q

18 τίνι ὁμοία ἐστὶν ἡ βασιλεία τοῦ θεοῦ καὶ τίνι ὁμοιώσω αὐτήν; **19** ὁμοία ἐστὶν κόκκῳ σινάπεως, ὃν λαβὼν ἄνθρωπος ἔβαλεν εἰς ⟦κῆπ⟧ον αὐτοῦ· καὶ ηὔξησεν καὶ ἐγένετο εἰς δένδρον, καὶ τὰ πετεινὰ τοῦ οὐρανοῦ κατεσκήνωσεν ἐν τοῖς κλάδοις αὐτοῦ.

18 What is the kingdom of God like, and with what am I to compare it? **19** It is like a seed of mustard, which a person took and threw into his ⟦garden⟧. And it grew and developed into a tree, and the birds of the sky nested in its branches.

Gos. Thom. 20 (Nag Hammadi II 2)

(1) Εἶπον οἱ μαθηταὶ τῷ Ἰησοῦ· εἰπὲ ἡμῖν, τίνι ὁμοία ἐστὶν ἡ βασιλεία τῶν οὐρανῶν. (2) εἶπεν αὐτοῖς· ὁμοία ἐστὶν κόκκῳ σινάπεως. (3) μικρός ἐστιν παρὰ πάντα τὰ σπέρματα. (4) ὅταν δὲ πέσῃ ἐπὶ τὴν γῆν τὴν ἐργαζομένην, ποιεῖ κλάδον μέγαν καὶ γίνεται σκέπη τοῖς πετεινοῖς τοῦ οὐρανοῦ.

(1) The disciples said to Jesus: Tell us, what is the kingdom of heaven like! (2) He said to them: It is like a seed of mustard. (3) <It>[1] is the smallest of all seeds. (4) But when it falls on cultivated soil, it (the soil) produces a large branch (and) becomes shelter for the birds of the sky.

[1] The conjugational element is missing in the Coptic text due to haplography.

Q 13:18-19

Luke 13:18-19	Mark 4:30-32	Ps 103:12a LXX	*Gos. Thom.* 20
κατ}[ε][13]{σκήν}[ωσεν][13] ἐν τοῖς {κλάδο}ις {αὐτοῦ}. ⸂[1]⇒ Luke 13:20-21 }[0]	κατασκηνοῦν.	κατασκηνώσει,	[1] Codex: ϲⲟⲃ̄ⲕ̄.

PH: ⟦()[12]⟧.

IQP 1994: **13:19** ()[14]… ()[14].

but only δένδρον in 𝔓[75] א B (D) L 070 (892) 1241 2542 *pc* it sy[s.c] sa bo[pt].

18 Wem ist das Reich Gottes gleich, und womit könnte ich es vergleichen? **19** Es ist gleich einem Senfkorn, das ein Mensch nahm und in seinen ⟦Garten⟧ warf. Und es wuchs und wurde zu einem Baum, und die Vögel des Himmels nisteten in seinen Zweigen.

18 A quoi le royaume de Dieu est-il comparable et à quoi le comparerai-je? **19** Il est comparable à un grain de moutarde qu'un homme a pris et jeté dans son ⟦jardin⟧. Et il poussa et devint un arbre et les oiseaux du ciel nichèrent dans ses branches.

(1) Die Jünger sprachen zu Jesus: Sage uns, wem das Königreich der Himmel gleicht! (2) Er sprach zu ihnen: Es ist gleich einem Senfkorn. (3) <Es>[2] ist der kleinste von allen Samen. (4) Wenn es aber auf die Erde fällt, die bearbeitet wird, bringt sie einen großen Zweig hervor (und) wird zum Schutz für die Vögel des Himmels.

[2] Das Fehlen des Konjugationselements im koptischen Text ist durch Haplographie verursacht.

(1) Les disciples dirent à Jésus: Dis-nous à quoi est comparable le royaume des cieux. (2) Il leur dit: Il est comparable à un grain de moutarde. (3) <Il>[3] est plus petit que toutes les semences. (4) Mais quand il tombe sur le sol qu'on a travaillé, il (le sol) produit une grande branche (et) devient un abri pour les oiseaux du ciel.

[3] L'absence du pronom sujet dans le texte copte est probablement imputable à une haplographie.

Q 13:20-21

Markan Parallel	Matthean Doublet	Matt 13:33	Q 13:20-21
		(Ἄλλην παραβολὴν)[1]	**13:20** ⟦[καὶ πάλιν][1]⟧
		ἐ(λάλησ)[2]εν	⟦~~ε~~[][2]~~εν~~⟧
		(αὐτοῖς)[3]·	⟦()[3]⟧·
		[ ][4]	[τίνι ὁμοιώσω][4]
		ʃ ʅ4	4ʃ [τ][4]ὴ[ν][4] βασιλεία[ν][4]
			τ[οῦ θεοῦ][5] ʅ4;
		ὁμοία ἐστὶν	**13:21** ὁμοία ἐστὶν
		4ʃ [ ][4]ἡ[ ][4] βασιλεία[ ][4]	ʃʅ4
		τ(ῶν οὐρανῶν)[5] ʅ4	
		ζύμῃ, ἣν λαβοῦσα	ζύμῃ, ἣν λαβοῦσα
		γυνὴ ἐνέκρυψεν	γυνὴ ἐνέκρυψεν
		εἰς ἀλεύρου σάτα τρία	εἰς ἀλεύρου σάτα τρία
		ἕως οὗ ἐζυμώθη ὅλον.	ἕως οὗ ἐζυμώθη ὅλον.
		ʅMatt 13:31-32[1]	ʅQ 13:18-19[1]

IQP 1990: [καὶ πάλιν][1].

IQP 1990: ε[ἶπ][2]εν.

Text Critical Note (see the discussion in the front matter): In Luke 13:21 ἔκρυψεν is in B K L N 892 1424 2542 *al*, but ἐνέκρυψεν in 𝔓[75]

[1] Luke's καὶ πάλιν or Matthew's ἄλλην παραβολήν.

[2] Luke's εἶπεν or Matthew's ἐλάλησεν.

[3] Matthew's αὐτοῖς.

[4] Luke's τίνι ὁμοιώσω and the resultant position of the refer-

Q

20 ⟦καὶ πάλιν⟧· τίνι ὁμοιώσω τὴν βασιλείαν τοῦ θεοῦ; **21** ὁμοία ἐστὶν ζύμῃ, ἣν λαβοῦσα γυνὴ ἐνέκρυψεν εἰς ἀλεύρου σάτα τρία ἕως οὗ ἐζυμώθη ὅλον.

20 ⟦And again⟧: With what am I to compare the kingdom of God? **21** It is like yeast, which a woman took and hid in three measures of flour until it was fully fermented.

Gos. Thom. 96.1-2 (Nag Hammadi II 2)

(1) Λ[έγε]ι Ἰησοῦς· ἡ βασιλεία τοῦ πατρὸς ὁμοία ἐστὶν γυναικί [τινι]. (2) ἔλαβεν μικρόν τι ζύμης (καὶ) ἔκρυ[ψεν] αὐτὴν εἰς ἄλευρον (καὶ) ἐποίησεν αὐτὸ ἄρτους μεγάλους.

(1) Jesus [says]: The kingdom of the Father is like [a] woman. (2) She took a little bit of yeast. [She] hid it in dough (and) made it into huge loaves of bread.

Q 13:20-21

Luke 13:20-21	Lukan Doublet	Markan Parallel	*Gos. Thom.* 96.1-2
13:20 [Καὶ πάλιν][1]			
ε[ἶπ][2]εν			96.1 π̣[ⲉϫ]ⲉ ⲓ̅ⲥ̅ ϫⲉ
( )[3]·			
[τίνι ὁμοιώσω][4]			
[4]⸉ [τ][4]ὴ[ν][4] βασιλεία[ν][4]			ⲧⲙ̅ⲛ̅ⲧⲉⲣⲟ
τ[οῦ θεοῦ][5] ⸊[4];			ⲙ̄ⲡⲉⲓⲱⲧ'
13:21 ὁμοία ἐστὶν			ⲉⲥⲧⲛ̄ⲧⲱ[ⲛ ⲁⲩ]ⲥϩⲓⲙⲉ
⸉ ⸊[4]			
ζύμῃ, ἣν λαβοῦσα			96.2 ⲁⲥϫⲓ ⲛ̄ⲟⲩⲕⲟⲩⲉⲓ
γυνὴ ἐνέκρυψεν			ⲛ̄ⲥⲁⲉⲓⲣ ⲁ̣[ⲥϩ]ⲟ̣ⲡϥ'
εἰς ἀλεύρου σάτα τρία			ϩⲛ̄ ⲟⲩϣⲱⲧⲉ
ἕως οὗ ἐζυμώθη ὅλον.			ⲁⲥⲁⲁϥ ⲛ̄ϩⲛ̄ⲛⲟ[ϭ ⲛ̄]ⲛⲟⲉⲓⲕ'
⸊Luke 13:18-19[1]			

IQP 1990: ( )[3]: Not in Q {D}.

א A D W Θ Ψ 070 f^{13} 1 𝔐.

ence to the kingdom prior to (Luke) or at the beginning of (Matthew) the parable.

[5] Luke's τοῦ θεοῦ or Matthew's τῶν οὐρανῶν.

20 ⟦Und wiederum⟧: Womit könnte ich das Reich Gottes vergleichen? **21** Es ist Sauerteig gleich, den eine Frau nahm und in drei Sat Weizenmehl verbarg, bis es ganz durchsäuert war.

20 ⟦Et encore⟧: A quoi comparerai-je le royaume de Dieu? **21** Il est comparable à du levain qu'une femme a pris et enfoui dans trois mesures de farine, jusqu'à ce qu'il ait parfaitement fermenté.

(1) Jesus [spricht]: Das Königreich des Vaters gleicht [einer] Frau. (2) Sie nahm ein wenig Sauerteig. [Sie] verbarg ihn im Mehl (und) machte daraus große Brote.

(1) Jésus [dit]: Le royaume du Père, est comparable [à une] femme. (2) Elle prit un peu de levain. [Elle] l'enfouit dans de la pâte (et) en fit de gros pains.

Q 13:24

Markan Parallel	Matthean Doublet	Matt 7:13-14	Q 13:24
		[0]/	[0]/
		[1]ʃ	[1]ʃ
		7:13 [ ][2]	**13:24** [][2]
		Εἰσέλθ(ατε)[2]	εἰσέλθ(ατε)[2]
		διὰ τῆς στενῆς (πύλης)[3]·	διὰ τῆς στενῆς [θύρας][3],
		ὅτι (πλατεῖα ἡ πύλη	ὅτι ()[4]
		καὶ εὐρύχωρος ἡ ὁδὸς	
		ἡ ἀπάγουσα εἰς τὴν	
		ἀπώλειαν καὶ)[4] πολλοί	πολλοὶ
		[ ][5]	⟦[][5]⟧
		(εἰ)[6]σιν	[ζητήσου][6]σιν
		(οἱ)[6] εἰσε(ρχόμενοι)[6]	()[6] εἰσε[λθεῖν][6]
		(δι' αὐτῆς)[7]·	( )[7]
		7:14 (τί στενὴ ἡ πύλη	()[8]
		καὶ τεθλιμμένη ἡ ὁδὸς	
		ἡ ἀπάγουσα εἰς τὴν ζωὴν)[8]	
		καὶ	καὶ
		(ὀλίγοι)[9]	(ὀλίγοι)[9]
		(εἰσὶν οἱ εὑρίσκοντες	⟦(εἰσὶν οἱ <εἰσέρχοντες
		αὐτήν)[10].	δι'>[10] (αὐτῇ)[10]<ς>)[10]⟧.
		ʅ[1]	ʅ[1]
		\[0]	\[0]

IQP 1992: ⟦[][2]⟧ εἰσέλθ⟦(ατε)[2]⟧ διὰ τῆς στενῆς ⟦[θύρας][3]⟧.

IQP 1992: ⟦[ζητήσου][6]⟧σιν ⟦()[6]⟧ εἰσε⟦[λθεῖν][6] ()[7]⟧.

[0] Is Luke 13:24 par. Matt 7:13-14 in Q?

[1] The position of Q 13:24 in Q: After Q 13:21 and before Q 13:25 (Lukan order); or after Q 6:31 (Matt 7:12) and before Q 6:43 (Matt 7:18) (Matthean order).

[2] Luke's ἀγωνίζεσθε εἰσελθεῖν or Matthew's εἰσέλθατε.

[3] Luke's θύρας or Matthew's πύλης.

[4] Matthew's πλατεῖα ἡ πύλη καὶ εὐρύχωρος ἡ ὁδὸς ἡ ἀπάγουσα εἰς τὴν ἀπώλειαν καί.

Q

εἰσέλθατε διὰ τῆς στενῆς θύρας, ὅτι πολλοὶ ζητήσουσιν εἰσελθεῖν καὶ ὀλίγοι ⟦εἰσὶν οἱ <εἰσέρχοντες δι'> αὐτῆ<ς>⟧.

Enter through the narrow door, for many will seek to enter and few ⟦are those who <enter through> it⟧.

Q 13:24

Luke 13:23-24	Luke 13:23	Markan Parallel	Gospel of Thomas
0/ 1⸂ **13:24** [ἀγωνίζεσθε][2] εἰσελθ[εῖν][2] διὰ τῆς στενῆς [θύρας][3], ὅτι ( )[4]			
πολλοί, [λέγω ὑμῖν,][5] [ζητήσου][6]σιν ( )[6] εἰσε[λθεῖν][6] ( )[7] ( )[8]			
καὶ ( )[9] [οὐκ ἰσχύσουσιν][10] . ⸃1 \0	**13:23** Εἶπεν δέ τις αὐτῷ· κύριε, εἰ (ὀλίγοι) (οἱ) σῳζόμενοι; ὁ δὲ εἶπεν πρὸς αὐτούς·		

JMR, PH, JSK: ( )[7] indeterminate.

IQP 1992: (εὐρ)[10]<ήσουσιν>[10] (αὐτήν)[10] {D}; JMR: Indeterminate.

[5] Luke's λέγω ὑμῖν.
[6] Luke's ζητήσουσιν εἰσελθεῖν or Matthew's εἰσιν οἱ εἰσερχόμενοι.
[7] Matthew's δι' αὐτῆς.
[8] Matthew's τί στενὴ ἡ πύλη καὶ τεθλιμμένη ἡ ὁδὸς ἡ ἀπάγουσα εἰς τὴν ζωήν.

[9] Matthew's ὀλίγοι.
[10] Luke's οὐκ ἰσχύσουσιν or Matthew's εἰσὶν οἱ εὑρίσκοντες αὐτήν, or an emendation <εἰσέρχοντες δι'> αὐτῆ<ς>. (See Matt 7:13 at variation units [6] and [7].)

Tretet ein durch die enge Tür, denn viele werden suchen einzutreten, und wenige ⟦sind es, die <durch> sie <eintreten>⟧.

Entrez par la porte étroite, parce que beaucoup chercheront à entrer et peu nombreux ⟦sont ceux qui la <franchissent>⟧.

Q 13:25

Markan Parallel	Matthean Doublet	Matt 25:10-12	Q 13:25
		0/	0/
		1⸂	1⸂
		25:10 (ἀπερχομένων δὲ αὐτῶν ἀγοράσαι)[2]	[ἀφ' οὗ ἄν][2]
		(ἦλθεν)[3]	⟦[ἐγερθῇ][3]⟧
		ὁ (νυμφίος, καὶ αἱ ἕτοιμοι εἰσῆλθον μετ' αὐτοῦ εἰς τοὺς γάμους)[4]	ὁ ⟦[οἰκοδεσπότης][4]⟧
		καὶ [ ][5](ἐ)[6]κλείσ(θη)[6]	καὶ [][5]⟦()[6]⟧κλείσ⟦[η][6]
		[ ][6]ἡ[ ][6] θύρα[ ][6].	[τ][6]⟧ἡ⟦[ν][6]⟧ θύρα⟦[ν][6]⟧
		25:11 (ὕστερον δὲ ἔρχονται καὶ αἱ λοιπαὶ παρθένοι)[7]	()[7]
		[ ][8]	⟦[καὶ ἄρξησθε ἔξω ἑστάναι καὶ κρούειν τὴν θύραν][8]⟧
		λέγο(υσαι)[9]·	λέγο[ντες][9]·
		κύριε (κύριε)[10], ἄνοιξον ἡμῖν.	κύριε ()[10], ἄνοιξον ἡμῖν,
		25:12 (ὁ δὲ)[11] ἀποκριθεὶς	[καὶ][11] ἀποκριθεὶς
		(εἶπεν)[12]·	[ἐρεῖ][12]
		(ἀμὴν λέγω)[13] ὑμῖν,	()[13] ὑμῖν·
		οὐκ οἶδα ὑμᾶς	οὐκ οἶδα ὑμᾶς
		[ ][14].	⟦[][14]⟧,
		⸃1	⸃1
		\0	\0

PH: Q 13:⟦25⟧.
PH: [()][3]… ~~καί~~.

IQP 1994: ⟦[ἀφ' οὗ ἄν][2]⟧ [ ][3] ὁ ⟦[οἰκοδεσπότης][4]⟧ ~~καὶ~~ ⟦[ἀπο][5]()[6]⟧κλείσ⟦[η][6] [τ][6]⟧ἡ⟦[ν][6]⟧ θύρα⟦[ν][6]⟧ ()[7] ⟦[καὶ ἄρξησθε][8]⟧

0 Is Luke 13:25 par. Matt 25:10-12 in Q?

1 The position of Q 13:25 in Q: After Q 13:24 and before Q 13:26 (Lukan order); or after Q 12:46 (Matt 24:51) and before Q 19:12 (Matt 25:14) (Matthean order).

2 Luke's ἀφ' οὗ ἄν or Matthew's ἀπερχομένων δὲ αὐτῶν ἀγοράσαι.

3 Luke's ἐγερθῇ or Matthew's ἦλθεν.

4 Luke's οἰκοδεσπότης or Matthew's νυμφίος … γάμους.

5 Luke's ἀπο-.

Q

ἀφ' οὗ ἄν ⟦ἐγερθῇ⟧ ὁ ⟦οἰκοδεσπότης⟧ καὶ κλείσ⟦η τ⟧ἡ⟦ν⟧ θύρα⟦ν καὶ ἄρξησθε ἔξω ἑστάναι καὶ κρούειν τὴν θύραν⟧ λέγοντες· κύριε, ἄνοιξον ἡμῖν, καὶ ἀποκριθεὶς ἐρεῖ ὑμῖν· οὐκ οἶδα ὑμᾶς,	When the ⟦householder has arisen⟧ and locked the door, ⟦and you begin to stand outside and knock on the door,⟧ saying: Master, open for us, and he will answer you: I do not know you,

Q 13:25

Luke 13:25	Lukan Doublet	Markan Parallel	Gospel of Thomas
⁰/ ¹ʃ [ἀφ' οὗ ἂν]² [ἐγερθῇ]³ ὁ [οἰκοδεσπότης]⁴ καὶ [ἀπο]⁵( )⁶κλείσ[η]⁶ [τ]⁶ὴ[ν]⁶ θύρα[ν]⁶ ( )⁷ [καὶ ἄρξησθε ἔξω ἑστάναι καὶ κρούειν τὴν θύραν]⁸ λέγο[ντες]⁹· κύριε ( )¹⁰, ἄνοιξον ἡμῖν, [καὶ]¹¹ ἀποκριθεὶς [ἐρεῖ]¹² ( )¹³ ὑμῖν· οὐκ οἶδα ὑμᾶς [πόθεν ἐστέ]¹⁴. ʅ¹ \⁰			

[ ]⁸ ⟦[κρούειν]⁸⟧ [ ]⁸ λέγο⟦[ντες]⁹⟧·.

PH: [καὶ ἄρξησθε]⁸ [ ]⁸ (= ἔξω ἑστάναι καί indeterminate) [κρούειν τὴν θύραν]⁸.

⁶ Luke's active or Matthew's passive formulation.
⁷ Matthew's ὕστερον δὲ ἔρχονται καὶ αἱ λοιπαὶ παρθένοι.
⁸ Luke's καὶ ἄρξησθε ἔξω ἑστάναι καὶ κρούειν τὴν θύραν.
⁹ Luke's λέγοντες or Matthew's λέγουσαι.

¹⁰ Matthew's duplication of κύριε.
¹¹ Luke's καί or Matthew's ὁ δέ.
¹² Luke's ἐρεῖ or Matthew's εἶπεν.
¹³ Matthew's ἀμὴν λέγω.
¹⁴ Luke's πόθεν ἐστέ.

Wenn der ⟦Hausherr sich erhoben⟧ und die Tür verschlossen hat, ⟦und ihr anfangen werdet draußen zu stehen und an die Tür zu klopfen⟧ «und» zu sagen: Herr, öffne uns, so wird er euch antworten und sagen: Ich kenne euch nicht,

Après que le ⟦maître de la maison se sera levé⟧ et aura fermé la porte, ⟦et que vous aurez commencé à rester dehors et à frapper à la porte,⟧ en disant: Seigneur, ouvre-nous, et qu'il vous aura dit en réponse: Je ne vous connais pas,

Q 13:26

Markan Parallel	Matthean Doublet	Matt 7:22	Q 13:26
		^{0}/	^{0}/
		^{1}ʃ	^{1}ʃ
		^{2}ʃ (πολλοὶ ἐροῦσίν μοι)^{3} ʅ^{2}	^{2}ʃ ()^{3} ʅ^{2}
		(ἐν ἐκείνῃ τῇ ἡμέρᾳ·)^{2}	[τότε]^{2}
		^{2}ʃ [ ]^{3} ʅ^{2}	^{2}ʃ [ἄρξεσθε λέγειν·]^{3} ʅ^{2}
		(κύριε κύριε,)^{4}	()^{4}
		(οὐ)^{5}	()^{5}
		(τῷ σῷ ὀνόματι)^{6}	()^{6}
		ἐ(προφητεύσα)^{6}μεν [ ]^{6},	ἐ[φάγο]^{6}μεν [ἐνώπιόν σου]^{6}
		καὶ (τῷ σῷ ὀνόματι	καὶ ()^{6}
		δαιμόνια)^{6} ἐ(ξεβάλ)^{6}ομεν,	ἐ[πί]^{6}ομεν
		καὶ (τῷ σῷ ὀνόματι δυνάμεις	καὶ [ἐν ταῖς πλατείαις ἡμῶν
		πολλὰς ἐποιήσαμεν)^{6}(;)^{5}	ἐδίδαξας]^{6}·
		ʅ^{1}⇒ Matt 7:23	ʅ^{1}⇒ Q 13:27
		\\$^{0}$⇒ Matt 7:23	\\$^{0}$⇒ Q 13:27

IQP 1994: ⟦^{2}ʃ ()^{3} ʅ^{2} [τότε]^{2} ^{2}ʃ [ἄρξεσθε λέγειν·]^{3} ʅ^{2}⟧.

IQP 1994: ἐ[φάγο]^{6}μεν ⟦[ἐνώπιόν σου]^{6}⟧ καὶ ()^{6} ἐ[πί]^{6}ομεν καὶ ⟦[ἐν ταῖς πλατείαις ἡμῶν ἐδίδαξας]^{6}⟧.

^{0} Is Luke 13:26-27 par. Matt 7:22-23 in Q?

^{1} The position of 13:26-27 in Q: After Q 13:25 and before Q 13:28 (Lukan order); or after Q 6:46 (Matt 7:21) and before Q 6:47-49 (Matt 7:24-27) (Matthean order).

^{2} Luke's τότε or Matthew's ἐν ἐκείνῃ τῇ ἡμέρᾳ, and the resultant divergence of word order.

^{3} Luke's ἄρξεσθε λέγειν or Matthew's πολλοὶ ἐροῦσίν μοι.

Q

τότε ἄρξεσθε λέγειν· ἐφάγομεν ἐνώπιόν σου καὶ ἐπίομεν καὶ ἐν ταῖς πλατείαις ἡμῶν ἐδίδαξας·

then you will begin saying: We ate in your presence and drank, and «it was» in our streets you taught.

Q 13:26

Luke 13:26	Lukan Doublet	Markan Parallel	Gospel of Thomas
⁰/ ¹ʃ ²ʃ ( )³ ʅ² [τότε]² ²ʃ [ἄρξεσθε λέγειν·]³ ʅ² ( )⁴ ( )⁵ ( )⁶ ἐ[φάγο]⁶μεν [ἐνώπιόν σου]⁶ καὶ ( )⁶ ἐ[πί]⁶ομεν καὶ [ἐν ταῖς πλατείαις ἡμῶν ἐδίδαξας]⁶· ʅ¹⇒ Luke 13:27 \⁰⇒ Luke 13:27			

[4] Matthew's κύριε κύριε.
[5] Matthew's formulation as a question with οὐ.
[6] Luke's statements not indicating that the speakers are disciples or Matthew's statements indicating that the speakers are disciples.

dann werdet ihr anfangen zu sagen: Wir aßen und tranken vor dir, und du hast in unseren Straßen gelehrt.

alors vous vous mettrez à dire: Nous avons mangé en ta présence et bu et «c'est» dans nos rues «que» tu as enseigné.

Q 13:27

Ps 6:9a LXX	Matthean Doublet	Matt 7:23	Q 13:27
ἀπόστητε ἀπ' ἐμοῦ, πάντες οἱ ἐργαζόμενοι τὴν ἀνομίαν		καὶ (τότε ὁμολογήσω αὐτοῖς ὅτι)[1] οὐ(δέποτε ἔγνων)[2] ὑμᾶς [ ][3]· ἀπο(χωρεῖ)[4]τε ἀπ' ἐμοῦ (οἱ)[5] ἐργα(ζόμενοι τὴν)[6] ἀ(νομ)[7]ία(ν)[6]. ⸂Matt 7:22[1] \Matt 7:22[0]	καὶ [ἐρεῖ λέγων ὑμῖν][1]· οὐ[κ οἶδα][2] ὑμᾶς ⟦[][3]⟧· ἀπό[στη][4]τε ἀπ' ἐμοῦ ⟦(οἱ)[5]⟧ ἐργα(ζόμενοι τὴν)[6] ἀ(νομ)[7]ία(ν)[6]. ⸂Q 13:26[1] \Q 13:26[0]

IQP 1994: ⟦[ὑμῖν][1]⟧.
IQP 1994: [ ][3] {D}.

IQP 1994: ἀπό[ ][4]τε {D}; JMR: ἀπο⟦(χωρεῖ)[4]⟧τε.

Text Critical Note (see the discussion in the front matter): In Luke 13:27 ἐρεῖ ὑμῖν only is in ℵ 579 *pc* lat sy^p sa bo^pt, but only ἐρεῖ is in 1195 *pc* bo^pt; ἐρεῖ· λέγω ὑμῖν is in 𝔓^75* A D L W Θ Ψ 070 *f*^1.13 𝔐 sy^s.c.h (bo^ms); ἐρεῖ λέγων ὑμῖν is in 𝔓^75c B 892 *pc*.

[1] Luke's ἐρεῖ λέγων ὑμῖν or Matthew's τότε ὁμολογήσω αὐτοῖς ὅτι.
[2] Luke's οὐκ οἶδα or Matthew's οὐδέποτε ἔγνων.
[3] Luke's πόθεν ἐστέ.
[4] Luke's ἀπόστητε or Matthew's ἀποχωρεῖτε.

Q

καὶ ἐρεῖ λέγων ὑμῖν· οὐκ οἶδα ὑμᾶς· ἀπόστητε ἀπ' ἐμοῦ ⟦οἱ⟧ ἐργαζόμενοι τὴν ἀνομίαν.

And he will say to you: I do not know you! Get away from me, ⟦«you» who⟧ do lawlessness!

Q 13:27

Luke 13:27	Lukan Doublet	Markan Parallel	Ps 6:9a LXX
καὶ [ἐρεῖ λέγων ὑμῖν][1]· οὐ[κ οἶδα][2] ὑμᾶς [πόθεν ἐστέ][3]· ἀπό[στη][4]τε ἀπ' ἐμοῦ [πάντες][5] ἐργά[ται][6] ἀ[δικ][7]ία[ς][6]. ˀLuke 13:26[1] \Luke 13:26[0]			ἀπόστητε ἀπ' ἐμοῦ, πάντες οἱ ἐργαζόμενοι τὴν ἀνομίαν,

IQP 1994: ( )[5].

IQP 1994: ἐργα( )[6] ἀ(νομ)[7]ία( )[6].

Text Critical Note (see the discussion in the front matter): In Luke 13:27 οὐκ οἶδα πόθεν ἐστέ is in 𝔓[75] B L 070 1241 2542 *pc* b ff[2] i l; οὐδέποτε εἶδον ὑμᾶς is in D (e); οὐκ οἶδα ὑμᾶς πόθεν ἐστέ is in א A W Θ Ψ *f*[1.13] 𝔐 lat sy; *2 Clem* Or *Did.*

[5] Luke's πάντες or Matthew's οἱ.

[6] Luke's ἐργάται with the genitive or Matthew's ἐργαζόμενοι with the article and the accusative.

[7] Luke's ἀδικίας or Matthew's ἀνομίαν.

Und er wird euch sagen: Ich kenne euch nicht! Geht weg von mir, ⟦«ihr,» die «ihr»⟧ die Gesetzwidriges tut!

Et il vous dira: Je ne vous connais pas! Éloignez-vous de moi, ⟦«vous» qui⟧ commettez l'iniquité!

Q 13:29, 28

Markan Parallel	Matthean Doublet	Matt 8:11-12	Q 13:29, 28
		[0]/	[0]/
		[1]⸂	[1]⸂
		⸂ ⸃[2]	⸂⸃[2]
		8:11 [3]⸂ (λέγω δὲ ὑμῖν ὅτι)[4]	**13:29** [3]⸂ ⟦[καὶ][4]
		(πολλοὶ)[5]	(πολλοὶ)[5]⟧
		⸂ ⸃[6] ἀπὸ ἀνατολῶν	⸂⸃[6] ἀπὸ ἀνατολῶν
		καὶ δυσμῶν	καὶ δυσμῶν
		[ ][7]	[][7]
		⸂ἥξουσιν⸃[6]	⸂ἥξουσιν⸃[6]
		καὶ ἀνακλιθήσονται	καὶ ἀνακλιθήσονται
		[ ][8] ⸃[3]	[][8] ⸃[3]
		(μετὰ)[9]	**13:28** (μετὰ)[9]
		Ἀβραὰμ καὶ Ἰσαὰκ	Ἀβραὰμ καὶ Ἰσαὰκ
		καὶ Ἰακὼβ	καὶ Ἰακὼβ
		[ ][10]	[][10]
		ἐν τῇ βασιλείᾳ	ἐν τῇ βασιλείᾳ
		τ(ῶν οὐρανῶν)[11],	τ[οῦ θεοῦ][11],
		8:12 (οἱ)[12] δὲ	⟦[ὑμ<εῖ>ς][12]⟧ δὲ
		(υἱοὶ τῆς βασιλείας)[12]	⟦()[12]⟧
		ἐκβ[ ][13]λ(ηθήσονται)[13]	ἐκβ[][13]λ⟦(ηθήσ)[13]<εσθε>[13]
		(εἰς τὸ σκότος τὸ)[14]	(εἰς τὸ σκότος τὸ)[14]⟧
		ἐξώ(τερον)[14].	ἐξώ⟦(τερον)[14]⟧·
		⸂ἐκεῖ ἔσται ὁ κλαυθμὸς	⸂ἐκεῖ ἔσται ὁ κλαυθμὸς
		καὶ ὁ βρυγμὸς	καὶ ὁ βρυγμὸς
		τῶν ὀδόντων.⸃[2]	τῶν ὀδόντων.⸃[2]
		⸂ ⸃[3]	⸂⸃[3]

[0] Is Luke 13:28-29 par. Matt 8:11-12 in Q?

[1] The position of Q 13:29, 28 in Q: After Q 13:27 and before Q 13:30 (Lukan order); or after Q 7:9 (Matt 8:10) and before Q 7:?10?; 9:57 (Matt 8:13, 19) (Matthean order).

[2] The position of ἐκεῖ ἔσται ὁ κλαυθμὸς καὶ ὁ βρυγμὸς τῶν ὀδόντων at the beginning (Luke) or the end (Matthew).

[3] The position of the clause about coming from different directions and reclining, at the end (Luke) or the beginning (Matthew).

[4] Luke's καί or Matthew's λέγω δὲ ὑμῖν ὅτι.

Q 13:29, 28

Luke 13:28-29	Lukan Doublet	Markan Parallel	Gospel of Thomas
⁰/ ¹ʃ **13:28** ʃἐκεῖ ἔσται ὁ κλαυθμὸς καὶ ὁ βρυγμὸς τῶν ὀδόντων,ʅ² ʃ ʅ³ [ὅταν ὄψησθε][9] Ἀβραὰμ καὶ Ἰσαὰκ καὶ Ἰακὼβ [καὶ πάντας τοὺς προφήτας][10] ἐν τῇ βασιλείᾳ τ[οῦ θεοῦ][11], [ὑμᾶς][12] δὲ ( )[12] ἐκβ[α][13]λ[λομένους][13] ( )[14] ἔξω( )[14]. ʃ ʅ² **13:29** ³ʃ [καὶ][4] ( )[5] ʃἥξουσινʅ⁶ ἀπὸ ἀνατολῶν καὶ δυσμῶν [καὶ ἀπὸ βορρᾶ καὶ νότου][7]			

⁵ Matthew's πολλοί.

⁶ The position of ἥξουσιν before ἀπὸ ἀνατολῶν καὶ δυσμῶν (Luke) or after (Matthew).

⁷ Luke's καὶ ἀπὸ βορρᾶ καὶ νότου.

⁸ Luke's repetition of ἐν τῇ βασιλείᾳ τοῦ θεοῦ. (See also τῆς βασιλείας in Matt 8:12 at variation unit [12].)

⁹ Luke's ὅταν ὄψησθε or Matthew's μετά.

¹⁰ Luke's καὶ πάντας τοὺς προφήτας.

¹¹ Luke's τοῦ θεοῦ or Matthew's τῶν οὐρανῶν.

¹² Luke's ὑμᾶς or Matthew's οἱ … υἱοὶ τῆς βασιλείας.

¹³ Luke's ἐκβαλλομένους or Matthew's ἐκβληθήσονται.

¹⁴ Luke's ἔξω or Matthew's εἰς τὸ σκότος τὸ ἐξώτερον.

Q 13:29, 28

Markan Parallel	Matthean Doublet	Matt 8:11-12	Q 13:29, 28
		ʅ^{1} \$^{0}$	ʅ^{1} \$^{0}$

PH: [( )]^{4}: Indeterminate.

IQP 1990: ⟦[]^{8}⟧.

Q

29 ⟦καὶ πολλοὶ⟧ ἀπὸ ἀνατολῶν καὶ δυσμῶν ἥξουσιν καὶ ἀνακλιθήσονται **28** μετὰ Ἀβραὰμ καὶ Ἰσαὰκ καὶ Ἰακὼβ ἐν τῇ βασιλείᾳ τοῦ θεοῦ, ⟦ὑμ<εῖ>ς⟧ δὲ ἐκβλ⟦ηθήσ<εσθε> εἰς τὸ σκότος τὸ⟧ ἐξώ⟦τερον⟧· ἐκεῖ ἔσται ὁ κλαυθμὸς καὶ ὁ βρυγμὸς τῶν ὀδόντων.

29 ⟦And many⟧ shall come from Sunrise and Sunset and recline **28** with Abraham and Isaac and Jacob in the kingdom of God, but ⟦you will be⟧ thrown out ⟦into the⟧ out⟦er darkness⟧, where there will be wailing and grinding of teeth.

Q 13:29, 28

Luke 13:28-29	Lukan Doublet	Markan Parallel	Gospel of Thomas
ʃ ʅ[6] καὶ ἀνακλιθήσονται [ἐν τῇ βασιλείᾳ τοῦ θεοῦ.][8] ʅ[3] ʅ[1] \[0]			

PH: **13:28** ⟦(οἱ)[12]⟧ δὲ ⟦(υἱοὶ τῆς βασιλείας)[12]⟧ ἐκβ⟦[][13]⟧λ⟦(ηθήσονται)[13]⟧.

IQP 1990: **13:28** ()[14] ἔξω()[14]; JSK: ⟦()[14]⟧ ἔξω⟦()[14]⟧; PH: (εἰς τὸ σκότος τὸ)[14] ἐξώ(τερον)[14]; JMR: ⟦(εἰς τὸ σκότος τὸ)[14]⟧ ἐξώ⟦(τερον)[14]⟧.

29 ⟦Und viele⟧ werden vom Osten und Westen kommen und zu Tisch liegen **28** mit Abraham und Isaak und Jakob im Reich Gottes, ⟦ihr⟧ aber ⟦werdet in die⟧ äußer⟦ste Finsternis⟧ geworfen ⟦werden⟧; dort wird Weinen und Zähneklappern sein.

29 ⟦Et beaucoup⟧ viendront de l'Orient et de l'Occident et s'attableront **28** avec Abraham et Isaac et Jacob dans le royaume de Dieu, mais ⟦vous, vous serez⟧ chassés ⟦dans les ténèbres du⟧ dehors; il y aura là pleur et grincement de dents.

Q 13:⟦30⟧

Mark 10:31	Matt 19:30	Matt 20:16	Q 13:⟦30⟧
		⁰{	⟦⁰{
		¹∫	¹∫
πολλοὶ δὲ	{πολλοὶ δὲ	(οὕτως) [2]	[< >][2]
		[ ][3]	[][3]
ἔσονται	(ἔσονται)	∫ {ἔσονται} ≀3	∫ {ἔσονται} ≀3
		(οἱ)[3]	(οἱ)[3]
πρῶτοι	[(πρῶτοι)]	∫ {ἔσχατοι} ≀3	∫ ἔσχατοι} ≀3
ἔσχατοι	[(ἔσχατοι)]	{πρῶτοι}	{πρῶτοι}
καὶ	καὶ}	{καὶ} [ ][3]	{καὶ} [][3]
		∫ ≀3	∫≀3
οἱ		{(οἱ)}[3]	{(οἱ)}[3]
ἔσχατοι	{[(ἔσχατοι)]	∫ {πρῶτοι} ≀3	∫ {πρῶτοι} ≀3
		[ ][4]	[][4]
πρῶτοι.	[(πρῶτοι)]}.	{ἔσχατοι}.	{ἔσχατοι}.
		≀1	≀1
		}⁰	}⁰⟧

PH: In Q indeterminate.

PH: The position is indeterminate; IQP 1992: Luke = Q {B}; JMR, JSK: Luke = Q {C}.

⁰ Is Luke 13:30 par. Matt 20:16 in Q or from Mark?

¹ The position of Q 13:30 in Q: After Q 13:29, 28 and before Q 13:34 (Lukan order); or after Q 22:28, 30 (Matt 19:28) and before Q 7:⟦29-30⟧; 14:16 (Matt 21:32; 22:2) (Matthean order).

² Luke's καὶ ἰδού or Matthew's οὕτως.

Q

⟦.. ἔσονται οἱ ἔσχατοι πρῶτοι καὶ οἱ πρῶτοι ἔσχατοι.⟧	⟦.. The last will be first, and the first last.⟧

Gos. Thom. 4.2 (Nag Hammadi II 2)

ὅτι πολλοὶ ἔσονται πρῶτοι ἔσχατοι

For many who are first will become last,

Gos. Thom. 4.2 (P. Oxy. 654)

ὅτι πολλοὶ ἔσονται π[ρῶτοι ἔσχατοι καὶ] οἱ ἔσχατοι πρῶτοι,

For many «of the» [first] will become [last, and] the last will be first,

Q 13:⟦30⟧

Luke 13:30	Lukan Doublet	Mark 10:31	*Gos. Thom.* 4.2
[0]{			
[1]ʃ			
[καὶ ἰδοὺ][2]		πολλοὶ δὲ	
[εἰσὶν][3]			
ʃ {ἔσχατοι} ʅ[3]		ἔσονται	
[οἳ][3]			
ʃ {ἔσονται} ʅ[3]		πρῶτοι	
{πρῶτοι}		ἔσχατοι	
{καὶ} [εἰσὶν][3]		καὶ	ϫⲉ ⲟⲩⲛ̄
ʃ {πρῶτοι} ʅ[3]			
{[οἳ]}[3]		οἱ	
		ἔσχατοι	ϩⲁϩ ⲛ̄ϣⲟⲣⲡ'
[ἔσονται][4]			ⲛⲁⲣ̄
{ἔσχατοι}.		πρῶτοι.	ϩⲁⲉ
ʅ[1]			
}[0]			

IQP 1992: [( )][2]; PH: Neither Luke nor Matthew in Q; JSK: < >[2]; JMR: ⟦[καὶ ἰδού][2]⟧.

IQP 1992: Variation unit [3] indeterminate.

[3] Luke's use of οἳ … οἳ as relative pronouns preceded by εἰσὶν ἔσχατοι … εἰσὶν πρῶτοι and followed by ἔσονται or Matthew's use of οἱ … οἱ as definite articles preceded by ἔσονται (explicit in the first instance only) and followed by ἔσχατοι … πρῶτοι.

[4] Luke's repetition of ἔσονται.

⟦.. Es werden die Letzten Erste und die Ersten Letzte sein.⟧

⟦.. Les derniers seront les premiers et les premiers seront les derniers.⟧

Denn viele Erste werden Letzte sein,

Car beaucoup de premiers seront derniers,

Denn viele [Erste] werden [Letzte] sein, [und] die Letzten werden Erste sein,

Car beaucoup de [premiers] seront [derniers, et] les derniers seront premiers,

Q 13:34

Markan Parallel	Matthean Doublet	Matt 23:37	Q 13:34
		¹ʃ	¹ʃ
		Ἰερουσαλὴμ Ἰερουσαλήμ,	Ἰερουσαλὴμ Ἰερουσαλήμ,
		ἡ ἀποκτείνουσα	ἡ ἀποκτείνουσα
		τοὺς προφήτας	τοὺς προφήτας
		καὶ λιθοβολοῦσα	καὶ λιθοβολοῦσα
		τοὺς ἀπεσταλμένους	τοὺς ἀπεσταλμένους
		πρὸς αὐτήν,	πρὸς αὐτήν,
		ποσάκις ἠθέλησα	ποσάκις ἠθέλησα
		ἐπισυνα(γαγεῖν)²	ἐπισυνα(γαγεῖν)²
		τὰ τέκνα σου,	τὰ τέκνα σου,
		ὃν τρόπον ὄρνις	ὃν τρόπον ὄρνις
		(ἐπισυνάγει)³	(ἐπισυνάγει)³
		τ(ὰ)⁴	τ⟦(ὰ)⁴⟧
		ʃ ʅ⁵	ʃʅ⁵
		νοσσία[ ]⁴	νοσσία⟦[]⁴⟧
		ʃ [ ]⁵αὐτῆςʅ⁵	ʃ []⁵αὐτῆςʅ⁵
		ὑπὸ τὰς πτέρυγας,	ὑπὸ τὰς πτέρυγας,
		καὶ οὐκ ἠθελήσατε.	καὶ οὐκ ἠθελήσατε.
		ʅ¹⇒ Matt 23:38-39	ʅ¹⇒ Q 13:35

JMR: Q **13:34-35** is between Q **11:49-51** and Q **17:⟦21⟧, 23** (Matthean order) {B}.

IQP 1994: ἐπισυνά[ξαι]²... ⟦(ἐπισυνάγει)³⟧.

¹ The position of Q 13:34-35 in Q: After Q 13:28, ⟦30⟧ and before Q 14:~~5~~, 11 (Lukan order); or after Q 11:49-51 (Matt 23:34-36) and before Q 17:⟦21⟧, 23 (Matt 24:23, 26) (Matthean order).

² Luke's ἐπισυνάξαι or Matthew's ἐπισυναγαγεῖν.

³ Matthew's ἐπισυνάγει.

⁴ Luke's τὴν ... νοσσιάν or Matthew's τὰ νοσσία.

Q

Ἰερουσαλὴμ Ἰερουσαλήμ, ἡ ἀποκτείνουσα τοὺς προφήτας καὶ λιθοβολοῦσα τοὺς ἀπεσταλμένους πρὸς αὐτήν, ποσάκις ἠθέλησα ἐπισυναγαγεῖν τὰ τέκνα σου, ὃν τρόπον ὄρνις ἐπισυνάγει τ⟦ὰ⟧ νοσσία αὐτῆς ὑπὸ τὰς πτέρυγας, καὶ οὐκ ἠθελήσατε.

O Jerusalem, Jerusalem, who kills the prophets and stones those sent to her! How often I wanted to gather your children together, as a hen gathers her nestlings under her wings, but you were not willing!

Q 13:34

Luke 13:34	Lukan Doublet	Markan Parallel	Gospel of Thomas
[1]⸂ Ἰερουσαλὴμ Ἰερουσαλήμ, ἡ ἀποκτείνουσα τοὺς προφήτας καὶ λιθοβολοῦσα τοὺς ἀπεσταλμένους πρὸς αὐτήν, ποσάκις ἠθέλησα ἐπισυνά[ξαι][2] τὰ τέκνα σου ὃν τρόπον ὄρνις ( )[3] τ[ὴν][4] ⸂ [ἑ][5]αυτῆς⸃[5] νοσσιὰ[ν][4] ⸂ ⸃[5] ὑπὸ τὰς πτέρυγας, καὶ οὐκ ἠθελήσατε. ⸃[1]⇒ Luke 13:35			

IQP 1994: ⸂ ⸃[5]... ⸂ ⟦[][5]⟧αὐτῆς⸃[5].

[5] Luke's ἑαυτῆς or Matthew's αὐτῆς and the resultant position of the pronoun before (Luke) or after (Matthew) the noun.

Jerusalem, Jerusalem, du tötest die Propheten und steinigst die zu dir Gesandten! Wie oft wollte ich deine Kinder sammeln, wie eine Henne ihre Küken unter die Flügel sammelt, aber ihr habt nicht gewollt.

Jérusalem, Jérusalem, toi qui tues les prophètes et lapides ceux qui t'ont été envoyés! Combien de fois ai-je voulu rassembler tes enfants à la manière d'une poule qui rassemble ses poussins sous ses ailes, mais vous n'avez pas voulu.

Q 13:35

Mark 11:9b-10; Ps 117:26a LXX	Jer 22:5 LXX; Matt 21:9b	Matt 23:38-39	Q 13:35
	Jer 22:5 LXX ἐὰν δὲ μὴ ποιήσητε τοὺς λόγους τούτους, κατ' ἐμαυτοῦ ὤμοσα, λέγει κύριος, ὅτι εἰς ἐρήμωσιν ἔσται ὁ οἶκος οὗτος.	**23:38** ἰδοὺ ἀφίεται ὑμῖν ὁ οἶκος ὑμῶν (ἔρημος)¹. **23:39** λέγω (γὰρ)² ὑμῖν, οὐ μή ⸉ ⸊³ με ⸉ἴδητε⸊³ (ἀπ' ἄρτι)⁴ ἕως (ἂν)⁵ εἴπητε·	ἰδοὺ ἀφίεται ὑμῖν ὁ οἶκος ὑμῶν ()¹. λέγω [ ]² ὑμῖν, οὐ μὴ ⸉ἴδητέ⸊³ με ⸉ ⸊³ ()⁴ ἕως ⟦[ἥξει ὅτε]⁵⟧ εἴπητε·
11:9b ἔκραζον· ὡσαννά· **11:9c = Ps 117:26a LXX** εὐλογημένος ὁ ἐρχόμενος ἐν ὀνόματι κυρίου· **11:10** εὐλογημένη ἡ ἐρχομένη βασιλεία τοῦ πατρὸς ἡμῶν Δαυίδ· ὡσαννὰ ἐν τοῖς ὑψίστοις.	**Matt. 21:9b** {ἔκραζον} λέγοντες· {ὡσαννὰ} τῷ υἱῷ {Δαυίδ}· [({εὐλογημένος ὁ ἐρχόμενος ἐν ὀνόματι κυρίου·})] {ὡσαννὰ ἐν τοῖς ὑψίστοις.}	{εὐλογημένος ὁ ἐρχόμενος ἐν ὀνόματι κυρίου}. ⸊Matt 23:37¹	{εὐλογημένος ὁ ἐρχόμενος ἐν ὀνόματι κυρίου}. ⸊Q 13:34¹

IQP 1994, JMR, PH, JSK: ⸉ἴδητε⸊³ με ⸉ ⸊³ {C}.

JSK: ⟦()⁴⟧.

Text Critical Note (see the discussion in the front matter): In Matt 23:38 ἔρημος is absent from B L ff² sy^s sa bo^pt, but present in 𝔓^77vid ℵ C D W Θ 0102 *f*^1.13 33 𝔐 lat sy^p.h mae bo^pt Cl Eus. In Luke 13:35 ἔρημος is present in D N Δ Θ Ψ *f*^13 33 700 892 1241 1424 *pm* it vg^cl sy^c.p.h. Ir^lat, but absent from 𝔓^45vid.75 ℵ A B K L W Γ *f*^1 565 579 2542 *pm* lat sy^s sa Ir^lat *u.l.*.

Text Critical Note (see the discussion in the front matter): In Luke 13:35 δέ is absent from 𝔓^45 ℵ* L 2542 *pc* it sy^c sa bo^mss, but present in 𝔓^75 ℵ² A B D W Θ Ψ *f*^1.13 𝔐 lat sy^(p).h bo.

¹ Matthew's ἔρημος.

² Luke's δέ or Matthew's γάρ.

Q

ἰδοὺ ἀφίεται ὑμῖν ὁ οἶκος ὑμῶν. λέγω .. ὑμῖν, οὐ μὴ ἴδητέ με ἕως ⟦ἥξει ὅτε⟧ εἴπητε· εὐλογημένος ὁ ἐρχόμενος ἐν ὀνόματι κυρίου.

Look, your house is forsaken! .. I tell you, you will not see me until ⟦«the time» comes when⟧ you say: Blessed is the one who comes in the name of the Lord!

Q 13:35

Luke 13:35	Luke 19:38	Mark 11:9b-10; Ps 117:26a LXX	John 12:13b
ἰδοὺ ἀφίεται ὑμῖν			
ὁ οἶκος ὑμῶν			
( )[1].			
λέγω [δὲ][2] ὑμῖν,			
οὐ μὴ ⸉ἴδητέ⸊[3] με ⸉ ⸊[3]			
( )[4]			
ἕως [ἥξει ὅτε][5]			
εἴπητε·	λέγοντες·	**11:9b** ἔκραζον·	ἐκραύγαζον·
		ὡσαννά·	ὡσαννά·
		11:9c = Ps 117:26a LXX	
{εὐλογημένος	[({εὐλογημένος	εὐλογημένος	εὐλογημένος
ὁ ἐρχόμενος	ὁ ἐρχόμενος})],	ὁ ἐρχόμενος	ὁ ἐρχόμενος
ἐν ὀνόματι	ὁ {βασιλ}εὺς [({ἐν ὀνόματι	ἐν ὀνόματι	ἐν ὀνόματι
κυρίου}.	κυρίου·})]	κυρίου·	κυρίου,
		11:10 εὐλογημένη	
		ἡ ἐρχομένη	
		βασιλεία τοῦ πατρὸς	καὶ ὁ βασιλεὺς
	ἐν οὐρανῷ εἰρήνη	ἡμῶν Δαυίδ·	τοῦ Ἰσραήλ.
	καὶ δόξα {ἐν} {ὑψίστοις}.	ὡσαννὰ ἐν τοῖς ὑψίστοις.	
⸊Luke 13:34[1]			

Text Critical Note (see the discussion in the front matter): In Luke 13:35 με ἴδητε is in 𝔓[45.75] D L Ψ f^1 𝔐, but ἴδητέ με in א B K W Θ (f^{13}) *al.*

Text Critical Note (see the discussion in the front matter): In Luke 13:35 ἥξει ὅτε is absent in 𝔓[75] B L 892 *pc*, and replaced by ἄν in 𝔓[45] א N (Θ) f^{13} (1241) 2542 *pc*, but conflated ἂν ἥξει ὅτε in A W (Ψ f^1) 𝔐, while ἥξει ὅτε only is in D.

[3] The position of ἴδητε before (Luke) or after (Matthew) με.
[4] Matthew's ἀπ' ἄρτι.
[5] Luke's ἥξει ὅτε or Matthew's ἄν.

Siehe, verlassen wird euch euer Haus. .. Ich sage euch, ihr werdet mich nicht mehr sehen, bis ⟦«die Zeit» kommen wird, daß⟧ ihr sagt: Gesegnet, der im Namen des Herrn kommt!

Voici qu'elle est laissée à l'abandon, votre maison. .. Je vous «le» dis: Vous ne me verrez pas jusqu'à ce que ⟦vienne «le temps» où⟧ vous direz: Bénis soit celui qui vient au nom du Seigneur!

Q 14:~~1-4~~, ~~5~~, ~~6~~

Mark 3:1-6	Matt 12:9-10, 12-14	Matt 12:11	Q 14:~~1-4~~, ~~5~~, ~~6~~
	[0]/	[0]/	
3:1 Καὶ	**12:9** {Καὶ} μεταβὰς		**14:~~1-4~~**
εἰσῆλθεν πάλιν εἰς τὴν συναγωγήν.	ἐκεῖθεν {ἦλθεν} {εἰς τὴν συναγωγὴν} αὐτῶν·		
καὶ ἦν ἐκεῖ ἄνθρωπος ἐξηραμμένην ἔχων τὴν χεῖρα.	**12:10** {καὶ} ἰδοὺ {ἄνθρωπος} {χεῖρα} {ἔχων} {ξηρά}ν.		
3:2 καὶ παρετήρουν αὐτὸν	{καὶ} ἐπηρώτησαν {αὐτὸν}		
εἰ τοῖς σάββασιν θεραπεύσει αὐτόν, ἵνα κατηγορήσωσιν αὐτοῦ.	λέγοντες· {εἰ} {ἔξεστιν} {τοῖς σάββασιν θεραπεῦ}σαι; {ἵνα κατηγορήσωσιν αὐτοῦ.}		
3:3 καὶ λέγει τῷ ἀνθρώπῳ τῷ τὴν ξηρὰν χεῖρα ἔχοντι· ἔγειρε εἰς τὸ μέσον.			
	\[0]		\[0]

[0] Is Luke 14:1-4, 6 or Matt 12:9-10, 12-14 in Q?

Q 14:~~1-4~~, ~~5~~, ~~6~~

Luke 14:1-4, 5, 6	Luke 6:6-8; 13:15b; 6:9-11	Mark 3:1-6	Gospel of Thomas
0/			
14:1 {Καὶ} ἐγένετο ἐν τῷ	**6:6** [᾿Ελέγετο] δὲ	**3:1** Καὶ	
	ἐν ἑτέρῳ σαββάτῳ		
ἐ{λθ}εῖν αὐτὸν {εἰς}	{εἰσ}[ε({λθ})εῖν αὐτὸν ({εἰς]	εἰσῆλθεν πάλιν εἰς	
οἶκόν τινος τῶν ἀρχόντων	τὴν συναγωγὴν})	τὴν συναγωγήν.	
τῶν Φαρισαίων σαββάτῳ	καὶ διδάσκειν.		
φαγεῖν ἄρτον			
καὶ αὐτοὶ ἦσαν			
{παρ}α{τηρ}ούμενοι {αὐτόν}.			
14:2 {Καὶ} ἰδοὺ	{([καὶ]) ἦν}	καὶ ἦν ἐκεῖ	
{ἄνθρωπός} τις	({[ἄνθρωπος]}) {ἐκεῖ}	ἄνθρωπος	
{ἦν} ὑδρωπικὸς ἔμπροσθεν	καὶ {ἡ} ({χεὶρ}) αὐτοῦ	ἐξηραμμένην ἔχων	
αὐτοῦ.	ἡ δεξιὰ ἦν ({ξηρά}).	τὴν χεῖρα.	
14:3 {καὶ} ἀποκριθεὶς	**6:7** {παρετηρ}οῦντο δὲ	**3:2** καὶ παρετήρουν	
ὁ ᾿Ιησοῦς	({αὐτὸν})	αὐτὸν	
εἶπεν πρὸς τοὺς νομικοὺς	οἱ γραμματεῖς		
καὶ Φαρισαίους λέγων·	[καὶ] οἱ [Φαρισαῖ]οι		
{ἔξεστιν}	({εἰ}) ἐν	εἰ	
{τ}ῷ {σαββά}τῳ	[({τ})ῷ ({σαββά})τῳ	τοῖς σάββασιν	
{θεραπεῦ}σαι ἢ οὔ;	({θεραπεύ})]ει,	θεραπεύσει αὐτόν,	
14:4 {οἱ δὲ} ἡσύχασαν.	({ἵνα}) εὕρ({ωσιν})	ἵνα	
	({κατηγορ})εῖν ({αὐτοῦ.})	κατηγορήσωσιν αὐτοῦ.	
	6:8 αὐτὸς δὲ ᾔδει		
	τοὺς διαλογισμοὺς αὐτῶν,		
	εἶπεν δὲ {τῷ} ἀνδρὶ	**3:3** καὶ λέγει τῷ ἀνθρώπῳ	
	{τῷ} {ζηρὰν}	τῷ τὴν ξηρὰν	
	{ἔχοντι} {τὴν} {χεῖρα·}	χεῖρα ἔχοντι·	
καὶ ἐπιλαβό{μενος} ἰάσατο	{ἔγειρε} καὶ στῆθι {εἰς τὸ	ἔγειρε εἰς τὸ	
αὐτὸν καὶ ἀπέλυσεν.	μέσον·} καὶ ἀναστὰς ἔστη.	μέσον.	
\0			

Q 14:~~1-4~~, ~~5~~, 6

Mark 3:1-6	Matt 12:9-10, 12-14	Matt 12:11	Q 14:~~1-4~~, ~~5~~, 6
		12:11 [1]/	**14:~~5~~** [1]/
		[2]ʃ	[2]ʃ
3:4 καὶ		(ὁ δὲ)[3]	[][3]
λέγει		ʃ ʅ[4] εἶπεν	[4]ʃ [()][5] {~~αὐτο~~()[5]~~ς~~ʅ[4]}
αὐτοῖς·		[4]ʃ [ ][5] {αὐτο(ῖ)[5]ς ʅ[4].}	~~εἶπεν~~ ʃʅ[4].
		τί(ς ἔσται ἐξ)[6] ὑμῶν	~~τί~~()[6] ~~ὑμῶν~~
		(ἄνθρωπος ὃς ἕξει)[7]	()[7]
		[ ][8]	[][8]
		(πρόβατον)[9]	[][9]
		(ἓν)[10]	()[10]
		(καὶ)[11]	()[11]
		ʃ ʅ12	[12]ʃ~~εἰς~~ ()[13] ʅ12
		(ἐὰν)[14]	()[14]
		(ἐμ)[15]πέσ(ῃ)[14]	()[15]~~πεσ~~[][14],
		(τοῦτο)[16]	()[16]
		[17]ʃ [ ][22]	ʃʅ17
		το(ῖς)[18] σάββα(σιν)[18] ʅ17	
		[12]ʃεἰς (βόθυνον)[13] ʅ12,	ʃʅ12,
		[ ][18]	[][18]
		οὐ(χὶ)[19]	~~οὐ~~[()][19]
		[ ][20]	[][20]
		(κρατή)[21]σει	[()][21]~~σει~~
		αὐτὸ[ ][9]	~~αὐτὸ~~[][9]
		ʃ ʅ17	[17]ʃ [][22]
			~~το~~()[22] ~~σάββα~~()[22] ʅ17
		(καὶ ἐγερεῖ)[23];	()[23];
		ʅ2	ʅ2
		\[1]	\[1]

[1] Is Luke 14:5 par. Matt 12:11 in Q?

[2] The position in Q: After Q 13:35 and before Q 14:11 (Lukan order); or after Q 10:22 (Matt 11:27) and before Q 11:14 (Matt 12:22) (Matthean order).

[3] Luke's *καί* or Matthew's ὁ δέ.

[4] The position of πρὸς αὐτούς before (Luke) or αὐτοῖς after (Matthew) εἶπεν.

[5] Luke's πρὸς αὐτούς or Matthew's αὐτοῖς.

[6] Luke's τίνος or Matthew's τίς ἔσται ἐξ.

[7] Matthew's ἄνθρωπος ὃς ἕξει.

[8] Luke's υἱὸς ἤ.

[9] Luke's βοῦς … αὐτόν or Matthew's πρόβατον … αὐτό.

[10] Matthew's ἕν.

[11] Matthew's *καί*.

Q 14:~~1-4~~, ~~5~~, ~~6~~

Luke 14:1-4, 5, 6	Luke 6:6-8; 13:15b; 6:9-11	Mark 3:1-6	Gospel of Thomas
14:5 [1]/			
[2]ʃ			
{[καὶ]}[3]		**3:4** καὶ	
[4]ʃ [πρὸς][5] {αὐτο}[ὺ][5]{ς} ʅ[4]	**6:9a** ([εἶπεν]) δὲ ὁ Ἰησοῦς	λέγει	
εἶπεν ʃ ʅ[4].	[πρὸς ({αὐτο})ύ({ς})]·	αὐτοῖς·	
τί[νος][6] ὑμῶν	**13:15b** ὑποκριταί, ἕκαστος ὑμῶν		
( )[7]	[{τ}ῷ {σαββά}τῳ) (οὐ) λύει		
[υἱὸς ἢ][8]	τὸν [βοῦν] αὐτοῦ [ἢ]		
[βοῦς][9]	τὸν ὄνον		
( )[10]	ἀπὸ τῆς φάτνης		
( )[11]			
[12]ʃεἰς [φρέαρ][13] ʅ[12]			
( )[14]			
( )[15]πεσ[εῖται][14],			
( )[16]			
ʃ ʅ[17]			
ʃ ʅ[12]			
[καὶ][18]	[(καὶ)]		
οὐ[κ][19]			
[εὐθέως][20]			
[ἀνασπά][21]σει	ἀπαγαγὼν ποτίζει;		
αὐτὸ[ν][9]			
[17]ʃ [ἐν ἡμέρᾳ][22]			
το[ῦ][22] σαββά[του][22] ʅ[17]			
( )[23];			
ʅ[2]			
\[1]			

12 The position of the prepositional phrase before (Luke) or after (Matthew) the verb.

13 Luke's φρέαρ or Matthew's βόθυνον.

14 Luke's πεσεῖται or Matthew's ἐὰν -πέσῃ.

15 Matthew's ἐμ-.

16 Matthew's τοῦτο.

17 The position of the reference to the sabbath at the end (Luke) or the center (Matthew) of the saying.

18 Luke's καί.

19 Luke's οὐκ or Matthew's οὐχί.

20 Luke's εὐθέως.

21 Luke's ἀνασπάσει or Matthew's κρατήσει.

22 Luke's ἐν ἡμέρᾳ τοῦ σαββάτου or Matthew's τοῖς σάββασιν.

23 Matthew's καὶ ἐγερεῖ.

Q 14:~~1-4~~, ~~5~~, ~~6~~

Mark 3:1-6	Matt 12:9-10, 12-14	Matt 12:11	Q 14:~~1-4~~, ~~5~~, ~~6~~
	^{0}/		^{0}/
	12:12 πόσῳ οὖν διαφέρει		
	ἄνθρωπος προβάτου.		
ἔξεστιν	ὥστε {ἔξεστιν		
τοῖς σάββασιν	τοῖς σάββασιν}		
ἀγαθὸν ποιῆσαι	καλῶς {ποι}εῖν.		
ἢ κακοποιῆσαι,			
ψυχὴν σῶσαι			
ἢ ἀποκτεῖναι;			
οἱ δὲ ἐσιώπων.			
3:5 καὶ περιβλεψάμενος			
αὐτοὺς μετ᾽ ὀργῆς,			
συλλυπούμενος			
ἐπὶ τῇ πωρώσει			
τῆς καρδίας αὐτῶν			
λέγει	**12:13** τότε {λέγει		
τῷ ἀνθρώπῳ·	τῷ ἀνθρώπῳ·		
ἔκτεινον τὴν χεῖρα.	ἔκτεινόν} σου {τὴν χεῖρα.		
καὶ ἐξέτεινεν	καὶ ἐξέτεινεν		
καὶ ἀπεκατεστάθη	καὶ ἀπεκατεστάθη} ὑγιὴς		
ἡ χεὶρ αὐτοῦ.	ὡς ἡ ἄλλη.		
3:6 καὶ ἐξελθόντες	**12:14** {ἐξελθόντες} δὲ		**14:~~6~~**
οἱ Φαρισαῖοι εὐθὺς	{οἱ Φαρισαῖοι}		
μετὰ τῶν Ἡρῳδιανῶν			
συμβούλιον ἐδίδουν	{συμβούλιον} ἔλαβον		
κατ᾽ αὐτοῦ	{κατ᾽ αὐτοῦ		
ὅπως αὐτὸν ἀπολέσωσιν.	ὅπως αὐτὸν ἀπολέσωσιν}.		
	\\$^{0}$		\\$^{0}$

IQP 1991, JMR: Q **14:5** is in Q {C}.
IQP 1991: Luke's position is that of Q {C}; JMR: The position in Q is indeterminate.

IQP 1991: **14:~~5~~** ⟦^{1}/ ^{2}⸂ [καὶ]^{3} ⸂⸃^{4} εἶπεν ^{4}⸂ []^{5} {αὐτο(ῖ)^{5}ς⸃^{4}·} τί(ς ἔσται ἐξ)^{6} ὑμῶν ()^{7} (ὃς ἕξει)^{7} []^{8} [βοῦ<ν>]^{9} ()^{10} (καὶ)^{11} ⸂ ⸃^{12} (ἐὰν)^{14} ()^{15}πέσ(ῃ)^{14} ()^{16} ^{17}⸂ []^{22} το(ῖς)^{22} σάββα(σιν)^{22} ⸃^{17} ^{12}⸂εἰς (βόθυνον)^{13} ⸃^{12}, ()^{18} οὐ[( )]^{19} []^{20} [( )]^{21}σει αὐτὸ[ν]^{9} ⸂⸃^{17} ( )^{23}; ⸃^{2} \\$^{1}$⟧.

Text Critical Note (see the discussion in the front matter): In Luke 14:5 ὄνος is in ℵ K L Ψ $f^{1.13}$ 33 579 892 1241 2542 *al* lat (sy^{s}) bo;

Q 14:~~1-4~~, ~~5~~, ~~6~~

Luke 14:1-4, 5, 6	Luke 6:6-8; 13:15b; 6:9-11	Mark 3:1-6	Gospel of Thomas
	6:9b ἐπερωτῶ ὑμᾶς		
	εἰ ({ἔξεστιν	ἔξεστιν	
	τ})ῷ ({σαββά})τῳ	τοῖς σάββασιν	
	{ἀγαθο}{(ποι)ῆσαι	ἀγαθὸν ποιῆσαι	
	ἢ κακοποιῆσαι,	ἢ κακοποιῆσαι,	
	ψυχὴν σῶσαι	ψυχὴν σῶσαι	
	ἢ ἀπο}λέσ{αι;}	ἢ ἀποκτεῖναι;	
		οἱ δὲ ἐσιώπων.	
	6:10 {καὶ περιβλεψάμενος}	**3:5** καὶ περιβλεψάμενος	
	πάντας {αὐτοὺς}	αὐτοὺς μετ' ὀργῆς,	
		συλλυπούμενος	
		ἐπὶ τῇ πωρώσει	
		τῆς καρδίας αὐτῶν	
	εἶπεν	λέγει	
	αὐτῷ·	τῷ ἀνθρώπῳ·	
	{(ἔκτεινον) (τὴν χεῖρά)}	ἔκτεινον τὴν χεῖρα.	
	(σου). ὁ δὲ ἐποίησεν	καὶ ἐξέτεινεν	
	{(καὶ ἀπεκατεστάθη)	καὶ ἀπεκατεστάθη	
	ἡ χεὶρ αὐτοῦ.}	ἡ χεὶρ αὐτοῦ.	
^{0}/			
14:6 {καὶ}	**6:11** αὐτοὶ (δὲ)	**3:6** καὶ ἐξελθόντες	
	ἐπλήσθησαν ἀνοίας	οἱ Φαρισαῖοι εὐθὺς	
		μετὰ τῶν Ἡρῳδιανῶν	
οὐκ ἴσχυσαν	καὶ διελάλουν	συμβούλιον ἐδίδουν	
	πρὸς ἀλλήλους	κατ' αὐτοῦ	
ἀνταποκριθῆναι πρὸς ταῦτα.	τί ἂν ποιήσαιεν τῷ Ἰησοῦ.	ὅπως αὐτὸν ἀπολέσωσιν.	
\ ^{0}			

JMR: **14:~~5~~** ⟦^{1}/ ^{2}ʃ []^{3} ʃʅ^{4} ~~εἶπεν~~ ^{4}ʃ [()]^{5} {~~αὐτο~~()^{5}ς ʅ^{4}·} τί(ς ἔσται ἐξ)^{6} ὑμῶν (ἄνθρωπος ὃς ἕξει)^{7} []^{8} [βοῦ<ν>]^{9} ()^{10} (καὶ)^{11} ʃ ʅ^{12} ()^{14} ()^{15}πεσ-[εῖται]^{14}, (<>^{16}οὗτο<ς>)^{16} ^{17}ʃ []^{17} το(ῖς)^{22} σάββα(σιν)^{22} ʅ^{17} ^{12}ʃεἰς (βόθυνον)^{13} ʅ^{12}, ()^{18} οὐ[()]^{19} []^{20} [( )]^{21}σει αὐτὸ[ν]^{9} ʃʅ^{17} ( )^{23}; ʅ^{2} \ ^{1}⟧.

ὄνος υἱός is in Θ (sy^{c}); πρόβατον is in D; and υἱός is in 𝔓$^{45.75}$ (A) B W 𝓜 e f q sy$^{p.h}$ sa.

Q 14:⟦11⟧

Markan Parallel	Matt 18:4	Matt 23:12	Q 14:⟦11⟧
		^{0}/	⟦^{0}/
		^{1}ʃ	^{1}ʃ
		ʃ [ ]^{2} ʅ^{2}	ʃ []^{2} ʅ^{2}
		(ὅστις)^{3}	[πᾶς ὁ]^{3}
		ʃ (δὲ)^{2} ʅ^{2}	ʃ ()^{2} ʅ^{2}
		ὑψώ(σει)^{3} ἑαυτὸν	ὑψῶ[ν]^{3} ἑαυτὸν
		ταπεινωθήσεται	ταπεινωθήσεται,
		καὶ	καὶ
	(ὅστις) οὖν	(ὅστις)^{3}	[ὁ]^{3}
	([ταπεινώ]σει [ἑαυτὸν])	ταπεινώ(σει)^{3} ἑαυτὸν	ταπεινῶ[ν]^{3} ἑαυτὸν
	ὡς τὸ παιδίον τοῦτο,		
	οὗτός ἐστιν ὁ μείζων	ὑψωθήσεται.	ὑψωθήσεται.
	ἐν τῇ βασιλείᾳ		
	τῶν οὐρανῶν.		
		ʅ^{1}	ʅ^{1}
		$\backslash^{0}$	$\backslash^{0}$⟧

IQP 1992: Q **14:11** is in Q {B}.

IQP 1992, JMR, PH, JSK: The position is that of Luke {C}.

^{0} Is Luke 14:11 par. Matt 23:12 in Q?

^{1} The position of Q 14:11 in Q: After Q 13:35; 14:~~1-4~~, ~~5~~, ~~6~~ and before Q 14:16 (the Lukan order of Luke 14:11); or after Q 17:37 and before Q 19:12 (the Lukan order of Luke 18:14b); or after Q 11:43 (Matt 23:6-7) and before Q 11:52 (Matt 23:13) (Matthean order).

Q

⟦πᾶς ὁ ὑψῶν ἑαυτὸν ταπεινωθήσεται, καὶ ὁ ταπεινῶν ἑαυτὸν ὑψωθήσεται.⟧

⟦Everyone exalting oneself will be humbled, and the one humbling oneself will be exalted.⟧

Q 14:⟦11⟧

Luke 14:11	Luke 18:14b	Markan Parallel	Gospel of Thomas
^{0}/			
^{1}⸂			
⸂ [ὅτι]^{2} ⸃^{2}	[ὅτι]		
[πᾶς ὁ]^{3}	[πᾶς ὁ]		
⸂ ( )^{2} ⸃^{2}			
ὑψῶ[ν]^{3} ἑαυτὸν	[(ὑψῶ)ν (ἑαυτὸν		
ταπεινωθήσεται,	ταπεινωθήσεται)],		
καὶ			
[ὁ]^{3}	[ὁ] δὲ		
ταπεινῶ[ν]^{3} ἑαυτὸν	[(ταπεινῶ)ν (ἑαυτὸν		
ὑψωθήσεται.	ὑψωθήσεται)].		
⸃^{1}			
\\$^{0}$			

JMR: ⸂ [ ]^{2} ⸃^{2}… ⸂ ( )^{2} ⸃^{2} indeterminate.

2 Luke's ὅτι or Matthew's postpositive δέ.

3 Luke's πᾶς ὁ … ὁ with articular participles or Matthew's ὅστις … ὅστις with future finite verbs.

⟦Jeder, der sich selbst erhöht, wird erniedrigt werden, und der sich selbst erniedrigt, wird erhöht werden.⟧

⟦Quiconque s'élève sera abaissé et qui s'abaisse sera élevé.⟧

Q 14:~~15~~, 16-18, ?19-20?, 21, ~~22~~, 23, ~~24~~

Q 14:~~15~~, 16

Markan Parallel	Matthean Doublet	Matt 22:1-2	Q 14:~~15~~, 16
		^{0}/	^{0}/
		^{1}ʃ	^{1}ʃ
			14:~~15~~ []^{2}
		ʃ ʅ^{3}	ʃʅ^{3}
		22:1 (Καὶ ἀποκριθεὶς)^{2}	**14:16** ()^{2}
		ὁ (Ἰησοῦς πάλιν)^{2}	⟦~~ὁ~~ [()]^{2}
		εἶπεν (ἐν παραβολαῖς)^{2}	~~εἶπεν~~ ()^{2}
		αὐτ(οῖς λέγων·)^{2}	~~αὐτ~~[()]^{2}⟧
		22:2 (ὡμοιώθη)^{3}	()^{3}
		ʃ [ ]^{3}ἡ βασιλεία	ʃʅ^{3}
		τ(ῶν οὐρανῶν)^{3} ʅ^{3} ἀνθρώπ(ῳ)^{3}	ἄνθρωπ[ός]^{3}
		(βασιλεῖ)^{4},	()^{4}
		(ὅσ)^{3}τις	( )^{3}τις
		ἐποί(ησεν)^{5}	ἐποί[ει]^{5}
		(γάμους)^{6}	[δεῖπνον]^{6}
		[ ]^{7}	⟦[μέγα,]^{7}⟧
		(τῷ υἱῷ αὐτοῦ)^{8}	()^{8}
		[ ]^{9}.	⟦[καὶ ἐκάλεσεν πολλούς]^{9}⟧
		ʅ^{1}⇒ Matt 22:11-14	ʅ^{1}⇒ Q 14:~~24~~
		\$^{0}$⇒ Matt 22:11-14	\$^{0}$⇒ Q 14:~~24~~

IQP 1991: The Parable of the Invited Dinner Guests is in Q {C}; JMR, PH, JSK: {B}.

IQP 1991: **14:~~15~~** []^{2} ʃʅ^{3} **14:⟦16⟧** (καὶ)^{2} ⟦~~ὁ~~ [()]^{2} εἶπεν ()^{2} αὐτ(οῖς)^{2} ()^{2}· < >^{3} ^{3}ʃ []^{3}ἡ βασιλεία τ[οῦ θεοῦ]^{2} ʅ^{3} ἀνθρώπ(ῳ)^{3} ()^{4} (ὅσ)^{3}τις

0 Is the Parable of the Invited Dinner Guests in Q?

1 The position of Q 14:16-24 in Q: After Q 14:11 and before Q 14:26 (Lukan order); or after Q 22:28, 30 (Matt 19:28) and before Q 11:46 (Matt 23:4) (Matthean order).

2 Luke's introduction (Luke 14:15-16a: ἀκούσας … αὐτῷ·) or Matthew's (Matt 22:1: καὶ … λέγων·).

3 Luke's lack of an introduction in the parable itself or Matthew's introduction ὡμοιώθη ἡ βασιλεία τῶν οὐρανῶν

Q

16 ἄνθρωπός τις ἐποίει δεῖπνον ⟦μέγα, καὶ ἐκάλεσεν πολλούς⟧

16 A certain person prepared a ⟦large⟧ dinner, ⟦and invited many⟧.

Gos. Thom. 64.1a (Nag Hammadi II 2)

Λέγει Ἰησοῦς· ἀνθρώπῳ τινὶ ξένοι ἦσαν· καὶ ἑτοιμάσας τὸ δεῖπνον

Jesus says: A person had guests. And when he had prepared the dinner,

Q 14:~~15~~, 16

Luke 14:15, 16	Lukan Doublet	Markan Parallel	*Gos. Thom.* 64.1a
⁰/ ¹⸉ **14:15** [Ἀκούσας δέ τις τῶν συνανακειμένων ταῦτα εἶπεν αὐτῷ· μακάριος ὅστις φάγεται ἄρτον ἐν][2] ⸉ [τ][3]ῇ βασιλείᾳ τ[οῦ θεοῦ.][3] ⸊3			
14:16 ( )[2] Ὁ [δὲ][2] εἶπεν ( )[2] αὐτ[ῷ·][2] ( )[3] ⸉ ⸊3			ⲡⲉϫⲉ ⲓ̅ⲥ̅ ϫⲉ
ἄνθρωπ[ός][3] ( )[4] ( )[3]τις			ⲟⲩⲣⲱⲙⲉ ⲛⲉⲩⲛ̅ⲧⲁϥ ϩⲛ̅ϣⲙ̅ⲙⲟ
ἐποί[ει][5] [δεῖπνον][6] [μέγα,][7] ( )[8] [καὶ ἐκάλεσεν πολλούς][9] ⸊¹⇒ Luke 14:24 \⁰⇒ Luke 14:24			ⲁⲩⲱ ⲛ̅ⲧⲁⲣⲉϥⲥⲟⲃⲧⲉ ⲙ̅ⲡⲇⲓⲡⲛⲟⲛ

ἐποί[ει][5] [δεῖπνον][6] [μέγα,][7] ()[8] [][9]⟧.

PH: ⟦[][7]⟧ … ⟦[][9]⟧.

ἀνθρώπῳ βασιλεῖ ὅσ-, including the question of the reference to the kingdom: whether it is in Q, and, if so, its position, syntax, and modifying phrase τοῦ θεοῦ or τῶν οὐρανῶν.

4 Matthew's βασιλεῖ.

5 Luke's ἐποίει or Matthew's ἐποίησεν.

6 Luke's δεῖπνον or Matthew's γάμους. (See below, Q 14:23[8.13].)

7 Luke's μέγα.

8 Matthew's τῷ υἱῷ αὐτοῦ.

9 Luke's καὶ ἐκάλεσεν πολλούς. (See Matt 22:3 at Q 14:17[3].)

16 Ein Mensch bereitete ein ⟦großes⟧ Gastmahl ⟦und lud viele ein⟧.

16 «Il était» un homme «qui» préparait un ⟦somptueux⟧ dîner ⟦et invita beaucoup de monde⟧.

Jesus spricht: Ein Mensch hatte Gäste. Und als er das Mahl bereitet hatte,

Jésus dit: Un homme avait des hôtes. Et lorsqu'il eut préparé le dîner,

Q 14:17

Markan Parallel	Matthean Doublet	Matt 22:3-4	Q 14:17
		22:3 καὶ ἀπέστειλεν το(ὺς)[1] δούλο(υς)[1] αὐτοῦ [ ][2] (καλέσαι τοὺς κεκλημένους εἰς τοὺς γάμους, καὶ οὐκ ἤθελον ἐλθεῖν. **22:4** πάλιν ἀπέστειλεν ἄλλους δούλους λέγων·)[3]	καὶ ἀπέστειλεν τὸ[ν][1] δοῦλο[ν][1] αὐτοῦ ⟦[τῇ ὥρᾳ τοῦ δείπνου][2]⟧ ()[3]
		εἴπ(ατε)[4] τοῖς κεκλημένοις· ʃ ʅ[5]	εἰπ[εῖν][4] τοῖς κεκλημένοις· [5]ʃ [ἔρχεσθε][6] ()[6], ʅ[5] [ὅτι ἤδη][7]
		(ἰδοὺ τὸ ἄριστόν μου ἡτοίμακα, οἱ ταῦροί μου καὶ τὰ σιτιστὰ τεθυμένα καὶ πάντα)[7] ἕτοιμα [ ][7]· [5]ʃ (δεῦτε εἰς τοὺς γάμους)[6] ʅ[5].	ἕτοιμά [ἐστιν][7] ʃʅ[5].

IQP 1991: Q 14:⟦17⟧.

IQP 1991: [ ][2] indeterminate.

[1] Luke's τὸν δοῦλον or Matthew's τοὺς δούλους.

[2] Luke's τῇ ὥρᾳ τοῦ δείπνου.

[3] Matthew's καλέσαι τοὺς κεκλημένους εἰς τοὺς γάμους, καὶ οὐκ ἤθελον ἐλθεῖν. πάλιν ἀπέστειλεν ἄλλους δούλους λέγων·. (See also Q 14:16[9].20[3].)

Q

καὶ ἀπέστειλεν τὸν δοῦλον αὐτοῦ ⟦τῇ ὥρᾳ τοῦ δείπνου⟧ εἰπεῖν τοῖς κεκλημένοις· ἔρχεσθε, ὅτι ἤδη ἕτοιμά ἐστιν.	And he sent his slave ⟦at the time of the dinner⟧ to say to the invited: Come, for it is now ready.

Gos. Thom. 64.1b (Nag Hammadi II 2)

ἀπέστειλεν τὸν δοῦλον αὐτοῦ ἵνα καλέσῃ τοὺς ξένους.	he sent his slave so that he might invite the guests.

Q 14:17

Luke 14:17	Lukan Doublet	Markan Parallel	*Gos. Thom.* 64.1b
καὶ ἀπέστειλεν			ⲁϥϫⲟⲟⲩ
τὸ[ν][1] δοῦλο[ν][1] αὐτοῦ			ⲙ̄ⲡⲉϥϩⲙ̄ϩⲁⲗ
[τῇ ὥρᾳ τοῦ δείπνου][2]			
( )[3]			
εἰπ[εῖν][4] τοῖς κεκλημένοις·			ϣⲓⲛⲁ ⲉϥⲛⲁⲧⲱϩⲙ
[5]ʃ [ἔρχεσθε][6], ʅ[5]			ⲛ̄ⲛ̄ϣⲙ̄ⲙⲟⲉⲓ
[ὅτι ἤδη][7]			
ἕτοιμά [ἐστιν][7]			
ʃ ʅ[5].			

4 Luke's εἰπεῖν or Matthew's εἴπατε.

5 The position of the invitation before the reference to the dinner being ready (Luke) or after it (Matthew).

6 Luke's ἔρχεσθε or Matthew's δεῦτε εἰς τοὺς γάμους.

7 Luke's ὅτι ἤδη ... ἐστιν or Matthew's ἰδοὺ τὸ ἄριστόν μου ἡτοίμακα, οἱ ταῦροί μου καὶ τὰ σιτιστὰ τεθυμένα καὶ πάντα.

Und er sandte seinen Sklaven ⟦zur Stunde des Gastmahls⟧, um den Geladenen zu sagen: Kommt, denn es ist schon bereit.

Et il envoya son esclave ⟦à l'heure du dîner⟧ dire aux invités: Venez car voilà, c'est prêt.

sandte er seinen Sklafen, damit er die Gäste einlade.

il envoya son esclave inviter les hôtes.

Q 14:18, ?19-20?

Markan Parallel	Matthean Doublet	Matt 22:5-6	Q 14:18, ?19-20?
		22:5 (οἱ δὲ ἀμελήσαντες ἀπῆλθον,)[1] (ὃς μὲν εἰς τὸν ἴδιον)[2]	**14:18** [( )][1] [( )][2]
		ἀγρόν, [ ][2]	ἀγρόν, [ ][2]
		(ὃς δὲ ἐπὶ τὴν ἐμπορίαν αὐτοῦ·)[2]	**14:?19?** [( )][2]
		22:6 (οἱ δὲ λοιποὶ	**14:?20?** [ ][3]

IQP 1991: **14:⟦18⟧** [ ][1] [ ][2] ⟦ἀγρόν,⟧ [ ][2] **14:⟦19⟧** [ ][2] **14:⟦20⟧** [ ][3].

PH: **14:18** ⟦(οἱ δὲ ἀμελήσαντες ἀπῆλθον,)[1] (ὃς μὲν εἰς τὸν ἴδιον)[2]⟧ ἀγρόν, [][2] **14:⟦19⟧** ⟦(ὃς δὲ ἐπὶ τὴν ἐμπορίαν αὐτοῦ·)[2]⟧ **14:⟦20⟧** [()][3].

[1] The different general statements of the response.

[2] Luke's direct discourse, or Matthew's narration of the first two excuses.

Q

18 … ἀγρόν, .. **?19?** .. **?20?** ..

18 «One declined because of his» farm. **?19?** «Another declined because of his business.» **?20?** ..

Q 14:18, ?19-20?

Luke 14:18-20	Lukan Doublet	Markan Parallel	*Gos. Thom.* 64.2-5, 8-9, 6-7
14:18 [καὶ ἤρξαντο ἀπὸ μιᾶς πάντες παραιτεῖσθαι.][1] [ὁ πρῶτος εἶπεν αὐτῷ·][2]			64.2 ⲁϥⲃⲱ́ⲕ' ⲙ̄ⲡϣⲟⲣⲡ' ⲡⲉϫⲁϥ ⲛⲁϥ' ϫⲉ ⲡⲁϫⲟⲉⲓⲥ ⲧⲱϩⲙ̄ ⲙ̄ⲙⲟⲕ' 64.3 ⲡⲉϫⲁϥ ϫⲉ ⲟⲩⲛ̄ⲧⲁⲉⲓ ϩⲛ̄ϩⲟⲙⲧ' ⲁϩⲉⲛⲉⲙⲡⲟⲣⲟⲥ ⲥⲉⲛ̄ⲛⲏⲩ ϣⲁⲣⲟⲉⲓ ⲉⲣⲟⲩϩⲉ ϯⲛⲁⲃⲱⲕ' ⲛ̄ⲧⲁⲟⲩⲉϩ ⲥⲁϩⲛⲉ ⲛⲁⲩ ϯⲣ̄ⲡⲁⲣⲁⲓⲧⲉⲓ ⲙ̄ⲡⲇⲓⲡⲛⲟⲛ 64.4 ⲁϥⲃⲱⲕ' ϣⲁ ⲕⲉⲟⲩⲁ ⲡⲉϫⲁϥ ⲛⲁϥ' ϫⲉ ⲁⲡⲁϫⲟⲉⲓⲥ ⲧⲱϩⲙ̄ ⲙ̄ⲙⲟⲕ'
ἀγρὸν [ἠγόρασα καὶ ἔχω ἀνάγκην ἐξελθὼν ἰδεῖν αὐτόν· ἐρωτῶ σε, ἔχε με παρῃτημένον.][2]			64.5 ⲡⲉϫⲁϥ ⲛⲁϥ ϫⲉ ⲁⲉⲓⲧⲟⲟⲩ ⲟⲩⲏⲉⲓ ⲁⲩⲱ ⲥⲉⲣ̄ⲁⲓⲧⲉⲓ ⲙ̄ⲙⲟⲉⲓ ⲛ̄ⲟⲩϩⲏⲙⲉⲣⲁ ϯⲛⲁⲥⲣ̄ϥⲉ ⲁⲛ
14:19 [καὶ ἕτερος εἶπεν· ζεύγη βοῶν ἠγόρασα πέντε καὶ πορεύομαι δοκιμάσαι αὐτά· ἐρωτῶ σε, ἔχε με παρῃτημένον.][2]			64.8 ⲁϥ'ⲃⲱⲕ' ϣⲁ ⲕⲉⲟⲩⲁ ⲡⲉϫⲁϥ ⲛⲁϥ ϫⲉ ⲡⲁϫⲟⲉⲓⲥ ⲧⲱϩⲙ ⲙ̄ⲙⲟⲕ' 64.9 ⲡⲉϫⲁϥ ⲛⲁϥ' ϫⲉ ⲁⲉⲓⲧⲟⲟⲩ ⲛ̄ⲟⲩⲕⲱⲙⲏ ⲉⲉⲓⲃⲏⲕ' ⲁϫⲓ ⲛ̄ϣⲱⲙ ϯⲛⲁϣⲓ ⲁⲛ ϯⲣ̄ⲡⲁⲣⲁⲓⲧⲉⲓ
14:20 [καὶ ἕτερος εἶπεν·			64.6 ⲁϥⲉⲓ ϣⲁ ⲕⲉⲟⲩⲁ ⲡⲉϫⲁϥ ⲛⲁϥ' ϫⲉ ⲡⲁϫⲟ'ⲉⲓⲥ ⲧⲱϩⲙ̄ ⲙ̄ⲙⲟⲕ' 64.7 ⲡⲉϫⲁϥ ⲛⲁϥ ϫⲉ

JSK: Q **14:18-20** Luke = Q {B}; JMR: Q **14:18** [( )][1] [( )][2] ἀγρόν, [ ][2], indeterminate; Q **14:?19?** [( )][2]; **14:?20?** ()[3] [ ][3], Luke indeterminate.

[3] Luke's third excuse (see also Matt 22:3b καὶ οὐκ ἤθελον ἐλθεῖν at Q 14:17) or Matthew's violent response.

18 «Der eine weigerte sich wegen seines» Ackers, ?19? «der andere wegen seines Geschäfts.» ?20? ..

18 «L'un refusa à cause de son» champ. ?19? «Un autre refusa à cause de ses affaires.» ?20? ..

Q 14:18, ?19-20?

Markan Parallel	Matthean Doublet	Matt 22:5-6	Q 14:18, ?19-20?
		κρατήσαντες τοὺς δούλους αὐτοῦ ὕβρισαν καὶ ἀπέκτειναν.)[3]	

Gos. Thom. 64.2-5, 8, 9, 6, 7 (Nag Hammadi II 2)

(2) ἦλθεν πρὸς τὸν πρῶτον (καὶ) εἶπεν αὐτῷ· ὁ κύριός μου καλεῖ σε. (3) εἶπεν· ἀργύρια ἐδάνεισα ἐμπόροις, οἳ ἐλεύσονται τῆς ἑσπέρας· πορεύσομαι ἐπιτάσσειν αὐτοῖς, παραιτοῦμαι περὶ τοῦ δείπνου. (4) ἐλθὼν πρὸς ἕτερον εἶπεν αὐτῷ· ὁ κύριός μου ἐκάλεσέν σε. (5) εἶπεν αὐτῷ· οἰκίαν ἠγόρασα καὶ αἰτοῦσίν με ἡμέραν· οὐκ εὐκαιρῶ.

(2) He came to the first (and) said to him: My master invites you. (3) He said: I have bills for some merchants. They are coming to me this evening. I will go (and) give instructions to them. Excuse me for the dinner. (4) He came to another (and) said to him: My master has invited you. (5) He said to him: I have bought a house, and I have been called (away) for a day. I will not have time.

(8) ἐλθὼν πρὸς ἕτερον εἶπεν αὐτῷ· ὁ κύριός μου καλεῖ σε. (9) εἶπεν αὐτῷ· κώμην ἠγόρασα (καὶ) πορεύομαι λαβεῖν τὸν μισθόν· οὐ δυνήσομαι ἐλθεῖν, παραιτοῦμαι.

(8) He came to another (and) said to him: My master invites you. (9) He said to him: I have bought a village. Since I am going to collect the rent, I will not be able to come. Excuse me.

(6) ἐρχόμενος πρὸς ἕτερον εἶπεν αὐτῷ· ὁ κύριός μου καλεῖ σε. (7) εἶπεν αὐτῷ· ὁ φίλος μου γαμήσει καὶ ἐγὼ δεῖπνον ποιήσω· οὐ δυνήσομαι ἐλθεῖν, παραιτοῦμαι περὶ τοῦ δείπνου.

(6) He went to another (and) said to him: My master invites you. (7) He said to him: My friend is going to marry, and I am the one who is going to prepare the meal. I will not be able to come. Excuse me for the dinner.

Q 14:18, ?19-20?

Luke 14:18-20	Lukan Doublet	Markan Parallel	*Gos. Thom.* 64.2-5, 8-9, 6-7
γυναῖκα ἔγημα καὶ διὰ τοῦτο οὐ δύναμαι ἐλθεῖν.][3]			ⲡⲁϣⲃⲏⲣʼ ⲛⲁⲣ̄ ϣⲉⲗⲉⲉⲧ ⲁⲩⲱ ⲁⲛⲟⲕʼ ⲉⲧⲛⲁⲣ̄ ⲇⲓⲡⲛⲟⲛ ϯⲛⲁϣⲓ ⲁⲛ ϯⲣ̄ⲡⲁⲣⲁⲓⲧⲉⲓ ⲙ̄ⲡⲇⲓⲡⲛⲟⲛʼ

(2) Er kam zu dem ersten (und) sprach zu ihm: Mein Herr lädt dich ein. (3) Er sprach: Ich habe Geld(forderungen) gegenüber Kaufleuten. Sie kommen zu mir am Abend. Ich werde gehen (und) ihnen Anweisungen geben. Ich entschuldige mich für das Mahl. (4) Er kam zu einem anderen (und) sprach zu ihm: Mein Herr hat dich eingeladen. (5) Er sprach zu ihm: Ich habe ein Haus gekauft, und man bittet mich für einen Tag. Ich werde keine Zeit haben.

(8) Er kam zu einem anderen (und) sprach zu ihm: Mein Herr lädt dich ein. (9) Er sprach zu ihm: Ich habe ein Dorf gekauft. Da ich gehe, die Abgaben zu bekommen, werde ich nicht kommen können. Ich entschuldige mich.

(6) Er ging zu einem anderen (und) sprach zu ihm: Mein Herr lädt dich ein. (7) Er sprach zu ihm: Mein Freund wird heiraten, und ich bin es, der das Mahl bereiten wird. Ich werde nicht kommen können. Ich entschuldige mich für das Mahl.

(2) Il alla vers le premier (et) lui dit: Mon maître t'invite. (3) Il dit: J'ai de l'argent à des marchands. Ils doivent venir chez moi ce soir. J'irai leur donner des ordres. Je m'excuse pour le dîner. (4) Il alla vers un autre (et) lui dit: Mon maître t'a invité. (5) Il lui dit: J'ai acheté une maison et on me requiert pour la journée. Je ne serai pas libre.

(8) Il alla vers un autre (et) lui dit: Mon maître t'invite. (9) Il lui dit: J'ai acheté un village. Comme j'y vais pour percevoir les redevances, je ne pourrai pas venir. Je m'excuse.

(6) Il vint vers un autre (et) lui dit: Mon maître t'invite. (7) Il lui dit: Mon ami va se marier, et c'est moi qui ferai le dîner. Je ne pourrai pas venir. Je m'excuse pour le dîner.

Q 14:21

Markan Parallel	Matt 22:9	Matt 22:7-8	Q 14:21
		22:7 [ ][1]	«[καὶ < >
			ὁ δοῦλος < >
			τῷ κυρίῳ αὐτοῦ ταῦτα.][1]»
		⸂ ⸃[2]	⸂τότε⸃[2]
		⸂ ⸃[3]	[3]⸂ [ὀ][4]ργισθ[εὶς][4] ⸃[3]
		ὁ (δὲ)[2]	ὁ ()[2]
		(βασιλεὺς)[5]	[οἰκοδεσπότης][5]
		[3]⸂ (ὠ)[4]ργίσθ(η)[4] ⸃[3]	⸂⸃[3]
		(καὶ πέμψας τὰ στρατεύματα	()[2]
		αὐτοῦ ἀπώλεσεν τοὺς φονεῖς	
		ἐκείνους καὶ τὴν πόλιν αὐτῶν	
		ἐνέπρησεν)[2].	
		22:8 ⸂τότε⸃[2]	⸂⸃[2]
		(λέγει)[6]	[εἶπεν][6]
		τ(οῖς)[7] δούλ(οις)[7] αὐτοῦ·	τ[ῷ][7] δούλ[ῳ][7] αὐτοῦ·
		(ὁ μὲν γάμος ἕτοιμός ἐστιν,	()[8]
		οἱ δὲ κεκλημένοι	
		οὐκ ἦσαν ἄξιοι)[8]·	
	πορεύεσθε οὖν	[ ][9]	[][9]
	ἐπὶ [τὰς] διεξόδους		
	τῶν ὁδῶν		
	καὶ ὅσους		
	ἐὰν εὕρητε		
	καλέσατε		
	εἰς τοὺς γάμους.		

IQP 1991: The formatting of Q **14:21, 23** used by the IQP in 1991 differed basically from that used by the General Editors in 1999. The difficulty is as follows: Much the same language is found in Matt 22:9 and 10a for the master's command and the slave's compliance, and in Luke 14:21c and 23b for the master's two commands at the two missions of the slave; but in both cases only one instance is now assumed to be in Q, whereas in 1991 both the command and the compliance were assumed to be in Q at **14:21c** and **23b** respectively. Hence in 1991 Matt 22:9 was formatted parallel to Luke 14:21c and Matt 22:10a parallel to Luke 14:23b, whereas in 1999

[1] Luke's καὶ παραγενόμενος ὁ δοῦλος ἀπήγγειλεν τῷ κυρίῳ αὐτοῦ ταῦτα.

[2] Matthew's καὶ πέμψας ... ἐνέπρησεν, which determines the late placement of the τότε and the use of δέ at the beginning.

[3] The participle preceding the subject (Luke) or the finite verb following the subject (Matthew).

[4] Luke's ὀργισθείς or Matthew's ὠργίσθη.

Q 14:21

Luke 14:21	Luke 14:23a-b	Luke 14:13b	*Gos. Thom.* 64.10-11a
[καὶ παραγενόμενος			64.10 ⲁϥⲉⲓ ⲛ̄ϭⲓ
ὁ δοῦλος ἀπήγγειλεν			ⲡϩⲙ̄ϩⲁⲗ ⲁϥϫⲟⲟⲥ
τῷ κυρίῳ αὐτοῦ ταῦτα.][1]			ⲁⲡⲉϥϫⲟⲉⲓⲥ ϫⲉ
⸂τότε⸃[2]			ⲛⲉⲛⲧⲁⲕ'ⲧⲁϩⲙⲟⲩ
[3]⸂ [ὀ][4]ργισθ[εὶς][4] ⸃[3]			ⲁⲡⲇⲓⲡⲛⲟⲛ
ὁ ( )[2]			ⲁⲩⲡⲁⲣⲁⲓⲧⲉⲓ
[οἰκοδεσπότης][5]			
⸂ ⸃[3]			
( )[2]			
⸂ ⸃[2]	καὶ		
[εἶπεν][6]	[εἶπεν] [ὁ] κύριος		64.11a ⲡⲉϫⲉ ⲡϫⲟⲉⲓⲥ
τ[ῷ][7] δούλ[ῳ][7] αὐτοῦ·	πρὸς [(τ)]ὸν [(δοῦλ)]ον		ⲙ̄ⲡⲉϥϩⲙ̄ϩⲁⲗ ϫⲉ
( )[8]			
[ἔξελθε ταχέως	[ἔξελθε]	κάλει	
εἰς τὰς πλατείας καὶ ῥύμας	[εἰς τὰς] ὁδοὺς		
τῆς πόλεως	καὶ φραγμούς		
καὶ τοὺς πτωχοὺς	καὶ	[πτωχούς],	
καὶ ἀναπείρους		[ἀναπείρους],	
καὶ τυφλοὺς καὶ χωλοὺς		[χωλούς], [τυφλούς]·	
εἰσάγαγε ὧδε][9].	ἀνάγκασον [εἰσ]ελθεῖν,		

Matt 22:10a and Luke 14:21c are formatted without parallel in the other Gospel (resulting in no text in Q); rather Matt 22:9 is formatted parallel to Luke 14:23b. Either formatting alternative is possible. The (unformatted) text of Q **14:21** read in 1991: ⟦[καὶ παραγενόμενος ὁ δοῦλος ἀπήγγειλεν τῷ κυρίῳ αὐτοῦ ταῦτα. τότε ὀργισθεὶς ὁ οἰκοδεσπότης εἶπεν τῷ δούλῳ αὐτοῦ· ἔξελθε ταχέως εἰς τὰς <>ὁδοὺς καὶ ὅσους ἐὰν εὕρητε καλέσατε⟧ … .
PH: ⟦[][1]⟧.

[5] Luke's οἰκοδεσπότης or Matthew's βασιλεύς.
[6] Luke's εἶπεν or Matthew's λέγει.
[7] Luke's τῷ δούλῳ or Matthew's τοῖς δούλοις.
[8] Matthew's ὁ μὲν γάμος ἕτοιμός ἐστιν, οἱ δὲ κεκλημένοι οὐκ ἦσαν ἄξιοι. (See Luke 14:24 τῶν κεκλημένων.)
[9] Luke's ἔξελθε ταχέως … εἰσάγαγε ὧδε.

Q 14:21

Markan Parallel	Matt 22:9	Matt 22:7-8	Q 14:21

Q

«καὶ < > ὁ δοῦλος < > τῷ κυρίῳ αὐτοῦ ταῦτα.» τότε ὀργισθεὶς ὁ οἰκοδεσπότης εἶπεν τῷ δούλῳ αὐτοῦ·

«And the slave went away. He said> these things to his master.» Then the householder, enraged, said to his slave:

Gos. Thom. 64.10-11a (Nag Hammadi II 2)

(10) ἐρχόμενος ὁ δοῦλος εἶπεν τῷ κυρίῳ αὐτοῦ· οὓς ἐκάλεσας εἰς τὸ δεῖπνον παρῃτήσαντο. (11a) εἶπεν ὁ κύριος τῷ δούλῳ αὐτοῦ·

(10) The slave went away. He said to his master: Those whom you invited to dinner have asked to be excused. (11a) The master said to his slave:

Q 14:21

Luke 14:21	Luke 14:23a-b	Luke 14:13b	*Gos. Thom.* 64.10-11a

«Und der Sklave <kam und berichtete> dies seinem Herrn.» Da wurde der Hausherr zornig «und» sagte seinem Sklaven:

«Et, <de retour>, l'esclave <rapporta> cela à son maître.» Alors le maître de maison, en colère, dit à son esclave:

(10) Der Sklave ging. Er sagte seinem Herrn: Die, die du zum Mahl eingeladen hast, haben sich entschuldigt. (11a) Der Herr sprach zu seinem Sklave:

(10) L'esclave s'en vint. Il dit à son maître: Ceux que tu as invités au dîner se sont excusés. (11a) Le maître dit à son esclave:

Q 14:~~22~~

Markan Parallel	Matthean Doublet	Matthew	Q 14:~~22~~
		[ ][1]	[][1]

[1] Is Luke 14:22 in Q?

Q 14:~~22~~

Luke 14:22	Lukan Doublet	Markan Parallel	Gospel of Thomas
[καὶ εἶπεν ὁ δοῦλος· κύριε, γέγονεν ὃ ἐπέταξας, καὶ ἔτι τόπος ἐστίν.][1]			

Q 14:23

Markan Parallel	Matt 22:10a	Matt 22:9-10	Q 14:23
		[ ][1]	[][1]
	[καὶ] [ἐξελθ]όντες	**22:9** (πορεύεσθε)[2]	[ἔξελθε][2]
	οἱ [δοῦλο]ι ἐκεῖνοι	(οὖν)[3]	()[3]
	[εἰς (τὰς) (ὁδοὺς)]	(ἐπὶ)[4] τὰς (διεξ)[5]όδους	[εἰς][4] τὰς ()[5]ὁδοὺς
		(τῶν ὁδῶν)[5]	()[5]
	συνήγαγον	[ ][6]	[][6]
	πάντας οὓς (εὗρ)ον,	καὶ (ὅσους ἐὰν εὕρητε)[7]	καὶ (ὅσους ἐὰν εὕρ)[7]<ῃς>[7]
	πονηρούς τε καὶ ἀγαθούς·		
		(καλέσατε)[7]	(καλέσ)[7]<ον>[7],
		(εἰς τοὺς γάμους)[8].	()[8]
		22:10 (καὶ ἐξελθόντες	()[9]
		οἱ δοῦλοι ἐκεῖνοι	
		εἰς τὰς ὁδοὺς συνήγαγον	
		πάντας οὓς εὗρον,	
		πονηρούς τε καὶ ἀγαθούς·)[9]	
		(καὶ)[10]	[ἵνα][10]
		(ἐπλήσθη)[11]	[γεμισθῇ][11]
		[ ][12]	[μου][12]
		ὁ (γάμ)[13]ος	ὁ [οἶκ][13]ος
		(ἀνακειμένων)[14].	()[14].

IQP 1991 unformatted (see the note in the critical apparatus of Q 14:21): ⟦καὶ ἐξελθ<ὼν> ὁ<> δοῦλο<ς> εἰς τὰς ὁδοὺς συνήγαγ<ε>ν

1 Luke's καὶ εἶπεν ὁ κύριος πρὸς τὸν δοῦλον.
2 Luke's ἔξελθε or Matthew's πορεύεσθε.
3 Matthew's οὖν.
4 Luke's εἰς or Matthew's ἐπί.
5 Luke's ὁδούς or Matthew's διεξόδους τῶν ὁδῶν.
6 Luke's καὶ φραγμούς.
7 Luke's ἀνάγκασον εἰσελθεῖν or Matthew's ὅσους ἐὰν εὕρητε καλέσατε.

Q

ἔξελθε εἰς τὰς ὁδοὺς καὶ ὅσους ἐὰν εὕρ<ῃς> καλέσ<ον>, ἵνα γεμισθῇ μου ὁ οἶκος.

Go out on the roads, and whomever you find, invite, so that my house may be filled.

Gos. Thom. 64.11b (Nag Hammadi II 2)

ἔξελθε ἔξω εἰς τὰς ὁδοὺς (καὶ) ὅσους ἐὰν εὕρῃς εἰσάγαγε ἵνα δειπνήσωσιν.

Go out on the roads. Bring (back) whomever you find, so that they might have dinner.

Q 14:23

Luke 14:23	Luke 14:21b-c	Markan Parallel	*Gos. Thom.* 64.11b
	τότε ὀργισθεὶς		
[καὶ εἶπεν ὁ κύριος	[ὁ] οἰκοδεσπότης [εἶπεν]		
πρὸς τὸν δοῦλον][1]·	[τ]ῷ [(δούλ)]ῳ αὐτοῦ·		
[ἔξελθε][2]	[ἔξελθε] ταχέως		ⲃⲱⲕʼ ⲉⲡⲥⲁ ⲛⲃⲟⲗ
( )[3]			
[εἰς][4] τὰς ( )[5]ὁδοὺς	[εἰς (τὰς)] πλατείας		ⲁⲛϩⲓⲟⲟⲩⲉ
( )[5]	καὶ ῥύμας τῆς πόλεως		
[καὶ φραγμοὺς][6]	[(καὶ)] τοὺς πτωχοὺς		
καὶ ( )[7]	καὶ ἀναπείρους		ⲛⲉⲧⲕⲛⲁϩⲉ ⲉⲣⲟⲟⲩ
	καὶ τυφλοὺς καὶ χωλοὺς		ⲉⲛⲓⲟⲩ
[ἀνάγκασον εἰσελθεῖν][7],	[εἰσ]άγαγε ὧδε.		
( )[8]			
( )[9]			
[ἵνα][10]			ϫⲉⲕⲁⲁⲥ
[γεμισθῇ][11]			ⲉⲩⲛⲁⲣ̄ⲇⲓⲡⲛⲉⲓ
[μου][12]			
ὁ [οἶκ][13]ος			
( )[14].			

πάντας οὓς εὕρ<ε>ν· καὶ <ἐ>γεμίσθη ὁ οἶκος⟧ <..>.

PH: ⟦(ἐπὶ)[4]⟧ τὰς ⟦(διεξ)[5]⟧ὁδους ⟦(τῶν ὁδῶν)[5]⟧.

8 Matthew's εἰς τοὺς γάμους. (See above, Q 14:~~15~~, 16.)

9 Matthew's καὶ ἐξελθόντες οἱ δοῦλοι ἐκεῖνοι εἰς τὰς ὁδοὺς συνήγαγον πάντας οὓς εὗρον, πονηρούς τε καὶ ἀγαθούς.

10 Luke's ἵνα or Matthew's καί.

11 Luke's γεμισθῇ or Matthew's ἐπλήσθη.

12 Luke's μου.

13 Luke's οἶκος or Matthew's γάμος. (See above, Q 14:~~15~~, 16.)

14 Matthew's ἀνακειμένων.

Gehe hinaus auf die Wege, und wen auch immer du findest, lade ein, damit mein Haus voll werde.

Va-t-en par les routes et tous ceux que tu trouveras, invite «-les», pour que ma maison soit remplie.

Gehe hinaus auf die Wege. Die, die du finden wirst, bringe mit, damit sie Mahl halten.

Va-t-en par les routes et tous ceux que tu trouveras, invites les, pour que ma maison soit remplie.

Q 14:~~24~~

Markan Parallel	Matthean Doublet	Matthew 22:11-14	Q 14:~~24~~
		22:11 (εἰσελθὼν δὲ ὁ βασιλεὺς θεάσασθαι τοὺς ἀνακειμένους εἶδεν ἐκεῖ ἄνθρωπον οὐκ ἐνδεδυμένον ἔνδυμα γάμου, **22:12** καὶ λέγει αὐτῷ· ἑταῖρε, πῶς εἰσῆλθες ὧδε μὴ ἔχων ἔνδυμα γάμου; ὁ δὲ ἐφιμώθη. **22:13** τότε ὁ βασιλεὺς εἶπεν τοῖς διακόνοις· δήσαντες αὐτοῦ πόδας καὶ χεῖρας ἐκβάλετε αὐτὸν εἰς τὸ σκότος τὸ ἐξώτερον· ἐκεῖ ἔσται ὁ κλαυθμὸς καὶ ὁ βρυγμὸς τῶν ὀδόντων. **22:14** πολλοί)^{0} γάρ (εἰσιν)^{0}	()^{0} ~~γάρ~~ ([])^{0}
		κλη(τοί, ὀλίγοι δὲ ἐκλεκτοί.)^{0}	~~κλη~~([])^{0}
		≀Matt 22:1-2^{1} \Matt 22:1-2^{0}	≀Q 14:15-16^{1} \Q 14:15-16^{0}

IQP 1991: < >^{0} {D}.

^{0} Is Luke 14:24 or Matt 22:11-14 in Q?

Gos. Thom. 64.12 (Nag Hammadi II 2)

οἱ ἀγοράζοντες καὶ οἱ ἔμποροι οὐ μὴ εἰσ[έ]λθ[ωσιν] εἰς τοὺς τόπους τοῦ πατρός μου.

Dealers and merchants [will] not enter the places of my Father.

Q 14:~~24~~

Luke 14:24	Lukan Doublet	Markan Parallel	*Gos. Thom.* 64.12
[λέγω]^{0} γὰρ [ὑμῖν ὅτι οὐδεὶς τῶν ἀνδρῶν ἐκείνων τῶν κε]^{0}κλη[μένων γεύσεταί μου τοῦ δείπνου.]^{0} ʅLuke 14:15-16^{1} \Luke 14:15-16^{0}			ⲛ̄ⲣⲉϥⲧⲟⲟⲩ ⲙⲛ̄ ⲛⲉϣⲟⲧ̣[ⲉ ⲥⲉⲛⲁⲃ]ⲱ̣ⲕ ⲁⲛ’ ⲉϩⲟⲩⲛ’ ⲉⲛⲧⲟⲡⲟⲥ ⲙ̄ⲡⲁϊⲱⲧ’

Die Käufer und die Händler [werden] nicht eingehen zu den Orten meines Vaters.

Les acheteurs et les marchands n'entr[eront] pas dans les lieux de mon Père.

Q 14:26

Mark 10:29b	Matt 19:29a	Matt 10:37	Q 14:26
		[1]ʃ	[1]ʃ
οὐδείς ἐστιν ὃς	καὶ πᾶς {ὅσ}τις	(Ὁ)[2]	⟦<{ὃς}>[2]⟧
		[ ][3]	[][3]
ἀφῆκεν οἰκίαν	{ἀφῆκεν οἰκία}ς	(φιλῶν)[4]	[οὐ μισεῖ][4]
ἢ ἀδελφοὺς	{ἢ ἀδελφοὺς		
ἢ ἀδελφὰς	ἢ ἀδελφὰς}		
ἢ μητέρα	{ἢ ([πατέρα]}	[ ][5] {πατέρα}	[τὸν][5] {πατέρα}
		[ ][6]	⟦[][6]⟧
		{(ἢ)[7]	[καὶ][7]
ἢ πατέρα	{ἢ [μητέρα])}	[ ][5] μητέρα}	[τὴν][5] {μητέρα}
		[8]((ὑπὲρ ἐμὲ)[4]	[8](()[4]
		οὐ(κ ἔστιν)[9]	οὐ <δύναται εἶναί>[9]
		μου (ἄξιος)[9],	μου <μαθητής>[9],
		καὶ	καὶ
		(ὁ)[2]	⟦<ὃς>[2]⟧
		(φιλῶν)[4])[8]	<οὐ μισεῖ>[4])[8]
		[ ][7]	[][7]
		[ ][5] (υἱὸν)[10]	[τ][5]<ὸ>[10][ν][5] (υἱὸν)[10]
		{(ἢ)}[7]	[καὶ][7]
ἢ τέκνα	{ἢ [τέκνα]	[ ][5] (θυγατέρα)[10]	[τ][5]<ὴν>[10] (θυγατέρα)[10]
		[ ][7]	[][7]
		[ ][5] [ ][10]	[][5] [][10]
		[ ][7]	[][7]
		[ ][5] [ ][10]	[][5] [][10]
ἢ ἀγροὺς	ἢ ἀγροὺς	[ ][11]	[][11]
ἕνεκεν ἐμοῦ	ἕνεκεν}	(ὑπὲρ {ἐμ}ὲ)[4]	()[4]
καὶ ἕνεκεν			

IQP 1991: ⟦[εἴ τις][2]⟧.

IQP 1991: ⟦[ἑ][6]⟧[αυτοῦ][6].

Text Critical Note (see the discussion in the front matter): In Luke 14:26 αὐτοῦ is in 𝔓[45] א A D W Θ *f*[1.13] *𝔐*; αὐτοῦ is omitted in 579 2542 e; and ἑαυτοῦ is in 𝔓[75] B L Ψ *pc*.

[1] The position of Q 14:26-27 in Q: After Q 14:23 and before Q 14:34 (Lukan order); or after Q 12:53 (Matt 10:35) and before Q 17:33 (Matt 10:39) (Matthean order).

[2] Luke's εἴ τις or Matthew's ὁ (*bis*).

[3] Luke's ἔρχεται πρός με καί.

[4] Luke's οὐ μισεῖ or Matthew's φιλῶν … ὑπὲρ ἐμέ (*bis*).

[5] Luke's definite articles with the family members.

[6] Luke's ἑαυτοῦ.

Q 14:26

Luke 14:26	Luke 18:29b	*Gos. Thom.* 55	*Gos. Thom.* 101.1-2
[1]ʃ		55.1 ⲡⲉϫⲉ ⲓ̅ⲥ̅ ϫⲉ	
[εἴ τις][2]	{οὐδείς ἐστιν ὃς		
[ἔρχεται πρός με καὶ][3]			
[οὐ μισεῖ][4]	ἀφῆκεν οἰκίαν}	ⲡⲉⲧⲁⲙⲉⲥⲧⲉ	101.1 ⲡⲉⲧⲁⲙⲉⲥⲧⲉ
[τὸν][5] {πατέρα}		ⲡⲉϥʼⲉⲓⲱⲧʼ ⲁⲛʼ	ⲡⲉϥⲉⲓ̣[ⲱⲧ]ʼ ⲁ̣ⲛ
[ἑαυτοῦ][6]			
[καὶ][7]		ⲙⲛ̄	ⲙⲛ̄
[τὴν][5] {μητέρα}		ⲧⲉϥⲙⲁⲁⲩ	ⲧⲉϥʼⲙⲁⲁⲩ
( )[8]			ⲛ̄ⲧⲁϩⲉ
		ϥⲛⲁϣⲣ̄	ϥⲛⲁϣⲣ̄
		ⲙⲁⲑⲏⲧⲏⲥ ⲁⲛ ⲛⲁⲉⲓʼ	ⲙ[ⲁⲑⲏⲧ]ⲏ̣ⲥ ⲛ̣ⲁⲉⲓ ⲁⲛ
		55.2 ⲁⲩⲱ	101.2 ⲁⲩⲱ
		ⲛ̄ϥⲙⲉⲥⲧⲉ	
			ⲡⲉⲧⲁⲙⲣ̄ⲣⲉ
[καὶ][7]			
[τὴν][5] [γυναῖκα][10]	ἢ [γυναῖκα]		
[καὶ][7]			ⲡⲉϥ[ⲉⲓⲱⲧ ⲁⲛ
[τὰ][5] [{τέκνα}][10]			ⲙ]ⲛ̣
[καὶ][7]			ⲧⲉϥⲙⲁⲁⲩ
[τοὺς][5] {[ἀδελφοὺς]}[10]	{ἢ [ἀδελφοὺς]}	ⲛⲉϥʼⲥⲛⲏⲩʼ	
[καὶ][7]	ἢ γονεῖς	ⲙⲛ̄	
[τὰς][5] {[ἀδελφὰς]}[10]	{ἢ τέκνα}	ⲛⲉϥⲥⲱⲛⲉ	
[ἔτι τε καὶ τὴν ψυχὴν		ⲛ̄ϥϥⲉⲓ ⲙ̄ⲡⲉϥⲥⳁⲟⲥ	
ἑαυτοῦ][11],		ⲛ̄ⲧⲁϩⲉ	ⲛ̄ⲧⲁϩⲉ
( )[4]	{ἕνεκεν}		

IQP 1991: ⟦[8](()[4] (οὐ <δύναται εἶναί>[9] μου <μαθητής>[9],⟧ καὶ ⟦<εἴ τις>[2] <οὐ μισεῖ>[4])[8] [][7] [τ][5]<ὸ>[10][ν][5] (υἱὸν)[10] [καὶ][7] [τ][5]<ὴν>[10] (θυγατέρα)[10] [][7] [][5] [][10] [][7] [][5] [][10]⟧.

[7] Luke's repetitive *καί* or Matthew's *ἤ* (*bis*).

[8] Matthew's anticipation of the conclusion and repetition of the beginning at the middle, producing two statements connected by *καί*.

[9] Luke's οὐ δύναται εἶναί μου μαθητής or Matthew's οὐκ ἔστιν μου ἄξιος (*bis*). (See below, Q 14:27[6].)

[10] Luke's list of additional family members or Matthew's.

[11] Luke's inclusion of ἔτι τε καὶ τὴν ψυχὴν ἑαυτοῦ. (See Matt 10:39 and Mark 8:35 at Q 17:33.)

Q 14:26

Mark 10:29b	Matt 19:29a	Matt 10:37	Q 14:26
τοῦ εὐαγγελίου,	{τοῦ} ὀνόματός {(μ)ου},	οὐ(κ ἔστιν)[9] μου (ἄξιος)[9]. ʅ[1]⇒ Matt 10:38	οὐ()[9] [δύναται εἶναί][9] μου [μαθητής][9]. ʅ[1]⇒ Q 14:27

Q

⟦<ὅς>⟧ οὐ μισεῖ τὸν πατέρα καὶ τὴν μητέρα οὐ <δύναται εἶναί> μου <μαθητής>, καὶ ⟦<ὅς>⟧ <οὐ μισεῖ> τ<ὸ>ν υἱὸν καὶ τ<ὴν> θυγατέρα οὐ δύναται εἶναί μου μαθητής.

⟦<The one who>⟧ does not hate father and mother <can>not <be> my <disciple>; and ⟦<the one who>⟧ <does not hate> son and daughter cannot be my disciple.

Gos. Thom. 55 (Nag Hammadi II 2)

(1) Λέγει Ἰησοῦς· ὅστις οὐ μισήσει τὸν πατέρα αὐτοῦ καὶ τὴν μητέρα αὐτοῦ οὐ δυνήσεται εἶναί μου μαθητής. (2) καὶ ὅστις οὐ μισήσει τοὺς ἀδελφοὺς αὐτοῦ καὶ τὰς ἀδελφὰς αὐτοῦ καὶ οὐ βαστάσει τὸν σταυρὸν αὐτοῦ ὡς ἐγώ, οὐ γενήσεταί μου ἄξιος.

(1) Jesus says: Whoever will not hate one's father and one's mother will not be able to become a disciple of mine. (2) And whoever will not hate one's brothers and one's sisters and will not take up one's cross as I do, will not be worthy of me.

Gos. Thom. 101.1-2 (Nag Hammadi II 2)

(1) Ὅστις οὐ μισήσει τὸν πα[τέρα] αὐτοῦ καὶ τὴν μητέρα αὐτοῦ ὡς ἐγὼ οὐ δυνήσεται εἶναί μου μ[αθητ]ής. (2) καὶ ὅστις [οὐ] φιλήσει τὸν [πατέρα] αὐτοῦ [κα]ὶ τὴν μητέρα αὐτοῦ ὡς ἐγὼ οὐ δυνήσεται εἶναί μου μ[αθητής].

(1) Whoever will not hate his [father] and his mother as I do, cannot be my [disciple]. (2) And whoever will [not] love his [father and] his mother as I do, cannot become a [disciple] of mine.

Q 14:26

Luke 14:26	Luke 18:29b	*Gos. Thom.* 55	*Gos. Thom.* 101.1-2
	τῆς βασιλείας τοῦ θεοῦ,	ϥⲛⲁϣⲱⲡⲉ ⲁⲛ	ϥⲛⲁϣⲣ̄
οὐ [δύναται εἶναί][9]		ⲉϥⲟ	
μου [μαθητής][9].		ⲛ̄ⲁⲝⲓⲟⲥ ⲛⲁⲉⲓ	ⲙ[ⲁⲑⲏⲧⲏⲥ ⲛⲁ]ⲉⲓ ⲁⲛ
ι[1]⇒ Luke 14:27			

⟦<Wer>⟧ den Vater und die Mutter nicht hasst, <kann> nicht mein <Jünger sein>; und ⟦<wer>⟧ <den> Sohn und <die> Tochter <nicht hasst>, kann nicht mein Jünger sein.

⟦<Celui qui>⟧ ne hait pas père et mère, ne <peut> pas <être> mon <disciple>; et ⟦<celui qui>⟧ <ne hait pas> fils et fille ne pourra pas être mon disciple.

(1) Jesus spricht: Wer nicht seinen Vater hassen wird und seine Mutter, wird mir kein Jünger sein können. (2) Und wer nicht seine Brüder und seine Schwestern hassen wird und nicht sein Kreuz tragen wird wie ich, wird meiner nicht würdig sein.

(1) Jésus dit: Celui qui ne haïra pas son père et sa mère ne pourra être mon disciple. (2) Et celui qui ne haïra pas ses frères et ses sœurs, et ne portera sa croix comme moi ne sera pas digne de moi.

(1) Wer nicht seinen [Vater] und seine Mutter hassen wird wie ich, wird nicht mein [Jünger] sein können. (2) Und wer seinen [Vater und] seine Mutter [nicht] lieben wird wie ich, wird mir kein [Jünger] sein können.

(1) Celui qui ne haïra pas son [père] et sa mère comme moi ne pourra être mon [disciple]. (2) Et celui qui [n']aimera [pas] son [père et] sa mère comme moi ne pourra être mon [disciple].

Q 14:27

Mark 8:34b	Matt 16:24b	Matt 10:38	Q 14:27
		(καὶ)[1]	( )[1]
εἴ τις θέλει	{εἴ τις θέλει	ὃς[ ][2]	ὃς[][2]
ὀπίσω μου ἀκολουθεῖν,	ὀπίσω μου} ἐλθ{εῖν},		
ἀπαρνησάσθω ἑαυτὸν	{ἀπαρνησάσθω ἑαυτὸν		
καὶ ἀράτω τὸν σταυρὸν	καὶ ἀράτω ([τὸν σταυρὸν]	οὐ (λαμβάν)[3]ει {τὸν σταυρὸν	οὐ (λαμβάν)[3]ει {τὸν σταυρὸν
αὐτοῦ	[αὐτοῦ]	[ ][4]αὐτοῦ	[][4]αὐτοῦ
καὶ ἀκολουθείτω	καὶ ἀκολουθ)είτω	καὶ (ἀκολουθεῖ)}[5] ὀπίσω	καὶ (ἀκολουθεῖ)}[5] ὀπίσω
μοι.	([μο])ι}.	{μο}υ, οὐ(κ ἔστιν)[6]	{μο}υ, οὐ [δύναται εἶναί][6]
		μου (ἄξιος)[6].	μου [μαθητής][6].
		⸀Matt 10:37[1]	⸀Q 14:26[1]
		\Matt 10:37[0]	\Q 14:26[0]

IQP 1991: ()[1]; JMR, PH, JSK: Indeterminate.

IQP 1991: ⟦[][4]⟧αὐτοῦ.

Text Critical Note (see the discussion in the front matter): In Luke 14:27 αὐτοῦ is in 𝔓[45.75] ℵ D L* Θ $f^{1.13}$ 33 892 1006 1342 𝔐, but ἑαυτοῦ is in A B L[c] W Δ Ψ.

[1] Matthew's καί.
[2] Luke's ὅστις or Matthew's ὅς.
[3] Luke's βαστάζει or Matthew's λαμβάνει.
[4] Luke's ἑαυτοῦ or Matthew's αὐτοῦ.

Q

.. ὃς οὐ λαμβάνει τὸν σταυρὸν αὐτοῦ καὶ ἀκολουθεῖ ὀπίσω μου, οὐ δύναται εἶναί μου μαθητής.	.. The one who does not take one's cross and follow after me cannot be my disciple.

Gos. Thom. 55.2 (Nag Hammadi II 2)

καὶ ὅστις οὐ μισήσεῖ τοὺς ἀδελφοὺς αὐτοῦ καὶ τὰς ἀδελφὰς αὐτοῦ καὶ οὐ βαστάσει τὸν σταυρὸν αὐτοῦ ὡς ἐγώ, οὐκ γενήσεταί μου ἄξιος.

And whoever does not hate one's brothers and one's sisters and does not take up one's cross as I do, will not be worthy of me.

Q 14:34 is to be found below, between Q 17:33 and Q 14:35.

Q 14:27

Luke 14:27	Luke 9:23b	Mark 8:34b	*Gos. Thom.* 55.2
( )[1]			ⲁⲩⲱ
ὅσ[τις][2]	{εἴ [τις] θέλει	εἴ τις θέλει	ⲛ̄ϥⲙⲉⲥⲧⲉ ⲛⲉϥ'ⲥⲛⲏⲩ'
	ὀπίσω μου} [ἔρχ]εσθαι,	ὀπίσω μου ἀκολουθεῖν,	ⲙⲛ̄ ⲛⲉϥⲥⲱⲛⲉ
	{ἀρνησάσθω ἑαυτὸν	ἀπαρνησάσθω ἑαυτὸν	
οὐ [βαστάζ][3]ει {τὸν σταυρὸν}	καὶ ἀράτω ([τὸν σταυρὸν]	καὶ ἀράτω τὸν σταυρὸν	ⲛ̄ϥϥⲉⲓ ⲙ̄ⲡⲉϥⲥ⳨ⲟⲥ
[ἑ][4]{αυτοῦ}	[αὐτοῦ])} καθ' ἡμέραν	αὐτοῦ	
{καὶ} [ἔρχεται][5] ὀπίσω	{([καὶ] ἀκολουθ)είτω	καὶ ἀκολουθείτω	ⲛ̄ⲧⲁϩⲉ
{μο}υ, οὐ [δύναται εἶναί][6]	[μο]ι}.	μοι.	ϥⲛⲁϣⲱⲡⲉ ⲁⲛ
μου [μαθητής][6].			ⲉϥⲟ ⲛ̄ⲁⲝⲓⲟⲥ ⲛⲁⲉⲓ
ʅLuke 14:26[1]			
\Luke 14:26[0]			

[5] Luke's ἔρχεται or Matthew's ἀκολουθεῖ.

[6] Luke's οὐ δύναται εἶναί μου μαθητής or Matthew's οὐκ ἔστιν μου ἄξιος. (See above, Q 14:26[9].)

.. Wer sein Kreuz nicht auf sich nimmt und mir nachfolgt, kann nicht mein Jünger sein.

.. Celui qui ne prend pas sa croix et se met à ma suite ne peut pas être mon disciple.

Und wer nicht seine Brüder und seine Schwestern hassen wird (und) nicht sein Kreuz tragen wird wie ich, wird meiner nicht würdig sein.

Et celui qui ne haïra pas ses frères et ses sœurs, et ne portera sa croix comme moi, il ne sera pas digne de moi.

Q 14:34 is to be found below, between Q 17:33 and Q 14:35.

Q 17:33

Mark 8:35	Matt 16:25	Matt 10:39	Q 17:33
		⁰{	⁰{
		¹ʃ	¹ʃ
ὃς γὰρ	{[ὃς] γὰρ	(ὁ)²	⟦(ὁ)²⟧
ἐὰν θέλῃ	[ἐὰν] θέλ[ῃ	(εὑρ)³(ὼν)²	(εὑρ)³⟦(ὼν)²⟧
τὴν ψυχὴν αὐτοῦ	τὴν ψυχὴν αὐτοῦ]	{τὴν ψυχὴν αὐτοῦ}	{τὴν ψυχὴν αὐτοῦ}
σῶσαι	σῶσαι	[ ]³	⟦[]³⟧
ἀπολέσει αὐτήν·	[ἀπολέσει αὐτήν]·	{ἀπολέσει αὐτήν},	{ἀπολέσει αὐτήν},
ὃς δ' ἂν	[ὃς δ' ἂν	ʃ (καὶ)⁴ ʅ⁴ (ὁ)² ʃ ʅ⁴	ʃ (καὶ)⁴ ʅ⁴ ⟦(ὁ)²⟧ ʃʅ⁴
ἀπολέσει	ἀπολέσ}ῃ]	{ἀπολέσ}(ας)²	{ἀπολέσ}⟦(ας)²⟧
τὴν ψυχὴν αὐτοῦ	{(τὴν ψυχὴν αὐτοῦ)	{(τὴν ψυχὴν αὐτοῦ)⁵	({τὴν ψυχὴν αὐτοῦ})⁵
ἕνεκεν ἐμοῦ	(ἕνεκεν ἐμοῦ)}	(ἕνεκεν ἐμοῦ)}⁶	⟦({ἕνεκεν ἐμοῦ})⁶⟧
καὶ τοῦ εὐαγγελίου			
σώσει αὐτήν.	(εὑρ[ή{σει αὐτήν}]).	(εὑρ)³ή{σει αὐτήν}.	(εὑρ)³ή{σει αὐτήν}.
		ʅ¹	ʅ¹
		}⁰	}⁰

JMR: In Q {C}.

IQP 1994: (ὁ)² ... (ὁ)².

⁰ Is Luke 17:33 par. Matt 10:39 in Q or from Mark?

¹ The position of Luke 17:33 in Q: After Q 17:30 and before Q 17:34-35 (the Lukan order of Luke 17:33); or after Q 7:35 and before Q 9: 57 (the Lukan order of Luke 9:24); or after Q 14:27 (Matt 10:38) and before Q 10:16 (Matt 10:40) (Matthean order).

² Luke's ὃς ἐὰν ... ὃς ... ἄν with finite verb forms or Matthew's ὁ ... ὁ with participles.

Q

⟦ὁ⟧ εὑρ⟦ὼν⟧ τὴν ψυχὴν αὐτοῦ ἀπολέσει αὐτήν, καὶ ⟦ὁ⟧ ἀπολέσ⟦ας⟧ τὴν ψυχὴν αὐτοῦ ⟦ἕνεκεν ἐμοῦ⟧ εὑρήσει αὐτήν.

⟦The one who⟧ finds one's life will lose it, and ⟦the one who⟧ loses one's life ⟦for my sake⟧ will find it.

Q 17:34-35 is to be found below, between Q 17:30, ~~31-32~~ and Q 19:12.

Q 17:33

Luke 17:33	Luke 9:24	Mark 8:35	John 12:25
[0]{			
[1]ʃ			
[{ὃς}	{[ὃς] γὰρ}	ὃς γὰρ	ὁ
{ἐὰν}][2] [ζητήσ][3]{[η]}[2]	{[ἂν] θέλ[η]	ἐὰν θέλῃ	φιλῶν
τὴν ψυχὴν αὐτοῦ}	[(τὴν ψυχὴν αὐτοῦ)]	τὴν ψυχὴν αὐτοῦ	τὴν ψυχὴν αὐτοῦ
[περιποιήσασθαι][3]	σῶσαι	σῶσαι	
{ἀπολέσει αὐτήν,	[(ἀπολέσει αὐτήν)·	ἀπολέσει αὐτήν·	ἀπολλύει αὐτήν,
ʃ ʅ[4] [ὃς][2] ʃ [δ’][4] ʅ[4] [ἂν][2]	ὃς δ’ ἂν	ὃς δ’ ἂν	καὶ ὁ
ἀπολέσ}[η][2]	ἀπολέσ}η]	ἀπολέσει	μισῶν
({ })[5]	{(τὴν ψυχὴν αὐτοῦ	τὴν ψυχὴν αὐτοῦ	τὴν ψυχὴν αὐτοῦ
({ })[6]	ἕνεκεν ἐμοῦ)}	ἕνεκεν ἐμοῦ	ἐν τῷ κόσμῳ τούτῳ
		καὶ τοῦ εὐαγγελίου	εἰς ζωὴν αἰώνιον
[ζῳογον][3]ή{σει αὐτήν}.	οὗτος {σώ[(σει αὐτήν)]}.	σώσει αὐτήν.	φυλάξει αὐτήν.
ʅ[1]			
}[0]			

[3] Luke's verbs ζητέω, περιποιέω, ζῳογονέω or Matthew's εὑρίσκω (*bis*).

[4] Luke's postpositive δ’ or Matthew's καί.

[5] Matthew's second τὴν ψυχὴν αὐτοῦ.

[6] Matthew's ἕνεκεν ἐμοῦ.

⟦Wer⟧ sein Leben findet, wird es verlieren, und ⟦wer⟧ sein Leben ⟦meinetwegen⟧ verliert, wird es finden.

⟦Celui qui⟧ aura trouvé sa vie la perdra et ⟦celui qui⟧ aura perdu sa vie ⟦à cause de moi⟧ la trouvera.

Q 17:34-35 is to be found below, between Q 17:30, ~~31-32~~ and Q 19:12.

Q 14:34

Mark 9:49-50a	Matthean Doublet	Matt 5:13a	Q 14:34
9:49 Πᾶς γὰρ πυρὶ ἁλισθήσεται. 9:50a καλὸν τὸ ἅλας· ἐὰν δὲ τὸ ἅλας ἄναλον γένηται, ἐν τίνι αὐτὸ ἀρτύσετε;		⁰{ ¹ʃ (Ὑμεῖς ἐστε)² [ ]³ {τὸ ἅλας} (τῆς γῆς)⁴· {ἐὰν δὲ [ ]⁵ τὸ ἅλας} μωρανθῇ, {ἐν τίνι} (ἁλισ)⁶θήσεται; }⁰ ℓ¹⇒ Matt 5:13b	⁰{ ¹ʃ ⟦[{καλὸν}]²⟧ []³ {τὸ ἅλας} ()⁴· {ἐὰν δὲ []⁵ τὸ ἅλας} μωρανθῇ, {ἐν τίνι} ⟦[{ἀρτυ}]⁶⟧θήσεται; }⁰ ℓ¹⇒ Q 14:35

IQP 1990:The position is that of Luke {A}; JMR, PH, JSK: {C}. IQP 1990: [{ }]⁶θήσεται.

⁰ Is Luke 14:34 par. Matt 5:13a in Q or from Mark?

¹ The position of Q 14:34-35 in Q: After Q 14:27 and before Q 15:4 (Lukan order); or after Q 6:23 (Matt 5:12) and before Q 11:33 (Matt 5:15) (Matthean order).

² Luke's καλόν or Matthew's ὑμεῖς ἐστε.

³ Luke's οὖν.

Q

⟦καλὸν⟧ τὸ ἅλας· ἐὰν δὲ τὸ ἅλας μωρανθῇ, ἐν τίνι ⟦ἀρτυ⟧θήσεται;	Salt ⟦is good⟧; but if salt becomes insipid, with what will it be ⟦seasoned⟧?

Q 14:34

Luke 14:34	Lukan Doublet	Mark 9:49-50a	Gospel of Thomas
[0]{ [1]⸀ [{Καλὸν}][2] [οὖν][3] {τὸ ἅλας} ( )[4]. {ἐὰν δὲ} [καὶ][5] {τὸ ἅλας} μωρανθῇ, {ἐν τίνι} [{ἀρτυ}][6]θήσεται; }[0] ⸃[1]⇒ Luke 14:35		9:49 Πᾶς γὰρ πυρὶ ἁλισθήσεται. 9:50a καλὸν τὸ ἅλας· ἐὰν δὲ τὸ ἅλας ἄναλον γένηται, ἐν τίνι αὐτὸ ἀρτύσετε;	

4 Matthew's τῆς γῆς.
5 Luke's καί.

6 Luke's ἀρτυθήσεται or Matthew's ἁλισθήσεται.

⟦Gut⟧ ist das Salz; wenn jedoch das Salz fad wird, womit soll es ⟦gewürzt⟧ werden?

Le sel ⟦est bon⟧. Mais si le sel devient insipide, avec quoi l'⟦assaisonne⟧ra-t-on?

Q 14:35

Markan Parallel	Matthean Doublet	Matt 5:13b	Q 14:35
		[ ]¹ εἰς [ ]¹	[οὔτε]¹ εἰς [γῆν]¹
		οὐ(δ)¹ἐ(ν)¹	οὔ[τ]¹ε [εἰς κοπρίαν]¹
		(ἰσχύει)²	⟦[εὔθετόν ἐστιν]²⟧,
		(ἔτι εἰ μὴ)¹	()¹
		⸉ ⸊³	⸉ἔξω⸊³
		β[ ]⁴λ(ηθὲν)⁴	β[ά]⁴λ[λουσιν]⁴
		⸉ἔξω⸊³	⸉⸊³
		[ ]⁴	[αὐτό]⁴
		(καταπατεῖσθαι ὑπὸ τῶν ἀνθρώπων)⁵.	()⁵.
		[ ]⁶	[]⁶
		⸊Matt 5:13a¹	⸊Q 14:34¹

PH: ⟦[]¹ εἰς []¹ οὐ(δ)¹ἐ(ν)¹⟧.

IQP 1990: [εὔθετόν ἐστιν]²; PH ⟦(ἰσχύει)²⟧.

¹ Luke's οὔτε εἰς γῆν οὔτε εἰς κοπρίαν or Matthew's εἰς οὐδὲν … ἔτι εἰ μή.

² Luke's εὔθετόν ἐστιν or Matthew's ἰσχύει.

³ The position of ἔξω before (Luke) or after (Matthew) the verb.

Q

οὔτε εἰς γῆν οὔτε εἰς κοπρίαν ⟦εὔθετόν ἐστιν⟧, ἔξω βάλλουσιν αὐτό.	Neither for the earth nor for the dunghill ⟦is it fit⟧ – it gets thrown out.

Q 15:4-5a, ~~5b-6~~, 7, ⟦8-10⟧ is to be found below, between Q 17:1-2 and Q 17:3-4.

Q 14:35

Luke 14:35	Lukan Doublet	Markan Parallel	Gospel of Thomas
[οὔτε][1] εἰς [γῆν][1] οὔ[τ][1]ε [εἰς κοπρίαν][1] [εὔθετόν ἐστιν][2], ( )[1] ⸉ἔξω⸊[3] β[ά][4]λ[λουσιν][4] ⸉ ⸊[3] [αὐτό][4] ( )[5]. [ὁ ἔχων ὦτα ἀκούειν ἀκουέτω.][6] ⸊Luke 14:34[1]			

[4] Luke's βάλλουσιν αὐτό or Matthew's βληθέν.
[5] Matthew's καταπατεῖσθαι ὑπὸ τῶν ἀνθρώπων.
[6] Luke's ὁ ἔχων ὦτα ἀκούειν ἀκουέτω.

⟦Es ist⟧ weder für die Erde noch für den Misthaufen ⟦brauchbar⟧, man wirft es hinaus.

⟦Il⟧ ne ⟦profite⟧ ni à la terre, ni au fumier; on le jette dehors.

Q 15:4-5a, ~~5b-6~~, 7, ⟦8-10⟧ is to be found below, between Q 17:1-2 and Q 17:3-4.

Q 16:13

Markan Parallel	Matthean Doublet	Matt 6:24	Q 16:13
		[1]⸂	[1]⸂
		Οὐδεὶς [ ][2]	οὐδεὶς [][2]
		δύναται δυσὶ κυρίοις δουλεύειν·	δύναται δυσὶ κυρίοις δουλεύειν·
		ἢ γὰρ τὸν ἕνα μισήσει	ἢ γὰρ τὸν ἕνα μισήσει
		καὶ τὸν ἕτερον ἀγαπήσει,	καὶ τὸν ἕτερον ἀγαπήσει,
		ἢ ἑνὸς ἀνθέξεται	ἢ ἑνὸς ἀνθέξεται
		καὶ τοῦ ἑτέρου καταφρονήσει.	καὶ τοῦ ἑτέρου καταφρονήσει.
		οὐ δύνασθε θεῷ δουλεύειν	οὐ δύνασθε θεῷ δουλεύειν
		καὶ μαμωνᾷ.	καὶ μαμωνᾷ.
		⸃[1]	⸃[1]

The Lukan position: IQP 1989, JSK: {C}; IQP 1995 {D}; between Q 14:35 and 16:16: PH: {C}; JMR: Indeterminate.

[1] The position of Q 16:13 in Q: After Q 15:7, ⟦8-10⟧ and before Q 16:16 (Lukan order); or after Q 11:35 (Matt 6:23) and before Q 12:22b (Matt 6:25) (Matthean order); or a conjectured position between Q 14:35 and Q 16:16.

Q

οὐδεὶς δύναται δυσὶ κυρίοις δουλεύειν· ἢ γὰρ τὸν ἕνα μισήσει καὶ τὸν ἕτερον ἀγαπήσει, ἢ ἑνὸς ἀνθέξεται καὶ τοῦ ἑτέρου καταφρονήσει. οὐ δύνασθε θεῷ δουλεύειν καὶ μαμωνᾷ.

Nobody can serve two masters; for a person will either hate the one and love the other, or be devoted to the one and despise the other. You cannot serve God and Mammon.

Gos. Thom. 47.2 (Nag Hammadi II 2)

καὶ οὐ δύναται δοῦλος[1] δυσὶ κυρίοις λατρεύειν. ἢ τὸν ἕνα τιμήσει καὶ τὸν ἕτερον ὑβρίσει.

And it is not possible that a slave serve two masters. Either[2] he will honor the one and insult the other.

[1] Or: οἰκέτης.

[2] One could also read: Or else....

Q 16:13

Luke 16:13	Lukan Doublet	2 Clem. 6.1	*Gos. Thom.* 47.2
1⸤		Λέγει δὲ ὁ κύριος·	
Οὐδεὶς [οἰκέτης]2		Οὐδεὶς οἰκέτης	ⲁⲩⲱ
δύναται δυσὶ κυρίοις δουλεύειν·		δύναται δυσὶ κυρίοις δουλεύειν.	ⲙⲛ̄ ϭⲟⲙ’ ⲛ̄ⲧⲉ ⲟⲩϩⲙϩ̄ⲁ̄ⲗ̄
ἢ γὰρ τὸν ἕνα μισήσει			ϣⲙ̄ϣⲉ ϫⲟⲉⲓⲥ ⲥⲛⲁⲩ
καὶ τὸν ἕτερον ἀγαπήσει,			ⲏ ϥⲛⲁⲣ̄ⲧⲓⲙⲁ ⲙ̄ⲡⲟⲩⲁ’
ἢ ἑνὸς ἀνθέξεται			ⲁⲩⲱ ⲡⲕⲉⲟⲩⲁ
καὶ τοῦ ἑτέρου καταφρονήσει.		ἐὰν ἡμεῖς θέλωμεν	ϥⲛⲁⲣ̄ϩⲩⲃⲣⲓⲍⲉ ⲙ̄ⲙⲟϥ’
οὐ δύνασθε θεῷ δουλεύειν		καὶ θεῷ δουλεύειν	
καὶ μαμωνᾷ.		καὶ μαμωνᾷ,	
⸥1		ἀσύμφορον ἡμῖν ἐστίν.	

IQP 1989: ⟦[]2⟧.

2 Luke's οἰκέτης.

Keiner kann zwei Herren dienen; denn entweder wird er den einen hassen und den anderen lieben, oder er wird dem einen anhängen und den anderen verachten. Ihr könnt nicht Gott dienen und «dem» Mammon.

Personne ne peut servir deux maîtres; car soit il haïra l'un et aimera l'autre, soit il s'attachera à l'un et méprisera l'autre. Vous ne pouvez pas servir Dieu et Mammon.

Und es ist nicht möglich, dass ein Knecht zwei Herren dient. Entweder[3] wird er den einen ehren und den anderen wird er schmähen.

3 Oder man kann lesen: Sonst wird er….

Et il n'est pas possible qu'un esclave serve deux maîtres. Ou bien[4] il honorera l'un, et il outragera l'autre.

4 On pourrait aussi lire: Sinon….

Q 16:16

Markan Parallel	Matthean Doublet	Matt 11:12-13	Q 16:16
		[1]⸂	[1]⸂
		11:12 ⸂ ⸃[2]	[2]⸂
			[3]⸂ὁ ( )[4] νόμος⸃[3]
			καὶ
			[3]⸂ ()[5]
			οἱ προφῆται⸃[3]
			⟦(ἕως)[6]⟧
			Ἰωάννου ()[7]·
			()[8]
			⸃[2]
		ἀπὸ (δὲ τῶν ἡμερῶν Ἰωάννου)[9]	ἀπὸ [τότε][9]
		(τοῦ βαπτιστοῦ)[7]	()[7]
		(ἕως ἄρτι)[10]	()[10]
		ἡ βασιλεία τ(ῶν οὐρανῶν)[11]	ἡ βασιλεία τ[οῦ θεοῦ][11]
		(βιά)[12]ζεται	(βιά)[12]ζεται
		καὶ ⸂βια(σ)[13]ταὶ⸃[13]	καὶ ⸂βια(σ)[13]ταὶ⸃[13]
		(ἁρπάζουσιν)[13] αὐτήν ⸂ ⸃[13].	(ἁρπάζουσιν)[13] αὐτήν ⸂⸃[13].
		11:13 [2]⸂	⸂⸃[2]
		[3]⸂ (πάντες)[5]	
		(γὰρ)[4] οἱ προφῆται⸃[3]	
		καὶ	
		⸂ὁ νόμος⸃[3]	
		(ἕως)[6]	
		Ἰωάννου	
		(ἐπροφήτευσαν)[8].	
		⸃[2]	
		⸃[1]	⸃[1]

IQP 1993: The position of Q **16:16** is between Q **16:13** and Q **16:17** {D}; PH, JSK: {C}; IQP 1995, JMR: The position of Q **16:16(-18)** is indeterminate.
IQP 1993, 1995: The position of the law and the prophets is at the beginning (Luke) {C}; JMR, PH {B}; JSK: at the end (Matthew) {B}.
IQP 1993, 1995: ὁ νόμος precedes οἱ προφῆται {C}; JMR, PH: {B}; JSK: οἱ προφῆται precedes ὁ νόμος {B}.
IQP 1993: ⟦()[4]⟧; IQP 1995, JMR, JSK: ( )[4], indeterminate; PH: ()[4].

[1] The position of Q 16:16 in Q: After Q 16:13 and before Q 16:17 (Lukan order); or after Q 7:28 (Matt 11:11) and before Q 7:31 (Matt 11:16) (Matthean order).

[2] The position of the reference of scripture in relation to John: at the beginning (Luke) or end (Matthew) of the saying.

[3] The position of ὁ νόμος before (Luke) or after (Matthew) οἱ προφῆται.

[4] Matthew's γάρ.

[5] Matthew's πάντες.

[6] Luke's μέχρι or Matthew's ἕως.

Q 16:16

Luke 16:16	Lukan Doublet	Markan Parallel	Justin, *Dial.* 51.3a
^{1}⸂			
^{2}⸂			
^{3}⸂Ὁ ( )^{4} νόμος⸃^{3}			Ὁ νόμος
καὶ			καὶ
^{3}⸂ ( )^{5}			
οἱ προφῆται⸃^{3}			οἱ προφῆται
[μέχρι]^{6}			μέχρι
Ἰωάννου ( )^{7}·			Ἰωάννου τοῦ βαπτιστοῦ.
( )^{8}			
⸃^{2}			
ἀπὸ [τότε]^{9}			ἐξ ὅτου
( )^{7}			
( )^{10}			
ἡ βασιλεία τ[οῦ θεοῦ]^{11}			ἡ βασιλεία τῶν οὐρανῶν
[εὐαγγελί]^{12}ζεται			βιάζεται
καὶ ⸂ ⸃^{13} [πᾶς εἰς]^{13}			καὶ βιασταὶ
αὐτὴν ⸂βιά[ζε]^{13}ται⸃^{13}.			ἁρπάζουσιν αὐτήν·
⸂ ⸃^{2}			
⸃^{1}			⸃^{1}

IQP 1995: ⟦()^{5}⟧.
IQP 1993: [ ]^{6}; IQP 1995: ⟦[μέχρι]^{6}⟧.
IQP 1995: ⟦()^{7}⟧.
IQP 1993: ⟦()^{8}⟧.

IQP 1993: ἀπὸ ⟦[τότε]^{9}⟧; PH: ἀπὸ ⟦(δὲ τῶν ἡμερῶν Ἰωάννου)^{9}⟧; JSK: ἀπὸ (δὲ τῶν ἡμερῶν Ἰωάννου)^{9}, but if the position of the law and the prophets is at the beginning (Luke), then ἀπὸ [τότε]^{9}.
IQP 1993, PH: ⟦()^{10}⟧.

7 Matthew's τοῦ βαπτιστοῦ.
8 Matthew's ἐπροφήτευσαν.
9 Luke's τότε or Matthew's δὲ τῶν ἡμερῶν Ἰωάννου. The decision is influenced by variation unit ^{2}.
10 Matthew's ἕως ἄρτι.

11 Luke's τοῦ θεοῦ or Matthew's τῶν οὐρανῶν.
12 Luke's εὐαγγελίζεται or Matthew's βιάζεται.
13 Luke's πᾶς εἰς αὐτὴν βιάζεται or Matthew's βιασταὶ ἁρπάζουσιν αὐτήν. The position of the verb after (Luke) or before (Matthew) αὐτήν.

Q 16:16

Markan Parallel	Matthean Doublet	Matt 11:12-13	Q 16:16

Q

ὁ .. νόμος καὶ οἱ προφῆται ⟦ἕως⟧ Ἰωάννου· ἀπὸ τότε ἡ βασιλεία τοῦ θεοῦ βιάζεται καὶ βιασταὶ ἁρπάζουσιν αὐτήν.	.. The law and the prophets «were» until John. From then on the kingdom of God is violated and the violent plunder it.

Q 16:16

Luke 16:16	**Lukan Doublet**	**Markan Parallel**	**Justin, *Dial.* 51.3a**

.. Das Gesetz und die Propheten «sind» bis Johannes. Von da an erleidet das Reich Gottes Gewalt, und Gewalttäter rauben es.	.. La loi et les prophètes «vont» jusqu'à Jean. Depuis lors, le royaume de Dieu est violenté et ce sont des violents qui le pillent.

Q 16:17

Mark 13:30a, 31, 30b	Matt 24:34a, 35, 34b	Matt 5:18	Q 16:17
		¹ʃ	¹ʃ
13:30a Ἀμὴν λέγω ὑμῖν	**24:34a** {(ἀμὴν) (λέγω ὑμῖν)	({ἀμὴν} γὰρ {λέγω ὑμῖν})²·	()²
ὅτι οὐ μὴ	ὅτι οὐ μὴ	(ἕως ἂν)³	⟦[εὐκοπώτερον δέ ἐστιν]³
παρέλθῃ	(παρέλθῃ)	⁴ʃ {παρέλ}θ(ῃ)³ ˥⁴	ʃ ˥⁴
ἡ γενεὰ αὕτη	ἡ γενεὰ αὕτη}		
13:31 ὁ οὐρανὸς	**24:35** {(ὁ [οὐρανὸ]ς	{(ὁ)³ οὐρανὸ(ς)³	[τὸν]³⟧ {οὐρανὸ}⟦[ν]³⟧
καὶ	[καὶ]	καὶ	{καὶ}
ἡ γῆ	ἡ [γῆ])	(ἡ)³ γῆ}[ ]³	⟦[τὴν]³⟧ {γῆ}⟦[ν]³⟧
παρελεύσονται,	([παρελ])εύσ}ε{ται,	ʃ ˥⁴,	⁴ʃ {παρελ}θ⟦[εῖν]³ ˥⁴
		[ ]³	[ἢ]³
		(ἰῶτα ἓν ἢ)⁵	(ἰῶτα ἓν ἢ)⁵⟧
		ʃ ˥⁶	ʃ ˥⁶
οἱ δὲ λόγοι μου	οἱ δὲ λόγοι μου	μία[ ]³ κεραία[ ]³	μία⟦[ν]³⟧ κεραία⟦[ν]³
			⁶ʃ ()⁷⟧ τοῦ νόμου˥⁶
οὐ μὴ παρελεύσονται.	(οὐ μὴ παρέλ}θ)ωσιν.	{(οὐ μὴ παρέλ}θ)⁸(ῃ)³	⟦[πεσ]⁸[εῖν]³
		⁶ʃ (ἀπὸ)⁷ τοῦ νόμου˥⁶,	ʃ ˥⁶⟧
13:30b μέχρις οὗ	**24:34b** (ἕως ἂν	(ἕως ἂν	()⁹.
ταῦτα πάντα γένηται.	{πάντα)} {ταῦτα} {(γένηται)}.	{πάντα} {γένηται})⁹.	
		˥¹	˥¹

IQP 1989, IQP 1995: Q **16:17** is between Q **16:16** and Q **16:18** {C}; JMR, PH: {B}; JSK: {A}.
IQP 1989: Variation units ³ and ⁴, Luke = Q {B}; PH: Matt = Q {C}.

PH: ⟦(ἕως ἂν)³⟧ ⁴ʃ {παρέλ}θ⟦(ῃ)³ ˥⁴ {(ὁ)³⟧ οὐρανὸ⟦(ς)³⟧ καὶ ⟦(ἡ)³⟧ γῆ}⟦[]³ ʃ ˥⁴, []³ (ἰῶτα ἓν ἢ)⁵⟧ ʃ ˥⁶ μία⟦[]³⟧ κεραία⟦[]³ {(οὐ μὴ παρέλ}θῃ)⁸ ⁶ʃ (ἀπὸ)⁷⟧ τοῦ νόμου˥⁶.

¹ The position of Q 16:17 in Q: After Q 16:16 and before Q 16:18 (Lukan order); or after Q 11:33 (Matt 5:15) and before Q 12:58 (Matt 5:25) (Matthean order).

² Matthew's ἀμὴν γὰρ λέγω ὑμῖν.

³ Luke's εὐκοπώτερον δέ ἐστιν … παρελθεῖν ἢ … -εῖν with the accusative or Matthew's ἕως ἂν παρέλθῃ … -ῃ with the nominative.

Q

⟦εὐκοπώτερον δέ ἐστιν τὸν⟧ οὐρανὸ⟦ν⟧ καὶ ⟦τὴν⟧ γῆ⟦ν⟧ παρελθ⟦εῖν ἢ ἰῶτα ἓν ἢ⟧ μία⟦ν⟧ κεραία⟦ν⟧ τοῦ νόμου ⟦πεσεῖν⟧.	⟦But it is easier for⟧ heaven and earth ⟦to⟧ pass away ⟦than for one iota or⟧ one serif of the law ⟦to fall⟧.

Q 16:17

Luke 16:17	Luke 21:32a, 33, 32b	Mark 13:30a, 31, 30b	Gospel of Thomas
⸂[1]			
( )[2]	**21:32a** {(ἀμὴν) (λέγω ὑμῖν)	**13:30a** Ἀμὴν λέγω ὑμῖν	
[εὐκοπώτερον δέ ἐστιν][3]	ὅτι οὐ μὴ	ὅτι οὐ μὴ	
⸂ ⸃[4]	παρέλθῃ	παρέλθῃ	
	ἡ γενεὰ αὕτη}	ἡ γενεὰ αὕτη	
[τὸν][3] {οὐρανὸ}[ν][3]	**21:33**{([ὁ] [οὐρανὸ]ς	**13:31** ὁ οὐρανὸς	
{καὶ}	[καὶ]	καὶ	
[τὴν][3] {γῆ}[ν][3]	[ἡ] [γῆ])	ἡ γῆ	
[4]⸂ {παρελ}θ[εῖν][3] ⸃[4]	[(παρελ)]εύσονται,	παρελεύσονται,	
[ἢ][3]			
( )[5]			
[6]⸂ ( )[7] τοῦ νόμου⸃[6]			
μία[ν][3] κεραία[ν][3] ( )[3]	οἱ δὲ λόγοι μου	οἱ δὲ λόγοι μου	
[πεσ][8][εῖν][3]	(οὐ μὴ παρελ)εύσονται.}	οὐ μὴ παρελεύσονται.	
⸂ ⸃[6]			
( )[9].	**21:32b** (ἕως ἂν	**13:30b** μέχρις οὗ	
	{πάντα γένηται}).	ταῦτα πάντα γένηται.	
⸃[1]			

IQP 1989: [6]⸂ ()[7] τοῦ νόμου ⸃[6] μίαν κεραίαν ⸂ ⸃[6].
IQP 1989, 1995: ( )[7] not in Q {D}; PH: ⟦(ἀπὸ)[7]⟧.

IQP 1989: Variation unit [8]: The choice between πίπτω and παρέρχομαι is indeterminate.

[4] The position of παρελθ- after (Luke) or before (Matthew) "heaven and earth."
[5] Matthew's ἰῶτα ἓν ἤ.
[6] The position of τοῦ νόμου (Luke) or ἀπὸ τοῦ νόμου (Matthew).
[7] Matthew's ἀπό.
[8] Luke's πεσεῖν or Matthew's οὐ μὴ παρέλθῃ.
[9] Matthew's ἕως ἂν πάντα γένηται.

⟦Es ist aber leichter, dass⟧ der Himmel und die Erde vergehen, ⟦als dass ein Jota oder⟧ ein Häkchen des Gesetzes ⟦fällt⟧.

⟦Mais il est plus facile au⟧ ciel et ⟦à⟧ la terre de passer ⟦qu'à un iota ou⟧ à un serif de la Loi de ⟦tomber⟧.

Q 16:18

Mark 10:11-12	Matt 19:9	Matt 5:32	Q 16:18
		[0]{	[0]{
		[1]⸂	[1]⸂
10:11 καὶ λέγει αὐτοῖς·	({λέγ}ω) (δὲ) (ὑμῖν ὅτι)	**5:32** (ἐγὼ δὲ {λέγ}ω ὑμῖν ὅτι)[2]	()[2]
ὃς ἂν ἀπολύσῃ	{ὃς ἂν [(ἀπολύ)]σῃ[3]	πᾶς ὁ {ἀπολύ}ων	πᾶς ὁ {ἀπολύ}ων
τὴν γυναῖκα αὐτοῦ	[(τὴν γυναῖκα αὐτοῦ)]}	{τὴν γυναῖκα αὐτοῦ}	{τὴν γυναῖκα αὐτοῦ
	μὴ ἐπὶ (πορνείᾳ)	(παρεκτὸς λόγου πορνείας)[3]	()[3]
καὶ γαμήσῃ ἄλλην	[{καὶ γαμ]ήσῃ ἄλλην	[ ][4]	⟦[καὶ γαμ}ῶν <{ἄλλην}>][4]⟧
		(ποιεῖ {αὐτὴν})[5]	()[5]
μοιχᾶται ἐπ' αὐτήν·	[(μοιχ)]ᾶται}.	{μοιχ}ευ(θῆναι)[5],	{μοιχ}εύ[ει][5],
10:12 καὶ ἐὰν αὐτὴ		{καὶ} (ὃς {ἐὰν})[6]	{καὶ} [ὁ][6]
ἀπολύσασα		{ἀπο}λε{λυ}μένην	{ἀπο}λε{λυ}μένην
τὸν ἄνδρα αὐτῆς		[{ }][7]	[{}][7]
γαμήσῃ ἄλλον		{γαμ(ήσῃ)}[6],	{γαμ}[ῶν][6]
μοιχᾶται.		{μοιχ(ᾶται)}[8].	{μοιχ}⟦[εύει]⟧[8].
		⸃[1]	⸃[1]
		}[0]	}[0]

IQP 1989, JMR, PH, JSK: The Lukan position {B}; IQP 1995: {C}.

IQP 1989, 1995: [{}][4] ⟦({})[5]⟧ {μοιχ}εύ⟦[ει][5]⟧.

[0] Is Luke 16:18 par. Matt 5:32 in Q or from Mark?

[1] The position of Q 16:18 in Q: After Q 16:17 and before Q 17:1 (Lukan order); or after Q 12:59 (Matt 5:26) and before Q 6:29 (Matt 5:39) (Matthean order).

[2] Matthew's ἐγὼ δὲ λέγω ὑμῖν ὅτι.

[3] Matthew's παρεκτὸς λόγου πορνείας.

Q

πᾶς ὁ ἀπολύων τὴν γυναῖκα αὐτοῦ ⟦καὶ γαμῶν <ἄλλην>⟧ μοιχεύει, καὶ ὁ ἀπολελυμένην γαμῶν μοιχ⟦εύει⟧.

Everyone who divorces his wife ⟦and marries another⟧ commits adultery, and the one who marries a divorcée commits adultery.

Q 16:18

Luke 16:18	1 Cor 7:10-11	Mark 10:11-12	Herm. Man. 4.1.6c
[0]{	**7:10** Τοῖς δὲ γεγαμηκόσιν		
[1]⸀	παραγγέλλω,		
( )[2]	οὐκ ἐγὼ ἀλλὰ ὁ κύριος,	**10:11** καὶ λέγει αὐτοῖς·	
Πᾶς ὁ {ἀπολύ}ων	γυναῖκα ἀπὸ ἀνδρὸς	ὃς ἂν ἀπολύσῃ	ἐὰν δὲ ἀπολύσας
{τὴν γυναῖκα αὐτοῦ	μὴ χωρισθῆναι,	τὴν γυναῖκα αὐτοῦ	τὴν γυναῖκα
( )[3]			
[καὶ γαμ}ῶν ἑτέραν][4]		καὶ γαμήσῃ ἄλλην	ἑτέραν γαμήσῃ,
({ })[5]			καὶ αὐτὸς
{μοιχ}εύ[ει][5],	**7:11** - ἐὰν δὲ καὶ χωρισθῇ,	μοιχᾶται ἐπ' αὐτήν·	μοιχᾶται.
{καὶ} [ὁ][6]	μενέτω ἄγαμος	**10:12** καὶ ἐὰν αὐτὴ	
{ἀπο}λε{λυ}μένην	ἢ τῷ ἀνδρὶ καταλλαγήτω, -	ἀπολύσασα	
[ἀπὸ {ἀνδρ}ὸς][7]	καὶ ἄνδρα γυναῖκα	τὸν ἄνδρα αὐτῆς	
{γαμ}[ῶν][6]	μὴ ἀφιέναι.	γαμήσῃ ἄλλον	
{μοιχ}[εύει][8].		μοιχᾶται.	
⸁[1]			
}[0]			

IQP 1989, 1995: ⟦[ὁ][6]⟧ {ἀπο}λε{λυ}μένην ⟦[{}][7]⟧ {γαμ}⟦[ῶν][6]⟧ {μοιχ}[ ][8].

[4] Luke's καὶ γαμῶν ἑτέραν.
[5] Luke's μοιχεύει, or Matthew's ποιεῖ αὐτὴν μοιχευθῆναι.
[6] Luke's ὁ … γαμῶν or Matthew's ὃς ἐὰν … γαμήσῃ.
[7] Luke's ἀπὸ ἀνδρός.
[8] Luke's μοιχεύει or Matthew's μοιχᾶται.

Jeder, der seine Frau entlässt ⟦und eine andere heiratet⟧, begeht Ehebruch, und wer eine Entlassene heiratet, begeht Ehebruch.

Quiconque répudie sa femme ⟦et en épouse une autre⟧ commet un adultère et celui qui épouse une répudiée commet un adultère.

Q 17:1

Markan Parallel	Matthean Doublet	Matt 18:7	Q 17:1
		[0]/	[0]/
		[1]ʃ	[1]ʃ
		[ ][2]	[][2]
		(Οὐαὶ τῷ κόσμῳ ἀπὸ τῶν σκανδάλων·)[3]	()[3]
		(ἀνάγκη)[4]	(ἀνάγκη)[4]
		(γὰρ)[3]	()[3]
		ʃἐλθεῖνʅ[5]	ʃἐλθεῖνʅ[5]
		τὰ σκάνδαλα [ ][4],	τὰ σκάνδαλα [][4],
		ʃ ʅ[5]	ʃ ʅ[5]
		πλὴν οὐαὶ	πλὴν οὐαὶ
		(τῷ ἀνθρώπῳ)[6] δι᾽ οὗ	⟦()[6]⟧ δι᾽ οὗ
		(τὸ σκάνδαλον)[7] ἔρχεται.	⟦()[7]⟧ ἔρχεται.
		ʅ[1]	ʅ[1]
		\[0]	\[0]

IQP 1990: < >[2] {D}.

IQP 1990: ()[7].

[0] Is Luke 17:1 par. Matt 18:7 in Q?

[1] The position of Q 17:1: After Q 16:18 and before Q 17:2 (Lukan order); or after Q 17:2 (Matt 18:6) and before Q 15:4 (Matt 18:12) (Matthean order).

[2] Luke's εἶπεν δὲ πρὸς τοὺς μαθητὰς αὐτοῦ·.

[3] Matthew's οὐαὶ τῷ κόσμῳ ἀπὸ τῶν σκανδάλων· ... γάρ.

[4] Luke's ἀνένδεκτόν ἐστιν τοῦ ... μή or Matthew's ἀνάγκη.

Q

ἀνάγκη ἐλθεῖν τὰ σκάνδαλα, πλὴν οὐαὶ δι᾽ οὗ ἔρχεται.

It is necessary for enticements to come, but woe «to the one» through whom they come!

Q 17:1

Luke 17:1	Lukan Doublet	Markan Parallel	1 Clem. 46.8a
⁰/			
¹⸉			
[Εἶπεν δὲ πρὸς τοὺς μαθητὰς αὐτοῦ·][2]			εἶπεν γάρ·
( )[3]			
[ἀνένδεκτόν ἐστιν τοῦ][4]			
( )[3]			
⸉ ⸊⁵			
τὰ σκάνδαλα [μὴ][4]			
⸉ἐλθεῖν⸊⁵,			
πλὴν οὐαὶ			Οὐαὶ
( )[6] δι' οὗ			τῷ ἀνθρώπῳ ἐκείνῳ·
( )[7] ἔρχεται·			
⸊¹			
\⁰			

[5] The position of ἐλθεῖν after (Luke) or before (Matthew) τὰ σκάνδαλα.

[6] Matthew's τῷ ἀνθρώπῳ.

[7] Matthew's τὸ σκάνδαλον.

Es ist notwendig, dass Verführungen kommen, aber wehe «dem», durch den sie kommen!

Il est nécessaire que les scandales arrivent, mais malheur «à celui» par qui ils arrivent.

Q 17:2

Mark 9:42	Matthean Doublet	Matt 18:6	Q 17:2
		[0]{	[0]{
		[1]ʃ	[1]ʃ
		ʃ ʅ[2]	[2]ʃ [λυσιτελεῖ][3]
			{αὐτῷ} ⟦{[εἰ]}[4]⟧
			[5]ʃ [λίθος {μυλ}{ικὸς}][6] ʅ[5]
			[{περίκειται}][7]
			ʃ ʅ[5]
			{περὶ τὸν τράχηλον αὐτοῦ
			καὶ} [ἔρριπ{ται}][8]
			[εἰς τὴν][9]
			θάλασσ[αν]}[9] ʅ[2]
Καὶ ὃς ἂν		({῞Ος} δ᾽ {ἂν})[10]	[ἢ ἵνα][10]
σκανδαλίσῃ		{σκανδαλίσῃ	{σκανδαλίσῃ}
ἕνα		ʃἕναʅ[11]	ʃ ʅ[11]
τῶν μικρῶν τούτων		τῶν μικρῶν τούτων	{τῶν μικρῶν τούτων}
		ʃ ʅ[11]	ʃ {ἕνα} ʅ[11]
τῶν πιστευόντων εἰς ἐμέ,		(τῶν πιστευόντων εἰς ἐμέ})[12],	({})[12]
καλόν ἐστιν		[2]ʃ (συμφέρει)[3]	ʃ ʅ[2]
αὐτῷ μᾶλλον εἰ		{αὐτῷ} (ἵνα)[4]	
		ʃ ʅ[5]	
περίκειται		(κρεμασθῇ)[7]	
μύλος ὀνικὸς		[5]ʃ {(μύλος ὀνικὸς)[6] ʅ[5]	
περὶ τὸν τράχηλον αὐτοῦ		περὶ τὸν τράχηλον αὐτοῦ	
καὶ βέβληται		καὶ} (καταποντισθῇ)[8]	
εἰς		(ἐν τῷ πελάγει)[9]	
τὴν θάλασσαν.		{τ}ῆ(ς)[9] {θαλάσσ}(ης)[9] ʅ[2].	.
		ʅ[1]	ʅ[1]
		}[0]	}[0]

PH: Q 17:2 is in Q {C}.
PH: The order of the two clauses: Matt = Q {B}; IQP 1990: Luke = Q {A}; JMR, JSK: Luke = Q {C}.

PH: ⟦<{καλόν ἐστιν}>[3]⟧.
IQP 1990: ({μύλος ὀνικός})[6]; PH: ⟦({μύλος ὀνικός})[6]⟧.

0 Is Luke 17:2 par. Matt 18:6 in Q or from Mark?
1 Is Q 17:2 after (Luke) or before (Matthew) Q 17:1?
2 The converse order of the two clauses.
3 Luke's λυσιτελεῖ or Matthew's συμφέρει.
4 Luke's εἰ with the indicative or Matthew's ἵνα with the subjunctive.
5 The position of "millstone" before (Luke) or after (Matthew) the verb.
6 Luke's λίθος μυλικός or Matthew's μύλος ὀνικός.
7 The choice of verbs: Luke's περίκειμαι or Matthew's κρεμάννυμαι.

Q 17:2

Luke 17:2	Lukan Doublet	Mark 9:42b, a	1 Clem. 46.8b-c
[0]{			
[1]ʃ			
[2]ʃ [λυσιτελεῖ][3]		**9:42b** καλόν ἐστιν	καλὸν ἦν
{αὐτῷ} {[εἰ]}[4]		αὐτῷ μᾶλλον εἰ	αὐτῷ, εἰ οὐκ ἐγεννήθη,
[5]ʃ [λίθος {μυλ}{ικὸς}][6] ≀[5]		περίκειται	ἢ ἕνα τῶν ἐκλεκτῶν μου
[{περίκειται}][7]		μύλος ὀνικὸς	σκανδαλίσαι·
ʃ ≀[5]			κρεῖττον ἦν αὐτῷ
{περὶ τὸν τράχηλον αὐτοῦ		περὶ τὸν τράχηλον αὐτοῦ	περιτεθῆναι μύλον
καὶ} [ἔρριπ{ται}][8]		καὶ βέβληται	καὶ καταποντισθῆναι
[εἰς][9] τὴ[ν][9]		εἰς τὴν	εἰς τὴν
θάλασσ[αν]}[9] ≀[2]		θάλασσαν.	θάλασσαν,
[ἢ ἵνα][10]		**9:42a** Καὶ ὃς ἂν	
{σκανδαλίσῃ}		σκανδαλίσῃ	
ʃ ≀[11]		ἕνα	ἢ ἕνα
{τῶν μικρῶν τούτων}		τῶν μικρῶν τούτων	τῶν ἐκλεκτῶν μου
ʃ {ἕνα} ≀[11]			διαστρέψαι.
({ })[12]		τῶν πιστευόντων εἰς ἐμέ,	
ʃ ≀[2]			
.			
≀[1]			
}[0]			

PH: ⟦<{βέβληται}>[8]⟧.
IQP 1990: ⟦[εἰς τὴν][9]⟧ θάλασσ⟦[αν}][9]⟧.

PH: ⟦({ὃς} δ' {ἄν})[10]⟧.
PH: ʃἕνα≀[11] τῶν μικρῶν τούτων ʃ ≀[11].

[8] Luke's ῥίπτομαι or Matthew's καταποντίζομαι.

[9] Luke's εἰς τὴν θάλασσαν or Matthew's ἐν τῷ πελάγει τῆς θαλάσσης.

[10] Luke's ἢ ἵνα or Matthew's ὃς δ' ἄν.

[11] The position of ἕνα after (Luke) or before (Matthew) τῶν μικρῶν τούτων.

[12] Matthew's τῶν πιστευόντων εἰς ἐμέ.

Q 17:2

Mark 9:42	Matthean Doublet	Matt 18:6	Q 17:2

Q

λυσιτελεῖ αὐτῷ ⟦εἰ⟧ λίθος μυλικὸς περίκειται περὶ τὸν τράχηλον αὐτοῦ καὶ ἔρριπται εἰς τὴν θάλασσαν ἢ ἵνα σκανδαλίσῃ τῶν μικρῶν τούτων ἕνα.

It is better for him ⟦if⟧ a millstone is put around his neck and he is thrown into the sea, than that he should entice one of these little ones.

Q 17:3-4 is to be found below, between Q 15:4-5a, ~~5b-6~~, 7, ⟦8-10⟧ and Q 17:6.

Q 17:2

Luke 17:2	Lukan Doublet	Mark 9:42b, a	Gospel of Thomas

Es ist besser für ihn, ⟦wenn⟧ ein Mühlstein um seinen Hals gelegt und er in das Meer geworfen wird, als dass er von diesen Kleinen einen verführt.	Il vaut mieux pour lui d'avoir une pierre meulière passée à son cou et d'être jeté à la mer que d'être une occasion de scandale pour l'un de ces petits.

Q 17:3-4 is to be found below, between Q 15:4-5a, ~~5b-6~~, 7, ⟦8-10⟧ and Q 17:6.

Q 15:4-5a, ~~5b-6~~, 7

Markan Parallel	Matt 18:10	Matt 18:12-14	Q 15:4-5a, ~~5b-6~~, 7
		[0]/	[0]/
		[1]ʃ	[1]ʃ
		18:12 (Τί ὑμῖν δοκεῖ;)[2]	**15:4** ()[2]
		(ἐὰν γένηταί)[3]	()[3]
		τι(νι)[3] ἀνθρώπ(ῳ)[3]	τί[ς][3] < >[3] ἄνθρωπ[ος
		[ ][3]	ἐξ ὑμῶν][3] < >[3] [ἔχ][3]< >[3]
		ἑκατὸν πρόβατα	ἑκατὸν πρόβατα
		καὶ (πλανηθῇ)[4]	καὶ ⟦[ἀπολέσας][4]⟧
		ʃἓνʅ[5] ἐξ αὐτῶν ʃ ʅ[5],	ʃἓνʅ[5] ἐξ αὐτῶν ʃ ʅ[5],
		οὐ(χὶ)[6]	οὐ⟦(χὶ)[6]
		(ἀφήσ)[7]ει	(ἀφήσ)[7]⟧ει
		τὰ ἐνενήκοντα ἐννέα	τὰ ἐνενήκοντα ἐννέα
		(ἐπὶ τὰ ὄρη)[8]	⟦(ἐπὶ τὰ ὄρη)[8]⟧
		καὶ πορευ(θεὶς ζητεῖ)[9]	καὶ πορευ⟦(θεὶς ζητεῖ)[9]⟧
		τὸ (πλανώμενον)[4]	τὸ ⟦[ἀπολωλός][4]⟧
		[ ][9]	[][9]
		ʃ ʅ[10];	ʃʅ[10];
		18:13 καὶ (ἐὰν γένηται)[10]	**15:5a** καὶ (ἐὰν γένηται)[10]
		εὑρ(εῖν)[10] ʃαὐτόʅ[10],	εὑρ(εῖν)[10] ʃαὐτόʅ[10],
		[ ][11]	**15:~~5b~~** [][11]
			15:~~6~~ [][11]

[0] Is Luke 15:4-7 par. Matt 18:12-14 in Q?

[1] The position of Q 15:4-10 in Q: After Q 14:35 and before Q 16:13 (Lukan order); or (Q 15:4-7 only) after Q 17:2, 1 (Matt 18:6-7) and before Q 17:3 (Matt 18:15) (Matthean order).

[2] Matthew's τί ὑμῖν δοκεῖ;

[3] Luke's τίς ἄνθρωπος ἐξ ὑμῶν ἔχων or Matthew's ἐὰν γένηταί τινι ἀνθρώπῳ.

[4] Luke's ἀπολέσας ... ἀπολωλός or Matthew's πλανηθῇ ... πλανώμενον. (See ἀπόληται in Matt 18:14.)

[5] The position of ἕν after (Luke) or before (Matthew) ἐξ αὐτῶν.

Q 15:4-5a, ~~5b-6~~, 7

Luke 15:4-7	Luke 15:8-10	Markan Parallel	*Gos. Thom.* 107
[0]/			
[1]ʃ			
15:4 ( )[2]	**15:8**		107.1 ⲡⲉϫⲉ ⲓ̅ⲥ̅ ϫⲉ
( )[3]	"Η		ⲧⲙⲛ̅ⲧⲉⲣⲟ ⲉⲥⲧⲛ̅ⲧⲱⲛ
τί[ς][3] ἄνθρωπ[ος	[(τί)ς] γυνὴ		ⲉⲩⲣⲱⲙⲉ ⲛ̅ϣⲱⲥ
ἐξ ὑμῶν ἔχων][3]	δραχμὰς [ἔχ]ουσα		ⲉⲩⲛ̅ⲧⲁϥ' ⲙ̅ⲙⲁⲩ
ἑκατὸν πρόβατα	δέκα		ⲛ̅ϣⲉ ⲛ̅ⲉⲥⲟⲟⲩ
καὶ [ἀπολέσας][4]	ἐὰν [ἀπολέσ]ῃ		107.2 ⲁⲟⲩⲁ ⲛ̅ϩⲏⲧⲟⲩ
ʃ ʅ[5] ἐξ αὐτῶν ʃἓνʅ[5]	δραχμὴν μίαν,		ⲥⲱⲣⲙ' ⲉⲡⲛⲟϭ ⲡⲉ
οὐ( )[6]	[(οὐ]χὶ)		
[καταλείπ][7]ει	ἅπτ[(ει)]		ⲁϥⲕⲱ
τὰ ἐνενήκοντα ἐννέα	λύχνον		ⲙ̅ⲡⲥⲧⲉⲯⲓⲧ
[ἐν τῇ ἐρήμῳ][8]	καὶ σαροῖ τὴν οἰκίαν		
καὶ πορεύ[εται ἐπὶ][9]	[(καὶ)] (ζητεῖ)		ⲁϥϣⲓⲛⲉ ⲛ̅ⲥⲁ
τὸ [ἀπολωλὸς][4]	ἐπιμελῶς		ⲡⲓⲟⲩⲁ'
[ἕως εὕρῃ][9]	[ἕως] οὗ [εὕρῃ];		ϣⲁⲛⲧⲉϥϩⲉ
ʃαὐτόʅ[10];			ⲉⲣⲟϥ
15:5a καὶ ( )[10]	**15:9** [(καὶ)		
εὑρ[ὼν][10] ʃ ʅ[10]	(εὑρ)]οῦσα		107.3 ⲛ̅ⲧⲁⲣⲉϥϩⲓⲥⲉ
15:5b [ἐπιτίθησιν			
ἐπὶ τοὺς ὤμους αὐτοῦ			
χαίρων			
15:6 καὶ ἐλθὼν			
εἰς τὸν οἶκον			
συγκαλεῖ τοὺς φίλους	[συγκαλεῖ τ]ὰς [φίλ]ας		
καὶ τοὺς γείτονας	[καὶ] [γείτονας		
λέγων αὐτοῖς·	λέγ]ουσα·		ⲡⲉϫⲁϥ'
συγχάρητέ μοι,	[συγχάρητέ μοι,		
ὅτι εὗρον	ὅτι εὗρον		
τὸ πρόβατόν μου	τ]ὴν δραχμὴν		ⲙ̅ⲡⲉⲥⲟⲟⲩ
τὸ ἀπολωλός.][11]	ἣν [ἀπ][ώλ]εσα.		

[6] Luke's οὐ<κ> or Matthew's οὐχί. (See also οὐχί in Luke 15:8.)

[7] Luke's καταλείπει or Matthew's ἀφήσει.

[8] Luke's ἐν τῇ ἐρήμῳ or Matthew's ἐπὶ τὰ ὄρη.

[9] Luke's πορεύεται ἐπὶ … ἕως εὕρῃ or Matthew's πορευθεὶς ζητεῖ.

[10] Luke's repetitious ἕως εὕρῃ αὐτό; καὶ εὑρὼν and the resultant positioning of αὐτό after the first occurrence of εὑρίσκω, or Matthew's ἐὰν γένηται and single εὑρεῖν followed by αὐτό, parallel to the second Lukan occurrence.

[11] Is Luke 15:5b-6 in Q?

Q 15:4-5a, ~~5b-6~~, 7

Markan Parallel	Matt 18:10	Matt 18:12-14	Q 15:4-5a, ~~5b-6~~, 7
		(ἀμὴν)[12] λέγω ὑμῖν ὅτι	**15:7** ()[12] λέγω ὑμῖν ὅτι
		⸉ ⸊[13]	⸉⸊[13]
		χα(ί)[14]ρ(ει)[14]	χα(ί)[14]ρ(ει)[14]
		ἐπ' (αὐτῷ)[14]	ἐπ' (αὐτῷ)[14]
		(μᾶλλον)[15] ἤ	(μᾶλλον)[15] ἤ
		ἐπὶ (τοῖς)[16]	ἐπὶ (τοῖς)[16]
		ἐνενήκοντα ἐννέα	ἐνενήκοντα ἐννέα
		[ ][17]	[][17]
		(τοῖς μὴ	(τοῖς μὴ
		πεπλανημένοις)[18].	πεπλανημένοις)[18].
	18:10 Ὁρᾶτε	**18:14** ⸉οὕτως⸊[13]	⸉⸊[13]
	μὴ καταφρονήσητε	(οὐκ ἔστιν θέλημα	()[19]
	[(ἑν)]ὸς (τῶν μικρῶν τούτων)·	ἔμπροσθεν τοῦ πατρὸς	
	[(λέγω)] γὰρ [(ὑμῖν ὅτι)]	ὑμῶν τοῦ ἐν οὐρανοῖς	
	οἱ ἄγγελοι αὐτῶν	ἵνα ἀπόληται	
	[ἐν] [οὐραν]οῖς	ἓν τῶν μικρῶν τούτων)[19].	
	διὰ παντὸς βλέπουσι		
	τὸ πρόσωπον		
	(τοῦ πατρός) μου		
	(τοῦ ἐν οὐρανοῖς).		
		⸊[1]	⸊[1]⇒ Q 15:10
		\[0]	\[0]

Q 15:4-5a, ~~5b-6~~, 7, ⟦8-10⟧ is between Q 14:35 and Q 16:13: IQP 1994: {D}; JSK: {C}; Q 15:4-5a, ~~5b-6~~, 7 is between Q 17:1-2 and Q 17:3: JMR, PH: {C}.
IQP 1994: τί[ς][3] ἄνθρωπ[ος ἐξ ὑμῶν ἔχων][3]; JMR, PH, JSK: The conjectural emendations τί[ς][3] <ἐστιν>[3] ἄνθρωπ[ος ἐξ ὑμῶν][3] <ὃς>[3] [ἔχ][3]<ει>[3] are indeterminate.
IQP 1994: ⟦[ἀπολέσας][4]⟧ ... ⟦[ἀπολωλός][4]⟧; JMR: [( )][4]... [( )][4]; JSK: [ἀπολέσας][4]... [ἀπολωλός][4]; PH: ⟦(πλανηθῇ)[4]⟧ ... ⟦(πλανώμενον)[4]⟧.

[12] Matthew's ἀμήν.

[13] Is the position of οὕτως before (Luke) or after (Matthew) the comparison, if in Q at all?

[14] Luke's χαρὰ ἐν τῷ οὐρανῷ ἔσται ἐπὶ ἑνὶ ἁμαρτωλῷ μετανοοῦντι or Matthew's χαίρει ἐπ' αὐτῷ. (See χαίρων also in Luke 15:5; and see οὐκ ἔστιν ... ἐν οὐρανοῖς ... ἓν τῶν μικρῶν τούτων in Matt 18:14.)

[15] Matthew's μᾶλλον.

Text Critical Note (see the discussion in the front matter): Matt 18:11 is absent from ℵ B L* Θ* $f^{1.13}$ 33 892* *pc* e ff[1] sy[s] sa mae bo[pt] Or Eus,

Q 15:4-5a, ~~5b-6~~, 7

Luke 15:4-7	Luke 15:8-10	Markan Parallel	*Gos. Thom.* 107
15:7 ( )[12] λέγω ὑμῖν ὅτι ⸉οὕτως⸊[13] [χα( )[14]ρὰ ἐν τῷ οὐρανῷ ἔσται][14] ἐπ[ὶ ἑνὶ ἁμαρτωλῷ μετανοοῦντι][14] ( )[15] ἢ ἐπὶ ( )[16] ἐνενήκοντα ἐννέα [δικαίοις][17] [οἵτινες οὐ χρείαν ἔχουσιν μετανοίας][18]. ⸉ ⸊[13] ( )[19] ⸊[1]⇒ Luke 15:10 \[0]	**15:10** [οὕτως,] [(λέγω ὑμῖν)], γίνεται [(χα)(ρ)ὰ] ἐνώπιον τῶν ἀγγέλων τοῦ θεοῦ [(ἐπ)ὶ ἑνὶ ἁμαρτωλῷ μετανοοῦντι].		ϫⲉ ϯⲟⲩⲟϣⲕʼ ⲡⲁⲣⲁ ⲡⲥⲧⲉⲯⲓⲧʼ

IQP 1994: ⸉ἓν⸊[5] ἐξ αὐτῶν ⸉ ⸊[5] {D}; JMR, PH, JSK: {C}.
IQP 1994: οὐ<κ>[6].
IQP 1994: [( )][8] καὶ πορεύ⟦[εται ἐπὶ][9]⟧ τὸ ⟦[ἀπολωλὸς][4]⟧ [ἕως εὕρῃ][9] ⸉αὐτό⸊[10]; **15:~~5a~~** ~~καὶ~~ ()[10] ~~εὑρ~~()[10] ⸉⸊[10] **15:~~5b~~** [][11] **15:~~6~~** [][11] **15:7** ⟦()[12]⟧.

IQP 1994: **15:7** οὕτως is in Q, but its position is indeterminate; JMR, PH, JSK: **15:7** οὕτως is not in Q {B}.
IQP 1994: ⟦( )[15]⟧ ἢ ἐπὶ ⟦(τοῖς)[16]⟧ ἐνενήκοντα ἐννέα [][17] ()[18].

16 Matthew's τοῖς.
17 Luke's δικαίοις.
18 Luke's οἵτινες οὐ χρείαν ἔχουσιν μετανοίας or Matthew's τοῖς μὴ πεπλανημένοις.

19 Matthew's οὐκ ἔστιν θέλημα ἔμπροσθεν τοῦ πατρὸς ὑμῶν τοῦ ἐν οὐρανοῖς ἵνα ἀπόληται ἓν τῶν μικρῶν τούτων. (See also Luke 15:8-10.)

but ἦλθεν γὰρ ὁ υἱὸς τοῦ ἀνθρώπου (+ζητῆσαι καὶ (L[mg]) 579 892[c] *al* c sy[h] bo[pt]) σῶσαι τὸ ἀπολωλός is in D L[mg] W Θ[c] 078[vid] *𝔐* lat sy[c.p.h] bo[pt].

Q 15:4-5a, ~~5b-6~~, 7

Markan Parallel	Matthean Doublet	Matt 18:10, 12-14	Q 15:4-5a, ~~5b-6~~, 7

Q

4 τίς < > ἄνθρωπος ἐξ ὑμῶν < > ἔχ< > ἑκατὸν πρόβατα καὶ ⟦ἀπολέσας⟧ ἓν ἐξ αὐτῶν, οὐ⟦χὶ ἀφήσ⟧ει τὰ ἐνενήκοντα ἐννέα ⟦ἐπὶ τὰ ὄρη⟧ καὶ πορευ⟦θεὶς ζητεῖ⟧ τὸ ⟦ἀπολωλός⟧; **5a** καὶ ἐὰν γένηται εὑρεῖν αὐτό, 7 λέγω ὑμῖν ὅτι χαίρει ἐπ' αὐτῷ μᾶλλον ἢ ἐπὶ τοῖς ἐνενήκοντα ἐννέα τοῖς μὴ πεπλανημένοις.

4 Which person «is there» among you «who» has a hundred sheep, ⟦on losing⟧ one of them, ⟦will⟧ not leave the ninety-nine ⟦in the mountains⟧ and go ⟦hunt for⟧ the ⟦lost one⟧? **5a** And if it should happen that he finds it, 7 I say to you that he rejoices over it more than over the ninety-nine that did not go astray.

Gos. Thom. 107 (Nag Hammadi II 2)

(1) Λέγει Ἰησοῦς· ἡ βασιλεία ὁμοία ἐστὶν ἀνθρώπῳ ποιμένι ἔχοντι ἑκατὸν πρόβατα. (2) ἓν ἐν αὐτοῖς, τὸ μέγιστον, ἐπλανήθη. κατέλιπεν τὰ ἐνενήκοντα ἐννέα (καὶ) ἐζήτησεν τὸ ἕν, ἕως εὕρῃ αὐτό. (3) κοπιάσας εἶπεν τῷ προβάτῳ· θέλω[1] σε παρὰ τὰ ἐνενήκοντα ἐννέα.

(1) Jesus says: The kingdom is like a shepherd who has a hundred sheep. (2) One of them went astray, the largest. He left the ninety-nine (and) sought the one until he found it. (3) Exhausted, he said to the sheep: I love you more than the ninety-nine.

[1] Or: εὐδοκῶ.

Q 15:4-5a, ~~5b-6~~, 7

Luke 15:4-7	Luke 15:8-10	Markan Parallel	*Gos. Thom.* 107

4 Welcher Mensch von euch, «der» hundert Schafe hat und eines von ihnen ⟦verliert, wird⟧ nicht die neunundneunzig ⟦in den Bergen⟧ lassen und losgehen und das ⟦Verlorene suchen⟧? **5a** Und wenn es geschieht, dass er es findet, 7 ich sage euch: Er freut sich über dieses mehr als über die neunundneunzig, die sich nicht verirrt haben.

4 Quel homme parmi vous «qui» a cent brebis et ⟦viendrait à perdre⟧ l'une d'entre elles ne laisse⟦ra⟧ pas les quatre-vingt-dix-neuf ⟦dans les montagnes⟧ et partir⟦a à la recherche de⟧ celle qui ⟦est perdue⟧? **5a** Et s'il arrive qu'il la trouve, 7 je vous dis qu'il se réjouit plus pour ⟦elle⟧ que pour les quatre-vingt-dix-neuf qui ne se sont pas égarées.

(1) Jesus spricht: Das Königreich gleicht einem Hirten, der hundert Schafe hat. (2) Eines von ihnen verirrte sich, das größte. Er ließ die neunundneunzig, (und) er suchte nach dem einen, bis er es fand. (3) Nachdem er sich abgeplagt hatte, sprach er zu dem Schaf: Ich liebe dich mehr als die neunundneunzig.

(1) Jésus dit: Le royaume ressemble à un berger qui a cent brebis. (2) L'une d'entre elles se perdit, qui était la plus grosse. Il laissa les quatre-vingt-dix-neuf (et) il chercha l'unique jusqu'à ce qu'il l'eût trouvée. (3) Après avoir peiné, il dit à la brebis: Je t'aime plus que les quatre-vingt-dix-neuf.

Q 15:⟦8-10⟧

Markan Parallel	Matthew 18:10, 12-14	Matthew	Q 15:⟦8-10⟧
	18:10 Ὁρᾶτε μὴ καταφρονήσητε [ἑν]ὸς τῶν μικρῶν τούτων· [λέγω] γὰρ [ὑμῖν] ὅτι οἱ [ἄγγελ]οι αὐτῶν ἐν οὐρανοῖς διὰ παντὸς βλέπουσι τὸ πρόσωπον τοῦ πατρός μου τοῦ ἐν οὐρανοῖς.		
	18:12 Τί ὑμῖν δοκεῖ;	[ ][0]	**15:⟦8⟧** ⟦«[0][[ἢ τίς γυνὴ][1] ʃ ʅ[2] [ἔχουσα][1]
	ἐὰν γένηταί τινι ἀνθρώπῳ ἑκατὸν πρόβατα καὶ πλανηθῇ ἓν ἐξ αὐτῶν, οὐχὶ ἀφήσει τὰ ἐνενήκοντα ἐννέα ἐπὶ τὰ ὄρη καὶ πορευθεὶς ζητεῖ τὸ πλανώμενον;		δέκα ʃδραχμὰςʅ[2] ἐὰν ἀπολέσῃ δραχμὴν μίαν, οὐχὶ ἅπτει λύχνον καὶ σαροῖ τὴν οἰκίαν καὶ ζητεῖ [][3] ἕως [][4] εὕρῃ;⟧
	18:13 καὶ ἐὰν γένηται εὑρεῖν αὐτό,		**15:⟦9⟧** ⟦καὶ εὑροῦσα
			[][5][καλεῖ][5] [τὰς φίλας καὶ γείτονας][6]

IQP 1993: Luke 15:8-10 is not in Q {D}; PH: {B}; IQP 1995: Luke 15:8-10 is in Q {D}; JMR: {C}; JSK: **15:8-9** (emended) {B}, **15:10** (emended) {C}.

[0] Is Luke 15:8-9 in Q?

[1] Does the parable begin ἢ τίς γυνὴ .. ἔχουσα? (See ἐάν with the subjunctive in Matt 18:12.)

[2] Does δραχμάς precede ἔχουσα δέκα (Luke) or (conjecturally) follow δέκα in Q?

Q 15:⟦8-10⟧

Luke 15:8-10	Luke 15:4-7	Markan Parallel	Gospel of Thomas
15:8 [0][			
[Ἢ τίς γυνὴ][1]	**15:4** [τίς] ἄνθρωπος ἐξ ὑμῶν		
⸉δραχμὰς⸊[2] [ἔχουσα][1]	[ἔχ]ων		
δέκα ⸉ ⸊[2]	ἑκατὸν πρόβατα		
ἐὰν ἀπολέσῃ	καὶ [ἀπολέσ]ας		
δραχμὴν μίαν,	ἐξ αὐτῶν ἓν		
οὐχὶ	[οὐ]		
ἅπτει	καταλείπ[ει]		
λύχνον	τὰ ἐνενήκοντα ἐννέα		
καὶ σαροῖ τὴν οἰκίαν	ἐν τῇ ἐρήμῳ		
καὶ ζητεῖ	[καὶ] πορεύεται ἐπὶ		
[ἐπιμελῶς][3]	τὸ ἀπολωλὸς		
ἕως [οὗ][4] εὕρῃ;	[ἕως] [εὕρῃ] αὐτό;		
15:9 καὶ	**15:5** [καὶ		
εὑροῦσα	εὑρ]ὼν		
	ἐπιτίθησιν		
	ἐπὶ τοὺς ὤμους αὐτοῦ		
	χαίρων		
	15:6 καὶ ἐλθὼν		
	εἰς τὸν οἶκον		
[συγκαλεῖ][5]	[συγκαλεῖ		
[τὰς φίλας	τ]οὺς [φίλ]ους		
καὶ γείτονας][6]	[καὶ] τοὺς [γείτονας]		

JSK: The sequence is ⸉ ⸊[2] [ἔχουσα][1] δέκα ⸉δραχμάς⸊[2] {C}.

JSK: ⟦[][3]⟧ ἕως ⟦[][4]⟧.

[3] Luke's ἐπιμελῶς.

[4] Luke's οὗ.

[5] Luke's συγκαλεῖ and συγχάρητέ μοι.

[6] Luke's τὰς φίλας καὶ γείτονας.

Q 15:⟦8-10⟧

Markan Parallel	Matthew 18:10, 12-14	Matthew	Q 15:⟦8-10⟧
	ἀμὴν λέγω ὑμῖν ὅτι χαίρει ἐπ' αὐτῷ μᾶλλον ἢ ἐπὶ τοῖς ἐνενήκοντα ἐννέα τοῖς μὴ πεπλανημένοις. **18:14** οὕτως οὐκ ἔστιν θέλημα ἔμπροσθεν τοῦ πατρὸς ὑμῶν τοῦ ἐν οὐρανοῖς ἵνα ἀπόληται ἓν τῶν μικρῶν τούτων.	 [ ][7] ↷ ⇒ Matt 18:12-14[1]	λέγουσα· [][5][χάρητέ μοι][5], ὅτι εὗρον τὴν δραχμὴν ἣν ἀπώλεσα.][0]»⟧ **15:⟦10⟧** ⟦«[οὕτως, λέγω ὑμῖν, γίνεται χαρὰ <ἔμπροσθεν> τῶν ἀγγέλων][7] [][7] [ἐπὶ ἑνὶ ἁμαρτωλῷ μετανοοῦντι.][7]»⟧ ↷ ⇒ Q 15:4-5a, ~~5b-6~~, 7[1]

[7] Is Luke 15:10 in Q?

Q

⟦8⟧ ⟦«ἢ τίς γυνὴ ἔχουσα δέκα δραχμὰς ἐὰν ἀπολέσῃ δραχμὴν μίαν, οὐχὶ ἅπτει λύχνον καὶ σαροῖ τὴν οἰκίαν καὶ ζητεῖ ἕως εὕρῃ;»⟧ ⟦9⟧ ⟦«καὶ εὑροῦσα καλεῖ τὰς φίλας καὶ γείτονας λέγουσα· χάρητέ μοι, ὅτι εὗρον τὴν δραχμὴν ἣν ἀπώλεσα.»⟧ ⟦10⟧ ⟦«οὕτως, λέγω ὑμῖν, γίνεται χαρὰ <ἔμπροσθεν> τῶν ἀγγέλων ἐπὶ ἑνὶ ἁμαρτωλῷ μετανοοῦντι.»⟧

⟦8⟧ ⟦«Or what woman who has ten coins, if she were to lose one coin, would not light a lamp and sweep the house and hunt until she finds?»⟧ ⟦9⟧ ⟦«And on finding she calls the friends and neighbors, saying: Rejoice with me, for I found the coin which I had lost.»⟧ ⟦10⟧ ⟦«Just so, I tell you, there is joy before the angels over one repenting sinner.»⟧

Q 16:13, 16-18 is above, between Q 14:34-35 and Q 17:1-2.

Q 15:⟦8-10⟧

Luke 15:8-10	Luke 15:4-7	Markan Parallel	Gospel of Thomas
λέγουσα· [συγχάρητέ μοι][5], ὅτι εὗρον τὴν δραχμὴν ἣν ἀπώλεσα.][0] **15:10** [οὕτως, λέγω ὑμῖν, γίνεται χαρὰ ἐνώπιον τῶν ἀγγέλων τοῦ θεοῦ ἐπὶ ἑνὶ ἁμαρτωλῷ μετανοοῦντι.][7] ʅ ⇒ Luke 15:4-7[1]	[λέγ]ων αὐτοῖς· [συγχάρητέ μοι, ὅτι εὗρον τ]ὸ πρόβατόν μου τὸ [ἀπ]ολ[ωλ]ός. **15:7** [λέγω ὑμῖν] ὅτι [οὕτως] [χαρὰ] ἐν τῷ οὐρανῷ ἔσται [ἐπὶ ἑνὶ ἁμαρτωλῷ μετανοοῦντι] ἢ ἐπὶ ἐνενήκοντα ἐννέα δικαίοις οἵτινες οὐ χρείαν ἔχουσιν μετανοίας.		

⟦8⟧ ⟦«Oder welche Frau, die zehn Münzen hat, wird nicht, wenn sie eine Münze verliert, eine Lampe anzünden und das Haus ausfegen und suchen, bis sie sie findet?»⟧ ⟦9⟧ ⟦«Und wenn sie sie findet, ruft sie ihre Freundinnen und Nachbarinnen und sagt: Freut euch mit mir, denn ich habe die Münze gefunden, die ich verloren hatte.»⟧ ⟦10⟧ ⟦«Genau so, sage ich euch, wird Freude vor den Engeln sein über einen Sünder, der umkehrt.»⟧

⟦8⟧ ⟦«Ou quelle femme qui a dix drachmes, si elle perd une drachme, n'allume-t-elle pas une lampe, ne balaie la maison et ne cherche jusqu'à ce qu'elle trouve?»⟧ ⟦9⟧ ⟦«Et quand elle l'a retrouvée, elle appelle ses amies et ses voisines en disant: Réjouissez-vous avec moi, parce que j'ai retrouvé la drachme que j'avais perdue»⟧ ⟦10⟧ ⟦«Ainsi, je vous dis, il y a de la joie devant les anges pour un seul pécheur qui se repent.»⟧

Q 16:13, 16-18 is above, between Q 14:34-35 and Q 17:1-2.

Q 17:3

Markan Parallel	Matthean Doublet	Matt 18:15	Q 17:3
		⁰/	⁰/
		¹ʃ	¹ʃ
		[ ]²	[]²
		Ἐὰν (δὲ)³	ἐὰν ()³
		ἁμαρτ(ήσ)⁴η	ἁμαρτ(ήσ)⁴η
		(εἰς σὲ)⁵	⟦(εἰς σὲ)⁵⟧
		ὁ ἀδελφός σου,	ὁ ἀδελφός σου,
		(ὕπαγε)⁶	()⁶
		(ἔλεγξ)⁷ον αὐτ(ὸν)⁷	[ἐπιτίμησ]⁷ον αὐτ[ῷ]⁷,
		(μεταξὺ σοῦ καὶ αὐτοῦ μόνου)⁸.	()⁸
		[ ]⁹	[καὶ]⁹
		ἐάν (σου ἀκούσῃ,)¹⁰	ἐὰν ⟦[μετανοήσῃ]¹⁰⟧,
		(ἐκέρδησας τὸν ἀδελφόν σου)¹¹.	[ἄφες αὐτῷ]¹¹.
		ʅ¹ ⇒ Matt 18:21-22	ʅ¹⇒ Q 17:4
		\⁰ ⇒ Matt 18:21-22	\⁰⇒ Q 17:4

JMR, PH: Q **17:3-4** is between Q **17:2**; **15:4-5a**, ~~**5b-6**~~, 7, ⟦**8-10**⟧ and Q **17:6** {C}; IQP 1990: Q **17:3-4** follows directly upon Q **17:2** {A}; JSK: {C}.

IQP 1990, JSK: ()⁵.

⁰ Is Luke 17:3-4 par. Matt 18:15 in Q?

¹ The position of Q 17:3-4 in Q: After 17:1-2 and before Q 17:6 (Lukan order); or after Q 15:4-7 (Matt 18:12-14) [plus Q 15:8-10 only in Luke] and before Q 22:28, 30 (Matt 19:28) (Matthean order).

² Luke's προσέχετε ἑαυτοῖς·.

³ Matthew's δέ.

⁴ Luke's ἁμάρτῃ or Matthew's ἁμαρτήσῃ.

⁵ Matthew's εἰς σέ.

Q

ἐὰν ἁμαρτήσῃ ⟦εἰς σὲ⟧ ὁ ἀδελφός σου, ἐπιτίμησον αὐτῷ, καὶ ἐὰν ⟦μετανοήσῃ⟧, ἄφες αὐτῷ.

If your brother sins ⟦against you⟧, rebuke him; and if ⟦he repents⟧, forgive him.

Q 17:3

Luke 17:3	Lukan Doublet	Markan Parallel	Gospel of Thomas
⁰/ ¹ʃ [προσέχετε ἑαυτοῖς·]² ᾿Εὰν ( )³ ἁμάρτ( )⁴η ( )⁵ ὁ ἀδελφός σου ( )⁶ [ἐπιτίμησ]⁷ον αὐτ[ῷ]⁷, ( )⁸ [καὶ]⁹ ἐὰν [μετανοήσῃ]¹⁰ [ἄφες αὐτῷ]¹¹. ʅ¹⇒ Luke 17:4 \⁰⇒ Luke 17:4			

IQP 1990, PH: ⟦(σου ἀκούσῃ,)¹⁰⟧.

IQP 1990: ⟦[ἄφες αὐτῷ]¹¹⟧.

6 Matthew's ὕπαγε.
7 Luke's ἐπιτίμησον αὐτῷ or Matthew's ἔλεγξον αὐτόν.
8 Matthew's μεταξὺ σοῦ καὶ αὐτοῦ μόνου.

9 Luke's καί.
10 Luke's μετανοήσῃ or Matthew's σου ἀκούσῃ.
11 Luke's ἄφες αὐτῷ or Matthew's ἐκέρδησας τὸν ἀδελφόν σου.

Wenn dein Bruder ⟦gegen dich⟧ sündigt, weise ihn zurecht, und wenn ⟦er umkehrt⟧, vergib ihm!

Si ton frère pèche ⟦contre toi⟧, reprends-le, et s'⟦il se repent⟧, pardonne-lui.

Q 17:4

Markan Parallel	Matthean Doublet	Matt 18:21-22	Q 17:4
		18:21 (Τότε προσελθὼν	()^{1}
		ὁ Πέτρος εἶπεν αὐτῷ·)^{1}	
		(κύριε,)^{2}	()^{2}
		(ποσ)^{3}άκις	[καὶ ἐὰν ἑπτ]^{3}άκις
			[τῆς ἡμέρας]^{3}
		ἁμαρτ(ήσει)^{3}	ἁμαρτ[ήσῃ]^{3}
		εἰς (ἐμὲ)^{1}	εἰς [σὲ]^{1}
		(ὁ ἀδελφός μου)^{4}	()^{4}
		καὶ ʃ ʅ^{5}	καὶ ^{5}ʃ ()^{6} ἑπτάκιςʅ^{5}
		[ ]^{7}	[]^{7}
		ἀφήσ(ω)^{1} αὐτῷ;	ἀφήσ[εις]^{1} αὐτῷ.
		^{5}ʃ (ἕως)^{6} ἑπτάκις; ʅ^{5}	ʃʅ^{5}
		18:22 (λέγει αὐτῷ ὁ Ἰησοῦς·	()^{1}
		οὐ λέγω σοι ἕως ἑπτάκις	
		ἀλλὰ ἕως ἑβδομηκοντάκις	
		ἑπτά.)^{1}	
		ʅMatt 18:15^{1}	ʅQ 17:3^{1}
		\Matt 18:15^{0}	\Q 17:3^{0}

IQP 1990: ⟦[]^{7}⟧.

^{1} Luke's... σὲ ... ἀφήσεις or Matthew's τότε προσελθὼν ὁ Πέτρος εἶπεν αὐτῷ· ... ἐμὲ ... ἀφήσω ... λέγει αὐτῷ ὁ Ἰησοῦς· οὐ λέγω σοι ἕως ἑπτάκις ἀλλὰ ἕως ἑβδομηκοντάκις ἑπτά.

^{2} Matthew's κύριε.

^{3} Luke's καὶ ἐὰν ἑπτάκις τῆς ἡμέρας ἁμαρτήσῃ or Matthew's ποσάκις ἁμαρτήσει.

Q

καὶ ἐὰν ἑπτάκις τῆς ἡμέρας ἁμαρτήσῃ εἰς σὲ καὶ ἑπτάκις ἀφήσεις αὐτῷ.	And if seven times a day he sins against you, also seven times shall you forgive him.

Q 17:4

Luke 17:4	Lukan Doublet	Markan Parallel	Gospel of Thomas
( )[1] ( )[2] [καὶ ἐὰν ἑπτ][3]άκις [τῆς ἡμέρας][3] ἁμαρτ[ήσῃ][3] εἰς [σὲ][1] ( )[4] καὶ [5]ʃ ( )[6] ἑπτάκιςʅ[5] [ἐπιστρέψῃ πρὸς σὲ λέγων· μετανοῶ,][7] ἀφήσ[εις][1] αὐτῷ. ʃ ʅ[5] ( )[1] ʅLuke 17:3[1] \Luke 17:3[0]			

[4] Matthew's ὁ ἀδελφός μου.

[5] The position of (ἕως) ἑπτάκις.

[6] Matthew's ἕως.

[7] Luke's ἐπιστρέψῃ πρὸς σὲ λέγων· μετανοῶ.

Und wenn er siebenmal am Tag gegen dich sündigt, sollst du auch siebenmal ihm vergeben.

Et s'il pèche sept fois par jour contre toi, alors sept fois tu lui pardonneras.

Q 17:6

Mark 11:22-23	Matt 21:21	Matt 17:20b	Q 17:6
		[0]{	[0]{
11:22 καὶ ἀποκριθεὶς	{ἀποκριθεὶς} [δὲ]	[1]ʃ	[1]ʃ
ὁ Ἰησοῦς λέγει αὐτοῖς·	{[ὁ] Ἰησοῦς} [εἶπεν] {αὐτοῖς·}	[ ][2]	[][2]
	{(ἀμὴν) (λέγω ὑμῖν},	({ἀμὴν} γὰρ {λέγω ὑμῖν},)[3]	()[3]
ἔχετε πίστιν θεοῦ.	[ἐ]ὰν {[ἔχ]}η{[τε πίστιν]})	ἐ(ὰν)[4] {ἔχ}(η)[4]{τε} {πίστιν}	ε[ἰ][4] {ἔχ}[ε][4]{τε} {πίστιν}
		ὡς κόκκον σινάπεως,	ὡς κόκκον σινάπεως,
11:23 ἀμὴν λέγω ὑμῖν ὅτι	(καὶ μὴ διακριθῆτε,		
	οὐ μόνον τὸ τῆς συκῆς		
	ποιήσετε, ἀλλὰ κ{[ἂν]})		
ὃς ἂν εἴπῃ	({[τ]ῷ ὄρει [τ]ο[ύτ]ῳ})	(ἐρεῖτε)[5]	[ἐλέγετε ἂν][5]
τῷ ὄρει τούτῳ·	{εἴπ}η[(τε)]·	{(τῷ ὄρει)[6] τ(ο)[6]ύτ(ῳ)}[6]·	[τῇ συκαμίνῳ {τ}[α{ύτ}ῃ][6]·
ἄρθητι	{ἄρ[θητι	(μετάβα ἔνθεν	[ἐκριζώ{θητι}
καὶ βλήθητι	καὶ] βλή[θητι]		{καὶ} φυτεύ{θητι}
εἰς τὴν θάλασσαν,	εἰς [τὴ]ν [θάλασσ]αν,}	ἐκεῖ,)[7]	ἐν {τῇ} {θαλάσσ}ῃ·][7]
καὶ μὴ διακριθῇ			
ἐν τῇ καρδίᾳ αὐτοῦ			
ἀλλὰ πιστεύῃ ὅτι			
ὃ λαλεῖ γίνεται,			
ἔσται αὐτῷ.	{γ}ε{ν}ήσε{ται}	καὶ (μεταβήσε{ται})[8]·	καὶ [ὑπήκουσεν ἂν][8]
		(καὶ οὐδὲν ἀδυνατήσει)[9]	()[9]
	.	ὑμῖν.	ὑμῖν.
		ʅ[1]	ʅ[1]
		}[0]	}[0]

[0] Is Luke 17:6 par. Matt 17:20b in Q or from Mark?

[1] The position of Q 17:6 in Q: After Q 17:4 and before Q 17:⟦20-21⟧, 23 (Lukan order); or after Q 12:56 (Matt 16:3) and before Q 17:2 (Matt 18:6) (Matthean order).

[2] Luke's εἶπεν δὲ ὁ κύριος·.

[3] Matthew's ἀμὴν γὰρ λέγω ὑμῖν.

Q

εἰ ἔχετε πίστιν ὡς κόκκον σινάπεως, ἐλέγετε ἂν τῇ συκαμίνῳ ταύτῃ· ἐκριζώθητι καὶ φυτεύθητι ἐν τῇ θαλάσσῃ· καὶ ὑπήκουσεν ἂν ὑμῖν.	If you have faith like a mustard seed, you might say to this mulberry tree: Be uprooted and planted in the sea! And it would obey you.

Gos. Thom. 48 (Nag Hammadi II 2)

Λέγει Ἰησοῦς· ἐὰν δύο εἰρηνεύσωσιν ἐν ἀλλήλοις ἐν μιᾷ καὶ τῇ αὐτῇ οἰκίᾳ, ἐροῦσιν τῷ ὄρει· μετάβα, καὶ μεταβήσεται.	Jesus says: If two make peace with one another in one and the same house, (then) they will say to the mountain: Move away, and it will move away.

Q 17:6

Luke 17:6	Lukan Doublet	Mark 11:22-23	*Gos. Thom.* 48
^{0}{			
^{1}⸢		11:22 καὶ ἀποκριθεὶς	
[εἶπεν δὲ ὁ κύριος·]^{2}		ὁ Ἰησοῦς λέγει αὐτοῖς·	ⲡⲉϫⲉ ⲓ̅ⲥ̅ ϫⲉ
( )^{3}			
ε[ἰ {ἔχ}ε{τε}]^{4} {πίστιν}		ἔχετε πίστιν θεοῦ.	ⲉⲣϣⲁ ⲥⲛⲁⲩ ⲣ̄ ⲉⲓⲣⲏⲛⲏ
ὡς κόκκον σινάπεως,			ⲙⲛ̄ ⲛⲟⲩⲉⲣⲏⲩ ϩⲙ̄
		11:23 ἀμὴν λέγω ὑμῖν ὅτι	ⲡⲉⲓⲏⲉⲓ ⲟⲩⲱⲧ'
[ἐλέγετε ἂν]^{5}		ὃς ἂν εἴπῃ	ⲥⲉⲛⲁϫⲟⲟⲥ
[τῇ συκαμίνῳ {τ}[α{ύτ}ῃ]^{6}·		τῷ ὄρει τούτῳ·	ⲙ̄ⲡⲧⲁⲩ ϫⲉ
[ἐκριζώ{θητι		ἄρθητι	ⲡⲱⲱⲛⲉ ⲉⲃⲟⲗ
καὶ} φυτεύ{θητι}		καὶ βλήθητι	ⲁⲩⲱ ϥⲛⲁⲡⲱⲱⲛⲉ
ἐν {τῇ} {θαλάσσ}ῃ·]^{7}		εἰς τὴν θάλασσαν,	
		καὶ μὴ διακριθῇ	
		ἐν τῇ καρδίᾳ αὐτοῦ	
		ἀλλὰ πιστεύῃ ὅτι	
		ὃ λαλεῖ γίνεται,	
καὶ [ὑπήκουσεν ἂν]^{8}		ἔσται αὐτῷ.	
( )^{9}			
ὑμῖν.			
⸣^{1}			
}^{0}			

4 Luke's εἰ ἔχετε or Matthew's ἐὰν ἔχητε.
5 Luke's ἐλέγετε ἄν or Matthew's ἐρεῖτε.
6 Luke's τῇ συκαμίνῳ ταύτῃ or Matthew's τῷ ὄρει τούτῳ.
7 Luke's ἐκριζώθητι καὶ φυτεύθητι ἐν τῇ θαλάσσῃ or Matthew's μετάβα ἔνθεν ἐκεῖ.
8 Luke's ὑπήκουσεν ἄν or Matthew's μεταβήσεται.
9 Matthew's καὶ οὐδὲν ἀδυνατήσει.

Wenn ihr Glaube habt wie ein Senfkorn, könntet ihr diesem Maulbeerbaum sagen: Entwurzle dich und pflanze dich in das Meer! Und er würde euch gehorchen.

Si vous aviez une foi comme un grain de moutarde, vous diriez à ce mûrier: Déracine-toi et plante-toi dans la mer! Et il vous obéirait.

Jesus spricht: Wenn zwei miteinander Frieden schließen in ein und demselben Hause, (dann) werden sie zum Berg sagen: Hebe dich weg, und er wird sich wegheben.

Jésus dit: Si deux font la paix l'un avec l'autre dans la même maison, ils diront à la montagne: Déplace-toi, et elle se déplacera.

Q 17:⟦20⟧

Markan Parallel	Matthean Doublet	Matthew	Q 17:⟦20⟧
		[ ][0]	⟦[0][[1]ʃ [«'Επερωτηθεὶς δὲ»][0] [][2] [«πότε ἔρχεται ἡ βασιλεία τοῦ θεοῦ ἀπεκρίθη αὐτοῖς καὶ εἶπεν· οὐκ ἔρχεται ἡ βασιλεία τοῦ θεοῦ μετὰ παρατηρήσεως,»][0] ʅ[1]][0]⟧

IQP 1994: Luke 17:20 in Q: Indeterminate.

PH: Luke 17:20 is not in Q {B}.

[0] Is Luke 17:20 in Q?

[1] Is the position of Q 17:20 after Q 17:6 and before Q 17:⟦21⟧, 23 (Lukan order)?

Q

⟦«'Επερωτηθεὶς δὲ πότε ἔρχεται ἡ βασιλεία τοῦ θεοῦ ἀπεκρίθη αὐτοῖς καὶ εἶπεν· οὐκ ἔρχεται ἡ βασιλεία τοῦ θεοῦ μετὰ παρατηρήσεως,»⟧

⟦«But on being asked when the kingdom of God is coming, he answered them and said: The kingdom of God is not coming visibly,»⟧

Gos. Thom. 113.1-2 (Nag Hammadi II 2)

(1) Εἶπον αὐτῷ οἱ μαθηταὶ αὐτοῦ· ποίᾳ ἡμέρᾳ ἔρχεται ἡ βασιλεία; (2) οὐκ ἔρχεται μετὰ ἀποκαραδοκίας.

(1) His disciples said to him: The kingdom – on what day will it come? (2) It will not come by watching (and waiting for) it.

Q 17:⟦20⟧

Luke 17:20	Lukan Doublet	Markan Parallel	*Gos. Thom.* 113.1-2
[0]⟦ [1]⟅ ['Επερωτηθεὶς δὲ][0] [ὑπὸ τῶν Φαρισαίων][2] [πότε ἔρχεται ἡ βασιλεία τοῦ θεοῦ ἀπεκρίθη αὐτοῖς καὶ εἶπεν· οὐκ ἔρχεται ἡ βασιλεία τοῦ θεοῦ μετὰ παρατηρήσεως,][0] ⟆[1] ⟧[0]			113.1 πεϫαγ ναq ν̄6ι νεqμαθητης ϫε τμν̄τερο εсν̄νηγ ν̄αϣ ν̄ϩοογ 113.2 εсν̄νηγ αν ϩν̄ ογ6ωϣτ' εβολ'

[2] Is ὑπὸ τῶν Φαρισαίων in Q or is it Lukan redaction?

⟦«Als er aber gefragt wurde, wann das Reich Gottes komme, antwortete er ihnen und sagte: Das Reich Gottes kommt nicht so, dass man es beobachten könnte.»⟧

⟦«Tandis qu'on lui demandait quand viendrait le royaume de Dieu, il leur répondit et dit: Le royaume de Dieu ne vient pas comme un fait observable»⟧

(1) Seine Jünger sprachen zu ihm: Das Königreich – an welchem Tage wird es kommen? (2) Nicht im Erwarten wird es kommen!

(1) Ses disciples lui dirent: Le royaume, quel jour viendra-t-il? (2) Ce n'est pas à force de (l')attendre qu'il viendra.

Q 17:⟦21⟧

Mark 13:21	Matt 24:26	Matt 24:23	Q 17:⟦21⟧
		⁰{	⟦⁰{
		¹/	¹/
Καὶ τότε ἐάν τις	({ἐὰν}) οὖν	{(Τότε ἐάν τις	[ ]²
ὑμῖν εἴπῃ·	({εἴπ})ω[σιν] ({ὑμῖν·})	ὑμῖν εἴπῃ)²·	
ἴδε	[({ἰδ}οὺ)]	ἰδ}οὺ	{ἰδ}οὺ
ὧδε	ἐν τῇ ἐρήμῳ ἐστίν,	{ὧδε	{ὧδε
ὁ χριστός,		(ὁ χριστός)³},	()³}
	μὴ ἐξέλθητε·		
		ἤ·	ἤ·
ἴδε	{ἰδ}οὺ		
ἐκεῖ,	ἐν τοῖς ταμείοις,	(ὧδε)⁴,	{[ ]}⁴,
μὴ πιστεύετε·	({μὴ πιστεύ}ση{τε})·	({μὴ πιστεύ}ση{τε})⁵·	({})⁵
		[ ]⁶	[«ἰδοὺ γὰρ
			ἡ βασιλεία τοῦ θεοῦ
			ἐντὸς ὑμῶν ἐστιν»]⁶.
		\¹	\¹
		}⁰	}⁰⟧

IQP 1994: Q **17:21** in Q: Indeterminate.

PH: Q **17:21** is not in Q {B}.

Text Critical Note (see the discussion in the front matter): In Luke 17:21 ἤ· ἰδοὺ ἐκεῖ is in A D (W) Ψ $f^{1.13}$ 𝔐 lat sy^c.p.h.^, ηκει (sic!)

⁰ Is Luke 17:21 in Q or from Mark?

¹ Is Q 17:21 after Q 17:20 and before Q 17:23 (Lukan order) or after Q 11:51 (Matt 23:36) and before Q 17:23 (Matt 24:26) (Matthean order)?

² Luke's οὐδὲ ἐροῦσιν or Matthew's τότε ἐάν τις ὑμῖν εἴπῃ.

Q

⟦.. ἰδοὺ ὧδε ἤ· …, «ἰδοὺ γὰρ ἡ βασιλεία τοῦ θεοῦ ἐντὸς ὑμῶν ἐστιν.»⟧

⟦«Nor will one say:» Look, here! or: «There! For, look, the kingdom of God is within you!»⟧

Q 17:⟦21⟧

Luke 17:21	Luke 17:23	*Gos. Thom.* 113.3-4	*Gos. Thom.* 3.1-3
[0]{			
[1]/			3.1 ⲡⲉϫⲉ ⲓ̅ⲥ̅ ϫⲉ
[οὐδὲ	{καὶ}		
ἐροῦσιν][2]·	[ἐροῦσιν] ({ὑμῖν·})	113.3 ⲉⲩⲛⲁϫⲟⲟⲥ ⲁⲛ ϫⲉ	ⲉⲩϣⲁϫⲟⲟⲥ ⲛⲏⲧⲛ̅ ⲛ̅ϭⲓ
			ⲛⲉⲧ'ⲥⲱⲕ ϩⲏⲧ'ⲧⲏⲩⲧⲛ̅ ϫⲉ
{ἰδ}ού	[({ἰδ}ού)]	ⲉⲓⲥϩⲏⲏⲧⲉ	ⲉⲓⲥϩⲏⲏⲧⲉ ⲉⲧ'ⲙⲛ̅ⲧⲉⲣⲟ
{ὧδε	{[ἐκεῖ]},	ⲙ̅ⲡⲓⲥⲁ	ϩⲛ̅ ⲧⲡⲉ
( )[3]}			ⲉⲉⲓⲉ ⲛ̅ϩⲁⲗⲏⲧ' ⲛⲁⲣ̅
			ϣⲟⲣⲡ' ⲉⲣⲱⲧⲛ̅ ⲛ̅ⲧⲉ
			ⲧⲡⲉ
ἤ·	[(ἤ)]·	ⲏ	3.2 ⲉⲩϣⲁⲛϫⲟⲟⲥ
			ⲛⲏⲧⲛ̅
	{ἰδ}ού	ⲉⲓⲥϩⲏⲏⲧⲉ	ϫⲉ
{[ἐκεῖ]}[4],	{[(ὧδε]}·	ⲧⲏ	ⲥϩⲛ̅ ⲑⲁⲗⲁⲥⲥⲁ
	{μὴ)} ἀπέλθη{(τε)}		ⲉⲉⲓⲉ ⲛ̅ⲧⲃⲧ'
({ })[5]	μηδὲ διώξητε.		ⲛⲁⲣ̅ ϣⲟⲣⲡ' ⲉⲣⲱⲧⲛ̅
[ἰδοὺ γὰρ		113.4 ⲁⲗⲗⲁ	3.3 ⲁⲗⲗⲁ
ἡ βασιλεία τοῦ θεοῦ		ⲧⲙⲛ̅ⲧⲉⲣⲟ ⲙ̅ⲡⲉⲓⲱⲧ'	ⲧⲙⲛ̅ⲧⲉⲣⲟ
ἐντὸς ὑμῶν ἐστιν][6].			ⲥⲙ̅ⲡⲉⲧⲛ̅ϩⲟⲩⲛ'
\\[1]		ⲉⲥⲡⲟⲣϣ' ⲉⲃⲟⲗ	ⲁⲩⲱ ⲥⲙ̅ⲡⲉⲧⲛ̅ⲃⲁⲗ'
}[0]		ϩⲓϫⲙ̅ ⲡⲕⲁϩ	
		ⲁⲩⲱ ⲣ̅ⲣⲱⲙⲉ	
		ⲛⲁⲩ ⲁⲛ ⲉⲣⲟⲥ	

in Θ, and ἤ· ἐκεῖ in 𝔓[75] ℵ B L 1241 2542 *pc* e ff[2] i l s sy[s].

[3] Matthew's ὁ χριστός.

[4] Luke's ἐκεῖ or Matthew's second ὧδε.

[5] Matthew's μὴ πιστεύσητε.

[6] Luke's ἰδοὺ γὰρ ἡ βασιλεία τοῦ θεοῦ ἐντὸς ὑμῶν ἐστιν.

⟦«Noch wird man sagen:» Siehe, hier! oder: «Dort! Denn, siehe, das Reich Gottes ist in eurer Mitte.»⟧

⟦«et on ne dira pas:» Le voici! ou: «Le voilà! Car, voyez-vous, le royaume de Dieu est en vous!»⟧

Q 17:⟦21⟧

Mark 13:21	Matt 24:26	Matt 24:23	Q 17:⟦21⟧

Gos. Thom. 113.3-4 (Nag Hammadi II 2)

(3) οὐκ ἐροῦσιν· ἰδοὺ ὧδε ἤ ἰδοὺ ἐκεῖ. (4) ἀλλὰ ἡ βασιλεία τοῦ πατρὸς ἐστρωμένη ἐστὶν ἐπὶ τῆς γῆς καὶ οἱ ἄνθρωποι οὐ βλέπουσιν αὐτήν.

(3) They will not say: Look, here! or: Look, there! (4) Rather the kingdom of the Father is spread out upon the earth, and people do not see it.

Gos. Thom. 3.1-3 (Nag Hammadi II 2)

(1) Λέγει Ἰησοῦς· ἐὰν οἱ ἡγούμενοι ὑμᾶς εἴπωσιν ὑμῖν· ἰδοὺ ἡ βασιλεία ἐν τῷ οὐρανῷ ἐστιν, φθήσεται ὑμᾶς τὰ πετεινὰ τοῦ οὐρανοῦ. (2) ἐὰν (δ') εἴπωσιν ὑμῖν· ἐν τῇ θαλάσσῃ ἐστίν, φθήσονται ὑμᾶς οἱ ἰχθύες. (3) ἀλλὰ ἡ βασιλεία ἐντὸς ὑμῶν ἐστιν καὶ ἐκτὸς ὑμῶν.

(1) Jesus says: If those who lead you say to you: Look, the kingdom is in the sky, then the birds of the sky will precede you. (2) If they say to you: It is in the sea, then the fish will precede you. (3) Rather, the kingdom is within you, and outside of you.

Gos. Thom. 3.1-3 (P. Oxy. 654)

(1) λέγει Ἰ[η(σοῦ)ς· ἐὰν] οἱ ἕλκοντες <ὑ>μᾶς [εἴπωσιν ὑμῖν· ἰδοὺ] ἡ βασιλεία ἐν οὐρα[νῷ, ὑμᾶς φθήσεται] τὰ πετεινὰ τοῦ οὐρ[ανοῦ· (2) ἐὰν δ' εἴπωσιν ὅ]τι ὑπὸ τὴν γῆν ἐστ[ιν, εἰσελεύσονται] οἱ ἰχθύες τῆς θαλά[σσης προφθάσαν]τες ὑμᾶς· (3) καὶ ἡ βασ[ιλεία τοῦ θεοῦ] ἐντὸς ὑμῶν [ἐσ]τι [κἀκτός.]

(1) Jesus says: [If] those who entice <you> [say to you: Look,] the kingdom is in the sky, [there will precede you] the birds of the sky. (2) [But if they say]: It is under the earth, [there will enter it] the fish of the sea [ahead of] you. (3) And the kingdom [of God] is within you, [and outside.]

Q 17:⟦21⟧

Luke 17:21	Luke 17:23	*Gos. Thom.* 113.3-4	*Gos. Thom.* 3.1-3

(3) Sie werden nicht sagen: Siehe, hier! oder: Siehe, dort! (4) Vielmehr ist das Königreich des Vaters ausgebreitet über die Erde, und die Menschen sehen es nicht.

(3) On ne dira pas: Le voici ici! ou: Le voici là! (4) Mais le royaume du Père, c'est sur la terre qu'il est déployé et les gens ne le voient pas.

(1) Jesus spricht: Wenn die, die euch vorangehen, zu euch sagen: Siehe, im Himmel ist das Königreich, dann werden euch die Vögel des Himmels zuvorkommen. (2) Wenn sie zu euch sagen: Es ist im Meer, dann werden euch die Fische zuvorkommen. (3) Vielmehr: Das Königreich ist innerhalb von euch und außerhalb von euch.

(1) Jésus dit: Si ceux qui vous conduisent vous disent: Voici que le royaume est dans le ciel, alors les oiseaux du ciel vous précéderont. (2) S'ils vous disent: Il est dans la mer, alors les poissons vous précéderont. (3) Mais le royaume, il est à l'intérieur de vous et à l'extérieur de vous.

(1) Jesus spricht: [Wenn] die, die <euch> verführen, [zu euch sagen: Siehe,] im Himmel ist das Königreich, [werden euch] die Vögel des Himmels [zuvorkommen. (2) Wenn aber sie sagen:] Es ist unter der Erde, [werden] die Fische des Meeres [eingehen], euch [zuvorkommend]. (3) Das Königreich [Gottes] ist innerhalb von euch [und außerhalb.]

(1) Jésus dit: [Si] ceux qui <vous> entraînent [vous disent: Voici que] le royaume est dans le ciel, les oiseaux du ciel [vous précéderont. (2) S'ils vous disent:] Il est sous la terre, les poissons de la mer (y) entreront, vous [précédant]. (3) Et le royaume [de Dieu] est à l'intérieur de vous [et à l'extérieur.]

Q 17:~~22~~

Markan Parallel	Matthean Doublet	Matthew	Q 17:~~22~~
		[ ][0]	[][0]

[0] Is Luke 17:22 in Q?

Q 17:~~22~~

Luke 17:22	Lukan Doublet	Markan Parallel	Gospel of Thomas
[Εἶπεν δὲ πρὸς τοὺς μαθητάς· ἐλεύσονται ἡμέραι ὅτε ἐπιθυμήσετε μίαν τῶν ἡμερῶν τοῦ υἱοῦ τοῦ ἀνθρώπου ἰδεῖν καὶ οὐκ ὄψεσθε.]⁰			

Q 17:23

Mark 13:21	Matt 24:23	Matt 24:26	Q 17:23
		^{0}{	^{0}{
		^{1}⸂	^{1}⸂
Καὶ τότε ἐάν τις	{Τότε (ἐάν) τις	({ἐὰν})^{2}	({ἐὰν})^{2}
		(οὖν)^{3}	{[()]}^{3}
ὑμῖν εἴπῃ·	[(ὑμῖν)] (εἴπ)ῃ·	({εἴπ}ω)^{2}σιν {ὑμῖν}·	({εἴπ}ω)^{2}σιν {ὑμῖν}·
ἴδε	[(ἰδ}οὺ)]	{ἰδ}οὺ	{ἰδ}οὺ
ὧδε	{ὧδε	(ἐν τῇ ἐρήμῳ ἐστίν)^{4},	(ἐν τῇ ἐρήμῳ ἐστίν)^{4},
ὁ χριστός,	ὁ χριστός,}		
		^{5}⸂μὴ (ἐξ)^{6}έλθητε⸃^{5}	^{5}⸂μὴ (ἐξ)^{6}έλθητε⸃^{5}
	[ἤ]·	[ ]^{7}·	[]^{7}·
ἴδε		{ἰδ}οὺ	{ἰδ}οὺ
ἐκεῖ,	[ὧδε],	(ἐν τοῖς ταμείοις)^{4},	(ἐν τοῖς ταμείοις)^{4},
		⸂ ⸃^{5}	⸂⸃^{5}
μὴ πιστεύετε·	({[μὴ] πιστεύ}σ[η{τε}]).	{μὴ[ ]^{8} (πιστεύ}σ)^{9}η{τε}·	{μὴ}[]^{8} [διώξ]^{9}η{τε}·
		⸃^{1}⇒ Mt 24:27	⸃^{1}⇒ Q 17:24
		}^{0}	}^{0}

PH: Q **17:23-24** follows Q **17:6** and precedes Q **17:37** {B}.

IQP 1994: ({ })^{2} {[( )]}^{3} ({ })^{2}σιν.

Text Critical Note (see the discussion in the front matter): In Luke 17:23 ἐκεῖ, (+ *καί* ℵ) ἰδοὺ ὧδε is in ℵ L *pc* (sy$^{s.c.}$); ὧδε, ἰδοὺ ἐκεῖ (+ ὁ Χριστός K 2542 *pc*) in D K W 33 2542 *al* lat (sy^{p}); ὧδε, ἤ· ἰδοὺ (- *f*^{13}) ἐκεῖ (+ ὁ Χριστός N sy^{h**}) in A Θ Ψ *f*^{13} 𝔐 it vg^{mss} sy^{h}; ὧδε, μὴ διώξητε· ἤ· ἰδοὺ ἐκεῖ ὁ Χριστός, in *f*^{1}; and ἐκεῖ, ἤ· ἰδοὺ ὧδε in 𝔓^{75} B 579.

^{0} Is Luke 17:23 par. Matt 24:26 in Q or from Mark?

^{1} The position of Q 17:23-24 in Q: After Q 17:6, ⟦20-21⟧ and before Q 17:26 (Lukan order); or after Q 13:34-35; 17:⟦21⟧ (Matt 23:37-39; 24:23) and before Q 17:37 (Matt 24:28) (Matthean order).

^{2} Luke's ἐροῦσιν or Matthew's ἐὰν … εἴπωσιν.

^{3} Luke's *καί* or Matthew's οὖν.

^{4} Luke's ἐκεῖ … ὧδε or Matthew's ἐν τῇ ἐρήμῳ ἐστίν … ἐν τοῖς ταμείοις.

Q

ἐὰν εἴπωσιν ὑμῖν· ἰδοὺ ἐν τῇ ἐρήμῳ ἐστίν, μὴ ἐξέλθητε· ἰδοὺ ἐν τοῖς ταμείοις, μὴ διώξητε·	If they say to you: Look, he is in the wilderness, do not go out; look, he is indoors, do not follow.

Q 17:23

Luke 17:23	Luke 17:21	Mark 13:21	*Gos. Thom.* 3.1-2
[0]{			
[1]ʃ			
( )[2]		Καὶ τότε ἐάν τις	3.1 ⲡⲉϫⲉ ⲓ̅ⲥ̅ ϫⲉ
{[καὶ]}[3]	οὐδὲ		
[ἐροῦ][2]σιν {ὑμῖν}·	[ἐροῦ(σιν)]·	ὑμῖν εἴπῃ·	ⲉⲩϣⲁϫⲟⲟⲥ ⲛⲏⲧⲛ̅ ⲛ̅ϭⲓ
			ⲛⲉⲧ'ⲥⲱⲕ ϩⲏⲧ' ⲧⲏⲩⲧⲛ̅ ϫⲉ
{ἰδ}οὺ	[({ἰδ}οὺ)]	ἴδε	ⲉⲓⲥϩⲏⲏⲧⲉ ⲉⲧ'ⲙⲛ̅ⲧⲉⲣⲟ
{[ἐκεῖ]}[4],	[{ὧδε}]	ὧδε	ϩⲛ̅ ⲧⲡⲉ
		ὁ χριστός,	ⲉⲉⲓⲉ ⲛ̅ϩⲁⲗⲏⲧ' ⲛⲁⲣ̅
ʃ ʅ[5]			ϣⲟⲣⲡ' ⲉⲣⲱⲧⲛ̅ ⲛ̅ⲧⲉ ⲧⲡⲉ
[ἤ][7]·	[ἤ]·		3.2 ⲉⲩϣⲁⲛϫⲟⲟⲥ ⲛⲏⲧⲛ̅
{ἰδ}οὺ		ἴδε	ϫⲉ
{[ὧδε]}[4]·	[{ἐκεῖ}],	ἐκεῖ,	ⲥϩⲛ̅ ⲑⲁⲗⲁⲥⲥⲁ
[5]ʃμὴ [ἀπ][6]έλθητεʅ[5]			ⲉⲉⲓⲉ ⲛ̅ⲧⲃⲧ'
{μη}[δὲ][8] [διώξ][9]η{τε}.		μὴ πιστεύετε·	ⲛⲁⲣ̅ ϣⲟⲣⲡ' ⲉⲣⲱⲧⲛ̅
ʅ[1]⇒ Luke 17:24	[({ἰδ}οὺ)] γὰρ		
}[0]	ἡ βασιλεία		
	τοῦ θεοῦ ἐντὸς ὑμῶν ἐστιν.		

IQP 1994: ⟦(ἐν τῇ ἐρήμῳ ἐστίν)[4]⟧ … ⟦(ἐν τοῖς ταμείοις)[4]⟧.

IQP 1994: {μη[ ][8].

Text Critical Note (see the discussion in the front matter): In Luke 17:23 μὴ διώξητε ($\mathfrak{P}^{75}$ f^{13}: -ξετε) is in B sa, μὴ πιστεύσητε in f^{1} sy^{hmg}, μὴ ἀπέλθητε μηδὲ διώξετε in L Δ *al*, and μὴ ἐξέλθητε μηδὲ διώξητε in 579 *pc*.

5 The position of the first prohibition just after the second (Luke) or between the two alternate places proposed (Matthew).

6 Luke's ἀπέλθητε or Matthew's ἐξέλθητε.

7 Luke's ἤ.

8 Luke's μηδέ or Matthew's μή.

9 Luke's διώξητε or Matthew's πιστεύσητε.

Wenn sie euch sagen: Siehe, er ist in der Wüste, geht nicht hinaus; siehe, er ist drinnen in den Häusern, folgt «ihnen» nicht.

Et si on vous dit: Voici, il est dans le désert, n'y sortez pas; voici, il est dans les chambres, ne vous lancez pas à «sa» poursuite.

Q 17:23

Mark 13:21	Matt 24:23	Matt 24:26	Q 17:23

Gos. Thom. 3.1-2 (Nag Hammadi II 2)

(1) Λέγει Ἰησοῦς· ἐὰν οἱ ἡγούμενοι ὑμᾶς εἴπωσιν ὑμῖν· ἰδοὺ ἡ βασιλεία ἐν τῷ οὐρανῷ ἐστιν, φθήσεται ὑμᾶς τὰ πετεινὰ τοῦ οὐρανοῦ. (2) ἐὰν εἴπωσιν ὑμῖν· ἐν τῇ θαλάσσῃ ἐστίν, φθήσονται ὑμᾶς οἱ ἰχθύες.

(1) Jesus says: If those who lead you say to you: Look, the kingdom is in the sky, then the birds of the sky will precede you. (2) If they say to you: It is in the sea, then the fish will precede you.

Gos. Thom. 3.1-2 (P. Oxy. 654)

(1) λέγει Ἰ[η(σοῦ)ς· ἐὰν] οἱ ἕλκοντες <ὑ>μᾶς [εἴπωσιν ὑμῖν· ἰδοὺ] ἡ βασιλεία ἐν οὐρα[νῷ, ὑμᾶς φθήσεται] τὰ πετεινὰ τοῦ οὐρ[ανοῦ· (2) ἐὰν δ' εἴπωσιν ὅ]τι ὑπὸ τὴν γῆν ἐστ[ιν, εἰσελεύσονται] οἱ ἰχθύες τῆς θαλά[σσης προφθάσαν]τες ὑμᾶς·

(1) Jesus says: [If] those who entice <you> [say to you: Look,] the kingdom is in the sky, [there will precede you] the birds of the sky. (2) [But if they say]: It is under the earth, [there will enter it] the fish of the sea, [preceding] you.

Q 17:23

Luke 17:23	**Luke 17:21**	**Mark 13:21**	***Gos. Thom.* 3.1-2**

(1) Jesus spricht: Wenn die, die euch vorangehen, zu euch sagen: Siehe, im Himmel ist das Königreich, dann werden euch die Vögel des Himmels zuvorkommen. (2) Wenn sie zu euch sagen: Es ist im Meer, dann werden euch die Fische zuvorkommen.

(1) Jésus dit: Si ceux qui vous conduisent vous disent: Voici que le royaume est dans le ciel, alors les oiseaux du ciel vous précéderont. (2) S'ils vous disent: Il est dans la mer, alors les poissons vous précéderont.

(1) Jesus spricht: [Wenn] die, die <euch> verführen, [zu euch sagen: Siehe,] im Himmel ist das Königreich, [werden euch] die Vögel des Himmels [zuvorkommen. (2) Wenn aber sie sagen:] Es ist unter der Erde, [werden] die Fische des Meeres [eingehen], euch [zuvorkommend].

(1) Jésus dit: [Si] ceux qui <vous> entraînent [vous disent: Voici que] le royaume est dans le ciel, les oiseaux du ciel [vous précéderont. (2) S'ils vous disent:] Il est sous la terre, les poissons de la mer (y) entreront, vous [précédant].

Q 17:24

Markan Parallel	Matthean Doublet	Matt 24:27	Q 17:24
		[0]/	[0]/
		ὥσπερ γὰρ ἡ ἀστραπὴ	ὥσπερ γὰρ ἡ ἀστραπὴ
		(ἐξέρχεται)[1]	(ἐξέρχεται)[1]
		(ἀπὸ ἀνατολῶν)[2]	(ἀπὸ ἀνατολῶν)[2]
		(καὶ)[1]	(καὶ)[1]
		[3]ʃ (φαίνεται)[1] ʅ[3]	[3]ʃ (φαίνεται)[1] ʅ[3]
		(ἕως δυσμῶν)[2]	(ἕως δυσμῶν)[2]
		ʃ ʅ[3],	ʃʅ[3],
		οὕτως ἔσται	οὕτως ἔσται
		(ἡ παρουσία)[4]	⟦()[4]
		(τοῦ)[4] υἱο(ῦ)[4]	[ὁ][4]⟧ υἱὸ⟦[ς][4]⟧
		τοῦ ἀνθρώπου	τοῦ ἀνθρώπου
		[ ][4].	⟦[ἐν τῇ ἡμέρᾳ αὐτοῦ][4]⟧.
		ʅ Matt 24:26[1]	ʅ Q 17:23[1]
		\[0]	\[0]

IQP 1991: ⟦(ἀπὸ ἀνατολῶν)[2]⟧ (καί)[1] ⟦[3]ʃ (φαίνεται)[1] ʅ[3] (ἕως δυσμῶν)[2]⟧ ʃʅ[3], οὕτως ἔσται ⟦(ἡ)[4] <[ἡμέρα][4]>⟧ (τοῦ)[4] υἱο(ῦ)[4] τοῦ

Text Critical Note (see the discussion in the front matter): In Luke 17:24 ἐν τῇ ἡμέρᾳ αὐτοῦ is lacking in 𝔓[75] B D it sa, but present in א

[0] Is Luke 17:24 par. Matt 24:27 in Q?

[1] Luke's ἀστράπτουσα … λάμπει or Matthew's ἐξέρχεται … καί φαίνεται.

[2] Luke's ἐκ τῆς ὑπὸ τὸν οὐρανὸν εἰς τὴν ὑπ' οὐρανόν or Matthew's ἀπὸ ἀνατολῶν … ἕως δυσμῶν.

Q

ὥσπερ γὰρ ἡ ἀστραπὴ ἐξέρχεται ἀπὸ ἀνατολῶν καὶ φαίνεται ἕως δυσμῶν, οὕτως ἔσται ⟦ὁ⟧ υἱὸ⟦ς⟧ τοῦ ἀνθρώπου ⟦ἐν τῇ ἡμέρᾳ αὐτοῦ⟧.	For as the lightning streaks from Sunrise and flashes as far as Sunset, so will be the Son of Humanity ⟦on his day⟧.

Q 17:24

Luke 17:24	Luke 17:30	Markan Parallel	Gospel of Thomas
⁰/ ὥσπερ γὰρ ἡ ἀστραπὴ [ἀστράπτουσα][1] [ἐκ τῆς ὑπὸ τὸν οὐρανὸν][2] ( )[1] ʃ ʅ[3] [εἰς τὴν ὑπ' οὐρανὸν][2] [3]ʃ [λάμπει][1] ʅ[3], οὕτως ἔσται ( )[4] [ὁ][4] υἱὸ[ς][4] τοῦ ἀνθρώπου [ἐν τῇ ἡμέρᾳ αὐτοῦ][4]. ʅ Luke 17:23[1] \⁰	 κατὰ τὰ αὐτὰ ἔσται ᾗ ἡμέρᾳ ὁ υἱὸς τοῦ ἀνθρώπου ἀποκαλύπτεται.		

ἀνθρώπου [][4].

A L W Θ Ψ $f^{1.13}$ 𝔐 lat sy bo.

[3] The position of the second verb in Q 17:24a after (Luke) or before (Matthew) the second direction.

[4] Luke's ὁ υἱὸς τοῦ ἀνθρώπου ἐν τῇ ἡμέρᾳ αὐτοῦ or Matthew's ἡ παρουσία τοῦ υἱοῦ τοῦ ἀνθρώπου.

Denn wie der Blitz vom Osten ausgeht und bis zum Westen leuchtet, so wird der Menschensohn ⟦an seinem Tag⟧ sein.

Car tel un éclair qui surgit de l'Orient et étincelle jusqu'à l'Occident, ainsi sera le Fils de l'homme ⟦lors de son jour⟧.

Q 17:~~25~~

Markan Parallel	Matthean Doublet	Matthew	Q 17:~~25~~
		[ ][0]	[][0]

[0] Is Luke 17:25 in Q or from Mark?

Q 17:26 is to be found below, between Q 17:37 and Q 17:27

Q 17:~~25~~

Luke 17:25	Luke 9:22	Mark 8:31	Gospel of Thomas
	εἰπὼν {ὅτι	Καὶ ἤρξατο διδάσκειν	
[πρῶτον δὲ {δεῖ} αὐτὸν	[δεῖ] τὸν υἱὸν τοῦ	αὐτοὺς ὅτι δεῖ τὸν υἱὸν τοῦ	
{πολλὰ παθεῖν	ἀνθρώπου [πολλὰ παθεῖν	ἀνθρώπου πολλὰ παθεῖν	
καὶ ἀποδοκιμασθῆναι} ἀπὸ	καὶ ἀποδοκιμασθῆναι} ἀπὸ]	καὶ ἀποδοκιμασθῆναι ὑπὸ	
τῆς γενεᾶς ταύτης.]^{0}	{τῶν πρεσβυτέρων}	τῶν πρεσβυτέρων	
	{τῶν ἀρχιερέων	καὶ τῶν ἀρχιερέων	
	καὶ} {γραμματέων	καὶ τῶν γραμματέων	
	καὶ ἀποκτανθῆναι καὶ}	καὶ ἀποκτανθῆναι καὶ μετὰ	
	τῇ {τρ}ίτῃ {ἡμέρ}α ἐγερθῆναι.	τρεῖς ἡμέρας ἀναστῆναι·	

Q 17:26 is to be found below, between Q 17:37 and Q 17:27

Q 17:37

Markan Parallel	Matthean Doublet	Matt 24:28	Q 17:37
		^{0}/	^{0}/
		^{1}ʃ	^{1}ʃ
		[ ]^{2}	[]^{2}
		ὅπου (ἐὰν ᾖ)^{3}	ὅπου ()^{3}
		τὸ (πτῶμα)^{4},	τὸ (πτῶμα)^{4},
		ἐκεῖ	ἐκεῖ
		^{5}ʃ [ ]^{6}συναχθήσονταιʅ^{5}	^{5}ʃ []^{6}συναχθήσονταιʅ^{5}
		[ ]^{7}	[]^{7}
		οἱ ἀετοί	οἱ ἀετοί
		ʃ ʅ^{5}.	ʃʅ^{5}.
		ʅ^{1}	ʅ^{1}
		\\$^{0}$	\\$^{0}$

0 Is Luke 17:37 par. Matt 24:28 in Q?
1 The position of Q 17:37 in Q: After Q 17:34-35 and before Q 19:12 (Lukan order); or after Q 17:24 (Matt 24:27) and before Q 17:26 (Matt 24:37) (Matthean order).
2 Is Luke 17:37a in Q?
3 Matthew's ἐὰν ᾖ.

Q

ὅπου τὸ πτῶμα, ἐκεῖ συναχθήσονται οἱ ἀετοί.	Wherever the corpse, there the vultures will gather.

Q 19:12 is to be found below, between Q 17:34-35 and Q 19:13.

Q 17:37

Luke 17:37	Lukan Doublet	Markan Parallel	Gospel of Thomas
⁰/ ¹ʃ [καὶ ἀποκριθέντες λέγουσιν αὐτῷ· ποῦ, κύριε; ὁ δὲ εἶπεν αὐτοῖς·]² ὅπου ( )³ τὸ [σῶμα]⁴, ἐκεῖ ʃ ʅ⁵ [καὶ]⁷ οἱ ἀετοὶ ⁵ʃ [ἐπι]⁶συναχθήσονται ʅ⁵. ʅ¹ \⁰			

[4] Luke's σῶμα or Matthew's πτῶμα.
[5] The position of the verb after (Luke) or before (Matthew) οἱ ἀετοί.
[6] Luke's ἐπισυναχθήσονται or Matthew's συναχθήσονται.
[7] Luke's καί.

Wo das Aas «ist», dort werden sich die Geier versammeln.

Où que «soit» le cadavre, là se rassembleront les vautours.

Q 19:12 is to be found below, between Q 17:34-35 and Q 19:13.

Q 17:26

Markan Parallel	Matthean Doublet	Matt 24:37	Q 17:26
		[0]/	[0]/
		ʃ [ ][1] ʅ[1]	ʃ [ ][1] ʅ[1]
		(Ὥσπερ)[2]	⟦[καθὼς][2]⟧
		ʃ (γὰρ)[1] ʅ[1]	ʃ ( )[1] ʅ[1]
		[ ][3]	⟦[ἐγένετο][3]⟧
		[ ][4]αἱ[ ][4] ἡμέραι[ ][4]	[ἐν τ][4]⟧αῖ⟦[ς][4]⟧ ἡμέραι⟦[ς][4]⟧
		(τοῦ)[5] Νῶε,	()[5] Νῶε,
		οὕτως ἔσται	οὕτως ἔσται
		(ἡ παρουσία)[6]	⟦[][6] [ἐν τ<ῇ>[6] ἡμέρ<α>][6]⟧
		τοῦ υἱοῦ τοῦ ἀνθρώπου.	τοῦ υἱοῦ τοῦ ἀνθρώπου·
		\[0]	\[0]

JMR, PH, JSK: [ ][1]… ( )[1], indeterminate.

IQP 1991: (ὥσ)[2]⟦(περ)[2] (γάρ)[1]⟧ [][3].

Text Critical Note (see the discussion in the front matter): In Matt 24:37 καί follows ἔσται in D W Θ 067 *f* [1.13] 𝔐 lat sy[h], but is absent in

[0] Is Luke 17:26 par. Matt 24:37 in Q?

[1] Luke's καί or Matthew's postpositive γάρ.

[2] Luke's καθώς or Matthew's ὥσπερ.

[3] Luke's ἐγένετο.

Q

.. ⟦καθὼς⟧ .. ⟦ἐγένετο ἐν τ⟧αῖ⟦ς⟧ ἡμέραι⟦ς⟧ Νῶε, οὕτως ἔσται ⟦ἐν τ<ῇ> ἡμέρ<α>⟧ τοῦ υἱοῦ τοῦ ἀνθρώπου.

.. As ⟦it took place in⟧ the days of Noah, so will it be ⟦in the day<>⟧ of the Son of Humanity.

Q 17:26

Luke 17:26	Luke 17:28a	Markan Parallel	Gospel of Thomas
0/			
ʃ [καὶ][1] ʅ[1]	ὁμοίως		
[καθὼς][2]	καθὼς		
ʃ ( )[1] ʅ[1]	ἐγένετο		
[ἐγένετο][3]			
[ἐν τ][4]αῖ[ς][4] ἡμέραι[ς][4]	ἐν ταῖς ἡμέραις		
( )[5] Νῶε,	Λώτ·		
οὕτως ἔσται			
[καὶ ἐν ταῖς ἡμέραις][6]			
τοῦ υἱοῦ τοῦ ἀνθρώπου·			
\0			

IQP 1991: [καὶ][6] ⟦[ἐν ταῖς ἡμέραις][6]⟧.

א B L Γ 33 700 892 *pc* it vg^{mss} sy$^{s.p}$ co.

4 Luke's ἐν ταῖς ἡμέραις or Matthew's αἱ ἡμέραι.
5 Matthew's τοῦ.

6 Luke's καὶ ἐν ταῖς ἡμέραις or Matthew's ἡ παρουσία.

.. Wie ⟦es geschah in⟧ den Tagen Noachs, so wird es auch ⟦ a<m> Tag<>⟧ des Menschensohns sein.

.. Comme ⟦ce fut le cas aux⟧ jours de Noé, ainsi en sera-t-il ⟦au<> jour<>⟧ du Fils de l'homme.

Q 17:27

Markan Parallel	Matthean Doublet	Matt 24:38-39a	Q 17:27
		0/	0/
		24:38 (ὡς γὰρ ἦσαν	⟦(ὡς γὰρ ἦσαν
		ἐν ταῖς ἡμέραις ἐκείναις	ἐν ταῖς ἡμέραις ἐκείναις)[1]
		ταῖς πρὸ τοῦ	()[1]⟧
		κατακλυσμοῦ)[1]	
		(τρώγοντες)[2.3]	(τρώγοντες)[2.3]
		(καὶ)[4]	(καὶ)[4]
		(πίνοντες)[2],	(πίνοντες)[2],
		(γαμοῦντες)[2]	(γαμοῦντες)[2]
		(καὶ)[4]	(καὶ)[4]
		γαμίζ(οντες)[2.5],	γαμίζ⟦(οντες)[2.5]⟧,
		ἄχρι ἧς ἡμέρας	ἄχρι ἧς ἡμέρας
		εἰσῆλθεν Νῶε	εἰσῆλθεν Νῶε
		εἰς τὴν κιβωτόν,	εἰς τὴν κιβωτόν,
		24:39a καὶ (οὐκ ἔγνωσαν	καὶ ()[6]
		ἕως)[6] ἦλθεν ὁ κατακλυσμὸς	ἦλθεν ὁ κατακλυσμὸς
		καὶ (ἦρεν)[7]	καὶ (ἦρεν)[7]
		(ἅ)[8]παντας,	(ἅ)[8]παντας,
		\0	\0

IQP 1991: ⟦‹ἔ›[2](τρωγ)[3]‹ον›[2]⟧, ()[4] ⟦[ἔ]πιν⟦ον⟧[2], [ἐ]γάμ⟦ουν⟧[2]⟧, ()[4] ⟦[ἐ]γαμίζ⟦οντο⟧[2.5]⟧ {C}; JSK: {B} except ⟦‹ἔ›[2](τρωγ)[3]‹ον›[2]⟧.

Text Critical Note (see the discussion in the front matter): In Matt 24:38 τοῦ Νῶε replaces ἐκείναις in 1424 Chr; ἐκείναις is simply absent in ℵ L W Θ 067 *f*[1.13] 33 𝔐 lat mae bo; and ἐκείναις is in B D 579 *pc* it sa sy[h].

[0] Is Luke 17:27 par. Matt 24:38-39a in Q?
[1] Matthew's protasis of the flood correlative.
[2] Luke's imperfect finite tenses or Matthew's present participles.
[3] Luke's ἐσθίω or Matthew's τρώγω.
[4] Matthew's καί *bis*.

Q

⟦ὡς γὰρ ἦσαν ἐν ταῖς ἡμέραις ἐκείναις⟧ τρώγοντες καὶ πίνοντες, γαμοῦντες καὶ γαμίζ⟦οντες⟧, ἄχρι ἧς ἡμέρας εἰσῆλθεν Νῶε εἰς τὴν κιβωτόν, καὶ ἦλθεν ὁ κατακλυσμὸς καὶ ἦρεν ἅπαντας,

⟦For as in those days they were⟧ eating and drinking, marrying and giving in marriage, until the day Noah entered the ark and the flood came and took them all,

Q 17:27

Luke 17:27	Luke 17:28b-29	Markan Parallel	Gospel of Thomas
0/			
( )1			
[ἤσθιον]2.3,	**17:28b** [ἤσθιον,		
( )4			
[ἔπινον]2,	ἔ(πιν)ον],		
[ἐγάμουν]2,	ἠγόραζον, ἐπώλουν,		
( )4	ἐφύτευον,		
[ἐ]2γαμίζ[οντο]2.5,	ᾠκοδόμουν·		
ἄχρι ἧς ἡμέρας	**17:29** ᾗ δὲ [(ἡμέρᾳ)]		
εἰσῆλθεν Νῶε	ἐξ[(ῆλθεν)] Λὼτ		
εἰς τὴν κιβωτὸν	ἀπὸ Σοδόμων,		
καὶ ( )6	ἔβρεξεν		
ἦλθεν ὁ κατακλυσμὸς	πῦρ καὶ θεῖον ἀπ᾽ οὐρανοῦ		
καὶ [ἀπώλεσεν]7	[(καὶ) ἀπώλεσεν		
( )8πάντας.	(πάντας)].		
\0			

Text Critical Note (see the discussion in the front matter): In Matt 24:38 γαμίσκοντες is in B *pc*, ἐκγαμίσκοντες in W 1424 *pc*, ἐκγαμίζοντες in L Θ 067 *f*[1] 33 *M*, ἐγγαμίζοντες in Σ *f*[13] 892 1241 *al*, and γαμίζοντες in א D 33 *pc*.

5 Luke's γαμίζομαι or Matthew's γαμίζω.
6 Matthew's οὐκ ἔγνωσαν ἕως.
7 Luke's ἀπόλλυμι or Matthew's αἴρω.
8 Luke's πάντας or Matthew's ἅπαντας.

⟦Denn wie sie in jenen Tagen⟧ aßen und tranken, heirateten und verheirateten bis zu dem Tag, an dem Noach in die Arche ging und die Flut kam und alle wegraffte,

⟦Car de même que ces jours, on les passait⟧ à manger et à boire, à prendre femme et à marier jusqu'au jour où Noé entra dans l'arche, où le déluge vint et les emporta tous,

Q 17:?28-29?

Markan Parallel	Matthean Doublet	Matthew	Q 17:?28-29?
		[ ][0]	[ ][0]

IQP 1991, PH: Luke 17:28-29 is not in Q {B}; JMR: Indeterminate; JSK: In Q {C}.

[0] Is Luke 17:28-29 in Q?

Q

..	..

Q 17:?28-29?

Luke 17:28-29	Luke 17:26a, 27	Markan Parallel	Gen 19:24 LXX
[**17:28** ὁμοίως καθὼς ἐγένετο	**17:26a** καὶ [καθὼς ἐγένετο		
ἐν ταῖς ἡμέραις Λώτ·	ἐν ταῖς ἡμέραις] Νῶε,		
ἤσθιον, ἔπινον,	**17:27** [ἤσθιον, ἔπινον,]		
ἠγόραζον, ἐπώλουν,			
ἐφύτευον, ᾠκοδόμουν·	ἐγάμουν, ἐγαμίζοντο,		
17:29 ᾗ δὲ ἡμέρᾳ ἐξῆλθεν	ἄχρι ἧς [ἡμέρα]ς εἰσ[ῆλθεν]		
Λὼτ ἀπὸ Σοδόμων,	Νῶε εἰς τὴν κιβωτὸν		
ἔβρεξεν	καὶ ἦλθεν		καὶ κύριος ἔβρεξεν
			ἐπὶ Σοδομα καὶ Γομορρα
πῦρ καὶ θεῖον	ὁ κατακλυσμὸς		θεῖον καὶ πῦρ
ἀπ' οὐρανοῦ καὶ ἀπώλεσεν	[καὶ ἀπώλεσεν		παρὰ κυρίου ἐκ τοῦ οὐρανοῦ
πάντας.][0]	πάντας].		

..

..

Q 17:30

Markan Parallel	Matthean Doublet	Matt 24:39b	Q 17:30
		⁰/ (οὕτως)¹ ἔσται (καὶ)¹ (ἡ)² (παρουσία)³ (τοῦ)² υἱο(ῦ)² τοῦ ἀνθρώπου [ ]². \⁰	⁰/ (οὕτως)¹ ἔσται (καὶ)¹ [ᾗ]² [ἡμέρα]³ [ὁ]² υἱὸ[ς]² τοῦ ἀνθρώπου [ἀποκαλύπτεται]². \⁰

IQP 1991: ⟦[ᾗ]² [ἡμέρα]³ [ὁ]²⟧ υἱὸ⟦[ς]²⟧ τοῦ ἀνθρώπου ⟦[ἀποκαλύπτεται]²⟧.

Text Critical Note (see the discussion in the front matter): In Matt 24:39b καί is absent in B D 892 *l* 2211 *pc* it vg[mss] sy[s.p] co, but present

⁰ Is Luke 17:30 par. Matt 24:39b in Q?

¹ Luke's κατὰ τὰ αὐτά or Matthew's οὕτως … καί.

Q

οὕτως ἔσται καὶ ᾗ ἡμέρᾳ ὁ υἱὸς τοῦ ἀνθρώπου ἀποκαλύπτεται.	so will it also be on the day the Son of Humanity is revealed.

Q 17:30

Luke 17:30	Luke 17:26b	Luke 17:24b	Gospel of Thomas
⁰/			
[κατὰ τὰ αὐτὰ]¹ ἔσται	(οὕτως [ἔσται]	(οὕτως [ἔσται])	
( )¹			
[ᾗ]² [ἡμέρᾳ]³	καὶ) ἐν ταῖς [ἡμέρα]ις		
[ὁ]² υἱὸ[ς]² τοῦ ἀνθρώπου	(τοῦ [υἱο]ῦ [τοῦ ἀνθρώπου])·	[ὁ (υἱὸ)ς (τοῦ ἀνθρώπου)]	
[ἀποκαλύπτεται]².		ἐν τῇ [ἡμέρᾳ] αὐτοῦ.	
\⁰			

in ℵ A L W Θ 067 $f^{1.13}$ 33 𝔐 lat sy[h].

[2] Luke's ᾗ … ὁ υἱὸς … ἀποκαλύπτεται or Matthew's ἡ … τοῦ υἱοῦ … .

[3] Luke's ἡμέρᾳ or Matthew's παρουσία.

so wird es auch an dem Tag sein, an dem der Menschensohn offenbart wird.	de même en sera-t-il aussi le jour où le Fils de l'homme se se révélera.

Q 17:~~31-32~~

Mark 13:15-16	Matthean Doublet	Matt 24:17-18	Q 17:~~31-32~~
		[0]{	{}[0]
			17:~~31~~ [][1]
13:15 ὁ δὲ		**24:17** ({ὁ})[1]	()[1]
ἐπὶ τοῦ δώματος		{ἐπὶ τοῦ δώματος	{~~ἐπὶ τοῦ δώματος~~}
		[ ][2]	ʃ [ ][2] ʅ[2]
μὴ καταβάτω		ʃμὴ καταβάτω}	ʃ {~~μὴ καταβάτω~~}
μηδὲ εἰσελθάτω ἆραί		{ἆραι ʅ[2]	{~~ἆραι~~} ʅ[2]
τι ἐκ τῆς οἰκίας αὐτοῦ,		ʃ (τ}ὰ {ἐκ τῆς οἰκίας αὐτοῦ)[2] ʅ[2],	[()][2]
13:16 καὶ ὁ		**24:18** καὶ ὁ}	{~~καὶ ὁ~~}
εἰς τὸν ἀγρὸν		ἐν ({τ}ῷ)[3] {ἀγρ}ῷ	~~ἐν~~ ()[3] {~~ἀγρ~~}~~ῷ~~
		[ ][4]	[][4]
μὴ ἐπιστρεψάτω		{μὴ ἐπιστρεψάτω}	{~~μὴ ἐπιστρεψάτω~~
εἰς τὰ ὀπίσω		[ ][5] {ὀπίσω	[][5] ~~ὀπίσω~~}
ἆραι τὸ ἱμάτιον αὐτοῦ.		(ἆραι τὸ ἱμάτιον αὐτοῦ.)[6]}	()[6]
		[ ][7]	**17:~~32~~** [][7]
		}[0]	

[0] Is Luke 17:31-32 par. Matt 24:17-18 in Q or from Mark and Lukan redaction?

[1] Luke's ἐν ἐκείνῃ τῇ ἡμέρᾳ ὃς ἔσται or Matthew's ὁ.

[2] Luke's καὶ τὰ σκεύη αὐτοῦ ἐν τῇ οἰκίᾳ prior to μὴ καταβάτω ἆραι, necessitating αὐτά, or Matthew's τὰ ἐκ τῆς οἰκίας αὐτοῦ following μὴ καταβάτω ἆραι.

Q 17:33 is to be found above, between Q 14:26-27 and Q 14:34-35.

Q 17:~~31-32~~

Luke 17:31-32	Lukan Doublet	Mark 13:15-16	Gen 19:26 LXX
[0]{			
17:31 [ἐν ἐκείνῃ τῇ ἡμέρᾳ			
ὃς ἔσται][1]		**13:15** ὁ δὲ	
{ἐπὶ τοῦ δώματος}		ἐπὶ τοῦ δώματος	
ʃ [καὶ τὰ σκεύη αὐτοῦ			
ἐν {τ}ῇ {οἰκί}ᾳ,][2] ʅ[2]			
ʃ {μὴ καταβάτω}		μὴ καταβάτω	
{ἆραι} ʅ[2]		μηδὲ εἰσελθάτω ἆραί	
[αὐτά][2],		τι ἐκ τῆς οἰκίας αὐτοῦ,	
{καὶ ὁ}		**13:16** καὶ ὁ	καὶ
ἐν ( )[3] {ἀγρ}ῷ		εἰς τὸν ἀγρὸν	ἐπέβλεψεν
[ὁμοίως][4]			
{μὴ ἐπιστρεψάτω		μὴ ἐπιστρεψάτω	ἡ γυνὴ αὐτοῦ
[εἰς τὰ][5] ὀπίσω.}		εἰς τὰ ὀπίσω	εἰς τὰ ὀπίσω
( )[6]		ἆραι τὸ ἱμάτιον αὐτοῦ.	καὶ ἐγένετο στήλη ἁλός.
17:32 [μνημονεύετε			
τῆς γυναικὸς Λώτ.][7]			
}[0]			

3 Matthew's τῷ.
4 Luke's ὁμοίως.
5 Luke's εἰς τά.

6 Matthew's ἆραι τὸ ἱμάτιον αὐτοῦ.
7 Luke's μνημονεύετε τῆς γυναικὸς Λώτ.

Q 17:33 is to be found above, between Q 14:26-27 and Q 14:34-35.

Q 17:34-35

Mark 13:16	Matt 24:18	Matt 24:40-41	Q 17:34-35
  καὶ ὁ εἰς τὸν ἀγρὸν μὴ ἐπιστρεψάτω εἰς τὰ ὀπίσω ἆραι τὸ ἱμάτιον αὐτοῦ.	 {καὶ ὁ} (ἐν {τ}ῷ {ἀγρ}ῷ) {μὴ ἐπιστρεψάτω} {ὀπίσω ἆραι τὸ ἱμάτιον αὐτοῦ.}	0/ **24:40** [ ][1] (τότε)[2] ⸉ ⸊[3] δύο ⸉ἔσονται⸊[3] (ἐν τῷ ἀγρῷ)[4], [ ][5] εἷς παραλ(αμβάν)[6]εται καὶ [ ][5] (εἷς)[7] ἀφ(ί)[6]εται· **24:41** [ ][8] δύο ἀλήθουσαι (ἐν τῷ μύλῳ)[9], [ ][5] μία παραλ(αμβάν)[6]εται [ ][5] (καὶ)[10] (μία)[7] ἀφ(ί)[6]εται. \0	0/ **17:34** [λέγω ὑμῖν,][1] [()][2] ⸉ἔσονται⸊[3] δύο ⸉ ⸊[3] ⟦(ἐν τῷ ἀγρῷ)[4]⟧, [][5] εἷς παραλ(αμβάν)[6]εται καὶ [][5] (εἷς)[7] ἀφ(ί)[6]εται· **17:35** [][8] δύο ἀλήθουσαι (ἐν τῷ μύλῳ)[9], [][5] μία παραλ(αμβάν)[6]εται [][5] (καὶ)[10] (μία)[7] ἀφ(ί)[6]εται. \0

IQP 1991:⟦[λέγω ὑμῖν,][1]⟧ [()][2].

IQP 1991: ⸉ἔσονται⸊[3] δύο ⸉⸊[3] {B}; JMR, PH, JSK: Indeterminate.

Text Critical Note (see the discussion in the front matter): In Luke 17:34 ὁ just prior to εἷς is absent in A D L W Ψ 𝔐, but present in 𝔓[75] א B Θ *f*[1.13] 579 892 2542 *pc*.

[0] Is Luke 17:34-35 par. Matt 24:40-41 in Q?
[1] Luke's λέγω ὑμῖν.
[2] Luke's ταύτῃ τῇ νυκτί or Matthew's τότε.
[3] Is ἔσονται before (Luke) or after (Matthew) δύο?
[4] Luke's ἐπὶ κλίνης μιᾶς or Matthew's ἐν τῷ ἀγρῷ.
[5] Luke's ὁ (*bis*) and ἡ (*bis*).

Q

34 λέγω ὑμῖν, ἔσονται δύο ⟦ἐν τῷ ἀγρῷ⟧, εἷς παραλαμβάνεται καὶ εἷς ἀφίεται· 35 δύο ἀλήθουσαι ἐν τῷ μύλῳ, μία παραλαμβάνεται καὶ μία ἀφίεται.

34 I tell you, there will be two «men» ⟦in the field⟧; one is taken and one is left. 35 Two «women» will be grinding at the mill; one is taken and one is left.

Gos. Thom. 61.1 (Nag Hammadi II 2)

Λέγει Ἰησοῦς· δύο ἀναπαύσονται ἐπὶ κλίνης, ὁ εἷς ἀποθανεῖται, ὁ εἷς ζήσεται.

Jesus said: Two will rest on a bed. The one will die, the other will live.

Q 17:37 is to be found above, between Q 17:23-24, ~~25~~ and Q 17:26-27.

Q 17:34-35

Luke 17:34-35	Lukan Doublet	Markan Parallel	*Gos. Thom.* 61.1
0/ **17:34** [λέγω ὑμῖν,][1] [ταύτῃ τῇ νυκτὶ][2] ⸉ἔσονται⸊[3] δύο ⸉ ⸊[3] [ἐπὶ κλίνης μιᾶς][4], [ὁ][5] εἷς παραλ[ημφθήσ][6]εται καὶ [ὁ][5] [ἕτερος][7] ἀφ[εθήσ][6]εται· **17:35** [ἔσονται][8] δύο ἀλήθουσαι [ἐπὶ τὸ αὐτό][9], [ἡ][5] μία παραλ[ημφθήσ][6]εται [ἡ][5] [δὲ][10] [ἑτέρα][7] ἀφ[εθήσ][6]εται. \0			пеҳе ⲓ̅ⲥ̅ ⲟⲩⲛ̄ ⲥⲛⲁⲩ ⲛⲁⲙ̄ⲧⲟⲛ' ⲙ̄ⲙⲁⲩ ϩⲓ ⲟⲩϭⲗⲟϭ ⲡⲟⲩⲁ ⲛⲁⲙⲟⲩ ⲡⲟⲩⲁ ⲛⲁⲱⲛϩ

IQP 1991: [ἐπὶ κλίνης μιᾶς][4].

Text Critical Note (see the discussion in the front matter): Luke 17:36 is attested only in some manuscripts: δύο ἔσονται (- D 579 *pc*) ἐν τῷ ἀγρῷ· εἷς παραλη(μ)φθήσεται καὶ ὁ ἕτερος (ἡ δὲ ἕτερα *f*[13]) ἀφεθήσεται D *f*[13] (579) 700 *al* lat sy.

[6] Luke's παραλημφθήσεται ... ἀφεθήσεται or Matthew's παραλαμβάνεται ... ἀφίεται.

[7] Luke's ἕτερος ... ἑτέρα or Matthew's εἷς ... μία.

[8] Luke's second ἔσονται.

[9] Luke's ἐπὶ τὸ αὐτό or Matthew's ἐν τῷ μύλῳ.

[10] Luke's δέ or Matthew's καί.

34 Ich sage euch, zwei «Männer» werden ⟦auf dem Acker⟧ sein; einer wird weggenommen und einer wird zurückgelassen. **35** Zwei «Frauen» werden an der Mühle mahlen, eine wird weggenommen und eine wird zurückgelassen.

34 Je vous «le» dis: Il y aura deux «hommes» ⟦dans le champ⟧; un est pris et un est laissé. **35** Il y aura deux «femmes» en train de moudre au moulin; une est prise et une est laissée.

Jesus sprach: Zwei werden ruhen auf einem Bett. Der eine wird sterben, der andere wird leben.

Jésus dit: Deux reposeront sur un lit. L'un mourra, l'autre vivra.

Q 17:37 is to be found above, between Q 17:23-24, ~~25~~ and Q 17:26-27.

Q 19:12

Mark 13:34a	Matthean Doublet	Matt 25:14a	Q 19:12
		[0]/	[0]/
		[1]ʃ	[1]ʃ
Ὡς		({Ὥσ}περ)[2]	[ ][2]
		(γὰρ)[3]	([])[3]
ἄνθρωπος		{ἄνθρωπος	{ἄνθρωπός} [τις][4]
ἀπόδημος		(ἀποδημ}ῶν)[5]	({ἀποδημ}ῶν)[5]
ἀφεὶς τὴν οἰκίαν αὐτοῦ			
		[ ][6]	[][6]
		ʅ[1]⇒ Matt 25:30	ʅ[1]⇒ Q 19:⟦~~27~~⟧
		\[0]⇒ Matt 25:30	\[0]⇒ Q 19:⟦~~27~~⟧

IQP 1994: ⟦[][4] ({ἀποδημ}ῶν)[5]⟧.

[0] Is the parable in Q?

[1] The position of the parable in Q: After Q 17:35, 37 and before Q 22:28 (Lukan order); or, as the end of Q, after Q 12:42-46; 13:25-27 (Matt 24:45-51; 25:10-12, but see Matt 7:22-23) (Matthean order).

[2] Luke's εἶπεν or Matthew's ὥσπερ.

Q

.. ἄνθρωπός τις ἀποδημῶν	.. A certain person, on taking a trip,

Q 19:12

Luke 19:12	Lukan Doublet	Mark 13:34a	Gospel of Thomas
⁰/			
¹ʃ			
[εἶπεν]²		Ὡς	
[οὖν]³·			
{ἄνθρωπός} [τις]⁴		ἄνθρωπος	
[εὐγενὴς ἐπορεύθη		ἀπόδημος	
εἰς χώραν μακρὰν]⁵		ἀφεὶς τὴν οἰκίαν αὐτοῦ	
[λαβεῖν ἑαυτῷ βασιλείαν			
καὶ ὑποστρέψαι]⁶.			
ɩ¹⇒ Luke 19:27			
\⁰⇒ Luke 19:27			

3 Luke's οὖν or Matthew's γάρ.
4 Luke's τις.

5 Luke's εὐγενὴς ἐπορεύθη εἰς χώραν μακράν or Matthew's ἀποδημῶν.
6 Luke's λαβεῖν ἑαυτῷ βασιλείαν καὶ ὑποστρέψαι.

.. Ein Mensch, der auf Reisen gehen «wollte»,

«Il était» un homme «qui», partant en voyage,

Q 19:13

Mark 13:34b	Matthean Doublet	Matt 25:14b-15b	Q 19:13
		25:14b (ἐ)^{1}κάλεσ(εν)^{1}	(ἐ)^{1}κάλεσ(εν)^{1}
		[ ]^{2}	[]^{2}
		({το}ὺ{ς})^{3}	[δέκα]^{3}
		⸉ (ἰδίους)^{4} ⸊4	⸉ ()^{4} ⸊4
		{δούλο}υ{ς}	{δούλο}υ{ς}
		⸉ [ ]^{4} ⸊4	⸉ [ἑ{αυτοῦ}]^{4} ⸊4
καὶ		{(καὶ)}^{1}	{(καὶ)}^{1}
δοὺς τοῖς δούλοις αὐτοῦ		(παρ)^{5}έ{δ}ωκεν αὐτοῖς	()^{5}ἔ{δ}ωκεν αὐτοῖς
τὴν ἐξουσίαν		({τ}ὰ ὑπάρχοντα {αὐτοῦ},	[δέκα μνᾶς]^{6}
		25:15a-b καὶ ᾧ μὲν	
		ἔδωκεν πέντε τάλαντα,	
		ᾧ δὲ δύο, ᾧ δὲ ἕν,)^{6}	
ἑκάστῳ τὸ ἔργον αὐτοῦ		({ἑκάστῳ}	⟦[καὶ εἶπεν]^{7} []^{7} [αὐτο]^{7}<ῖ>^{7}[ς·
καὶ τῷ θυρωρῷ ἐνετείλατο		κατὰ {τ}ὴν ἰδίαν δύναμιν,)^{7}	πραγματεύσασθε
ἵνα γρηγορῇ.			ἐν ᾧ ἔρχομαι]^{7}
		(καὶ ἀπεδήμησεν)^{8}.	()^{8}⟧.

IQP 1994: ({το}ὺ{ς})^{3}.

IQP 1994: []^{6} [ ]^{7} ()^{8}.

^{1} Luke's καλέσας or Matthew's ἐκάλεσεν … καί.
^{2} Luke's δέ.
^{3} Luke's δέκα or Matthew's τούς.

^{4} Luke's ἑαυτοῦ after δούλους or Matthew's ἰδίους before δούλους.

Q

ἐκάλεσεν δέκα δούλους ἑαυτοῦ καὶ ἔδωκεν αὐτοῖς δέκα μνᾶς ⟦καὶ εἶπεν αὐτο<ῖ>ς· πραγματεύσασθε ἐν ᾧ ἔρχομαι⟧.

called ten of his slaves and gave them ten minas ⟦and said to them: Do business until I come⟧.

Q 19:13

Luke 19:13	Lukan Doublet	Mark 13:34b	Gospel of Thomas
( )¹καλέσ[ας]¹			
[δὲ]²			
[δέκα]³			
ʃ ( )⁴ ʅ⁴			
{δούλο}υ{ς}			
ʃ [ἑ{αυτοῦ}]⁴ ʅ⁴			
( )¹		καὶ	
( )⁵ἔ{δ}ωκεν αὐτοῖς		δοὺς τοῖς δούλοις αὐτοῦ	
[δέκα μνᾶς]⁶		τὴν ἐξουσίαν	
[καὶ εἶπεν πρὸς αὐτούς·		ἑκάστῳ τὸ ἔργον αὐτοῦ	
πραγματεύσασθε		καὶ τῷ θυρωρῷ ἐνετείλατο	
ἐν ᾧ ἔρχομαι]⁷		ἵνα γρηγορῇ.	
( )⁸.			

[5] Matthew's παρ-. (See ἔδωκεν in Matt 25:15a.)

[6] Luke's δέκα μνᾶς or Matthew's τὰ ὑπάρχοντα αὐτοῦ, καὶ ᾧ μὲν ἔδωκεν πέντε τάλαντα, ᾧ δὲ δύο ᾧ δὲ ἕν.

[7] Luke's καὶ εἶπεν πρὸς αὐτούς· πραγματεύσασθε ἐν ᾧ ἔρχομαι or Matthew's ἑκάστῳ κατὰ τὴν ἰδίαν δύναμιν.

[8] Matthew's καὶ ἀπεδήμησεν.

rief zehn seiner Sklaven und gab ihnen zehn Minen ⟦und sagte ihnen: Macht Geschäfte «damit», bis ich komme⟧.

appela dix de ses esclaves et leur confia dix mines. ⟦Et il leur dit: Faites des affaires jusqu'à ce que je revienne.⟧.

Q 19:~~13↔15/Matt 25:15c-18~~

Markan Parallel	Matthean Doublet	Matt 25:15c-18	Q 19:13↔15/Matt 25:15c-18
		(**25:15c** εὐθέως **25:16** πορευθεὶς ὁ τὰ πέντε τάλαντα λαβὼν ἠργάσατο ἐν αὐτοῖς καὶ ἐκέρδησεν ἄλλα πέντε· **25:17** ὡσαύτως ὁ τὰ δύο ἐκέρδησεν ἄλλα δύο. **25:18** ὁ δὲ τὸ ἓν λαβὼν ἀπελθὼν ὤρυξεν γῆν καὶ ἔκρυψεν τὸ ἀργύριον τοῦ κυρίου αὐτοῦ.)[0]	()[0]

[0] Is Matthew 25:15c-18 in Q? (See also Q 19:16[9] and Q 19:18[9] [Matt 25:20, 22: both ἐκέρδησα], and Q 19:20-21

Q 19:~~13↔15/Matt 25:15c-18~~

Luke	Lukan Doublet	Markan Parallel	Gospel of Thomas
( )⁰			

[Matt 25:25: ἔκρυψα … ἐν τῇ γῇ].)

Q 19:~~14~~

Markan Parallel	Matthean Doublet	Matthew	Q 19:~~14~~
		[ ][0]	[][0]

[0] Is Luke 19:14 in Q? (See also Luke 19:27.)

Q 19:~~14~~

Luke 19:14	Lukan Doublet	Markan Parallel	Gospel of Thomas
[οἱ δὲ πολῖται αὐτοῦ ἐμίσουν αὐτὸν καὶ ἀπέστειλαν πρεσβείαν ὀπίσω αὐτοῦ λέγοντες· οὐ θέλομεν τοῦτον βασιλεῦσαι ἐφ' ἡμᾶς.][0]			

Q 19:15

Markan Parallel	Matthean Doublet	Matt 25:19	Q 19:15
		ʃ [ ][1] ʅ[1]	ʃ [ ][1] ʅ[1]
		(μετὰ)[2] ʃ (δὲ)[1] ʅ[1]	⟦(μετὰ)[2]⟧ ʃ ( )[1] ʅ[1]
		(πολὺν χρόνον)[2]	⟦(πολὺν χρόνον)[2]⟧
		(ἔρχεται)[3]	(ἔρχεται)[3]
		[ ][4]	[][4]
		(ὁ κύριος)[5]	(ὁ κύριος)[5]
		ʃ ʅ[6]	ʃʅ[6]
		τ(ῶν)[7] δούλ(ων)[7]	τ(ῶν)[7] δούλ(ων)[7]
		(ἐκείνων)[8]	(ἐκείνων)[8]
		[6]ʃκαὶ (συναίρει λόγον μετ' αὐτῶν)[9] ʅ[6]	[6]ʃκαὶ (συναίρει λόγον μετ' αὐτῶν)[9] ʅ[6]
		[ ][9]	[][9]
		.	.

IQP 1994: [][1]… ()[1].

[1] Luke's καί or Matthew's postpositive δέ.

[2] Matthew's μετὰ … πολὺν χρόνον.

[3] Luke's ἐγένετο ἐν τῷ ἐπανελθεῖν or Matthew's ἔρχεται.

[4] Luke's αὐτὸν λαβόντα τὴν βασιλείαν.

[5] Matthew's ὁ κύριος.

[6] The position of the master's summons before (Luke) or after (Matthew) mentioning the slaves.

Q

.. ⟦μετὰ⟧ .. ⟦πολὺν χρόνον⟧ ἔρχεται ὁ κύριος τῶν δούλων ἐκείνων καὶ συναίρει λόγον μετ' αὐτῶν.

.. ⟦After a long time⟧ the master of those slaves comes and settles accounts with them.

Q 19:15

Luke 19:15	Lukan Doublet	Markan Parallel	Gospel of Thomas
ʃ [καὶ][1] ʅ[1] ( )[2] ʃ ( )[1] ʅ[1] ( )[2] [ἐγένετο ἐν τῷ ἐπανελθεῖν][3] [αὐτὸν λαβόντα τὴν βασιλείαν][4] ( )[5] [6]ʃκαὶ [εἶπεν φωνηθῆναι αὐτῷ][9] ʅ[6] τ[οὺς][7] δούλ[ους][7] [τούτους οἷς δεδώκει τὸ ἀργύριον][8], ʃ ʅ[6] [ἵνα γνοῖ τί διεπραγματεύσαντο][9].			

[7] Luke's τοὺς δούλους or Matthew's τῶν δούλων. (The decision depends on variation units [5] and [9].)

[8] Luke's τούτους οἷς δεδώκει τὸ ἀργύριον (see also τὸ ἀργύριον in Matt 25:18) or Matthew's ἐκείνων.

[9] Luke's εἶπεν φωνηθῆναι αὐτῷ … ἵνα γνοῖ τί διεπραγματεύσαντο or Matthew's συναίρει λόγον μετ' αὐτῶν.

.. ⟦Nach langer Zeit⟧ kommt der Herr jener Sklaven und hält Abrechnung mit ihnen.

.. ⟦Longtemps après,⟧ le maître de ces esclaves revient et règle ses comptes avec eux.

Q 19:16

Matt 25:24a, 25	Matt 25:22	Matt 25:20	Q 19:16
		ʃ (καὶ)[1] ʅ[1]	ʃ (καὶ)[1] ʅ[1]
25:24a (προσελθὼν)	(προσελθὼν)	(προσελθὼν)[2]	⟦<ἦ>[2](λθ)[2]<εν>[2]⟧
[δὲ] (καὶ)	[δὲ] (καὶ)	ʃ [ ][1] ʅ[1]	ʃ [][1] ʅ[1]
([ὁ] τ)ὸ ἓν (τάλαντ)ον	([ὁ] τὰ) δύο (τάλαντα)	ὁ (τὰ πέντε τάλαντα	ὁ [πρῶτος][3]
εἰληφὼς		λαβὼν προσήνεγκεν	
		ἄλλα πέντε τάλαντα)[3]	
εἶπεν·	εἶπεν·	λέγων·	λέγων·
([κύριε,])…	([κύριε,])	κύριε,	κύριε,
25:25 καὶ φοβηθεὶς ἀπελθὼν	δύο (τάλαντά	(πέντε τάλαντά)[4]	[ἡ μνᾶ][4]
ἔκρυψα τὸ (τάλαντ)όν [σου]	μοι παρέδωκας·	(μοι παρέδωκας)[5]·	[σου][5]
ἐν τῇ γῇ· (ἴδε)	ἴδε	(ἴδε)[6]	()[6]
ἔχεις	ἄλλα) δύο	(ἄλλα πέντε)[7]	[δέκα][7]
τὸ σόν.	(τάλαντα	[8]ʃ (τάλαντα)[4] ʅ[8]	ʃʅ[8]
	ἐκέρδησα).	(ἐκέρδησα)[9].	[προσηργάσατο][9]
		ʃ ʅ[8]	[8]ʃ [μνᾶς][4] ʅ[8].

IQP 1994: ( )[1] < >[2]( )[2]< >[2] [][1] ὁ ⟦[πρῶτος][3]⟧.

IQP 1994: [ ][3] ⟦[σου δέκα προσηργάσατο][3]⟧ [ ][3].

[1] Luke's postpositive δέ or Matthew's καί.

[2] Luke's παρεγένετο or Matthew's προσελθών followed by a finite verb form.

[3] Luke's πρῶτος or Matthew's τὰ πέντε τάλαντα λαβὼν προσήνεγκεν ἄλλα πέντε τάλαντα. (The decision depends on the decision at Q 19:13[6].)

[4] Luke's ἡ μνᾶ … μνᾶς or Matthew's πέντε τάλαντα … τάλαντα. (The decision depends on the decision at Q 19:13[6].)

Q

καὶ ⟦<ἦ>λθ<εν>⟧ ὁ πρῶτος λέγων· κύριε, ἡ μνᾶ σου δέκα προσηργάσατο μνᾶς.	And the first ⟦came⟧ saying: Master, your mina has produced ten more minas.

Q 19:16

Luke 19:16	Luke 19:18	Luke 19:20	Gospel of Thomas
ʃ ( )[1] ʅ[1]	(καὶ)	(καὶ) ([ὁ]) ἕτερος	
[παρεγένετο][2]	ἦ(λθ)εν	ἦ(λθ)εν	
ʃ [δὲ][1] ʅ[1]			
ὁ [πρῶτος][3]	[(ὁ)] δεύτερος		
λέγων·	[(λέγων·)]	[(λέγων·	
κύριε,		κύριε,)]	
[ἡ μνᾶ][4]	[ἡ μνᾶ	(ἰδ)οὺ [ἡ μνᾶ	
[σου][5]	σου],	σου]	
( )[6]	[(κύριε,)]	ἣν εἶχον	
[δέκα][7]			
ʃ ʅ[8]			
[προσηργάσατο][9]	ἐποίησεν	ἀποκειμένην	
[8]ʃ [μνᾶς][4] ʅ[8].	(πέντε) [μνᾶς].	ἐν σουδαρίῳ·	

5 Luke's σου or Matthew's μοι παρέδωκας.
6 Matthew's ἴδε.
7 Luke's δέκα or Matthew's ἄλλα πέντε.

8 The position of the currency after (Luke) or before (Matthew) the verb.
9 Luke's προσηργάσατο (see ἠργάσατο in Matt 25:16) or Matthew's ἐκέρδησα. (See ἐκέρδησεν in Matt 25:16, 17.)

Und der erste [[kam]] «und» sagte: Herr, deine Mine hat zehn Minen hinzuerworben.

Et le premier [[vint]] en disant: Maître, ta mine a rapporté dix mines.

Q 19:17

Matt 25:26	Matt 25:23	Matt 25:21	Q 19:17
ἀποκριθεὶς δὲ (ὁ κύριος		[ ][1]	[καὶ][1]
αὐτοῦ) [εἶπεν (αὐτῷ)]·	(ἔφη [αὐτῷ]	(ἔφη)[2] αὐτῷ	[εἶπεν][2] αὐτῷ
	ὁ κύριος αὐτοῦ·	(ὁ κύριος αὐτοῦ)[3]·	⟦()[3]⟧·
	εὖ,	εὖ[ ][4],	εὖ[][4],
πονηρὲ [(δοῦλε)]	[δοῦλε] [ἀγαθὲ]	ʃ ʅ[5] δοῦλε ʃἀγαθὲʅ[5]	ʃἀγαθὲʅ[5] δοῦλε ʃ ʅ[5]
(καὶ) ὀκνηρέ,	καὶ πιστέ,	(καὶ πιστέ)[6],	()[6],
ᾔδεις [ὅτι]		[ ][7]	⟦[][7]⟧
θερίζω	ἐπὶ ὀλίγα	(ἐπὶ ὀλίγα)[8]	(ἐπὶ ὀλίγα)[8]
ὅπου	ἦς [πιστός],	ʃ (ἦς)[9] ʅ[9] πιστός ʃ [ ][9] ʅ[9],	ʃ (ἦς)[9] ʅ[9] πιστός ʃ [][9] ʅ[9],
οὐκ ἔσπειρα	[ἐπ]ὶ πολλῶν	[10]ʃ (ἐπὶ πολλῶν)[11] ʅ[10]	[10]ʃ (ἐπὶ πολλῶν)[11] ʅ[10]
καὶ	σε καταστήσω·	(σε καταστήσω)[12]·	(σε καταστήσω)[12]·
συνάγω		ʃ ʅ[10]	ʃʅ[10]
ὅθεν	εἴσελθε εἰς τὴν χαρὰν	(εἴσελθε εἰς τὴν χαρὰν	()[13]
οὐ διεσκόρπισα;	τοῦ κυρίου σου).	τοῦ κυρίου σου)[13].	

IQP 1994: ( )[3] omit {D}.

IQP 1994: ( )[8].

[1] Luke's καί.
[2] Luke's εἶπεν or Matthew's ἔφη.
[3] Matthew's ὁ κύριος αὐτοῦ.
[4] Luke's εὖγε or Matthew's εὖ.
[5] The position of ἀγαθέ before (Luke) or after (Matthew) δοῦλε.
[6] Matthew's καὶ πιστέ.
[7] Luke's ὅτι.
[8] Luke's ἐν ἐλαχίστῳ or Matthew's ἐπὶ ὀλίγα.
[9] Luke's ἐγένου or Matthew's ἦς, and the position of the verb after (Luke) or before (Matthew) πιστός.

Q

καὶ εἶπεν αὐτῷ· εὖ, ἀγαθὲ δοῦλε, ἐπὶ ὀλίγα ἦς πιστός, ἐπὶ πολλῶν σε καταστήσω.

And he said to him: Well done, good slave, you have been faithful over a pittance, I will set you over much.

Q 19:17

Luke 19:17	Luke 19:19	Luke 19:22	Luke 16:10a
[καὶ][1]			
[εἶπεν][2] αὐτῷ	[εἶπεν] δὲ [καὶ] τούτ[(ῳ)]·	λέγει [(αὐτῷ)]·	
( )[3]·		ἐκ τοῦ στόματός σου	
εὖ[γε][4],	καὶ	κρινῶ σε,	
⸉ἀγαθὲ⸊[5] δοῦλε⸉ ⸊[5]		πονηρὲ [(δοῦλε)].	
( )[6],			
[ὅτι][7]		ᾔδεις [ὅτι] ἐγὼ	
[ἐν ἐλαχίστῳ][8]		ἄνθρωπος αὐστηρός εἰμι,	
⸉ ( )[9] ⸊[9] πιστὸς ⸉ [ἐγένου][9] ⸊[9],		αἴρων	Ὁ [(πιστὸς)]
⸉ ⸊[10]		ὃ οὐκ ἔθηκα	[ἐν ἐλαχίστῳ]
[ἴσθι ἐξουσίαν ἔχων][12]	(σ)ὺ	καὶ	καὶ ἐν (πολλ)ῷ
[10]⸉ [ἐπάνω δέκα	[ἐπάνω] γίνου πέντε	θερίζων	πιστός ἐστιν,
πόλεων][11]. ⸊[10]	[πόλεων].	ὃ	
( )[13]		οὐκ ἔσπειρα;	

[10] Does the prepositional phrase follow (Luke) or precede (Matthew) the verbal expression?

[11] Luke's ἐπάνω δέκα πόλεων or Matthew's ἐπὶ πολλῶν. (The decision depends on the decision at Q 19:13[6].)

[12] Luke's ἴσθι ἐξουσίαν ἔχων or Matthew's σε καταστήσω. (See also κατέστησεν in Luke 12:42 and καταστήσει in Luke 12:44.)

[13] Matthew's εἴσελθε εἰς τὴν χαρὰν τοῦ κυρίου σου.

Und er sagte ihm: «Sehr» gut, du guter Sklave, mit Wenigem warst du zuverlässig, über Vieles werde ich dich stellen.

Et il lui dit: C'est bien, bon esclave, tu as été digne de confiance avec peu, je vais t'établir sur de nombreux biens.

Q 19:18

Matt 25:24a, 25	Matt 25:20	Matt 25:22	Q 19:18
	([καὶ])	⸂ ⸃[1]	⸂καὶ⸃[1]
25:24a (προσε[λθ]ὼν	(προσελθὼν)	(προσε)[2]λθ(ὼ)[2]ν	[ἦ][2]λθ[ε][2]ν
δὲ [καὶ]		⸂ (δὲ)[1] καὶ⸃[1]	⸂ ()[1] ⸃[1]
[ὁ] τ)ὸ ἓν (τάλαντ)ον	([ὁ] τὰ) πέντε (τάλαντα)	ὁ (τὰ δύο τάλαντα)[3]	ὁ ⟦[δεύτερος][3]⟧
εἰληφὼς	λαβὼν προσήνεγκεν		
	ἄλλα πέντε τάλαντα		
(εἶπεν·	[λέγων]·	(εἶπεν)[2]·	[λέγων][2]·
[κύριε,])…	[(κύριε,)]	⸂κύριε,⸃[4]	⸂κύριε,⸃[4]
25:25 καὶ φοβηθεὶς ἀπελθὼν	πέντε (τάλαντά	(δύο τάλαντά)[5]	[ἡ μνᾶ][5]
ἔκρυψα τὸ (τάλαντ)όν [σου]	μοι παρέδωκας·	(μοι παρέδωκας)[6]·	[σου][6]
ἐν τῇ γῇ·		⸂ ⸃[4]	⸂⸃[4]
(ἴδε)	ἴδε	(ἴδε)[7]	()[7]
ἔχεις	ἄλλα) [πέντε] (τάλαντα)	[8]⸂ (ἄλλα δύο τάλαντα)[5] ⸃[8]	⸂⸃[8]
τὸ σόν	ἐκέρδησα)	ἐ(κέρδ)[9]ησ(α)[10]	ἐ[ποί][9]ησ[εν][10]
.	.	⸂ ⸃[8].	[8]⸂ [πέντε μνᾶς][5] ⸃[8].

IQP 1994: ⟦[ ][5] [ ][6] ⸂⸃[4] ( )[7] ⸂ ⸃[8] ἐ[ ][9]ησ[ ][10] [8]⸂ [ ][5] ⸃[8].

[1] Luke's use of καί as a conjunction or Matthew's use of postpositive δέ as a conjunction followed by καί as an adverb. (See Q 19:19[3], 20-21[1].)

[2] Luke's ἦλθεν … λέγων or Matthew's προσελθὼν … εἶπεν.

[3] Luke's δεύτερος or Matthew's τὰ δύο τάλαντα.

[4] Does κύριε occur in the middle of the statement (Luke) or at its beginning (Matthew)?

[5] Luke's ἡ μνᾶ … πέντε μνᾶς or Matthew's δύο τάλαντά … ἄλλα δύο τάλαντα. (The decision depends on the decision at Q 19:13[6].)

Q

καὶ ἦλθεν ὁ ⟦δεύτερος⟧ λέγων· κύριε, ἡ μνᾶ σου ἐποίησεν πέντε μνᾶς.	And the ⟦second⟧ came saying: Master, your mina has earned five minas.

Q 19:18

Luke 19:18	Luke 19:16	Luke 19:20	Gospel of Thomas
ʃκαὶʅ[1]		καὶ ὁ ἕτερος	
[ἦ][2]λθ[ε][2]ν	παρεγένετο	ἦ(λθ)εν	
ʃ ( )[1] ʅ[1]	(δὲ)		
ὁ [δεύτερος][3]	([ὁ)] πρῶτος		
[λέγων][2]·	[λέγων]·	[λέγων]·	
ʃ ʅ[4]	[(κύριε,)]	[(κύριε,)]	
[ἡ μνᾶ][5]	[ἡ μνᾶ	ἰδοὺ [ἡ μνᾶ	
[σου][6],	σου]	σου]	
ʃκύριε,ʅ[4]		ἣν εἶχον	
( )[7]			
ʃ ʅ[8]	δέκα		
ἐ[ποί][9]ησ[εν][10]	προσηργάσατο	ἀποκειμένην	
[8]ʃ [πέντε μνᾶς][5] ʅ[8].	[μνᾶς].	ἐν σουδαρίῳ·	

6 Luke's σου or Matthew's μοι παρέδωκας.

7 Matthew's ἴδε.

8 The position of the quantity and of the currency after (Luke) or before (Matthew) the verb.

9 Luke's ἐποίησεν or Matthew's ἐκέρδησα. (See ἐκέρδησεν in Matt 25:16, 17.)

10 Luke's third person formulation or Matthew's first person.

Und der ⟦zweite⟧ kam «und» sagte: Herr, deine Mine hat fünf Minen gemacht.

Puis le ⟦second⟧ vint en disant: Maître, ta mine a produit cinq mines.

Q 19:19

Matt 25:26	Matt 25:21	Matt 25:23	Q 19:19
ἀποκριθεὶς [δὲ] (ὁ κύριος	(ἔφη	(ἔφη)[1]	[εἶπεν][1]
αὐτοῦ) [εἶπεν]		[ ][2]	[][2]
		[ ][3]	⟦[][3]
(αὐτ[ῷ])·	αὐτ[ῷ]	(αὐτ)[4]ῷ	(αὐτ)[4]⟧ῷ
πονηρὲ (δοῦλε)	ὁ κύριος αὐτοῦ·	(ὁ κύριος αὐτοῦ)[5]·	⟦()[5]·
(καὶ) ὀκνηρέ,	εὖ, δοῦλε ἀγαθὲ	(εὖ, ⸉ ⸊ δοῦλε ⸉ἀγαθὲ⸊)[6]	(εὖ, ⸉ἀγαθὲ⸊ δοῦλε ⸉ ⸊)[6]
ᾔδεις ὅτι	καὶ πιστέ,	(καὶ πιστέ)[6],	()[6],
θερίζω	[ἐπ]ὶ ὀλίγα	(ἐπὶ ὀλίγα	(ἐπὶ ὀλίγα
ὅπου	ἦς πιστός,	ἦς πιστός,)[6]	ἦς πιστός,)[6]⟧
οὐκ ἔσπειρα		⸉ ⸊[7]	⸉ ⸊[7]
καὶ	ἐπὶ	ἐπ(ὶ)[8]	ἐπ(ὶ)[8]
συνάγω		⸉ ⸊[9]	⸉⸊[9]
ὅθεν	πολλῶν	(πολλῶν)[8]	(πολλῶν)[8]
οὐ διεσκόρπισα;	σε	[7]⸉σ(ε)[10] ⸊[7]	⸉σ(ε)[10] ⸊[7]
	καταστήσω·	[9]⸉ (καταστήσω)[10] ⸊[9].	[9]⸉ (καταστήσω)[10] ⸊[9]
	εἴσελθε εἰς τὴν χαρὰν	(εἴσελθε εἰς τὴν χαρὰν	()[11]
	τοῦ κυρίου σου).	τοῦ κυρίου σου)[11].	.

IQP 1994: ⟦[δὲ][2] [καὶ][3]⟧ [ ][4]ῳ ()[5]· ⟦[καὶ][6]⟧ [7]⸉σ(ε)[8] ⸊[7] [9]⸉ (καταστήσω)[8] ⸊[9] (ἐπὶ)[10] ⸉ ⸊[9] (πολλῶν)[10] ⸉ ⸊[7].

1 Luke's εἶπεν or Matthew's ἔφη.

2 Luke's δέ.

3 Luke's καί. (See variation unit 6 and Q 19:18[1], 20-21[1].)

4 Luke's τούτῳ or Matthew's αὐτῷ.

5 Matthew's ὁ κύριος αὐτοῦ.

6 Luke's καί or Matthew's εὖ, δοῦλε ἀγαθὲ καὶ πιστέ, ἐπὶ ὀλίγα ἦς πιστός, or emended to read (see Q 19:17[5.6]): εὖ, ἀγαθὲ δοῦλε, ἐπὶ ὀλίγα ἦς πιστός.

Q

εἶπεν ⟦αὐτ⟧ῷ· ⟦εὖ, ἀγαθὲ δοῦλε, ἐπὶ ὀλίγα ἦς πιστός,⟧ ἐπὶ πολλῶν σε καταστήσω.	He said to ⟦him: Well done, good slave, you have been faithful over a pittance,⟧ I will set you over much.

Q 19:19

Luke 19:19	Luke 19:17	Luke 19:22	Luke 16:10a
[εἶπεν][1]	[καὶ] [εἶπεν]	λέγει	
[δὲ][2]			
[καὶ][3]			
[τούτ][4]ῳ	(αὐτ[ῷ])	(αὐτ[ῷ])·	
( )[5]·	·		
[καὶ][6]	(εὖ)γε, (ἀγαθὲ) (δοῦλε),	ἐκ τοῦ στόματός σου	
( )[6]		κρινῶ [σ]ε,	
( )[6]	ὅτι ἐν ἐλαχίστῳ		Ὁ (πιστὸς)
	πιστὸς ἐ[γ]έ[νου],	πονηρὲ (δοῦλε).	ἐν ἐλαχίστῳ
[7]⸂σ[ὺ][10] ⸃[7]	ἴσθι ἐξουσίαν ἔχων	ᾔδεις	
ἐπ[άνω][8]	[(ἐπ)άνω]	ὅτι ἐγὼ ἄνθρωπος	καὶ ἐν (πολλ)ῷ
[9]⸂ [γίνου][10] ⸃[9]		αὐστηρός εἰμι,	πιστός ἐστιν,
[πέντε πόλεων][8]	δέκα [πόλεων]	αἴρων	
⸂ ⸃[7]		ὃ οὐκ ἔθηκα	
⸂ ⸃[9]		καὶ θερίζων	
( )[11]		ὃ οὐκ ἔσπειρα;	
.	.		

[7] The position of the second person pronoun before (Luke) or after (Matthew) the prepositional phrase.

[8] Luke's ἐπάνω … πέντε πόλεων or Matthew's ἐπὶ πολλῶν. (The decision depends on the decision at Q 19:13[6].)

[9] The position of the verb in the middle (Luke) or after (Matthew) the prepositional phrase.

[10] Luke's σὺ … γίνου or Matthew's σε καταστήσω.

[11] Matthew's εἴσελθε εἰς τὴν χαρὰν τοῦ κυρίου σου.

Er sagte zu ⟦ihm: «Sehr» gut, du guter Sklave, mit wenigem warst du zuverlässig,⟧ über vieles werde ich dich stellen.

Il ⟦lui⟧ dit: ⟦C'est bien, bon esclave, tu as été digne de confiance avec peu,⟧ je vais t'établir sur de nombreux biens.

Q 19:20-21

Matt 25:20	Matt 25:22a, 26b, 22b	Matt 25:24-25	Q 19:20-21
[(καὶ)]		**25:24** ʃ ʅ[1]	**19:20** ʃκαὶʅ[1]
		ʃ ʅ[2]	ʃ ʅ[2]
(προσε[λθ]ὼν)	**25:22a** (προσε[λθ]ὼν	(προσε)[4]λθ(ὼν)[4]	[ἦ][4]λθ[εν][4]
	δὲ [καὶ	ʃ (δὲ)[1] καὶʅ[1]	ʃ ()[1] ʅ[1]
(ὁ τ)ὰ πέντε (τάλαντ)α	ὁ] τ)ὰ δύο (τάλαντ)α	[2]ʃὁ (τὸ ἓν τάλαντον	[2]ʃὁ [ἕτερος][3] ʅ[2]
λαβὼν προσήνεγκεν		εἰληφὼς)[3] ʅ[2]	
ἄλλα πέντε τάλαντα	(εἶπεν·	(εἶπεν)[4]·	[λέγων][4]·
[λέγων· (κύριε)],	[κύριε]),	κύριε,	κύριε,
		ʃ ʅ[5]	ʃʅ[5]
		ʃ ʅ[6]	ʃʅ[6]
	25:26b πονηρὲ δοῦλε		
	καὶ ὀκνηρέ, ᾔδεις	(ἔγνων)[7]	**19:21** ⟦(ἔγνων)[7]⟧
		ʃ ʅ[8] σε	ʃ ʅ[8] σε
	([ὅτι])	ὅτι ʃ ʅ[9]	ὅτι ʃ ʅ[9]
		(σκλ)[10]ηρὸς εἶ	(σκλ)[10]ηρὸς εἶ
		ʃἄνθρωποςʅ[9],	ʃἄνθρωποςʅ[9],
	([θερίζ]ω)	[11]ʃθερίζ(ων)[12]	[11]ʃθερίζ(ων)[12]
	(ὅπου	(ὅπου)[13]	(ὅπου)[13]

IQP 1994: ʃκαὶʅ[1] [2]ʃὁ ⟦[ἕτερος][3]⟧ ʅ[2] [ἦ][4]λθ[εν][4] ʃ ()[1] ʅ[1] ʃʅ[2].
IQP 1994: ʃ ʅ[5].

IQP 1994: **19:21** [11]ʃθερίζ[εις][12]… (συνάγ)[14]<εις>[12].
IQP 1994: **19:21** ⟦(καί)[8]⟧.

[1] Luke's use of καί as a conjunction or Matthew's use of the postpositive δέ as a conjunction followed by καί as an adverb. (See Q 19:18[1], 19[3].)

[2] The position of the reference to the third slave before (Luke) or after (Matthew) the verb of motion.

[3] Luke's reference to the slave as ὁ ἕτερος or Matthew's ὁ τὸ ἓν τάλαντον εἰληφώς. (The decision depends on the decision at Q 19:13[6].)

[4] Luke's ἦλθεν λέγων or Matthew's προσελθὼν … εἶπεν.

[5] The position of the return of the money before (Luke) or after (Matthew) the slave's explanation of where he had kept it.

[6] The position of the slave's explanation of where he had kept the

Q 19:20-21

Luke 19:20-21	Luke 19:22b	Luke 19:16	Luke 19:18
19:20 ʃκαὶʅ[1]			[(καὶ)]
[2]ʃὁ [ἕτερος][3] ʅ[2]		παρεγένετο (δὲ)	
[ἦ][4]λθ[εν][4]		ὁ πρῶτος	[ἦ(λθ)εν]
ʃ ( )[1] ʅ[1]			
ʃ ʅ[2]			[(ὁ)] δεύτερος
[λέγων][4]·		[λέγων·	[λέγων]·
κύριε,		(κύριε)],	
[5]ʃ			
ἰδ[οὺ][19]			
( )[20]			
[ἡ μνᾶ][21] σ[ου][21]		ἡ μνᾶ σου	ἡ μνᾶ σου, [(κύριε)],
ʅ[5]			
[6]ʃ			
( )[15]			
[ἣν εἶχον ἀποκειμένην][16]			
( )[17]			
ἐν [σουδαρίῳ][18]	ἐκ τοῦ στόματός σου		
ʅ[6].	κρινῶ σε,		
	πονηρὲ δοῦλε.		
19:21 [ἐ][7]φοβ[ούμην][7]	ᾔδεις		
ʃ [γάρ][8] ʅ[8] σε,			
ὅτι ʃἄνθρωποςʅ[9]	[(ὅτι)] ἐγὼ [ἄνθρωπος		
[αὐστ][10]ηρὸς εἶ	αὐστ(ηρός)] εἰμι,		
ʃ ʅ[9],			
[11]ʃ [αἴρ][14][εις][12]	[αἴρ](ων)		
[ὃ][13]	[ὃ		

IQP 1994, JMR, JSK: The Matthean sequence: **19:21** ὅτι ʃ ʅ[9] (σκλ)[10]ηρὸς εἶ ʃἄνθρωποςʅ[9] {D}; PH {C}.

IQP 1994: **19:21** (ἀπ)[15]⟦(ελθὼν)[15] (ἔκρυψα)[16]⟧ < >[17] (σου)[17].
IQP 1994: **19:21** ἴδ(ε)[19] (ἔχ)[20]⟦(εις)[20] (τὸ)[21] σ(όν)[21]⟧.

money before (Luke) or after (Matthew) he gives the reason.

7 Luke's ἐφοβούμην or Matthew's ἔγνων … φοβηθείς.

8 Luke's postpositive γάρ or Matthew's καί deferred by the construction ἔγνων … φοβηθείς.

9 The position of ἄνθρωπος before (Luke) or after (Matthew) the adjective and verb.

10 Luke's αὐστηρός or Matthew's σκληρός.

11 Is θερίζω/σπείρω the second (Luke) or the first (Matthew) metaphor?

12 Luke's construction with two finite verbs or Matthew's with two participles.

13 Luke's ὃ … ὅ or Matthew's ὅπου … ὅθεν.

Q 19:20-21

Matt 25:20	Matt 25:22a, 26b, 22b	Matt 25:24-25	Q 19:20-21
	([οὐκ] ἔσπειρα)	οὐκ ἔσπειραςʅ[11]	οὐκ ἔσπειραςʅ[11]
	([καὶ] συνάγ)ω	καὶ [11]ʃ (συνάγ)[14](ων)[12]	καὶ [11]ʃ (συνάγ)[14](ων)[12]
	(ὅθεν	(ὅθεν)[13]	(ὅθεν)[13]
	[οὐ] διεσκόρπισα);	οὐ (διεσκόρπισ)[14]ας,ʅ[11]	οὐ (διεσκόρπισ)[14]ας,ʅ[11]
		25:25 ʃ (καὶ)[8] ʅ[8]	ʃ (καὶ)[8] ʅ[8]
		φοβ(ηθεὶς)[7]	φοβ⟦(ηθεὶς)[7]⟧
		[6]ʃ	[6]ʃ
		(ἀπελθὼν)[15]	⟦(ἀπελθὼν)[15]⟧
		(ἔκρυψα)[16]	(ἔκρυψα)[16]
πέντε (τάλαντ)ά	**25:22b** δύο (τάλαντ)ά	(τὸ τάλαντόν σου)[17]	⟦<τὴν μνᾶν>[17] (σου)[17]⟧
μοι παρέδωκας·	μοι παρέδωκας·	ἐν (τῇ γῇ)[18]·	ἐν ⟦(τῇ γῇ)[18]⟧·
		ʅ[6]	ʅ[6]
		[5]ʃ	[5]ʃ
(ἴδε)	(ἴδε)	ἴδ(ε)[19]	ἴδ⟦(ε)[19]⟧
		(ἔχεις)[20]	(ἔχεις)[20]
ἄλλα πέντε τάλαντα	ἄλλα δύο τάλαντα	(τὸ)[21] σ(όν)[21]	(τὸ)[21] σ(όν)[21]
ἐκέρδησα.	ἐκέρδησα.	ʅ[5].	ʅ[5].

[14] The choice of verbs: Luke's αἴρω and τίθημι or Matthew's συνάγω and διασκορπίζω, involving Luke's οὐκ or Matthew's οὐ.

[15] Matthew's ἀπελθών.

[16] Luke's ἣν εἶχον ἀποκειμένην or Matthew's ἔκρυψα. (See also Q 19:~~13↔15/Matt 25:15c-18~~: ἔκρυψεν.)

Q

20 καὶ ἦλθεν ὁ ἕτερος λέγων· κύριε, **21** ⟦ἔγνων⟧ σε ὅτι σκληρὸς εἶ ἄνθρωπος, θερίζων ὅπου οὐκ ἔσπειρας καὶ συνάγων ὅθεν οὐ διεσκόρπισας, καὶ φοβ⟦ηθεὶς ἀπελθὼν⟧ ἔκρυψα ⟦<τὴν μνᾶν> σου⟧ ἐν ⟦τῇ γῇ⟧· ἴδ⟦ε⟧ ἔχεις τὸ σόν.

20 And the other came saying: Master, **21** ⟦I knew⟧ you, that you are a hard person, reaping where you did not sow and gathering up from where you did not winnow; and, scared, I ⟦went «and»⟧ hid ⟦your <mina>⟧ in ⟦the ground⟧. Here, you have what belongs to you.

Q 19:20-21

Luke 19:20-21	Luke 19:22b	Luke 19:16	Luke 19:18
οὐ[κ ἔθηκ][14]ας⸃[11]	(οὐ)κ ἔθηκα]		
καὶ [11]⸂θερίζ[εις][12]	[(καὶ) (θερίζ]ων)		
[ὃ][13]	[ὃ		
οὐκ ἔσπειρας⸃[11]	(οὐκ ἔσπειρα)];		
⸂ ⸃[8]			
( )[7]			
⸂ ⸃[6]			
⸂ ⸃[5]			
		δέκα	
		προσηργάσατο	ἐποίησεν
		μνᾶς.	πέντε μνᾶς.
.			

[17] Matthew's τὸ τάλαντόν σου. (The decision depends on the decision at 19:13[6]. See also variation unit [21].)

[18] Luke's σουδαρίῳ or Matthew's τῇ γῇ. (See also Q 19:~~13⟨ ⟩15/Matt 25:15c-18~~: γῆν.)

[19] Luke's ἰδού or Matthew's ἴδε.

[20] Matthew's ἔχεις.

[21] Luke's ἡ μνᾶ σου or Matthew's τὸ σόν.

20 Und der dritte kam «und» sagte: Herr, **21** ⟦ich wußte⟧ von dir, dass du ein harter Mensch bist, du erntest, wo du nicht gesät hast, und sammelst ein von dort, wo du nicht ausgestreut hast; und aus Furcht ⟦ging ich hin «und»⟧ verbarg ⟦deine <Mine>⟧ in ⟦der Erde⟧. Sieh, «hier» hast du das Deine.

20 Et un autre vint en disant: Seigneur, **21** ⟦je savais⟧ que tu étais une personne dure, qui moissonnes où tu n'a pas semé et qui ramasses où tu n'as pas répandu; et, par crainte, ⟦je suis allé⟧ cacher ⟦ta <mine>⟧ dans ⟦la terre⟧; «la» voici, tu as ton bien.

Q 19:22

Matt 25:21 = 25:23	Matt 25:24	Matt 25:26	Q 19:22
	προσελθὼν (δὲ) καὶ	(ἀποκριθεὶς δὲ	
ἔφη ([αὐτῷ])	ὁ τὸ ἓν τάλαντον εἰληφὼς	ὁ κύριος αὐτοῦ	
(ὁ κύριος αὐτοῦ)·	(εἶπεν)·	εἶπεν)[1] αὐτῷ·	[λέγει][1] αὐτῷ·
		[ ][2]	[][2]
εὖ, ([δοῦλε]) ἀγαθὲ	κύριε,	πονηρὲ δοῦλε (καὶ ὀκνηρέ)[3],	πονηρὲ δοῦλε ()[3],
(καὶ) πιστέ,	ἔγνων σε ([ὅτι])	ᾔδεις ὅτι	ᾔδεις ὅτι
	σκληρὸς εἶ [ἄνθρωπος],	[ ][4]	[][4]
ἐπὶ ὀλίγα	[(θερίζ)ων]	[5]ʃθερίζ(ω)[4]	[5]ʃθερίζ(ω)[4]
ἦς πιστός,	(ὅπου	(ὅπου)[6]	(ὅπου)[6]
ἐπὶ πολλῶν	[οὐκ ἔσπειρα)]ς	οὐκ ἔσπειραʅ[5]	οὐκ ἔσπειραʅ[5]
σε καταστήσω·	([καὶ]	καὶ	καὶ
εἴσελθε εἰς τὴν χαρὰν	συνάγ)[ων]	[5]ʃ (συνάγ)[7](ω)[4]	[5]ʃ (συνάγ)[7](ω)[4]
τοῦ κυρίου σου.	(ὅθεν	(ὅθεν)[6]	(ὅθεν)[6]
	[οὐ] διεσκόρπισα)ς,	οὐ (διεσκόρπισα)[6] ʅ[5];	οὐ (διεσκόρπισα)[6] ʅ[5];

IQP 1994: ⟦[][4]⟧ [5]ʃθερίζ(ω)[4] … (συνάγ)[6](ω)[4].

1 Luke's λέγει or Matthew's ἀποκριθεὶς δὲ ὁ κύριος αὐτοῦ εἶπεν.
2 Luke's ἐκ τοῦ στόματός σου κρινῶ σε.
3 Matthew's καὶ ὀκνηρέ.
4 Luke's ἐγὼ ἄνθρωπος αὐστηρός εἰμι followed by participles, or the absence of the clause and hence the indicatives (Matthew).

Q

λέγει αὐτῳ· πονηρὲ δοῦλε, ᾔδεις ὅτι θερίζω ὅπου οὐκ ἔσπειρα καὶ συνάγω ὅθεν οὐ διεσκόρπισα;	He said to him: Wicked slave! You knew that I reap where I have not sown, and gather up from where I have not winnowed?

Q 19:22

Luke 19:22	Luke 19:19	Luke 19:17	Luke 19:21
		καὶ	
[λέγει][1] αὐτῷ·	(εἶπεν) (δὲ)	(εἶπεν [αὐτῷ])·	
[ἐκ τοῦ στόματός σου	καὶ τούτ[(ῳ)]·		
κρινῶ σε][2],			
πονηρὲ δοῦλε ( )[3].	καὶ σύ	εὖγε, ἀγαθὲ [(δοῦλε)],	
ᾔδεις ὅτι [ἐγὼ		ὅτι ἐν ἐλαχίστῳ	ἐφοβούμην γάρ σε, [(ὅτι)]
ἄνθρωπος αὐστηρός εἰμι][4],		πιστὸς ἐγένου,	[ἄνθρωπος αὐστηρὸς] εἶ,
[5]ʃ [αἴρ][7][ων][4]			[αἴρ]εις
[ὃ][6]			[ὃ
οὐ[κ ἔθηκα][6] ʅ[5]	ἐπάνω γίνου	ἴσθι ἐξουσίαν ἔχων	οὐκ ἔθηκα]ς
καὶ	πέντε πόλεων.	ἐπάνω δέκα πόλεων.	[(καὶ)
[5]ʃθερίζ[ων][4]			(θερίζ)]εις
[ὃ][6]			[ὃ
οὐκ ἔσπειρα ʅ[5];			(οὐκ ἔσπειρα)]ς

[5] Is θερίζω/σπείρω the second (Luke) or the first (Matthew) metaphor?

[6] Luke's ὃ … ὅ or Matthew's ὅπου … ὅθεν.

[7] The choice of verbs: Luke's αἴρω and τίθημι or Matthew's συνάγω and διασκορπίζω, involving Luke's οὐκ and Matthew's οὐ.

Er sagte ihm: Du böser Sklave! Du wusstest, dass ich ernte, wo ich nicht gesät habe, und von dort einsammle, wo ich nicht ausgestreut habe?

Il lui dit: Méchant esclave, tu savais que je moissonnais où je n'avais pas semé et que je ramassais où je n'avais pas répandu?

Q 19:23

Markan Parallel	Matthean Doublet	Matt 25:27	Q 19:23
		(ἔδει σε οὖν βαλεῖν)¹ ʃ ʅ² τ(ὰ)³ ἀργύρι(ά)³ ʃμουʅ² (τοῖς)⁴ τραπεζ(ίταις)⁴, κα(ὶ)⁵ ʃἐλθὼνʅ⁵ (ἐ)⁵γὼ ʃ ʅ⁵ ⁶ʃἐ(κομισάμην)⁷ ʅ⁶ ἂν (τὸ ἐμὸν)⁸ ʃσὺν τόκῳʅ⁶.	⟦(ἔδει σε οὖν βαλεῖν)¹⟧ ʃμουʅ² τ⟦(ὰ)³⟧ ἀργύρι⟦(ά)³⟧ ʃ ʅ² ⟦(τοῖς)⁴⟧ τραπεζ⟦(ίταις)⁴⟧, κα(ὶ)⁵ ʃἐλθὼνʅ⁵ (ἐ)⁵γὼ ʃ ʅ⁵ ⁶ʃἐ(κομισάμην)⁷ ʅ⁶ ἂν (τὸ ἐμὸν)⁸ ʃσὺν τόκῳʅ⁶.

IQP 1994: ⟦[καὶ διὰ τί οὐκ ἔδωκάς]¹⟧ ʃμουʅ² τ⟦[ὸ]³⟧ ἀργύρι⟦[ον]³⟧ ʃʅ² ⟦[ἐπὶ]⁴⟧ τράπεζ⟦[αν]⁴;⟧.

JMR, PH, JSK: The position of μου is indeterminate; as a convention it is put in Lukan position.

¹ Luke's καὶ διὰ τί οὐκ ἔδωκας or Matthew's ἔδει σε οὖν βαλεῖν.

² The position of μου before (Luke) or after (Matthew) the reference to money.

³ Luke's τὸ ἀργύριον (see Luke 19:15) or Matthew's τὰ ἀργύρια.

⁴ Luke's ἐπὶ τράπεζαν or Matthew's τοῖς τραπεζίταις.

Q

⟦ἔδει σε οὖν βαλεῖν⟧ τ⟦ὰ⟧ ἀργύρι⟦ά⟧ μου ⟦τοῖς⟧ τραπεζ⟦ίταις⟧, καὶ ἐλθὼν ἐγὼ ἐκομισάμην ἂν τὸ ἐμὸν σὺν τόκῳ.

⟦Then you had to invest⟧ my money ⟦with the⟧ money ⟦changers⟧! And at my coming I would have received what belongs to me plus interest.

Q 19:23

Luke 19:23	Lukan Doublet	Markan Parallel	Gospel of Thomas
[καὶ διὰ τί οὐκ ἔδωκάς][1] ⸂μου⸃[2] τ[ὸ][3] ἀργύρι[ον][3] ⸂ ⸃[2] [ἐπὶ][4] τράπεζ[αν][4]; κἀ( ) [5]⸂ ⸃[5] ( )[5]γὼ ⸂ἐλθὼν⸃[5] ⸂σὺν τόκῳ⸃[6] ἂν [αὐτὸ][8] [6]⸂ἔ[πραξα][7] ⸃[6].			

IQP 1994: ⟦(τὸ ἐμόν)[8]⟧.

[5] The position of ἐλθών after κἀγώ (Luke) or between καί and ἐγώ (Matthew), involving in Luke a contraction not in Matthew.

[6] The interchanged positions of the finite verb and σὺν τόκῳ.

[7] Luke's ἄν ... ἔπραξα or Matthew's ἐκομισάμην ἄν.

[8] Luke's αὐτό or Matthew's τὸ ἐμόν. (See Q 19:20-21[21].)

⟦Dann hättest du⟧ mein Geld ⟦zu den⟧ Geld⟦wechslern⟧ bringen ⟦müssen⟧! Und bei meinem Kommen hätte ich das Meine mit Zins zurückerhalten.

⟦Il te fallait donc placer⟧ mon argent ⟦chez les⟧ chang⟦eurs⟧! Et à mon retour, j'aurais retiré mon bien avec un intérêt.

Q 19:24

Markan Parallel	Matthean Doublet	Matt 25:28	Q 19:24
		[ ][1] ἄρατε (οὖν)[2] ἀπ' αὐτοῦ τ(ὸ τάλαντον)[3] καὶ δότε τῷ ʃἔχοντιʅ[4] τὰ[ ][3] δέκα (τάλαντα)[3] ʃ ʅ[4].	[][1] ἄρατε (οὖν)[2] ἀπ' αὐτοῦ τ[ὴν μνᾶν][3] καὶ δότε τῷ ʃἔχοντιʅ[4] τὰ[ς][3] δέκα [μνᾶς][3] ʃʅ[4].

IQP 1994: ( )[2]... τ[ ][3]... τὰ[ ][3] δέκα [ ][3].

[1] Luke's καὶ τοῖς παρεστῶσιν εἶπεν·.

[2] Matthew's οὖν.

Q

ἄρατε οὖν ἀπ' αὐτοῦ τὴν μνᾶν καὶ δότε τῷ ἔχοντι τὰς δέκα μνᾶς·	So take from him the mina and give «it» to the one who has the ten minas.

Q 19:24

Luke 19:24	Lukan Doublet	Markan Parallel	Gospel of Thomas
[καὶ τοῖς παρεστῶσιν εἶπεν][1]· ἄρατε ( )[2] ἀπ' αὐτοῦ τ[ὴν μνᾶν][3] καὶ δότε τῷ ⸉ ⸊[4] τὰ[ς][3] δέκα [μνᾶς][3] ⸉ἔχοντι⸊[4]			

[3] The monetary unit ἡ μνᾶ (Luke) or τὸ τάλαντον (Matthew). (The decision depends on the decision at Q 19:13[6].)

[4] The position of ἔχοντι after (Luke) or before (Matthew) the reference to the money.

Nehmt ihm daher die Mine weg und gebt «sie» dem, der die zehn Minen hat.

Enlevez-lui donc cette mine et donnez«-la» à celui qui a les dix mines.

Q 19:~~25~~

Markan Parallel	Matthean Doublet	Matthew	Q 19:~~25~~
		[ ][0]	[][0]

Text Critical Note (see the discussion in the front matter): Luke 19:25 is omitted in D W 69 *pc* b e ff^{2} $\text{sy}^{s.c}$ bo^{ms}.

[0] Is Luke 19:25 in Q?

Q 19:~~25~~

Luke 19:25	Lukan Doublet	Markan Parallel	Gospel of Thomas
[- καὶ εἶπαν αὐτῷ· κύριε, ἔχει δέκα μνᾶς -][0]			

Q 19:26

Mark 4:25	Matt 13:12	Matt 25:29	Q 19:26
		[ ][1]	⟦[][1]⟧
		ʃ ʅ[2]	ʃʅ[2]
ὃς γὰρ ἔχει,	{ὅσ}τις {(γὰρ [ἔχ])ει,	τῷ {(γὰρ)[3] ἔχ}οντι	τῷ ⟦{(γὰρ)[3]⟧ ἔχ}οντι
δοθήσεται αὐτῷ·	[(δοθήσεται)] αὐτῷ}	ʃπαντὶʅ[2] {δοθήσεται}	ʃπαντὶʅ[2] {δοθήσεται},
	(καὶ περισσευθήσεται)·	(καὶ περισσευθήσεται)[4],	()[4]
		ʃ ʅ[5]	ʃʅ[5]
καὶ ὃς οὐκ ἔχει,	{ὅσ}τις [(δὲ)] {οὐκ [(ἔχ)]ει,	ʃ ʅ[6] τοῦ ʃδὲʅ[6] μὴ {ἔχ}οντος	ʃʅ[6] τοῦ ʃδὲʅ[6] μὴ {ἔχ}οντος
καὶ ὃ ἔχει	([καὶ ὃ ἔχει	{καὶ ὃ ἔχει	{καὶ ὃ ἔχει
ἀρθήσεται	ἀρθήσεται]	ἀρθήσεται	ἀρθήσεται
ἀπ' αὐτοῦ.	[ἀπ'] αὐτοῦ)}.	ʃἀπ' (αὐτοῦ)}[5] ʅ[5].	ʃἀπ' (αὐτοῦ)}[5] ʅ[5].

IQP 1994: [ ][1] ʃʅ[2] τῷ ()[1] ἔχοντι.

1 Luke's λέγω ὑμῖν ὅτι.
2 The position of παντί before (Luke) or after (Matthew) τῷ ἔχοντι.
3 Matthew's postpositive γάρ.
4 Matthew's καὶ περισσευθήσεται.

Q

τῷ ⟦γὰρ⟧ ἔχοντι παντὶ δοθήσεται, τοῦ δὲ μὴ ἔχοντος καὶ ὃ ἔχει ἀρθήσεται ἀπ' αὐτοῦ.

⟦For⟧ to everyone who has will be given; but from the one who does not have, even what he has will be taken from him.

Gos. Thom. 41 (Nag Hammadi II 2)

(1) Λέγει Ἰησοῦς· ὅστις ἔχει ἐν τῇ χειρὶ αὐτοῦ, δοθήσεται αὐτῷ· (2) καὶ ὅστις οὐκ ἔχει, καὶ τὸ μικρὸν ὃ ἔχει ἀρθήσεται ἀπ' αὐτοῦ.

(1) Jesus says: Whoever has (something) in his hand, (something more) will be given to him. (2) And whoever has nothing, even the little he has will be taken from him.

Q 19:26

Luke 19:26	Luke 8:18	Mark 4:25	*Gos. Thom.* 41
[λέγω ὑμῖν ὅτι][1]	Βλέπετε οὖν πῶς ἀκούετε·		41.1 ⲡⲉϫⲉ ⲓ̅ⲥ̅ ϫⲉ
ʃπαντὶʅ[2]			
τῷ ( )[3] {ἔχ}οντι	{ὃς} ἂν ({γὰρ [ἔχ]})η,	ὃς γὰρ ἔχει,	ⲡⲉⲧⲉⲩⲛ̄ⲧⲁϥʼ ϩⲛ̄ ⲧⲉϥʼϭⲓϫ
ʃ ʅ[2] {δοθήσεται},	{[(δοθήσεται)] αὐτῷ·	δοθήσεται αὐτῷ·	ⲥⲉⲛⲁϯ ⲛⲁϥʼ
( )[4]			
ʃἀπ[ὸ][5] ʅ[5]			
ʃδὲʅ[6] τοῦ ʃ ʅ[6] μὴ {ἔχ}οντος	καὶ ὃς} ἂν ([μὴ {ἔχ}])η,	καὶ ὃς οὐκ ἔχει,	41.2 ⲁⲩⲱ ⲡⲉⲧⲉ ⲙⲛ̄ⲧⲁϥ
{καὶ ὃ ἔχει	{([καὶ ὃ])} δοκεῖ {([ἔχ])}ειν	καὶ ὃ ἔχει	ⲡⲕⲉϣⲏⲙ ⲉⲧⲟⲩⲛ̄ⲧⲁϥʼ
ἀρθήσεται}	{([ἀρθήσεται]	ἀρθήσεται	ⲥⲉⲛⲁϥⲓⲧϥ̄
ʃ ʅ[5].	ἀπ' αὐτοῦ)}.	ἀπ' αὐτοῦ.	ⲛ̄ⲧⲟⲟⲧϥʼ

[5] The position of the preposition, and the resultant choice between Luke's τοῦ μὴ ἔχοντος or Matthew's αὐτοῦ as its object.

[6] The position of the postpositive δέ. The decision depends on variation unit[5].

⟦Denn⟧ jedem, der hat, wird gegeben werden, von dem jedoch, der nichts hat, von dem wird auch das, was er hat, weggenommen werden.

⟦Car⟧ à tout homme qui a, on donnera, mais à celui qui n'a pas, même ce qu'il a lui sera enlevé.

(1) Jesus spricht: Wer (etwas) in seiner Hand hat – ihm wird gegeben werden. (2) Und wer nichts hat – auch das Wenige, was er hat, wird von ihm weggenommen werden.

(1) Jésus dit: Celui qui a (quelque chose) dans sa main, on lui donnera. (2) Et celui qui n'a rien, même le peu qu'il a lui sera enlevé.

Q 19:⟦~~27~~⟧

Matt 22:13b-c	Matt 8:12	Matt 25:30	Q 19⟦~~27~~⟧
	οἱ δὲ	(καὶ τὸν	⟦[()]⁰⟧
δήσαντες αὐτοῦ	υἱοὶ	ἀχρεῖον	
πόδας καὶ χεῖρας	τῆς βασιλείας	δοῦλον	
ἐκβάλετε αὐτὸν	ἐκβληθήσονται	ἐκβάλετε	
εἰς τὸ σκότος τὸ ἐξώτερον·	εἰς τὸ σκότος τὸ ἐξώτερον·	εἰς τὸ σκότος τὸ ἐξώτερον·	
ἐκεῖ ἔσται ὁ κλαυθμὸς	ἐκεῖ ἔσται ὁ κλαυθμὸς	ἐκεῖ ἔσται ὁ κλαυθμὸς	
καὶ ὁ βρυγμὸς τῶν ὀδόντων.	καὶ ὁ βρυγμὸς τῶν ὀδόντων.	καὶ ὁ βρυγμὸς τῶν ὀδόντων.)⁰	
		≀Matt 25:14a[1]	≀Q 19:12[1]
		\Matt 25:14a[0]	\Q 19:12[0]

IQP 1994: [( )]⁰.

[0] Does a saying of judgment follow Q 19:26? (See also Luke 19:14.)

Q 19:⟦~~27~~⟧

Luke 19:27	Lukan Doublet	Markan Parallel	Gospel of Thomas
[πλὴν τοὺς ἐχθρούς μου τούτους τοὺς μὴ θελήσαντάς με βασιλεῦσαι ἐπ' αὐτοὺς ἀγάγετε ὧδε καὶ κατασφάξατε αὐτοὺς ἔμπροσθέν μου.][0] ˀLuke 19:12[1] \Luke 19:12[0]			

Q 22:28

Mark 10:29a	Matthean Doublet	Matt 19:28a	Q 22:28
		^{0}/	^{0}/
		^{1}ʃ	^{1}ʃ
ἔφη ὁ Ἰησοῦς·		({ὁ} δὲ {Ἰησοῦς} εἶπεν αὐτοῖς·	()^2
ἀμὴν λέγω ὑμῖν,		{ἀμὴν λέγω ὑμῖν} ὅτι)^2	
		ὑμεῖς [ ]^3	ὑμεῖς [ ]^3
		[ ]^4 οἱ (ἀκολουθήσαν)^{4}τές	[]^4 οἱ (ἀκολουθήσαν)^{4}τές
		[ ]^{4}μο(ι)^4	[]^{4}μο(ι)^4
		[ ]^5	[]^5
		ʅ^1⇒ Matt 19:28b	ʅ^1⇒ Q 22:~~29~~, 30
		\ ^{0}⇒ Matt 19:28b	\ ^{0}⇒ Q 22:~~29~~, 30

IQP 1994: ( )^2, indeterminate.

PH: ⟦()^2⟧ ⟦({λέγω ὑμῖν} ὅτι)^2⟧ ὑμεῖς ⟦[]^3⟧.

^{0} Is Luke 22:28-30 par. Matt 19:28 in Q?

^{1} The position of Q 22:28-30 in Q: After Q 19:26, ⟦~~27~~⟧ (Lukan order); or after Q 17:4 (Matt 18:22) and before Q 13:30 (Matt 20:16) (Matthean order).

^{2} Is Matthew's ὁ δὲ Ἰησοῦς εἶπεν αὐτοῖς· ἀμὴν λέγω ὑμῖν ὅτι in Q or from Mark?

^{3} Luke's δέ.

Q

ὑμεῖς .. οἱ ἀκολουθήσαντές μοι	.. You who have followed me

Q 22:28

Luke 22:28	Luke 18:29a	Mark 10:29a	Gospel of Thomas
⁰/ ¹⸢			
( )²	({ὁ} δὲ) (εἶπεν αὐτοῖς· {ἀμὴν λέγω ὑμῖν} ὅτι)	ἔφη ὁ Ἰησοῦς· ἀμὴν λέγω ὑμῖν,	
Ὑμεῖς [δέ]³ [ἔστε]⁴ οἱ [διαμεμενηκό]⁴τες [μετ' ἐ]⁴μο[ῦ]⁴ [ἐν τοῖς πειρασμοῖς μου]⁵· ⸣¹⇒ Luke 22:29-30 \⁰⇒ Luke 22:29-30			

IQP 1994: ⟦[]⁴⟧ οἱ ⟦(ἀκολουθήσαν)⁴⟧τές ⟦[]⁴⟧μο⟦(ι)⁴⟧.

⁴ The sentence structure (Luke's ἔστε), the choice of the verb and of the tense for the participle, and the dependent constructions.

⁵ Luke's ἐν τοῖς πειρασμοῖς μου.

Ihr .., die ihr mir nachgefolgt seid,

.. Vous qui m'avez suivi

Q 22:~~29~~, 30

Markan Parallel	Matt 25:31	Matt 19:28b	Q 22:~~29~~, 30
		[ ]^{0}	[]^{0}
			22:30
		[ ]^{0}	[]^{0}
		ἐν τῇ (παλιγγενεσίᾳ,)^{1}	~~ἐν τῇ~~ [ ]^{1} < >^{1}
	("Οταν) δὲ ἔλθῃ	(ὅταν καθίσῃ	()^{2},
	(ὁ υἱὸς τοῦ ἀνθρώπου)	ὁ υἱὸς τοῦ ἀνθρώπου	
	ἐν τῇ (δόξῃ) (αὐτοῦ)		
	καὶ πάντες οἱ ἄγγελοι		
	μετ' αὐτοῦ, τότε ([καθ])ίσει		
	([ἐπὶ θρόν]ου δόξης αὐτοῦ)·	ἐπὶ θρόνου δόξης αὐτοῦ)^{2},	
		[ ]^{0} καθήσεσθε	[]^{0} καθήσεσθε
		(καὶ ὑμεῖς)^{2}	()^{2}
		ἐπὶ (δώδεκα)^{3}	ἐπὶ ⟦()^{3}⟧
		θρόν(ους)^{4}	θρόν⟦(ους)^{4}⟧
		⸂κρίνοντες⸃^{5}	⸂κρίνοντες⸃^{5}
		τὰς δώδεκα φυλὰς ⸂ ⸃^{5}	τὰς δώδεκα φυλὰς ⸂⸃^{5}
		τοῦ Ἰσραήλ.	τοῦ Ἰσραήλ.
		⸃Matt 19:28a^{1}	⸃Q 22:28^{1}
		\Matt 19:28a^{0}	\Q 22:28^{0}

IQP 1994, JMR: **22:30** ἐν τῇ ⟦[βασιλείᾳ]^{1}⟧ < >^{1}, i.e. <τοῦ θεοῦ>^{1} {D}; PH, JSK: **22:30** ~~ἐν τῇ~~ [ ]^{1} < >^{1}, indeterminate.

IQP 1994, JMR: ()^{3}.

^{0} Is Luke 22:29 κἀγὼ διατίθεμαι ὑμῖν καθὼς διέθετό μοι ὁ πατήρ μου βασιλείαν, **22:30** ἵνα ἔσθητε καὶ πίνητε ἐπὶ τῆς τραπέζης μου …, καί in Q?

^{1} Is ἐν τῇ and its object βασιλείᾳ μου (Luke) or παλιγγενεσίᾳ (Matthew) in Q?

Q

.. καθήσεσθε ἐπὶ θρόν⟦ους⟧ κρίνοντες τὰς δώδεκα φυλὰς τοῦ Ἰσραήλ.	will sit .. on thrones judging the twelve tribes of Israel.

Q 22:~~29~~, 30

Luke 22:29-30	Luke 12:32	Markan Parallel	Gospel of Thomas
 [**22:29** κἀγὼ διατίθεμαι ὑμῖν καθὼς διέθετό μοι ὁ πατήρ μου βασιλείαν, **22:30** ἵνα ἔσθητε καὶ πίνητε ἐπὶ τῆς τραπέζης μου][0] ἐν τῇ [βασιλείᾳ μου][1] ( )[2], [καὶ][0] καθήσεσθε ( )[2] ἐπὶ ( )[3] θρόν[ων][4] ⸂ ⸃[5] τὰς δώδεκα φυλὰς ⸂κρίνοντες⸃[5] τοῦ Ἰσραήλ. ⸃Luke 22:28[1] \Luke 22:28[0]	Μὴ φοβοῦ, τὸ μικρὸν ποίμνιον, ὅτι εὐδόκησεν ὁ πατὴρ ὑμῶν δοῦναι ὑμῖν τὴν βασιλείαν.		

IQP 1994, PH: **22:30** θρόν(ους)[4].

JSK: **22:30** ⸂κρίνοντες⸃[5] τὰς δώδεκα φυλάς ⸂ ⸃[5].

[2] Matthew's ὅταν clause and καὶ ὑμεῖς.
[3] Matthew's δώδεκα.
[4] Luke's ἐπὶ θρόνων or Matthew's ἐπὶ … θρόνους.

[5] The position of κρίνοντες after (Luke) or before (Matthew) τὰς δώδεκα φυλάς.

werdet .. auf Thronen sitzen und die zwölf Stämme Israels richten.

vous siégerez .. sur des trônes pour juger les douze tribus d'Israël.

Concordance of Q

Introduction

The concordance indexes all of the vocabulary found in the Q column of *The Critical Edition of Q*, apart from definite articles. Q has a total vocabulary of some 760 words, and a size of 3519 words, excluding at least 400 occurrences of the definite article.

The presentation of data in the Concordance allows for a simple visual identification of the various types of vocabulary present in Q:

3:7 **Bold** font marks vocabulary that occurs in both Matthew and Luke, and hence constitutes "minimal Q" vocabulary. It is not necessarily the case, however, that bolded words appear in the same inflection in Matthew and Luke. Only in the case of pronouns does the use of bold font imply agreement in dictionary form and inflection.

3:7 Normal font is used for vocabulary found in either Matthew or Luke and which the International Q Project has assigned to Q with a probability of either {A} or {B}.

⟦3:7⟧ Double square brackets designate {C} vocabulary in *The Critical Edition* and hence in the concordance. Since it is possible for an entire verse to be assigned to Q with a probability of {C} *and* that Matthew and Luke agree on the use of the same lexeme, there are some occurrences of **bolded** numerals in double square brackets, for example, λέγω *Q* **⟦12:54⟧**. Here both Matthew and Luke have λέγετε, but because the entire verse is not securely in Q, it is enclosed in ⟦ ⟧.

«12:33» Guillemets mark the vocabulary belonging to phrases for which there seems to be a Q origin, but which only reflect in a general sense what Q contained. This siglum appears normally for phrases and verses that are found in only one gospel (⟦«Q/Matt 5:41»⟧; «12:33»; ⟦«12:49»⟧; «14:21a»; ⟦«15:8-10»⟧; «17:20, 21b»). Although the verse or phrase appears to come from Q, it is impossible to achieve a fully formatted text or to determine with any degree of probability the exact wording of Q lying behind the evangelist's redaction.

3:7 *Italic* font designates vocabulary that is not printed in the Q column because it has been assigned either a {D} or a {U} probability. No visual distinction is made between {D} and {U} vocabulary, but the reader of *The Critical Edition* can easily determine whether the lexeme in question is only in Matthew or only in Luke, since its place will be marked with ( ) in the Q column if the word is found only in Matthew and by [ ] if it occurs only in Luke. {U} passages, since they are indeterminate, are marked by [( )] in the Q column when there is text in both Matthew and Luke. In these cases, the Matthaean {D} and Lukan {D} vocabulary is included in the concordance, and both Matthew's and Luke's words in the case of {U} vocabulary where there is text in Matthew and Luke.

The decision to include {D} and {U} vocabulary, while obviously running the risk of including redactional items in the concordance, errs on the side of inclusiveness and is preferable to excluding both sets of vocabulary. There are points at which the *sense* of Q is clear enough, even though the IQP has not been able to decide between Matthew and Luke. For example, at Q 4:2, Matthew has νηστεύσας while Luke has οὐκ ἔφαγεν οὐδέν, but the IQP found no grounds to decide between the two and so registered the variant as {U}, printing [( )][11] in the Q column. Since there is an agreement in basic meaning between Matthew and Luke, it seems better to include both sets of vocabulary in the concordance than to exclude both and hence to exclude a basic agreement in sense.

<7:3> The editors of *The Critical Edition* have occasionally found it necessary to propose conjectural readings, which appear in the critical text of Q and the concordance marked with pointed brackets. In most cases, such conjectures have some basis in either Matthew or Luke. For example, at Q 7:3, Matthew has προσῆλθεν, a strongly Matthaean word, while Luke uses ἀπέστειλεν, probably also redactional. While the IQP favored Matthew's stem over the Lukan term, the Matthaean form is suspect, and hence ἦλθεν was conjectured as Q's reading.

As indicated above, articles are not included in the concordance. Personal pronouns, however, are listed at the end of the concordance by inflected form.

Concordance

Ἄβελ
Q **11:51.**
Ἀβρααμ
Q **3:8; 3:8; 13:28.**
ἀγαθός
Q ⟦6:35⟧; **6:45; 6:45; 6:45; 11:13;** 11:13; **19:17;** ⟦19:19⟧.
ἀγαλλιάω
Q ⟦6:22⟧.
ἀγαπάω
Q 6:27; **6:32; 6:32; 16:13.**
ἀγγαρεύω
Q ⟦«Q/Matt 5:41»⟧.
ἄγγελος
Q **4:10;** 7:27; 12:8; 12:9; ⟦«15:10»⟧.
ἁγιάζω
Q **11:2.**
ἅγιος
Q ⟦**3:16**⟧; ⟦*3:22*⟧; **12:10;** ⟦12:12⟧.
ἀγορά
Q **7:32; 11:43.**
ἀγοράζω
Q 14:18; 14:19; 17:28.
ἀγρός
Q **12:28; 14:18;** ⟦17:34⟧.
ἀδελφός
Q **6:41; 6:42; 6:42; 17:3.**
ἄδηλος
Q 11:44.
ᾅδης
Q **10:15.**
ἄδικος
Q ⟦6:35⟧.
ἀετός
Q 17:37.
ἀθετέω
Q ⟦*7:30*⟧.
αἷμα
Q **11:50; 11:51; 11:51.**
αἴρω
Q **4:11;** 17:27; **19:24; 19:26.**
αἰτέω
Q **6:30; 11:9; 11:10; 11:11; 11:12; 11:13.**
ἀκάθαρτος
Q **11:24.**
ἄκανθα
Q **6:44.**
ἀκολουθέω
Q 7:9; **9:57; 9:60;** 14:27; 22:28.
ἀκούω
Q **6:47; 6:49; 7:9;** ⟦7:18⟧;7:22; 7:22; ⟦*7:29*⟧; **10:24; 10:24; 10:24;** *11:28*; **11:31; 12:3.**
ἀκρασία
Q 11:39.
ἅλας
Q **14:34; 14:34.**
ἄλευρον
Q **13:21.**
ἀλήθω
Q **17:35.**
ἀλλά
Q 7:7; **7:25; 7:26; 11:33; 12:51.**
ἄλλος
Q **6:29; 7:8;** <16:18>.
ἅλων
Q 3:17.
ἀλώπηξ
Q **9:58.**
ἁμαρτάνω
Q **17:3; 17:4.**
ἁμαρτωλός
Q **7:34;** ⟦«15:10»⟧.
ἀμελέω
Q 14:18.
ἀμήν
Q ⟦12:44⟧.
ἄμμος
Q 6:49.
ἀμφιέννυμι
Q **7:25;** ⟦12:28⟧.
ἀμφότεροι
Q **6:39.**
ἄν
Q 10:5; **10:8; 10:10; 10:13;** ⟦12:8⟧; 12:9; 12:10; **12:39;** 13:25; 17:6; 17:6; **19:23.**
ἀναβλέπω
Q **7:22.**
ἀνάγκη
Q 14:18; 17:1.
ἀνάγω
Q ⟦4:1⟧.
ἀνακλίνω
Q **13:29.**
ἀνάπαυσις
Q **11:24.**
ἀνάπτω
Q ⟦«12:49»⟧.
ἀνατέλλω
Q 6:35.

ἀνατολή
Q **13:29**; 17:24.
ἀνεκτός
Q **10:12**; **10:14**.
ἄνεμος
Q ⟦6:48⟧; ⟦6:49⟧; **7:24**.
ἄνευ
Q 12:6.
ἄνηθον
Q 11:42.
ἀνήρ
Q **11:32**.
ἄνθρωπος
Q **4:4**; 6:22; **6:31**; **6:45**; ⟦6:45⟧; 6:48; 6:49; 7:8; 7:25; 7:34; 7:34; **9:58**; 11:11; **11:24**; **11:26**; **11:30**; 11:44; ⟦**11:46**⟧; ⟦11:52⟧; **12:8**; ⟦12:8⟧; **12:9**; **12:10**; **12:40**; **13:19**; **14:16**; **15:4**; **17:24**; **17:26**; **17:30**; **19:12**; **19:21**.
ἀνίστημι
Q **11:32**.
ἀνοίγω
Q ⟦3:21⟧; **11:9**; **11:10**; 13:25.
ἀνομία
Q 13:27.
ἀντέχω
Q **16:13**.
ἀντίδικος
Q **12:58**; ⟦12:58⟧.
ἄνυδρος
Q **11:24**.
ἀξίνη
Q **3:9**.
ἄξιος
Q **3:8**; **10:7**.
ἀπαγγέλλω
Q 7:22.
ἀπαιτέω
Q ⟦6:30⟧.
ἀπαλλάσσω
Q 12:58.
ἅπας
Q ⟦*3:21*⟧; ⟦12:30⟧; 17:27.
ἀπέρχομαι
Q 7:24; **9:57**; **9:59**; *14:18*; ⟦19:21⟧.
ἄπιστος
Q 12:46.
ἁπλοῦς
Q **11:34**.
ἀπό
Q **3:7**; ⟦*3:21*⟧; ⟦**6:30**⟧; **7:35**; **10:21**; **11:24**; 11:50; 11:50; **11:51**; 11:51; **12:4**; 12:58; 13:25; **13:27**; **13:29**; *14:18*; **16:16**; 17:24; *17:29; 17:29;* **19:24**; **19:26**.
ἀποδεκατόω
Q **11:42**.
ἀποδημέω
Q 19:12.
ἀποδίδωμι
Q **12:59**.
ἀποθήκη
Q **3:17**; **12:24**.
ἀποκαλύπτω
Q **10:21**; **10:22**; **12:2**; 17:30.
ἀποκρίνομαι
Q **4:4**; ⟦4:8⟧; ⟦4:12⟧; 7:6; 7:22; *11:29*; 13:25; ⟦«17:20»⟧.
ἀποκτείνω
Q 11:47; *11:48*; **11:49**; **12:4**; 12:4; **13:34**.
ἀπόλλυμι
Q 11:51; 12:5; ⟦15:4⟧; ⟦15:4⟧; ⟦«15:8»⟧; ⟦«15:9»⟧; *17:29;* **17:33**; **17:33**.
ἀπολύω
Q **16:18**; **16:18**.
ἀποστέλλω
Q **7:27**; **10:3**; **10:16**; **11:49**; **13:34**; **14:17**.
ἅπτω
Q ⟦«15:8»⟧.
ἄρα
Q **11:20**; *11:48*; **12:42**.
ἀργύριον
Q **19:23**.
ἀριθμέω
Q **12:7**.
ἀρκετός
Q ⟦6:40⟧.
ἀρνέομαι
Q **12:9**; 12:9.
ἁρπαγή
Q **11:39**.
ἁρπάζω
Q 16:16.
ἄρτος
Q **4:3**; **4:4**; **11:3**; 11:11.
ἀρτύω
Q ⟦14:34⟧.
ἄρχομαι
Q **7:24**; **12:45**; ⟦13:25⟧; 13:26; *14:18*.
ἄρχων
Q **11:15**.
ἄσβεστος
Q **3:17**.
ἀσθενέω
Q ⟦10:9⟧.
ἀσπάζομαι
Q 10:4.
ἀσπασμός
Q **11:43**.
ἀσσάριον
Q **12:6**.
ἀστραπή
Q **17:24**.
αὐλέω
Q **7:32**.
αὐξάνω
Q **12:27**; **13:19**.
αὔριον
Q **12:28**.
ἀφανίζω
Q «12:33»; 12:33.

ἀφίημι
Q 4:13; ⟦6:29⟧; **6:42**; **9:60**; **11:4**; **11:4**; ⟦11:42⟧; ⟦11:42⟧; 11:52; **12:10**; **12:10**; **13:35**; 15:4; 17:3; **17:4**; **17:34**; **17:35**.

ἀφίστημι
Q 13:27.

ἄχρι
Q **17:27**.

ἄχυρον
Q **3:17**.

βαλλάντιον
Q ⟦10:4⟧.

βάλλω
Q **3:9**; **4:9**; **12:28**; ⟦«12:49»⟧; 12:51; 12:51; **12:58**; 13:19; **14:35**; ⟦19:23⟧.

βαπτίζω
Q 3:7; **3:16**; **3:16**; ⟦*3:21*⟧; ⟦*3:21*⟧; ⟦3:21⟧; ⟦*7:29*⟧; ⟦*7:30*⟧.

βάπτισμα
Q ⟦*7:29*⟧.

βαρύς
Q *11:46*.

βασιλεία
Q **4:5**; **6:20**; **7:28**; **10:9**; **11:2**; **11:17**; **11:18**; **11:20**; 11:52; **12:31**; **13:18**; **13:20**; **13:28**; **16:16**; ⟦«17:20»⟧; ⟦«17:20»⟧; ⟦«17:21»⟧; *22:30*.

βασιλεύς
Q 7:25; 10:24.

βασίλισσα
Q **11:31**.

βαστάζω
Q 3:16; 10:4; *11:27*.

Βεελζεβούλ
Q **11:15**; **11:19**.

Βηθσαϊδά(ν)
Q **10:13**.

βιάζω
Q **16:16**.

βιαστής
Q 16:16.

βλέπω
Q **6:41**; 7:22; **10:23**; 10:23; **10:24**.

βόθυνος
Q **6:39**.

βουλή
Q ⟦*7:30*⟧.

βούλομαι
Q **10:22**.

βοῦς
Q *14:19*.

βρέχω
Q ⟦6:35⟧; *17:29*.

βροχή
Q 6:48; 6:49.

βρυγμός
Q **13:28**.

βρῶσις
Q «12:33»; 12:33.

Γαλιλαία
Q ⟦*3:21*⟧.

γαμέω
Q *14:20*; ⟦16:18⟧; **16:18**; **17:27**.

γαμίζω
Q **17:27**.

γάρ
Q **3:8**; **4:10**; **6:23**; *6:32*; ⟦6:37⟧; **6:45**; 6:48; 7:8; ⟦7:29⟧; **7:33**; **10:7**; **10:24**; **11:10**; **11:30**; **12:12**; **12:30**; ⟦12:30⟧; **12:34**; 12:53; ⟦12:54⟧; ⟦12:55⟧; **16:13**; *16:16*; ⟦«17:21»⟧; **17:24**; *17:26*; ⟦17:27⟧; ⟦19:26⟧.

γέεννα
Q **12:5**.

γείτων
Q ⟦«15:9»⟧.

γεμίζω
Q 14:23.

γέμω
Q **11:39**.

γενεά
Q 7:31; 11:29; **11:29**; 11:30; **11:31**; **11:32**; 11:50; **11:51**.

γέννημα
Q 3:7.

γεννητός
Q 7:28.

γῆ
Q **10:21**; **11:31**; 12:6; «12:33»; ⟦«12:49»⟧; **12:51**; 14:35; **16:17**; ⟦19:21⟧.

γίνομαι
Q ⟦*3:21*⟧; **4:3**; 6:35; ⟦6:36⟧; ⟦6:40⟧; ⟦7:1⟧; **10:13**; **10:13**; **10:21**; **11:26**; *11:27*; 11:30; *11:41*; **12:40**; ⟦12:54⟧; **13:19**; 15:5; ⟦«15:10»⟧; ⟦17:26⟧; *17:28*.

γινώσκω
Q **6:44**; 10:22; ⟦10:22⟧; **12:2**; **12:39**; **12:46**; ⟦19:21⟧.

γραμματεύς
Q *11:16*.

γράφω
Q **4:4**; **4:8**; **4:10**; 4:12; 7:27.

γυνή
Q **7:28**; *11:27*; **13:21**; *14:20*; ⟦«15:8»⟧; **16:18**.

δαιμόνιον
Q **7:33**; 11:14; **11:14**; **11:15**; **11:15**; **11:19**; **11:20**.

δάκτυλος
Q 11:20; **11:46**.

δαν(ε)ίζω
Q ⟦6:30⟧; ⟦6:34⟧.

δέ
Q **3:9**; **3:16**; **3:17**; ⟦*3:21*⟧; 4:1; *4:9*; **6:41**;

6:41; *6:46*; **7:9**; *7:18*; **7:24**; **7:28**; ⟦7:29⟧; **⟦7:30⟧**; ⟦*7:31*⟧; **9:58**; **9:59**; **9:60**; **10:2**; **10:5**; **10:6**; ⟦10:7⟧; 10:10; **11:15**; ⟦11:16⟧; **11:17**; **11:20**; *11:27*; *11:28*; **11:29**; **11:34**; *11:39*; **11:39**; **11:42**; ⟦11:46⟧; 11:47; *11:48*; 12:4; 12:5; ⟦12:7⟧; **12:9**; **12:10**; **12:11**; **12:25**; **12:27**; **12:28**; 12:31; 12:33; **12:39**; **12:45**; 12:45; **⟦12:56⟧**; 13:28; *13:35*; *14:18*; *14:19*; **14:34**; ⟦16:17⟧; ⟦«17:20»⟧; *17:29*; *19:15*; **19:26**.

δεῖ
Q **11:42**; ⟦19:23⟧.

δείκνυμι
Q 4:5.

δεῖπνον
Q ⟦11:43⟧; 14:16; ⟦14:17⟧.

δέκα
Q ⟦«15:8»⟧; 19:13; 19:13; 19:16; **19:24**.

δένδρον
Q **3:9**; **3:9**; *6:43*; *6:43*; **6:43**; **6:43**; **6:44**; **13:19**.

δέομαι
Q **10:2**.

δεσμεύω
Q ⟦11:46⟧.

δεσμωτήριον
Q *7:18*.

δεύτερος
Q ⟦19:18⟧.

δέχομαι
Q 10:8; **10:10**; 10:16; 10:16; 10:16; 10:16.

διά
Q 7:18; **11:19**; **11:24**; **11:49**; **12:22**; **13:24**; *13:24*; ⟦<13:24>⟧; *14:20*; **17:1**.

διαβλέπω
Q **6:42**.

διάβολος
Q **4:2**; 4:3; 4:5; ⟦4:9⟧; **4:13**.

διακαθαρίζω
Q 3:17.

διακρίνω
Q ⟦12:56⟧.

διανόημα
Q 11:17.

διασκορπίζω
Q 19:21; 19:22.

διαφέρω
Q **12:7**; **12:24**.

διδάσκαλος
Q **6:40**; **6:40**.

διδάσκω
Q 12:12; 13:26.

δίδωμι
Q **4:6**; **6:30**; **11:3**; **11:9**; **11:13**; **11:13**; **11:29**; **12:42**; 12:58; **19:13**; **19:24**; **19:26**.

διέρχομαι
Q **11:24**.

δίκαιος
Q ⟦6:35⟧.

δικαιόω
Q ⟦*7:29*⟧; **7:35**.

διορύσσω
Q «12:33»; 12:33; **12:39**.

διχάζω
Q 12:53.

διχοτομέω
Q **12:46**.

διώκω
Q ⟦6:22⟧; ⟦6:23⟧; ⟦6:28⟧; **11:49**; 17:23.

δοκέω
Q 3:8; **12:40**; ⟦12:51⟧.

δοκιμάζω
Q *14:19*.

δοκός
Q **6:41**; **6:42**; **6:42**.

δόμα
Q **11:13**.

δόξα
Q **4:5**; **12:27**.

δουλεύω
Q **16:13**; **16:13**.

δοῦλος
Q *6:40*; *6:40*; **7:8**; 12:42; **12:43**; **12:45**; **12:46**; **14:17**; «14:21»; **14:21**; **19:13**; **19:15**; **19:17**; ⟦19:19⟧; **19:22**.

δραχμή
Q ⟦«15:8»⟧; ⟦«15:8»⟧; ⟦«15:9»⟧.

δύναμαι
Q **3:8**; 6:39; *6:42*; 12:4; 12:5; **12:25**; ⟦12:56⟧; *14:20*; <14:26>; 14:26; 14:27; **16:13**; **16:13**.

δύναμις
Q **10:13**.

δύο
Q ⟦«Q/Matt 5:41»⟧; ⟦12:6⟧; **16:13**; **17:34**; **17:35**.

δυσβάστακτος
Q *11:46*.

δυσμή
Q **13:29**; 17:24.

δώδεκα
Q **22:30**.

δῶμα
Q **12:3**.

ἐάν
Q 4:7; **6:34**; 7:23; **9:57**; **10:6**; **10:22**; *11:34*; *11:34*; 12:10; **12:45**; 14:23; **14:34**; 15:5; ⟦«15:8»⟧; **17:3**; **17:3**; 17:4; 17:23.

ἑαυτός
Q **3:8**; ⟦*7:30*⟧; **9:60**; **11:17**; 11:17; **11:18**; 11:26; **11:26**; ⟦11:48⟧; **⟦14:11⟧**; **⟦14:11⟧**; 14:23; 19:13.

ἐάω
Q ⟦12:39⟧.
ἐγγίζω
Q **10:9**.
ἐγείρω
Q **3:8**; 7:22; 7:28; **11:31**; ⟦13:25⟧.
ἐγκρύπτω
Q **13:21**.
ἐθνικός
Q ⟦6:34⟧.
ἔθνος
Q **12:30**.
εἰ
Q **4:3**; **4:9**; ⟦6:32⟧; ⟦10:6⟧; **10:13**; **10:22**; **10:22**; **11:13**; **11:18**; **11:19**; **11:20**; **11:29**; 11:35; **12:28**; **12:39**; ⟦«12:49»⟧; ⟦17:2⟧; 17:6.
εἰμί
Q 3:16; **3:16**; ⟦*3:22*⟧; **4:3**; **4:9**; **6:20**; **6:22**; **6:36**; **6:40**; 6:43; 6:48; 6:49; 6:49; **7:6**; **7:8**; **7:19**; **7:23**; **7:25**; 7:27; **7:28**; 7:31; **7:32**; **10:6**; **10:12**; **10:14**; 11:11; 11:13; **11:19**; **11:23**; **11:23**; 11:29; **11:30**; **11:34**; **11:34**; **11:34**; **11:34**; **11:35**; *11:41;* ⟦11:44⟧; **11:48**; **12:2**; ⟦12:7⟧; **12:23**; **12:28**; **12:34**; **12:34**; **12:42**; ⟦*12:58*⟧; **13:18**; 13:19; **13:21**; ⟦13:24⟧; **13:28**; ⟦**13:30**⟧; 14:17; <14:26>; **14:26**; **14:27**; ⟦14:35⟧; ⟦16:17⟧; ⟦«17:21»⟧; 17:23; **17:24**; **17:26**; ⟦17:27⟧; **17:30**; **17:34**; 19:17; ⟦19:19⟧; **19:21**.
εἶπον
Q ⟦3:7⟧; **4:3**; **4:3**; **4:6**; 4:8; 4:9; 4:12; ⟦6:22⟧; 6:42; 7:7; **7:9**; ⟦7:19⟧; **7:22**; **9:57**; 9:58; **9:59**; 9:60; **10:21**; **11:15**; **11:17**; *11:27*; *11:28*; ⟦11:29⟧; *11:39*; 11:49; **12:3**; **12:10**; ⟦12:10⟧; 12:11; 12:12; **12:45**; *12:54*; 13:25; 13:27; **13:35**; **14:17**; *14:18*; *14:19*; *14:20*; 14:21; ⟦«17:20»⟧; ⟦*17:21*⟧; **17:23**; 19:12; ⟦19:13⟧; 19:17; 19:19.
εἰρήνη
Q 10:5; 10:6; **10:6**; 10:6; **12:51**; 12:51.
εἰς
Q **3:9**; **3:17**; ⟦4:1⟧; 4:5; **4:9**; *4:16*; ⟦6:20⟧; 6:29; **6:39**; 7:1; **7:24**; ⟦*7:30*⟧; **10:2**; **10:5**; ⟦10:7⟧; **10:8**; 10:10; **11:4**; **11:24**; **11:32**; ⟦11:33⟧; 12:3; 12:10; 12:10; ⟦<12:11>⟧; 12:24; **12:28**; **12:58**; 13:19; 13:19; **13:21**; ⟦13:28⟧; *14:18*; **14:23**; **14:35**; 14:35; 17:2; ⟦17:3⟧; **17:4**; **17:27**.
εἷς
Q ⟦«Q/Matt 5:41»⟧; **12:6**; *12:25*; **12:27**; **15:4**; ⟦«15:8»⟧; ⟦«15:10»⟧; *14:18*; **16:13**; **16:13**; **16:17**; 16:17; **17:2**; **17:34**; 17:34; **17:35**; 17:35.
εἰσέρχομαι
Q **7:1**; 7:6; **10:5**; ⟦10:8⟧; 10:10; **11:26**; **11:52**; **11:52**; 11:52; **13:24**; **13:24**; <13:24>; **17:27**.
εἰσφέρω
Q **11:4**; 12:11.
ἐκ
Q **3:8**; ⟦6:42⟧; **6:42**; **6:44**; 6:44; 6:44; **6:45**; **6:45**; **6:45**; ⟦10:7⟧; **11:11**; 11:13; *11:27*; **11:31**; 11:39; **11:49**; **12:6**; **12:25**; 15:4; **15:4**.
ἑκατόν
Q **15:4**.
ἑκατοντάρχος
Q **7:3**; 7:6.
ἐκβάλλω
Q **6:42**; **6:42**; **6:42**; 6:45; 6:45; **10:2**; 11:14; 11:14; **11:15**; **11:19**; **11:19**; **11:20**; **13:28**.
ἐκεῖ
Q 10:6; **11:26**; **12:34**; **13:28**; ⟦*17:21*⟧; 17:37.
ἐκεῖθεν
Q **12:59**.
ἐκεῖνος
Q **6:48**; **6:49**; 10:10; 10:12; **10:12**; *10:21*; **11:26**; *12:12*; ⟦12:39⟧; **12:43**; **12:45**; **12:46**; ⟦17:27⟧; 19:15.
ἐκζητέω
Q 11:50; 11:51.
ἐκκόπτω
Q **3:9**.
ἐκπειράζω
Q **4:12**.
ἐκριζόω
Q 17:6.
ἐκτινάσσω
Q 10:11.
ἐκτός
Q 11:41.
ἐκχέω
Q **11:50**.
ἔλεος
Q 11:42.
ἐλπίζω
Q ⟦6:34⟧.
ἐμαυτοῦ
Q **7:8**.
ἐμός
Q 19:23.

ἐμπορία
Q *14:19*.

ἔμπροσθεν
Q 7:27; **10:21**; 11:52; **12:8**; **12:8**; 12:9; 12:9; ⟦<«15:10»>⟧.

ἐν
Q **3:8**; ⟦3:16⟧; **3:16**; **3:17**; ⟦*3:21*⟧; **6:23**; ⟦6:37⟧; ⟦6:38⟧; **6:41**; **6:41**; **6:42**; *6:42*; 7:9; *7:18*; 7:23; 7:25; 7:25; 7:28; 7:28; 7:32; **10:3**; ⟦10:7⟧; 10:9; **10:12**; **10:13**; **10:13**; **10:13**; **10:14**; **10:21**; **11:15**; **11:19**; **11:19**; **11:20**; *11:27*; **11:31**; **11:32**; 11:33; **11:35**; ⟦11:43⟧; **11:43**; **11:43**; **12:3**; **12:3**; *12:3*; 12:5; **12:8**; **12:8**; **12:12**; **12:27**; 12:28; **12:33**; **12:42**; **12:45**; **12:46**; **12:46**; **12:58**; **13:19**; 13:26; 13:28; **13:35**; **14:34**; 17:6; 17:23; 17:23; ⟦17:24⟧; ⟦17:26⟧; ⟦17:26⟧; ⟦17:27⟧; *17:28;* ⟦17:34⟧; 17:35; 19:13; 19:21.

ἔνδυμα
Q **12:23**; 12:26.

ἐνδύω
Q **12:22**.

ἕνεκα -εν
Q **6:22**; ⟦17:33⟧.

ἐνενήκοντα
Q **15:4**; **15:7**.

ἐννέα
Q **15:4**; **15:7**.

ἐντέλλω
Q **4:10**.

ἐντός
Q 11:41; ⟦«17:21»⟧.

ἐνώπιον
Q 13:26.

ἐξέρχομαι
Q 7:24; 7:25; **7:26**; **10:10**; **11:24**; **11:24**; **12:59**; *14:18*; **14:23**; 17:23; 17:24; *17:29*.

ἐξομολογέω
Q **10:21**.

ἐξουσία
Q 7:8.

ἔξω
Q ⟦10:10⟧; ⟦13:25⟧; **14:35**.

ἔξωθεν
Q **11:39**.

ἐξώτερος
Q ⟦13:28⟧.

ἐπαθροίζω
Q *11:29*.

ἐπαίρω
Q ⟦6:20⟧; *11:27*.

ἐπάν
Q *11:34*.

ἐπάνω
Q 11:44.

ἐπερωτάω
Q ⟦«17:20»⟧.

ἐπί
Q ⟦*3:21*⟧; ⟦3:22⟧; **4:4**; **4:9**; **4:11**; **6:35**; ⟦6:35⟧; **6:48**; 6:48; **6:49**; **10:6**; ⟦10:6⟧; 10:9; **11:18**; **11:20**; **11:33**; ⟦11:46⟧; **12:3**; 12:6; **12:25**; «12:33»; **12:42**; **12:44**; ⟦«12:49»⟧; 12:51; *14:19*; ⟦15:4⟧; **15:7**; **15:7**; ⟦«15:10»⟧; 19:17; 19:17; ⟦19:19⟧; 19:19; **22:30**.

ἐπιδίδωμι
Q **11:11**; **11:12**.

ἐπιζητέω
Q **12:30**.

ἐπιθυμέω
Q *10:24*.

ἐπιούσιος
Q **11:3**.

ἐπιστρέφω
Q ⟦10:6⟧; 11:24.

ἐπισυνάγω
Q **13:34**; 13:34.

ἐπιτίθημι
Q ⟦11:46⟧.

ἐπιτιμάω
Q 17:3.

ἐπιτρέπω
Q **9:59**.

ἑπτά
Q **11:26**.

ἑπτάκις
Q **17:4**; **17:4**.

ἐργάζομαι
Q 13:27.

ἐργασία
Q 12:58.

ἐργάτης
Q **10:2**; **10:2**; **10:7**.

ἔρημος
Q 4:1; **7:24**; 17:23.

ἐρημόω
Q **11:17**.

ἔρχομαι
Q ⟦3:7⟧; **3:16**; ⟦*3:22*⟧; *4:16*; 6:48; 6:49; <7:3>; **7:3**; **7:8**; **7:8**; **7:19**; ⟦7:29⟧; **7:33**; **7:34**; **11:2**; **11:25**; **11:31**; **12:39**; **12:40**; **12:43**; ⟦«12:49»⟧; 12:51; 12:51; 12:53; **13:35**; 14:17; *14:20*; **17:1**; **17:1**; ⟦«17:20»⟧; ⟦«17:20»⟧; **17:27**; 19:13; 19:15; ⟦<19:16>⟧; 19:18; 19:20; **19:23**.

ἐρωτάω
Q *14:18*; *14:19*.

ἐσθίω
Q ⟦*4:2*⟧; **7:33**; **7:34**; 10:7; ⟦10:8⟧; **12:22**; **12:29**; **12:45**; 13:26; *17:28*.

ἔσχατος
Q **11:26**; **12:59**; ⟦**13:30**⟧; ⟦**13:30**⟧.

ἔσωθεν
Q **11:39**.
ἕτερος
Q ⟦7:19⟧; ⟦7:32⟧; **9:59**; **11:26**; *14:19*; *14:20*; **16:13**; **16:13**; 19:20.
ἕτοιμος
Q **12:40**; **14:17**.
εὖ
Q 19:17; ⟦19:19⟧.
εὐαγγελίζω
Q 7:22.
εὐδία
Q ⟦12:54⟧.
εὐδοκία
Q **10:21**.
εὔθετος
Q ⟦14:35⟧.
εὐθύς
Q 6:49.
εὔκοπος
Q ⟦16:17⟧.
εὐλογέω
Q **13:35**.
εὑρίσκω
Q 7:9; **11:9**; **11:10**; **11:24**; **11:25**; **12:43**; 14:23; **15:5**; ⟦«15:8»⟧; ⟦«15:9»⟧; ⟦«15:9»⟧; 17:33; 17:33.
ἐχθρός
Q **6:27**.
ἔχιδνα
Q 3:7.
ἔχω
Q **3:8**; 6:32; 7:3; **7:8**; **7:33**; **9:58**; **9:58**; *14:18*; *14:18*; *14:19*; 15:4; ⟦«15:8»⟧; **17:6**; 19:21; **19:24**; **19:26**; **19:26**; **19:26**.
ἕως
Q **10:15**; **10:15**; **11:51**; ⟦12:58⟧; **12:59**; **13:21**; **13:35**; ⟦«15:8»⟧; ⟦16:16⟧; 17:24.
Ζαχαρίας
Q **11:51**.
ζάω
Q **4:4**.
ζεύγη
Q *14:19*.
ζητέω
Q **11:9**; **11:10**; 11:16; **11:24**; 11:29; **12:31**; 13:24; ⟦15:4⟧; ⟦«15:8»⟧.
ζύμη
Q **13:21**.
ζυμόω
Q **13:21**.
ἤ
Q *6:43*; 6:44; **7:19**; **10:12**; **10:14**; *11:11*; **11:12**; **12:11**; ⟦12:29⟧; ⟦12:29⟧; **15:7**; ⟦«15:8»⟧; **16:13**; **16:13**; **16:17**; 17:2.
ἤδη
Q **3:9**; ⟦«12:49»⟧; 14:17.
ἡδύοσμον
Q **11:42**.
ἥκω
Q **12:46**; **13:29**; ⟦13:35⟧.
ἡλικία
Q **12:25**.
ἥλιος
Q 6:35.
ἡμέρα
Q **4:2**; **10:12**; **12:46**; 17:4; ⟦17:24⟧; **17:26**; ⟦17:26⟧; ⟦17:27⟧; **17:27**; *17:28; 17:29;* 17:30.
θάλασσα
Q **17:2**; 17:6.
θάπτω
Q **9:59**; **9:60**.
θαυμάζω
Q **7:9**; **11:14**.
θεάομαι
Q **7:24**.
θεῖον
Q *17:29*.
θέλω
Q ⟦6:29⟧; **6:31**; *10:24*; ⟦11:46⟧; ⟦«12:49»⟧; **13:34**; **13:34**.
θεμελιόω
Q 6:48.
θεός
Q **3:8**; ⟦*3:22*⟧; **4:3**; **4:8**; **4:9**; **4:12**; 6:20; 7:28; ⟦*7:30*⟧; ⟦*7:30*⟧; 10:9; **11:20**; **11:20**; *11:28*; *11:49*; <11:52>; *12:8*; *12:9*; 12:24; **12:28**; 13:18; 13:20; 13:28; **16:13**; 16:16; ⟦«17:20»⟧; ⟦«17:20»⟧; ⟦«17:21»⟧.
θεραπεύω
Q 7:3; **10:9**.
θερίζω
Q **12:24**; **19:21**; **19:22**.
θερισμός
Q **10:2**; **10:2**; **10:2**.
θηλάζω
Q *11:27.*
θησαυρίζω
Q «12:33»; 12:33.
θησαυρός
Q **6:45**; ⟦6:45⟧; «12:33»; **12:33**; **12:34**.
θρηνέω
Q **7:32**.
θρίξ
Q **12:7**.
θρόνος
Q **22:30**.
θυγάτηρ
Q **12:53**; 14:26.
θύρα
Q 13:24; **13:25**; ⟦13:25⟧.
θυσιαστήριον
Q **11:51**.
Ἰακώβ
Q **13:28**.
ἰάομαι
Q 7:7.

ἴδε
Q ⟦19:21⟧.
ἴδιος
Q *14:18*.
ἰδού
Q ⟦*3:22*⟧; 6:42; **7:25**; 7:27; **7:34**; **10:3**; **11:31**; **11:32**; *11:41*; **13:35**; ⟦17:21⟧; ⟦«17:21»⟧; **17:23**; **17:23**.
ἱερόν
Q **4:9**.
Ἰερουσαλήμ
Q 4:9; **13:34**; **13:34**.
Ἰησοῦς
Q ⟦<3:0>⟧; ⟦*3:21*⟧; ⟦**3:21**⟧; 4:1; 4:4; **4:8**; 4:12; *7:1*; 7:9; **9:58**; *11:39*.
ἱκανός
Q **3:16**; **7:6**.
ἱμάτιον
Q **6:29**.
ἵνα
Q 4:3; **6:31**; *6:37*; ⟦6:40⟧; **7:6**; *11:41*; ⟦11:50⟧; 14:23; 17:2.
Ἰορδάνης
Q 3:3; ⟦*3:21*⟧.
Ἰσαάκ
Q **13:28**.
Ἰσραήλ
Q 7:9; **22:30**.
ἵστημι
Q **4:9**; 11:17; **11:18**; ⟦13:25⟧.
ἰσχυρός
Q **3:16**.
ἰχθύς
Q **11:12**.
Ἰωάννης
Q 3:2; ⟦*3:21*⟧; 7:18; 7:22; 7:24; 7:28; ⟦7:29⟧; ⟦*7:29*⟧; **7:33**; **16:16**.
Ἰωνᾶς
Q **11:29**; **11:30**; **11:32**; **11:32**.
ἰῶτα
Q 16:17.
καθαρίζω
Q 7:22; **11:39**; ⟦11:41⟧.
καθαρός
Q **11:41**.
κάθημαι
Q 7:32; **22:30**.
καθίστημι
Q **12:42**; **12:44**; 19:17; 19:19.
καθώς
Q 6:31; ⟦11:30⟧; ⟦17:26⟧; *17:28*.
καί
Q **3:8**; **3:9**; **3:16**; 3:17; **3:17**; ⟦*3:21*⟧; ⟦**3:22**⟧; **4:2**; 4:3; 4:4; 4:5; **4:5**; 4:5; **4:6**; 4:8; **4:8**; **4:9**; 4:9; **4:11**; 4:12; 4:13; ***4:16***; **6:20**; **6:22**; **6:22**; **6:23**; 6:28; **6:29**; **6:29**; ⟦6:29⟧; **6:29**; ⟦«Q/Matt 5:41»⟧; **6:30**; 6:31; *6:32*; **6:32**; **6:34**; **6:34**; **6:35**; ⟦6:35⟧; ⟦6:35⟧; *6:36*; *6:37*; *6:37*; ⟦6:38⟧; *6:40*; 6:42; **6:42**; *6:43*; *6:43*; **6:45**; 6:46; **6:47**; 6:48; 6:48; 6:48; 6:48; **6:48**; 6:49; **6:49**; 6:49; 6:49; ⟦6:49⟧; 6:49; **6:49**; **6:49**; ⟦7:1⟧; ⟦7:3⟧; 7:3; 7:6; 7:7; **7:8**; **7:8**; **7:8**; **7:8**; **7:8**; **7:8**; **7:8**; **7:9**; *7:18*; **7:22**; **7:22**; 7:22; **7:22**; 7:22; 7:22; **7:23**; **7:26**; ⟦*7:29*⟧; ⟦*7:29*⟧; ⟦**7:29**⟧; ⟦*7:30*⟧; 7:31; **7:32**; **7:32**; **7:33**; **7:34**; **7:34**; **7:34**; **7:34**; **7:35**; **9:57**; **9:58**; **9:58**; 9:59; 9:60; 10:4; **10:6**; 10:7; 10:8; 10:8; 10:9; 10:9; 10:10; **10:13**; **10:13**; **10:14**; **10:15**; ⟦10:16⟧; **10:21**; **10:21**; **10:21**; **10:22**; **10:22**; **10:24**; **10:24**; **10:24**; **10:24**; **11:4**; **11:4**; **11:4**; **11:9**; **11:9**; **11:9**; **11:10**; **11:10**; **11:12**; 11:14; 11:14; **11:14**; *11:16*; **11:17**; **11:18**; 11:19; **11:23**; **11:24**; **11:25**; **11:25**; **11:26**; **11:26**; **11:26**; *11:27*; *11:28*; *11:29*; **11:29**; ⟦11:30⟧; **11:31**; **11:31**; **11:32**; **11:32**; 11:33; ⟦11:33⟧; *11:39*; **11:39**; **11:39**; **11:41**; **11:42**; **11:42**; **11:42**; **11:42**; 11:42; ⟦**11:43**⟧; **11:43**; 11:44; ⟦**11:46**⟧; *11:46*; ⟦11:46⟧; 11:49; **11:49**; 11:49; **11:49**; **11:51**; **12:2**; **12:3**; 12:4; 12:5; 12:5; **12:6**; **12:7**; 12:8; **12:10**; **12:23**; **12:24**; 12:26; **12:28**; **12:31**; «12:33»; «12:33»; «12:33»; 12:33; **12:34**; **12:40**; ⟦12:42⟧; **12:45**; **12:45**; **12:46**; **12:46**; **12:46**; ⟦«12:49»⟧; ⟦12:53⟧; ⟦12:53⟧; ⟦**12:55**⟧; **12:58**; **12:58**; 13:18; 13:19; **13:19**; 13:19; ⟦13:20⟧; **13:24**; **13:25**; ⟦13:25⟧; ⟦13:25⟧; 13:25; **13:26**; **13:26**; **13:27**; **13:28**; **13:28**; **13:28**; ⟦13:29⟧; **13:29**; **13:29**; ⟦13:30⟧; **13:34**; **13:34**; ⟦14:11⟧; ⟦14:16⟧; **14:17**; *14:18*; *14:18*; *14:19*; *14:19*; *14:20*; *14:20*; «14:21»; **14:23**; 14:26; 14:26; 14:26; *14:27*; **14:27**; **15:4**; **15:4**; **15:5**; ⟦«15:8»⟧; ⟦«15:8»⟧; ⟦«15:9»⟧; ⟦«15:9»⟧; **16:13**; **16:13**; **16:13**;

16:16; **16:16**; **16:17**; ⟦16:18⟧; **16:18**; **17:2**; 17:3; 17:4; **17:4**; 17:6; **17:6**; ⟦«17:20»⟧; 17:24; *17:26*; 17:27; 17:27; **17:27**; **17:27**; *17:29*; *17:29*; 17:30; 17:33; **17:34**; 17:35; 19:13; ⟦19:13⟧; *19:15*; **19:15**; 19:16; 19:17; **19:18**; **19:20**; **19:21**; 19:21; **19:22**; **19:23**; **19:24**; **19:26**.

καιρός
Q *10:21*; **12:42**; ⟦**12:56**⟧.

καίω
Q 11:33.

κἀκεῖνος
Q **11:42**.

κακῶς
Q ⟦7:3⟧.

κάλαμος
Q **7:24**.

καλέω
Q 6:46; ⟦14:16⟧; **14:17**; 14:23; ⟦<«15:9»>⟧; **19:13**.

καλός
Q **3:9**; *6:43*; *6:43*; 6:43; **6:43**; ⟦14:34⟧.

καλύπτω
Q 12:2.

καρδία
Q **6:45**; **12:34**; **12:45**.

καρπός
Q **3:8**; **3:9**; *6:43*; *6:43*; **6:43**; **6:43**; **6:44**.

κάρφος
Q **6:41**; **6:42**; **6:42**.

κατά
Q ⟦6:22⟧; 10:4; ⟦11:17⟧; 11:17; **11:23**; ⟦12:53⟧; ⟦12:53⟧; ⟦12:53⟧.

καταβαίνω
Q 6:48; 6:49; **10:15**.

καταβολή
Q 11:50.

κατακαίω
Q **3:17**.

κατακλυσμός
Q **17:27**.

κατακρίνω
Q **11:31**; **11:32**.

καταλείπω
Q *4:16*.

καταμανθάνω
Q ⟦12:27⟧.

κατανοέω
Q **6:41**; 12:24.

κατασκευάζω
Q 7:27.

κατασκηνόω
Q **13:19**.

κατασκήνωσις
Q **9:58**.

καταφρονέω
Q **16:13**.

κατοικέω
Q **11:26**.

κάτω
Q **4:9**.

καύσων
Q ⟦12:55⟧.

Καφαρναούμ
Q 7:1; **10:15**.

κεῖμαι
Q **3:9**.

κεραία
Q **16:17**.

κεφαλή
Q **9:58**; **12:7**.

κῆπος
Q ⟦13:19⟧.

κήρυγμα
Q **11:32**.

κηρύσσω
Q **12:3**.

κιβωτός
Q **17:27**.

κινέω
Q ⟦11:46⟧.

κλάδος
Q **13:19**.

κλαίω
Q 7:32.

κλαυθμός
Q **13:28**.

κλείω
Q 11:52; ⟦13:25⟧.

κλέπτης
Q «12:33»; **12:33**; **12:39**.

κλέπτω
Q «12:33»; 12:33.

κλίβανος
Q **12:28**.

κλίνω
Q **9:58**.

κοδράντης
Q ⟦12:59⟧.

κόκκος
Q **13:19**; **17:6**.

κοιλία
Q *11:27*.

κομίζω
Q 19:23.

κονιορτός
Q **10:11**.

κοπιάω
Q 12:27.

κοπρία
Q 14:35.

κόραξ
Q 12:24.

κοσμέω
Q **11:25**.

κόσμος
Q 4:5; 11:50.

κρίμα
Q ⟦6:37⟧.

κρίνον
Q 12:27.

κρίνω
Q ⟦6:29⟧; **6:37**; **6:37**; ⟦6:37⟧; ⟦6:37⟧; **22:30**.

κρίσις
Q **10:14**; **11:31**; **11:32**; **11:42**.

κριτής
Q **11:19**; **12:58**; **12:58**.

κρούω
Q **11:9**; **11:10**; ⟦13:25⟧.
κρύπτη
Q ⟦11:33⟧.
κρυπτός
Q **12:2**.
κρύπτω
Q 10:21; 19:21.
κύμινον
Q 11:42.
κύριος
Q **4:8**; **4:12**; *6:40*; *6:40*; **6:46**; **6:46**; **7:6**; **9:59**; **10:2**; **10:21**; *11:39*; **12:42**; **12:43**; **12:45**; **12:46**; 13:25; **13:35**; «14:21»; **16:13**; 19:15; **19:16**; **19:18**; **19:20**.
κωφός
Q **7:22**; **11:14**; **11:14**.
λαλέω
Q **6:45**; **11:14**; *11:39*.
λαμβάνω
Q ⟦6:29⟧; ⟦6:34⟧; **11:10**; **13:19**; **13:21**; 14:27.
λάμπω
Q ⟦11:33⟧.
λαός
Q ⟦*3:21*⟧; ⟦*7:29*⟧.
λατρεύω
Q **4:8**.
λέγω
Q **3:8**; **3:8**; ⟦*3:22*⟧; **6:27**; *6:42*; 6:46; ⟦7:3⟧; ⟦7:3⟧; **7:8**; **7:9**; **7:24**; **7:26**; **7:28**; **7:32**; **7:33**; **7:34**; **10:2**; 10:5; **10:9**; **10:12**; **10:24**; ⟦11:2⟧; 11:9; **11:24**; *11:27*; *11:39*; **11:51**; 12:3; **12:22**; **12:27**; 12:29; **12:44**; ⟦*12:54*⟧; ⟦**12:54**⟧; **12:59**; 13:25; 13:26; 13:27; **13:35**; **15:7**; ⟦«15:9»⟧; ⟦«15:10»⟧; 17:6; 17:34; **19:16**; 19:18; 19:20; 19:22.
λεπρός
Q **7:22**.
λίαν
Q ⟦4:5⟧.
λιθοβολέω
Q **13:34**.
λίθος
Q **3:8**; **4:3**; **4:11**; 11:11; 17:2.
λόγος
Q **6:47**; ⟦6:49⟧; 7:1; 7:7; *11:28*; **12:10**; 19:15.
λύκος
Q **10:3**.
λυσιτελέω
Q 17:2.
λυχνία
Q **11:33**.
λύχνος
Q **11:33**; **11:34**; ⟦«15:8»⟧.
Λώτ
Q 17:28; 17:29.
μαθητής
Q 6:20; **6:40**; ⟦6:40⟧; **7:18**; 10:2; *11:39*; <14:26>; 14:26; 14:27.
μακάριος
Q **6:20**; **6:21**; **6:21**; **6:22**; **7:23**; **10:23**; *11:27*; *11:28*; **12:43**.
μαλακός
Q **7:25**; 7:25.
μᾶλλον
Q **11:13**; *12:5*; **12:24**; **12:28**; 15:7.
μαμωνᾶς
Q **16:13**.
μαρτυρέω
Q ⟦11:48⟧.
μαστός
Q 11:27.
μάχαιρα
Q 12:51.
μέγας
Q **6:49**; 7:28; **7:28**; ⟦14:16⟧.
μεθύω
Q ⟦12:45⟧.
μέλλω
Q 3:7.
μέν
Q **3:16**; **10:2**; 10:6; *11:48*; *14:18*.
μενοῦν
Q 11:28.
μένω
Q **10:7**.
μερίζω
Q 11:17; 11:17; 11:18.
μεριμνάω
Q **12:11**; **12:22**; **12:25**; **12:26**; 12:29.
μέρος
Q **12:46**.
μέσος
Q **10:3**.
μετά
Q ⟦«Q/Matt 5:41»⟧; **11:23**; **11:23**; 11:26; **11:31**; **11:32**; 12:45; **12:46**; **12:58**; 13:28; ⟦«17:20»⟧; ⟦19:15⟧; 19:15.
μεταβαίνω
Q ⟦10:7⟧.
μεταμέλομαι
Q ⟦*7:30*⟧.
μετανοέω
Q **10:13**; **11:32**; ⟦«15:10»⟧; ⟦17:3⟧.
μετάνοια
Q **3:8**.
μεταξύ
Q **11:51**.
μετρέω
Q **6:38**; **6:38**.
μέτρον
Q **6:38**.
μή
Q **3:8**; **3:9**; **6:30**; **6:37**; **6:37**; **6:49**; **7:23**; *7:33*; ⟦*7:30*⟧; **10:4**; **10:4**; 10:4; **10:6**; ⟦10:7⟧; **10:10**;

10:15; 10:22; 10:22; 11:4; 11:11; 11:12; **11:23; 11:23; 11:29; 11:42; 12:4; 12:4; 12:7; 12:11; 12:22; 12:29**; «12:33»; **12:59; 13:35**; 15:7; **17:23**; 17:23; **19:26.**

μηδέ
Q 10:4; **12:22.**

μηδείς
Q 10:4.

μήποτε
Q **4:11; 12:58.**

μήτε
Q *7:33*; **7:33.**

μητήρ
Q **12:53; 14:26.**

μήτι
Q 6:39; 6:44.

μικρός
Q **7:28; 17:2.**

μίλιον
Q ⟦«Q/Matt 5:41»⟧.

μισέω
Q 14:26; <14:26>; **16:13.**

μισθός
Q **6:23**; 6:32; ⟦6:34⟧; 10:7.

μνᾶ
Q 19:13; 19:16; 19:16; 19:18; 19:18; ⟦<19:21>⟧; 19:24; 19:24.

μνημεῖον
Q 11:44; **11:47.**

μοιχαλίς
Q *11:29.*

μοιχεύω
Q **16:18**; ⟦16:18⟧.

μόνος
Q **4:4; 4:8.**

μυλικός
Q 17:2.

μύλος
Q 17:35.

μωραίνω
Q **14:34.**

Ναζαρα
Q 4:16.

ναί
Q **7:26; 10:21**; 11:51.

νεκρός
Q 7:22; **9:60; 9:60.**

νήθω
Q **12:27.**

νήπιος
Q **10:21.**

νηστεύω
Q ⟦*4:2*⟧.

Νινευίτης
Q 11:30; **11:32.**

νομικός
Q ⟦*7:30*⟧; ⟦11:46⟧; ⟦11:52⟧.

νόμος
Q **16:16; 16:17.**

νοσσίον
Q 13:34.

νότος
Q **11:31**; ⟦12:55⟧.

νύμφη
Q **12:53.**

Νῶε
Q **17:26; 17:27.**

ὁδηγέω
Q **6:39.**

ὁδός
Q **7:27**; 10:4; **12:58; 14:23.**

ὀδούς
Q **13:28.**

ὅθεν
Q **11:24**; 19:21; 19:22.

οἶδα
Q ⟦*7:30*⟧; **11:13; 11:17**; 11:44; **12:30; 12:39**; ⟦12:56⟧; 13:25; 13:27; **19:22.**

οἰκετεία
Q 12:42.

οἰκία
Q **6:48; 6:48; 6:49; 6:49; 10:5**; ⟦10:7⟧; ⟦10:7⟧; ⟦10:7⟧; 11:17; ⟦11:33⟧; ⟦«15:8»⟧.

οἰκοδεσπότης
Q **12:39**; ⟦13:25⟧; 14:21.

οἰκοδομέω
Q **6:48; 6:49; 11:47**; *11:48*; *17:28.*

οἶκος
Q 7:25; ⟦10:5⟧; **11:24**; 11:51; 12:39; **13:35**; 14:23.

οἰκτρίμων
Q 6:36; 6:36.

οἰνοπότης
Q **7:34.**

ὀλιγόπιστος
Q **12:28.**

ὀλίγος
Q **10:2**; 13:24; 19:17; ⟦19:19⟧.

ὅλος
Q **11:34**; 11:34; **13:21.**

ὅμοιος
Q 6:48; 6:49; 7:31; **7:32; 13:18**; 13:19; **13:21.**

ὁμοιόω
Q **7:31**; 13:18; 13:20.

ὁμοίως
Q *17:28.*

ὁμολογέω
Q **12:8; 12:8.**

ὀνειδίζω
Q **6:22.**

ὄνομα
Q **11:2; 13:35.**

ὀπίσω
Q 3:16; **14:27.**

ὅπου
Q **9:57**; «12:33»; «12:33»; **12:33**; 12:33; **12:34; 17:37**; 19:21; 19:22.

ὅπως
Q 6:35; *7:3*; **10:2.**

ὁράω
Q 7:25; **7:26; 10:24; 10:24; 13:35**; *14:18.*

ὀργή
Q 3:7.

ὀργίζω
Q **14:21.**

ὄρνις
Q **13:34.**

ὄρος
Q 4:5; ⟦15:4⟧.

ὀρχέομαι
Q **7:32.**

ὅς, ἥ, ὅ
Q **3:16; 3:17;** ⟦*3:22*⟧; ⟦6:34⟧; ⟦6:37⟧; **6:38;** 6:46; 6:48; 6:49; **7:22; 7:23;** 7:27; 7:27; 7:32; 10:5; **10:8; 10:10; 10:22;** 10:23; **10:24; 10:24;** 11:11; *11:27*; **12:2; 12:2;** 12:3; **12:3;** 12:8; 12:9; **12:10;** 12:10; **12:40; 12:42; 12:43; 12:46; 12:46; 13:19; 13:21; 13:21;** 13:25; **13:34;** *14:18*; *14:19*; ⟦<14:26>⟧; ⟦<14:26>⟧; 14:27; ⟦«15:9»⟧; **17:1; 17:27;** *17:29;* 17:30; 19:13; **19:26.**

ὅσος
Q 14:23.

ὅστις
Q ⟦6:29⟧; ⟦«Q/Matt 5:41»⟧; ⟦12:58⟧; *14:16*; 14:27.

ὅταν
Q **6:22;** ⟦11:2⟧; **11:24;** *11:34*; **12:11.**

ὅτε
Q ⟦7:1⟧; ⟦13:35⟧.

ὅτι
Q **3:8;** 4:4; **4:10; 6:20; 6:21; 6:21;** 6:23; **6:35;** *10:9*; ⟦10:12⟧; **10:13; 10:21; 10:21; 10:24; 11:31; 11:32;** 11:39; **11:42;** 11:43; **11:44;** 11:46; **11:47;** ⟦11:48⟧; *11:48*; **11:52; 12:24; 12:30; 12:39; 12:40; 12:44; 12:51; 13:24;** 14:17; **15:7;** ⟦«15:9»⟧; **19:21; 19:22.**

οὐ, οὐκ, οὐχ
Q **3:16;** ⟦*4:2*⟧; **4:4; 4:12;** *6:37*; **6:40; 6:41; 6:43;** 6:46; **6:48; 7:6;** 7:28; ⟦*7:29*⟧; 7:32; 7:32; **9:58; 10:24; 10:24;** 11:17; 11:24; **11:29;** 11:44; **11:46; 11:52; 12:2; 12:2; 12:6; 12:10; 12:24;** 12:24; **12:27;** 12:28; 12:33; **12:39; 12:40; 12:46; 12:46;** 12:51; ⟦**12:56**⟧; **12:59;** 13:25; 13:27; **13:34; 13:35;** *14:20*; 14:26; 14:26; <14:26>; **14:26; 14:27; 14:27; 16:13;** ⟦«17:20»⟧; **19:21; 19:21; 19:22; 19:22.**

οὐαί
Q **10:13; 10:13;** 11:39; **11:42;** 11:43; **11:44;** 11:46; **11:47; 11:52; 17:1.**

οὐδέ
Q *6:40*; **6:43;** 7:9; ⟦*7:30*⟧; 10:22; ⟦11:52⟧; **12:24; 12:24; 12:27; 12:27;** 12:33; ⟦*17:21*⟧.

οὐδείς
Q ⟦*4:2*⟧; **10:22;** 11:33; **12:2; 16:13.**

οὖν
Q **3:8; 3:9;** ⟦*7:31*⟧; **10:2; 11:13; 11:35;** ⟦12:29⟧; ⟦19:23⟧; 19:24.

οὐρανός
Q ⟦3:21⟧; **6:23; 9:58; 10:15; 10:21; 11:13; 12:33;** ⟦12:54⟧; ⟦12:55⟧; ⟦**12:56**⟧; **13:19; 16:17;** *17:29.*

οὖς
Q **12:3.**

οὔτε
Q 12:33; 12:33; 14:35; 14:35.

οὗτος
Q **3:8;** ⟦*3:22*⟧; **4:3; 4:6;** 7:1; **7:8; 7:8;** ⟦7:18⟧; 7:24; 7:27; 7:31; ⟦10:5⟧; *10:21*; **10:21; 11:19;** *11:27*; 11:29; 11:30; **11:31; 11:32; 11:42; 11:49;** 11:50; **11:51;** *12:12*; **12:22; 12:27; 12:30; 12:30; 12:31;** *14:20*; «14:21»; **17:2; 17:6.**

οὕτως
Q 6:23; 6:31; **10:21; 11:30; 12:28; 12:43;** ⟦«15:10»⟧; **17:24; 17:26;** 17:30.

οὐχί
Q 6:32; 6:34; 6:39; **12:6;** 12:23; ⟦15:4⟧; ⟦«15:8»⟧.

ὀφειλέτης
Q 11:4.

ὀφείλημα
Q 11:4.

ὀφθαλμός
Q ⟦6:20⟧; **6:41; 6:41; 6:42; 6:42; 6:42; 6:42; 10:23; 11:34; 11:34;** 11:34.

ὄφις
Q **11:12.**

ὄχλος
Q ⟦3:7⟧; 7:24; **11:14;** *11:27*; *11:29*; *11:39*; ⟦*12:54*⟧.

ὄψιος
Q ⟦12:54⟧.

παιδίον
Q **7:32.**

παῖς
Q 7:3; 7:7.